BURNSIDE

1824,

Happy Birthday, Feb. 16, 1972, de
to John Ambrose Burnside,
since Ambrose Burnside
was Great-Grandfather
Solomon's commander June 3,
from Spring 1827 pentil follow
his story Rudisill help to to
Solomon Rudisill Civil War.
With much love for my
dear Winifred Rudisill

BURNSIDE

WILLIAM MARVEL

The University of North Carolina Press   Chapel Hill & London

© 1991 The University of North Carolina Press

All rights reserved

Manufactured in the United States of America

95 94 93 92 91   5 4 3 2 1

Library of Congress Cataloging-in-Publication Data

Marvel, William.

Burnside / by William Marvel.

p.   cm.

Includes bibliographical references and index.

ISBN 0-8078-1983-2 (cloth : alk. paper)

1. Burnside, Ambrose Everett, 1824–1881.   2. Generals—
United States—Biography.   3. United States. Army—Biography.
4. United States—History—Civil War, 1861–1865—Campaigns.

I. Title.

E467.1.B8M37   1991

973.7′3—dc20

[B]   91-8419

CIP

FOR ELIZABETH,

who bore more for Burnside than I

CONTENTS

A section of illustrations will be found following page 217.

MAPS

PREFACE

During the latter half of the last century, Joel Headley supplemented his income by writing popular histories and biographies. He began composing an account of the Civil War while it was in progress. The conflict outgrew his expectations, however, and by November 1, 1862, he closed volume one and sent it to the publisher, concluding it with the events of June. In that first volume, written during the final days of George McClellan's military career, Headley spoke very highly of Ambrose Burnside, referring to his "accustomed energy," which secured the coast of North Carolina in a dazzling campaign. The frontispiece consisted of a collection of generals' portraits, arranged in an oval around McClellan's. Burnside's image occupied the second place of honor, at top center. By contrast, Henry Halleck's cameo was at bottom center, and U. S. Grant's at the upper left.

Volume two of Headley's *Great Rebellion* did not go to press until 1866. Early in that work the author roundly criticized Burnside's "lethargy" at Antietam, a battle fought six weeks before that same writer released the laudatory passages of volume one. Headley then lay all the blame for the repulse at Fredericksburg on Burnside, after which he hardly mentioned that general throughout the rest of the book. What could have wrought such a transformation in his treatment of the man? Was Headley temporarily blinded by Burnside's initial success, or did the soldier spiral into deserved obscurity through his own shortcomings?

The timing of the publication of Headley's first volume could not have been more telling, for it implies Burnside was not found wanting at Antietam: that indictment was manufactured in 1863, by the deposed George McClellan. Little Mac's accusations, now demonstrably false, seemed perfectly plausible by then, for the costly setback at Fredericksburg was fresh in the public memory. Burnside had publicly accepted responsibility for the defeat, though it was not altogether his, and that extraordinary act of generosity became the watchword of those subordinates who felt it necessary to defend their own performance. Burnside's humble demeanor spawned a seed of distrust when he inherited the army, and his insistence on assuming blame for the lost battle fertilized that seed, which blossomed into a cabal that foiled his next campaign and finally turned most of the army against him. The Army of the Potomac never again had any faith in Burnside, and that poor opinion was itself part and parcel of his other great defeat, at the Crater.

Burnside never defended himself against his critics, save through the medium of official inquiries. A public controversy, he feared, would create discord out of all proportion to any benefit that might accrue to his reputation. He sincerely believed—as he stubbornly believed in the natural goodness of men—that history would vindicate him. He was wrong on both counts, and his silence has worked against him. Though he spent but nine of his forty months of Civil War service with them, it was the sneering officers of the Army of the Potomac who most often wrote about him, and the modern perspective of Burnside is framed by their biased remarks and often-unsubstantiated recollections, almost none of which were published until the man was dead.

Historians who should have known better have used this chorus of contempt without questioning its accuracy, painting a dark portrait with strokes of bitter sarcasm. The myth of Burnside the Incapable has thus become self-perpetuating, and modern Civil War seminars abound with speakers who delight in finding ever-more-humorous means of expressing his capacity for failure. Ambrose Burnside may be the most maligned figure of the war, and anyone who has studied it enough to undertake his biography has been thoroughly indoctrinated in this negative mystique. Indeed, this effort began with the underlying expectation that a hundred years of accumulated criticism could not prove wrong, but the further the investigation progressed the clearer it became that Burnside's legendary incompetence was, like most legends, largely apocryphal. A real man emerged at last who was neither genius nor blockhead, who blundered in ways no different from some of the great heroes of his age—whom he occasionally outsmarted—and whose downfall may have been his own honest, humble, and trusting manner.

BURNSIDE

It is better to trust in the Lord than

to put confidence in man.

Psalms 118:8

PROLOGUE: THE RIVER

As the steamboat pulled away from Cincinnati, two young subalterns stood on the passenger deck in fresh blue single-breasted coats and visored army caps. In this early autumn of 1847 word had yet to reach the Ohio River country of Winfield Scott's victories around Mexico City, so the two eager officers had no idea that the battles in which they had dreamed of distinguishing themselves would never occur.

The larger of the two soldiers stood fully six feet tall, with a deep chest and broad shoulders decorated with the blank scarlet straps of a brevet second lieutenant of artillery. He cultivated a bushy new pair of muttonchop whiskers that met his moustache on either side, but despite his twenty-three years his bright brown hair was particularly thin on top. Though his size was intimidating, he greeted people with such habitual good humor that they were drawn to him in a crowd, almost magnetically. One man, so drawn, invited the brawny lieutenant to a game of euchre. The stranger also asked a third traveler, who agreed to join them in apparent indifference.

At first the officer won everything. After a time he began to lose a hand or two, then his luck turned inexorably bad. Perhaps everyone but the young soldier realized that the two sharps had conspired to clean him out, and by the time the boat docked at Louisville, they had done so.[1]

This was not the first time Ambrose Burnside's optimistic view of human nature had brought him trouble. He found it nearly impossible to believe another person could wish him harm until the evidence fairly knocked him on the head, and sometimes not then. It was equally characteristic of him, though, to lay the blame on himself rather than on the card cheats. As at every occasion in his life when adversity assailed him, he accepted personal responsibility for the misfortune and set out to find his own way out of the difficulty.

He came of honest, independent stock. His great-grandfather, Robert Burnside, had been one of those outnumbered Scots who swung a claymore for Bonnie Prince Charlie: thus had he taken part in that final spectacle of Celtic courage, the battle on Culloden Moor. Escaping the massacre that followed, he fled Scotland for the backwoods of South Carolina, to begin life anew. There the Burnsides partook of a great cultural irony. With other Highland Scots who had fought the hated English in the 1740s, they resisted the insurrection against the English king in the 1770s. At the commencement of the American Revolution Robert Burnside declared for the crown—against the wealthier Lowland rebels, which explained much of the contradiction—and his oldest son commanded a Tory company. By war's end Robert was dead, and James disbanded his Loyalist troop; the former captain escaped with his wife and children to Jamaica, to avoid the persecution meted out by the victors. Within a few years political animosities withered away, and the family returned to South Carolina to begin pioneering again in the Laurens District.

James Burnside died in 1798, leaving seven sons and daughters. The widow, daughter of her husband's Tory colonel, sought to improve her family's situation by migrating to new territory. Her son Edghill, influenced by Quaker neighbors, had developed a distaste for slavery and wished to move to a place where it was already prohibited, so the entire family (save two married daughters) made the arduous journey to Indiana. For most of them this new frontier was too difficult a transition from the moderate circumstances they had come to enjoy in South Carolina. After only two years, the matriarch and all but two of her sons returned South. Her oldest son gravitated to Illinois and, later, Wisconsin, leaving Edghill to find his way in a new town named, appropriately enough, Liberty.[2]

In 1814 Edghill Burnside married Pamelia Brown, daughter of another Scottish expatriate from Laurens County. Over the next two dozen years she bore him nine children, though the last three died in infancy. Burnside was hard pressed to support the growing brood. At one point he won election to the bench of the circuit court as an associate justice, and forever after people called him Judge Burnside, but for most of his life he worked as clerk of the county court. In 1842 an influential friend noted he paid close attention to his duties and was very honest and respectable, but, the friend confided, "he has not managed to be over thrifty." At a time when he had but three children at home, two of whom were able to contribute to the family income, Judge Burnside's economic condition could not be described as any better than moderate.[3]

Ambrose Everts Burnside was the fourth of those nine children. Born May 23, 1824, he was named after the dead son of the doctor who delivered him. The boy grew strong with agricultural labor, for even the court clerk had to supplement his income by farming. Ambrose's schooling came from a source agreeable to his father's intellectual persuasion. William Haughton, a gentle Quaker and so great a self-educated scholar that folks nicknamed him "Doctor," taught the rudiments of language and arithmetic in a one-room school that grew to become Beech Grove Academy. Here, as much as at home, did Ambrose develop the strict honesty and kindliness for which he became famous. In later years he took further instruction from Samuel Bigger, a future Indiana governor, who remembered the boy as particularly intelligent.[4]

Intelligence alone could not insure success in the Indiana of the 1830s. Continued education was a luxury Edghill Burnside could not provide his sons, and by late 1840 Ambrose felt pressured to take an immediate occupation. That winter he apprenticed himself to a tailor in Centreville, a dozen miles from his home.

Pamelia Burnside died the following spring, in her early forties. The next year Ambrose came back to Liberty and opened a shop of his own, with one partner. Though pleased to be able to support himself, he quickly realized it would not satisfy him to spend his life crosslegged on a tailor's board. In 1842 his father happened to be serving in the state legislature, and he took that opportunity to gratify his son's ambitions. He asked the governor to write Senator Albert White on the subject of an appointment to West Point; the senator referred the letter to the commander of the U.S. Army Engineer Department, which administered the military academy. The chief of engineers explained that some appointments could be awarded to the sons of dedicated public officials who could not otherwise afford an education. Judge Burnside was certainly dedicated, was surely unable to send any of his children to college, and was apparently quite popular. Forty-five members of the Indiana legislature signed a petition recommending his son, the state's two U.S. senators endorsed that recommendation, and in March of 1843 the appointment arrived in the Liberty post office.[5]

Young Burnside reported at West Point June 1, 1843, with twenty-five dollars in his pocket. The term did not begin until the first day of July, when the new cadets began the rigorous and strictly disciplined routine of academy life. Their every movement solicited a punishment if · not performed on command. A cadet—or plebe, as a harried first-year man was called—accumulated demerits for every infraction, the number of demerits varying with the perceived severity of the offense. If he tallied 200 demerits in a single year, it was back to the farm for him. Burnside earned his first demerit on the third morning of the term, for seating himself at the breakfast table before the command was given. The fifth day he came late for drill, and the demerits mounted steadily from there. A gregarious fellow, he scored 5 demerits for each of many instances of unauthorized "visiting," 4 for talking while on guard, 4 for allowing friends in his quarters at noontime, and 2 for "playing" in the sickroom. On his birthday he ignored his duties in order to celebrate—to the tune of 11 demerits. By June he had 198 demerits. Of 211 cadets at the academy, he ranked 207 in general conduct: the 4 below him were dismissed. Academically, however, he fared better. Though in the bottom third of his class in French, he ranked in the upper third in mathematics, a discipline more important to the military profession.[6]

During his second year Cadet Burnside improved greatly, advancing to the top quarter of his class in mathematics and doing very well in English grammar, hinting that Doctor Haughton's efforts had not been wasted. His standing in conduct rose noticeably as well, for he earned only 133 demerits.

The summer after their second year, the cadets went on furlough, and Burnside rode the train, coach, and steamers back to Indiana. The reintroduction to farm drudgery may have reminded him of the consequences of dismissal, for his third year was his best at the academy. He became a cadet lieutenant, stood twelfth in general merit in a class of forty, and shaved his demerits to a respectable sixty-nine. During his last year he confidently jeopardized all those accomplishments by cavorting with his beloved roommate, Henry Heth, slipping away to Benny Havens's notorious groggery. Havens admired Burnside above any cadet he ever knew, but an 1846 alumnus discounted him as one of those few who wanted only to do enough to graduate, caring nothing for class standing.[7] Burnside was reprimanded often for absence at breakfast (and for trying to replace the lost meal with an unauthorized snack from the kitchen). One gay afternoon in September he disappeared from the post altogether and did not come back to his room until the following night. Strangely enough, academy officials deemed it a much worse transgression a month later when they caught him outside the barracks after taps. For that late-night jaunt he drew eight demerits, the heaviest single punishment of his cadet years.

Burnside took up smoking early in 1847, a violation anytime and anywhere on the post; with that, with his incurably hospitable nature, and with numerous violations of the uncomfortable uniform code, he sat on the brink of dismissal again as graduation approached. He had shown great promise in such fields as tactics and "natural philosophy"—mostly physics—and the superintendent excused a couple of violations on one pretext or another. Burnside thus reduced his demerit load to 190, graduating eighteenth among only thirty-eight survivors of his class. Henry Heth came in dead last.[8]

The uppermost graduates earned the right to choose their assignments, and most chose the engineers. After the engineers the most popular branch was the artillery. On July 1, 1847, his middle name permanently perverted by an administrative error at the academy, Ambrose Everett Burnside accepted a commission in the 3rd U.S. Artillery. His battery was fighting just then in Mexico. When his summer-long furlough ended, he joined fellow graduate Egbert Viele, and it was with him that he boarded the Louisville packet at Cincinnati.

Once ashore at Louisville, the pair of fledgling lieutenants encountered a man named John Gill, who astonished the destitute Burnside by lending him cash enough to carry him to New Orleans. The generous stranger even took the soldiers home for dinner and introduced them to his family.[9] At the army's rendezvous in New Orleans a paymaster reimbursed Burnside his travel expenses, which he dutifully mailed to Mr. Gill before joining a glut of other soldiers aboard a transport bound for Vera Cruz. With a detachment of recruits for his regiment he followed the long, dangerous route Scott had marched, from Vera Cruz to Mexico City. He passed the battlefield of Cerro Gordo, the ancient city of Jalapa, and came at last to the captured capital.

Though officially assigned to Company C of the 3rd Artillery, commanded by Braxton Bragg of Buena Vista fame, Burnside began active duty with another regiment in the battered walls of the Citadel. All the fighting, save that against brigands, was over by December 9, the day he reported. Duty in Mexico presented no more occasion for a young officer to gain notoriety; it turned dreadfully tedious. Some soldiers washed their boredom away with excessive quantities of the native equivalent of forty-rod, but when Ambrose Burnside left the Chapultepec bastion, it was to pass his time in the gambling houses, where he became known by his dangerous penchant for increasing the stakes whenever the cards went against him: he would wager again and again, until his last dollar had gone across the table. When the war officially ended in the spring of 1848, he owed six months' pay. All that saved him from disgrace was a transfer to Fort Adams, in Rhode Island's Narragansett Bay, which offered no opportunity for gambling and, with an active social agenda, no need for it.[10]

1

ARM'D YEAR—YEAR OF THE STRUGGLE

I

Dawn had yet to come. The trees and the flaps of the tent still dripped from a midnight shower when an orderly slipped inside to wake his regimental commander. He shook the solid shoulder and murmured something about orders from General Patterson. Ambrose Burnside opened his dark eyes and read the dispatch by flickering candlelight: he was to march with his command for Washington, in all haste. Within seconds the colonel sat upright on his cot, pushing his bald head through the neck of the baggy pullover blouse he had designed for his 1st Rhode Island Infantry. Outside, in the twilight of June 17, 1861, his regiment dozed along the banks of the Potomac River near Williamsport, Maryland. Attached to it was a battery of artillery, two sections of which he had sent across the river into Virginia the day before. To retrieve those four guns, the colonel turned to a rabbit-toothed man several years his junior, a babyfaced assistant wearing all but the shoulder straps of a major general's uniform—William Sprague, the Boy Governor of Rhode Island. The governor bounded into the saddle and splashed through the chilly ford, his cape billowing behind him.[1]

Soon the twelve hundred men of Burnside's mixed column stumbled away from Williamsport in a lurching, drowsy column. The detached artillerymen soon came clattering up behind with their guns, and while the force marched through Hagerstown, Burnside paused to report his progress to Robert Patterson, the septuagenarian general in charge of Union troops on the upper Potomac. Patterson told him General Scott had personally requested the presence of the Rhode Islanders in the capital and advised him there was rail transportation available at Frederick, another twenty miles and more away. Burnside's men were still footsore from a punishing march two days back, but before calling a two-hour break for lunch he drove them on under the hot sun to Boonsborough, fifteen miles from the morning's starting place.

The moment the bugles sounded the halt, the column disintegrated into impromptu messes along either side of the old National Road, where the men cooked, ate, and napped a bit or tended their burning feet. A few members of Company D took the time to shred a Confederate flag some inattentive partisan had left atop his building. Then the bugles blared again, and officers herded their men reluctantly into a line that jerked into motion. The road climbed immediately up the side of South Mountain, cutting a steep swath over that imposing ridge at Turner's Gap. The descent was even more precipitous, and brutally hard on sore feet and cramped calves. Little knots of ignorant, isolated mountain folk stood transfixed by the roadside, awed by the sight of so impressive a horde of strangers in such good clothes. As the road twisted to the bottom of the mountain, some homesick New Englanders compared the rugged scenery to that of New Hampshire's White Mountains.

Deceptively gentler hills still taunted the weary troops. One officer's boots hurt him so that he marched barefoot for four miles, and numbers of men had to be carried in the baggage wagons when they gave out entirely. At the wooden bridge over Catoctin Creek, scores bounded for the clear water of that shallow stream, but company officers waved them back into the ranks with bared swords. At Middletown the citizens gathered on the narrow main street to greet the soldiers in the fading summer light, but their encouragement did little to compensate the infantrymen for the agonizing climb out of that village. A mile or so beyond stood the slopes of the Catoctins, every bit as difficult as South Mountain. As the vanguard topped Braddock Heights—the local name for the crest there—the windows of Frederick twinkled in the moonlight, teasing the exhausted soldiers for several more miles. It was well after midnight when Burnside turned his regiment into the fields near the town, more than thirty miles from the morning campsite. Early the next day, while his yawning troops marched into the railroad yard to board welcome cattle cars, the colonel and his staff called on Governor Hicks, who treated them to a meal.[2]

Ambrose Burnside had just turned thirty-seven. At an age when most of his contemporaries had established themselves, he had but recently redeemed himself from a sudden and total failure. Three short years before he had been bankrupt, his military career long since pawned on the altar of entrepreneurialism.

The delightful duty at Fort Adams was a long way behind him. After less than a year there, Lieutenant Burnside returned to his own company in the spring of 1849. By then Company C had transferred to the desolate post of Las Vegas, New Mexico, on the Santa Fe Trail and about forty miles east of that town: eight years later a passing officer found Las Vegas "a dirty hamlet of adobe and jacal habitations, alive with yelping dogs and swarthy blanketed 'greasers.'" Burnside reported to his stark assignment on the Gallinas River the last day of June, to discover that Captain Bragg—reputedly a quarrelsome fussbudget—had departed on staff duty. Happily, detached duty had kept them apart in Mexico City; nor did Burnside see much of his company commander all the time he served in New Mexico.

Almost all the enlisted men at Las Vegas were of Mexican descent. Within a few weeks after Burnside came to the post, though certainly not because he came, the great preponderance of those Spanish surnames disappeared from the rolls, to be replaced by those of Germans, Irish, and Englishmen.[3]

The principal duty of these artillerymen was escorting U.S. mail shipments, for which they unhitched the gun teams and rode as cavalry. Due to a shortage of officers, Burnside also had to moonlight as the post commissary and quartermaster, but because he frequently followed the mail for a month at a time, he submitted to a risky arrangement to assure the fort enough food and supplies during his absences. Each time he prepared to leave with an escort, he would sign an advance requisition for Captain Alexander W. Reynolds, the department quartermaster in Santa Fe. These requisitions amounted to as much as six thousand dollars, on which the post could draw whatever it needed. Burnside relied upon Captain Reynolds to enter only the expended portion of these receipts in the record. Once again his faith in his fellow man would bring him to grief.[4]

The enemy around Las Vegas was no longer the Mexican army, but the more fierce and effective Apache Indians, and during months of service against them Burnside began to contemplate the inefficiency of the carbines issued to U.S. horse soldiers. On August 23, 1849, less than eight weeks into his tour in New Mexico, he led a score of his company in an attack on a party of sixty Indians, in which the only weapon his men could use was the saber. Revolvers were not yet in general issue, and it was too awkward and time-consuming for a mounted man to reload a muzzle-loading firearm in the midst of a swirling fray. Burnside came away from the fight with an arrow in his neck and the germ of an idea. He began thinking about a light, breechloading carbine during the monotonous off-duty hours, improving upon some rough mental designs in secret during the remaining four years of his Regular Army career.[5]

At times during his stay at Las Vegas, Burnside found himself in command of the unprotected fort, and for the entire summer of 1850 he took charge of a detachment, chasing one particularly murderous war party. That fall he proceeded to Jefferson Barracks, Missouri, taking the opportunity to visit his home on an extended leave. Like many veterans of the Mexican campaign, Burnside had suffered ever since from a recurring intestinal ailment, which may explain how he managed to secure a twenty-day leave, followed by a subsequently excused absence without leave and, finally, another sixty-day furlough. He left the army two days before Christmas, 1850, and did not return to duty until sometime in May, 1851.[6]

It was perhaps during this long sojourn at Liberty—if it ever happened at all—that Burnside wooed and lost Charlotte Moon, a feisty and fickle young lady who lived just across the Ohio state line. As local legend insists, Burnside proposed to this descendant of Virginia emigrants. She is supposed to have accepted, and the wedding feast was prepared in the home of a relative—whether Miss Moon's relative or Burnside's is not recorded. All went well until the minister asked if she would take Ambrose for her husband, when she allegedly snapped "No, sirree, Bob, I won't," and fled. A continuation of the tale has it that she later agreed to marry an Ohio lawyer, who unholstered a pistol at the ceremony and announced there would either be "a wedding tonight or a funeral tomorrow."[7]

By the time of his twenty-seventh birthday, Burnside had returned to the Mexican border, where he spent the next ten months with a commission delineating that boundary as the Treaty of Guadaloupe had stipulated. For Christmas he received his promotion to first lieutenant. As the winter drew to a close, his superior officer on the commission charged him with a packet of dispatches to deliver in Washington, on his way back to the fondly remembered comfort of Fort Adams. Exactly thirty days after he reported to that fort he married Mary Richmond Bishop, a twenty-three-year-old Providence girl he must have known during his first assignment in Rhode Island. After a sixty-day leave, they set up housekeeping in a bricked-up casemate at the fort.[8]

Burnside did not have long to enjoy his honeymoon before he learned that something was amiss with his financial accounts from Las Vegas. Quartermaster Reynolds complained the lieutenant had failed to return $5,700 in unexpended army funds when he left New Mexico. Burnside went to Washington to set the record straight, and when Reynolds came East he met him there, and again at Philadelphia, to go over his papers. Reynolds admitted, at least to Burnside, that the error must have resulted from one of those highly irregular receipts for undelivered funds, but Reynolds failed to make the same disclosure to the federal auditors, who continued to hold Burnside personally responsible for the money. Eventually they tacked on another discrepancy of $557.14 and presented the astonished young man with a bill for the total. Burnside was not the first, however, to run afoul of Reynolds. The captain was either a hopelessly disorganized keeper of records or a brazen embezzler; Franklin Pierce dismissed him in 1855 for what the U.S. comptroller described as "great irregularity and palpable fraud." Word of that turn of events did not reach the auditors dunning Burnside; the mistaken debt remained a blight on his reputation for more than a decade.[9]

In the midst of this imbroglio, but for reasons unrelated to it, Burnside forwarded his resignation. The War Department accepted it in October, 1853, and Mr. and Mrs. Burnside left Fort Adams for the town of Bristol, a dozen miles up the bay. With the approach of his thirtieth birthday, Burnside decided the time had come to improve his situation; he based his hopes for that improvement on the design of his breechloading rifle, which he had finally perfected. He borrowed money, equipped a drab brick building with the necessary machinery, and went into business as the Bristol Rifle Works.

The weapon worked very simply. The barrel broke down at the receiver, and when a brass cartridge had been inserted, the barrel snapped back in place. A separate primer ignited the charge through a hole in the base of the cartridge; this brass round, with its swollen neck that prevented gas from escaping, was the most easily recognizable feature of the arm. Unlike many mass-produced pieces, all Burnside's military carbines and rifles were well made, as were his sporterized guns. The Burnside carbine has been called the best of all cavalry carbines issued during the war that was to come, in which more than 55,000 saw service.

At first sales were slow, but adequate to cover expenses. Secretary of War Jefferson Davis bought a couple of hundred carbines for the army, but most of the early productions went to sportsmen—including a few ornately engraved pieces hand-finished for Persian potentates.[10]

His military service had been of such relative obscurity that Burnside was genuinely surprised to find the public held his experience a valuable commodity. In 1855 he accepted an appointment as the major general of Rhode Island militia, a grand leap for the erstwhile chief of a two-gun section of artillery. There were some differences between the militia and the Regular Army, though, which tended to offset the honor of the position, and two years later he resigned his commission when the governor interfered with his attempt to discipline a blueblooded subordinate. President Pierce also called upon him for his military expertise in 1856, asking him to serve on the annual Board of Visitors for West Point. In June of that year he returned to his alma mater on that duty, where he joined the debate over the curriculum and made his plea for the enhancement of the mathematics department, in which he had done so well.

Just after Buchanan's inauguration, the Democrats of Burnside's district nominated him for Congress. It was a hopeless race in which the candidate had no heart, and his commitments to a War Department contract left him unable to campaign for the seat. He finally lost to a Know-Nothing rival by more than a two-to-one margin. This would be the only election Burnside ever lost, but any distress the defeat gave him was overshadowed by growing financial woes that arose from one government contract he had supposed secure.[11]

In 1857 the secretary of war was a Virginian named John B. Floyd. Floyd seems to have made certain verbal assurances to Burnside about his carbines, specifically that he would purchase them for the army to the extent of $90,000 if they successfully withstood testing. In August Burnside went back to the military academy with a dozen other inventors, to submit his weapon. The six officers who test-fired the pieces, one of whom was his old roommate Henry Heth, judged Burnside's to be the best model. Guided apparently by Floyd's personal promise, the gratified inventor went back to Bristol and began turning out carbines by the hundreds, going deep into debt just as the Panic of 1857 made cash scarce. His own debtors were already beginning to default on their notes, and federal auditors hounded him repeatedly over the missing quartermaster funds; Burnside was therefore shocked when the War Department notified him it had suspended its order pending a second test of the weapon.

His carbine emerged the victor in the second competition, and he fully expected Floyd to respond according to his word, but the secretary appears to have had some second thoughts. After another personal interview with Floyd—whose poltroonery during the war lends credence to Burnside's suspicions—the novice industrialist realized the Virginian had broken their agreement in favor of some crony. Floyd said he would buy only a few token carbines, rather than enough to rearm the entire United States Cavalry. This blow fell early in 1858, by which time Burnside's finances had been stretched beyond recovery. Disdaining formal bankruptcy proceedings that might have made the failure easier, he assigned everything he owned to the investors in his company, including his uniform, sword, and his firearm patent, and set about earning enough cash to repay the balance of his company's debts. Boarding his wife with relatives, he started west.[12]

Railroads were booming beyond the Alleghenies, and it was there the ruined inventor intended to find work. He went directly to St. Paul, Minnesota, taking a room at the Fuller House while he hunted for work and scratched at new inventions. One year earlier, he had obtained a patent on a leather or malleable-metal cap for artillery projectiles, to assist the round in reacting to the rifling in a gun tube, but he never carried the idea through to development; while he stayed at the Fuller House he modified the invention by designing a leather shoe for the same purpose and applied for a new patent.[13]

The most productive work Burnside did at St. Paul was to borrow a piece of hotel stationery and write to his old classmate and friend George B. McClellan. "Mac," as Burnside called him, had just resigned from the army to take an executive position with the Illinois Central Railroad. Burnside explained that, between the "infernal rascality" of the secretary of war and the money crisis, he was out of business. Did McClellan know of any railroad jobs open in Iowa, Illinois, or Wisconsin? McClellan certainly did: Burnside could be cashier for his own railroad's land department. The bewhiskered Burnside fairly exploded with gratitude, but McClellan confided to his fiancée that it gave him great satisfaction to be able to help "such a noble man" as Burnside.[14]

For two years Burnside remained in Chicago, paying debts and living frugally, lodging with McClellan. By 1860 he had been promoted to treasurer of the railroad office in New York, where he and his wife were at last able to afford their own accommodations—though she flitted constantly between New York and Providence to care for her ailing parents. Her father died two months before the national election.

By the time the Civil War began, Burnside's obligations from the Bristol Rifle Works had all been retired. Ironically, those who took over his company soon enjoyed substantial profits. As early as 1858 they met a frustratingly tardy War Department contract amounting to more than $21,000, the quality of Burnside's initial manufactures having won the demand of the men who had to use them. The gun's mere reputation maintained sales until the outbreak of the war, when orders began rolling in for thousands at a time. Only an acute economic downturn and Burnside's unjustified faith in another man's integrity prevented him from sharing a single dollar of the wealth his enterprise generated.[15]

New York City knew of the fall of Fort Sumter within hours of its surrender. Burnside immediately began arranging his paperwork with a view toward offering his services in the contest that was bound to follow, but his chance came sooner than he expected. April 15, as President Lincoln called for militia to suppress the rebellion, Burnside opened a telegram from Rhode Island's young millionaire governor, asking the former militia general if he would take charge of a regiment from that state. Burnside arrived in Providence the next morning.

The tailor-become-soldier outfitted his regiment in grey trousers and a loose blue pullover blouse with long tails that hung like a frock coat. Instead of issuing overcoats, he drew on his Mexican War observations and ordered blankets slit for wear like ponchos, thus saving his soldiers the extra burden of a heavy coat. He accepted a battery of brass field-pieces to accompany the regiment, accommodating his old fondness for the long arm. Four days after he arrived in the state, about half the companies were equipped for the field, and Burnside led them to Washington by way of New York and Annapolis. The giddy young governor followed this advance battalion, dragging his own staff along so as to play out his ex officio role as commander-in-chief of the state militia.

Each of the two halves of the 1st Rhode Island had to transfer to different steamers in New York. While Burnside stood on the Gotham wharf watching the troops re-embark, someone in the crowd recognized him and called for a speech. The colonel was neither trained for nor fond of public speaking. "I'll make a speech when I come back," he promised, and made his way up the gangplank.[16]

At first the Rhode Islanders slept in makeshift bunks in the Patent Office, but soon the reunited companies found new quarters on a farm in the northeastern suburbs of the city. Burnside named this Washington campsite for his impish governor, but it is difficult to determine how much he appreciated Sprague; the young man was forever in the way, strutting about in his custom-made uniform. He had appointed numerous surplus officers to Burnside's regiment, including a paymaster, an assistant chaplain, a staff engineer, and an ordnance sergeant, none of them necessary at the regimental level. Burnside's 1st Rhode Island and its battery had, like many of these early militia units, a cumbersome wagon train, all provided at Sprague's profligate behest.

On May 2 the unit was mustered into federal service for ninety days by Major Irvin McDowell, who had been the adjutant of the U.S. Military Academy when Cadet Burnside entered. The now-official soldiers responded well to their colonel's blend of strict discipline and paternal devotion; he toured the hospital, kitchen, and quarters regularly to monitor the health of the troops. He kept a close eye on these details throughout his military career, and his men grew to love him for it.[17]

Washington remained secure and rather quiet into early June despite constant rumors and scattered panics, and Winfield Scott felt safe planning a campaign against Harpers Ferry from the corseted waist of Maryland. On June 10 the aging general-in-chief ordered Burnside's regiment and battery to take railroad cars for Robert Patterson's army, then congregating in southern Pennsylvania.

Governor Sprague had left camp nearly three weeks before, in a state of ennui, and Burnside made no effort to notify him as the Rhode Islanders marched to the Washington depot. The regiment made the roundabout journey to Chambersburg without the young chief executive, but no one complained that his absence caused any problems. A second train unloaded the men at Greencastle, near the Maryland line, and there the unmistakable cape and buck teeth caught up with them a few days later—Sprague had read about the impending invasion in the newspapers.

Responding to Scott's instructions, Patterson ordered Burnside below Williamsport on June 15, to threaten Harpers Ferry. Moving his own headquarters to Hagerstown, Patterson considered sending the Rhode Island regiment to Cumberland, to relieve a detachment he feared was under attack. So matters had stood at midday of June 16. A few hours later Scott telegraphed Patterson that the Confederates had evacuated Harpers Ferry, rendering part of Patterson's force unnecessary; Scott wanted some of those troops back for defense of the capital, and he named Burnside and all Patterson's Regulars in particular.[18] It may well have been a token of Scott's opinion of Burnside—arrived at during inspections and reviews since the end of April—that he lumped the Rhode Island regiment with Regular troops and took them from the lackadaisical commander in western Maryland.

If, indeed, General Scott had developed a high regard for Burnside, he was not the only professional officer who had. Patterson's assistant adjutant general, Fitz John Porter, was one West Point classmate of George McClellan's who thought of Burnside as one of the top soldiers in the country. On the day of Lincoln's call for troops, the same day Burnside accepted command of the First Rhode Island, Porter wrote McClellan to urge him back into uniform. Citing the danger to the country, he told his old friend "such men as you and Cump Sherman and Burnside are required to counterbalance the influence of Davis, Bragg, & Bearegard [sic]." Many months would pass before Porter changed his mind about Burnside's capabilities, and when he did, it would have little to do with the man's performance.[19]

II

When Burnside's men had returned to Camp Sprague from Frederick, they noticed a degree of organization that had not been evident when they departed for Pennsylvania. Someone had finally been appointed to field command of all the troops around the capital: that someone was

Brigadier General Irvin McDowell, the same stocky West Pointer who had mustered in the 1st Rhode Island a few weeks before.

No sooner had the well-traveled regiment snuggled into its tents than some newcomers came visiting: on June 22, the 2nd Rhode Island Volunteers marched in from the train depot, fresh from Camp Burnside, in Providence. The commander of this new three-year regiment was Colonel John Slocum, formerly Burnside's major in the 1st. The three-months men shared their breakfast with these reinforcements, who afterward sidled off into some nearby woods to pitch their own tents. The two units drilled and ate together thereafter and constituted an informal brigade. With the 2nd came a battery of six James rifles, which arrived just in time to fill a void: the three-months battery in Burnside's regiment soon packed up to return to Patterson, on the upper Potomac.[1]

On the same day the militia battery departed for Williamsport, July 9, the 2nd Rhode Island's battery went out on the parade field for drill; during that exercise a poorly packed ammunition chest exploded. The corporal responsible for that caisson died in the blast, a few privates were maimed, and the entire Rhode Island contingent learned a rough lesson. Until that moment, they had seen no soldier die a violent death; a bit of the allure faded from their war as they reflected that anyone among them could be as readily mutilated.

The coming of the new regiment was a personal relief to Ambrose Burnside, for the officious Governor Sprague took up new quarters with Colonel Slocum. The impetuous young man had journeyed to Washington in order to be commander of his state's forces, but discovered he could exercise no real command. In his attempt to act as a brigadier, he emerged as more of a bothersome volunteer aide, ready to do the bidding of anyone of rank who ventured within range.[2]

President Lincoln and General Winfield Scott, the senior officer of the U.S. Army, had been badgering McDowell, for political reasons, to make a movement against the enemy. McDowell dutifully decided to attack the Confederate army at Manassas Junction, under P. G. T. Beauregard, though he would much rather have taken more time to train his own new troops. As July opened, McDowell had about seventeen thousand men, with more coming all the time. Most of those present were ninety-day regiments like the 1st Rhode Island, whose terms expired late in July or early in August, so it behooved the new commander to do something quickly, if he were to do anything at all. He grouped the assorted regiments into brigades, mixing the militia and the long-term volunteers together, then lumped these brigades into lopsided divisions.

The army that grew thus, after the Fourth of July celebration, was one led by field officers. Two division commanders and one brigadier wore stars by virtue of state commissions tendered by their governors; only McDowell was a "real" general, by the hand of the president and Congress. All the rest of the high command consisted of colonels, many of them beyond middle age. The Rhode Island regiments found themselves brigaded under Colonel David Hunter, who soon ascended to division command. Hunter was just short of fifty-nine years old. He had graduated from West Point a couple of years before Burnside drew breath; but for one ten-year lapse he had been in the army ever since. Later, like many of the officers in McDowell's army, he would earn a retroactive promotion to brigadier general, but for the upcoming campaign he was officially the colonel of the 3rd U.S. Cavalry, doing detached duty.[3]

At its final organization, Hunter's division included only two brigades, the first under Colonel Andrew Porter of the 16th U.S. Infantry and the second under Colonel Burnside. Burnside's contained four regiments: the two from Rhode Island, the 2nd New Hampshire, and the 71st New York Militia.

Burnside's brigade typified an untidy diversification of arms and equipment in that infant national army. His Rhode Islanders, though dressed similarly in blue blouses and grey trousers, with broadbrimmed black hats, were not armed the same: the 1st regiment carried new Springfield rifles, while the 2nd had had to settle for old .69 caliber smoothbores. The 2nd New Hampshire, in its grey uniforms and forage caps, could have passed for Confederate troops; it also shouldered the short-range smoothbores, except for Company B: courtesy of the private donations of Concord citizens, Company B went to war equipped with the new Sharps breechloading rifles. The 71st New York wore its own version of the antebellum militia uniform, dressed down for the field, but the weapons it carried remain a mystery.[4]

Ironically, the two militia organizations were much better prepared for an active campaign, particularly Burnside's own. When McDowell finally issued his marching orders, those two regiments had been in uniform nearly three months, improving themselves with constant drill these ten weeks. The 1st Rhode Island had already had a taste of the killing marches that would be required and had made a good showing. The 2nd Rhode Island and 2nd New Hampshire, on the other hand, had been in Washington barely three weeks. For the only time during the war, the militiamen would be more dependable than the three-year volunteers.

Each of these regiments lined up July 16 to collect marching rations—salt pork and hardtack. In the afternoon they filed toward their rendezvous across the Potomac, marching between sidewalks littered with curious citizens, some of whom rushed the news that McDowell was on the move to the Confederates, while others lavished garlands of flowers on the troops. Burnside's brigade came together from three different camps and formed ranks for the first time; over the Long Bridge they went, the bands playing "Dixie" and Burnside loaded down with bouquets as the first man stepped on Virginia soil. They marched no farther than Bailey's Cross Roads that first day, five miles from Washington and three miles short of the Little River Turnpike. Rail fences bordering that intersection disappeared as these jubilant soldiers roasted their rations, the fat pork sizzling by the pound at the end of several thousand ramrods. Most of the men ate provisions intended for an entire day at this single sitting, going to bed on rubber blankets under an open sky. There were no tents—these remained standing in Washington, under the care of that inevitable percentage of invalids. Ten miles ahead lay Fairfax Court House, where McDowell expected to have to fight.[5]

A heavy dew saturated the men as they awoke, but before they fell in once more they were dry from breakfast fires and the heat of the morning sun. McDowell put Burnside's brigade in the lead that morning—a decision suggesting particular confidence, considering that the general anticipated an engagement in the vicinity of Fairfax Court House. About four miles out on the Little River Turnpike Burnside began to find primitive impediments the enemy had left for him: nothing more imaginative than a tree across the road here and there, to give the obviously forewarned Confederates time to concentrate and prepare. Axmen from the New Hampshire regiment quickly cleared the obstructions.

One feature that did slow the Union column was a border of blackberry bushes alongside the road. In deference to the holiday atmosphere of the march, men stopped at will to gorge themselves on the ripe fruit. From the foremost company in Burnside's brigade to the last one in the army, captains and lieutenants screamed in vain as men left the ranks. Sometimes officers picked a few berries themselves.

The atmosphere turned a tad more sober when Confederate earthworks loomed ahead. Burnside signalled his men to load their weapons, then trotted out in front to deliver the speech every soldier expected in 1861, warning them that danger lay ahead but reminding them their country was watching—wives, mothers, sisters, sweethearts, and so on—or words to that effect. It all ended rather melodramatically when the lead regiment deployed and rolled into town to find it abandoned by the enemy. The Stars and Bars flew from the courthouse cupola, but the anxious Yankees could not raise a single armed Confederate. The perennial flag-catchers from Rhode Island stormed up the courthouse steps to tear down the Southern emblem, running up the colors of the 2nd New Hampshire in its place.[6]

Burnside did not take the lead the next morning. His brigade had camped east of the village, and followed Andrew Porter's brigade back through town the next day. Considerable looting had evidently taken place. That sort of thing disturbed the old soldier in Burnside; pillage could debilitate an invading army, for it tended to demoralize the troops, shifting their attention from duty to plunder. But nearly as important to Burnside was the point that Southern property ought to be respected if, as the government maintained, this rebellion had been imposed on most Southerners by a vocal and active minority. Now, and for some time to come, Burnside adhered to the conservative doctrine that distinguished between what he called rebels and people who merely resided in states that had seceded—between slaveholders and participating Confederates. When he had seen a bit more of the Confederacy and a good deal more of the war, he would finally come to perceive that the elimination of slavery was a necessary prerequisite to restoration of the union, but never would he approve of the wanton vandalism or theft of civilian property. Still, he witnessed much in that line today. By the time he reached the next village, Germantown, Union soldiers had reduced it to ashes.

The cinders of Germantown marked the spot where the road divided. The Warrenton Turnpike veered slightly south of west from here, toward the little settlement of Centreville and a stream called Bull Run. This was the route the army followed.

The Confederates sat behind Bull Run, waiting for the Yankees. At first McDowell thought to turn Beauregard's right, and toward that end he sent a reconnaissance to Blackburn's Ford under Daniel Tyler—one of the two militia generals still with the army. What ought to have been a simple movement to draw the enemy's fire resulted in a sharp fight and a near rout, one New York regiment coming back helter-skelter, and the affair cooled the army's enthusiasm. There had not been a hundred casualties, but the little thrashing discouraged these green troops disproportionately.

Burnside's men could hear the sound of the fighting. Later, few of them would have called it a battle, but now they reacted to every minor conflict, and the repulse had a commensurate effect on morale; they went gloomily into camp on the north side of the pike, a mile short of Centreville, to cook the remnants of their provisions and nurse their sore feet.[7]

Some had no food left. Unaccustomed to stinting themselves, they had disposed of this third day's ration long ago. McDowell knew his men would fight poorly if they were hungry; he wished to give himself every advantage, and it was partly to allow time for bringing up commissary stores that he kept his army sitting at Centreville more than two full days. Tyler's division squatted across the turnpike a mile west of town while three other divisions camped behind the ridge that bisected the village. McDowell left his fifth division several miles back, commanded by another homegrown brigadier who would not again be heard from during this war.

After the fiasco at Blackburn's Ford, the brawny new army chief conducted his own reconnaissances. He satisfied himself that he could not turn Beauregard's right and so determined to go around his left. His engineer, Major John Barnard, led several staff officers on a survey of the roads northwest of the Warrenton Turnpike. The ubiquitous Governor Sprague accompanied him. Barnard encountered Confederate videttes and decided not to finish his expedition for fear of arousing their suspicion, but with help from a loyal citizen he sketched out a route for a turning movement.

About eight o'clock on the evening of July 20, McDowell illuminated his tent with lanterns and candles, spread out his maps, and called in sixteen brigade and division commanders, who elbowed together while he explained his new strategy: a feint at Beauregard's front with a simultaneous attack on his left. Dixon Miles would cover Centreville and Blackburn's Ford against any threat from the Confederate right while Tyler's four brigades moved up the turnpike to Bull Run and engaged the enemy's attention at the stone bridge there. McDowell's other two divisions would turn northwest along the farm road to Sudley's Ford: Hunter's division would lead that column, with Burnside's brigade in front.

McDowell wanted to advance his flanking column toward Sudley's that evening, to put it in better position for an early assault the morning of the twenty-first. If Burnside's brigade was to lead that flank march, it would have to cover the greatest distance, so the colonel asked McDowell if he might start for his objective the next morning. Major Barnard represented the route as only six miles, and the men would tire less if they could make a single march, after a solid six hours of sleep. Burnside may also have been worried about the confusion that could result from camping and subsequently reforming on unfamiliar ground in total darkness. McDowell, equally concerned about the freshness of his flanking column, readily agreed.[8]

Burnside roused his troops at one o'clock in the morning and wrestled them into line. He fully intended to move them down the Warrenton Turnpike at two, with the expectation that Tyler's division would be in motion soon enough to be out of his way. Tyler, however, was extremely slow: he had three miles to go, but spent three and a half hours reaching his position. One of his batteries hauled along a 30-pounder Parrott rifle, a behemoth that rolled like a Trojan horse; it threatened to cave in the old wooden bridge over Cub Run. While Tyler put construction crews to work bracing up that structure, Burnside's force stood impatiently in ranks, shifting from one foot to the other. A blazing summer's sun crept nearer the horizon.[9]

Tyler's lumbering column finally cleared the way sometime before six, and Burnside was able to turn his brigade off the turnpike on the road to Sudley Ford. In the interest of greater speed, he brought his command into columns abreast on the road and in the adjoining fields, the New York regiment following the troika formed by the others, but soon the vaunted flanking road narrowed to a virtual cowpath, and the brigade had to string out in single file again. To make matters worse, the engineer officer guiding the movement passed a couple of shortcuts out of concern that they would bring the troops too close to the enemy and give the maneuver away. Thus, with the division already late and the men beginning to suffer from the heat and dust, the journey stretched from the anticipated six miles to more than ten.[10]

When the foremost regiments emerged from the woods and found Sudley Ford, the officers' watches averaged nine o'clock. The parched soldiers broke column and lined up at the run, gulping the turgid water and refilling their canteens. They could hardly be dissuaded, so Burnside allowed them a brief rest, joining Colonel Hunter for a little luncheon under a tree. Just then General McDowell himself galloped up, having shouldered his way up the crowded road to see what was holding up his program: Tyler's diversion had already been under way for hours.

The cautious engineer officer with the flanking force, Captain Daniel Woodbury, had led the column several extra miles to no avail, for while the New England troops lounged along the creek and the New Yorkers came dragging in, a Confederate officer in a signal tower at Beauregard's headquarters turned his binoculars on them. His signalman wigwagged news of the sighting to another tower near the stone bridge, and within minutes the message lay in the hands of Colonel Nathan Evans, a South Carolinian in charge of a demi-brigade at the bridge. This bold young man—he was the same age as Ambrose Burnside and had been a year behind him at the military academy—left four companies to stall Tyler's entire division and took the rest of his troops to stunt the Union thrust. With the balance of the 4th South Carolina, Major Roberdeau Wheat's battalion of Louisiana zouaves, and a squadron of cavalry, Evans marched to an elevated position perpendicular to the Sudley Springs Road. He strung these thousand-or-so men and a brace of fieldpieces along the crest of Matthews Hill and bid them lay down to wait.[11]

Signal flags were not the only innovation aiding the Confederates that day: Beauregard's somewhat outnumbered army was drawing reinforcements by railroad, the first wartime use of that sort of logistics. As McDowell had long feared, General Patterson had been unable to contain Joe Johnston's Confederate force at Winchester. Johnston sat in Beauregard's headquarters that very moment, while his regiments unloaded at regular intervals on the Manassas Gap Railroad.

Lest such reinforcements come into line soon enough to repel his flank attack, McDowell urged Hunter and his division ahead. Burnside put the 2nd Rhode Island in the van again, but warned Colonel Slocum to fan out some flankers and skirmishers. Within a few moments, Evans's Confederates opened up on these reluctant harbingers and stopped the column cold. Burnside ordered Slocum to deploy his entire regiment and battery and pushed him ahead, but Evans maintained such a fierce fire that the Rhode Islanders and their smoothbores could get nowhere.

Hunter rode ahead to see what was happening, while Burnside formed the New Hampshire and New York regiments in a line of battle. A few minutes later Hunter came back wounded, telling Burnside to take charge of the action. Burnside immediately tried to bring the 71st New York and 2nd New Hampshire to the front, but the green Granite Staters were still having trouble with his earlier commands and confounded the militiamen in their own confusion, so Burnside turned to his old 1st Rhode Island and hurried it to the side of the 2nd. With the additional pressure of these hundreds of Springfield muskets, the Confederates began to soften a little. Presently the New Yorkers untangled themselves from the New Hampshire regiment and went into action; in the midst of all this, Governor Sprague bothered Burnside for something to do. The busy colonel told him he might see to the battery, which Colonel Slocum had apparently not yet unlimbered, and position it where it might bring the most effective fire to bear. The continued survival of Evans's two little guns and the stubborn resistance of his infantry testified to the poverty of that spunky but inept little politician's performance that day.[12]

Despite an initial superiority of numbers, Burnside's brigade took a severe beating. Colonel Slocum fell, shot through skull and ankle; his major's leg was smashed by a solid shot, and two of his captains were killed. So convoluted did the New Hampshire regiment become in the execution of another complicated maneuver that it left the Rhode Island battery without support in a dangerous position; Burnside finally raced across the Sudley Road to ask Colonel Porter for the use of his battalion of Regulars. Porter obliged, afraid that Burnside's collapse would leave him cut off, and the Rhode Islander coaxed the Regulars into a trot.

At last the clumsy New Hampshiremen squeezed into the firing line, but by now Colonel Evans had greeted some help. General Barnard Bee rode up at the head of two of his regiments, the 4th Alabama and the 2nd Mississippi—part of Johnston's Winchester army. Attached to Bee's 2nd were two companies of the 11th Mississippi, in which served six of Ambrose Burnside's westering cousins.[13]

These fresh Confederates trotted up just in time. Major Wheat had led his battalion in a reckless charge only moments before: he shook Burnside's line but did not break it; Wheat had been desperately wounded, and his fancifully clad Louisiana Tigers had been thrown back.

At this moment there was great potential for confusion. Wheat's zouaves wore striped trousers, shell jackets, and red fezzes: they looked as though they might have come from the Barbary Coast, or from either army; Burnside's men were variously clad in grey, blue, or a combination; other Confederates, at least those of the 11th Mississippi, wore light trousers, dark blue bib-front blouses, and broadbrimmed black hats that rendered them indistinguishable from either of the Rhode Island regiments. As the 27th New York, of Porter's brigade, came up on Burnside's right, it ran into a strong force of men in grey uniforms. Thinking this might be the 8th New York Militia, they held their fire; the newcomers were Confederates, however, as a withering volley soon testified.[14]

Porter had fully deployed his brigade on Burnside's right now, and Heintzelman's division began arriving on the field. McDowell ordered Heintzelman to extend Burnside's left with a regiment, so he sent in the 1st Minnesota. Under all this weight the Confederates reeled farther back toward the Warrenton Turnpike, despite the arrival of another half-brigade of Georgians under Colonel Francis Bartow. As the Southern line gave ground, it uncovered a ford upstream from the stone bridge, and William Sherman's brigade of Tyler's division waded across. Another brigade, under Colonel Erasmus Keyes, followed Sherman. This demolished the Confederate resistance, and the six Southern regiments scampered beyond the turnpike, up the slope of Henry House Hill. Union forces swept ahead.[15]

No Union brigade had been in close combat so long as Burnside's, and his men were rapidly running out of ammunition. Only the last regiment to reach the firing line, the 2nd New Hampshire, had much of a supply. Burnside represented his problem to McDowell, who directed him to pull back and replenish his cartridge boxes. The Rhode Islander left the 2nd New Hampshire to support his battery, but his three other

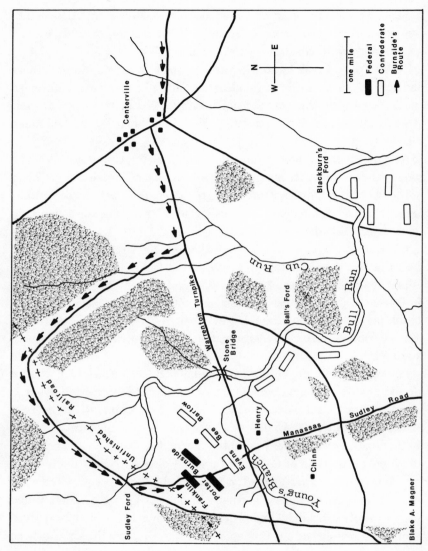

Map 1.
First Bull Run

regiments took cover in an oak thicket on Matthew's Hill, watching as their comrades drove the enemy to the top of the opposite eminence. While the battle swirled around widow Henry's house, the men who had opened the fight cared for their wounded and waited for the ammunition wagons.

Replenishing ammunition was a slow process, as each company lined up at the wagon and took two prefilled tins per man. Not much longer than an hour after Burnside had fallen back, a courier brought him word that Heintzelman needed the support of one of his regiments, but as none of the other three had been fully resupplied, he ordered up the 2nd New Hampshire. The Granite Staters started down the Sudley Road under their lieutenant colonel: their colonel had long since been carried away with a shoulder wound.[16]

Back when General Bee's regiments were falling apart and Burnside's men ambled toward the rear for cartridges, Brigadier General Thomas Jackson had formed his Virginia brigade atop Henry House Hill. His determined defense there earned him the nickname of "Stonewall" almost with Bee's dying breath, and now both Beauregard and Joe Johnston came on the field. A semblance of order materialized in the Confederate ranks. For more than two hours the outnumbered Southerners had held their ground, till reinforcements arrived. Heintzelman, whom the 2nd New Hampshire never found, failed in each of several attempts to smash this new line, until one regiment after another began fleeing in disorder. The 11th New York—the Ellsworth Zouaves—virtually disintegrated. The New Hampshire regiment approached as near the embattled hill as it could, suffering a few casualties from the devastatingly accurate Confederate cannon, and took cover under the brow of the hill as fighting continued along the plateau.

Confederate infantry worked its way around the Union right, behind the 2nd New Hampshire. Atop the hill, the confusion in uniforms allowed a Virginia regiment to approach a double battery of Union fieldpieces and mow down the gunners, at which point the Federal battle line collapsed. Militiamen and volunteers alike swarmed back down Henry House Hill, a battalion here or there in wavering cohesion but most of the men running. The 2nd New Hampshire, without orders and unaware of the peril, would have been captured to a man had Ambrose Burnside not come, personally, to look for his lost lambs. The novice soldiers hid themselves in the woods alongside the Sudley Road until

Burnside's majestic mounted form appeared in front of them, on the road, alone and undaunted. He rode a little way east on the road, took in the situation there, and trotted back to direct the New Hampshiremen into the safety of a ravine cut by a branch of Bull Run. A bit later they filed crosscountry toward the scene of the morning's fighting. With fresh ammunition, the rest of Burnside's brigade had just thrown itself across the Sudley Road to block the enemy's pursuit, and the 2nd New Hampshire fell in alongside.

Knots of wild-eyed men were stumbling toward Sudley's Ford, following the long road by which they had come. Cavalry officers and Governor Sprague cantered about futilely, trying to rally them. When Burnside's brigade finally fell into the line of retreat, these stragglers disrupted his command, but he began his withdrawal in better order than most of the brigadiers. A company of the 2nd U.S. Dragoons spread out to protect the tail of his column.[17]

All went well, considering the sudden reverse, until the brigade reached Cub Run. There, just ahead of Burnside's foremost regiment, Confederate artillery that had contributed so much to the victory struck the coup de grâce. A direct hit on the bridge overturned a wagon in the middle of the span, and the retreating column began piling up at the bottleneck. Southern guns concentrated their fire on this glut of traffic, and panic erupted on the western bank of Cub Run. Dusk at last pledged to close the steaming summer day, but these men who had marched so far and fought so long without food faced the awful prospect of a night attack on their defenseless mass. Shell and case shot played upon the piano wire their nerves had become, and those who had been brave by day succumbed to the anonymity of the growing darkness. They bolted, abandoning arms, ammunition, and supply wagons. One of the Rhode Island guns had already fallen into enemy hands, and now the artillerymen deserted the rest of the battery. Every man undertook to save himself.[18]

The retreat went on into the night and the next morning. The organized and unfought brigades of Israel Richardson and Louis Blenker formed solid pillars on either side of the Warrenton Turnpike as the wet pantlegs of defeated men fled by. Gunners without cannon and captains without companies all hurried, bleary-eyed, straight through Centreville. A large fragment of what had been Burnside's brigade collected itself on the site of the pre-battle camp and lay down for a blessed hour, but real rest was not to be had. At ten o'clock Colonel Burnside gathered what men he could, mounted his horse, and started for Washington with a thin grey-blue line trailing behind him.

The sun was several hours high Monday morning when these hungry, stumbling survivors reached the toll booth on the Long Bridge and thudded across. As the remnants of regiments veered away to their farflung former encampments, Burnside's six-day-old brigade ceased to exist.[19]

Many of the fleetfooted already loafed sheepishly about Camp Sprague when the last stalwarts arrived, and a few others who had thought to hide somewhere came dribbling in afterward. Burnside scribbled a rough draft of his report on Wednesday, and the next morning the adjutant general's office reminded him that his regiment had but a week remaining in its federal service. Ordered to prepare his men immediately for the return to Rhode Island, Burnside offered to persuade the regiment to stay on so long as the capital was in danger. General Scott personally assured him there was no immediate threat, and on the evening of July 25 the 1st Rhode Island boarded trains at the Washington depot.

Their cars left at midnight, but the regiment did not step down in Providence until July 28, one week after the battle. Four fancy militia companies met the veterans at the station and escorted them to Exchange Place, where everyone crowded into Railroad Hall to hear speeches and accolades. Five days later the 1st Rhode Island disbanded, and Ambrose Burnside became a civilian again.[20]

Some trouble developed over the first draft of Burnside's report, which he had submitted to Colonel Hunter the moment he was ordered to leave Washington. In it, Burnside recorded the colonel had told him, as Hunter left the battlefield wounded, "to take charge of the formation of the division in the presence of the enemy." Doubtless Hunter had said something very much like that, or Burnside would not have dared return such a report to him. Still, Colonel Andrew Porter thought this challenged his succession to the command of the division, although at that juncture he had not yet arrived on the field. Apparently mounting a little vendetta on that unintended slight, Porter employed subtle sarcasm in his own report to imply that Burnside's brigade had done but little fighting. He disputed Burnside's remark that his brigade had acted as the army's rear guard during the retreat and suggested his men had departed the field ahead of Porter's own brigade. Burnside replied that he had not meant to overlook Porter, but that in writing under the pressure of time, he had inadvertently phrased the sentence ambiguously. What he had meant to say was that Hunter told him to form "that part of the division in the presence of the enemy." That explanation is perfectly plausible, for nowhere else in his battle report does Burnside suggest that he had command of anything more than his own brigade. Porter's complaint evinced the oversensitivity not uncommon among Old Army martinets, and his other criticisms were altogether unfounded. While most of Burnside's brigade left the fighting during the latter half of the battle, it seems to have done heavier service than Porter's: Porter's brigade was about 20 percent larger than Burnside's, which nevertheless suffered 87 percent the number of killed and wounded Porter reported; but Porter's loss in captured and missing was 50 percent greater than Burnside's.

If, amid the confusion of the rout, Burnside's brigade did precede Porter's from the field, it may be that Burnside mistook Porter's men for the enemy, or he may have been altogether unable to see them through the smoke and the swarming wreckage of other regiments. He had, besides, been specifically ordered to guard the rear. Everyone, in fact, had been ordered to cover the retreat, and no fewer than four brigadiers besides Burnside claimed to have been the last from the field. One even pointed to the profusion of officers quoted in the newspapers as having claimed the honor of guarding the retreat before asserting that he, alone, was the man who had done so.[21] The problem lay not in the honesty of the disputants—necessarily—but in the absolute pandemonium of the rout of an untrained army. Porter's specious accusation was but the first of many officers' attempts to salvage or embellish their own reputations at the expense of Ambrose Burnside.

Despite a sound performance, Burnside made one major contribution (albeit an indirect one) to Union defeat on July 21. On Saturday evening, when McDowell ordered a nighttime advance on the Confederate left, it had been only Burnside's appeal that persuaded him to postpone the march until early morning. Logical as Burnside's idea was, considering the available information, that delay set the stage for

a tardy flank attack, which allowed Nathan Evans the leisure to suspect
Tyler's feint and gave Beauregard time enough to bolster his left and
land the haymaker.

III

On the same day Ambrose Burnside marched his regiment out of Camp
Sprague, his old friend George McClellan assumed command of all the
troops around Washington. Mac arrived in the city less than twenty-four
hours after Burnside had left. The newly mustered-out colonel must
have been quite gratified to read this news in the *Providence Journal*
and even more pleased when, on August 6, he received from Lincoln's
desk a commission as brigadier general of United States Volunteers,
with orders to report to McClellan at the capital. It should have been
most frustrating for Governor Sprague: only four days before, he had
written General McClellan asking if he could not be of some service—at
division level—but while Burnside donned an unsolicited star, no commission came for Sprague. To the detriment of Rhode Island and the
benefit of the army, William Sprague remained in politics and, for the
most part, out of field operations.[1]

In Burnside's first assignment, he replaced Fitz John Porter as commander of the provisional brigades. These were the rawest troops, confined in camps of instruction on the Washington side of the river until
they were armed, equipped, and sufficiently trained to go into battle
without shooting too many of their friends, after which they were transferred to the advanced camps in Virginia. The commander of these
new men did little more than a glorified quartermaster and drillmaster;
Burnside quickly tired of the job.[2]

Less than a week after he arrived on the Potomac, Burnside had
his first taste of that backstabbing spirit that would become endemic
in the Army of the Potomac, as McClellan named his new command.
The specifics of the attack are not clear; McClellan merely referred to
it as "some slanders," but it was probably associated with a lingering
grudge on the part of Andrew Porter, who now served as McClellan's
provost marshal. The matter itself was of so little importance that no
one ever remembered it afterward—and people usually recalled any-

thing slanderous about General Burnside—but it revealed something about George McClellan's attitude toward old friends, now that he was a national figure. In just seventeen words of a letter to his wife, the new major general divulged how bored he was with "Burn's" brief attempt to explain his side of the story.[3] One can fairly see McClellan's fingers drumming on the desk.

For all of McClellan's preoccupation, Burnside gained his attention long enough to unfold an idea he had about an amphibious division. Discussion about combined service operations had recently become the rage in Washington: General Thomas W. Sherman, formerly captain of the company to which Burnside was attached at Fort Adams, had just won authorization to raise a division for use in conjunction with a naval force, and a political general from Massachusetts named Ben Butler had recently joined with Flag Officer Silas Stringham to capture Hatteras Inlet, on the Outer Banks of North Carolina. Burnside's notion was to recruit a few brigades specifically for such enterprises, including veteran seamen among them who could readily man their own boats and ships, if necessary. McClellan immediately liked the idea (so much so that he took full credit for it, two years later), and he told Burnside to reduce it to a formal proposal. With his usual inability to set aside an interesting project, Burnside submitted a detailed plan the next day.[4]

Having lived both in the pioneer West and the industrializing East, Burnside had an image of the occupational skills of the residents of those respective areas. From his years in Rhode Island and New York he had learned how great a proportion of sailors and mechanics there were in those places; he theorized that a division raised from those coastal states would, by the mere luck of the draw, include men with all the skills necessary to navigate and maintain light-draft ships in Southern waters, capturing inlets here and there, from which they could also conduct future operations against the Confederate interior. Technological self-sufficiency was an essential ingredient to the success of isolated coastal expeditions.

As soon as the War Department approved the plan, Burnside went to New York to recruit troops and arrange for the purchase or charter of the vessels necessary for such a venture. First, he made the rounds of the New York and New England governors to ask for troops. Thomas Sherman simultaneously pressured them for men, but they all promised a regiment or two apiece. Burnside established a temporary camp for his prospective division at Hempstead, Long Island, but he left most of the subsequent recruiting to Simon Cameron, secretary of war, who ordered each of the promised regiments to him once they were mustered into federal service. As it happened, the only governor who resisted Burnside was William Sprague, who made the odd complaint that detailing the 4th Rhode Island to coast duty would be detrimental to its organization. Burnside took no part in this little tempest; for the moment he had turned his attention to the search for suitable craft to carry his waterborne army, the target of which remained unchosen. Finding ships that could weather the open sea and still surmount shallow bars was no mean feat and proved expensive: one small but particularly desirable steamer was offered at $175 per day, and a few months after the contract had been agreed upon, the owners howled for more. Burnside also needed a few score of surf boats, for loading large contingents quickly, and he bought a number of canal boats, in connection with a design he had developed for converting them to floating batteries. He pursued the material for his flotilla personally, inspecting the craft closely and failing only to crawl into a diving suit to check the depth of their keels. So vigorously did he go about the work that he sprained his ankle while bounding around one potential craft.[5]

General Sherman's force took ship from Annapolis October 21, and Burnside immediately began transferring his accumulated troops there. Now that the regiments were actually gathering, the time had come to consider where they might be used. At one point Burnside asked for a detailed report on affairs in Texas from a man familiar with that state, supposing that its sparsely inhabited Gulf Coast might be inviting, but early in November a visitor came to Washington whose testimony narrowed the focus of consideration.[6]

That visitor was Rush Hawkins, colonel of the 9th New York Volunteers, a dapper regiment that wore a high-toned zouave uniform. Hawkins had participated in the capture of the two forts guarding Hatteras Inlet, and for a time thereafter he had commanded Union forces on Hatteras Island. His haughty pride and condescending attitude had already caused much trouble. He had not been at Hatteras ten days before he offended another colonel, whose men he characterized as "vandals" for pillaging Confederate camps and private homes. True though that may have been, Hawkins insinuated the other officer was a party to the looting, and he threatened to turn Fort Clark's guns on his men if they did not behave. A month later, when a brigadier general traveled down to take over Hawkins's command, the New York colonel scribbled a nasty note to the department commander who had sent him, accusing that general of a personal slight and damning an ungrateful government. "I do not seek promotion," he protested, with bitter disappointment. "Brigadier-generals are made of such queer stuff nowadays, that I should not esteem it any very great honor to be made one." The letter found its way to Winfield Scott, bearing the redundant endorsement that it was insubordinate, but no formal action resulted. Within a matter of a few more weeks, the new post commander arrested Hawkins for refusing to assign a captain whose qualifications he challenged, but he survived that controversy as well. Despite his belligerence, Hawkins's superiors sent him by special boat to see President Lincoln: Hawkins had made some suggestions in his early dispatches that intrigued Lincoln, and both he and George McClellan seated themselves behind a conference table to hear what the opinionated aristocrat thought.[7]

Hawkins thought, among other things, that the counties around Pamlico Sound were brimming with citizens loyal to the government of the United States. He thought federal authorities could easily recruit troops there to suppress the rebellion. These were theories Abraham Lincoln desperately wanted to believe, for the reestablishment of loyal state governments was a subject dear to his heart. McClellan, whom the president had just named to supersede Winfield Scott as commander of all the nation's armies, found more interest in the colonel's strategic suggestions. Two months before, Hawkins had proposed the capture of Roanoke Island and the occupation of both the Neuse and Pamlico rivers, plus the town of Beaufort. He must have reiterated those plans at the Washington conference, for when McClellan finally discussed the specifics of the operation with Burnside, the goals and the order of their achievement remained identical.[8]

The interview with Hawkins occurred on Tuesday, November 5. Two days later, in New York, the Cooper Institute hosted a benefit lecture for the Union citizens of North Carolina. Historian George Bancroft introduced two ministers straight from there, who described the sufferings of loyal people along the Outer Banks. After an address by the president of the institute, Ambrose Burnside rose to the sound of three cheers and the greatest applause of the evening: his strong, bald form was well known in New York, and now he struggled to give the speech

he had promised on the wharf, in April. Briefly, he appealed for money
for the coastal Unionists; the rest of his words concerned the new commander of the armies, for whom he asked forbearance and confidence.
He lauded McClellan's competence, honesty, and selflessness to a degree he might have modified two years hence, and it was with difficulty
that subsequent speakers brought the direction of the affair back to the
destitute Tarheels. William Cullen Bryant took the podium after the
general sat down, and the evening ultimately produced a satisfactory
purse. Some of those funds paid the passage of one of the ministers back
to Hatteras: ten days later a rump convention chartered a provisional
state government there, with the Reverend Marble Nash Taylor—one
of the Cooper Institute guests—as governor.[9]

Burnside's appearance at the benefit may have had no relation to the
meeting between Hawkins, Lincoln, and McClellan, but the New York
colonel's special delivery to Washington indicated that the administration had a wide eye cast on North Carolina. While Burnside addressed
the New York audience, General Sherman's soldiers settled into battered Confederate works around the harbor of Port Royal, South Carolina. That augured well for another base of operations between Port
Royal and Fort Monroe. A few days later, Secretary of the Navy Gideon
Welles received a memorial from Flag Officer Louis M. Goldsborough,
commander of the North Atlantic Squadron, outlining a plan to secure
Pamlico Sound by means of a joint army-navy effort. That seems to
have decided the matter.[10]

The day after the benefit lecture, Mary Burnside took a room at the
Astor House. She was a dainty creature who befriended people as easily
as her husband. Her friends knew her as Molly, but though she never
bore any children, her towering husband habitually called her Mother.
The general was still shuttling back and forth between New York and
Washington; he had no time for detours to Providence now, so his wife
resolved to await him at least on one end of the rail corridor.[11]

Burnside was a devoted family man, and even amid this ceaseless
activity he found time for his own. His relatives by both blood and
marriage looked upon him as the patriarch. In Providence, Molly's wid-
owed mother depended more on her son-in-law than on her son, whose
brood of daughters occupied most of his attention and resources, and
back in Indiana his father's death had left him the clan leader by a sort
of silent acclamation. He provided most of the support for his ailing,

unmarried sister Ellen, who still lived on the family farm, and it was Treasurer Burnside's influence with the president of the Illinois Central that landed his younger brother—Benjamin Franklin Burnside—a job on that line.

Since the summer of 1859, Ben had lived at Freeport, Illinois, acting as the company's agent for land sales and earning what seemed to him a comfortable commission. He had also been doubling as something of an agent for "Brose," as he called his elder brother, overseeing the management of a section of prairie the general had bought in Monee, twenty-five miles south of Chicago, and handling some of his remaining Chicago bank accounts. The final months of 1861 were not very productive for Ben, though, and as his more famous brother entered his last few weeks of preparation for the amphibious expedition, Ben began sending none-too-subtle hints that he could use Brose's help. To begin with, Illinois Central president William H. Osborn had transferred him from the lucrative main line to a branch, where his commissions barely exceeded his expenses. The company's surplus land, or the demand for it, had dwindled to the point where the land agent's services were superfluous, and though Osborn eventually sent him back to the main trunk, it was only for a couple of months: then, with a sheaf of handsomely worded recommendations, the board of directors let him go altogether. On top of this, both Ben and Ellen had been sick, and Ben supposed his coffers might turn up empty before winter was over. Neither had he had much success with the Monee farm. After putting in a hundred and twenty acres of wheat, he had reaped far fewer than the twelve hundred bushels he expected, at a cost of more than nine hundred dollars for planting and harvesting. At one point he even considered joining the army, from which his brother dissuaded him with the argument that he had too large a family. General Burnside, who had the benefit of both his salaries as a brigadier general and treasurer of the railroad, as well as some remunerative investments in Illinois and New York, characteristically told Ben that his pocketbook was open to him.[12]

Nor was Ben the only Burnside who relied upon the general. His aging Uncle Andrew, who also lived in Freeport, kept himself supplied with railroad passes through Burnside's capacity with the Illinois Central. Nephew Ambrose did not seem averse to using his private position for the benefit of his kin, but his public office was another matter: when Uncle Andrew pressed for a staff job for his son Edward, General Burnside would give him nothing of the kind, sending Edward unceremoniously back home. Nor, later, would he even endorse his cousin James's Treasury Department application for a routine trading permit. Familial benevolence ended where the public trust began.[13]

Less than two weeks after Mrs. Burnside arranged family quarters at the Astor House, William Sprague followed her there. Not yet discouraged from basking in the glory of Rhode Island's favorite son, the governor may have promised to pose too great an interruption during the general's weekend visits with his wife: the day after Sprague's arrival, Mr. and Mrs. Burnside transferred their lodgings to the Fifth Avenue Hotel.[14]

Toward the end of the year, Burnside had to reinterest himself in the assignment of brigadiers and acceptable troops. The men he wanted to command his brigades were all West Point classmates and, aside from McClellan, perhaps his closest friends. He first sought the services of John G. Foster, class of '46. Later, he petitioned for Jesse Reno and John Parke. Like Foster, Reno had come out of the military academy in 1846 and had fought in Mexico; Parke graduated second in his class the year after that war ended, but despite his lack of combat experience, he impressed Burnside with technical competence and an unselfish devotion to duty.[15] Burnside asked for what troops the New England states were raising in predominantly coastal areas, though many of the companies that reached him were inlanders to a man. In most cases he had to take regiments just as they rolled out of the various recruiting camps, with the result that their numbers ran almost consecutively. The 4th and 5th Rhode Island Volunteers joined his division, the 8th, 10th, and (after much pleading) the 11th Connecticut, and all but two of the 21st through 27th Massachusetts regiments.[16]

Burnside tried to compose his staff of officers whose qualifications he knew as well as those of his brigadiers. He applied for Lieutenant Charles J. Turnbull for his topographical engineer, but General Butler had already spoken for him, and he took Lieutenant W. S. Andrews instead. For an ordnance officer he preferred Henry W. Kingsbury. Kingsbury was a native of Connecticut and an honor graduate of the military academy—he had been under fire at Bull Run barely a month after his graduation—but he was also a family friend of Burnside's. Mrs. Burnside was somehow a beneficiary of his father, Julius Kingsbury, who died in Chicago about 1860, and Burnside himself had been asked to be an executor of the estate. Mr. Kingsbury's only other child had married Simon Bolivar Buckner, of Kentucky, now a Confederate general: she conveyed her inheritance to Henry as soon as the war began, and years later Burnside would have to unravel a tangle of documents to determine whether she did so to protect her interest or because she meant for her brother to have her share. He made a faithful and diligent executor, and Burnside expected Lieutenant Kingsbury would offer the same qualities as a member of his staff. Just for now, the War Department had other plans for Kingsbury and gave the position to Daniel Flagler, who had not yet completed his final year at West Point.[17]

Most of the rest of Burnside's staff appointments went to Rhode Islanders he had previously measured, or who came recommended by acquaintances whose judgment he trusted. The most visible position was that of assistant adjutant general, who was somewhat of an executive secretary, with the duties of overseeing the clerks and correspondence for commanders of brigades and larger units. The name of the AAG became synonymous with that of the general he served, and for that role Burnside chose Lewis Richmond, a thirty-seven-year-old dry goods merchant from Providence who had served as a private in the 1st Rhode Island.[18] He also attached two private secretaries, who temporarily agreed to serve without rank. One of them, Daniel Larned, came to him almost by accident. He was a younger son of another old Rhode Island family, and like many later children in the age of primogeniture, he had left home to seek his fortune. By the age of thirty-three he had achieved prominence in a New Haven banking house. His brother-in-law, a New York businessman, visited Burnside's office on Bowling Green Street one day in December—apparently on a whim. He asked if the general did not need another private secretary, suggesting Daniel's name. Burnside expressed some interest, but said he would leave in a day or so and could not pay much, as his staff was nearly complete, but if Larned was willing to chance a poor salary and could be in New York by the following morning, he would take him along. The brother-in-law wrote Daniel, promising the Burnside expedition would offer excitement: "The Genl is a man of action," he said, "and is on the go the whole time." With commendable speed, the post office delivered the letter in New Haven the same day, and the prospective secretary appeared at breakfast the next morning, glowing letters of introduction in hand. He had declined a quartermaster's straps in a new regiment to work for the general; in a few months he would be one of Burnside's closest friends and most loyal supporters.[19]

The New York headquarters was aflutter the day Larned arrived, as the staff prepared to transfer to Annapolis. Burnside himself set a frenzied pace as he readied the fleet for the run down from New York. He wanted all the vessels at sea by December 14 and planned to be in Washington himself by the sixteenth; the newspapers prognosticated the imminent departure of his expedition. In the bustle, he forgot to arrange passage for his servant, whom he left stranded in Providence with his horse. An auditor in the Treasury Department had to shell out five dollars to get the horse and man aboard a train.[20]

The staff ordnance position remained unclaimed by December 16, Henry Kingsbury having been neither approved nor rejected, and with his myriad other concerns Burnside had been unable to attend sufficiently to the armament of his chartered vessels. He sent his transports to Annapolis on that date, but he lingered behind to see the heavy ordnance bolted to the decks of his makeshift gunboats. It was not until Tuesday, December 17, that Mr. Larned stowed the headquarters baggage on one of the Annapolis-bound craft and joined the general for a tedious fourteen-hour train ride to Washington.

A few days before Christmas the entire headquarters family finally gathered at Annapolis—wives included. The general and Molly took room 52 at the City Hotel, and there they held a party for the staff on December 20, celebrating Christmas ahead of time in anticipation of the imminent commencement of what was—to everyone but General Burnside, now—a mysterious voyage. They might as well have waited, for the holiday passed with three green brigades continually practicing their marching, facing, wheeling, and filing under the bleak Maryland skies. Burnside occasionally reviewed them, delighting the men with the fine figure he cut atop Major, his strong (and strong-willed) gelding. He spent most of his time squinting at paperwork, though. His desk disappeared beneath requests to consider uniforms, guns, steamboats, and clerks, and he gave all this correspondence his personal eye. The two secretaries and Captain Richmond drafted his replies, but it was he who considered every detail, and daily he worked late into the evening in Larned's hotel room, so his wife might sleep. Mr. Larned soon decided Burnside pushed himself too hard, noting he had been "on the stretch" ever since they left New York. Once, well after midnight, as

Larned passed him letter after letter to sign, the general dozed off in the very act of scratching his name. Later still, as Burnside stood behind him, the secretary asked him a question; he heard no reply, and turned to find his chief leaning against the wall, literally asleep on his feet.[21]

Burnside visited Washington again the last Sunday of 1861. He, President Lincoln, and McClellan (suffering a bout of typhoid fever) made more specific plans for the campaign. Burnside reported his force ready to go, after which he returned to Annapolis to confer with Flag Officer Goldsborough. Goldsborough had been one of the early advocates of the mission about to commence, and he would escort the flotilla as well as co-operate with the land forces in battle. On January 2, fresh from one final conference at Washington, Burnside wired the flag officer that he was ready to depart, asking him to send back a big steamer he had loaned the navy. The telegram took a roundabout route through Baltimore and finally went down to Fort Monroe by boat. Goldsborough, away on blockade duty, did not read it until three days later, and three crucial days of calm weather were thus lost. Meanwhile, Burnside went back to the City Hotel. Everyone there expected sailing orders momentarily, and Mrs. Burnside (whom Larned found "quite delicate") consumed the anxious hours embroidering her husband's blankets with his initials; Mr. Larned was a bachelor, so she did the same for him. With increasing excitement and a certain measure of sadness, they awaited news from Goldsborough.[22]

2

THE CAROLINA SHORE

I

Long queues of dark blue overcoats and gun barrels corrugated the fresh down of snow at the Annapolis wharves the morning of January 6, 1862. Dories and lighters flitted back and forth, ferrying the little army from the docks to what one observer characterized as "a large city afloat." Nearly a hundred sailing vessels, steam transports, propeller gunboats, floating batteries, and U.S. Navy gunboats awaited this impatient population, which stood stamping its twenty thousand feet against the raw cold of a Chesapeake winter.[1]

The insemination of Burnside's armada had begun rather clumsily the day before; only now did the process achieve a graceful, satisfactory flow. The majority of the troops collapsed their camps or, if they had been fortunate, filed out of the brick naval academy buildings this morning, marching to the waterfront behind fluttering flags and the shrill, frostbitten notes of brass bands. Annapolis citizens contributed to the chill, either ignoring the spectacle or affording it unenthusiastic eyes. Some of the slaveowners among them missed servants this morning, and in succeeding days Ambrose Burnside would be pelted with complaints that his outward-bound soldiers had coaxed away the property of people who were at least nominally loyal. These tidewater Marylanders quickly learned the score: Union armies threatened the very warp of their social fabric, whether or not those armies were led by sound Democrats.[2]

The embarkation continued throughout January 6 and 7, the troops resting uncomfortably in place all night. Some of the more daring field officers commandeered nearby cordwood piles and had bonfires built for their men, while news of Burnside's departure radiated north and south with the smoke. The entire country seemed to be wondering at the destination of what was then considered a major expedition. One man carried his curiosity all the way to the White House and put the question to Abraham Lincoln. The harried president finally agreed to tell the petitioner where the force was headed if he swore to keep the information to himself. The man eagerly swore, and the lanky Westerner leaned melodramatically close to whisper that the expedition was "going to sea."[3]

Hostile hands—and there were many around Chesapeake Bay—carried word of the flotilla's formation to Norfolk, Richmond, and beyond. Confederate operatives may have been more resourceful than any in the North, for on the very day the first of Burnside's men bounded onto the deck of a transport, the governor of North Carolina notified Richmond of their precise destination: Pamlico Sound. The "reliable information" on which he said he based that warning was unavailable to any of the officers or men waiting in the snow on the banks of the Severn River. Besides Burnside, his three brigadiers, and a couple of staff officers, every Union soldier was contentedly ignorant of where he would next feel land beneath his shoes. Even the captains in that shoal of ships carried sealed orders, which would remain sealed until every vessel was on the open sea.[4]

General-in-Chief McClellan issued written orders January 7, confirming the discussions Burnside had had with him. This missive from McClellan's sickbed outlined the crossing of Hatteras Inlet, the seizure of Roanoke Island, the capture of Newbern, and the reduction of Fort Macon; the ailing general treated future movements upon Goldsborough, Raleigh, and Wilmington less specifically, and ended with an admonition against such provocative proclamations as the general emancipation John C. Frémont had seen fit to publish in Missouri. Included with these orders was Burnside's appointment as commander of the newly created Department of North Carolina.[5]

Wednesday, January 8, Burnside watched a final regiment of tardy New Hampshiremen clamber aboard the last empty transport, whereupon he said goodbye to Mrs. Burnside and checked out of their hotel room. Down in his new department, three full regiments of North Carolinians simultaneously started for Newbern from the interior; a fourth waited outside Goldsborough only long enough for its muskets to catch up.[6]

Burnside and his staff had reserved quarters on the *George Peabody*, one of the heavier steamers in the squadron. Such a vessel seemed appropriate to the dignity of the commander of the expedition, and the relative steadiness of her decks lent themselves to the writing of legible orders. But Larned the scrivener had hardly spread his freshly monogrammed blankets on a cabin bunk when General Burnside changed his mind. Rumors wafting through the fleet insisted the preponderance of ships were unseaworthy, and there was bad weather in the wind: in order to foster both courage and confidence by personal example, Burnside shifted his headquarters to the propeller-driven gunboat *Picket*, the smallest and most vulnerable craft within his command.[7]

The next morning, Thursday, January 9, Burnside toured the floating division in his launch, exchanging a word with each ship's captain while soldiers leaned over the rails to cheer him. He acknowledged these serial tributes by removing his hat—despite a light drizzle; by the time the *Picket* led the procession out of Annapolis harbor, his head was drenched.[8]

By Friday evening the last of the teeming transports had slipped down the bay to Fort Monroe, where the nervous steerage soldiers could climb up on deck to see the Confederate flag rippling on the far side of Hampton Roads. That night they held an illumination, a pretty sentimentality of that era: scores of glowing vessels rang with a cacophony of brassy tunes as regimental bands vied with the vocal efforts of those without instruments. The stirring little demonstration offered expression to the somber sense that these men had begun a dangerous and momentous adventure, but it was an outburst of restlessness as well. Some regiments had been crowded on board for five days now, and they wanted to get on with it, little dreaming how much longer they would be required to endure the stale air and unsavory rations belowdecks: the cramped troops already worked on each other's nerves.

A single improvised cabin, deep in one of the holds of the *Satterly*, quartered all the officers of Burnside's Signal Corps detachment. Three Regular Army lieutenants had come from Washington to organize a branch of this new service for Burnside's division, selecting two officers and four men from each regiment. The two dozen officers and half-a-hundred men had spent their last days in Annapolis "learning the flags," and they had already memorized most of the alphabetic code. Their esoteric profession was so new and mysterious that the signalmen involuntarily inclined to supercilious behavior, but once herded into their cargolike accommodations, they shed such pretensions and found one another just as irritating as their more plebeian brethren. One nineteen-year-old lieutenant complained that his fellow flagwaggers were whiling away their abundant shipboard leisure at blackjack and faro; the last words he heard each night were usually "Place your bets, gentlemen." To make matters worse, water was too scarce to allow for bathing, and what went into the canteens tasted disagreeably of the recycled whiskey barrels in which it was stored.[9]

In the darkness of January 11 the motley flotilla abandoned Fort Monroe and struck for the open Atlantic, ungainly as a cluster of pregnant women on promenade. As the ships turned in the only logical direction—south—eighty weatherworn fingers broke the wax on as many envelopes, and the name of Hatteras Inlet hissed its sibilant way down the companionways; what satisfaction the curious may have gained from the knowledge of their destination soon gave way, however, to concern over whether the argonauts would live to see the place. A few hours into the voyage the fleet encountered violent winds, and smaller vessels like the *Picket* floundered dangerously in the cradles of successive seas. Supplies and equipment pitched from their compartments and the men began to suffer from the ineluctable nausea. Only with the dawn did this turbulence subside, but there followed a thick fog that isolated each ship and rendered the intricate system of signals useless. At dusk a fresh breeze blew the meddlesome mists away, but that zephyr soon whipped itself into a greater gale than the night before. Even the big steamers hove frightfully, while those aboard the *Picket* and other small ships all but gave themselves up for lost.[10]

In the midst of this second night's tempest, the gargantuan *Eastern Queen* loomed out of the black seas off the *Picket*'s bow. The tiny ship popped one of its guns to warn the *Queen*, but she swung even closer, and the helmsman of the headquarters vessel spun his wheel desperately to avoid a collision but still maintain headway against the mountainous waves. The gale scattered the expedition the length of the coast between Cape Henry and Hatteras Light; only a fragment of it lay within Burnside's view the morning of the thirteenth. This advance guard, led by the *Picket*, lurched and lunged the final leg of the journey to the inlet, picking up strays along the way. By noon they reached Hatteras, and while those who had the stomach for it forced down some lunch, a guard boat fought its way out to offer greetings. That afternoon the little craft led the *Picket* through the breakers and over the bar. One by one, the rest of the smaller ships began to work their way in.[11]

In the fluid geography of the Outer Banks, Hatteras Inlet was somewhat new. During the 1730s a British ship grounded in an old channel, a few miles to the south, and for three decades sand, silt, and flotsam gathered around the hulk until, by 1764, the inlet had completely closed. For more than eighty years, until Ambrose Burnside was a first classman at West Point, Ocracoke and Hatteras islands were one. The night of September 7, 1846, a tremendous storm lashed the entire coast of North Carolina. In the morning there were two new gaps in the Outer Banks: Oregon Inlet, almost abreast of Roanoke Island, and Hatteras, a few miles south of a fishing village of the same name. Hatteras Inlet was not very deep. Burnside had been aware of that, which was why he had insisted upon such light-draft vessels for his fleet, the deepest of which was supposed to draw about nine feet. Their laden draft was naturally greater, though, and the bar measured about eight feet deep—two feet shallower than Burnside had been told, and then only at high tide. Those craft that could easily cross the Swash (the flat shoals that topped the bar) did so as quickly as possible, thus avoiding the worst of another gale that buffeted the cape January 13 and 14. While these luckier boats continued to bump and bash each other and run aground in the crowded anchorage in Pamlico Sound, the bigger ships started across. The supply ship *City of New York* grounded on the bar to windward, and her crewmen swarmed into the rigging. There they lashed themselves until the next day, when others saw them and took them off the doomed steamer.[12]

Some of the troops were fortunate enough to be able to land: in order that their ships might mount the bar, the ten companies of the 24th Massachusetts unloaded on the tip of Hatteras Island. The enlisted men were so overjoyed to feel earth under them again that they scampered like toddlers in every direction. It was all the officers could do to form them in line and march them the six miles to the Union camps, near Hatteras village. The soft sand overworked their sea-crazy legs, so they arrived exhausted and pitched their tents indiscriminately on the beach. (A few nights later yet another gale forced them to relocate in the dark, and the dawn found them in the cemetery where the former Confederate occupants had hastily buried their dead; the surf washed away much of the sand during the night, and the morning stench left the Bay Staters retching.)[13]

The storms persisted for nearly a fortnight. Most of the farflung expedition eventually rendezvoused around the entrance to the sound, but the *Pocahontas* never arrived: she had been driven aground off the cape and lost, along with a hundred horses intended for the Hatteras endeavor. Miraculously, the crew and all the teamsters, with nineteen horses, managed to reach shore and avoid capture.

The *Colonel Satterly* was among the last transports to arrive. Her rather overcautious captain spotted the Hatteras Light the night of January 16, but he lay to instead of joining the fleet at the inlet. During the night the ship drifted out of sight of land. On the way back, the captain sighted what he feared might be a Confederate privateer and deliberately veered off course. Thereafter he was lost, and for five days he beat about, until provisions grew short and the whiskey-water gave way to a supply flavored by turpentine barrels, which made the passengers more nauseous than ever. Finally, on January 22, the signal officers in the makeshift stateroom amidships confronted the captain and demanded he strike for land, wherever it might bring them. He vowed that he would, but that night another storm began dragging the vessel by its anchor. The seasick signalmen could not keep to their bunks, and a foot of water sloshed about in the room, dousing their lamps. The young subaltern who had objected to the gambling could not stand the close air; he went to a hatch while the ship pitched and rolled. He poked his head out briefly, and the magnificent fury of nature momentarily overawed his fear of death. "Words cannot express the grandeur and sublimity of the scene," William Draper wrote his future wife. "The waves rolled mountain high and their crests seemed on fire from the phosphorescent light. Now, we were lifted up by some huge wave high above the surrounding waters, and then we plunged down into an almost unfathomable abyss, which seemed ready to engulf us." To add to the terror betweendecks, someone smelled smoke in the gloomy passageways. Even Lieutenant Draper blanched at this prospect, for the deepest and largest of the holds were full of gunpowder. A frantic search traced the scent to the captain's cabin, where the master had determined to meet his fate with a fire in both his stomach and his stove: once a bottle of brandy had kindled the former, he made a botch of the latter, which the officers extinguished.

Blown about four hundred miles in the course of two days, the *Satterly* was not able to limp back to Hatteras until January 27, food and water nearly gone, firing off an assortment of formal and improvised distress signals. The next day the signalmen learned that New York newspapers had written their ship off as lost, one imaginative journalist even counting sixty of her dead washed ashore north of the inlet.[14]

The other ships at Hatteras, meanwhile, still rode dangerously close to each other, both in the leeward harbor and in the inlet anchorage, short of the Swash. They battered each other mercilessly and went aground with alarming frequency. The gunboat *Zouave* sank inside the bar, and though her crew got off, there was nothing that could be done to raise the little warship. There were no tugs to rescue the grounded vessels: Burnside had chartered eight from Baltimore, but with the ferocious weather none had yet dared to leave Chesapeake Bay. Anxious officers from the ships offshore braved the seas to come in for orders, and at least one of their cutters capsized. The oarsmen knew enough to cling to its overturned hull, but their passengers—the colonel and surgeon of the 9th New Jersey—tried to swim for land. Raw surf dashed their bodies on the beach. They were the first human casualties of the expedition; remarkably, theirs were the only lives lost between Annapolis and Roanoke Island.[15]

Colonel Hawkins, the New Yorker who formerly commanded the garrison at Hatteras, had told General Burnside he would find local pilots quite helpful in leading his ships over the bar. Hawkins was mistaken, as he would eventually prove to be mistaken about many things: however much knowledge of the channel might have overcome keels too deep for the bar, the pilots never materialized. Yankee ingenuity was all Burnside could rely upon, but in the end it triumphed. Burnside unloaded most of the troops and supplies from the biggest transports, lightered them ashore, then directed the ships to steam deliberately aground in the Swash, against the outgoing tide. Boat crews carried the anchors to their full extension, so the vessels held fast while the strong channel current washed the sand from beneath their hulls. When this natural action had cleared a short passage, the engineers raised steam again and plowed deeper into the sand. Oarsmen dragged the anchors ahead once more, repeating the process until each vessel surmounted the bar. It was slow work: a Confederate civilian, training his spyglass on the fleet from an Ocracoke dune, counted only twenty ships inside the sound one day in late January; two days later he reported only sixteen more.[16]

Burnside detailed his difficulties in a letter to McClellan, which he entrusted to a civilian observer, a Mr. Sheldon. Sheldon not only delivered the letter, but verbally described the Hatteras situation to President Lincoln. The president grew thoroughly discouraged as he listened to the endless obstacles Burnside seemed to face, finally remarking it was "all a failure. . . . They had better come back at once." Not at all, Sheldon assured him, for despite the repeated impediments General Burnside was progressing surprisingly well, finding his way around every problem. At this Lincoln brightened.

Yet, for all the optimism he instilled in his subordinates and messengers, Ambrose Burnside later referred to this tedious ordeal as the most taxing period of his military career. The *Picket* maternally circled and traversed the huddled ships, and the commander went about his daily inspections with a face ever cheerful and confident, but in private and in his letters to "Dear Mac" he revealed an anxiety that approached despair. "I have never undertaken a work that has presented so many obstacles," he confessed to McClellan. A reporter from the *New York Tribune* pumped Burnside for the names of the contractors who had misrepresented the drafts of some of the transports, but the general refused to accommodate the journalist's thirst for a scandal. "It's all my fault," Burnside argued, evincing a deadly tendency to assume total responsibility for operations under his command. "I should have satisfied myself with my own eyes and hands that the vessels were as represented. I had no business to trust any man in such a matter." The correspondent, more generous than some Burnside later encountered, did not take advantage of his sense of accountability.[17]

Another crisis soon presented itself. The entire fleet's supply of fresh water had about run out, and although Burnside had arranged for one schooner a day to bring a supply from Baltimore, none had arrived by January 26. They, as well as several colliers, had been driven to sea by the endless bad weather. A primitive condensing apparatus aboard the steamer *Guide* could produce up to three thousand gallons a day, but that was too little to satisfy the throats of nearly twenty thousand soldiers and sailors, and the taste was terribly brackish. Armed guards went before all the water casks, and the Stars and Stripes flew upside down from scores of ships that ran completely out of water. Burnside surveyed these distress signals, turned his binoculars to the mastless horizon in search of the missing schooners, and at one point ventured alone to the prow of the *Picket*, certain only that all was lost. Without water he could not even give up the campaign, fight his way back over the bar, and return home, nor could the barren cape ever support his division. The enemy sensed his plight, and although a generous helping of wishful thinking attended the crowing over it, so too was there some justification when the Newbern *Daily Progress* discounted the Yankee expedition as a failure. Neither was it sheer gullibility that led the same newspaper to express credence in a rumor that Burnside had surrendered to Confederates at Hatteras—even though there were no Confederates at Hatteras. The possibility of surrender to an inferior force may well have occurred to the Rhode Islander as he leaned over the bow of the *Picket*, for how else could he have saved the lives of his men? At that moment of his most abject desolation, he noticed the black clouds of a squall drifting toward the inlet. With the thrill of a man reprieved from the gallows, he watched the signals run up to spread sail and collect water. The rain came in torrents, and soon the barrels overflowed again. In the next three days four of the Baltimore schooners beat their way in, and even one of the tugs. Five more tugs arrived January 30 and began dragging the biggest of the steamers over the Swash. Burnside at once became his usual optimistic self; never again did he want for hope.[18]

Those encamped on the island naturally fared better than those still aboard ship. Hatteras village was a poor community of some six hundred apolitical souls—the provisional government aside—who strained a meager living from the sea. The town had had a post office less than four years. Enough of the inhabitants kept geese and sheep, however, that the soldiers ashore managed a nourishing, if illicit, supplement to their diets. Others fried fish trapped in sand pockets when the storm waters receded. Whatever they ate was garnished with sand, but the air blew fresh and there was plenty of room to move around.

The island itself lay virtually barren, with miles of beach and dunes infrequently interrupted by scrub bushes and spiny little cacti that could go right through a shoddy brogan, but Hatteras offered more amusements than the transports. Chief among the sights were the abandoned Confederate forts, Hatteras and Clark, and the acres of variegated seashells that dressed the tide-smoothed beach. Hooded gulls provided a little circus when they hovered overhead, begging, and an occasional marsh rabbit or even a dwarfed deer might scurry from an unexpected hiding place. Most beautiful of all was the wavetop ballet of the brown pelicans, two or three abreast as they soared with their bellies brushing the whitecaps, heads tucked back, turning and dipping in perfect unison, the choreography of their little squadron still unbroken as they periodically maintained altitude with a single synchronized stroke of wings.[19]

Despite a renewal of the windy weather and rough seas, most of Burnside's vessels and more than nine thousand of his troops rode inside the harbor by the third day of February. Only one ship, a bark which arrived late, carrying the 53rd New York Volunteers, was found to draw too much water for even the tugs to pull. With its disappointed cargo— less the lieutenant colonel, who remained behind as a volunteer—the *John Trucks* turned back for Fort Monroe.[20]

Burnside got wind of strong Confederate reinforcements at Nag's Head, a seaside resort opposite Roanoke Island. He held a brief conference with Flag Officer Goldsborough, who feared the enemy might have used the delay in making the Swash to strengthen Roanoke to the point of impregnability; certainly they might have been expected to do so. Goldsborough ordered a frigate from the Wilmington blockade up to Nag's Head, thinking to bombard the place and its reputed garrison, and in a final frenzy of activity Burnside brought the rest of his forces together. He put even the Hatteras garrison, Colonel Hawkins's 9th New York, aboard a transport. The signalmen emerged from the bowels of the *Satterly* and scattered to assignments on the upper decks of various ships, Lieutenant Draper joining General Burnside. Draper—and Burnside's staff—seemed gratified when the general moved his headquarters back to the commodious quarters and epicurean galley of the *S. R. Spaulding* the next morning.[21]

When the troop-laden transports began chugging up the inside sleeve of the Outer Banks, they would intrude upon what the Confederate government recognized as the Chowan District, the southernmost quadrant of the Department of Norfolk. Commander of that district was

Henry Wise, one of the Civil War's greater anomalies. A native of Virginia's largely loyal Eastern Shore, Wise himself had been an ardent Whig and Unionist; he was in his mid-fifties now, and among his laurels were terms as foreign minister to Brazil and governor of Virginia. Despite his prewar antagonism toward the excesses of the slave power, the pugnacious Wise was a fervent Confederate now, and a brigadier general. He had taken over the command two days before Burnside's flotilla left Annapolis, complaining immediately that his troops were wholly inadequate for defense. He realized, as had the Yankees, that Roanoke Island was the gateway to his district, and there lay his entire force, poorly sheltered, indifferently clothed, and medievally equipped.

Henry Shaw, colonel of the 8th North Carolina, commanded at Roanoke. He had only three Tarheel units: his own regiment, the 31st, and three companies of the 17th, amounting to no more than fifteen hundred men, many of them armed with outdated flintlock smoothbores. Three forts guarded the island, all of them facing the mainland, where the enemy would most likely try to pass: these redoubts boasted a total of twenty-three guns, only three of them rifled. Across the channel lay a pitiful battery extemporized by beaching some armed barges. Except for a pair of smoothbores trained on Roanoke Sound and a ridiculous battery of mismatched fieldpieces without teams, this was the island's entire armament, and after manning his big guns Colonel Shaw had only eight hundred men left for use as infantry.[22]

General Wise went to work with a vengeance to bring his command up to snuff. He shipped in two pivot guns to beef up his lowermost fort and appealed to the navy for a midshipman to train his gun crews; he secured one of only two steam-operated pile drivers in the department to begin a line of obstructions across Croatan Sound and assigned an engineer lieutenant named William Selden to supervise the work; he pleaded with the secretary of war and with Benjamin Huger (his department commander) for the return of Wise's Legion, his brigade of mixed infantry, cavalry, and artillery. In order to reinforce his requests, he left his post without orders and visited the War Department personally. Part of his own brigade arrived in dribbles, a regiment at first, then eight companies of another, and he gained the promised use of the five companies of the 2nd North Carolina Battalion. But the secretary of war took a dim view of this sort of lobbying, and he issued Wise a peremptory order to return to Roanoke Island. This the general did—

after a week's sojourn at his home in Norfolk—but virtually until the moment of Burnside's attack he could muster only the same men he had originally found on the island. The day he left Norfolk, he directed a composite battery of his legion artillery to join him at his headquarters, by way of the Outer Banks beaches, but General Huger rerouted the six guns that might have done Burnside some real damage, and they did not find Wise until a week after the battle for the island. The Richmond government even declined to send any artillery ammunition to fit the three oddball field guns at Roanoke, citing a nationwide shortage.[23]

Other than the weather, Henry Wise had but one ally in his district— Flag Officer William F. Lynch of the Confederate States Navy. His exalted rank did not match the fleet of little two-gun steamers and the single schooner he commanded, however, and in the general's eyes the naval officer did more harm than good. In order to increase his squadron to eight steamers, Lynch commandeered all but one of the island's tug-boats, transforming them into what Wise characterized as "perfectly imbecile gunboats." The resulting lack of transportation hampered the delivery of piles and supplies; with ultimately disastrous effects it also impeded Wise's ability to jockey what troops he had from one position to another.[24]

Signal flares arched away from the flagship *Philadelphia* the morning of February 5, 1862, and the aquatic ballet began, bulky gunboats and topheavy steamships working their tedious way into assigned columns. The amphibious Yankees watched without regret as Hatteras Inlet disappeared over eighty fantails. The size of the armada and Golds-borough's justifiable caution in navigating Long Shoal ate up most of the day; at dusk the lead vessels anchored off Stumpy Point, while a boat went ashore to abduct a civilian pilot known to live there. Six miles ahead lay Croatan Sound, much as Walter Raleigh's colonists had seen it nearly three centuries before. Fog came in thick the next morning, and Burnside dared venture no closer than the entrance to the sound; the Federals could make out the puny Confederate fleet off Pork Point, before the mists obscured it. It was there Burnside's information indi-cated the first enemy fort sat, and there he found it at 9:05 A.M. the following day, February 7. Fort Bartow (named after one of Burnside's antagonists at Bull Run) let fly at the foremost warships with three usable 32-pounder smoothbores and its single rifle, a beast hand-tooled by Confederate ordnancemen from another old smoothbore. The Union

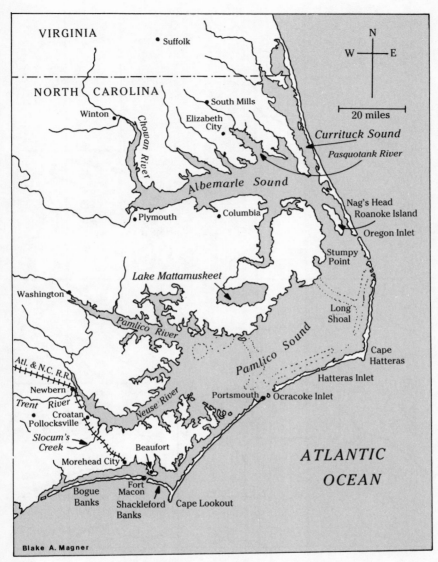

Map 2. The North Carolina Sounds

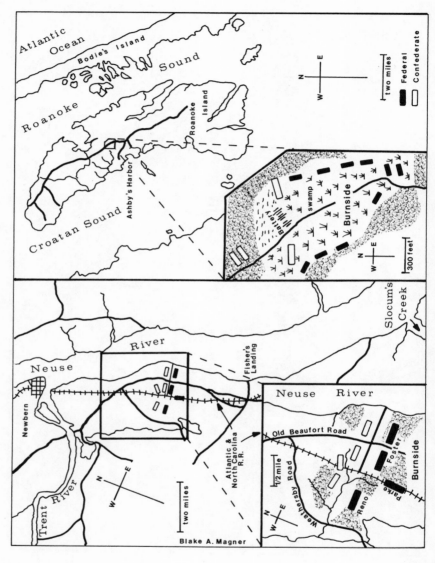

Map 3.
Battles of Roanoke
and Newbern

fleet returned fire, backing water to a position where still another of the fort's guns could not bear. Captain Samuel Hazard, directing the army-owned ships in Burnside's command, joined in the contest as much as he dared, though his crowded decks offered a vulnerable target for any stray shot. Even General Burnside had the *Spaulding* steam up from its place in line to fire a couple of token rounds before he dropped back to watch.[25]

This fight thundered across the otherwise calm waters for more than eight hours. Neither the Federal navy nor the Confederate artillery-men suffered terribly, but Lynch's mosquito fleet disintegrated be-fore Goldsborough's heavier and more accurate firepower. Of the seven brave little steamers that defended Lieutenant Selden's unfinished line of pilings, two were sunk, one was captured, and two were scuttled by their crews. The surviving pair fled back to Elizabeth City.

Burnside, meanwhile, poked the island for a spot to land his troops. From a teenaged contraband named Tom he had already learned of the attractiveness of Ashby's Harbor, in the hollow of Roanoke's cupped hand, and at spyglass distance it seemed a likely place to put the divi-sion ashore. To be certain, Burnside sent a boatload of gallant Rhode Islanders out under a zouave lieutenant, to take soundings and exam-ine the beach. Colonel Shaw had posted a couple of advance companies here, and after a run-in with these North Carolinians the impromptu survey team pulled oars for the ships—one of their number cradling his shattered jaw—and reported the harbor adequate for an amphibious landing.[26]

By now Burnside had conferred with Goldsborough about the disem-barkation, and he told General Foster to take his brigade in. Foster loaded five hundred of his men aboard the steamer *Pilot Boy*, with nearly a thousand more in a long queue of surfboats trailing from the stern. As the steamer started toward the harbor like the mother of an enormous brood of ducks, picking up speed, Foster caught the glint of some bayonets near farmer Ashby's ramshackle cabin. These belonged to the men who had shot the Rhode Islander—a few dozen infantry with those three antiquated fieldpieces. Foster ordered the captain to veer north of them, as if to cut them off. Driving close to a sandy jut that would take the name of Yankee Point, the shallow-draft *Pilot Boy* let go of the surfboats, which catapulted to the beach like so many children playing snap the whip. Two dozen men leaped from each boat, those aboard the *Pilot Boy* bounded over the side, and within the first twenty minutes some four thousand Union soldiers had secured what, in later years, would be called the beachhead. Burnside came ashore, perceived that things were going well, approved of the dispositions Foster and Reno had made, and returned to the *Spaulding*. There would be no battle that evening. Not only was it growing dark, these Yankees had been on shipboard so long it would take them a few hours to find their land legs. Skirmishers fanned out, and the three brigadiers did a little reconnoitering. It grew cold as the men lay down to sleep, blanketless as well as tentless, and then it began to rain.

One of Foster's men, hunched on a furrow in the mud and stubble of an old cornfield behind a Mr. Hammond's house, could not sleep. Neither could most of his comrades. Orders to the contrary notwithstanding, these men relieved Hammond of his fence, one rail at a time, and fed a reluctant fire in the midst of the deluge.[27]

When the *Pilot Boy* sheered away from the Confederate picket post at Ashby's house, the two companies of Carolinians had drawn their guns a mile back, to a meager prefabricated earthwork across the narrow road that crawled up the island's spine. Reinforcements came jangling up from the forts to meet them: no more than eight hundred more North Carolinians and recently arrived Virginians under Colonel Shaw himself. General Wise was flat on his back with pneumonia in his head-quarters at a resort hotel on Nag's Head, overlooking the Atlantic. The best he could do for Shaw was ferry over some more troops with his remaining tug and a couple of barges. He sent two companies of his 46th Virginia, including that under his own son, and eight companies of his 59th Virginia. Colonel Shaw, a renegade Rhode Islander who had departed the state about the time Burnside first visited it, positioned a third of his men behind these fieldworks—which did not extend far enough to shelter more—reserving the rest of his infantry force in two groups, a few hundred yards behind. His three guns gave small comfort. All of them were smoothbores, one an obsolete brass 6-pounder captured during the Mexican War, another a brass 18-pounder for which he had only 12-pounder ammunition, and the last a 24-pounder navy howitzer of little use beyond pointblank range. Only by scavenging a few saddle horses and mules did he collect a patchwork trio of teams for this comic battery, their harness woven from a variety of materials that did not include leather. The gunners fumbled, altogether untrained;

of the two officers who labored to give them a crash course only one, Lieutenant Selden, knew much more than the men.[28]

Shaw's confidence hinged on an advantage of position. The road his little fort commanded was well flanked by swamps and thick undergrowth, and as an earlier precaution he had cleared his field of fire for six or seven hundred yards, the felled trees imposing a tangled obstacle before the attacking enemy infantry.

At daybreak, February 8, Foster began moving his troops forward, according to a plan he and Burnside had agreed upon. The commanding general arrived after an early breakfast, just as Foster's third regiment filed onto the trail. It quickly became apparent that the vegetation was too thick for Burnside to oversee the entire battle. He therefore sent Foster, his senior brigadier, to the front of the column, where he could receive any attack and direct the deployment of whatever reinforcements his chief sent him. Burnside gave him a free hand to meet any crisis he came against, trusting both Foster's good judgment and the willingness of Reno and Parke to cooperate with him.[29]

By the primitive track from Ashby's Harbor and the central island road it was barely a mile to the breastworks, situated at a place called Suple's Hill. There was not the slightest hint of a hill to the location; it was nothing more than an island of dry ground amid a great bog, named for some mosquito-tormented unfortunate who had once lived there.[30] Foster had barely begun to move his attenuated column when he discovered Shaw's barricade. He saw the stength of the terrain at once: the road here appeared to him as a causeway, conjuring up visions of another waterbound highway he had charged across at Mexico City. He overestimated the number of Confederate defenders by two to one and dismissed any notion of a full-scale frontal attack, instead sending two Massachusetts regiments into the swamp to turn Shaw's left.[31] These men had barely begun to dry out from the previous night's downpour. They tried hopping from one tuft of ground to another, but their heavy clothing and equipment threw them off balance. After a few chilly tumbles they found it easier to immerse the skirts of their overcoats and simply wade through the more open watercourses. Company officers ranged ahead, hacking a path through dense vines and sweetbrier with swords bearing delicately engraved patriotic mottoes.[32]

Meanwhile, Foster placed a battery of Dahlgren guns in the road. These light naval howitzers were served—and pulled—by a detach-

ment of the 1st New York Marine Artillery, a unit representative of the
forces Burnside had initially wanted for his division. They were nearly
all sailors, and had been distributed among the crews of the various
transports on the voyage from Annapolis. Some of them carried short
Belgian muskets and served as infantry, while the gunners wore revolvers and cutlasses. Their officers sported double-breasted coats like
those of their navy counterparts, and the men were dressed from top to
bottom in dark blue, like seamen on a man of war.[33]

When Reno approached at the head of his brigade, he told Foster
he would try to outflank the Confederates' right. Foster approved, and
Reno's men also plunged into the marsh. Foster's other two regiments
and the battery occupied Shaw from the bowling-alley position created
by the road, losing a man every couple of minutes to either Shaw's few
riflemen or to the old Mexican 6-pounder, operated surprisingly well
by Lieutenant Selden. General Parke, whose 8th Connecticut and 5th
Rhode Island Battalion had been detailed to guard the landing site, arrived several hours after the fight began, leading the 4th Rhode Island
and the 9th New York Zouaves. Foster initially pointed both regiments
into the swamp east of the road, but when he thought he detected
some confusion in the rude fort, he countermanded those orders and redirected the zouaves straight up the causeway, down the throats of those
three cannon. He stopped the New York major, since Colonel Hawkins
had already bolted too far into the swamp to hear. As a preliminary,
the Civil War infantry charge seemed to require a stirring speech, in
the tradition of Henry V, but time was short and Foster offered only a
truncated little peroration.

"You are the very man," he told the major, fortissimo, "and this is the
very moment. Zouaves—Storm the battery!" The excited New Yorkers, half in the road and half in the bog, loosed a noisy volley—"in all
directions but the right one," as one Massachusetts man remembered—
their fire shaking up Reno's 9th New Jersey, which had just reached the
Confederate right flank. (One of their wild shots may also have killed
the lieutenant colonel of the 53rd New York, who did volunteer duty
as a sharpshooter.) Finally the zouaves backed out of the swamp and
swarmed like hornets over the narrow passageway toward the barricade, sounding like hornets as well with their battle chant, "zou-zou-
zou." Colonel Hawkins did not find his way out of the morass in time to
join them.

The zouaves did not have a bad time of it. The confusion Foster had seen among the Confederates had resulted from the progress of one of the flanking columns. Three of Reno's regiments, after nearly four hours of struggling in waist-deep water, had finally come up abreast of the fort. Pouring a crossfire into the enemy, the 51st New York, 21st Massachusetts, and 9th New Jersey scattered the Confederate reserves, which Shaw had sent to stop them, and drove most of the amateur gunners away, killing Lieutenant Selden when he tried to man his piece alone. These three Federal regiments were making their way into the rear of the barricade, and the Confederates were retreating, when the zouaves' red fezzes appeared in the road before the muzzles of those silent cannon. The teams had all been killed, so the defenders spiked the guns, and Colonel Shaw led his garrison on a wild retreat to the northern tip of the island, hoping against hope to find a transport with which he could evacuate.[34]

Burnside came up on foot in the wake of his division. He gave orders for the leading elements to begin the chase, but Foster and Reno had already anticipated him and began leapfrogging their brigades after the refugees, sweeping up prisoners on every trail that diverged from the main road. Small groups of Confederates gathered in Shallow Bag Bay, on the eastern side of the island, seeking escape by boat, but Reno sent the zouaves to scoop them up. Among the prisoners they brought back was Captain O. Jennings Wise of the Richmond Light Infantry Blues, General Wise's mortally wounded son.[35]

Left wounded on the field was another officer of the Blues, a lieutenant by the name of Carter. General Burnside noted Carter's condition and ordered a couple of men to help him aboard the *Picket*, where his staff physician could tend to him. The injured man stared at Burnside's disappearing figure in amazement, asking Mr. Larned who "that officer" was.

"General Burnside," replied the private secretary. Carter responded that he was a gentleman and a friend; Larned assured him he would never find a kinder one.[36]

Leaving the two senior brigadiers to bag the enemy infantry, Burnside took General Parke and two regiments to capture Fort Bartow, on Pork Point. Advancing from the bastion's undefended landward side, he found it empty, its guns spiked with rattail files. Officers on the gunboats saw one of Parke's men run up the Stars and Stripes, and surged

ahead to the other two forts and the remnants of the Southern fleet. The
U.S. flag had hardly been tethered to Bartow's pole when a messenger
from Foster announced that Colonel Shaw had surrendered every man
on the island, including four more companies of Virginians and the 2nd
North Carolina Battalion, which Wise had just shuttled across Roanoke
Sound to stiffen the defense.[37]

Burnside had captured more than twenty-five hundred men in all,
among them two full colonels. This was the first significant Union triumph on dry land in ten demoralizing months. Even U. S. Grant's victory at Fort Henry, two days before, had yielded fewer than a hundred
prisoners. Eight days later Grant would overshadow Burnside's coup
with the capture of Fort Donelson, but for a few days Ambrose Burnside was the nation's hero. News of his feat first reached the country
by way of Confederate sources, whereupon Burnside found himself besieged with letters of congratulation and gratitude. People wrote poems
praising him; one man even asked the general for his full name, that he
might christen his new son after him.[38]

Burnside's success created another advantage no Northerner could
recognize at the time, and which few realized later. Until Burnside
strode into Pamlico Sound and swallowed a small army, which had been
ordered to its defenseless and inescapable position through apparent
incompetence, the Southern people had relied contentedly on the military wisdom of the Richmond government to protect the country. As
one Richmond editor later noted, the capture of Roanoke and Shaw's
garrison marked the birth of that criticism and suspicion of the central government which ultimately undid the Confederacy. Certainly
General Wise's voluminous report, pointing blame at everyone above
him, helped foster and encourage the dissatisfied murmuring; fueled by
the editorials of sympathetic newspapers, it soon rose to a howl. How
much more faith would the Confederate government put in sand forts
(a rattled Newbern editor wanted to know), and how many more troops
would be sacrificed in traps like Roanoke Island?

The critical attitude spawned by Burnside's victory permeated the
Richmond government itself: a clerk in Judah Benjamin's War Department grumbled in his diary that Roanoke had fallen despite the presence
of fifteen thousand "idle troops at Norfolk within hearing of the battle.
The government would not interfere, and Gen. Huger refused to allow
the use of a few thousand of his troops." The truth of such allegations

was less important than their existence: the seed of doubt had germinated. As vital a strategic consideration as Roanoke was, its loss had disproportionately serious effects on Southern morale.[39]

In a situation that inhibited his overall command, Burnside had wisely delegated his authority, leaving the management of the actual fighting to the general at the front while he distributed troops and attended to the goals of the greater strategy. When he wrote his reports a few days later, he treated his own role with characteristic humility, giving the glory to his three able subordinates. He told McClellan, "I owe everything to Generals Foster, Reno, and Parke."[40]

II

The Monday after Shaw surrendered, Burnside dispatched Hawkins, the zouave colonel, to see what was left at Nag's Head. Hawkins took only two companies on his foray, indicating he thought the Confederates would be gone, and indeed he learned from residents that General Wise and his remaining troops—no more than a headquarters guard—had decamped the afternoon of the battle. In their wake they had left a number of buildings smouldering, including the hotel, some warehouses, and the homes of some people Hawkins believed to be loyal; the New Yorker therefore vilified Wise as a "Vandal" and "Barbarian."[1]

Burnside, on the other hand, exchanged some perfectly civilized letters on the subject of Confederate casualties and prisoners with Wise, who had taken up new lodgings at Currituck Bridge. Wise asked for news of wounded officers (wondering, without asking, whether his son had survived), and he offered to send surgeons to tend them; he also hoped the Union general would forward the effects of any officers who might have died. Burnside sympathetically described the death and burial of Captain Wise, declined the surgeons, and enclosed a letter he had drafted to General Huger, proposing to release his prisoners on parole—they pledging not to fight again until exchanged for prisoners of equal rank. This was not a new concept: it was based on a cartel with England during the War of 1812. Paroles had been administered to some U.S. Regulars captured in Texas the previous spring, but this was the first time during the present war that anyone had offered to parole a large command. The arrangement depended partly upon mutual trust between the antagonists and partly on the threat of execution, should a paroled prisoner be recaptured under arms. Aside from the potential for abuse, there were some logical arguments against the process, for while an unexchanged paroled prisoner could neither fight nor aid his armies in any direct manner, he was free to return to his farm or trade: the lack of such labor presented a significant problem in the South, and the release of an entire army could prove a boon to the Confederate economy. There was, in addition, the problem Ulysses Grant perceived two years later: if paroled men continued to reappear on the battlefield as exchanged prisoners, it might become necessary to kill or cripple every man on one side or the other to achieve victory.[2]

These objections would not gather expression for a couple of years, though, during which time Grant himself would parole thirty thousand Confederates. Right now there was something else to consider. The Confederacy still held hundreds of Union soldiers from the disasters at Bull Run and Ball's Bluff, among them a number from Burnside's 1st Rhode Island, and his own manservant, Robert Holloway; the Roanoke garrison provided more than enough prisoners to secure the release of all those men on an even trade. Burnside also harbored some ulterior motives for allowing his captives to go home. They were an embarrassment to him, since he could neither afford the guards nor spare the transports to send them North without weakening his force dangerously and interrupting his supplies. He guessed, too, that once they returned to a Confederate audience, the vanquished soldiers would be inclined to expound on the irresistible force of Union arms—to exaggerate it, in fact, in order to shine a better light on their defeat—and this would help erode the civilian population's will to fight. That, and the humanitarian gesture represented by the parole itself, would simultaneously encourage the loyal sentiment which Burnside had been led to believe rife in North Carolina.[3]

Burnside chose a young Brahmin, Lieutenant Colonel Francis Osborn, to work out the details of the parole. Osborn sailed a flag of truce up to Elizabeth City to arrange the repatriation, and on February 20 the Roanoke Confederates boarded five big steamers. Officers took their servants with them, slaves included, which might have raised a few abolitionists' eyebrows had they learned of it. Handshaking and a good deal of well-wishing passed between the Southerners and their captors before Osborn ordered the gangplanks drawn in and turned his charges back toward Elizabeth City; there he spent all the next day, counting off 2,580 prisoners with a Confederate officer and calculating, for purposes of future exchange, their exact rank.[4]

A week after the battle General Wise, whose district lay entirely in North Carolina, retreated into Virginia with the escort that now comprised his principal force. On February 17, Burnside sent Colonel Hawkins on a two-day jaunt up the Chowan River to Winton, to investigate a reputed conclave of loyalists. Hawkins boarded his zouaves on a convoy of gunboats and steamed up to Winton, taking a cabin on the *Delaware* for himself. Commander Stephen Rowan, who would soon take over naval forces in the sounds, commanded the vessels. The *Delaware* approached Winton with Hawkins clinging to the crosstrees as a lookout, and both he and Rowan came near being riddled when a Confederate rear guard ambushed their amphibious operation. Hawkins tumbled down the ratlines with (for once) no regard for his dignity, and the ships pulled out of range to reevaluate their mission. The next morning Commander Rowan sent his gunboats in to shell the place, after which Hawkins put his men ashore without incident. With a rationale that somehow excused him from the company of vandals and barbarians, he put the torch to the greater part of Winton. The resulting heat flushed no loyal citizens.[5]

The troops on Roanoke grew restive in the weeks following the engagement. One soldier wrote home to Massachusetts that his comrades killed anything that moved on the island in the way of food— in direct violation of orders—and it was partly to keep them in discipline that Burnside planned excursions to the mainland.[6] Little raids helped to hone the new men, on top of winning strategic goals, so he tried to spread the work through the division. While Colonel Hawkins watched Winton burn, John Parke sent the 5th Rhode Island Battalion cruising up Currituck Sound on a sternwheeler, in search of a major salt works. The Rhode Island major and his naval counterpart slipped ashore at several points, but found no commercial operation. The few family-sized distilling pots they discovered were of no use to anyone but the local inhabitants, whom they wished to befriend, and the boats returned without disembarking the infantry.[7]

Later, some of Foster's regiments steamed up Albemarle Sound to Columbia, to disperse a secessionist recruiting camp. With the usual accompaniment of naval muscle, the Yankees ascended the Scuppernong

River in the ubiquitous fog. The helmsman of the *Alice Price*, the lead boat, groped his way on the advice of a local pilot, who took his cue in turn from the muzzle of a revolver, which a Signal Corps lieutenant kept cocked at his ear. Fortunately for the pilot the squadron met with no mishap, but after a six-mile march inland, neither did the soldiers find any Confederate camp. At least in this instance, the field practice actually subverted the discipline Burnside wanted to instill: he entrusted the detachment to the colonel of a regiment that had never been under fire before, who proved unable to restrain his frustrated soldiers from looting the abandoned homes in the village.[8]

Before the last week in February General Wise and his depleted legion were transferred from the Department of Norfolk; Burnside would not meet these Virginians again until his final battle, two and a half years hence. Except for a regiment of Georgians General Huger positioned at South Mills, to guard the Dismal Swamp Canal, the Chowan District lay almost clear of Confederate troops by the end of the month.[9] This freed Burnside to begin the second phase of his campaign: the capture of Newbern.

Lawrence O'Bryan Branch, the Confederate brigadier commanding the District of the Pamlico, had his headquarters at Newbern. Below town, he had fringed the Neuse River with seven forts, five of them already complete and ready to turn thirty guns on any riverborne assault. The largest battery was Fort Thompson, with armament including three 32-pounder pivot guns that could also enfilade a land attack. Ten miles below Newbern, Branch had situated a strong line of fortifications between the mouth of Otter Creek and the swamps to the southwest: Croatan breastwork, he called it. It could easily be defended by a small brigade. These works would be costly to carry and virtually impossible to avoid for an enemy advancing from the southeast. More rifle pits covered a mile of bluffs at Fisher's Landing, above Otter Creek, to discourage any landing there—which would flank the Croatan breastwork. On his last monthly return, Branch had estimated he could put barely six thousand rifles in the field, and these must defend not only Newbern but his entire district, which yawned all the way from Cape Lookout to Washington, and across the Pamlico River into Hyde County.

Branch was still at work on his fortifications, but without much help from any of the citizens within his protectorate. When he called for laborers, only a squad of freedmen answered; when he advertised that he would rent hands from willing slaveowners, but one plantation responded, sending a single man. Each day the equivalent of a regiment of soldiers toiled on the works with a couple of hundred axes and spades— not a pick to share among them.[10]

Burnside and Commander Rowan developed a plan to bypass the batteries along the Neuse River. The army would land at the mouth of Slocum's Creek, several miles downstream from the Croatan breastwork, while the gunboats continued up the Neuse to a point from which they could rake the Confederate position with their huge guns. That should ease its capture considerably, after which the fleet would parallel Burnside's progress toward Newbern, shattering each fort in succession while the infantry assailed it from the front or flank. In order to avoid a tragedy, the two commanders concocted a simple fire direction code: a single rocket, fired straight up, would mark the advance of Burnside's army; two rockets meant the troops were about to advance, warning Rowan to swing his guns upriver; three rockets would tell Rowan his rounds were falling short; four were to indicate his range was long.

Burnside began loading some of his troops, particularly his artillery, as early as February 26, but successive storms forced him to postpone his movement for several days. He had to disembark the artillery to stretch and feed both man and beast, but he resumed loading a few days into March. By the ninth, the last man was aboard. The next day Burnside learned from Adjutant General Lorenzo Thomas that the Confederate army at Manassas seemed to be in retreat: at that he dared wait no longer, for the farther that army retreated, the more easily it could reinforce Branch. He issued orders for the expedition immediately.[11]

In a driving rain a thousand backs bent to the windlasses the morning of March 11; anchors crept from the murky water while all yards and rudders turned for Hatteras Inlet. Burnside detailed a garrison of three regiments on Roanoke. Two of them were new. The third was the 9th New York, and because of his seniority Colonel Hawkins had command of what was officially designated Burnside's fourth brigade. Doubtless Burnside left the untried regiments behind in order to have as veteran a fighting force as possible; he may have placed the zouaves among them as an experienced cadre, or simply to be free of Hawkins, who waxed troublesome once again.[12]

One transport spent the day aground; the rest of the fleet congregated at Hatteras that afternoon. Late that night the sole casualty steamed bashfully into the anchorage. The clouds had dispersed by dawn of March 12, and the uncharacteristically mirrorlike surface of the sound shone, as one man remembered, "like burnished gold" in the rose cast of the rising sun. In that glow the ships heaved forward once again. The pilot boats had not entered the broad mouth of the Neuse when black smoke began billowing up from signal fires Branch had prepared. Faster than the telegraph could have relayed news of the enemy's approach, the softwood bonfires carried it to Newbern.

The weather, Burnside's perpetual nemesis, stood ready to strike again when Slocum's Creek appeared around a reach of the river. The sky had grown black, and as the gunboats and transports hove to a stop, the rain began. In the dismal dusk came word of the fall of Nashville, and the same source brought the premature report that Burnside had been promoted to major general. The rumors leaped like a forest fire from the masts of one ship to another, cheers following in rapid succession, reverberating against the wall of the forest. Later the bands came out on deck and began tooting in the drizzle, as ten thousand voices serenaded the geese and the cottonmouths with songs of home and country. Half a dozen miles up the Neuse, nervous Confederates huddling in muddy rifle pits could hear them.[13]

The moon was only four nights shy of full that dreary night, but none aboard the ships could have seen it, even if they had been able to leave the muggy congestion of the passenger decks. Burnside and his brigadiers went over to Rowan's *Philadelphia* for a final council of war, in which they determined to land the men the next morning regardless of the weather.

The rain had tapered off to an uncomfortable mist as March 13 opened. At first light the preparatory signals fluttered up the halyards, and while the transports disgorged the endless platoons into surfboats, a pair of steamers crept into the narrow mouth of the creek. One, the *Delaware*, posted a daring leadsman on the bow, sounding the shallows. The other was the *Alice Price*, with Burnside himself on deck. A boat crew shoved off from the *Price* to reconnoiter the shoreline, with a man in the prow whose position and purpose remain somewhat nebulous. His name was Harvey H. Helper. A native of Rowan County, North Carolina, he had ostensibly left the state because of his sympathy with the federal government. That was not quite true, though. He had actually made his departure several years before, because of a book his brother had written. Hinton Rowan Helper, who condemned the economic and social effects of slavery on white people (but hated black people fervently), had published his infamous antislavery argument in 1857. The release of *The Impending Crisis of the South* precipitated both a furious indignation across the South and the author's sudden recognition of the salubrious climate of New York City, where he went to live in voluntary exile, the unwilling darling of Northern abolitionists. He held no sympathy with secession, a distinction that helped earn him the consulate at Buenos Aires, but his family suffered for his notoriety. Harvey, who shared his brother's abolitionist sentiments, had had to flee long before loyalty to the government became an issue, and he settled in Illinois. Eventually he became sergeant major of the 8th Illinois Cavalry. Both his colonel and Senator Henry Wilson, of Massachusetts, recommended him to Burnside as a man who might be of service in his native state; Helper himself referred to his duties as "secret service," but at this moment they seemed to include nothing more specialized than testing the depth of the mud.[14]

Helper and the coxswain's crew returned to the *Alice Price* unmolested. Meanwhile Commander Rowan continued upstream with the floating fortresses, scanning the shore for the works reputed to guard Newbern's back door. Somehow he missed the Croatan breastwork. The first target he saw was the string of rifle pits at Fisher's Landing. Here was a piece of luck, for the bluffs were held by a regiment that was not on the verge of earning a reputation for sticking—James Sinclair's 35th North Carolina. Even before Burnside's entire division waded ashore at Slocum's Creek, more than six miles below, Sinclair sent the 35th into abject flight, bearing tales of a phantom Union debarkation at Fisher's Landing. This false report led to the abandonment of the Croatan breastwork, relieving Burnside of what would have posed the worst difficulty in the taking of Newbern.[15]

Back at Slocum's Creek, the 51st Pennsylvania climbed down the sides of the *Alice Price* into the familiar landing boats. Rowing through a gap pioneers had sawn in the Confederate pilings, they vied with the 24th Massachusetts to be the first ashore; the hard-pulling Bay Staters had been the last to land at Roanoke. The Pennsylvanians had too much of a lead, and their keels grounded in the muck first. The infantrymen bounded into cold, brackish sea-and-river water rippling waist-deep. Mud rose to their shins, both beneath the water and out of it, sucking and dragging at the feet of men who had grown unaccustomed to marching. Cottonmouth moccasins slithered away as the troops sloshed up on the spongy banks of the creek, and some of these homebound Yankees shuddered at their eerie new surroundings. Dwarf palmettos greeted them, arranged on the bank like an escort of pygmies armed with ceremonial fans; clutching catbrier vines spiraled about the trunks of towering yellow pines. Even in this sodden forest the desert cactus and spiny, yucca-like bristles threatened their feet. One captain likened the thick, drooping Spanish moss to a witch's tresses.[16] It was, for the untraveled New Englander, a surrealistic landscape.

No beach lined the bank. The land rose abruptly to a low, flat shelf. The beginnings of a column of march started into the cathedrallike forest by eight o'clock, splashing through several inches of water: the ground was saturated, and the rain simply accumulated on the surface. Many feet soon whipped the trail into a spongy trough. Behind the foremost regiments came the Pennsylvanians, who had been so eager, assigned now as beasts of burden for the six guns of the Marine Artillery, while the 23rd Massachusetts followed them, alternate companies taking turns with the boat howitzer from one of the ships. The captain of the *Cossack* and some of his sailors manned the ropes on the eighth and last piece of Burnside's artillery train. A Massachusetts officer described the woods path as a "mortar-bed" after the troops and guns had passed, and when they emerged on a traveled road, the problem grew worse; he had charge of one of those shipboard howitzers, and to ease the strain on his men he scouted ahead for another route, through stumps and woods, parallel to the line of march. Skirmishers sent back a yoke of oxen to help twitch the gun through twelve and fourteen inches of "stiff, tenacious clay." The Pennsylvanians ran out of adjectives and metaphor, paying tribute to "the *muddiest* mud ever invented," and knee deep. These men finally encountered Captain Bennett, of the *Cossack*, with his heavy Wiard gun mired to its hubs. The captain begged them for help. They knew him from the weeks they had spent aboard his ship and had high regard for him, but they were spent from their own burdens; the first who passed him declined to lay a hand on his gun. Bennett finally spun himself into a frenzy, threatening to blow his own brains all over Carteret County if they refused him. The exhausted infantrymen feared he meant it and reluctantly took up the ropes or wrapped their fingers around the spokes.[17]

While his troops poured ashore, Burnside and the division staff stood among them, adjuring every man to conserve his equipment. It was common practice to jettison what seemed like excess baggage on the march, but once away from this landing site there would be no chance of resupply (short of retreat) until Newbern fell.[18]

The weather continued raw. One of those who recorded the day from the perspective of three decades recalled intermittent drizzle with periods of showers, but diarists on the spot spoke of heavy rain. Overcoats soaked up a quart or two of water apiece and grew dreadfully heavy, but even wet wool offered some warmth. No one shed them.[19]

In the early afternoon the sweeping Union skirmishers discovered the empty Croatan breastwork and Colonel Sinclair's rifle pits at Fisher's Landing. Here lay a camp, with barracks for troops, but no troops; here stood platforms for guns, but no guns. Nearby was an abandoned cavalry encampment—presumably identifiable by piles of manure—which had been vacated in such haste when Rowan's 64-pound shells came whistling through that breakfast still sat on the table. The foot soldiers gaped at the imposing Croatan work, simultaneously amazed and relieved it had not been defended. One man told his family, "We could have held it with 5000 troops against all the soldiers in North Carolina." A lieutenant wondered, since the Confederates had fled such an enviable position, whether they would resist at all.[20]

The advance rested here for a meal (perhaps partly from the Confederates' untouched breakfasts) while many privates scattered to inspect some farmers' nearby smokehouses. A few excited Rhode Islanders raided a barnyard full of squealing pigs; one man aiming for some midday pork accidentally killed his own sergeant. While these foragers slaughtered livestock and each other, signal officers found a prominence from which they could fire a pair of rockets for the gunboats.[21]

Burnside had sent two staff lieutenants and his new engineer, Captain Robert Williamson, to reconnoiter the enemy's movements from beyond the advance. A party of brigade staff officers rode with them. The general was cantering up to the head of the column that evening when he met Williamson and his impromptu escort returning to the

main body. They had ridden almost headlong into the tail of the retreating Confederate force and had dogged it until they drew fire from
Southern pickets. At this news, Burnside concluded he would soon
encounter the next fortified position. Growing darkness precluded an
attack, so he assigned his brigadiers their bivouacs. He placed Foster on
the right, across the old county road to Beaufort, and put Reno on the
left, astride the railroad that paralleled the Old Beaufort Road, farther
inland. Parke went into reserve behind Foster. A thick fog knitted itself
around the division like an old, familiar quilt, drawing a blind between
the soldiers and the fleet.[22]

Most of the drenched Yankees camped by 9:00 P.M., though the infantrymen hauling some of the howitzers did not reach their bivouac
until much later. A few cooked over hard-fought campfires, but the
greater portion of the army was too bone-tired to bother with food; they
lay down to sleep in chilly beds awash in puddles, but miraculously they
slept. At two o'clock in the morning, with the rain still pelting them
in solid sheets, the men who had charge of the guns awoke to prodding feet and voices that grumbled about their artillery. Under cover
of the predawn darkness the generals wanted those guns brought as
close to the enemy's position as possible, so the weary Pennsylvanians
rolled the iron felloes of the six deck guns within five hundred yards of
Branch's line.[23]

A fellow Rhode Islander later speculated that Burnside had formed
a rough impression of the Confederate defenses from the reports of
deserters and contraband refugees: there had been numerous such deserters since the first days of the Burnside expedition, many of them
Northern men whom the war fever had caught south of the Mason-
Dixon Line, and escaped slaves collected around every occupation force
like steel filings on a magnet. Burnside's information, this other Rhode
Islander supposed, may even have included knowledge of the fortified
line from Fort Thompson, on the Neuse, to the railroad tracks, but
he probably had no hint of a series of redans west of the railroad,
behind a tributary of Bryce Creek. Whatever he did know about his
enemy, Burnside apparently had no specific plan, beyond the landing at
Slocum's Creek, for the capture of Newbern. Thereafter, except for the
prearranged cooperation of the gunboats, everything could only have
been extemporized on the basis of information provided on the spot
by the engineer captain who roved ahead of him. Captain Williamson

started off again at dawn the next day, March 14; he had not gone far when he raised the Confederate pickets.[24]

Branch had scattered four North Carolina regiments in the works between Fort Thompson and the tracks of the Atlantic & North Carolina. At the railroad, his line swung back at a right angle. He seems not to have expected an attack beyond there, where the ground was broken by Butten's Creek and a snarl of slash, because he garrisoned that vulnerable angle with an untrained battalion of state militia. After a short run to the north, the Confederate line jogged west again, where two more regiments of regular North Carolina troops defended the near bank of the creek. Well to the rear, but within supporting distance, waited part of a cavalry regiment. Two field batteries and the gun crews in Fort Thompson completed Branch's little army. His artillery was not impressive, but at least it had been placed by a professional military engineer—Captain Richard K. Meade, an old friend of General Foster. A Virginian, and one of very few men to fight as an officer on both sides in this war, Meade had been on duty with Foster inside Fort Sumter during the bombardment that opened the hostilities.[25]

Rain stopped with daybreak, but dense fog lingered. General Burnside saddled up and trotted to Foster's headquarters fire in this cottony mist. He worried about his troops: he had driven them mercilessly yesterday, and they had enjoyed little sleep in unhealthy beds. Rolling cheers greeted him, though, as he passed each camp, and his reservations disappeared.

Foster would lead the attack. Most of his brigade—four Massachusetts regiments—materialized out of the fog on the Old Beaufort Road sometime after seven o'clock; a vigilant Tarheel jerked the lanyard on a fieldpiece, and the battle line erupted. Foster called up Captain Dayton, the transport skipper who had suffered the 23rd Massachusetts to wrestle his gun through the mire; a few Bostonians put the ropes over their shoulders once more and wheeled the little cannon into the middle of the county road, barely a thousand feet from the Confederate gun. Two more Southern pieces began throwing iron their way, but Dayton's gunners calmly opened their hand-carried ammunition chests. To the intense disgust of the men who had struggled from Slocum's Creek with these burdens, the chests were packed with projectiles alone: the only powder cartridges were those in the gun crew's passing cases, and they quickly expended these. Something—perhaps a spent bullet or a stone kicked up by a bounding shell—glanced off a button on Dayton's coat about the time his gunner fired the last round. With what must have been wry humor, one of his Massachusetts mulemen watched the captain turn for the rear to seek treatment "in spite of a determined effort to remain," while the infantrymen rolled his emasculated howitzer to a safer location. The Marine Artillery's battery of Dahlgren guns soon took the same ground, lighting the hazy roadway with its six blazing muzzles.[26]

Foster's brigade shouldered into a line of battle at the edge of a thousand-foot-wide swath of abatis—trees felled with their branches pointing toward the attackers. This was a simple but effective obstacle, for while it created a desperate tangle for troops trying to advance in formation, it afforded the defenders a clear field of fire. A similar precaution at Roanoke Island had decided Foster on a flank attack, and he did not care to make a frontal assault now. When the 10th Connecticut arrived, he added it to his line and later borrowed Parke's 11th Connecticut, but he did not advance. These six regiments simply found whatever cover they could and shot it out with the men behind the breastworks.[27]

Commander Rowan heard the battle begin ashore, and by gauging the sound (for fog still enshrouded everything) he was able to throw his nine-inch shells in the general direction of the Confederates. Tall pines snapped like matchsticks, but the effect of the naval guns was mostly psychological: what the ships could not see, neither could they hit.

Burnside observed all of this from horseback, near Parke's brigade, on the Old Beaufort Road. He and his staff had clustered beneath a tree when a stray solid shot dropped one of its boughs on top of them. Much to the amusement of the rank and file, the frightened horses reared into each other, dancing around for some time, but no one was hurt.[28]

On the left, Reno worked his brigade within range of that first jog in the Confederate line, which he mistook for their right flank. His men ached in foot, bone, and muscle—not unlike Foster's, perhaps, though the overworked 51st Pennsylvania awoke especially rheumatic that morning, with men falling in "as if they were walking on eggs." In addition to weariness, however, Reno's men also complained of unserviceable weapons: the Pennsylvanians' rifles had become too damp to fire, while a number of Enfields in the 21st Massachusetts had so swollen with the moisture that the ramrods stuck fast in the stocks.

Jammed ramrods or not, Reno sent the regiment to attack the inviting salient angle, which graced the corner of a brickyard.[29]

Fortunately for Union arms, the point Reno chose to attack happened to be that held by the militia battalion. The tubes of two 24-pounder howitzers emerged from the Confederate works here just as the Yankees swept forward, but they came too late to provide much punch. By coincidence, the attack pitted one Colonel Clark against another; the Massachusetts Clark struck the Confederate Clark fast and hard, and the militia bolted. Victory seemed thus easily won. While the panicky North Carolina citizen-soldiers were still spilling out of their rifle pits, Reno himself led one wing of the 21st up on the parapet, waving his sword while fire from down the line converged on him, dropping men all around him. Reno went back for his other three regiments, but just then the rest of the Confederate line (the part Reno had failed to detect) made its presence known. Zebulon Vance, colonel of the 26th North Carolina, opened a blistering volley from his infantry and artillery positions across Butten's Creek.[30]

While Reno spread his front out to the left, Burnside ordered Parke to the railroad with his remaining troops, then spurred his horse over to see how Reno was doing. Parke's weakened brigade, two and a half regiments, started forward with the 4th Rhode Island in the lead, which proved to be another instance of good luck. As that regiment reached the front, the 21st Massachusetts was just scrambling back from its dearly won parapet, driven out by an overwhelming force drawn from Foster's front. Lieutenant Colonel William Clark caught sight of the 4th Rhode Island as he withdrew the four battered companies that had followed him into the enemy works. He approached the Rhode Island colonel with a description of the position he had been forced to abandon: the Confederates had not yet reoccupied it, and if enough Union troops—say, a regiment—could dash in before they did, the Confederate line would be cut in half.[31]

It posed a wonderful opportunity, but if an officer were to take the risk without orders and fail, his head might roll. As it happened, the colonel of the 4th Rhode Island was Isaac Rodman, a personal friend of Ambrose Burnside. He knew, as did most of Burnside's friends, that the general would support anyone who acted in his behalf in good faith. They could not waste a moment if this advantage was not to be lost, but General Parke was nowhere in sight. Rodman decided to throw his men

in on his own hook. His regiment swarmed over the top of the entrenchments; when Parke came up, he pushed in his last two units to follow up
the blow.[32]

Who should Rodman's soldiers encounter on the other side but James
Sinclair and the 35th North Carolina, which promptly gave way, leaving
several brass cannon behind. Despite a spirited struggle by other North
Carolinians, Rodman began folding up their line like a hallway carpet.
These Yankees wore grey overcoats, though, and for a time they endured both a fire from the enemy in front and from their friends on the
right. It required a courageous display of the national flag from atop
the parapet to correct the problem, though the solution did not sit well
with the color guard.[33]

Foster saw Rodman's men coming down the enemy works. His exposed brigade had been taking a beating from the artillery in front,
especially from the river battery in Fort Thompson, but now he flung his
line of battle forward. Frustrated Massachusetts men sprang to their
feet and charged recklessly for the Confederate line. Water filled the
ditch in front of the parapet: some leaped over, surprised at their own
agility, while others fell short and dropped in, and still more dragged
logs across for a catwalk. The Tarheels here scudded for town. Foster's
men and Parke's congregated on the captured works either side of the
Old Beaufort Road, wondering what to do next as their brigadiers tried
to catch up.[34]

The sounds of musketry and light artillery still echoed from Reno's
direction, beyond the railroad; the two Confederate regiments there
continued to show fight. The five companies of the 5th Rhode Island Battalion, Parke's nearest troops, wheeled about and trotted to the brow
of a hill to Vance's left front, where they began to harass him with an
oblique fire. Parke scooped up the rest of his command and trudged back
up the blasted enemy line. He applied the full firepower of his other two
regiments to the flank of the Confederate fragment, while Reno simultaneously threw two regiments into the maze of felled trees that littered
the marshy ground in front of the North Carolinians. The pair of Southern regiments held strong positions on high ground north of the creek,
but they were sorely outnumbered. At last these final stalwarts fell
back, too, but some of Foster's men had already swung around behind
them, snagging a couple of hundred birds from the fleeing covey.[35]

Satisfied with events here, Burnside galloped back to Foster's brigade. The gunboats still lobbed great shells at Fort Thompson, with better results now that the fog had thinned, but there was no agreed-upon signal to cease fire, and none of the four prearranged instructions would apply. Another grim-faced set of color bearers had to climb up on the ramparts and unfurl Old Glory. Through the wisps of smoke and mist a naval officer could see the stripes with his glass, and the muffled din of cheers carried across the water. The flotilla belched a volley of coal smoke and started for Newbern, nonchalantly barging over some paltry obstructions.[36]

General Burnside's horse pranced on the color line of the 24th Massachusetts, which had arrived too late for a taste of the fighting on Roanoke. Today the 24th had taken the brunt of Foster's casualties.

"Well, boys," Burnside bellowed, "I gave you something to do this time, didn't I?" Men from the South Shore and the Berkshires glanced up from the stew pots and porridge the Confederates had left cooking, pausing with sticky fingers and gravy-stained mouths long enough to give Old Burn a wild cheer.[37]

The Old Beaufort Road and the railroad crossed just below Newbern. Riding with Foster behind the spearhead of the first brigade, Burnside met Reno and Parke at that junction. He diverted Parke up the county road, to save the bridge over the Trent River, but a dense plume spiraling skyward left little hope for its survival. Thanks to the abundance of pitch products in the city, the Confederates were well prepared to burn anything they wished to keep from the Yankees; the bridge was engulfed before Parke arrived, forcing him to try instead to save the buildings and stores in the infantry camps on the south side of the river.

With Foster and Reno at his elbows, Burnside continued up the tracks to the city. The railroad bridge was also in flames, and the staff horses had to stand before the columns, stamping their feet, while Burnside and Foster rowed across to the gunboats—already at Newbern's wharves—to ask for ferry service. A few bulky steamboats waddled over to pick up Foster's brigade.[38]

By now it was four o'clock in the afternoon. Evacuating Confederates had warned the citizens away and had fired the larger storehouses. This conflagration had begun to spread; navy officers scrambled ashore to organize fire teams among their own crewmen and residents who had remained behind. The commander of the first battalion into Newbern looked about him at the burning warehouses, homes, and stockpiles of flaming tar and turpentine on the docks. The pungent pine smell of that thick black smoke overhung the entire city. Beyond, the Confederates reached full flight, and the streets were jammed with the conveyances of panicked civilians. "As I looked upon it," that officer remembered, "I could think of nothing but Sodom and Gomorrah."[39]

General Burnside's secretary found that looting had already begun, for many of the inhabitants had fled. He saw one black girl, ten or eleven years old, scurrying away with a serving dish on her head, with a pail, a pitcher, and a box of notions balanced on top of it. She also carried a card table in front of her, with a basket of pilfered items on that, and a bundle of things under her arm. "With this load she walked off as rapidly as *I* want to walk usually," he observed. Larned would spend most of the next couple of days helping the provost guards recover property such as that, rummaging through the dank hovels those black people occupied.[40]

Except that General Branch managed to escape with the greater part of his command—in whatever state of rout and demoralization—Burnside had earned another complete victory. True, he had fielded twice as many troops as his opponent, but the contemporary wisdom called for nearly that proportion to carry fortified works. He had not only gained his objective, but had inflicted heavier causalties in the process: his own losses amounted to less than 5 percent of his available troops, while Branch's approached 15 percent, prisoners included.[41] At Roanoke, Burnside had avoided the conventional but costly frontal assaults that would have crippled his force and impeded the rest of his campaign, but in so doing he had also spurned the cautious, time-consuming siege approaches that would soon bring a national clamor on the head of his friend McClellan. His losses might have been curtailed even further had he had the leisure for more reconnaissance on Reno's front, but his limited supplies, the uncomfortable condition of his men, and the chance of Confederate reinforcements required that Burnside act quickly.

A measure of the success at Newbern was due to the cooperation of Commander Rowan's gunboats, for even if their fire played an insignificant part in the victory, their mere presence had uncovered the most imposing Confederate works. Tacit in the recognition of this factor is the presence of yet another of Burnside's allies—his own agreeable, unassuming demeanor. There was no system of interservice authority in the armed forces of 1862, such as came later, and no army general could demand anything of a navy lieutenant. The effectiveness of a joint operation depended in a large degree on the ability of the respective commanders to get along; like Ulysses Grant, Ambrose Burnside could get along well with almost anyone, and they both parlayed that simple congeniality into victories that spring.

III

The victory at Newbern precipitated another flurry of congratulations, complimentary memberships to secular and religious societies, and memorial poems. Oliver Wendell Holmes offered General Burnside a handwritten ode entitled "The Two Armies"; seven Boston schoolchildren signed a joint letter praising him; the Rhode Island legislature appropriated money to commission a fancy new sword from Tiffany's. Daniel Larned cramped his writing hand responding to all these encomia, but Burnside was not one to rest on his laurels: he had work to do.[1]

In 1862 Newbern was a city of five or six thousand souls, many of whom lived in circumstances one former resident of a communistic utopian society considered "luxurious." Its streets were a cornucopia of classical architecture, but the lovely seaport's charm vanished in smoke and disorder the evening of March 14. Townspeople who had the courage to face the invaders were nonetheless shaken by the sight of wide-eyed Confederate soldiers flooding toward the Kinston Road, some of them still naked from swimming the Trent; widespread pillage by roving blacks sent shock waves through a community based on Negro subservience. Burnside first concerned himself with the restoration of order.[2]

The first morning he awoke in the city, Burnside sent the Southern prisoners out to bury their dead, while Union details reciprocated. He assigned squads, under officers, to search for stolen property, and he posted guards to prevent further theft. He named General Foster Newbern's military governor, and within a week he was able to report the place "as quiet as a New England village." He made army rations available to the needy, among whom were numerous formerly wealthy planters. This class, he said, had only Confederate money that was now worthless, untilled land, "and negroes who refuse to acknowledge any debt of servitude." The phrasing of this last comment might have given pause to those Radicals who later championed Burnside on the assumption he was an abolitionist, but the unsupervised slaves created a major dilemma: Burnside told the War Department "nine-tenths of the depredations on the 14th, after the enemy and citizens fled from the town, were committed by the negroes before our troops reached the city. . . . They are now a source of very great anxiety to us." Contraband refugees poured into Newbern from the outlying districts, too. Burnside expressed a hope that he would be able to find an acceptable policy toward these runaways, hinting broadly at a strong desire for direction on this sensitive topic.[3]

There had been some changes in Washington since Burnside last visited the seat of government. For one thing, the hawk-faced old secretary of war had been deposed in favor of Edwin M. Stanton, an Ohio lawyer who, like Burnside, had worked for western railroads and who (again like Burnside) was an old-fashioned Democrat. Another administrative change threw Burnside into close association with this new secretary: just as the movement toward Newbern had begun, Lincoln relieved McClellan of his job as general-in-chief. For some months there would be no such overall position, and the army and department commanders would have to report directly to Stanton. Where McClellan might have offered advice—good or bad—Stanton responded to Burnside's letter with both praise and a commission as major general, but not a word did he say about the footloose blacks. The general therefore took a practical course, employing the men and older boys on the fortifications and putting the women to work as laundresses, allowing them small government stipends.[4]

While Foster superintended police duties within the city and Reno defended the perimeter, Burnside turned General Parke loose on Fort Macon, the last Confederate bastion on the sounds. Macon squatted on the eastern end of Bogue Banks, outside Beaufort and Morehead City. It represented the final phase of the plan McClellan and Burnside had decided upon. An old pentagonal masonry fort along the lines of Fort Sumter, Macon trained guns over the harbor entrance and provided safe haven to blockade runners. Even as Burnside's division landed at Slocum's Creek, less than twenty miles away, the Confederate steamer

Nashville unloaded its cargo at Morehead City; she slipped out before moonrise on March 17, in spite of interference from a United States bark. Had Fort Macon been in federal hands, she would never have escaped.[5]

Parke's brigade marched back down the Old Beaufort Road two days after the *Nashville* steamed away. He encountered almost no resistance as far as Morehead City—which surrendered to a couple of foolhardy Signal Corps lieutenants and a newspaper artist who scurried ahead of the column—but the fort itself promised no light work. It had a clear field of fire and was surrounded by a deep, dry moat; Colonel Moses White, a young West Pointer, retreated inside the place with several companies of heavy artillery and a month's supplies. Parke issued the obligatory call for surrender, White politely refused, and Parke began the arduous preparations for a siege. There was no other way.[6]

The forces Burnside had distributed held Newbern fairly secure, but he had too few troops left for any of the incursions into North Carolina's interior that McClellan had hoped for; the Army of the Potomac stirred just then for its campaign toward Richmond, up the peninsula between the York and James rivers, and a dash against Goldsborough or Raleigh would siphon off a good deal of pressure. Despite McClellan's fall from the top command, Stanton gave him leave to call on Burnside for just such a cooperative effort. Burnside appealed for reinforcements toward that end: he had not a single cavalry trooper and required a regiment of horse for reconnaissance; he would need at least two more batteries of field artillery; of infantry he asked for enough "to make a division out of each one of my brigades." That implied he wanted at least another dozen regiments of infantry alone, based on two average brigades per division. Until recently, the division had been the largest tactical unit in the United States Army, but now it adopted the notion of an army corps, consisting of two or more divisions. In part, Burnside desired such a corps to initiate field operations, but he also wanted to expand his force to reward his brigadiers and certain deserving colonels with promotion; the latter purpose could be realized with but a token fragment of the troops he had requested.[7]

Scouts and raids were the only operations Burnside could afford to conduct until his reinforcements arrived. Four days after the battle, he supervised one reconnaissance himself, with two companies of the

24th Massachusetts, aboard the *Alice Price*. A couple of days later he
sent one of Foster's regiments out to clear the Kinston Road and one of
Reno's up the Trent, burning every bridge within thirty miles.

With the assistance of the navy Burnside again chose the 24th Massachusetts to visit Washington, on the Pamlico, to show the flag. (The men
of the 24th considered themselves Burnside's pets, and he did hold them
in high regard, principally because of their colonel, Thomas Stevenson.)
Washington was easily vanquished: the mayor met Colonel Stevenson
in an open boat and escorted his soldiers through a cheering crowd
while the band played national airs. The only rebellious spirit in town
seemed to be manifested by a windowful of stiff-lipped girls scowling
from the second story of a boarding school, and even they relented when
handsome Yankee officers began flirting with them, ultimately blowing
kisses to the young men when they marched back to their boats.

"So much for 'Secesh' at that place," Mr. Larned noted. It all seemed
very encouraging.[8]

Even the little brigade on Roanoke Island shed a few hundred men
for an attack on Elizabeth City, coming away with six dozen militiamen
as prisoners. Colonel Hawkins, who organized the raid but did not accompany it, perhaps offered the little victory as atonement for his most
recent transgressions. A few days after Burnside settled in at Newbern,
he had felt it necessary to squelch some of Hawkins's more undesirable
traits. For one thing, the New York colonel had made some requisitions
for teams and wagons directly from the supply center at Hatteras without so much as mentioning it to the division quartermaster, and at a
time when horses were scarce in the department. He had also forwarded
some observations on his brigade surgeon that Burnside deemed "highly
improper and unsoldierlike." Then, on March 19, Hawkins wrote Burnside a letter in which the division commander perceived "a spirit of insubordination and disposition to complain which if persisted in will tend
to lessen your usefulness as a commanding officer." With his customary
good will the general declined filing the charges a more rigid discipli-
narian might have invoked. Instead, attributing Hawkins's failings to
his relative inexperience, he dictated a reply full of as much friendly
advice as formal reprimand. In the end he did not even send that, lest
it fall into the public domain of official correspondence, though he must
have transmitted his displeasure through some more casual means, for
Hawkins embarked on a brief spell of good behavior. This would not be

the last instance when General Burnside's benevolence was misspent on a subordinate, but only one other object of Burnside's good nature would prove so ungrateful as Rush Hawkins.[9]

Seldom would Burnside's staff enjoy more pleasant accommodations than in Newbern. His first headquarters filled a big Georgian manse on the corner of New and Middle streets, the home of an absent Southern officer. The upstairs bedrooms had seen the births of both Lewis Armistead, who became a Confederate general that spring, and his uncle, Edward Stanly, a four-term U.S. congressman. There were gas lights in every room, eight black servants and a white steward, and expansive yards front and back. On the first morning of spring, Mr. Larned saw roses, crocuses, hyacinths, and lilies in bloom, and tall sycamores assured shade for the hot days of midsummer. March nights yet turned cool, but each room offered a cozy fireplace cased in King-of-Prussia marble, and many a bootheel propped itself on those low mantels during late-night hours. Burnside was a creature of the night, and his hospitable personality attracted visitors until well after midnight most evenings; Foster, Reno, and Parke frequently played euchre with their commander until three o'clock of a Carolina morning. It was often only after his guests had chosen to leave that Burnside turned to his correspondence, dictating letters and orders at a furious pace, sometimes until the verge of daybreak.[10]

Now and then regimental bands came to serenade the general. Everyone's favorite was Gilmore's Band, of the 24th Massachusetts, which performed a complete concert one night in April, across the street from Burnside's headquarters. There the band introduced a composition of Mr. Larned's—"Burnside's Grand March." The secretary gave his chief a copy of the piece.

"By Jove," Burnside replied, "I'll send one of those to my wife." Mrs. Burnside had apparently suffered so miserably with music lessons that she absolutely hated music; her husband, who admitted he could play no better "than a cow," teased her with a demand that she play it for him when next they met.[11]

Some of the leisure disappeared from life at headquarters early in April, when a brigade of reinforcements arrived. Although the four regiments did not approach the numbers Burnside had requested, he seeded them through his command in order to sprout the corps he eventually wanted: by virtue of a general order he created three stripling divisions, awarding each of his brigadiers the nominal grade of "acting major general." Foster and Reno each took two of the new regiments while Parke, busy at Fort Macon, assumed command of a "division" virtually unchanged from his old brigade. Burnside left the Roanoke Island brigade independent: he seemed unwilling to impose Colonel Hawkins on any of his generals—Hawkins bridled so in a subordinate capacity—nor did he wish to increase the command on the island, lest the New Yorker fall in line for a promotion.

Among the recent arrivals was the 3rd New York Artillery, under Colonel James H. Ledlie. In the space of ten weeks in 1864, this man would manage to seal the stamp of failure on Burnside's reputation.[12]

With this nucleus of a corps, the department commander longed to launch some offensive enterprises. Still he had not a scrap of cavalry, but with a lesson taken from his frontier days he mounted a company of Rhode Island artillerymen on the battery's horses, and he put part of an infantry regiment aboard an assortment of animals.[13] These troopers roved a twenty-five-mile radius of Newbern in their new incarnation, improving both Burnside's knowledge of the surrounding countryside and his estimation of the enemy's resources. Over the previous three weeks, ignorance of the actual Confederate presence had occasionally sent a shiver coursing up the collective spine of the occupation force.

One such alarm had come the very day Burnside announced the formation of his corps. A brigade surgeon in Foster's division came pounding down the streets of Newbern, raving of a Confederate assault on his very heels. Thirty thousand of them, he said, lurked only four miles away, while another ten thousand headed for Beaufort to gobble up Parke's division. Drums rolled and soldiers began turning out of their blankets: a lot of people lost their sleep as a reconnaissance moved out to track down the report. Tracing the rumor back from Surgeon Thompson, no one could learn anything of an enemy attack beyond the fact that someone on the Kinston Road had seen a dozen Southern cavalry. The troops finally returned to their beds, and Burnside sent the embarrassed doctor back to Washington with the recommendation that he be summarily dismissed from the service as an alarmist.[14]

This did not mean that Surgeon Thompson's anxiety was unjustified. The deaf, aging Old Army man newly assigned to the Confederate Department of North Carolina, Theophilus Holmes, gradually united an army of twenty-five thousand men near Kinston, thirty miles west of Newbern. His infantry alone outnumbered Burnside's entire corps, even with those four new regiments; Holmes had, besides, the option to call on a detached brigade at Weldon, and he grew optimistic about the prospect of recapturing Newbern—with good reason. Only a lack of personal confidence prevented him from unleashing his eager troops. He asked President Davis's military advisor, Robert E. Lee, to come down and make the coup, but Lee demurred.[15]

Rumors, and even evidence of a Confederate assault, failed to enervate General Burnside in the way they did McClellan, though he wisely chose to postpone his invasion of the interior until more troops arrived. He nevertheless continued raiding at widespread points, both to keep the enemy off balance and to protect his own men from the softening inherent in garrison duty. Within twenty-five days his officers reported seven different engagements with Confederate troops.[16]

The largest clash flared at South Mills, near the Virginia state line. South Mills was the southern terminus of the Dismal Swamp Canal, the most direct route to Norfolk; in the aftermath of the gladiatorial contest between the *Monitor* and the *Virginia*, a story threaded its way through Dismal Swamp to the effect that Confederates were building two smaller ironclads at Norfolk, which might fit through the canal locks and wreak havoc on Burnside's naval bodyguard. Commander Rowan brought this inaccurate but unsettling news to Burnside, who accordingly arranged an expedition to destroy the locks and cave in the banks of both the Dismal Swamp Canal and the Albemarle and Chesapeake, which connected the North River with Currituck Sound. He ordered General Reno, with two of his own regiments and all three of Hawkins's, to converge on Elizabeth City and proceed to South Mills.[17] This undertaking would prove unique among Burnside's coastal operations because its objectives were not accomplished and because, thanks to the ever-contentious and self-important Hawkins, it resulted in an acrimonious flap between two of Burnside's subordinates.

Reno landed at Elizabeth City just after midnight, April 19, to find Hawkins's brigade unloading from its own steamers. Hawkins claimed surprise at the discovery he would not command the raid himself. Reno started him well before dawn for the Pasquotank Bridge below South Mills, sixteen miles upstream. Reno's own troops did not dock for another four hours, yet they overtook Hawkins twelve miles out of Elizabeth City, the independent brigade having come by a circuitous route that exhausted the men.[18] Reno ordered Hawkins to fall in behind, but his winded brigade lagged even more, and Reno encountered a small Confederate line of battle with nothing more than the two regiments of his own division. These he threw into a flank maneuver sometime after one o'clock, directing Hawkins to follow with two more regiments when his command finally came up. The remaining regiment would meanwhile create another enfilade from the other flank. Perhaps because of the jaded condition of his men (and himself), Hawkins did not begin to position his brigade until Reno prodded him personally, and before he had even reached his assigned position, he led a spirited attack on a Confederate battery with his own 9th New York. Unauthorized, premature, and unsupported, the charge was beaten back with frightful losses—about 10 percent of the regiment fell in two short minutes. Hawkins himself cradled a wounded wing, and his adjutant was killed. Sheer weight of numbers soon forced the enemy to withdraw despite the blow struck at Hawkins, but the Southern defenders marched away unmolested. Ammunition had run low at least in Reno's two regiments, and the 9th New York looked pretty demoralized; a pelting thunderstorm also chilled the men and softened the roads. Confederate reinforcements were rumored to be on their way, as in fact they were, so after permitting his command to build fires and rest until ten o'clock that night, Reno ordered a withdrawal to the transports at Elizabeth City.[19]

When everyone arrived home, Colonel Hawkins penned a report that included no mention of his tardiness, ignored the presence of either General Reno or any of his troops, and left the demonstrably false impression that his reckless charge was forced upon him by the terrain. As if to insult Reno further, Hawkins sent the report directly to General Burnside, while Hawkins or someone on his staff grumbled aloud that Reno's own ineptitude had turned a promising affair into a defeat. Hawkins simultaneously wrote Burnside a private letter bemoaning the fight as an "unfortunate occurrence." All of this soon reached Reno's ears, and he saw a copy of the New Yorker's scandalous report. Going straight to Burnside, Reno pulled no punches, calling Hawkins an "infernal scoundrel," asking the commanding general to publish a congratulatory order if he approved of Reno's performance. Burnside certainly did approve, for he had specifically cautioned Reno to take no great risks to accomplish his mission; he published the desired order two days later.[20]

Reno's own report, however, also contains what appears to be a deliberate misrepresentation. He referred to the withdrawal to Elizabeth City as something done after "having accomplished the principal object of the expedition, conveying the idea that the entire Burnside expedition was marching upon Norfolk."[21] Burnside probably did hope to feign such a demonstration against that city, in McClellan's favor: McClellan himself had inquired about a similar diversion toward Winton or Suffolk two weeks before, and the operation to South Mills was conducted precisely as McClellan then suggested. To say that this was the "principal object" of the movement, though, was a different thing: in a letter to McClellan written the day Reno departed Newbern, Burnside detailed his plans for the operation; in that letter he never mentioned the notion of a demonstration, noting only that he planned to destroy the Currituck canal and a lock of the Dismal Swamp Canal at South Mills. The diary of a soldier in the 21st Massachusetts, found on the battlefield by the Confederate relief force, corroborates the theory that the destruction of the canals was the only aim. Ironically, though, the raid did serve to make Confederates in Norfolk nervous, and Burnside's presence was a major factor in their decision to evacuate the city a few weeks later.[22]

Burnside, who endorsed and forwarded Reno's report, would seem to have lapsed from his customary scrupulous forthrightness by not correcting the error, but there are reasons to believe he ignored it from honest motives. First, the altercation between Reno and Hawkins erupted almost as soon as the steamers returned, which would have led Burnside to concentrate on the facts surrounding the movement, distracting him from any comments about the genesis of the operation. Or he may have allowed the distortion to stand deliberately, since it suggested more of an element of success than existed; to do otherwise would cast an adverse reflection upon Reno, whom Burnside considered blameless for the failure and for whom he had the greatest affection. Finally, Burnside may have regarded the overstatement as a legitimate means of avoiding a slump in morale, for he still commanded an army that was isolated and outnumbered in the midst of a hostile land.

Even before Reno's hackles had settled, Burnside relished news of Parke's progress at Fort Macon. He and some of his staff sailed down the Clubfoot Creek Canal on the *Alice Price* to have a look. As they approached Bogue Banks, their lookout spotted a sail pulling away. The *Alice Price* drew alongside, and Burnside hailed the boat in his booming baritone. It never slackened. For the only time during the war, Burnside unholstered his revolver, putting a ball across the bow of the suspicious vessel, and she hove to. Two nondescript characters climbed aboard. Burnside confronted them in the cabin, asking what news they had from Beaufort, their evident home. In that pinched Banks dialect, one of them offered that he had heard "the Old Ginral has come down to Caroline City sword in hand." The staff burst into laughter, and the two seamen glanced nervously around. The same man added that this was only what he had heard, and it might be true or not. The staff laughed some more, and the pair grew thoughtful.

"I don't know," said the spokesman, "but you is the man arter all." Just then Burnside took off his hat and put it on the table, revealing his hairless pate. "Now I knows ye," said the man, and he grabbed the general's hand, pumping vigorously. The staff exploded while first one sailor, then the other, shook long and hard. Getting what information the two could give, Burnside escorted them back to the deck. One of them leaned over the rail and shouted for the rest of the crew to come up and "give the Old Ginral a grip," and Burnside had to stand it some more while his amused aides looked on.

Having ascertained it was safe to continue, Burnside had the steamer anchor off Bogue Banks while he went ashore to speak with General Parke. Members of the staff expected to accompany him, anxious to glimpse the fort General Foster had helped build, but in the wake of their glee at his predicament with the overfriendly schoonermen Burnside impishly told them they had better stay aboard. They remained, in morose but dutiful silence, until after he had landed on the beach, when he directed some of Parke's signalmen to wigwag the ship for them. They piled into the *Price*'s other boats like so many schoolchildren, tripping over each other in their excitement.[23]

For five weeks a few hundred Confederates under Colonel White had sapped Burnside's strength by occupying an entire division—albeit a small one. Now Parke's siege artillery sat ready to open on the fort, and on April 23 Burnside sent in another demand for surrender. White refused. The Confederate who brought word of that refusal went back into

Macon with Burnside's personal appeal for a meeting with the young colonel on Shackleford Banks, across the bay. White appeared there the next morning, and the two of them paced the sand while Burnside tried to persuade his opponent of the futility of his resistance. White had achieved as much success as he could expect by distracting Parke's troops more than a month; another day or two would hardly be worth the slaughter of his garrison. But the Romantic tradition ran strong in the antebellum South; White may not have been able to resist a chance to fight to the death against overwhelming odds. Again he refused.

At 5:40 A.M. April 25, Parke opened on Fort Macon with two batteries of huge mortars and one consisting of 30-pounder rifles. For a time the fleet joined in, but rough seas threw their shots wild. Parke's fire, conversely, fell with such fearful accuracy that the white flag went up Macon's staff eleven hours after the barrage began. More than two dozen of Colonel White's men lay dead or wounded, but only three of Parke's.[24]

Burnside again chose to parole his prisoners in order to broadcast the gospel of Union strength that he considered "as good as a second victory." Some of Mr. Larned's relatives suggested the general played favorites with White, a fellow military academy graduate, but Larned assured the folks at home that sympathy had little to do with it: Burnside had been willing to "put the garrison to the sword," if necessary. Larned regretted only that he drew the laborious job of writing up the parole certificates.

The *Alice Price* cast off with ninety unarmed Confederates aboard, bound for Newbern. When she steamed into the harbor every whistle in the Union fleet greeted her.[25]

With the elimination of Fort Macon, Burnside at last enjoyed a deep-water port. No longer would shallow-draft little steamers have to ferry all his provisions over the Swash, subject to the vagaries of the weather; the railroad connecting Newbern and Morehead City made his supply line all the more convenient. Nearly as important, the North Atlantic Blockading Squadron (of which Commander Rowan's gunboats were a part) had another coaling station south of Fort Monroe.

In addition to all the time Burnside devoted to his department during those hectic days, he had to burn the stubs of many candles in the pursuit of private business and personal affairs. Early on, he had to attend to some of his duties as treasurer of the Illinois Central at inopportune moments, as when someone reminded him—the day he announced the commencement of his expedition—that the land office account ran too low to meet an immediate debt. The Kingsbury estate frequently brought him up short and required his attention, and people from every cranny of his past pressed him for favors. Some requests he could not ignore. One came from a mother in Louisville whose son had served as a mounted orderly until his horse dropped from under him at Shiloh; she asked Burnside if he could find a place for her boy, so his abilities and opportunities would not languish in the ranks. The woman thought the general might remember her husband, who had furnished Burnside "the temporary means to convey you to New Orleans," fifteen years before.

Another matter to which Burnside paid personal attention was a plea from Marie Willcox, whose husband had been captured at Bull Run. She believed him in a prison at Salisbury, North Carolina, but her letters failed to reach him. She asked Burnside to deliver a packet of correspondence through the lines, since Salisbury lay within his department. He not only did that, but attempted to make arrangements for Willcox's release with his Confederate counterpart, General Holmes: Orlando Bolivar Willcox and Burnside had been classmates at West Point, where they had been rather close.[26]

Though General McClellan no longer controlled Burnside's operations, he continued to ask the North Carolina commander to make diversions in favor of the Army of the Potomac, and Burnside still gave him unofficial reports of his progress, explaining that his troops were too few and too thoroughly occupied to engage in any significant demonstrations. With Parke's little division free of Fort Macon, though, Burnside could plan some of the collateral movements McClellan had looked for, but before Burnside could inaugurate anything, the secretary of war instructed him to avoid major confrontations until McClellan's situation stabilized before Yorktown. McClellan, lapsing into his chronic delusion of numerical inferiority, cautioned his old friend Burn that a Southern division reportedly moved against him from Richmond, further quieting Burnside's aggressive impulses. The phantom division never arrived, but because of the warnings (and a crippling lack of wagons) Burnside remained on the defensive. He nevertheless hankered to strike a blow: in one of his boyishly friendly letters to Mac he promised that when

McClellan chased the enemy from Yorktown, "I'll give them a kick in the flank that will make them see stars."[27]

One of Burnside's principal worries disappeared early in May, when the Confederates evacuated Norfolk. With Union troops threatening the city from Fort Monroe, and the danger of Burnside squeezing him from the south, General Huger moved out on the ninth of May. His hegira trailed a caravan of refugees from well to the south, looking over their shoulders in the direction of North Carolina. The specter of Southern ironclads in the canals ceased to disturb Burnside's sleep: he was grateful, now, that Reno's force had failed in its mission of destruction, since those canals supplied the only rapid communication with Fort Monroe.[28]

In the midst of an inspection tour of Roanoke Island and Elizabeth City, Burnside learned of the capture of Norfolk and Portsmouth. With this news came reports that McClellan had achieved some success on the Peninsula, notably in a battle at Williamsburg and in his advance to a new base on the Pamunkey River, nearer still to Richmond. Burnside hurried back to Newbern to plan that promised venture into the interior, to take advantage of (or take some of the heat off) McClellan's progress, but he found himself still hamstrung by a dearth of transportation. Wagons, locomotives, and railroad cars he had ordered in mid-March had not been delivered in mid-May. The infantry reinforcements he requisitioned had manifested themselves only in the four regiments of early April, and Burnside might reasonably have wondered whether he was strong enough to leave his secure base. However, it was not his strength—some seventeen thousand, all told—that stopped him: he must have wagons, and the two dozen he might have mustered were not sufficient for an ammunition train.[29]

Fever took a heavy toll on the troops in North Carolina that spring. Through April the general reported a growing sick list; it never swelled to the point that he feared for the security of Newbern, but it became a greater concern when Stanton's War Department closed the nation's recruiting offices. Burnside discovered, as so many generals did, that his army fared worse in camp than on an active campaign. In the beginning of May, just after the recruiting offices opened again, he noticed a gradual improvement in the health of his men, but then he came down with chills himself. In the course of another request for those horses and wagons, on May 16, he confided to Secretary Stanton, "I have not been

well for a few days past." That same day he apparently grew worse, retreating to his bed for a few days with a touch of the diarrhea and fever
that weakened his troops. His own attack may have been the relapse
of a fever he had first encountered in Mexico, which seemed to disable
most veterans of that conflict periodically; at any rate, he was confident
by May 19 that he had recovered.[30]

The burden of department command eased again toward the end of
May, when Burnside's supervision of the civilian population came to an
end. For nearly a month he had governed his territory under the strict
control of martial law, with arrest and confinement awaiting anyone who
challenged his authority or dared to "utter one word against the Government of these United States," but with the appointment of Edward
Stanly as military governor, Secretary Stanton relieved the general of
responsibility for those duties he had assumed out of necessity. Any
further civil authority he exercised would come through Stanly, which
pleased Burnside no end.

Stanly had been born fifty-two years before in the very house where
Burnside lodged; it may have been out of respect for the new governor's birthplace that the general moved his headquarters to a three-
story brick Federal at the corner of Johnson and East Front streets.
After eight years in the U.S. House of Representatives—during which
he once thrashed fellow Whig Henry Wise, right on the House floor—
Stanly moved to gold-rush California. He ran for governor there in 1857
and lost, but on May 14 of 1862 a clipper dropped him in New York, in response to Stanton's appointment. He arrived in Newbern in the middle
of a spring deluge, but Burnside rose from his sickbed to greet him.[31]

Despite his Republican proclivities, Stanly favored adherence to
North Carolina's Negro Code as a means of rejuvenating support for
the Union, but he was rabidly opposed to secession: unlike his former
sparring partner, General Wise, no act of the state legislature could
legitimize that course in his eyes. This opinion did not appear to enjoy
unanimity within his family, for Stanly's own brother idled with those
Burnside had imprisoned under the order against treasonable utterances. Stanly, the prewar Whig from the South, and Burnside, the
Northern Democrat of days gone by, were of a like mind on many issues
confronting them. The general, for instance, had reentered the army
with a definite distaste for abolitionists. Though he gravitated invol-

untarily to the belief emancipation might be a necessary ingredient to
victory, he retained his dislike for volatile antislavery men. The same
was true of Stanly.[32] Their common opinion came to light in the case of
Vincent Colyer, of Brooklyn.

Colyer was a minister affiliated with the Young Men's Christian Association, who had come to Newbern on his own authority to do the work
of the Lord. Burnside appointed him superintendent of the poor. Most
of the poor there were black, and Colyer established a microcosmic
forerunner of the Freedmen's Bureau, operating a school for Negro
children and finding work for contrabands. He employed one runaway
slave at his own residence. It happened that this woman belonged to
an old friend of Governor Stanly's, and since the man professed loyalty
to the Union, the governor allowed him to retrieve her. Stanly also reminded Colyer that it was illegal to teach black people to read in North
Carolina, as the minister was doing at his school.

Colyer flew into a righteous fit, flinging an angry resignation on Burnside's desk before hopping a steamer for home. Not content to leave the
issue at that, however, he stopped in Washington on his way North and
stirred up a hornets' nest. (Given the number of abolition-minded men
in powerful positions there, such nests hung waiting.) He charged that
Stanly had ordered him to shut down a Sunday school and had brutally
returned a slave to her heartless master, all of which fell on anxious
Radical ears; within a week there swirled a whirlwind of controversy.
The U.S. House of Representatives passed a resolution demanding to
know what Stanly meant by this. He responded that he merely wanted
to win over loyal citizens by upholding the laws: many North Carolinians
would gladly return to the union, once assured the war's aim was not
abolition, and the government at least professed to be interested only
in reunion—did it not? The stewardship of a divided state required cir-
cumspection enough without such a red herring drawn across the path,
and Stanly illustrated his aggravation when the "secret service" agent
Harvey Helper tried to show him which way the wind blew: Stanly listened to none of Helper's abolition propaganda, throwing him on a boat
for New York.[33]

For his part, Burnside advised the administration to back Stanly, and
when the smirking reverend resumed his mission in early June, Burnside took him into his office, blasting him liberally for his meddling in

the delicate politics of the department.[34] Other than his advice to Washington and his explosion at Colyer, however, Burnside kept clear of civil administration.

Secretary Stanton suggested that Burnside could cooperate with General John Dix, commander at Fort Monroe, in an offensive maneuver below the James River, and Burnside decided to see Dix in person to make detailed plans. The evening of June 8 he started up the canal in his headquarters boat, arriving at Fort Monroe about midnight. Dix quickly revealed what he might have made known by wire: that his forces were too weak to move offensively. When Burnside forwarded this information to the War Department, Stanton replied that, since he was near the Peninsula, Burnside might as well go up to McClellan's headquarters for a chat. Only too glad to see his old friend after so many months, Burnside started up the York River the morning of June 10, in the pouring rain. The road from the railhead to McClellan's advance headquarters was nothing less than a quagmire. Burnside made this last leg of the journey in a light wagon with a four-horse team, but those last nine miles took four and a half hours. On the way, he saw two mules drowning in the mud, unable to raise their heads. The journey served to impart a particular understanding of McClellan's difficulties, one that might have caused certain Washington bureaucrats to moderate their flagging opinion of the Peninsula commander.[35]

He found McClellan in a soggy camp at New Bridge, on the flooded Chickahominy River, and for five hours they discussed family, old times, and military affairs. Burnside did his best to encourage his friend, speaking of the capture of Richmond as though it were a foregone conclusion and promising that as soon as that happened, North Carolina would return to the union. He left McClellan with the decided impression that many good Union hearts still beat in that state, but considering Burnside would totally despair of Tarheel loyalty within another month, the remark sounded like one more attempt to raise McClellan's spirits; the senior general appeared convinced he was hopelessly outnumbered and harbored a fear that the government would not sufficiently support him. Perhaps they discussed Governor Stanly, a man of their own mind, who saw it as his duty to restore the old order of things. They toyed with the idea of Burnside moving his divisions on Petersburg, below Richmond—he could do that now, for transportation had begun to arrive for his troops—and they considered the possibility of transferring the greater part of his corps to the Army of the Potomac. Doubtless the old plan of a march on Goldsborough came up, but they concluded nothing, and finally Burnside rode away in the incessant downpour, leaving his friend to an irksome group of Spanish generals "observing" his army.

Mr. Larned gazed longingly after the comfortable tent McClellan had prepared for them, but Burnside had good reason to hurry back: he had telegraphed Mrs. Burnside when they first docked at Fort Monroe, and by the time they returned from the Chickahominy, she had arrived on a steamer from New York.[36]

No one recorded whether the general's wife played "Burnside's Grand March" for him. Probably she did not, for their reunion was short-lived. President Lincoln took advantage of Burnside's presence at Fort Monroe to ask him up to Washington for an interview; he sailed up with a few of his staff, and while he spent the day answering questions for Lincoln and the cabinet, the staff officers toured the city. Citizens recognized them as Burnside men even without their commander, just by the cut of their uniforms and the punched-out crowns of their regulation hats. It did not help to disguise them that several of the staff affected the general's unique style of whiskers.

Mr. Larned and the other officers took rooms at Willard's Hotel, Burnside's habitual Washington lodging, where he returned late in the evening. He had spent hours responding to whole batteries of questions, and his voice had worn down to a croak. Still, he had one judgment to offer.

"If there is an honest man on the face of the earth," he told his aides, "Lincoln is one."

During part of that marathon interrogation, Lincoln and Stanton alone had taken Burnside into a private conference. In their presence, he could not have failed to describe McClellan's transportation problems on those miserable Peninsula roads, and he elicited some sympathy for McClellan from two superiors otherwise growing increasingly intolerant of Little Mac's procrastination: Burnside later revealed, at least to McClellan, that they had both told him he could obey McClellan's orders directly, without reference to Washington, as an expression of their support for the benighted commander of the Army of the Potomac.[37]

His victories in North Carolina had earned Burnside many honors. The legislatures of several states had voted him their thanks, and President Lincoln and Stanton evinced considerable gratitude and admiration. At a time when the principal Union army was being criticized for its lassitude, and just after the devastating setbacks at Bull Run and Ball's Bluff, Burnside's uninhibited early successes had been important to Northern morale.

One tardy tribute came a week after Burnside returned to Newbern from Fort Monroe. The Tiffany sword ordered by the Rhode Island general assembly was finally ready, and a small delegation headed by Adjutant General Edward Mauran traveled down from Providence to make a formal presentation, which they carried off despite the embarrassment it caused the modest Burnside. The deputation was no little vexation to him. Their antics before the ceremony caused one staff officer to judge them "some of the biggest fools that I ever saw." Nevertheless, on June 18 the entire Burnside expedition trotted out in a shower and formed a hollow square. Every man not detailed for guard duty wore his parade best. The brigades came to attention, and just as the 4th and 5th Rhode Island regiments escorted Burnside onto the field the rainshower ended, a rainbow stretching behind the procession as though to form a triumphal arch. Battery F of the 1st Rhode Island Artillery thundered a salute. General Mauran made the presentation, Burnside thanked him with a little speech, characteristically throwing all the credit on the officers and men under him, and fifteen thousand soldiers raised a deafening cheer.[38]

The peaceful springtime in Newbern drew to a close. In a fortnight Burnside would leave the Old North State forever, having established there a reputation that was perhaps somewhat exaggerated but creditable nevertheless. The plan for his campaign had not really been his but McClellan's, adapted in turn from those of Hawkins and Goldsborough, but Burnside carried out every facet of that campaign without a hitch, up to the point where Stanton ordered him to revert to the defensive. The only other field commander who had so consistently met his superiors' expectations at this juncture was Grant.

The capture of the North Carolina sounds virtually eliminated them as a haven for blockade runners, and seriously hampered the movement of supplies to Norfolk. Burnside's presence there was also responsible for the retention of several thousand Confederate troops at Norfolk, relieving McClellan of that much pressure on the Peninsula (it was not Burnside's fault McClellan did not take advantage of the circumstance), and even the bungled affair at South Mills helped Richmond authorities decide to evacuate Norfolk in May, which afforded the Army of the Potomac the invaluable assistance of Union gunboats on the James River. Federal troops inside Cape Hatteras created a sanctuary for those of Union principles and maintained numerous bases from which future reconnaissance and offensive operations could be conducted.

Burnside's share of the credit is difficult to assess. His greatest contributions to the expedition's victories seem to have been his moral courage, his exhaustive attention to administrative detail, and his readiness to rely upon—and credit—his subordinates' abilities.

Burnside admitted that at one point his confidence eroded with all the ill luck he encountered. The weather so battered his fleet, the Swash at Hatteras so impeded it, and the shortage of drinking water brought it so near the brink of disaster that he despaired of success; but once inside Pamlico Sound he never lost hope.[39] He dashed his men ashore at Roanoke Island and at Newbern with only a vague notion of the forces arrayed against him, and carried out his assaults with but scanty information about the obstacles he would meet. George McClellan would have done well to take a lesson from his less timid friend.

Burnside's close supervision of his command amounted very nearly to a fault. While outfitting the expedition, he saw personally to the specifications of the vessels, chartered them, and inspected them. Almost daily he made the rounds of the ships, seeing to the comfort and health of the men, reviewing the plans for landings and assaults, and consulting with his immediate subordinates. In battle he often delivered orders in person. All of these duties could have been assigned to staff officers. Attending personally to so many details did eliminate much opportunity for misunderstanding (though it did not avoid the near fiasco with the deep-draft vessels), but the disinclination to share the labor with his staff often caused him to overwork himself. At a higher level of command, that tendency could be dangerous.

There was one place where Burnside volunteered to delegate authority, and that was on the battlefield. Generals Foster, Reno, and Parke were all old acquaintances; he trusted their wisdom and he could also trust them to refrain from exercising the self-serving politics that pervaded the officer corps of the Army of the Potomac. Each of them could dare to make independent decisions when the circumstances required it, without fear of undue blame if success did not follow. That policy of reasonable independence apparently trickled down from division level with beneficial results, a case in point the decisive charge of the 4th Rhode Island at Newbern, carried out on Colonel Rodman's own responsibility. (It was perhaps to preserve this policy that Burnside declined to censure Colonel Hawkins for his foolish mistake at South Mills.) The good relations between his brigade and division commanders were indispensable to the hearty cooperation required for the triumph of Burnside's isolated little army. The only recorded instance of upper-echelon disharmony was the tiff between Reno and Colonel Hawkins. Hawkins, an argumentative man who grew too fond of command on Roanoke, disliked subordinating himself to Reno and showed it. His impudent outburst coincided with Burnside's only failure in North Carolina, but it was no coincidence.

The strategy Burnside devised during the campaign was adequate, but only that; he had needed no brilliance, however, so heavily did he outnumber his enemy. In the fight for the three-gun battery on Roanoke, no more than nine hundred Confederates were engaged, while Burnside had something like seven thousand troops handy. At Newbern a dozen Union regiments went into the battle, one battalion, an independent company, and enough artillerymen to serve eight guns, while Union gunboats supported them from the river. Though he had the noteworthy advantage of earthen fieldworks, Branch put only six regiments on the field, a battalion of nearly useless militia, one independent company, and two batteries. Six additional companies of cavalry did not come under fire, and one other regiment arrived only in time to cover the retreat. The units Branch could muster were reduced by reenlistment furloughs as well. In both battles, the Confederates fought with generally inferior weapons, including an occasional assortment of shotguns and flintlocks.[40] With odds of about two to one, Newbern was certainly the more challenging battle, but much of the Confederate advantage of position evaporated because of the militia and incompetents like Colonel Sinclair. It is interesting to note that Burnside favored the same tactics in each situation: a frontal assault followed by the turning of the Confederate right. In each case it was the flank attack that won the day.

What stuck in people's minds was that Burnside had made no mistakes. Regardless of the limitations of his campaign, the men under him gave him their unqualified faith. To them he was invincible; wherever Ambrose Burnside went, victory should soon follow.

3

MY MARYLAND

I

Spurred by optimistic predictions like that of Colonel Hawkins, Burnside had come to North Carolina with the hope of uncovering a stifled reservoir of national fervor; like Governor Stanly, he chose to acknowledge the rights of slaveholders in order to foster such sentiments. For a time the predictions seemed accurate, such as when the mayor of Washington welcomed Burnside's troops as liberators, but much of the apparent loyalty was feigned, while those who were truly opposed to secession often dared not speak: even Union troops could not provide universal protection, and one night Confederate authorities spirited Washington's mayor away to a Richmond prison. Burnside managed to induce a single skeleton regiment of North Carolinians to don blue uniforms, but as that regiment mustered in, Governor Stanly made a steamboat tour of Union-held towns around the sounds, exhorting true patriots to rally round the flag: his appeals echoed in profound silence. Most of his unwilling constituents curled their lips at a man they thought a traitor. Burnside took the hint and finally advised the administration to abandon any plans to accommodate the loyalist element. It was probably about this time that he began to reevaluate the issue of slavery.[1]

During Governor Stanly's unavailing circuit of the sounds, Robert E. Lee wielded his Richmond army against McClellan's forces in a week-long series of attacks that uprooted the Union host from its supply base and slammed it against the James River, at Harrison's Landing.

From the start, everyone but McClellan seemed to sense the tables had turned, and any strategies that relied upon a Union threat to the Confederate capital went temporarily by the board. Just as the Southern offensive opened, McClellan directed Burnside to make an immediate diversion—the old plan of attack against Goldsborough. Unaware of this, President Lincoln telegraphed Burnside three days later to gather up as many men as he could and go directly to the relief of the Army of the Potomac. Burnside inquired which directive took precedence, but on the preliminary assumption that the commander-in-chief overruled a general in the field he began crowding his troops onto transports at Newbern.

Despite the promise Lincoln and Stanton had made a fortnight ago, regarding McClellan's control of the divisions in North Carolina, the War Department wasted a few days deciding whether Burnside should follow McClellan's orders or the president's. Another delay arose from the false report that Richmond had fallen, but finally Stanton told Burnside to go to McClellan with what men he could spare. By July 8 most of Reno's and Parke's divisions were standing off Fort Monroe, with Burnside's launch nosing from steamer to steamer like a border collie herding its flock. The general boarded at least one ship to reprimand its officers for not spreading their awnings to shield his men from the broiling sun, and the soldiers took grateful notice of his attention.[2]

Because of orders designed to expedite the rapid transfer of his troops, Burnside left his every battery of artillery in North Carolina, as well as all his cavalry. With them he left Foster's division, to garrison the occupied towns. By the time he arrived at Fort Monroe, he found McClellan's position more secure and the crisis essentially over, so he leisurely ferried his infantrymen (almost eight thousand of them) up to Newport News, where they made a peaceful camp within musket range of the wreck of one of the *C.S.S. Virginia*'s victims.

A few days later, two more small brigades arrived at Newport News and pitched their tents alongside the divisions of Reno and Parke. They were just up from the coast of South Carolina under the command of a prewar engineer officer, Isaac Ingalls Stevens. Burnside's virtually undefeated soldiers greeted these reinforcements with an uncharacteristic touch of scorn—"the force that got licked down at James Island," commented Walt Whitman's brother—but "the force that got licked" was only a few weeks away from acceptance into the fraternity; the initiation would not be easy.[3]

While the troops trained, and fattened on the abundant seafood, their commander began a month of almost constant travel. After a brief interview with President Lincoln at Fort Monroe, he proceeded to Baltimore to meet Mrs. Burnside, and during his stop there he and his staff collided with a mob of admiring soldiers. A dash to New York on railroad business led to a similar demonstration on the streets of Manhattan. Lincoln called him back from New York to meet the president's new general-in-chief, Henry Halleck.[4]

Lincoln had chosen this man from the western army, where he had been Grant's superior. Halleck was a slightly pudgy man with bulging eyes and a keen administrative mind, and like all good bureaucrats he had the habit of looking out for himself first—while maintaining a disinterested facade. Halleck must have been favorably impressed with Burnside, for he asked him to accompany him and Quartermaster General Meigs on a visit to McClellan's headquarters, to see for themselves the situation of his army. They all sailed down to Fort Monroe on the *Hero* the afternoon of July 24, dropping off Burnside's wife and staff before continuing to Harrison's Landing.

The next evening, after day-long discussions with McClellan, Halleck withdrew to another tent while Burnside participated in a council of McClellan's corps and division commanders. Burnside, Heintzelman, and General Edwin Sumner concluded that the army should remain on the James and try again at Richmond, while Fitz John Porter could not decide; nearly everyone else (McClellan excluded, for he too had retired) felt it should be removed to another field of operations before its health was fully undermined. McClellan had said he could renew his offensive with but twenty thousand more men; by the time Burnside and Halleck returned to Washington, Halleck had decided to give him the men and allow him to continue on his chosen line.[5]

That was not the administration's first choice, however. Somewhere between Burnside's arrival in Washington on July 22 and his departure from there, about July 27, the president escorted him into a closed office with Secretary Stanton. To the general's intense surprise and discomfort, Lincoln asked him if he would consent to replace McClellan at the head of the Army of the Potomac. Two humble sons of Midwestern pioneers faced each other across the desk, the one gently probing, the other modestly shaking his head. McClellan was the better general, Burnside argued, and only needed a fair opportunity to prove it. Perhaps he reminded the president of the soggy conditions on the Peninsula in June and pointed out that he, like McClellan, would prefer that the army remain on the line of the James. The president, unaccustomed to officers who pretended to limitations, seemed not to agree that McClellan was the better general, and he already knew that Burnside's energy produced results. Lincoln appears to have attributed Burnside's refusal less to an honest self-evaluation than to pure nobility of character, admiring him all the more for it. For the present he agreed not to remove McClellan, but he marked Burnside for greater things.[6]

Thus, by default, Lincoln approved a new grand strategy in Virginia. This latest design called for McClellan to attack Richmond from the southeast while another army struck from the north. This other force, styled the Army of Virginia, consisted of three corps that had been strewn between Fredericksburg and the Shenandoah Valley since the early spring. At its head rode John Pope, another western general, who almost immediately alienated every officer in his army with a pompous inaugural address that implied they had shown a want of courage and resolve. He simultaneously disturbed men like Burnside and McClellan with an antagonistic attitude toward noncombatants. Like many who disdained the chivalric notion of civilized warfare, he considered it perfectly fitting to subsist his troops on the civilian population in enemy territory. Many of Pope's subordinate generals expressed a thorough lack of confidence in their brash new commander, one of them growing particularly bitter about his spiteful policy toward civilians. On that count, at least, he elicited agreement from General Burnside.[7]

In the end, McClellan was not allowed to pursue even this combined campaign. More procrastination and appeals for still more reinforcements prompted the administration to order him back to Aquia Creek, much nearer Washington, to support Pope's line of attack. As if to fix his will, Lincoln ordered Burnside—whose men would have constituted most of the twenty thousand reinforcements—to precede McClellan to Aquia Creek Landing. Ironically, McClellan based his latest plea for more men on reports of Confederate troops swarming toward Richmond from North Carolina, where Burnside's departure had freed them.[8]

Burnside opened orders dated August 1. Unlike George McClellan,

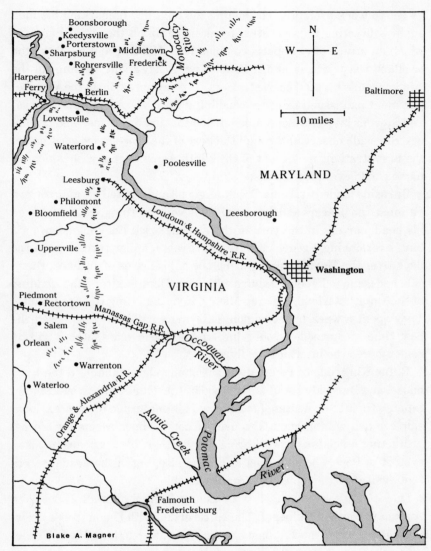

Boonsborough
Keedysville
Porterstown
Sharpsburg • Middletown
Rohrersville
Frederick

Monocacy River

Harpers Ferry
Berlin

Lovettsville

Waterford

Leesburg
Philomont
Bloomfield

Upperville

Piedmont
Rectortown

Salem

Orlean

Warrenton

Waterloo

N
W—E
S

10 miles

Baltimore

MARYLAND

Poolesville

Leesborough

Loudoun & Hampshire R.R.

Washington

VIRGINIA

Manassas Gap R.R.

Occoquan River

Orange & Alexandria R.R.

Aquia Creek

Potomac

River

Falmouth
Fredericksburg

Blake A. Magner

Map 4. The Eastern Theater, 1862

he set to work promptly, consuming the next day embarking his men again—directing the operation from his cabin on the *Alice Price*, to which an attack of erysipelas confined him. His foot and leg were too swollen to wear a boot, and he hobbled nervously about, looking out the window while his staff carried orders. Ten days previously the War Department had issued an order combining the divisions of Reno, Parke, and Stevens into a formal command, and that loading of men and trumpery Burnside observed through the port of the *Alice Price* constituted the first strategic movement of the Ninth Army Corps, with which his name would ever after be associated.[9]

Burnside landed at Aquia Creek August 3 and started his men toward Falmouth on boxcars and flatcars the following morning. He established his headquarters in the yard of the elegant brick Lacy mansion, on a bluff overlooking Fredericksburg. This was familiar territory. In the days after the Mexican War, during one of his leaves of absence, Burnside had come to Fredericksburg with Jesse Reno to attend the wedding of their mutual friend, Dabney Maury, in nearby King George County. They spent a week in the region, enjoying what Maury supposed the best time of Burnside's young life, and all these years later Burnside remembered the interlude fondly.[10]

Rufus King, one of Pope's division commanders, inhabited the Lacy house, and Burnside's staff fairly stood by their tents with arms akimbo, tapping their toes, waiting for King and his entourage to vacate. Burnside seemed willing enough to use the commodious rooms for offices, protecting official paperwork from the weather, but, perhaps in token protest of Pope's behavior, he continued sleeping in the headquarters tent even after the mansion became available.[11]

One of Pope's corps took a thrashing from Stonewall Jackson on August 9, south of Culpeper. The battle ended with Union troops drawing back toward the Rappahannock. Thereafter followed a few quiet days, the calm before the storm, during which Pope concentrated his forces on the north side of the Rapidan as Jackson and James Longstreet combined to crush him.

At the beginning of that same week, William Sprague journeyed to Falmouth to bathe in the reflected glow of Burnside's glory. The general had risen above Sprague's stratum by now, but the Boy Governor seems not to have recognized that. He seems not to have recognized many things, including the perils of meddling in the regular promotions of a regiment's officers: he had appointed an outsider to the command of the 4th Rhode Island when Colonel Rodman became a brigadier, with demoralization and mass resignations the fruits of his interference. Perhaps he expected to regain favor with a personal visit, and while the Rhode Islanders stood on parade one day he strutted before them like a field marshal. The men, rather than cheering according to the program, allowed him to pass in absolute silence.[12]

Halleck invested Burnside with general authority over not only his own corps but any part of McClellan's army that came north, from the moment it sailed from Harrison's Landing until sometime after it marched to Pope, but McClellan's first division was mighty slow about coming. Throughout much of August Burnside was no longer a field commander but simply the overseer of a replacement depot and reconnaissance base, relaying troops into the interior and information back to Washington. Every soldier with him anticipated marching to Pope's assistance and had no doubt there would be a fearful scrap when the time came. That time did not appear to be so very far in the future, either. King's division moved out August 9 and 10, leaving Burnside's impatient staff members the comfortable house.

At least one of King's brigadiers expressed a reluctance to join Pope. John P. Hatch noted just before marching that he and the other old Regular Army soldiers had no faith in Pope, though he said he felt perfectly safe under Burnside.[13]

On the twelfth of August Halleck urged Burnside to send Pope every man he dared strip from his line. Here again appeared the difference between George McClellan and Ambrose Burnside. When Little Mac read orders to reinforce Pope he would argue that it was not possible, then explain that it was impractical at any rate, and finally beg headquarters to understand that it was an imposition—veritably an insult to a general of his rank. Only when he knew his insubordination would be tolerated no longer would he grudgingly inch his various divisions toward the transports. By contrast, Halleck gave Burnside instructions to sift his corps for Pope's support August 12, and by seven o'clock that evening two of Burnside's three divisions started on their way.[14]

The column, which set out under Jesse Reno, consisted of his own division and that of Stevens—twelve infantry regiments and four newly arrived artillery batteries. Burnside also sent two of his scarce cavalry companies to provide some reconnaissance and so many of his corps surgeons that the Fredericksburg hospitals fell desperately short of doctors.

Reno's men marched under a "glorious" full moon with only light knapsacks and no tents, for greater speed, and they kept the road all night. Their advance left the second-ranking Union officer in all Virginia with only seven regiments of infantry and half-a-dozen cavalry companies to defend the supply base at Aquia Creek and patrol the entire Rappahannock River, from Fredericksburg to the Orange & Alexandria Railroad. Nor were Confederates his only worry: some of King's men had found a hogshead of whiskey and sparked a drunken brawl their first night out, and Burnside had to throw a guard over them until he could find the time to shave their heads and drum them out of camp.[15]

Conceit did not constitute the limit of John Pope's faults. As Burnside discovered, he was not a man easily pleased. To reach him, Reno's men plodded twenty-five miles in twenty-four hours, most of the time at a frustrating pace over roads clogged with artillery and supply wagons sent ahead earlier; then Reno put them on cattle cars for the last ten-mile leg of the distance. For all the haste exercised in his behalf, all Pope could say was that Reno's railroad ride disrupted his forage supply, unjustly and inaccurately claiming that the exhausted reinforcements might have marched the ten miles in the same two hours it had taken them to ride.[16]

The regiments remaining at Fredericksburg all belonged to Parke's division, and when Halleck summoned Burnside to Washington on August 14, Parke took over. Taking only Robert Holloway and his private secretary with him, the general was off before sunset. Just before galloping out of the neglected Lacy gardens, Burnside posted an order strictly prohibiting looting—lest any of his troops misapprehend that he endorsed the sort of pillage Pope appeared to encourage.

This order from Halleck had borne a peremptory tone: "Turn over your instructions to the officer next in rank and report in person to these headquarters." That sounded ominously like the message that had brought McClellan to Washington a little over a year before, and Burnside may have anticipated another difficult interview with the president about taking the army from McClellan. Such may have been Mr. Lincoln's underlying hope, but Burnside came away instead as something of a personal envoy between army headquarters and McClellan, with firm instructions to prod the Army of the Potomac into the withdrawal McClellan had been ordered to undertake more than ten days previously: afterward he would return and report privately. With his same two traveling companions at his elbows, Burnside returned to Fort Monroe on the sixteenth, where he transferred to a gunboat and went straight to McClellan's headquarters on the Chickahominy. The Army of the Potomac, Burnside was relieved to discover, was already in motion; the following day the two old friends stood together at one end of a 2,000-foot-long pontoon bridge as McClellan's five corps tramped across the river at routestep, bound for Old Point Comfort and Pope. It was a stirring sight to the little Romantic in shoulder straps; he could not eat, so moved was he by this view of his army.

"Look at them, Burn," he said. "Did you ever see finer men? Oh; I want to see those men beside of Pope's." The implied sneer at Pope's army betrayed a contempt rapidly becoming endemic among McClellan's friends and advisors, but Burnside innocently took the remark as an emotional accolade to the Army of the Potomac, missing the slur.[17]

Burnside sailed back to Fort Monroe that evening and left for Washington the next morning, August 18, for his prearranged conference with Halleck. This time he hobbled up and down the gangplank on a crutch: his ankle remained weak from the sprain he suffered in New York the previous winter, and he had turned it again in the swamps of the Peninsula.[18]

While Robert and Mr. Larned rested at Willard's, their chief gave Halleck his impressions of McClellan's army and McClellan's attitude. Certainly he had revealed to Mac Halleck's doubt of his willingness to obey orders quickly, and possibly he recounted the offer of command, for Burnside had no sooner spoken with McClellan than McClellan wired Halleck to rely on his "full cooperation." As a loyal friend of McClellan's, Burnside probably assured Halleck that that cooperation would be forthcoming; so devoid was he of envy or dishonesty that he must have believed it himself. Halleck relied more and more upon Burnside, and, as much as he wanted to relieve McClellan, he took a middle course by which he neither removed him nor retained him in command: Halleck simply took McClellan's army away a division at a time, giving Burnside authority over the pieces until he could forward them to Pope.[19]

Troops unloaded in such numbers that the few little wharves at Aquia Creek could not handle them; War Department telegraphers directed the excess to Alexandria, but before they did, John Reynolds's division of Pennsylvania Reserves swarmed ashore at Aquia, quickly followed by the rest of Fitz John Porter's Fifth Corps. The ailing Porter, touched with the ubiquitous fever, lodged in Burnside's tent, monitoring the movements of his corps from his cot. Porter was McClellan's particular confidant. Burnside himself might have expected to assume that capacity, so cordial were their relations and of such duration, but rather than regard Porter with jealousy he let their common affection for McClellan form the basis of their own friendship. Porter reciprocated with his brand of warmth, expressing himself openly and lauding the Young Napoleon at every opportunity.[20]

McClellan himself appeared at the Lacy house the evening of August 24. He remained there until well after midnight, sending or answering an occasional telegram but mostly reminiscing with Burnside over better days, reflecting on the apparent end of his once-promising military career. Neither general had a tangible command any longer. McClellan's army had scattered to the four winds, while Burnside was little more than a conduit for Pope's reinforcements. "I do not see that I can do anything here," McClellan wrote Halleck the next day, after which he took ship for Alexandria in search of the rest of his farflung corps.[21]

By this time John Pope had unwittingly encountered serious trouble. He had withdrawn the Army of Virginia north of the Rappahannock, concentrating on Warrenton, facing Longstreet's Confederate corps across the river. Meanwhile, Jackson's smaller half of Lee's army marched stealthily toward his rear, along the tracks of the Manassas Gap Railroad. Porter started from Fredericksburg to join Pope, but before he could reach him, Jackson fell on the immense store of military supplies at Manassas Junction. While ragamuffin Southerners gorged themselves on Union delicacies, Pope discovered that both his supply line and his direct telegraphic communication with Washington had been severed.

Tenuous communications survived through Burnside's key at Falmouth, and eventually that route came into use. Burnside asked Porter to send frequent reports from his front, as President Lincoln was in the habit of coming to the Washington end of the wire every morning for whatever news Burnside could give him.[22]

Porter, who shared McClellan's dim view of John Pope, phrased his reports in the same informal tone in which he and Burnside carried on normal conversation: his ill regard for Pope glowed in his dispatches, which came clicking into Falmouth on new lines Porter strung as he advanced. Beginning with a few sarcastic references to Pope's confused situation when the Fifth Corps neared the Army of Virginia on August 27, Porter tinted most of his more informative messages with undisguised scorn for the man who was then his immediate superior. He obviously assumed that Burnside, who shared some of his reservations about Pope, had taken McClellan's side in the almost open warfare between the two army commanders. That was hardly the case, and Burnside warned him of the indiscretion, wondering whether he ought to send the telegrams on to Washington. He consulted General Parke, who functioned as his chief of staff, whenever the more damaging memoranda arrived. In each case they determined to forward them to Washington verbatim: Parke felt it would be improper to withhold Washington's only word of Pope, while Burnside did not feel authorized to edit the dispatches if he did not withhold them entirely.[23]

Pope finally found Jackson—or rather, Jackson found him—August 28, and their troops clashed near the old Bull Run battlefield the rest of that day and the twenty-ninth. The Ninth Corps divisions under Reno suffered terribly. Pope ordered Porter up to his support, disregarding plain evidence that Longstreet's corps had arrived and would lay on Porter's flank if he advanced. Porter, accurately assessing the problem, chose not to obey; that hesitation eventually led Porter to a court-martial and dismissal from the army.[24]

What aided most in securing Porter's conviction was the sheaf of dispatches to Burnside, each more sarcastic and critical of Pope than the last. The messages plainly revealed Porter's uncontrolled disgust for his commander and hinted at a certain perverse amusement at Pope's self-induced predicament. His judges drew the conclusions—fairly or otherwise—that Porter never intended to help Pope and that he had deliberately disobeyed orders to assure his defeat for the purpose of restoring McClellan to command. Not until many years afterward, when political hatreds subsided and Confederate records became available, did Porter find at least nominal vindication.

The only information available to Washington during the fight continued to be that which came from Porter, so the compromising epistles kept winging regularly up the Potomac from Burnside's headquarters.

Their value at the capital became evident in a telegram from Halleck that came down to Falmouth: "I have heard nothing from Pope for four days, except through you." [25]

There were some moments of tension in Falmouth August 29 when someone reported a large body of the enemy across the river, a few miles outside of Fredericksburg. Burnside, who had already positioned his few remaining troops for a stubborn defense, sent cavalry scouts to confirm the reports. While he awaited their return he comforted Halleck (and perhaps himself) with the opinion that he could hold Falmouth against an assault coming from any direction but his right— toward where Pope was fighting. The heights along the Rappahannock lent themselves to artillery defense, and he had finally collected a preponderance of that arm.

The cavalry did not find a single Southern soldier in any direction. It seemed this was another panic caused by a nervous officer of the same stripe as Surgeon Thompson. [26]

Still, Halleck waxed anxious about the exposed garrison at Falmouth. For a time on Saturday, the thirtieth, it appeared that Pope might have gained a victory, but by Sunday the rumors began to drift in the other direction. Halleck wired Burnside to put his men on transports and hasten them to Alexandria, where they would join McClellan and the remnants of the Army of the Potomac.

It had rained August 31, and showers passed occasionally on the first of September. The road from Falmouth to Aquia Landing had been churned to jelly by the recent troop movements, and Burnside's march there dragged piteously. On more than one occasion he and his staff climbed out of the saddle to help free mired wagons. Behind the column, the bridges to Fredericksburg fell flaming into the Rappahannock: the general would presently have occasion to regret that precaution.

If Burnside found the withdrawal to Aquia a trial, loading his troops was even worse. He needed a dozen light-draft transports, but could not raise one. He embarked a few of his men by ferrying them out to deepwater steamers in tugs and lighters, but before long, coal ran low on those little boats. Figuratively looking over his shoulder for pursuing Confederates, he asked the Navy Department for some heavy gunboats to cover his evacuation. Some that happened by from Hampton Roads failed to stop on signal, and Gideon Welles had to write a midnight order to his Potomac commander to send the boats down, though from the comfort of his Washington bedroom he doubted the need.[27]

The transports arrived at long last two days later, and the movement resumed with the utmost urgency. By now Pope's battered army had backed into Fairfax Court House, not far from Washington, leaving Burnside's little fragment perfectly isolated.

Jackson had almost cut off Pope's retreat on Monday, at an intersection just north of Centreville, but portions of the Third and Ninth corps had held him back in a driving rainstorm while the Army of Virginia slipped by. Killed in that nasty affair, at the forefront of his charging division, was Isaac Stevens, the newest general in the Ninth Corps and probably one of the best it ever had.[28]

The next evening Pope and his surviving men bivouacked at Fairfax Court House, where there transpired a brief spat between Pope and General Porter that would wreak a significant, if indirect, effect on Ambrose Burnside. General headquarters had crowded into a comfortable house at the county seat. Officers were coming in and going out, relaying orders, when a dispatch arrived for Porter from McClellan, urging him and "all friends" to render Pope all the cooperation necessary to save the army. Porter felt the message must have come in response to some complaint from Pope, whom he asked what there had been about Porter's service that was unsatisfactory. Pope took that opportunity to vent his spleen, detailing Porter's instances of hesitation and noncompliance, and then he suggested that Porter had prejudged him, adding that he had heard of Porter's animosity in correspondence written before they even met on the field. The letter he cited was a private one, but revealed Porter's utter lack of confidence in Pope; Porter recoiled visibly at Pope's knowledge of it. He expressed his regret at having written of him so in even an unofficial missive, which seemed to satisfy Pope, but Porter must have reflected grimly on the denunciatory cables he had sent Burnside. Burnside had warned him about his indiscreet language, and if those insubordinate dispatches ever saw the light of day, they might corroborate Pope's accusation that he had not given him full support.[29] Within a few days Pope would know of these messages, too, and George McClellan's most influential friend would have great cause to regret his association with Ambrose Burnside.

II

By the glow of burning stores, the final remnant of the Ninth Corps still with Burnside boarded transports at the mouth of Aquia Creek near midnight on September 4. The personnel of the military railroad crowded onto the big, freshly finished wharf after Burnside and the last troops cast off, frantically transferring locomotives to the ships assigned to carry them. As these Federal officials prepared to abandon the landing, they burned five dozen railroad cars that could not be accommodated aboard ships and put even the storehouses and the expensive new wharf to the torch, for General Halleck had ordered nothing left behind that might be of use to the Confederates. When Burnside arrived at Washington, he discovered Halleck had undergone a change of heart on that point, and he wired the railroad men, too late, to spare the wharf and buildings if they could, but to destroy the rolling stock. Cars, wharf, and all sat simmering in the creek even as he composed the telegram.[1]

When the scattered fragments of the two Union armies gathered near the capital, they again fell under the command of General McClellan. General Pope was relieved of command, his reputation permanently tarnished, and those who took no part in the feud between him and McClellan could see that McClellan's partisans had had much to do with Pope's downfall. Lincoln seemed to understand as much himself, but he succumbed to the powerful argument of Little Mac's organizational abilities and agreed to let Halleck put him in charge of Washington's defenses, despite his suspicion that the general himself had lent a hand in the undermining of his competitor. Within hours after McClellan's appointment to that position, though, the president personally ordered Halleck to organize an army for the field, separate from and independent of the Washington defenses under McClellan.[2]

The need for such a field army arose sooner than anyone expected: as early as Friday morning, September 5, reports reached Washington of Confederates crossing into Maryland above Edward's Ferry, about forty miles up the Potomac. Halleck quickly named commanders for all the reorganized corps, assigning them positions around the city. General Burnside had arrived in the city from Aquia Creek that day, and President Lincoln called him to the White House again. A large proportion of Washington's defenders would have to pursue the invaders, Lincoln explained, and he wanted Burnside to lead that new army. McClellan's loyal old friend once again declined. He reiterated that he could not manage so large an army, but McClellan could. He seemed quite stubborn, so the president sighed and released him. Burnside returned to his old Ninth Corps, which had camped north of the city.[3]

That left only McClellan to head the new army; it was not something Lincoln could avoid. Sensing that inevitability, McClellan muttered something to Burnside in a midnight conversation about refusing the command until both Stanton and Halleck had resigned, but his friend convinced him after a long discussion to refrain from placing such conditions on his service to the country in its time of need. And so, as though by the hand of fate, McClellan glided back into control of the field army, too.[4]

Since the beginning of the war, the organization of American armies had expanded from the once-adequate brigade level to the creation of divisions and corps. In a logical extension of that trend, McClellan formed this latest army into left, center, and right wings, and he installed Burnside as the chief of the right wing, the largest. Official confirmation of his wing command lay a week away, but by virtue of a personal understanding, Burnside took charge of not only the twenty-nine regiments and seven batteries of the Ninth Corps but also of the corps under Joseph Hooker, which was stronger still by ten regiments and several batteries. Together, the two corps were twice as large as the army General McDowell had put under fire at First Bull Run. Hooker's corps, in fact, had been McDowell's until a day or so since, but McDowell fell out of favor again as a result of the second battle at Bull Run, so these veterans of the Army of Virginia became the First Corps of the Army of the Potomac and went under another general. "Fighting Joe" Hooker (so named by the misreading of a newspaper headline) was the very embodiment of ambitious intrigue. Thus he felt quite at home in the Army of the Potomac, and he could prove troublesome for a superior so patriotically disinterested as Ambrose Burnside.[5]

Under the wing arrangement, Reno stepped up to command of the Ninth Corps. The corps itself underwent a reorganization, adding half a dozen new regiments. The first division, that of the unfortunate Stevens, went to Orlando Bolivar Willcox, Burnside's old friend, who had recently been released from a Confederate prison. Reno's old second division was assigned to a profane career soldier, Samuel Sturgis. The original colonel of the 4th Rhode Island, Isaac Rodman, had lately returned from a convalescent leave with a brigadier's star on his shoulder, and he took over Parke's third division—Parke still serving as Burnside's chief of staff. These three commands rendezvoused at the hamlet of Leesborough, Maryland, six miles north of Washington City. A fourth, the Kanawha Division, moved through the city to join them, having just been assigned to the Ninth Corps. This was a unique organization, for unlike the original Ninth Corps—only one regiment of which had not hailed from the Atlantic Seaboard—these were all Westerners: six regiments of infantry and a battery of artillery from Ohio, a Bluegrass battery, and three companies of cavalry from Chicago and the soon-to-be state of West Virginia. Their experience had also been different from that of Burnside's other men: all the while the first three divisions fought their amphibious war in the Carolinas, the Kanawha Division had been tramping the guerrilla-infested hills between the Ohio River and the Alleghenies. One regiment in the first brigade, the 23rd Ohio, had two aspiring politicians in it—Lieutenant Colonel Rutherford B. Hayes and Commissary Sergeant William McKinley. Riding in the second brigade was Colonel George Crook, who achieved almost as great a notoriety for his exploits against various Indian tribes during the next quarter-century.

Jacob Dolson Cox, a veritable Renaissance man, commanded this western division. Born in Canada, Cox had had a successful political career in Ohio himself, and he showed a real talent for leading men. An Oberlin graduate, he was the youngest of the division commanders by five years, yet he had been a general before any of them—had taken a brigadier's commission before Burnside, in fact, when the war was barely a month old.

Cox's division was picking its way through the District of Columbia toward Leesborough when General Parke encountered it. Parke bivouacked the brigades on the future campus of Howard University and led the Ohio general to Burnside's headquarters. Burnside was absent at the time, at a meeting with the president, as Cox remembered (possibly the same meeting at which he refused the army command), but he soon returned and offered the expected stranger a warm greeting. Cox was impressed both by Burnside's air of athletic energy and his charming personality. "His large, fine eyes, his winning smile and cordial manners, bespoke a frank, sincere, and honorable character," Cox wrote later, "and these indications were never belied by more intimate acquaintance. The friendship then begun lasted as long as he lived."[6]

The two other wings of the new field army were equally informal, hinging on nothing more than verbal instructions until September 14. Sixty-five-year-old Edwin Sumner took the center wing, consisting of the Second Corps from the old Army of the Potomac and the Twelfth Corps, from Pope's army; William Franklin's Sixth Corps and an independent division made up the left wing, but Franklin's status as a wing commander never realized official recognition.[7]

Burnside enjoyed a brief chance in early September to renew old acquaintances in the recruit-swollen Ninth Corps as it camped around Leesborough. Not only had Reno, Parke, and Willcox been classmates of his at West Point, Sturgis had been there at the same time, and they all remembered each other well. Enoch Fellows, colonel of one of the new regiments, had also spent a couple of years at the military academy with them. Colonel Eliakim Scammon of the Kanawha Division, a stiff and aristocratic veteran of Winfield Scott's Mexican War staff, had taught all these former cadets ethics and English grammar. They met in an impromptu alumni gathering when Fellows's regiment arrived on September 7.[8] As it turned out, there was barely time for a shake of the hand and a glass around.

Lee's Confederates ambled freely through western Maryland by now, and on Sunday, September 7, McClellan chose to start after them. Halleck and Lincoln voiced no protest—having found no one with whom to replace him—so McClellan led the pursuit himself. His three wings radiated out of Washington's environs on roughly parallel roads running northwest, converging at or near Frederick. The cavalry fanned out in front of each column, groping for a sign of the enemy. The march was not particularly rapid, but the thousands of recruits in the big new regiments nevertheless suffered for their soft feet. The fresh, bright uniforms leaked backward like a streak of indigo in the river of faded soldier suits. A musician trailing after the 9th New Hampshire recorded the painful progress of his first campaign:

> Sept. 10 . . . Haveing marched some ten miles in our thin canvas shoes on the hard uneven turnpike, we feel footsore and weary, and are ready to sleep anywhere.

Sept. 11 . . . Everybodys footsore.

Sept. 12 . . . haveing marched some fifteen miles, with only a few ears of green corn for grub, with our feet covered with blisters, we retire, cross and ugly.[9]

The hard roads hurt everyone's feet, but the veterans found it different from marching through Virginia or North Carolina. Here, the people who gathered along the road cheered and occasionally set out buckets of cold water and lemonade. No longer were they the invaders; now they were truly the army of salvation. It helped to soften the pain in their shanks.

General Burnside could boast an extraordinary popularity among the foot soldiers of the right wing. They hailed him wherever he went. One freshly appointed officer later remembered the manner in which "vociferous cheering, first heard in the distance and increasing in apparent volume as it came nearer, was recognized as the sure announcement of the coming of Burnside."[10] These displays of affection took place along the National Road, the wagon route to the Ohio country that had been one of the Republic's early internal improvements. In places, it followed the old trail to Fort Duquesne, traveled by the doomed General Braddock and young George Washington in 1755. The first town of any size on that highway was Frederick, three miles beyond the Monocacy River. Confederates had been there for a week, but by September 12 most of their infantry had left. Only cavalry remained, and when Union troops crossed the Monocacy bridge at noon that day, they ran into mounted Southerners under Wade Hampton.

At first there was only a squadron of South Carolinians, pecking away with their inferior carbines at the leading regiments of Cox's Kanawha Division. Later, three fieldpieces contended with the Union host, inching back toward the town between rounds. Colonel Augustus Moor, commanding Cox's second brigade, spread his three Ohio regiments across the road and brought up one of the guns of his Kentucky battery. The colonel sat in the road, surrounded by the troop of Chicago dragoons assigned to his brigade, when one of General Reno's young staff officers commented rather snottily on the amount of time Moor's deployment was taking. The remark so stung Moor that, to everyone's surprise, he waved the dragoons into a headlong charge into the streets of Frederick, leading them personally while the gun bounced along behind.

Just inside the town the South Carolinians pounced on them, silencing the gun by killing its horses and scattering those Chicagoans who were not quickly killed or captured. They took Colonel Moor prisoner.

General Cox sent a regiment from Scammon's brigade into the melee, but by then the Confederates had withdrawn. Burnside's men filled the town to the music of a frenzied welcome, beaming in the moment of glory, swollen with the pride of the liberator. People crowded the streets, cheering and singing, and flags flew from nearly every window, still wrinkled from a week's hiding beneath mattresses or at the bottoms of trunks. Many of the citizens wept openly at their deliverance, and when General Burnside swam Major through the throng, a pretty young woman asked if she could kiss him. Never one to refuse a lady, Burnside freed a stirrup for her foot, drew her up, and steadied her with one arm about her waist while offering his bewhiskered face. Eventually the general worked his way out of the press of admirers and established camp on the Baltimore Pike. McClellan caught up with him there, and for a time the two of them reviewed the seemingly endless columns of Federal soldiers. It was almost dark before all Burnside's troops (stragglers aside) had filtered through town to find tent sites on the outskirts of Frederick.[11]

Early the next morning, the commander of the cavalry division rolling ahead of the Union army, Alfred Pleasonton, approached Burnside with a request for infantry support. The first of two major mountain ranges, the Catoctins, loomed just west of Frederick, and Confederate cavalry lingered along the roads to the passes there. Burnside gave him Rodman's division, and as Pleasonton trotted toward the mountains west of town, the rest of the Ninth Corps prepared to follow.

The Army of the Potomac traveled in two columns now. To the north, Burnside led the way on the National Road, followed by Sumner's center wing and most of Porter's Fifth Corps, which had been temporarily detained at Washington and which McClellan subordinated to no wing, withholding it as a reserve force. Some five or six miles south, Franklin took another road in the same direction. As Burnside's men started after the cavalry, Sumner's troops began making camp outside of Frederick, picking over the refuse of both the Confederate camps and Burnside's. Two noncommissioned officers in an Indiana regiment were thus employed when they found a package of cigars. The paper in which those cigars were wrapped had some flowery, official-looking script on it, which they thought worth showing to their captain. He recognized it, if they did not, as Lee's orders to his corps and division commanders, detailing the dispositions of his troops for the next few days. Early that afternoon the famous Lost Order reached McClellan's hands.[12]

If those four-day-old directions were still operative, the Confederate army lay dangerously divided. In an attempt to take Harpers Ferry and twelve thousand Union troops there, Jackson had countermarched across the Potomac into trans-Shenandoah Virginia; a single division had forded the Potomac downstream of Harpers Ferry and sat atop Loudoun Heights, east of the Shenandoah; two divisions under Lafayette McLaws were on Maryland Heights, across the Potomac from both these contingents, with the Union army virtually at their backs. The orders also revealed that D. H. Hill's division and most of Longstreet's corps guarded Boonsborough, but in reality Longstreet was at Hagerstown, even farther away.[13]

To crush the Army of Northern Virginia piecemeal, McClellan had only to cross the two long mountains that ran north and south beyond Frederick. Pleasonton's cavalry had already driven the Confederate horsemen over the Catoctins and had broken up two more rearguard stands east and west of Middletown by the time the Lost Order arrived at general headquarters. That left only South Mountain in the way of total victory, the base of which teemed with Union horse soldiers in the late afternoon of September 13. By nightfall Pleasonton had reconnoitered the precipitous roads leading to the crest, and during the evening Reno's Ninth Corps came up from Frederick. In the vesper warmth Reno's men struggled over the Catoctin range, and when they finally topped Braddock Heights, they could see the Middletown Valley spread green and gold before them, the village cradled "tidy and comfortable" in the saddle between the mountains. The long road wound toward South Mountain, dark and ominous in the twilight. The corps camped near Middletown, but many of Reno's troops did not spread their blankets until well after midnight.[14]

Three passes crossed South Mountain in the vicinity. Below the big dome of Lamb's Knoll, to the south, Crampton's Gap offered passage to Franklin's smaller wing. On the National Road, directly beyond Middletown, was Turner's Gap, and a mile south of there the Old Sharpsburg Road climbed Fox's Gap. Short of Turner's Gap, at a cluster of houses known as Bolivar, two roads broke left and right from the main pike. That to the left led to the Old Sharpsburg Road; the one on the right curled around to the hamlet of Frosttown before circling back—and steeply upward—to connect with the turnpike at Turner's Gap. To defend these three passes and the approaches to them, D. H. Hill had five small brigades—perhaps five thousand men. It was to Hill's advantage, though, that the Lost Order put Longstreet's corps at Boonsborough, just the other side of Turner's Gap: McClellan thought he faced more than thirty thousand of the enemy, and proceeded with commensurate caution.[15]

Back at Frederick, Burnside and his staff prepared somewhat leisurely to advance headquarters to a site nearer Middletown, issuing routine orders to Hooker to start his corps from Frederick at daylight. The army commander had intimated no sense of urgency, and the commander of the right wing understood none. He tarried in Frederick long enough to chat with a brigadier riding in the middle of Hooker's column, then spurred his wild bobtail down the National Road. He had not gone far when he met one of Pleasonton's couriers galloping back to ask for more infantry support. Burnside gave him an order for Cox, whose division marched nearest the front, to send up a brigade.[16]

Cox cut out Eliakim Scammon's three regiments and hurried them ahead, riding alongside them. They had just forded Catoctin Creek (retreating Confederates had burned the bridge) when they came upon a Union officer on foot. It was Colonel Moor, the captured commander of Cox's other brigade. He had just been released on parole. The rather humbled colonel asked whither the brigade was bound, and Cox told him Turner's Gap.

"My God!" Moor exclaimed. "Be careful!" At that he clapped his mouth shut, remembering he had just given his oath against aiding Union forces, but the single involuntary utterance convinced Cox to canter back for the other Kanawha brigade and to send a man back to warn Reno. Reno, who rode with Burnside, was approaching Middletown now. They both bade their staffs erect the headquarters tents in a field on the edge of town.

At Bolivar, Pleasonton steered the infantry down the road to the left, toward the Old Sharpsburg Road and Fox's Gap. Cox soon returned to the front to confer with him, and Pleasonton agreed to demonstrate with his cavalry on the main highway while Cox tried to flank the enemy by way of Fox's Gap. Cox followed his Ohioans up the Old Sharpsburg Road while Pleasonton directed operations on the turnpike from a knoll on the southeast quadrant of the intersection.[17]

The six Ohio regiments, numbering nearly three thousand men when they all came together, encountered five North Carolina regiments totaling fewer than one thousand. Owing to the rugged terrain, Cox fussed with his arrangements till nine o'clock. Then, after a fierce charge in which future-president Hayes was wounded, the Kanawha Division swept the Carolinians over the crest, killing their brigadier and scattering his regiments to the north, west, and south. A second brigade of Tarheels came to the rescue, however, and fought Cox's men to a standstill on the ridgeline. Southern prisoners slyly reported that Longstreet lay right behind; Colonel Moor's spontaneous caveat led Cox to believe them. Moor's warning now proved more of a hindrance than a help, for Longstreet was still many miles away. His men were only then forming up for a forced march to the battle and would not arrive for nearly four hours. Falling victim to this Confederate bluff, Cox drew back his forwardmost regiments and dug his heels in to await the rest of the Ninth Corps, which Reno had promised to send to his support.[18]

Willcox's division was the first reinforcement to come tramping into Bolivar. Willcox had been told to get his directions from Pleasonton— that is, his directions to Cox's position. Willcox interpreted this to mean he should apply to Pleasonton for orders, and when he greeted the puzzled cavalryman in that spirit, Pleasonton suggested he try flanking the enemy's left, pointing him up the Frosttown Road. The division was long gone up that country lane when Burnside and Reno rode up from Middletown, learned of the misunderstanding, and sent a messenger racing toward Frosttown to set Willcox aright. Once the division had begun its countermarch, the two major generals joined Pleasonton on his knoll, where he briefed them on developments since morning.

Burnside had seen this country before. He had come this way by coach on his journey to West Point in May of 1843, and fifteen months before he had brought his Rhode Island regiment over this very highway. Two hours had they rested during that march, just beyond that precipice held by the enemy.

Burnside was bringing his divisions up deliberately, but with no real haste. There is no evidence that McClellan ever shared the revelations of the Lost Order with him, so Burnside was unaware of Lee's precarious situation. Besides, McClellan's almost lethargic leapfrogging of divisions so far in the campaign, to which he later alluded himself, created a lackadaisical atmosphere in which even this day's work seemed extraordinary.[19]

Sturgis's division, and Rodman's (which had been sidetracked the day before), plodded up early in the afternoon, some of the new recruits loading their rifles for the first time. These men were the only Union reserves available until Hooker arrived, so Burnside stood them near the observation knoll against any threat that developed along the turnpike or the Frosttown Road. He wanted to create a diversion up there where Willcox had first gone astray—once Cox had enough help—but, in the event Hooker met a delay, he may have considered using Sturgis or Rodman for that diversion. When the head of Hooker's corps finally did come into view, Burnside composed orders for him to send one brigade straight up the National Road and march with the balance of his column around the Frosttown Road to assault Hill's left flank, just as Pleasonton proposed Willcox should do, but with a sufficient force to face the numbers expected by both the secretive McClellan and the uninformed Burnside.[20]

While he waited for Hooker to get under way, Burnside sent the rest of the Ninth Corps to Fox's Gap. Reno vaulted into the saddle to lead his last two divisions to the fray, and Burnside gave his favorite lieutenant a hearty farewell. It was the last time he ever saw him alive.

Willcox ran into more bad luck, caused by confusing and conflicting orders from Cox, in his front, and Reno, to his rear. For a time he endured a vicious enfilading fire when he faced a brigade the wrong way, but he swung two regiments to neutralize that fire. The larger of the two regiments was a brand-new one from Michigan, and Willcox seemed quite surprised when their line held.

Midafternoon came before Reno and the van of Sturgis's division rose into sight at Fox's Gap. By now Longstreet's brigades had actually begun to reach the field, and they flew furiously at the Union line. Reno squeezed Sturgis's division between Cox and Willcox, dividing Rodman's brigades to support either flank. Thus reunited, the Ninth

Corps waited for Hooker to go into action beyond the turnpike, when Burnside planned to make a general advance with his entire wing, forcing the enemy to defend both gaps at once, on three fronts.

Burnside had trouble budging Hooker, who chafed at having to submit to a wing commander. Burnside represented but one more rung between Hooker and the top of the ladder, where he fervently wished to sit. In a manner reminiscent of Rush Hawkins, Hooker haughtily reported directly back to the army commander, as though Burnside did not exist. He ignored three of Burnside's orders to proceed up the Frosttown Road, stirring only after one came to the front from McClellan's own hand—written either at Burnside's request or in base deference to Hooker's obvious preference for independent corps command. This order had probably just arrived when Burnside finally collared both Hooker and General Meade, commander of his third division, and propelled Meade up the road to Frosttown, closely followed by Hooker's two other divisions, under James Ricketts and John Hatch—the same Hatch who had expressed unbounded confidence in Burnside: he had succeeded to the command of Rufus King's division only an hour or two before.[21]

Hooker's men faced an elevation of Tyrolean proportions. By the time they had maneuvered half the grueling slope north of the pike, they flushed Robert Rodes's Alabama brigade. Soon thereafter three more Confederate brigades arrived from Longstreet, and Meade's division had to do some tall mountaineering to get around them. Hatch's division deployed in awful grandeur, marched straight up the mountain, and struck the enemy head-on. Hatch was wounded; the Alabamians put up such a fearful scrap that Meade called for aid from Ricketts, as did Hatch's successor, and only with immense difficulty were the Confederates forced back.[22]

The only engagement that involved nearly equal forces was on the turnpike itself, where Alfred Colquitt's Georgia and Alabama brigade held the highway against John Gibbon's slightly stronger Iron Brigade. Gibbon shot it out toe-to-toe with Colquitt well into the darkness without carrying the crest. Had Burnside sent a second brigade the road might well have been cleared, but Gibbon did good service by occupying Colquitt's men all evening, while Reno and Hooker barely drove in the two flanks with Union odds of as much as three to one.[23]

The beginning of Hooker's late-afternoon contest was the trigger

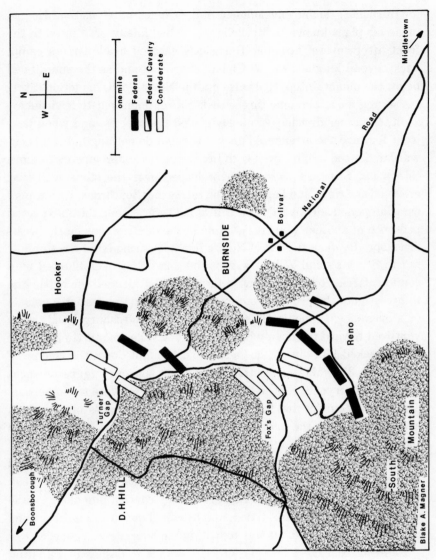

Map 5.
South Mountain

for Burnside's double envelopment of the Confederate position. He had made his plans known to McClellan, who had finally gravitated to the front after several hours at Burnside's vacated headquarters camp, back beyond Middletown. McClellan approved, and as the sun dipped below the mountaintop, Reno also put the Ninth Corps in motion. Sturgis strung a cumbersome three-week-old regiment out to lead the assault, the other divisions similarly girded themselves, and when they went forward the attenuated grey line could do nothing but fall backward under the weight, even with Longstreet's reinforcements to shore things up. Sturgis's new regiment leaped over the stone wall that crowned the ridge and kept after the retreating Southrons, its enthusiasm dampened only by the shouts of its field officers and the unexpected presence of another Confederate line in the dense woods on the western slope. By dusk the left of Reno's line had surmounted the summit, but in Sturgis's and Willcox's front the thrust had been blunted by a counterattack. Reno rode down a farm lane that defined the battle line to investigate the problem, stopping occasionally to question a colonel or a brigadier. Immediately south of the Old Sharpsburg Road, as he ventured toward the enemy lines, he drew a volley of startling volume that knocked him out of the saddle and brought down the colonel of the novice 35th Massachusetts. The sudden spasm of aggressiveness surprised everyone, especially the new men, who were so numerous. The green regiment that had so impetuously led Sturgis's advance fired a wild volley into the backs of some of their own men and bolted for the rear.[24]

Reno was shot through the chest. Four sad privates found a litter and carried their commander down the road, laying him beneath a big oak tree. He recognized General Sturgis as they carried him along, while the day's light—and his—faded, and he called out in astonishing good cheer: "Sam, I'm dead." It was so; within the hour, he was gone.[25]

Fighting continued into the night, the muzzle flashes illuminating the mountain range like a plague of angry fireflies, but little territory changed hands after dark. Under cover of night the Confederates withdrew toward Boonsborough and Sharpsburg, while equally exhausted Federal soldiers stared somnolently after them.

After passing the late afternoon on the same knoll as McClellan, Burnside joined him for the night in a brick house on the National Road, a short way toward Middletown. The generals sat in one room, discussing the day's events, while surgeons amputated arms and legs in a downstairs parlor. McClellan drew up a telegram to Halleck, outlining the results of the battle with his customary melodramatic touch; before he passed it on to the operator he asked Burnside to look it over. Nowhere in the dispatch did Burnside's name appear, but if he was stung by the omission his humility prevented him from saying so. Probably he was satisfied with the reference to Reno and Hooker, since it implied Burnside's participation, or possibly he thought he was merely being asked to review it for factual errors; whatever his personal impression, he endorsed the communication with the appearance of pleasure. His staff, however, was outraged that McClellan failed to give even routine recognition to the contribution of their chief, whom they knew to have fought most of the battle himself.[26] If Burnside was not offended by the lapses of the telegram, he would soon wince from another apparent insult dealt him by McClellan.

Only that day had McClellan issued the formal order assigning Burnside both the First and Ninth corps, perhaps in response to Hooker's disinclination to observe the informal chain of command. McClellan ought to have whipped the recalcitrant Hooker into shape; instead he effectively rewarded him now for what amounted to disobedience of orders in the face of the enemy. The suggestion has been made that the commanding general decided at this point that he had promoted Burnside beyond his level of competence, but the evidence does not really support that conclusion: McClellan himself said he approved Burnside's every order that day, a fact rather damning to McClellan if Burnside showed incompetence, nor has anyone since been able to criticize Burnside's South Mountain performance much, except insofar as he acted on the selected information McClellan gave him. True, McClellan wrote his wife on September 29 that Burnside was not fit to command anything larger than a regiment, but fourteen days later he assigned him to the command of three full corps, raising the question of how much he believed his own self-serving statement. Whatever his rationale, McClellan decided to take Hooker's corps from Burnside the next morning. He disguised it as a logistical necessity, but a march of less than a mile would have joined the First Corps with the Ninth, on either road, while Porter and Sumner could have taken the remaining route with equal ease. Instead, McClellan reduced Burnside to his old corps, planned for Porter to follow him, and freed the scheming Hooker to advance with—but not under—Sumner.

It did Burnside little good that Fitz John Porter had arrived at head-quarters the night of September 14. Justifiably concerned about an impending court of inquiry in the matter of Pope, he may already have held Burnside accountable for his predicament. If Burnside had won any accolades during the day, Porter might be inclined to belittle them before McClellan; if there was the least reason to criticize him, Porter could be expected to capitalize upon it. It necessarily remains a point of speculation to what degree Porter jaundiced McClellan's attitude toward his devoted friend Burnside, but he had a motive for doing so and he had his chief's ear.[27]

The morning of the fifteenth McClellan awaited word from Franklin, who had won a limited success against even less resistance at Cramp-ton's Gap than Hill had been able to produce farther north. McClellan wanted Burnside to wait with him for this news, he said later, but one wonders why, if Burnside was now no more than a corps commander. At any rate, Burnside seemed anxious to get away. With Reno's death he had lost his most trusted subordinate and probably wished to be with the corps in case it ran into trouble. The only person he could install to command the corps without insulting General Cox's rank was Parke, but Parke was indispensable as chief of staff and had, besides, begun to feel ill: in a few days he would require medical leave.[28]

When McClellan released him, about eight o'clock, Burnside trotted up to Fox's Gap and found the Ninth Corps at breakfast. Cox told him he had received orders to bury the dead and send the wounded back to Middletown, and the troops were completely exhausted: not only had many of them marched long distances the day before over very rough country, they had fought all day and into the night without stopping for food or replenishing their water. Some of the men had lost all their rations as well, when they stripped for action. Burnside permitted his men to finish cooking what food and coffee they had, and watched as they buried both their own dead and the enemy's. According to one story, he even refereed a dispute between a local farmer and soldiers who were dumping dead Confederates down his well.

The new troops who had lost their supplies—and most such unfor-tunates were new men, whose officers were too inexperienced to post guards over their shucked equipment—wandered about the battlefield. Some shuddered at the destruction they had wrought, counting bodies and bulletholes. Others, undaunted by the carnage, tried to beg food from friends in other regiments.[29]

At nine o'clock, an hour after Burnside left headquarters, McClellan dictated an order for Burnside to pursue the enemy with "the utmost vigor," but for all McClellan's supposed impatience to move, that order did not reach Fox's Gap until nearly noon, by which time Porter's Fifth Corps had crowded up the Old Sharpsburg Road. The Ninth Corps blocked the way, and Porter frowned theatrically, complaining of the delay to McClellan with obvious satisfaction. McClellan gave Porter immediate instructions to march through the Ninth Corps. With the redundant observation that Burnside was three hours late, Porter— who had himself been criticized for tardiness at Bull Run—barged self-righteously through the gap. The volunteers who had fought the battle sneered at Porter's Regular Army division, which had not been engaged. A Massachusetts man commented in a stage whisper that he saw nothing special about Regular troops. A sergeant among the Regulars brandished a spotless rifle, slapped the gleaming stock, and announced indignantly, "Here's where the difference comes in!"

"Yes," hooted the volunteer, "we use ours to fight with."[30]

McClellan directed an aide to inquire why Burnside seemed to be so slow, but the aide's message does not appear to have been delivered: a witness to the mutually affectionate greeting between Burnside and McClellan later that day records a scene that hardly suggests the encounter of a chastised subordinate and his dissatisfied commander, and on September 16 McClellan reiterated his demand for an explanation as though the first dispatch had never been written, casting more doubt on Burnside's receipt of the September 15 note. With that second communication, McClellan implied he had not forgiven the apparent lack of promptness, though he had found it unnecessary to mention it in conversation. He does not seem to have made any remarks to his staff about undue sluggishness on Burnside's part, either. It was as though McClellan, the master of procrastination, was deliberately fabricating a secret indictment for impunctuality against his friend.[31]

Strangely enough, while McClellan later claimed he expected Burnside to have his battle-weary corps moving at first light (his actual orders notwithstanding), he specifically allowed Hooker's troops time to take provisions. And when Hooker also failed to confront the enemy as quickly as he might have that afternoon, McClellan said not a word to him. Burnside presently sensed his friend had wronged him, but he could hardly imagine why. At a distance of a century and a quarter the reason is more readily apparent.

Two months before, Burn had warned Mac of his many enemies. That was no news to McClellan, but now he may have wondered whether Burnside were not one of those enemies.[32] Certainly Burnside's handling of Porter's incriminating telegrams must have smacked of perfidy—for the bulk of the army had polarized into pro-McClellan and anti-McClellan factions—but even if McClellan did not suspect Burnside of going over to the other side, he knew by now that he had twice refused command of the army: he learned of it from Burnside himself.[33] Instead of considering the information from the perspective of his friend's loyalty, though, he took it as evidence of how eagerly Lincoln and Stanton wanted to replace him, and with whom they wished to do so. Now the main Confederate army seemed to be in full retreat, on the verge of defeat and destruction, after a battle directed largely by Burnside. McClellan's reputation would suffer if his reluctant rival continued in so prominent a role as commander of the army's largest wing. The notion of sacrificing Burnside as a scapegoat in the event of disaster was perhaps not yet part of McClellan's design, nor did he actively pursue that course until he had actually been deposed; then circumstances had already made Burnside ripe for the character, and the carefully crafted dossier of delay became extremely convenient. For the moment, McClellan simply needed to reduce Burnside's part in the play. Logistical imperative provided the initial pretense for relieving him of a significant force, the imagined failure to move his remaining corps on demand seemed to justify retaining him in the reduced capacity, and in the next three days McClellan would use every available pretext to vindicate his treachery.

There is no doubt he liked Burnside: "such a noble man," he had once sincerely called him.[34] But the thought of having his thunder stolen at the brink of the great battle of the war was more than Little Mac could stand, and Burnside fell, like Germanicus, his reputation slowly poisoned by the one closest to him.

III

The Ninth Corps wound down the Old Sharpsburg Road in the early afternoon of September 15, leaving behind the half-buried cordwood piles of dead Confederates. It was hard marching, eating the dust raised by Porter's men, with the road taking the numerous hills and gullies head-on.

McClellan sent Burnside word that the Confederate army was at bay behind Antietam Creek. "If not too late," he suggested somewhat sarcastically, Burnside could advance on Rohrersville and make contact with Franklin, who struggled up from Crampton's Gap; Porter would go straight on toward Sharpsburg, by way of Keedysville.[1]

The temporal precaution within McClellan's message was altogether gratuitous. Early in the day he might have hoped to use Burnside to cut off Lee's retreat—although it appears now that McClellan was content to let the Confederates escape without another battle—but even if he did hope to corner the enemy, it was no longer possible: Lee was already beyond Burnside's front.[2] Since the enemy was known to be in line of battle behind Antietam Creek, Rohrersville must necessarily have been free to occupy, leaving Burnside to wonder how the term "too late" could apply to any advance upon it. Disguised as an essential condition of the order, which it was not, the flippancy was probably meant for another round in McClellan's personal ammunition chest.

While their troops marched toward Rohrersville—and Porterstown, as a later order directed—Burnside and Cox rode ahead to see McClellan. They found him at the home of Samuel Pry, the most elegant farmhouse between Keedysville and Sharpsburg, discussing the positions of the opposing armies with General Porter. This was the first time Cox had seen Burnside and McClellan together, and from his description of their warm greeting it did not appear McClellan had any open criticism for his subordinate on the subject of tardy departures. The growing klatch of generals in Mr. Pry's pasture gravitated to the top of a hill to view the Confederate lines, but Little Mac decided they would draw artillery fire if they remained in so large a group; he insisted everyone return to the farmhouse but himself and one other. His senior wing commander might have expected to be chosen for that conference, but Burnside was one of those waved back to the house. So was Sumner, commander of the other large wing. Predictably, it was Fitz John Porter who stayed to reconnoiter with his chief.[3] For a general who had so recently been considered for command of the army, such an obvious rebuff in front of his colleagues must have been humiliating to Burnside; for one who had declined that command in favor of the very man who now snubbed him, it must have been particularly painful.

The next day a dense fog hampered the movements of the entire Army of the Potomac. A few pickets invited shots, which announced that Lee had not used this opportunity to retreat, but an hour and a half after sunrise McClellan could still not see his own lines, much less the enemy's. When daylight finally burned through, he commenced another reconnaissance of the Confederate position.

He began this inspection on the Union right, with three staff officers. By the time he reached the left of the line, Burnside had joined him, and they strolled their horses about a mile beyond Burnside's headquarters near Porterstown. There were Confederates across Antietam Creek as far downstream as they went, indicating a significant shift in their defenses; to George McClellan that called for a reorganization of his own position.

The Ninth Corps lay a mile or so back from the creek, out of sight. McClellan wanted it nearer, behind the cover of hills and ridges immediately east of the stream, close to a stone bridge and a ford that was reputedly half a mile downstream. About noontime the army commander cantered back to headquarters, leaving behind the senior engineer officer on the general staff, Captain James Duane, to post Burnside's divisions. It was as though he did not trust Burnside to do it himself. Possibly McClellan meant no particular offense by this, for General Cox observed the habit of delegating field commanders' duties to members of the general staff was all too common in McClellan's army: Cox disliked it because it tended to rob the various generals of self-confidence and independence of spirit.

Duane did not care to spend much time locating Burnside's big corps. Later in the war this same Duane would demonstrate regular contempt for Burnside, his ideas, and his men; for now he proposed that Burnside lend him three of his own staff, so he could quickly show each of them the positions desired by McClellan. The three, in turn, could guide the divisions simultaneously into place while Captain Duane attended to work he considered more important. Burnside acceded, and Duane departed with the three assistants.[4]

During the intervening hours, in a continued effort to reduce Burnside's potential role, McClellan marched Hooker's corps to the extreme right of the line, well beyond Burnside's control. When Cox became aware of this, he offered to go back to his own division so Burnside could handle the Ninth Corps personally. He was a stranger to the corps itself, Cox argued, while the men looked to Burnside as their true master. Logical as that sounded, Burnside declined. He attributed the detachment of the First Corps to Hooker's ambitious lobbying for independent command, but he had no reason to believe the assignment was permanent, and he did not wish to believe McClellan would so abruptly deprive him of his new position. Some doubt must already have rooted in his mind, however, for he admitted that stepping back to the corps command would imply acquiescence, making it easier for McClellan to leave it so. At this point even so trusting a man as Ambrose Burnside could no longer ignore his friend's serial affronts.

Cox countered by complaining that his staff was too small for corps duty, but Burnside responded by lending him most of his own. If McClellan eventually returned him to wing command, as Burnside fully expected, Cox might find himself leading the Ninth Corps indefinitely; Burnside may have considered this a good opportunity for him to gain some battle experience at that level, while an older hand was free to monitor his performance. Cox relented, permitting Colonel Scammon to retain command of the Kanawha Division, but either because he did not think his Westerners would respond well to that generally disliked martinet or because he wanted to reduce the number of divisions under his control, he parceled his two brigades out to Rodman and Sturgis. Burnside interfered only to the extent of specifying that the Ohio brigade now under George Crook lead any attack that was ordered, as a tribute to its effectiveness and gallantry at South Mountain.[5] That compliment was probably intended equally for General Cox, who had overseen much of the fight at Fox's Gap, to help bolster his own confidence.

At least one person has hypothesized that Burnside began to pout, or sulk, about this time.[6] Certainly he had some cause, for he had recently suffered a temporary demotion which, coming with no apparent reason from the man he considered his good friend, hurt all the more. But his heart was too much in the war effort for him to have consciously allowed pure pique to affect his performance: he demonstrated his selflessness too many times for that argument to carry. If flagging morale impaired him, it was involuntary. He had just lost his most trusted advisor, Reno, who had been to him what Porter was to McClellan, and with Porter and Hooker working successfully against him he had additional occasion to feel discouraged. Yet even discouragement was not apparent in his demeanor, let alone the less creditable emotion of deliberate resentment: Burnside's only evident reactions to the situation were perplexity and an understandable air of caution in his dealings with headquarters.

When the three proxy guides returned from their jaunt with Captain Duane at midafternoon, the Ninth Corps divisions formed and started, one by one, from the vicinity of Porterstown to their designated campsites; the good idea of simultaneously posting them proved unworkable, since they all had to travel the same road in any case. Burnside positioned his headquarters on a prominent knoll a mile southeast of the stone bridge, from which he could see the entire field occupied by his troops and most of the terrain they might be expected to confront. Messengers soon learned they could find him near a conspicuous battery of 20-pounder Parrott rifles—guns served by a babyfaced lieutenant just a year out of West Point who happened to be a wizard with artillery: Samuel Benjamin had just been assigned to the Ninth Corps, to Burnside's great good fortune, and the general soon recognized the young man's talent.

Rodman's brigades moved to the extreme left late in the afternoon, near where Captain Duane had indicated the ford would be. Sturgis and Willcox followed, putting their men in place between dusk and dark, Sturgis lining up on Rodman's right and Willcox hanging back in reserve.[7]

While Burnside's men were still in motion they could hear the sound of battle grumbling to the northeast, where Hooker had crossed the creek and run into Lee's left wing. At this time, about six o'clock, Burnside noticed a column of enemy infantry moving across his own front toward the sound of the fighting. He nodded for Benjamin to open the Parrotts on them, and they had just scurried into the safety of a ravine when a curious thing happened. An officer from McClellan's staff galloped up to say the commanding general was not sure he had properly situated the Ninth Corps; better wait, the aide said, until he could get final word from McClellan himself. With that the mysterious officer sped away, his name lost to history.

The troop movement Burnside saw meant the Confederates might be weakening their right to meet Hooker's challenge, which could offer an opportunity to crush their right flank, but McClellan had evinced a certain unpredictability these past thirty hours, such that Burnside dared not attack on his own initiative. He spurred his horse to army headquarters, but McClellan was not there, nor could Burnside find him elsewhere, so he returned to the left and finished the dispositions he and Cox had originally undertaken.

Unlike Burnside, the nameless staff officer did catch up with McClellan, sometime after dark. He reported that only Rodman's division had been in place at sunset, which gave Little Mac yet another opportunity to find fault. Late that night another of McClellan's messengers rode the circuitous route to Burnside's knoll, carrying a reproof as severe as might have been expected for a serious failure. The reprimand was phrased so as to enhance the appearance of negligence, creating the impression Burnside had been ordered to have the Ninth Corps in position by noon—when in fact the order had not even been handed to him until shortly after that time. It was doubly frustrating to Burnside that most of the delay he was asked to justify was the fault of McClellan's own trusted staff engineer.[8]

That evening a steady rain softened the sounds of the armies, drenching and chilling the soldiers who could not, by virtue of McClellan's sudden wish to conceal his position, build fires to warm themselves. Even General Burnside slept, cold and wet, in a haystack that might have been safe in someone's barn, but for the whim of roving armies.[9]

Confederate artillery began to play upon the Ninth Corps at daylight, taking a particular toll on Rodman's division, parts of which the slowly melting fog exposed. His troops scrambled for cover, but it was almost an hour before McClellan sent orders to move forward to sheltered positions and prepare for an attack. Rodman moved nearer the creek, where he was screened from artillery fire by a steep bluff on the opposite bank, but that bluff was topped by Southern sharpshooters who began to wring a different tribute from these Union soldiers, picking them off all too regularly. Cox also advanced Sturgis's division, parking it immediately behind a long hill that faced the stone bridge, where his men relaxed in relative safety while Confederate shells passed long overhead.

After he had positioned the corps, Cox rejoined Burnside on his hill. The two waited anxiously for orders to attack, for they both understood they were to provide a diversion while the main attack emanated from the Union right. That was the way McClellan had explained it to them, and so he still claimed his plan to have been when he wrote his first— and more reliable—report of the battle. Yet the two top officers on the left of the line could plainly see that main attack in progress, with nary a word from McClellan for two hours and more.[10] Burnside, expecting orders every minute and wary of further irritating his strangely peevish commander, did not seem inclined to question the delay.

At daybreak on September 17, John G. Walker's Confederate division—which included the 35th North Carolina, of Burnside's Newbern acquaintance—sprawled across the property of farmer Snavely, who owned the fords in front of the Ninth Corps. From that time until shortly after nine, when Lee ordered Walker to his left to confront the Twelfth Corps, those fords were impassable to any but the largest forces. Walker's departure, though, left but five hundred Georgians to defend the stone bridge and the fords. These men operated under the same bifurcated command structure as the Ninth Corps: they were part of General Robert Toombs's brigade, but Toombs had been temporarily elevated to the command of a provisional division; his other two brigades had been ordered to stay with the main body of the army when he moved to Sharpsburg, however, and two regiments had been detailed away from his original brigade. His provisional division had effectually been disbanded. Still, he insisted upon retaining his empty title as a division commander while the demi-brigade left to him marched under the orders of the senior colonel.

Toombs's line stretched from the bridge to the bend in Antietam Creek, about three hundred yards downstream. He was able to spread fewer than three hundred men of the 20th Georgia and somewhat more than a hundred of the 2nd Georgia over that distance, in what was little more than a strong skirmish line. Around the bend, to their right, sat the fragmentary 50th Georgia—another hundred men covering the ford Duane had indicated on Rodman's front. All three of these regiments perched atop the wooded bluff high above the creek, while all the approaches to the bridge and the first ford coursed low, open ground, ex-

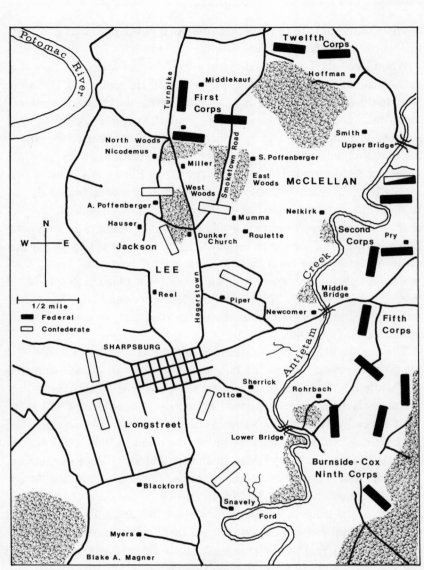

Map 6. Antietam

tremely vulnerable to Confederate fire. As it developed, that skirmish line would be almost enough.

When Lee called Walker's division away, Toombs asked the loan of a single company from a South Carolina brigade. He posted half the company in the gap between the 2nd and 50th regiments; the rest he placed a mile and more downstream from the bridge, astraddle Mr. Snavely's shallowest ford. This tiny platoon, under a lieutenant, covered the crossing that Rodman's division would eventually be forced to take.[11]

Just as Walker guided his brigades away from Burnside's front, one of McClellan's assistants was copying an order for Burnside to assault the bridge. The order promised support from other troops once he cleared that passageway: support that would come, "if necessary, on your own line of attack."[12] There were no signal stations ready yet by which the message could have been relayed, and even if there had been, that would have required transmitting and decoding it twice in the plodding vernacular of the flags. McClellan's headquarters were less than three miles from Burnside's by indirect country roads, so the dispatch went by the hand of an aide.

The timing of this order became a matter of needless dispute. In his original report, completed before he was relieved of his command and while he still believed Antietam was perceived as a victory—*his* victory—McClellan remembered having given the order at 10:00 A.M. That agreed with Burnside's recollection of less than two weeks after the battle. Cox first reported receiving the order at 9:00, but later he admitted he was probably mistaken and presented evidence suggesting it had arrived about 10:00. After his forced departure from the Army of the Potomac, however, McClellan turned to the task of absolving himself for the incompleteness of his victory in Maryland. The attempt can be tracked like a wounded animal through the various drafts of his autobiography. But even the final manuscript records the timing of the attack order as 10:00; in the published version, whether by McClellan's instruction or the whim of his posthumous editor, it is arbitrarily changed to 8:00. That matched McClellan's revised 1863 report, adding two important hours to Burnside's "delay" in carrying the bridge. It conjured up the image of the Ninth Corps dawdling during the bloody assaults of the First and Twelfth corps on the Union right. Burnside, by then in disfavor because of his defeats of December and January, made an easy mark.

Actually, an assault at 8:00 would have been more consistent with McClellan's original idea of using the Ninth Corps for a "diversion, with the hope of something more." It would certainly not have succeeded: the bridge could not be taken except by a flanking force over the fords, and Walker's division still held the usable ford at 8:00 A.M.—but an attack then would have detained Walker from Lee when the Twelfth Corps advanced, and that might have been decisive. Thanks to McClellan's corruption of the facts, the truth did not emerge until the last volumes of the *Official Records* went to press, years after both Burnside and McClellan were dead: therein appears a copy of McClellan's order, bearing a heading of 9:10 A.M. [13]

If the message was copied down at 9:10, it was probably finished and in the courier's hand by 9:20. Given the urgency of a pitched battle, and assuming the horseman was familiar with the haphazard road network (which was not necessarily so), he would have covered the distance to Burnside's position at a moderate gallop, breaking gait for at least six turns of ninety degrees or more. That would have brought him to the vicinity of Benjamin's battery no earlier than 9:35. If he had to ask directions or double back from a wrong turn, he could easily have been delayed until 10:00. [14]

Burnside and Cox were together on the knoll by the 20-pounder Parrotts when the aide reined in and handed the order to Burnside, who read it and gave it to Cox, reminding him that he wanted Crook to lead the assault. Perhaps thirty seconds passed before Cox had the order.

The choreography required Crook's Ohioans to dash over the hill before the bridge, rush across the structure, and reform in line of battle before charging up the bluff on the Confederate side. At the same time, Rodman's division advanced toward its ford, but Burnside personally ordered the 11th Connecticut from Rodman's ranks to support Crook as skirmishers—apparently without notifying either Rodman or the brigade commander, for the responsible brigadier spent the rest of the battle wondering where the Connecticut regiment had gone.

Crook's attack went badly. The 11th Connecticut sidled a short way from its sheltered location and strung out along the creek bank to lay a covering fire, but when Crook's men broke over the top of the wooded ridge, they found themselves several hundred yards upstream from the bridge. They began sniping from behind fences at the nearest Georgians, who guessed their range with a most unsatisfactory ease, and their forward momentum withered. For the next two hours they stood their ground, but they could not safely edge their way down to the crossing, and the creek in front of them ran too deep to wade in brigade front.

The lad for whom Burnside acted as conservator, Henry Kingsbury, had become colonel of the 11th Connecticut. He courageously urged his men to cross the stream by wading into it himself, alone. Inevitably he was shot, and the assault fizzled altogether. Crook persistently tried to execute his orders, but with little success.[15]

Recognizing the futility of Crook's attempt early on, and without his own staff to assist him, Burnside rode himself to Sturgis and told him to try the bridge next, after which he cantered back to his headquarters knoll and warned Willcox to prepare to follow Sturgis, if he should carry the bridge. Willcox bugled his men to their feet and stood them in columns of march, but for the moment they remained where they were, under cover and roughly equidistant from the bridge and from Rodman's division, from which point they could most quickly support whichever general first gained a foothold.

Sturgis turned to James Nagle's brigade, gesturing the 2nd Maryland and the 6th New Hampshire out of line. The two units totaled only some three hundred men combined, but they were reliable veterans who could be depended upon to do the job if it was possible—which, at that time, it was not. In order to avoid going astray like Crook, Sturgis pointed his assault force through the rail fence three hundred yards downstream from the bridge. That would put them right on the Rohrersville Road, on the very bank of the Antietam, with their flank barely fifty yards from the muzzles of those deadly Southern rifles.

The two regiments formed out of sight of Toombs's marksmen, side by side, each unit in a column of twos. Colonel Simon Griffin of the 6th had them fix bayonets, faced them to the left, and launched them into a double quick. From behind a hill they entered a field bordered by the chestnut rail fence. The head of the column veered toward a narrow gap in the fenceline and squeezed through, pouring into the road. At that moment the Georgians opened on them. The leaders turned toward the bridge, their comrades swerving to the right four abreast, but the front third of the column was virtually annihilated. A pitiful few reached the ramp to the bridge, but there Confederate artillery on the outskirts of Sharpsburg took them in front: shell, solid shot, and case shot came

crashing down the shredded remnant of Griffin's forlorn hope. The survivors fell back, made one more courageous but feeble attempt, and
gave up. Those who were left took what cover they could and pecked
away at the malevolent bluff across the stream.[16]

Burnside's Bridge, as some already called it, was indeed a modern
Thermopylae. The assaulting columns had to reduce their fronts to a
breadth of four men, and since a wide front was essential for firepower
in the days of muzzle-loading rifles, the aggressors could hardly defend
themselves until they had crossed the bridge. For their part, the few
hundred Georgians were as great a force as could be effectively used
on the heights, and their concentrated fire upon their vulnerable adversaries (combined with raking artillery fire from near Sharpsburg)
proved enough to destroy any charge against the bridge.

There were but two methods of achieving Burnside's goal: attrition of
the enemy force or a flanking movement. Certainly the Georgia riflemen
gave better than they got—they inflicted casualties here greater than
their own number—but Toombs could not replace the men he lost, while
to a point Burnside could. The remains of Crook's brigade, Nagle's two
regiments, and the 11th Connecticut kept the Confederates busy between individual charges, and at least one of the spanking-new Union
regiments went to work against them from the top of the hill immediately adjacent to the bridge.[17] They helped the Southerners use up their
ammunition and took an inexorable toll on their numbers, reducing
Toombs's available firepower.

As in all his previous battles that year, General Burnside had been
pursuing a flanking maneuver since the early stages of his assault. He
had ordered Rodman to cross at the ford to which Captain Duane had
guided him, and Rodman had dutifully moved his men forward. That
ford, though, was impossible for him to cross without unreasonable
losses, and for the same reasons that the bridge was impassable. He
had to form his men in a narrow column; his troops would have been
without any cover while waiting to cross; and the enemy was well hidden in woods along the lip of a bluff too steep to scale, right at the
edge of the creek. On top of that, the creek was too deep for organized troops here, Georgia rifles aside. Had Rodman even managed to
wade his men over, they would have been trapped on the toe of that
bluff while the Georgians shot them like fish in a barrel. Captain Duane
had either botched his reconnaissance and indicated the wrong ford to

Burnside's staff officers or communications between those officers and
Duane had gone awry, which might have been avoided had the captain personally placed the Ninth Corps divisions the previous day—
as his chief had ordered him.[18] McClellan's machinations against Burnside also may have played a part in this costly error: had Burnside not
been apprehensive of his commander's suddenly hypercritical mood,
he might have exercised more initiative and actually tested the ford
beforehand, though it might have brought on an engagement or tipped
the Confederates to intentions McClellan wanted kept secret.

Thus foiled, Rodman drew his brigades together behind two companies detailed to pick their way downstream in search of another ford. It
was slow work for the two companies and even slower for the ponder-
ous division, but while Sturgis tried the bridge these wanderers groped
their way down the serpentine creek, periodically sounding the water
amid the diminishing splash of sharpshooters' bullets. The division ultimately filed into a great teardrop bend in the Antietam, at the apex of
which stood the Snavely farm and the better ford, from which a road led
behind Toombs's position to Sharpsburg. The tail end of the 50th Georgia, on the hostile bluff, had fired its last shots some distance upstream.
The bluff itself had softened to a gentler hill, parted in the middle by the
farm road, and no Confederate resistance loomed obvious. The dozen-
or-so South Carolinians and their lieutenant were still there, but did
not reveal themselves until the first Yankees waded into the shallows.

Rodman wiggled his sword at the ford and at the 4th Rhode Island—
his old regiment. A freshly commissioned second lieutenant in the 4th
found the water "breast deep." Perhaps he was below average height,
or possibly he crossed to one side of the ford to give his men the easier
passage, but chest-deep water was mighty high for a military ford.

As the first of the Rhode Islanders slogged up the soggy shelf of land
in front of the draw, the handful of South Carolinians commenced bang-
ing away. At least one man dropped in midstream. Rodman formed his
men as quickly as he could urge them across, but he had no idea how
many Confederates he would face, and he wanted every man available
before he advanced.[19] With the attached brigade from the Kanawha
Division he had upwards of four thousand men; it took some time to
ford that many troops in single file.

Upstream from the bridge, Crook had similarly searched for a shallow spot and had finally found a precarious location where he could ease

across a man at a time. He had a company or two on the other bank by now, but like Rodman he dared not show them in their vulnerable position until he could support them properly.[20]

Crook's and Nagle's assaults had consumed fully two hours, during which McClellan had sent additional aides to urge haste from Burnside. One of those aides, burly Colonel Delos B. Sacket, complained that Burnside snapped at him.

"McClellan seems to think I am not trying my best to carry this bridge," Sacket supposedly remembered him saying; "you are the third or fourth one who has been to me this morning with similar orders."[21]

Colonel Thomas Key came twice from McClellan on this mission. On the second visit—according to the questionable account of a mutual friend of Key and McClellan, who sat upon the juicy secret for more than thirty years—Key carried McClellan's own order for Burnside's removal; if he did not advance across the creek immediately, one of Porter's division commanders would take over the Ninth Corps.[22] It is altogether unlikely Key carried such an order or McClellan would have made great use of the fact in the course of discrediting his friend, but even if he held such a document he would not have needed to produce it, for Burnside promptly relayed desperate orders to Sturgis to attack the bridge again—this time to carry it at any cost. This was a liberal divergence from Burnside's earlier understanding of his instructions. Though the 9:10 orders made reference to his "attack," he had no reason to believe his verbal directions to create a diversion were changed. The flurry of couriers was naturally infected with McClellan's confusion about his alleged plan of battle: if McClellan did not even recognize the subtle alteration of Burnside's orders, his messengers could hardly impart it. Finally, however, the mere volume of communications convinced Burnside to go for broke.

Sturgis now looked to his second brigade, under a former dancing master named Edward Ferrero. Ferrero chose his pet regiments, the 51st Pennsylvania and the 51st New York, and they lined up as Crook's men had, behind the hill opposite the bridge. Sweating up the lee side in the stifling midday heat, the tandem regiments came under fire the instant they pounded over the crest. As with Nagle's assault, Confederate fire concentrated on the head of this column, and it seemed to melt away like a thread of solder before a blowtorch. The Yankees reached the bridge, but their officers shooed the shredded companies to cover along the creekbank, one regiment throwing itself along a fence down-stream while the other crouched behind a stone floodwall that turned upstream from the bridge. They added their fire to the steady fusillade, and the Georgians responded with effective—albeit decreasing—fire.

Toombs's own men were beginning to suffer. One of his regiments had lost half its men and its commander, while another was nearly as badly riddled. The remnant of the 50th Georgia still sat intact in its sheltered location around the bend, but messengers from that direction brought the news that Union troops were spilling across Snavely's ford: Toombs was about to be cut off. David Jones, to whose division Toombs actually belonged, had prearranged a position to which Toombs would withdraw in case he were flanked, and the Georgian began pulling his marksmen away from the bank. Jones, meanwhile, braced for an attack from the direction of the Harpers Ferry Road, though at that particular moment he had little with which to brace.

When the musketry died away on the bluff opposite their creekside cover, the twin 51sts gathered in a disorganized manner and charged over the arched earthen deck of the bridge; some sentimental soul in the New York regiment shouted "Remember Reno!" and the others picked it up. The rear guard of Toombs's brigade let fly a final volley before bolting to the rear.[23]

All of Sturgis's men began pushing across. Many of them had been fighting for three hours now—it neared one o'clock—and their car-tridge boxes gave that grim rattle, but their original orders had im-plied they should drive right over the bridge at the first opportunity. It might have been advisable for Sturgis's men to step aside while Will-cox's fresh division crossed instead, but Sturgis was nearest and no one knew when Confederate reinforcements would appear to recapture the heights; regiment after regiment therefore shouldered across, dressed their lines individually, and started up the bluffs.

Not until it became obvious the defenders were half a mile or more away did Cox order Sturgis's winded soldiers to lay down and rest in line of battle. A number of men in the division had rifled the cartridge boxes of the dead and wounded to supply themselves and their comrades with a few rounds. Cox sent back for ammunition and reinforcements; Willcox, whom Burnside had ordered after Sturgis as soon as the bridge opened up, put his men in line to cross the stream just as the ammu-nition wagons started over. Confederate artillery along the Harpers

Ferry and Keedysville roads complicated the maneuver: taking up the slack for the Southern infantry, the gunners caught the bridge in a crossfire. Other batteries kept Rodman down with a storm of shell.[24] For the time being, the Ninth Corps could go nowhere, though there was little to stop it but those guns.

Despite shells bursting all around, Burnside threaded the better part of five batteries through the glut at the bridge to respond to this barrage, and ultimately he rode across himself to straighten out the traffic jam and distribute the guns and men. He spoke with Cox, going over the details of the next step in their assault. Willcox would take the right, with Crook's brigade joining him; Rodman and Scammon would advance on the left. All should move on Sharpsburg together, rather than in fragmentary attacks the Southerners could destroy in detail, while Sturgis's exhausted brigades lay back in reserve, covering the bridge.[25]

General Toombs, settling in behind a low stone wall, welcomed the reinforcement of two and a half regiments. He said later he could not understand why the enemy did not come, but as he sent his jaded 2nd and 20th regiments to the rear he could have reasoned that the Yankees who had chased him away from the bluff were just as fatigued and depleted as his own troops, whom he felt needed to be replaced.

While Willcox's division deployed, the battle on the Union right ended. Only minutes after Burnside took his bridge, the last Federal assault on Bloody Lane sputtered out, and the roar there subsided to the crackling of skirmishers. Without simultaneous pressure there or on the Boonsborough Pike, Burnside's advance was pointless, but McClellan ordered it anyway. Later McClellan would falsely accuse Burnside of a lethargy during the morning's fighting that allowed Lee to defend his left with troops from his right; in fact it was McClellan whose abandonment of the battle in the afternoon permitted Confederate artillery to apply all its attention to Burnside and allowed the last Southern reserves to throw all their energies against him.

Had the Confederate center been pressed once more, as Burnside came at the right, Lee's line ought to have cracked. It might have broken in the center even without the cooperation of the Ninth Corps, but McClellan conserved his strength. Once again, he feared he was heavily outnumbered, if his dispatch of 1:20 P.M. to Washington was sincere, and he felt his only hope of overcoming the enemy was for Burnside to gain the high ground immediately south of Sharpsburg.[26] From there Union artillery could take Lee's left and center from behind. Perfectly situated for a devastating pincer movement, McClellan characteristically fought, instead, for position.

Willcox had had to advance a mile before he even reached Burnside's Bridge—a distance General Cox estimated would occupy the average division an hour—and with the tangle of ammunition wagons and the artillery train, it was three o'clock before he traversed the span and formed atop the bluffs, ready to advance, Christ's brigade on the right of the road to Sharpsburg and Welsh's on the left, with Crook trailing behind Welsh. Rodman's division had already prepared to advance parallel with Willcox, Fairchild on the right and Harland on the left. Scammon's Ohio brigade (under Hugh Ewing, because of the awkward step-up in corps and division command) lagged behind to serve as immediate support for Rodman.[27]

On this part of the field, at that time, Burnside probably outnumbered his opponents four to one. As at South Mountain, however, he suffered from Little Mac's overestimate of Confederate numbers. The army commander doubtless imparted this faulty information either directly or indirectly to Burnside, and from the caution he exhibited in preparing for the final advance, Burnside seems not to have discounted it.

The Confederates fought with a fury that lent credence to the myth of overpowering forces. As the Union line rolled ahead it was stung mercilessly by swarms of skirmishers hidden in cornfields that had yet to be gleaned. Artillery seemingly hit the Yankees from everywhere, and more cannon were unlimbering against them all the time. The lead elements of A. P. Hill's division staggered onto the field now, among them numerous batteries that had been reconditioned with new U.S. guns and horses taken at Harpers Ferry, two days before. Thanks to McClellan's concentration of his cavalry behind the center of the Union line, Burnside had no warning of Hill's approach.

One of those reconditioned batteries was the Pee Dee Light Artillery—South Carolinians. The guns outran their crews in the race to Sharpsburg, but three pieces rumbled into action immediately, with officers and drivers manning the rammers. So close were the Federals that these makeshift crews loaded with double canister.

David Jones's skeleton brigades stepped slowly backward before Willcox's firm effort. Union soldiers poured into the field where the National

Cemetery would later sit: they approached the very houses of Sharpsburg. But the important progress, to McClellan's mind, was on Rodman's front. Fairchild's brigade and part of Harland's neared the crest
of the ridgeline that commanded the town and the rest of Lee's position. By dint of short rushes, the Hawkinsless zouaves of the 9th New
York succeeded, with the 8th Connecticut, in overrunning the Pee Dee
battery, the South Carolinians crippling their guns by running off with
the sponges and riding away on their limbers.[28]

Still farther to the left, A. P. Hill's infantry brigades formed in numbers that could do real damage to the Ninth Corps flank. Willcox, Fairchild, and the 8th Connecticut of Harland's brigade were all busy on the
right, driving back Jones's division. Hill's men, deploying well south of
Jones, forced Rodman's remaining troops to veer somewhat to the left
as they pushed ahead, creating a gap between this fragment and the
main body.

Rodman saw this rupture from the corner of his eye and rode over to
swing the wandering regiments around to the right and cement the line
together again. He found even more of the enemy on his left, however,
and faced this wing to meet the new threat. His detached left consisted
of only two regiments—the 4th Rhode Island on the extreme flank and,
to its right, the 16th Connecticut. The veteran 4th was badly thinned;
the 16th had almost full ranks but was perfectly green—its men had
been in the army less than a month and had joined the division only the
day before. They could maneuver but awkwardly. Tall corn hampered
both vision and communication, and the new regiment began to contort
itself. About this time Rodman dropped out of the saddle with his death
wound; shortly afterward Colonel Harland sprinted up (his horse had
just been shot) and tried to straighten things out. With considerable
trouble he shook the 16th into a semblance of a line of battle, but just
then a line of troops in blue uniforms appeared, waving what looked
like the United States flag. The Yankees held fire, lest these turn out
to be the supports McClellan had promised Burnside long hours ago.
Soon a couple of Rhode Island officers and a color bearer crept ahead to
identify themselves, inviting a withering blast at short range: the blue
uniforms, like many of the Confederate guns and horses, were spoils of
war from Harpers Ferry.

The 16th Connecticut buckled and fled, carrying part of the 4th Rhode
Island with it. The Rhode Island colonel—the man Governor Sprague

had imposed on the regiment—shouted for his men to withdraw, but someone shot him before he could pass that order to his second battalion. When those men saw their comrades inexplicably leaving the field, they, too, broke and ran. The 8th Connecticut, up on the hill with the South Carolina guns, turned to confront the new assault, and Scammon's little Kanawha brigade strung out in the cornfields to hold Hill's men back.

Fairchild's brigade caught Hill's fire full in the flank and had to pull back from its precious ridge. On the bridge road, Willcox was also withdrawing now for want of ammunition. By the time Burnside's afternoon assault was two hours old, it had begun reeling backward.[29]

Now Burnside sent to McClellan for the support he had been guaranteed on his "own line of attack." Even those watching from McClellan's headquarters could see Burnside did not exaggerate his plight, but when the courier reached the Pry house General McClellan shook his head. "I have no infantry," he said. Standing beside him was Fitz John Porter, who had the better part of two divisions handy.[30]

Despite all promises and despite available support, Burnside was on his own. He hurried Sturgis's weary brigades into line to replace Rodman's shattered division and began sweeping up scattered regiments of the Kanawha Division to fill the last ditch.

Sturgis's eight regiments plunged ahead, diving behind fences and furrows half a mile west of the bridge. With little maneuvering necessary (or possible) thereafter, even the new regiments functioned well, loading and firing furiously. For a time they, alone, stood against two Confederate divisions, and by virtue of passionate effort they brought them to a near halt. Then more of Hill's troops came into line, and the Southern counterattack resumed. Yankees, many of them only three weeks from home and just getting the knack of this deadly game, redoubled their fire, jamming cartridges into their sizzling rifles with desperate rapidity. Too raw to withdraw in order, they did not want to run and so stood rooted to their meager breastworks of earth and rail. Wild eyes turned back in search of help that was not coming; here a man glanced hopefully at the setting sun before him; now an officer worried his men with "Pop away, boys! Pop away!" This newest surge of Confederate resilience winced, paused, and finally recoiled.

Again Union ammunition grew scarce, and the dreadful "ping" of empty cartridge tins bounced behind the firing line amid the sounds of wood, leather, and ramrod iron. Some regiments had fired their last shots. Others had the final round loaded, and the chilling noise of bayonets rang everywhere.[31]

In this nervous twilight came Burnside's answer from McClellan: keep his position if he could, but hold the bridge at all costs. Officers accordingly whispered Sturgis's and Scammon's men away from the ground they held and placed them nearer the ordnance wagons, on more defensible ground. At least one new regiment went overlooked in the withdrawal. When its colonel discovered he had been abandoned, he advised his petrified recruits to sell their lives as dearly as possible, but it did not come to that; after an hour or so of frantic silence these lost children were also found and guided home. The depleted blue line doubled itself on a narrower front closer to the bridge, the whole corps standing shoulder-to-shoulder in the darkness. Only Harland's beaten regiments won permission to cross the creek and reform their jumbled companies.[32]

Burnside satisfied himself that his dispositions were stable before going back to the Ninth Corps hospitals to visit with some of his wounded officers. One house sheltered General Rodman, a dying aide of his, and the mortally wounded Colonel Kingsbury of the 11th Connecticut. Kingsbury's lieutenant colonel, Griffin Stedman, sat at the colonel's bedside. More than twenty years later McClellan finally "revealed" that Stedman told him Burnside was beaten, discouraged, and advocating retreat that night. As with most of McClellan's witnesses for his memoirs, Stedman was not around to say: he had, rather conveniently, been killed in the last year of the war.

The story of Burnside's discouragement does not wash. He gave no indication to anyone (especially Cox, his immediate subordinate) that a retreat lay in the cards. One man who did hear Burnside's conversation with the wounded officers was a captain in Rodman's old 4th Rhode Island, who was tending his former commander. Aside from Burnside, he was the only man in the group to survive the war, and more than half a century later he volunteered to literally place his hand on the Bible and swear that Burnside was calm and confident that night. He remembered Rodman asking how the battle had gone, to which Burnside replied: "It has gone well today, General; tomorrow we will have it out with them again."[33]

Tired as he was, Burnside rode the two miles and more to McClellan's headquarters beneath the third-quarter moon. As he explained it to a congressional committee some weeks later, he wanted to borrow a division with which to renew the battle in the morning. It was late when he arrived at the Pry house, and Little Mac's staff ran interference for him. Burnside cooled his heels while an aide went in and announced him to the commanding general. McClellan, perhaps afraid his old friend had come to call him to account for withholding the promised supports, pleaded fatigue. The aide came out to mumble his apologies, and a puzzled Burnside had to climb back into the saddle for the long return to his hilltop haystack. If ever a man had cause for irritation, Burnside did then, but his own staff, furious at what they perceived as a deliberate attempt to sacrifice their chief, marveled at Burnside's continued loyalty to McClellan.[34]

Afterward McClellan denied Burnside had wanted to renew the contest. Ignoring whatever Burnside had actually said, he recorded that the Ninth Corps commander gave him the "impression" his men would not be able to hold out against superior numbers. He admitted that Burnside came to him early on the eighteenth and asked for five thousand fresh men, which was true, but he maintained Burnside wanted them for defense, not offense.

Colonel Sacket alleged that a discouraged Burnside came to McClellan's headquarters attesting to the destruction and demoralization of his corps in front of McClellan and numerous other general officers. None of those generals ever mentioned the incident, perhaps because it did not happen: Sacket's convenient memory dated it the night after the battle, when McClellan declined to see Burnside.

If any general in the Union army felt beaten as September 17 ended it was George McClellan. David Strother, one of his staff, went to bed convinced Lee had suffered a thrashing, but in the wee hours of the eighteenth he awakened to the sound of McClellan's voice, admonishing some aggressive officer that his troops were to remain on the defensive. McClellan's tone upset Strother, for it suggested a certain unwarranted diffidence; the officer to whom McClellan spoke may have been Burnside himself, for it was in the early morning that Burnside finally penetrated the jealous palace guard around the Pry house to ask McClellan for fresh troops. After breakfast McClellan rode over to see for himself what shape the Ninth Corps was in and agreed to send a single division of Porter's corps. Emphasizing his own disinclination to resume the battle, McClellan ordered him to keep that division on the eastern bank. Colonel Strother even heard the commanding general direct Burnside to withdraw his entire force to that side of the creek, if he could do it without inviting an attack. Either because it could not be safely done or because Burnside did not share his commander's insecurity, the west bank of the Antietam remained in Federal hands.

Skirmisher firing continued most of September 18, and in the afternoon the troops on both sides hunched beneath a driving shower. The men in the front lines had not had a warm meal in nearly thirty-six hours, and with the prospect of sleeping wet through the cold night they rejoiced when Burnside sent a brigade of the borrowed division over to relieve them. They fell back to the bridge in the dusk and huddled around little fires. In his 1863 report, McClellan inflated this temporary substitution to include a wholesale withdrawal of the Ninth Corps and its replacement with the entire Fifth Corps division.[35] Whether that exaggeration was intended to demonstrate insubordination on Burnside's part or to reflect his supposed lack of confidence in his own corps is not clear: either would have aided McClellan's attempt to blame Burnside for the marred victory.

It is difficult to imagine Burnside, an honest and modest man who wished neither to malign McClellan nor supersede him, publicly inventing the story of his aggressiveness the night of September 17. Conversely, it is easy to comprehend McClellan's wish to squelch the tale. A good, solid tap Thursday morning probably would have finished Lee's army, and by late 1863 evidence of that was becoming available in the North. By 1885, when McClellan improved on his last version of the Maryland campaign, it was common knowledge that Lee had held his position on September 18 through sheer bluff. McClellan amplified every excuse to justify his hesitation: lack of ammunition, which he had considered insufficient cause for the delay of Burnside's afternoon attack; the allegedly demoralized condition of the left wing, and Burnside's employment of a fraction of one reserve corps to temporarily relieve it; and the tardy arrival of Andrew Humphreys's new division, which Humphreys himself angrily refuted. To have confessed that Burnside argued for an attack that day would have been to suggest qualities of perception and combativeness in that general that would have put the lie to his fancied derelictions of the seventeenth, upon which McClellan based his own exoneration from blame.[36]

By the morning of September 19, when McClellan finally made some tentative offensive overtures, the Confederate army had escaped. Mc-Clellan immediately telegraphed Washington that he had won a great victory, but one senses that, even then, he knew better.[37] Given time, so would the American people, and then it was up to George McClellan to salvage his place in history. The man he chose to sacrifice in his stead was none other than his own friend, the man who had been his paramount—if unwilling—rival for command. Typically, Burnside refused to defend himself against McClellan's accusations and innuendo, preferring to leave the judgment to history; that made him all the more effective a target.

McClellan's indictment charged that Burnside hesitated to attack and, once having attacked, lost confidence and wished to retreat. Historians' assessments have echoed McClellan's, adding the particularly damaging charge that Burnside was sulking, which helped delay the dissemination of orders to a degree that contributed to the lack of success. It has been demonstrated that McClellan deliberately exaggerated the amount of time it took to carry Burnside's Bridge. Less than three hours probably transpired between the receipt of the order and the accomplishment of what even McClellan admitted, early on, was a difficult job. (One of Hooker's brigadiers visited Burnside's front a couple of days after the battle and was amazed at the strength of the Confederate position.)[38] Two more hours, required to prepare a second assault with new troops brought into line over a narrow artery closely covered by enemy artillery, does not compare unfavorably with the marching time of supports using the uncontested crossings on the Union right, such as Joseph Mansfield's Twelfth Corps and Franklin's Sixth.

In regard to his attitude on the night of the seventeenth, Burnside himself—a man famous for strict honesty and a willingness to accept responsibility for failures not entirely his own—is perhaps the best witness. Soon after the battle, when the pertinent people were alive to correct any deviation from the truth, he testified publicly that he had wanted to renew the fight. He did not volunteer the information, but offered it when asked. There is no reason not to believe him, and other evidence supports him.

The charge that he was sulking is based solely upon his reluctance to yield his empty wing command. As he argued with General Cox, reverting to corps command would have made it appear he had been demoted. Since he had done nothing deserving of such a demotion, he had at first no reason to believe McClellan wished to remove him from command of his wing. Receipt of McClellan's bizarre rebuke just before the battle germinated an understandable concern, but Burnside's refusal to take the corps command from Cox at Antietam was not inspired by temper.[39] The relationship that resulted was not unlike the one he had shared with Foster, on Roanoke Island. In each case his forces had been attacking over a narrow, bullet-swept passageway; it was necessary that the column have a commander at both head and tail, the one to direct initial assaults and the other to feed up reinforcements and coordinate the whole. The Confederates defending the bluff managed very well under a similar command structure, though, in their case, unnecessarily.

Neither did this division of command cause the delays that have been attributed to it. The original attack order went directly from Burnside's hand to Cox's in a matter of seconds. Far from perfunctorily passing subsequent orders along to Cox, Burnside rode personally to Sturgis and Willcox with orders and instructions, coordinating troop movements for the nominal corps commander.

A rather more legitimate criticism concerns the failure to reconnoiter the fords. Burnside accepted Captain Duane's information on the subject; as events later indicated, Duane was not immune to error.[40] McClellan may have ordered Burnside to survey the crossings on the sixteenth, as he recorded in his self-exculpating 1863 report (even though such reconnaissance was generally the domain of the cavalry, which McClellan was hoarding), but by the time Duane's proxies had Burnside's divisions in place it was too dark for accurate scouting. Early the next morning Burnside's first orders from McClellan were to bring his troops near enough for a rapid assault but not close enough to suffer undue casualties. Any approach to the fords at that time would have been fatal for the individual who attempted it. Since Burnside had begun to feel his every movement was subject to censure, he may have reconciled these conflicting instructions by relying upon the reconnaissance of the general staff. He might, however, have sent a couple of platoons upstream and down to look for the tails of Toombs's flanks, where uncontested crossings might be made. Time may have discouraged him from such an endeavor, because even the existence of fords so distant would have entailed marches longer than Rodman's proved to be; expecting immediate orders to begin their diversion, Burnside and Cox anticipated no time for reconnaissance except in their immediate front. Noon had almost come before they began to understand they were to actually carry the bridge, rather than simply demonstrate against it "with the hope of something more"; until that point, further reconnaissance must have seemed a waste of valor. Still, a glance over the next hill might have prevented Crook from going so far astray; curious recruits ventured that much.[41]

At Antietam Burnside gave some evidence of a dangerous tendency to bypass the chain of command. Perhaps because he lacked his usual entourage of aides and orderlies, his removal of the 11th Connecticut from its assignment in support of a battery to the edge of Antietam Creek did not coincide with any notification of the brigade commander; when that brigadier sent an officer to gather it in for the move to Snavely's ford, the regiment had simply vanished. Thus detached, it did no measurable service after the bridge had been taken. Such an impropriety, though it may have been an honest oversight, could produce disastrous results if it were repeated frequently or committed on a larger scale.

Nonetheless, Burnside's performance at Antietam was superior to that of General McClellan and equal to that of any of the other corps or wing commanders. Afterward many looked back disapprovingly on his conduct there, but the ammunition used against him by his foremost critics came from stores accumulated by George McClellan, who gathered his best rounds from the banks of the Rappahannock River.

4

WINTER OF DISCONTENT

I

When Daniel Reed Larned returned to his job as General Burnside's secretary in the first days of October, the camp was in an uproar over a visit by President Lincoln. Generals and staff officers dragged the gangly chief executive up Loudoun Heights, all over Harpers Ferry, across the Potomac to Maryland Heights, and on October 3 they dangled his legs over the sides of a horse to review that part of the army perched on the banks of the Potomac at the mouth of Antietam Creek. Burnside, gracefully at home in the saddle, accompanied the president as he sauntered before the Ninth Corps. The general waved a voluminous gauntlet at the 9th New York, stopping to explain that these were the zouaves who had nearly won the day at Antietam. Lincoln nodded approvingly, while a private in the rear ranks took stock of the exalted visitor.

"Ain't the old bugger lean?" the zouave stage-whispered. "He wouldn't pay for skinnin'."

Later the president and McClellan climbed into an ambulance for a final circuit of the battlefield itself, where they had a chat before Lincoln returned to Washington. As the two departed, Burnside went back to his headquarters to greet a welcome guest.[1]

Mrs. Burnside had come from Baltimore under Mr. Larned's escort, and while she and the general secluded themselves in his quarters, the secretary dove into September's stack of unanswered correspondence.

As other staff officers drifted in and out of Larned's tent, he learned, piecemeal, of the injustices his chief had suffered at McClellan's hand: how he had directed most of the fighting at South Mountain, only to have Little Mac take all the credit, ignoring Burnside in the official dispatches; how he had been sent into the tempest at Antietam with the promise of support, only to be left to his own resources.[2] The staff remained convinced McClellan had meant to sacrifice Burnside and his men; some of them unburdened themselves to a *New York Tribune* correspondent on that subject, insisting McClellan had given Burnside the toughest job with the fewest men in hopes Burnside's reputation would suffer, as in fact it would. They were satisfied McClellan was jealous of his old friend—who, the correspondent admitted, "*is* a great favorite with the troops"—but the newspaperman thought McClellan would never stoop so low; he was obviously unaware the little general had stooped precisely that low only a few weeks previously, in the case of John Pope.[3]

Burnside himself confessed that his relations with the commanding general were very strained (McClellan had visited him but once in a fortnight) and that this had distressed him more than the considerable rigors of the campaign. Yet Burnside was not willing to turn against the man who had given him a job and a home when he most needed them. He would not reciprocate McClellan's chilly behavior; he would not confront him over the slights of Antietam; he would let no one know of their estrangement outside the immediate military family.[4]

Nor did McClellan seem disposed, then, to air any public grievance with his old friend. During the president's visit McClellan issued a general order congratulating the various corps for their performances at South Mountain and Antietam, this time stinting Burnside's praise not at all. And when the commander pondered an important dinner party about the same time, Burnside was one of the three special guests he invited.

Almost as they sat down to this meal, McClellan introduced the president's Emancipation Proclamation, which he had announced in the wake of Antietam. As an old-school Democrat McClellan was outraged at this reversal of war policy, and he considered making some sort of protest. The dinner had evidently been called that he might pump his guests for advice—or support, since two of the three were prewar Democrats—but he found no sympathy around the table. Jacob Cox, the sole Republican, warned him that he proposed a dangerous usurpation of civil authority and predicted he would not find a corporal's guard behind him. Burnside, from whom McClellan may have expected the greatest reinforcement, characteristically advised loyalty to the sitting government. Though he had earlier concurred with McClellan on this issue and had actively enforced slave laws to win over uncommitted North Carolinians, Burnside's observations had convinced him that no amount of such currying would lure the South back into the Union: slaveholders saw the Confederacy as their best hope of preserving their way of life. It would be more effective, he thought, to threaten them into a renunciation of secession on the penalty of total emancipation, while implying that slavery might continue (if it could) if the ordinance of secession were revoked. This the president had done, but even if Burnside had not supported him privately he could never have presumed to oppose him publicly, and so he told McClellan. If Little Mac had entertained any visions of a political coup, they were shaken by this unfriendly reception.

Emancipation remained a sore point for McClellan until the end of the war, and Burnside's change of opinion on the issue did nothing to eradicate the air of betrayal Fitz John Porter had insinuated upon Burnside's behavior. In McClellan's eyes, Burnside had demonstrated at least three times since late August that his duty to Abraham Lincoln outweighed his devotion to George McClellan, and the army commander may already have begun a final calculation of the value of Burnside's friendship as he and that Black Republican Cox rode back to their camp at the mouth of Antietam Creek.[5]

This campsite, surrounding a primitive industrial settlement called Antietam Iron Works, was a lovely spot, with another beautiful stone bridge like the one Sturgis had carried and an impressive stone aqueduct a hundred yards down the creek, where the Chesapeake and Ohio Canal crossed. It must have been romantic there, with the harvest moon of early October illuminating the placid Potomac below; it might have been eerie, too, if anyone learned of the mass grave nearby that contained the cholera-bloated bodies of five hundred Irish canal laborers who died in the epidemic of 1832. The army wasted no time polluting this pastoral scene, though. When Colonel Rush Hawkins came back to the army after the battle, he assumed command of Rodman's division and promptly distributed one of his bombastic orders, this time announcing: "Human excrement is so abundant and plentiful about the camp that a stranger would be led to believe that it is the natural element in which the officers and men of the 3^d Div had been reared from childhood." This may or may not have persuaded his men to clean up their bivouacs, but when Burnside read the preposterous circular he clapped Hawkins in arrest. The colonel wrote a penitent letter offering to request a transfer, and Burnside eventually released him, but it was a certain thing that Hawkins would not long remain at division headquarters.[6]

A week into October the Ninth Corps unseated itself from the vicinity of Antietam Iron Works and marched over Elk Ridge to a more salubrious camp in Pleasant Valley. Burnside accompanied his staff in its search for a new headquarters, his horse struggling with theirs up and down the merciless slopes of this extension of Maryland Heights. Once in the valley, the little troop drew up before a likely house owned by a Dr. Boteler. The doctor's seven lovely daughters gathered at the front door, whereupon the staff promptly voted to stay there. Burnside told them to keep to their saddles while he investigated the premises. Not wishing to discommode the family, he inquired only if they might pitch their tents in the orchard behind the house, to which the family readily agreed. Mr. Larned and the other bachelors on the staff were just as pleased. Burnside may have been gratified himself; for all his loyalty to Molly, he entertained a fondness for female companionship.

There was one large tent for headquarters business, and the staff officers paired off for living quarters. Burnside was no exception, sharing a tent with General Parke, who had returned from sick leave to resume his duties as chief of staff. Living with Burnside meant enduring his jovial antics, but Parke was devoted to him and enjoyed his playful company.[7]

Shortly after the Ninth Corps settled into its new camp, J. E. B. Stuart led Confederate cavalry on a raid that followed a wide arc around McClellan's entire army, stealing hundreds of horses in Pennsylvania before escaping cleanly back into Virginia. It was a terrible embarrassment to McClellan, who blamed the raiders' escape on the dearth of fresh horses in his own cavalry division. There is evidence to suggest the commanding general was away from the army at the commencement of the raid: if it was so, all of his relatives and friends—including Burnside—covered for him.[8]

Mrs. Burnside went home amid this clamor, passing dangerously close to the marauding Confederates, who crossed her path a few hours behind her. No sooner had she boarded the train than McClellan gave her husband command of the Second and Twelfth corps, as well as his own, with the officious title of Commander of the Defenses of Harpers Ferry, including responsibility for all the Potomac crossings from Harpers Ferry to the mouth of the Monocacy River. Low water that autumn made the river difficult to secure, as McClellan admitted: his appointment of Burnside indicated either grudging faith in his ability or a desire to transfer the censure to Burnside if the enemy came across again. No Confederate force passed on Burnside's front.[9]

Almost perfect weather prevailed through the end of September and most of October. The army had swollen to more than 140,000 by the attachment of other corps and scores of new regiments that stumbled in after Antietam. Burnside gradually reorganized the Ninth Corps during the fall, and his first order in that direction relieved Colonel Hawkins in favor of George Getty, a West Point brigadier whom Burnside had specially requested. In light of his own expanded duties, Burnside elevated Orlando Willcox to temporary corps command (Cox had been transferred west) and eventually gave Willcox's division to William Burns, another West Point classmate. He distributed nine new regiments among the three divisions, assigning three of them to Hawkins's brigade. That gave Hawkins the biggest and most inexperienced brigade in the corps, which would have been consistent with an intention to sideline either the brigade or its commander.[10]

The president again grew restless for a movement. He reduced some of his messages to McClellan to flagrant sarcasm in his anxiety for the general to use his expensive war machine. At last, on October 25, came evidence the great blue beast was stirring. Burnside's troops underwent an inspection that day by McClellan's chief engineer, Captain Duane. He snooped in their knapsacks, hefted their canteens, and tugged on their accoutrements to assure himself they were ready for an active campaign.

While the Ninth Corps patiently endured this poking and prodding, General Burnside cantered up to watch. He stopped in front of Colonel Hawkins's brigade, and presently the troublesome New Yorker trotted up beside him, as well as General Sturgis, the profane division commander. Next, some ladies riding sidesaddle came along, and the group ulti-

mately attracted three nondescript newspaper correspondents, intent
on learning the scuttlebutt. It was a raw day—a bad omen after so long
a fair spell—and Burnside had much to do. Neither did he care to remain within earshot of the journalists, for as soon as they arrived he
took leave of the little crowd. One bored private watched him peel off
his big floppy hat and bow, "holding down his head to show the ladies
the forehead on top." [11]

That same night, Burnside received his orders to cross an advance
guard over the river. After such fine weather in Pleasant Valley, it
was exasperating for the foot soldiers to have to strike their tents the
next day in a numbing rainstorm, the icy downpour driven into their
faces and through their clothing by vengeful winds. Burnside complied
with the orders: he rout-marched a couple of divisions over the pontoon
bridge at Berlin and settled them around Lovettsville, just inside Virginia. McClellan wanted all of his troops over, but Burnside's legendary
concern for the health and comfort of his men vied with his wish to
serve his friend satisfactorily; with the rebukes of mid-September dancing unforgotten behind his phrasing, he sent the commanding general
a friendly objection. Addressed to Dear Mac as in days of old, the letter appealed for a delay in crossing the bulk of the Ninth Corps, that
most of the men might weather the storm in their tents. He strained his
prose to assure McClellan he intended to comply with his every desire,
awkwardly promising not to get in the way of other troops. McClellan
directed one of his staff to give Burnside an impersonal note, consenting
to his request. [12]

The storm finally abated October 27, and the rest of the Ninth Corps
rumbled across the pontoon bridge, still wet and still cursing their
luck—and McClellan. Most of them would see those same pontoons in
another incarnation, six weeks hence.

The entire Army of the Potomac piled up behind Burnside's advance
corps, so on the twenty-ninth Burnside moved his divisions ahead to
Wheatland and Waterford, keeping his headquarters in the village at
Lovettsville. He and his staff may have wondered once again exactly
what his command entailed as the month of November approached: the
order placing him in control of the Second and Twelfth corps had never
been revoked, though he was obviously no longer in charge of the defenses of Harpers Ferry, but the Second Corps entered Virginia by a
very different route and most of the Twelfth Corps was staying be-

hind. At least one of Burnside's staff addressed his letters home from Headquarters of the Advance, and when General Parke communicated with McClellan's staff his dispatches were sent from Headquarters of the Left Wing. Certainly Burnside had the Ninth Corps, but beyond that his jurisdiction seemed to cover only a stray division under Amiel Whipple and George Stoneman's division of cavalry. McClellan had apparently bowed to Burnside's rank and prestige so far as to give him a command of nominal importance, but he stopped short of putting enough men in his power that he might have won a battle unassisted.[13]

On the second of November Burnside's men began their journey down the eastern edge of the Blue Ridge Mountains. Lee's army lay in the lower—that is to say, northern—end of the Shenandoah Valley, and this advance on his flank forced him to flee south with half his troops. Leaving Jackson in the valley, Lee skirted below the invaders, that he might confront them if they turned on Richmond.

When Union soldiers moved out of Wheatland and Waterford, they moved quickly. In the back of McClellan's mind (he later claimed) was the hope he could get in rear of the Confederates and cut them off from their supplies. It was an outside chance, but Burnside nonetheless urged his brigadiers to drive their men from the outset, and the march of November 2 was a severe trial to men who had just spent six sedentary weeks in camp.

Mounted officers found the march no less rigorous. Burnside rode his favorite, that horrid-looking creature, Major—a bony, highstepping, bobtailed grey with a malicious glare, and walleyed to boot. When the animal stood in a group, Jacob Cox remembered, he was always "keeping his white eye on the lookout for a chance to lash out at somebody." But with Burnside on his back, it was hard work to keep up with him. The staff left Lovettsville hours after the main body, but Burnside led off at a trot, trying to overtake the column. Much of their course ran crosscountry, through forests and fields, sometimes over fences, the horses splashing through frigid brooks up to their riders' boots, all at a pace one of them called "a John Gilpin speed." When they finally stopped for the night, they had come thirty miles and were abreast of the forwardmost brigades. They settled for the night in a house where, two days before, J. E. B. Stuart had slept; when Burnside's secretary took off his boots he found the insides of his knees raw from the day's race.[14]

Despite this rapid footwork, Confederates covered all the Blue Ridge passes ahead of the Yankees and worked some infantry in front of them as well. Union cavalry under Alfred Pleasonton met steady resistance to the south, and gunfire in the mountain gaps to the west indicated they were already defended. McClellan was thus limited to his basic plan of driving for the Orange & Alexandria Railroad, which could serve as his supply line in lieu of the bad roads over which his wagons presently carried the army's sustenance. Already his subordinates were asking where their next provisions could be had.

There seemed but one advantage to operating in this part of Virginia: an unexpected cavity of Union sympathizers. Pleasonton found he could forward a wide variety of valuable information from an assortment of inhabitants. This profusion of loyalists is best explained by the number of Quaker meetinghouses in the area; Burnside slept near one, outside of Union.[15]

On the third and fourth of November Burnside edged his divisions from the arc they occupied between Bloomfield and Philomont to the vicinity of Upperville: with the help of borrowed infantry and artillery, Pleasonton had finally pried Stuart out of that town. Burnside's men faced more tall marching November 5 and 6. By the evening of the first day they all slept south of the Manassas Gap Railroad, strung out between Piedmont and Salem, and the next day they started to Waterloo, on the main tributary of the Rappahannock.

Burnside was hamstrung by poor maps. Waterloo did not even appear on them, and his scouts had to hunt up a local citizen willing to tell them where it was. Once Burnside knew that, however, his troubles were only half over; Waterloo lay twenty miles away, and there were but two roads on which he could travel. One, following Carter's Run, was in bad shape. He sent Stoneman's cavalry down that one, figuring the speed of mounted troops would counterbalance the extra distance and difficult travel, but all four of his infantry divisions had to follow the road through Orlean. Not all of them reached Waterloo by the appointed time. Sturgis's division finally collapsed, well after dark, camping "on a desolate waste" near Orlean. Whipple trailed even farther behind. The wing stretched from there to Waterloo and beyond, where George Getty's division took position on the riverbank.[16]

A northeaster began the next morning. Snow fell heavy but dry, driven by bitter winds. Burnside closed up his column as best he could, but the bad weather and poor maps worked against him. He saw Sturgis's division slog through Orlean that afternoon, and these men gave him hearty cheers, regiment after regiment, as they passed. He stood with his hat in his hand, waving, his bald head bared to the snow. Later the column took a bad turn in the blizzard and marched two miles in the wrong direction before a courier caught up with it; back it came, the ordeal only begun, and marched another nine miles after the leaders regained the way. When these two brigades scattered into a forest near Waterloo, miles of Virginia fence rails disappeared in the twinkling of hundreds of campfires.[17]

General Burnside felt uncomfortable about the position of his troops that night. The storm and the movements of the army had churned the roads to mush. Wagon trains could hardly move, and supplies coming from the rear traveled the most dilapidated highways of all. Stoneman's cavalry and Whipple's infantry were extremely low on provisions; in other parts of the army the men were completely out of rations. Every evening before going to bed, Burnside took from his Bible several photographs of his wife that she had sent him in North Carolina. Though he doubtless glanced at them the evening of November 7, as he retired early, his last cogent thoughts before he dropped off to sleep were probably connected with supply lines.[18]

When the general awoke, it was to an unheralded intruder, General Catharinus Putnam Buckingham, a white-bearded Ohioan who had graduated four places behind Robert E. Lee at West Point. Buckingham was on a special assignment from the War Department, and he had a most unwelcome document for Ambrose Burnside; when the younger man was fully awake Buckingham gave it to him. Burnside unfolded a paper headed General Orders, No. 182, which announced the removal of George McClellan from command of the Army of the Potomac and the appointment of Burnside in his place.

As those in Washington had anticipated, Burnside immediately objected. He declared himself unprepared to handle the 120,000 men McClellan had brought with him. McClellan was a perfectly good commander, he again argued; besides, it was poor policy to change generals in the middle of an active campaign. Buckingham then explained that McClellan would be relieved regardless, and perhaps Burnside had better accept the command rather than let it go to someone even more undesirable, such as Hooker. Burnside, who disliked very few people, was one of many who disliked Joe Hooker very much. He found him arrogant, devious, and dangerously selfish, partly because of his habit of criticizing everyone above him, but especially perhaps because of his insubordinate procrastination at South Mountain. Had Hooker moved when Burnside first ordered him, the victory at that battle might have been more spectacular, and Jesse Reno would probably still be alive. Conferring at length with Parke and Lewis Richmond, Burnside finally relented: he would take the command.

Buckingham suggested they go immediately to McClellan. It was already very late, but the two rode into the storm several roundabout miles to Salem, where they sheltered their horses and took a military train to Rectortown. Headquarters lay silent when they arrived, but a lantern still illuminated the inside of McClellan's tent. His day's work finished, he leaned over a letter to his wife. Buckingham rapped on the tentpole and at McClellan's invitation the two other generals entered. Both seemed quite glum to McClellan, who later claimed to have divined their purpose, but he greeted them with some small talk; before long, however, Buckingham brought up the subject of their visit, handing Little Mac the order that ended his military career. He read the orders quickly, then turned to his distressed friend.

"Well, Burnside," he said, "I turn the command over to you." With those words vanished whatever satisfaction Burnside took in his army service.[19]

At Burnside's request, McClellan stayed on a couple of days to familiarize him with the army's situation. In years to come McClellan would insist he had asked Burnside to keep abreast of such details from the start of the campaign because, as next-senior officer, he would be in charge if McClellan became a casualty. Surviving correspondence does not bear out this claim, with its implication that Burnside neglected to heed McClellan's prophetic advice. Throughout the campaign, and for weeks preceding it, the principal communicants with general headquarters were Fitz John Porter and William Franklin. Burnside is perhaps the least frequently consulted corps commander. As Burnside's and McClellan's headquarters were usually many miles apart, the dearth of correspondence cannot be construed as evidence the two conferred regularly in person, and Burnside's comment on their personal estrangement casts even more doubt on that theory.[20] McClellan's claim is merely another in a sad accumulation of poisoned recollections that followed his descent from prominence.

To give McClellan his due, it was a bitter conclusion to his fifteen-month tenure with the Army of the Potomac. It is not altogether clear what motive provoked his replacement at that particular time. For seven weeks he had been urged to advance, and when the desired advance was respectably begun, the axe fell. One popular theory concerned the New York elections, the last important balloting of 1862. They had been held November 4, with the Democratic candidate winning the gubernatorial race. Some in the army speculated Lincoln would remove McClellan as soon as he no longer needed Democratic support; one officer in the First Corps wondered even as Burnside thumbed through his wife's photographs, just before Buckingham's arrival, whether McClellan would not go now that the returns were in. The passing of those elections did free Lincoln of a great impediment to the removal of McClellan the Democrat, but Lincoln's secretary of the navy hinted at a more immediate incentive in his diary: Edwin Stanton fervently wished McClellan replaced. On November 4, at a cabinet meeting, Stanton expressed growing dissatisfaction with McClellan's stubborn independence, which he considered perfectly insubordinate. Later at the same meeting, Lincoln announced that whenever Halleck required McClellan's removal it would be forthcoming as though by presidential decision. Little imagination is necessary to picture Halleck buckling under the pressure of his immediate superior, the secretary of war; Lincoln wrote the order the next day.[21]

On the tenth of November Burnside graciously organized a final review of the army for its deposed commander—a glorious farewell. The various corps—not including Burnside's old Ninth—lined up scores deep, the men cheering mightily for their beloved Mac as he cantered hat in hand before them. His staff rode behind him, and behind them, Burnside, already looking a little worn.

There was a giddy, bittersweet touch to that autumn day near Warrenton. McClellan had given this army a taste of glamor in spite of all the cold, mud, and snow, and it loved him for it. Hats flew into the air and color bearers waved their flags in a frenzy uncommon off the battlefield. Grown men wept as he rode before them. When he had passed them all and turned back toward headquarters, entire brigades broke ranks and poured after him. It was, as one line officer noted, more of a triumphal procession than anything else. This was as much as Burnside could do for his old friend, and perhaps it was enough: "The scenes of today," McClellan wrote that evening, "repay me for all that I have endured."[22]

Back in Providence, cannon on the state house lawn boomed a hundred-gun salute to Burnside's promotion, but in the Warrenton Hotel spirits were not so bright. A great many officers of the various headquarters drowned their sorrow at McClellan's departure in whiskey. The next day there was a tearful goodbye at the railroad station, after which those same officers turned out to receive Burnside, "handsomely—but not enthusiastically," as one of them phrased it. That same general judged that Burnside was good enough, but admitted "all seemed to think there was one they liked much better." It did not improve Burnside's relations with McClellan's admirers that the train now carrying the deposed commander away had brought General James Wadsworth to Warrenton. Wadsworth was the Republican who had lost the race against Horatio Seymour for governor of New York; most perceived him as representative of the abolitionist Republican element, so when he told people the government had sent him down to advise Burnside, it seemed to confirm the political motivation behind the change of commanders. Even worse, for Burnside, was the resulting insinuation that he had aligned himself with the administration against McClellan. Such must have been the suspicion around McClellan's tent since the Porter affair, or at least since the dinner discussion of the Emancipation Proclamation, and this apparent corroboration did nothing to endear the glamorous little general's partisans to his successor.[23]

So grief-stricken and indignant were some soldiers at McClellan's fall that rumors of a general mutiny worked their way north in the maws of the mail pouches, but that feeling never rooted well—nor was everyone in the army sad to see McClellan go. Despite having served under Hooker, who constantly belittled Burnside, one officer in the 19th Indiana was quite pleased with the change. Little Mac, he thought, was "below par." "We are well pleased with Burnside," he went on: "Thank God for the prospect ahead now, our soldiers will fight as well under B. as McC." Many in the ranks professed outright confidence.[24]

Fighting might be in the cards, but there would be precious little glamor under Ambrose Burnside. For all his playful temperament, he had not the flamboyant arrogance with which McClellan had inspired his men. His early upbringing among Quaker families had becalmed his speech with the tone of understatement so typical of that sect; West

Point had failed to eradicate the trait, so the romantic pomposity of McClellan's orders and dispatches disappeared from headquarters.

Mostly, however, Burnside did not have time for glamor. McClellan had not only been a brilliant organizer, he had been adept at delegating authority and choosing competent subordinates, which is partly the same thing. Burnside not only judged men generously rather than well, he found it next to impossible to apportion staff labor and digest the resulting information with so extensive an organization. Worst of all, he was a slow thinker. He had no leisure for bounding in front of parading troops on a picture-book stallion: so seriously did he take his duties, he had no stomach for it, either.

Not only did Burnside spend his entire day on headquarters business now, but most of the night as well. Oliver O. Howard, a one-armed division commander in the Second Corps, saw him two days after his appointment; he found Burnside already looking haggard, and somewhat lugubrious. He made it plain he considered his promotion a misfortune—just as he had implied to Howard's corps commander the day before—and that he had accepted it only from a sense of duty.[25] In addition to familiarizing himself with the position and condition of the army, arranging supply logistics, determining the whereabouts of the enemy, and reorganizing his own staff and staff duties throughout the army, Burnside was expected to devise a plan of campaign and report it to General Halleck at once.

One of Burnside's last messages to McClellan as his subordinate mentioned the need to repair the Orange & Alexandria Railroad, given the impossibility of feeding the army by way of Virginia's bottomless roads. On inspection, the Orange & Alexandria proved totally inadequate for such a massive undertaking so far in the interior. Even if it had not been, that long an umbilical would be a serious liability to an invading army. John Pope had discovered as much on the same line, even closer to Washington. As George McClellan observed, that left the army in a convenient position to either advance on Richmond via Fredericksburg or take ship from the coast to return to the James River. How McClellan hoped to convince the War Department, or President Lincoln, to allow him to return to the Peninsula is a mystery which he permitted to endure; that left Fredericksburg. The six corps would march southeast to that point and advance from there to Richmond along the heads of navigation of the several parallel rivers that intervened: supplies could be

ferried to each base and forwarded by rail to the army until it secured
the next river. It was a simple but relatively safe plan. It put most of the
army's lifeline under control of the dominant U.S. Navy and freed the
invading force—nearly—from the mercy of the weather.

This, then, was the route Burnside chose, and though he was responsible for making the choice it may not have been his idea. McClellan
had previously regarded the Fredericksburg option as an alternative to
his inland course if the railroad turned out to be inadequate; it turned
out to be just that, and though critics assailed Burnside for squander-
ing McClellan's "strategic advantage," McClellan's own logic indicates
that he would have headed for Fredericksburg, too.[26] His enormous influence with Burnside, even after McClellan's friendliness toward him
had stiffened, allows for the possibility that the departing commander
advised the change of base. The tragedy that followed explains why
McClellan would have avoided any outright claim for that credit.

Getting to Fredericksburg was half the trick. The Rappahannock
surged unfordable at its upper tributary, where the Ninth Corps
awaited Burnside's decision, so it could be supposed that it was even
deeper, wider, and swifter thirty or forty miles downstream.[27] The general therefore proposed to bring the pontoon bridges down from the
upper Potomac and land them at Aquia Creek, then transport them
overland to Falmouth, opposite Fredericksburg. The Army of the Potomac would be across the river and in a commanding position before Lee
even knew it was gone from Warrenton.

Halleck reflected Lincoln's preference for inland maneuver, taking
the short road to Richmond while forcing Lee to use the longer route.
One problem with that idea was Lee's new position, with half his army,
at Culpeper: he had that short road blocked. Another hitch, of course,
was the difficulty of supply. In the end Halleck made the journey—a
wearisome one, for so softened a Washington official—to the Warrenton
Hotel. He brought with him two very efficient staff brigadiers, Quartermaster General Montgomery Meigs and Henry Haupt, superintendent
of military railroads. With these experts to back him up, Halleck probably hoped to sway his new field commander.

They held something of a soirée when the generals first arrived.
These officebound soldiers seldom saw their old friends serving at the
front, and they ate dinner at the hotel with numerous former acquaintances. To be sure, Hooker was there, ingratiating himself to Halleck,

but finally they all drifted away, leaving Burnside, Halleck, and the two department heads to discuss business.

Burnside began by repeating his assessment that he was not fit for so large a command, while many others beneath him were. Halleck waved his objections aside rather impatiently, however, and invited him to reveal the details of his Fredericksburg plan. After the new commander had done that, Halleck presented his arguments against it. Perhaps to Halleck's surprise, and certainly to his consternation, General Haupt preferred Burnside's proposal. They discussed it into the early hours. The next morning Halleck wired Washington for the pontoons, in case the campaign were decided upon; then he, Haupt, and Meigs went back to the capital, where Halleck remained as lukewarm over the idea as he had been about McClellan's, on his return from the Harrison's Landing conference. Haupt still favored it, though; considering that Lincoln ultimately approved it, the quartermaster general must have offered no serious objections.[28]

Halleck forwarded the president's consent November 14. Lincoln felt confident of success if Burnside moved quickly, Halleck commented, "otherwise not." Burnside already understood the need for rapid movement: before nightfall his first units had orders to march.

Only that day, Burnside had reorganized the Army of the Potomac into his image of a more manageable weapon. He grouped the six corps gathered about Warrenton into three McClellanlike wings: the Left Grand Division, as he called it, consisted of the First and Sixth corps, under William Franklin; the Center Grand Division was made up of the newly arrived Third Corps and the Fifth Corps, placed under Joe Hooker if only because his rank required a command of such stature; and the Second and Ninth corps constituted the Right Grand Division, with sixty-five-year-old Edwin Sumner in charge. Though technically under Burnside's orders, Franz Sigel's Eleventh Corps remained behind, outside Washington.[29]

It was "Bull" Sumner's right wing that led off early on November 15. The Confederates detected his movement and ineffectually shelled his trains, but Sumner pushed his men hard, his infantry struggling cross-country while his supply wagons and artillery filled the roads.

Before letting Sumner go, Burnside sent his staff engineer to check on those pontoons again. It was only after Sumner was on his way, though, that word came back from Washington of a delay in the plan

Burnside and Halleck had agreed upon. Burnside expected Halleck to take care of such details when he returned to his Washington office: after all, the engineer brigade was in Washington, while Burnside would be fifty miles away and on the move, out of telegraphic reach. Unfortunately, though McClellan had ordered the pontoons to Washington the day before he was relieved, most of them were still on the upper Potomac when Burnside's man inquired about them nine days later. That was Henry Halleck's fault; he had not made his own engineer officer privy to the importance of the bridges, nor had he followed their progress. They were supposed to have been on their way to Falmouth by the morning of November 15, but the commander of the engineer brigade—Daniel Woodbury—could not now promise to even start them until November 17. That, too, turned out to be overly optimistic. Woodbury (the same man who had led the flanking column astray at First Bull Run) might have deduced that some schedule depended upon the pontoons when Halleck specifically instructed him to telegraph news of their departure, but the principal blame rested with Halleck.[30]

The Confederates were now aware of the movement toward the Tidewater, Lee already guessing that Fredericksburg might be the destination, so it was too late to simply call Sumner back. Fredericksburg was in enemy control, as well as Falmouth and Aquia Creek; therefore it would not be a bad idea to have Union infantry there ahead of the pontoons, which Burnside could still expect as early as November 19. Still, he held the rest of his army at Warrenton a couple of days longer, to give his opponent room to doubt his intentions.

The officer in charge of the pontoons ran into more trouble. An officious quartermaster department, from which he needed horses, harness, and teamsters, put him off. Woodbury, still unaware the movement requiring his pontoons had already begun, dutifully telegraphed that the departure would be delayed at least until November 18. It was ultimately not until November 19 that the first bridge train left Washington. By that time, Sumner had been in front of Fredericksburg a day and a half. He drew his two corps up along Stafford Heights, opposite the city, to await the pontoons and the balance of the army.

Burnside rode in on the nineteenth. Sumner asked permission to cross at one of the fords upstream, but Burnside shook his head. As much as he wanted to occupy Fredericksburg in its meagerly defended condition, the ford Sumner spoke of had been described as impassable for infantry and artillery; even if he could swim a sufficient force of cavalry across, it might quickly become stranded. Instead, Burnside dashed off a note to Halleck, reminding him—among other things—of the missing pontoons.[31]

A year later, Halleck tried to wriggle from beneath his considerable share of the responsibility by arguing that Burnside had verbally agreed to travel on the south bank of the Rappahannock all the way from his position near Warrenton. Such an idea was preposterous. Apparently there had been discussion, during the command conference at the Warrenton Hotel, of crossing a portion of the army well above Fredericksburg; but even if Halleck had construed that to mean the entire army would cross, he ought to have recognized the dangerous supply situation that would have resulted. As it was, Burnside opted against fording even a small force, for fear of having it isolated and destroyed. The Rappahannock was known to rise quickly in a storm, as Burnside had been somewhat redundantly warned by an officer who had also been there the previous summer. Rain came quickly and furiously in a Virginia winter, and the Army of the Potomac was already suffering enough from shortages of food and forage without putting an impassable river across the difficult roads faced by the teamsters.

Burnside's wisdom in keeping to the north bank was borne out before he established his headquarters adjacent to Fredericksburg. The night of November 18 a heavy rain began to fall, continuing throughout the next day and—with even greater force—into the twentieth. Had he permitted any unit to cross, it would have been trapped.[32]

Though the storm had already begun, Hooker proposed crossing his grand division at United States Ford and sweeping south, alone, toward Richmond. A number of people supposed Burnside's appointment over the army was only meant to be temporary, until Hooker had sufficiently recovered from his Antietam wound to assume the command. Evidently Joe Hooker was one of those who thought that, and in order to assist the prophecy he did not wait for Burnside's response to his proposal, writing directly to the secretary of war to suggest arrangements, taking the opportunity to criticize his commanding officer's management of the change of base. Burnside, unaware of Hooker's insubordinate intrigue, rejected his plan as diplomatically as possible: considering Hooker's poor showing with the entire army in a similar campaign the next spring, it was just as well he did.[33]

The storm came and passed, the rivers rose, and still they had no sign
of the pontoons. Burnside wrote Halleck again on the twenty-second to
say he was no longer so confident of success. Confederate soldiers moved
into camp beyond Fredericksburg in ever-greater numbers, while the
Union army sat idle, unable to cross a man. By November 21, the city's
original little garrison had been reinforced by two divisions of Longstreet's corps.

One pontoon train, sent by land, became mired in the storm, wallow-
ing a mere five miles a day. At the Occoquan progress stopped entirely
until engineers rebuilt the bridge, after which they divided the train,
sending half of it on to Falmouth by land and half to Belle Plain, on
Potomac Creek, behind a tug. Other bridge materials went by barge
directly from Washington to Belle Plain and Aquia Creek. The first to
reach the vicinity of the Army of the Potomac arrived at Belle Plain
November 22, but the major in charge there knew no more of the need
for dispatch than had his superiors; therefore, when the quartermaster
department again neglected to supply teams and drivers on demand, the
major waited patiently until they were provided. Between that delay
and emergency road repairs, he did not deliver that partial bridge to
Falmouth until the afternoon of November 24.[34]

Meanwhile, Burnside fell into a blue mood while his staff fumed. One
officer went up to Aquia Creek looking for pontoons but found only General Woodbury, who had none. The staff knew their commander was
not at fault, but knew equally well that he would catch the blame for
the setback they had all begun to anticipate. They were quite right:
as early as November 24, only ten days after he had approved Burnside's plan of campaign, President Lincoln lamented privately to one of
Sigel's generals that his new army commander seemed no faster than
his old one.[35]

Concerned about the army's hesitation, Lincoln made arrangements
to meet his general aboard the steamer *Baltimore* November 26, in the
middle of Aquia Creek. Burnside's secretary went aboard the boat with
him, but no one witnessed his conclave with the president. Burnside
complained of the missing pontoons, a few of which began to appear only
now, after Longstreet's entire corps had occupied the opposite bank.
Lincoln had a plan to put a corps or more of reinforcements ashore
at Port Royal, well downstream, and a similar force of new troops on
the north bank of the Pamunkey River, backed by gunboats. These two

could converge at or behind Fredericksburg while Burnside attacked head-on. It was not bad strategy, as it could prevent Lee from falling back on Richmond while forcing him to abandon his lines at Fredericksburg. Still, Burnside feared it would take too long to gather and deploy the other columns, which would put the campaign too far into winter; Halleck wanted Burnside to attack as soon as possible, or so he implied. Lincoln responded that he, as president, was in charge of such decisions, rather than Halleck. He added that Burnside might wait until he was ready: both he and the country were prepared to be patient. They parted with the understanding that Halleck would review the plan. He did, and he objected for the same reason as Burnside, so Lincoln shelved the idea.[36] Who, Burnside might then have wondered, was in charge now? And what did this say about the patience of either the country or the administration?

Burnside returned to Falmouth by omnibus and train the next day. On foot, and without the slightest indication of his rank, he waded through the mud from the depot to his headquarters with no entourage save his ubiquitous secretary—not the way George McClellan would have come back to camp.

He met good news, for once: his wife had reached Belle Plain by ship the previous evening. He immediately saddled a horse and rode to meet her for a Thanksgiving celebration.[37]

By now, Stonewall Jackson's corps of the Confederate army had started to Fredericksburg from the Shenandoah Valley. Burnside began to wonder whether he ought to provide for an alternate crossing; finally he did, choosing Skinker's Neck, more than a dozen miles below Fredericksburg. Preparations there, however, soon prompted Lee to send Jackson's corps in that direction, and before long the enemy had intimidating defenses in that location. The site had other limitations as well: fourteen miles of unimproved roads posed a major problem for the engineer, artillery, and supply wagons at that time of year, not to mention the infantry. It rained a light drizzle all of December 1, and for the next three days warm sun thawed each night's frozen mud; December 5 a drenching storm turned from rain to snow, and the roads became quagmires. Then came a hard freeze of three days' duration, followed by two relatively warm days that once again liquified the road system.

General Franklin believed it would be possible to cross at Skinker's Neck, but he expressed grave misgivings about advancing from there, with such strong positions as the enemy had for defending the neck. Taking all of this into consideration, Burnside determined at some time in early December to abandon that route and to bridge the river at the point where Lee would least expect it—smack in front of Fredericksburg, the most difficult spot. General Sumner had entertained reservations about that when the army first reached Falmouth: he feared bridging the river before Confederate artillery and Southern marksmen, posted in the houses along the waterfront. He suggested spanning the river below town, guarding the bridgehead with a shield of thirty heavy guns, and turning Lee's right by marching the entire army around it. Burnside eventually decided upon an amalgamation of his own plan and the one Sumner offered. The Union army would cross both at and below town, simultaneously driving at the enemy with a frontal assault and curling his right flank backward. He reasoned that the surprise crossing alone would catch the Confederates with half their forces a dozen miles away, at which the Army of the Potomac could leap between the two halves and defeat them in detail.[38]

Wherever it was to be done, Burnside felt compelled to attack somewhere, no matter how much patience the president professed: however prudent it might be to withdraw into winter quarters, the newspapers had denounced McClellan for doing so the previous year, and even Lincoln had joined in the chorus. McClellan's hesitation after Antietam had resurrected the journalistic tirade, and his removal implied the administration's recognition that the country wanted action. Editors were already urging Burnside to attack at once—editors who were friendly both to Lincoln and Burnside. There was also a psychological need within the army itself for some sort of offensive campaign. An officer who had been with Burnside in North Carolina evinced concern over army morale just as (though not because) McClellan was removed. "The men in the old regiments here are not very sanguine of success," he wrote home. "The general opinion is that if we don't take Richmond by spring the Southern Confederacy is a fixed fact."[39] The continued success and survival of the Army of Northern Virginia contributed to that attitude, and the Emancipation Proclamation may even have aggravated it. Those who had not sought to destroy slavery might have concluded the war needed to be won by January 1, to avoid the effects of the proclamation; the abolition-minded probably expected those War

Democrats in the army to cease giving their best effort after the first of the year, and they may have hoped for a battle on that account.

Discontent, however, was not limited to the prosecution of the war. To some degree—though not to that claimed subsequently—the men in the ranks had doubts about Ambrose Burnside's ability. A recruit in Rush Hawkins's 9th New York, who perhaps reflected a trickling-down of disrespect from the insufferable Hawkins, greeted the change of command with the comment that "Burnside has done well thus far but nothing to prove himself capable of maneuvering our 'Grand Army' successfully." The same lack of confidence in the upper echelons may have derived from the fact that Burnside had comparatively little military experience. Of his three grand division commanders, Hooker and Franklin had graduated from West Point years before Burnside, Franklin first in his class, and Sumner had been an officer long before Burnside was born. Four of the six corps commanders had preceded him at the Point, and Willcox had been ahead of him in the same class. More than two-thirds of the division commanders had also graduated before him, most of them having fought in Mexico and remained in the service ever since. Burnside's five years as a lieutenant had availed him only one brush with Apaches, even if he did get an arrow in the neck.[40] McClellan had been almost as junior among the West Pointers, but he had been next to the top of his class, had distinguished himself in Mexico, and had been out of the army but four years when the war began. He had, besides, exuded confidence. Burnside wore his heart on his sleeve, and his heart just then was very heavy.

A few days before he expected to throw his forces across the river, the commanding general learned of serious dissension among his subordinates. Hooker had already denounced Burnside's strategy, and at least among the corps and division commanders of Sumner's Right Grand Division there was almost unanimous disapproval of the plan to attack the enemy through Fredericksburg.

Burnside called Sumner's generals together at their grand division headquarters, in the largest room of the stately Lacy mansion, and outlined just what he planned to do: cross at and just below Fredericksburg in two columns, attacking both Marye's Heights, behind the city, and the Confederate right, below town, before Jackson's corps could reach the battlefield. He mentioned that he had heard of considerable disagreement with this plan and reprimanded the officers for "throwing cold water" on his operation.

General Sumner, who had sent the private note but had said nothing else against the proposed crossing, pledged himself to unquestioning obedience, as did Darius Couch, the Second Corps commander, who had openly objected to the idea. One by one, the other generals offered cheerful cooperation, regardless of their differences, and the meeting ended amiably enough.[41] Burnside had managed to quell the contention that threatened his position as commander of the army, but he had confirmed his suspicion that his subordinates were not terribly enthusiastic. For all their protestations to the contrary, he had good reason to believe their discouragement would infect the troops. And then of course there was Hooker, who had not recanted.

General Meade thought, with good cause, that Burnside's problem with his commanders was of his own manufacture, resulting from his frequent expressions of self-doubt. It mattered little whether that doubt was well founded: in the cutthroat atmosphere of the Army of the Potomac, merely letting it slip as much as fulfilled the prophecy. No one will ever know whether, under less antagonistic circumstances, Burnside could have handled the army efficiently. He was not a man afraid of doing things: he risked everything in business, lost, and eventually began anew; he recorded no qualms about going to sea with fifteen thousand men and scores of ships under his responsibility; nor, later in his career, did he shy away from deliberately jeopardizing himself and his command at Knoxville, to lure Longstreet away from Chattanooga. These undertakings required great personal confidence. Yet he seemed to dread stepping up from command of a wing to that of the army, and his native modesty and honesty led him to confide to several officers his belief that he could not manage it. There would have been nothing wrong with that in an army made up of men like himself, who stood ready to give their all to any man invested with the authority, whatever he said of himself. But here in Virginia Union generals were accustomed to looking out for themselves, covering their mistakes and carpeting their way to promotion with the shrouds of other men's reputations. Rather than endearing himself to his immediate subordinates (Sumner and a few others excepted), his admissions of doubt merely made him an easy mark for them and undermined any capacity he brought to the job. Few generals associated with him at Fredericksburg or afterward, wherever success was not complete, failed to relieve themselves of blame by pointing a finger at Burnside.[42]

In addition to the liability of certain officers who had little faith in him, Burnside carried an invisible but nonetheless burdensome weight of stress during the Fredericksburg campaign. Except for the trouble at Hatteras Inlet, the rigors of the North Carolina operation had been as nothing compared to the difficulties Burnside had endured since joining the Army of the Potomac. From July he had been subjected to an unusual amount of strain, and in the weeks preceding Fredericksburg the pressure became enormous. He had, at least once, been forced to visit his old friend McClellan with instructions to get Little Mac's army moving or, according to one source, supplant him as its chief. His devotion to McClellan made either chore painful, and he must also have suffered from McClellan's hinted-at suspicion that Burnside and the administration were conspiring against him.[43] July had also been the month of the steam-and-rail marathon up and down the East Coast, ending in Burnside's first assignment to Fredericksburg, where he arrived with an eruption of erysipelas so severe it flattened him. The skin disorder itself may have been a physical manifestation of accumulating stress.

Throughout the balance of August Burnside had had to picket most of the Rappahannock River with a single division, isolated most of the time from the protection of the main armies. The withdrawal from Falmouth had been something of a nightmare, with the specter of Lee's victorious battalions driving his troops into Aquia Creek, and the Antietam campaign had begun but a few days later. The physical attrition of another fortnight of active campaigning, two battles, and the deaths of two close friends immediately preceded the sensitive relations that developed between himself and McClellan, which continued through the next six weeks of what ought to have been relaxing camp routine. Unwilling to aggravate the rift in their friendship with a defense of his conduct at Antietam, Burnside was forced to watch his reputation sacrificed by McClellan's partisans, whose private gossip already foretold Burnside as the scapegoat there. In mid-October Burnside's medical director and personal friend, Dr. Church, wrote him to warn that he needed rest, reminding him that since the summer of 1861 he had not enjoyed one day of complete repose—"one day of relief from anxious thought & severe labor"—while most other generals had spent at least a couple of weeks or months at Washington or some other restful spot behind the lines.

Church suggested that Burnside had already begun to collapse when he added, "But for your great powers of endurance you would probably have broken down before this."[44]

It was in this sorely depleted condition that Burnside unhappily accepted responsibility for the Army of the Potomac. Summoning reserves of energy, he formulated and commenced a vigorous campaign that brought the army to Falmouth, then fretted for days as the negligence of others scuttled his grand design. Gathering himself for still another effort by way of Skinker's Neck, he was again frustrated by the weather and the arrival of Jackson's troops. Falling back to the original plan as a last resort, he encountered the almost solid opposition of his subordinates. Each of these operations consumed a massive amount of thought and preparation, and the successive discouragements must have been psychologically devastating to a man who felt he must do something and do it quickly.

Added to the emotional havoc wrought by his exertions was a noticeable physical deterioration. Due at least partly to his disinclination to delegate authority, Burnside had been working feverishly at all hours since General Buckingham consigned him that accursed appointment. General Howard noted that Burnside's first two nights as army commander were almost sleepless. Daniel Larned, his faithful secretary, complained that Burnside worked continually, day and night, sleeping little, ignoring his personal health, and Larned ominously mentioned at one point, "The general has been sick since he took command." While McClellan had screened himself from interruptions with a headquarters guard, Burnside scorned such pretensions and so suffered from an endless cycle of importuning visitors who distracted him and disturbed his rest.[45] The toll is evident in his photographs. The images of Burnside before he took command show determination and vigor; photographs taken afterward reveal a droopy sort of resignation, the eyes tired and dull, the famous whiskers heavily salted with grey.

The lack of sleep alone would have felled a less vibrant man in days, and anxiety over the support of subordinates only added to the strain; it is thus not surprising that most observers have misread the facts and credited Burnside with crumbling under the burden, yet he did not. He contrived a plan that should have worked, and modified it serially as circumstances rendered elements of it obsolete. On the brink of exhaustion he conducted a battle he ought to have won, despite the mistakes he made: a battle he would have won, but for the hesitation of his colleagues.

II

The engineers of the Army of the Potomac began dragging their pontoons into the frigid waters of the Rappahannock at three o'clock on the morning of December 11. Ambrose Burnside was awake already when the hollow thumping of their hammers alerted the Confederate pickets; he had roused his provost marshal, Marsena Patrick, to discuss the day's arrangements. General Patrick had commanded a brigade at Fredericksburg during most of the summer, and much of Burnside's information was based on Patrick's knowledge of the terrain. His old brigade would provide the guides for today's work.[1]

The bridge builders broke into two distinct teams: Woodbury's volunteer engineers started a couple of spans opposite Fredericksburg itself, while the Regulars worked more than a mile downstream, adjacent the plain below the city. Down at Skinker's Neck a regiment of Maine woodsmen had spent the whole night corduroying a thousand feet of road in an effort to decoy enemy troops in that direction. All three detachments suffered miserably in the severe cold. A half-inch of ice glazed the river, covering the entire breadth of the stream in some places, and the dampness of a heavy fog sank deep into aching bones.

At four o'clock the commanding general began composing attack orders for his grand division chiefs. They were simple to the point of vagueness, suggesting he had thoroughly reviewed the particulars with each of them in advance. Sumner and Hooker would cross into the city with the bulk of the army and carry Marye's Heights by sheer weight of numbers while Franklin followed the lower bridges onto the plain and moved "down the old Richmond road, in the direction of the railroad."[2] Franklin's goal at this point seemed twofold: to prevent Lee from stripping his right to reinforce Marye's Heights, and, if feasible, to turn the Confederate right as Sumner had previously advised. Burnside's orders do not specify that, but his description of Franklin's route suggests it. The Richmond road lay parallel to the railroad, and within Franklin's range there was no point at which it could be said to run "in the direction of the railroad." Just beyond Franklin's reach, though, a local road branched off to Hamilton's Crossing; at least one of Franklin's generals misconstrued this as the highway to Bowling Green—the next town on the Richmond road—and it would appear that Burnside intended Franklin to follow that approach, which would have led him to the enemy's extreme right flank.[3]

As clerks transcribed these orders, two signal guns echoed from Longstreet's front, beyond the city, warning the rest of the Southern forces the Yankees were finally coming across. For nearly three more hours the bridges crept steadily toward the indistinct city. Burnside had too much to do to think of it now, but his plan offered an opportunity for something of a clan gathering, for he was not the only Burnside who would participate in this battle. Going into its rifle pits behind Fredericksburg just then was the 3rd South Carolina Battalion, of Lafayette McLaws's division, which included Lieutenant A. W. Burnside; down at Port Royal, preparing to either defend Skinker's Neck or march to the fight at Fredericksburg, the 44th Georgia Infantry had an adjutant named Addison M. Burnside. It is doubtful that the general ever met these cousins, though he must have known their names through family letters, but it ought not to have surprised him to find representatives of his very Southern family in the Confederate service.[4]

It was only by chance that the 3rd South Carolina Battalion did not join the troops guarding the Fredericksburg waterfront: for no particular reason, McLaws had chosen William Barksdale's brigade to picket the riverside and delay the crossing. So thick was the fog that Barksdale's Mississippi and Florida riflemen could not see the Union engineers until they came a few rods short of completing their bridges. When the dark, scrambling shapes finally did loom from the lowering warp, the range was too short to miss.

The first volley erupted about six o'clock, dropping numerous men from the 50th New York Engineers. The survivors disappeared behind the foggy curtain. Union infantry at the bridgeheads tried to lay a covering fire, but could not see where they were shooting. When the engineers ventured back out, their infantry supports had to cease fire to avoid hitting them. The unarmed carpenters had struck but few blows when another crackling of musketry drove them back again, leaving more dead and wounded behind.

Downriver, the other bridges progressed more rapidly. One of those at the lower end of town neared the far bank at eight-thirty, with only token resistance, and the Regulars completed one of Franklin's by nine. Burnside seemed unwilling to jeopardize his army by crossing it all on that single lifeline, however. While Franklin might have crossed, wheeled to the right, and swept Barksdale from Fredericksburg, his left flank would have presented an inviting target for the Confederate artillery; the organization of his isolated force might also have disintegrated in the brushy ravines cut by Deep Run and Hazel Run. Burnside wanted both main bridges in place before he advanced (perhaps especially the upper set, that the trustworthy Sumner could reach any battle), and to disperse the enemy sharpshooters he ordered his artillery chief to open on the buildings. Artillerymen dragged three dozen fieldpieces down to the river's edge, from which they battered at the town for a while. When they ceased fire, General Woodbury gave it another try, but he could not coax his engineers back to work and so led a few score of infantry volunteers to the bridges, leading them personally. They had not even stepped on the planking when Southern marksmen shot some of them down. That was it for them; they refused to move another step, and Woodbury sent them back to their regiments.

It was almost noon now, the fog had lifted, and Burnside began to fret. His advantage of surprise was eluding him, and whatever portion of the Confederate army Lee had sent downstream would soon get wind of the Yankee ruse. With great regret he authorized Henry Hunt, his chief artilleryman, to pulverize the city. General Hunt had about 150 guns on Stafford Heights that would bear on the target, and shortly after midday he unleashed them all.

For two hours the heights belched fire at the empty homes and businesses along Water Street. Not a building in Fredericksburg escaped unscathed, but Barksdale's men holed up in the cellars and took the punishment well. At half past two the barrage ended and the cannoneers retired, exhausted and somewhat deaf, while smoke and dust rose languidly from the rubble. Confident engineers then dashed out to finish their work, but they had hardly lifted their hammers when the deadly sniper fire began anew. Back scurried the construction crews, and the bridges dangled a few frustrating yards short of the city.[5]

Henry Hunt had a better idea for cleaning out the hornets' nest. With the exasperated Burnside's permission he loaded some infantry into pontoons, sprinkled a few engineers among them for polemen, and sent them toward the opposite bank. The first detachment of engineer ferry-

men ran away, but more valiant gondoliers ferried across a few platoons
of Michigan and Massachusetts troops—and a hundred New Yorkers at
the lower end of town—who dashed at the troublesome buildings. They
found streets barricaded by barrels filled with stones and earth, but
the impromptu amphibious force formed ranks and confronted the Mississippians. The defenders fell back stubbornly. One sharp encounter
occurred between opposing companies commanded by former Harvard
classmates, ending only when the Confederate's colonel arrested him
for ignoring an order to retreat. The street fighting went door-to-door
until after dark, when Barksdale withdrew his brigade to the main line
along Marye's Heights.[6]

In the gathering darkness a brigade of the Ninth Corps thumped
across the completed bridges and occupied the city. O. O. Howard's division of the Second Corps followed them, and one of Franklin's brigades
crossed downstream.

For reasons he never explained, Burnside revised his orders to
Franklin and Sumner now, directing them to keep the preponderance of
their troops on the left bank of the river. The likeliest motive for this
change would have been the fear that moving large columns into the
city in the darkness would create confusion and crowding enough to
invite an attack—an attack disorganized troops might not be able to
resist. Additionally, Burnside may have hoped to keep the Confederate
leaders off balance, creating the impression that the day's work had all
been a diversion. In fact, Lee had not yet deduced his opponent's plan.
As Burnside had reasoned (and as his grand division commanders had
agreed), Fredericksburg was the least likely place to cross; Lee therefore could not believe he meant to strike there. That doubt had caused
Lee to keep D. H. Hill's division at Port Royal and Jubal Early's near
Skinker's Neck.[7] Still, it would have been better had Burnside crossed
all his troops during the night and made a vigorous attack early in the
morning, since his delay only gave Hill and Early even more time to
come up.

The Union commander meditated the need to rearrange his plan to
compensate for the delay in crossing. It might no longer do to simply
rush across and break Lee's lines by main strength: more inspired tactics could be necessary.

In actual numbers, the Army of the Potomac enjoyed a considerable
edge over the Army of Northern Virginia. Burnside's forces totaled

about 115,000 men of all arms, while Lee could only muster about 80,000. Lee's option to remain on the defensive seriously blunted that edge, as did the pressure to attack perceived by Burnside. One glaring deficiency in Burnside's army was the inexperience of so many of his men. He had, for instance, some 265 infantry regiments, most of which were sadly depleted by battle and months of disease and suffering, but 50 of these—and the largest of them, too—were brand-new units that had arrived since August. Most had never fired a shot or maneuvered under fire, and many had been with the army only a few days. A large number were short-term militia regiments. These novices could not have comprised fewer than 30,000 men.[8]

Burnside worked on his tactical modifications well into the night. After midnight General Franklin sent a note to headquarters that mentioned concern for Burnside's rest (suggesting his fatigue was already noticeable), but the commanding general was still at work when Franklin's late message came in. At that time, Burnside still contemplated the simultaneous frontal attack at and below town, nothing more complicated than Sumner assaulting Marye's Heights while Franklin hammered the Confederate right. However late Burnside went to bed, he was awake again by four the following morning, sitting by General Patrick's cot.[9]

At daylight the several bridges floating on the Rappahannock began to echo with the routestep thunder of 160,000 feet. The Second and Ninth corps rolled into the streets of Fredericksburg while the First and Sixth corps took position on the plain below town, separated from Sumner's Right Grand Division by two difficult streambeds. All morning the procession continued in thick fog.

In Fredericksburg, the soldiers stacked their arms in every thoroughfare. They broke ranks and began milling around, investigating the deserted houses, taking up a souvenir here and there, raiding pantries. The pillage soon escalated to the thievery of clothing, blankets, household furnishings, and family treasures; then it turned to wanton destruction. With the exception that the inhabitants had fled, it was like the sack of a medieval city: valuable books and colonial furniture went flying into the snowy streets; paintings were slashed with bayonets or cut from their frames and stuffed into knapsacks. A provost guard had to stand at every bridgehead to prevent troops from escaping to the rear with their loot. General Patrick personally laid his riding crop across one scavenger's back; he even found some mounted officers partaking of the spoil.[10]

The Southrons offered little opposition to the crossing now. Hawkins's brigade skirmished with some distant Confederate pickets on Hanover Street, and a couple of Stonewall Jackson's batteries opened on Franklin's men, but the Union host met no serious impediment. Still, it was three o'clock before the Left Grand Division took position for the proposed assault.

Burnside went over to the right bank with Franklin late that afternoon. It was too late to begin an attack, and the army commander feared it was also too late to catch Lee with his forces divided. As it happened, Lee was just then ordering up those last two divisions from Port Royal and Skinker's Neck.

Burnside, Franklin, and Franklin's two corps commanders, John Reynolds and William F. Smith, reconnoitered the ground in the dusk. They agreed upon a plan—ostensibly at Franklin's suggestion— whereby two divisions of Hooker's command would guard the bridges while the entire Left Grand Division formed on both sides of the Richmond Stage Road and stormed the heights on Lee's extreme right, taking the new military road known to connect the wings of the Confederate army. When the four generals seemed to understand his battle plan, Burnside went on to visit his other subordinates, promising to send orders.[11]

Burnside did not reach army headquarters until after midnight. There survives no testimony of the time he went to bed, but he could not have slept as long as four hours, and probably less, since he again personally woke the early-rising General Patrick the next morning. By six o'clock he had already formulated and dictated the battle orders for Franklin and Sumner. These two sets of orders, composed by a man with an enormous sleep deficit, served as the foundation for General Franklin's defense when others accused him of failing to support his commander.

Certainly those instructions were not models of technical clarity, but Franklin charged they indicated a different plan from that decided upon the previous evening, leaving him confused. Burnside ordered his left wing commander to put his "whole command in position for a rapid movement down the Old Richmond road" and to "send out at once a division at least to pass below Smithfield, to seize, if possible, the height

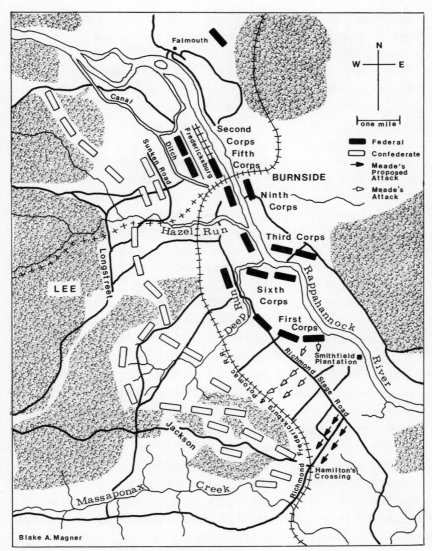

Map 7. Fredericksburg

near Captain Hamilton's, taking care to keep it well supported and its line of retreat open. . . . You will keep your whole command in readiness to move at once, as soon as the fog lifts."

Burnside chose James Hardie, of his staff, to carry the orders to Franklin, directing him to stay with the grand division commander during the rest of the day, acting as liaison between them. Hardie approached Burnside's tent about 5:30, but the transcribed copies were not ready. He came back a few minutes later, only to find the clerk still at work on them, but Burnside wanted to waste no more time. He gave Hardie the pencil copy of Franklin's orders, showed him a copy of Sumner's orders, and told him to go. The complete order, he added, would follow by telegraph. Hardie went straight for his horse, and by 6:00 he was on his way. It was still dark, and the roads were a perfect glaze of smooth, frozen mud, so he could hardly exceed a walk. The sun had just risen when he finally arrived at Franklin's headquarters, around 7:15 A.M. [12]

Franklin later argued that the orders reached him too late for him to deploy his men in time, implying he still waited for those two divisions of Hooker's to cross to his support. To an extent it is true the orders came too late, but for reasons unknown to Franklin. Daylight of December 13 found the Confederate divisions of Jubal Early and D. H. Hill resting at least three miles from Hamilton's Crossing, and the last of their brigades did not join the main Confederate body until after nine o'clock in the morning. Had Franklin had orders in the wee hours for a dawn movement, and had he followed the route he and Burnside discussed, he would have struck a vulnerable position on Lee's right flank. The complaint about Hooker's two divisions was not material to the delay Franklin wished to excuse, however, for his orders included the information that the two divisions already guarded the bridges, where they would stay. They had been there from the moment Franklin received his orders, and he need not have tarried further on that account. [13]

A Franklin crony later criticized Burnside for his use of the term *seize* in regard to the ridge at Hamilton's Crossing. *Seize*, he disputed, was a word used only in reference to an undefended position: for a fortified location, *carry* was the appropriate verb. Thus he backhandedly accused Burnside of being ignorant of any Confederate force on the heights, which was not true. The unfortunate choice of words provided Franklin with an excellent excuse for any failure to make his best effort.

At least one student of the battle has also pointed out that Burnside's caution about keeping the attacking force's line of retreat open tended to have a discouraging effect on Franklin. Taken with the heretofore common belief that Meade's frontal assault struck just where Burnside intended, a warning about lines of retreat certainly seems timid; but if Burnside meant for the attack to swing around Lee's right and strike Hamilton's Crossing (or "the height near Captain Hamilton's") from the east or southeast, the comment is hardly gratuitous and is in keeping with a bold plan of action.[14] Another historian, while citing Jubal Early's admission that this movement would have forced the Confederates to abandon their lines, points out that the Southern artillery position on Prospect Hill would have prevented Franklin from moving beyond Lee's right. That may have been true in clear weather (though the First Corps artillery commander thought otherwise), but the heavy fog on the morning of December 13 would have screened such a maneuver. That is probably why Burnside directed the capture of Prospect Hill immediately, but instructed Franklin to start the rest of his troops as soon as the fog lifted. It could have been a desire to assure himself of a covering fog that caused Burnside to withhold Franklin's orders until near daylight.[15] In his report, Franklin erroneously maintained that Hardie brought only verbal orders, and that the written version came by courier about 8:00, but the orders themselves were written at 5:55 A.M. and specified Hardie would carry them, as Hardie later insisted he did.[16]

General Franklin consulted briefly with his corps commanders, Reynolds and Smith. Afterward, Franklin and Smith claimed the orders seemed so radically different from Franklin's original suggestion that the generals wrangled at length over their meaning, coming to the conclusion that the use of the term *seize*—among other things—reduced the assault to a mere reconnaissance-in-force. Yet Hardie delivered the order between 7:10 and 7:15, the corps commanders convened, held their little caucus, argued over and interpreted the instructions, and Hardie telegraphed Burnside that Franklin had chosen Meade's division to make the assault—all by 7:40. That did not allow much time for the protracted debate Franklin and Smith claimed.

General Reynolds's orders to Meade offer added evidence that Burnside's phraseology had not contradicted his December 12 arrangements with his left wing subordinates: despite the commanding general's

choice of the word *seize*, Reynolds ordered Meade (and later Gibbon)
to *carry* the objective. Reynolds always held that Franklin interpreted
the orders too narrowly and ought to have put in his entire force; the
plan of December 12 was still in effect, as far as Ambrose Burnside and
John Reynolds were concerned. Reynolds's artillery chief hooted at the
notion of a reconnaissance, in force or otherwise, noting in his diary,
"Perhaps Burnside did not intend originally that we should attack at all.
If so, it is singular that he should use one-half of his army to make a mere
demonstration." Franklin thought differently—at least after the battle
had been lost. The rumors floating down through his grand division by
December 15 suggest a certain deliberate construction: Franklin was
telling subordinates by then that Burnside had ordered him to "attack
with *one* division," rather than with "a division at least." Franklin's interpretation conflicts with his control of a preponderance of the army,
with Burnside's failure to make the slightest mention of a change, and
with his own recorded opinion of what was best; it has the earmarks of
a strained conclusion drawn for personal defense.[17]

On the right, Sumner also drew orders to *seize* the Confederates'
strong position on the heights beyond Fredericksburg. This slope was
more formidably defended than the naked eye could detect, but under
no circumstances could it have been considered unoccupied; still, General Sumner seems not to have been confused by the absence of the
word *carry*. He knew just what Burnside expected of him. He should
delay his attack, however, until Franklin's was well under way: Burnside supposed Lee would strip his left to repel Franklin, which might
weaken it enough for Sumner's assault to crack the line and do some
real mischief.[18]

At Franklin's headquarters Meade complained that he could carry
the crest with his division, but not hold it. Franklin only replied that
those were Burnside's orders: attack with one division, supported by
one or more. Despite both his inherent and his implied authority to add
more strength if he deemed it necessary, Franklin chose to commit the
minimum number of troops his instructions permitted. Meade, who had
no illusions about a reconnaissance-in-force, immediately started his
fifteen regiments into motion. His was a battered little division, but
it was also the most respected on the left wing: the ranks had been
thinned in fighting all the way from the Peninsula, but the Pennsylvania
Reserves, augmented by two new regiments from that state, made a

logical choice to spearhead any assault. They were, besides, closest to
what Franklin imagined to be his objective.

Meade's division fell into line and marched downstream from Franklin's headquarters, veering toward the enemy in the vicinity of the
plantation known as Smithfield. The line of march took the troops perpendicularly across the Richmond Stage Road, and here the column had
to stop. A thick hedge fence lined the highway, and deep ditches would
need filling before supporting artillery could pass. Pioneers scurried
forward with axes and shovels to level the obstacles while the infantrymen stood in the thick fog stamping their feet.[19]

Franklin seems neither to have advanced Meade far enough nor to
have pointed him in the right direction before allowing him to begin his
assault. Burnside had ordered him to prepare for a movement "down
the old Richmond road, . . . to seize . . . the height near Captain Hamilton's." That implied Franklin should move southeast, in an arc around
Lee's right, and even as bitter a critic of Burnside as William F. Smith
later wrote that the plan of December 12 called for massing Franklin's
command "on the right and left of the Richmond road," suggesting the
same southeasterly sweep around the Confederate right. Burnside confirmed that this was his plan when he spoke to the Committee on the
Conduct of the War a few days later, and that theory is further corroborated by the letter in which Edwin Sumner originally proposed this
part of the choreography. After explaining how he would cross the river
on the plains below town, as Franklin had, and place thirty-or-so big
guns to protect the bridges, as Franklin had, Sumner said he would
"form our whole force in line of battle, and then by a determined march,
turn their right flank, . . . force them from the field, and after this
was done, we could occupy Fredericksburg, and reestablish our lines
of communication, making the city a depot." In order to reestablish
Union communications they first had to be broken. That, and Sumner's
description of the movement as "a determined march" rather than an
attack, make it obvious he proposed an end run down the stage road.
Sumner was the grand division commander whom Burnside trusted
and admired the most—he was devoted and obedient, if not brilliant—
and if Burnside adopted the mechanics of Sumner's plan, why would
he shun the goal? And if an attack to the southeast was practical the
afternoon of December 12, as Franklin, Smith, and the rest thought, it
was still practical on December 13. Stuart's cavalry defended that flank;

once through that, forty thousand Yankees could have turned down the road to Captain Hamilton's and threatened Lee's right and rear. John Esten Cooke, one of Stuart's staff, admitted as much, citing the ground between Hamilton's and the Massaponax as the only weak link in the Confederate line. Meade instead stopped at least half a mile short of the road to Hamilton's and turned southwest, to strike Stonewall Jackson's line head-on.[20]

Nine o'clock passed before Meade finished deploying his division. He strung it out between the stage road and the tracks of the Richmond, Fredericksburg & Potomac Railroad, two brigades deep, with the third brigade facing his left flank. John Gibbon's division stood to his right, opposite that same forested ridgeline, while Abner Doubleday's division lagged behind Meade and turned to the left, contending with Confederate artillery. Suddenly, out of the mist, shells began dropping into the Reserves from the stage road they had just crossed. Few things disturb troops more than a fire from the rear, and Meade moved quickly to counter it. He swung three batteries into position to drive away two fieldpieces the Southerners had run out dangerously close to his lines, and Doubleday turned a few cannon on them. These Confederate horse artillerymen, under Major John Pelham, simply changed position every time a Union battery got their range, lobbing periodic shells that Meade could not ignore. Franklin's cavalry stood idle while Pelham moved to ever-more-vulnerable positions. Some skirmishers advanced with Pelham's guns, but two companies of Pennsylvanians fanned out from Meade's left flank and stopped them. The fog began shredding apart now, and Union cannoneers could more readily see the troublesome section; they disabled one of the brace, and Stuart soon ordered Pelham to withdraw the other.[21] All this delay might have been avoided had Meade (and a couple more divisions) bulled directly through Stuart's videttes as Burnside seems to have wanted, instead of turning southwest that crucial half-mile too soon.

By now it was already eleven o'clock. Meade spent more time arranging his batteries and shelling the woods in front, and it was after noon when he finally pushed ahead. His first brigade swept into woods along the railroad, driving enemy skirmishers back to the tracks, where swampy ground had persuaded A. P. Hill's subordinates to overlook a 600-yard gap between the brigades of Lane and Archer. For all that Franklin's attack had gone astray, here was the sort of opportunity for which Burnside had been hoping. A division, thrust into that opening and supported on either flank by most of Franklin's command, would have forced Lee to either fall back or put everything he had into plugging the hole. The Pennsylvanians slogged through the boggy lapse with very little resistance at first, but the deeper they went the tougher it got.

As he penetrated the Confederate line, Meade scattered part of Archer's brigade on his left, taking one of its colors and several hundred prisoners, then he turned to face the fire of Lane's North Carolina brigade, on his right. Three hundred yards behind came his second brigade, which detached a regiment to forestall Lane while the rest of the brigade wheeled to the left and up the slope, to meet growing firepower from the remainder of Archer's men.[22]

The first brigade, invigorated by its good luck, followed the path of least resistance, which led to the coveted military road. Lounging in the middle of that road was a regiment of South Carolinians.

Maxcy Gregg, unaware of that disastrous rift at the front, knew only that his South Carolina brigade occupied the second line. To diminish the possibility of his troops firing into the backs of their own men, he had made them stack arms. They were resting in the vicinity of those stacked muskets when the Pennsylvania Reserves burst from the woods and leveled a volley at them. General Gregg rode straight into the fight to sort out his men, but he dropped from his horse with a bullet in the spine, and his panicked men in the road fled. The rest of his brigade stood firm, though, and henceforth Meade had to simply slug it out along the line of the military road, looking to the rear for supports that were nowhere in sight.[23]

Meanwhile, General Burnside trained his binoculars on Franklin's progress. He and the general staff stood on the roof of the Phillips house in the bitter air, gazing intently at the ribbonlike movement of the blue lines until smoke obscured them. General Hardie telegraphed an occasional report. The New Hampshire aeronaut, Thaddeus S. C. Lowe, even went up in his balloon during the fighting, shouting down his observations from far above the conflict. At 10:30 Burnside sent an aide to Franklin, to determine his exact situation.

It later became evident that Franklin was the last person on the left to know what his own situation was, but at eleven o'clock a telegram began clacking in from Hardie indicating that Franklin performed as expected: Meade had advanced half a mile and held his position; enemy infantry had begun to show up on Franklin's right and left; a brigadier had been wounded, but other casualties were insignificant. Given Burnside's expectation that Franklin's attack struck below Hamilton's Crossing, this news suggested the Confederates were shifting their forces to repel the assault. The message also implied that Smith's Sixth Corps, in which the wounded general commanded a brigade, was engaged. Such was not the case, but a postscript added that Reynolds had had "to develop his whole line" and reported suspicions of "an attack of some force on our left," which further convinced Burnside that Lee was weakening his own left.[24]

Aware that whatever advantage Franklin gained might be of short duration, Burnside had directed Sumner to form his leading divisions in the lee of Fredericksburg's outermost buildings. That position served three purposes: it offered the potential for quick deployment when the time was ripe; it gave the troops the comforting protection of those last few houses; and—perhaps most important—it concealed the strength of Sumner's column, a glimpse of which might have dissuaded Lee from reducing his left, as Burnside desired. He intended not merely to flank the Confederates out of their position, à la McClellan, but to do all the damage to their army that he could in the process—smashing their line rather than merely cracking it. It was for this that he had modified Sumner's plan of throwing the entire army on the left; after all, the possession of Fredericksburg could prove a hollow prize in the midst of muddy winter, while the destruction of Lee's army would be the greatest triumph of all.

Communications between Burnside and his two wings flickered with signal stations and glimmering wire, but despite these enhancements, Hardie might not be able to warn Burnside of the precise moment to launch Sumner until the chance was gone. Therefore the commanding general still had to guess, like a jockey in the final furlong, when to give rein and apply the whip. The winter day was already growing old; Burnside guessed that the time had come.

Sumner's Right Grand Division had spent an uncomfortable night in the city. The streets were jammed with men and stacked arms, and the weather had been brutally cold. A number of soldiers had awakened with their clothing clutched in the frozen mud, with a glaze of frost on their blankets. There had been no fires allowed—another symptom of intended surprise—and the crush of people forced the troops to remain still, enduring the cold without benefit of exercise. Significant numbers of men were absent from their commands, though, still busy looting Fredericksburg homes.[25]

French's division of the Second Corps had been waiting in place for the order to advance. Just as that order reached French, General Longstreet began shelling the edge of town to create some diversion in favor of the Confederate right. When blue troops began boiling out of the city a few moments later, Longstreet had the sensation of having upset a beehive. French's three brigades doublequicked up Hanover Street, across the open plain where the superintendent of Longstreet's artillery had said not even a chicken could live. Just beyond the town they encountered a canal ditch too deep for fording: two bridges passed over it, but Confederates had sabotaged one of them by stripping its deck. Under a fierce crossfire of shell and case shot, the Union troops pounded over the one bridge and scooted across the stringers of the other.[26]

Fortunately for the attacking force, an abrupt terrace offered protection on the far side of the canal. Barely out of sight of the Confederate gunners, French's already depleted regiments gathered in three columns of brigade, took a deep breath, and surged over the protective bluff, five hundred yards from the enemy line.

Now came a most unexpected impediment. Southern artillery had wrought enough havoc on the division, but they had anticipated that: those artillery positions were visible all the way from Stafford Heights. What neither visual reconnaissance nor the recollections of officers from General Patrick's old brigade had foretold was the sunken road that ran along the base of Marye's Heights. From a distance it appeared to be one uninterrupted incline, but a stone retaining wall supported the bank on either side of the road with no exterior indication, and in that deep roadbed waited twenty-five hundred of Longstreet's experienced marksmen. Union artillery had to find other targets once French ventured within a couple of hundred yards of the invisible trench, and his troops marched with their arms at a shoulder; when those sharpshooters appeared at the lip of their ready-made fort, the Yankees were helpless. They fell by scores, by hundreds, some still forging ahead after the first volley, but none coming within a hundred feet of the blazing line of battle. One youth in French's division recollected that the regiments were virtually blown from their feet, but staggered forward as though through a gale. A small regiment of skirmishers led the attack, escaping total annihilation by virtue of their more open formation, but even they lost a hundred men in the few minutes before they took cover. The close-packed brigades behind them suffered even more. Nine of French's regimental commanders and one of his brigadiers had been shot, and some twelve hundred of his men.[27]

As French's brigades piled up behind one another, the men began to lay down. It was their only hope of safety, and a slight depression gave cover to anyone who lay perfectly still.

Hancock's division came right after them; it was bigger than French's, but the mile of open plain, the bridges, and intervening fences so long delayed it that it was commensurately battered. Like French, Hancock chose to come over the protection of the bluff in three columns of brigades, which reached French's main body and even passed it. Each brigade, noted the commander of the Second Corps, melted "like snow coming down on warm ground." In the last of Hancock's brigades was a New Hampshire regiment that mustered only 268 officers and men. A piece of shell knocked the colonel down early in the charge, but the remnants of his command pressed on under the major, who disappeared into the smoke of Confederate rifles, never to be seen again. By nightfall the little regiment had lost 193 of its original number.[28]

From his aerie in the steeple of a Fredericksburg church it was clear to Darius Couch, commander of the Second Corps, that the stone wall could not be carried by frontal attack without tremendous loss. He therefore directed General Howard to throw his division against the northern end of the wall, on the Union right. Howard tried, but just as he deployed, French and Hancock implored Couch for help: he canceled Howard's orders and shifted him to support those beleaguered divisions. Sturgis's division of the Ninth Corps meanwhile went in to the left of French and Hancock.

Ferrero's brigade formed behind the railroad tracks on the south side of town. As soon as these troops came into sight, Confederates on the hills rained artillery on them. In one new regiment, men blanched to see a tall soldier's head taken off by a cannonball, a geyser of blood showering his comrades. A few moments later, in another regiment, the color guard was laid low by a shell, the color sergeant clasping the United States flag in the stumps of his arms when the smoke cleared; someone took the flag from him and was almost immediately killed, as was another who plucked the banner from his hands. Nearby a nervous private blurted, "Oh, dear! They'll kill every one of us. Not a damned one of us will be left to tell the story!" Companions laughed at him, though they fully shared his anxiety.

Ferrero's men bogged down a couple of hundred yards short of the first line of Confederate riflemen, and Sturgis sent in Nagle's brigade to help. These six regiments swept forward, stepping over the maimed and dead and rolling up to the bank of a railroad cut. Some of the men huddled in the illusion of safety there, but a battery had the range of that feature and commenced lobbing shells into it. As one officer described it, a "hurricane" of bullets buffeted the lip of the cut, but subalterns courageously stood on that lip and pulled men up by hand to get the advance moving again. Nagle's men suffered as Ferrero's had, color bearers dropping everywhere, and they threw themselves behind the same meager cover occupied by their predecessors. To some in a fragment of a Rhode Island regiment, isolated from the rest of Nagle's brigade, the sound of guns to the south offered hope that Franklin's men made better progress.[29]

The Rhode Islanders misread the sign; what they heard was probably the artillery Franklin had had to turn on a Confederate counterattack. Meade, struggling to maintain the hole he had punched in Jackson's line, never got the help he needed. The division to his left, Doubleday's, assisted only with its artillery—Doubleday's big division lost only 188 infantrymen all day long. On Meade's right, Gibbon's command accomplished little: two of his brigades were substantially thrown into "confusion"—meaning either the men or their leadership fell apart—and Meade's second flank fell open. Birney's division of the Third Corps, directly behind Meade, lay idle until the fought-out Reserves began streaming back out of the woods, repelled by superior numbers. Birney stopped the counterattack handily enough, but the good luck Meade had encountered was squandered. Outraged at the almost perfunctory assistance he had enjoyed from Doubleday and Gibbon, Meade railed at John Reynolds and the corps staff. Back at his headquarters General Franklin soon learned of Meade's fury. Revealing how ignorant he was of the fighting done by his own men, Franklin later admitted to Meade that this was his first inkling of any lack of support for Meade's assault.[30]

Franklin merely drew Doubleday, Birney, Meade's survivors, and the five inactive divisions on his right into a tight defensive line. He decided his day's work was over, despite the arrival just then of a courier with orders from Burnside. The commanding general, suspecting by now that Franklin may have committed too few troops, wished him to move forward on his right and front to take some of the pressure off Sumner's attack on the stone wall. As Franklin quoted it, the order mentioned, "Your instructions of this morning are so far modified as to require an advance upon the heights immediately in your front." Here is still more evidence that Franklin misdirected Meade's attack: if Burnside had not expected the assault of Prospect Hill to be made perpendicular to Lee's right flank, he would have been unlikely to characterize a frontal assault as a modification of Franklin's orders.

Burnside was asking for a grand assault, instantly. Franklin told the young captain carrying the order that he could not do that. The captain returned that reply. "But he must advance," said the perplexed Burnside, dispatching another aide with a peremptory order for Franklin to move forward on his entire front. Franklin put off this messenger with the excuse that eight of his nine divisions were already "engaged," with only Burns's borrowed Ninth Corps division remaining undisturbed between the two halves of the Union army. This was only technically true; all eight divisions were in line and under fire to one degree or another. But, for instance, Smith's entire corps took fewer casualties than any one of Meade's little brigades and could have used its considerable muscle to some advantage.[31]

Franklin perhaps thought he had done his best. A disciple of the George B. McClellan school of warfare, he felt he was outnumbered and must keep a large reserve to repel any surprise attack. The Sixth Corps, with Birney's and Sickles's divisions of the Third Corps, was that reserve. Had those five divisions supported Meade and Gibbon, the day would probably have ended differently. As it was, Franklin did nothing more than hold his original position from that moment forward.[32]

Back at headquarters, Burnside grew annoyed. He rode over to Sumner's command post in the garden of the Lacy mansion. Sumner sat there in an ambulance—Burnside had ordered him to keep this side of the river, lest he lose this trusted advisor—and a newspaper reporter lingering nearby heard the old soldier mutter once or twice about Franklin. "Everything depends on Franklin's coming up on the flank," said Sumner or one of his aides at one point. Burnside paced the garden quietly for a time before leaving instructions that the crest had to be carried that night, after which he strode through the bower to his horse and returned to the Phillips house.[33]

General Hooker, whose remaining troops Burnside had ordered to support Sumner, rode back about then to tell Burnside gruffly that the stone wall could not be taken. He was blunt to the point of insubordination in the telling. This, added to Burnside's general dislike and mistrust of "Fighting Joe," may have driven him to discount Hooker's judgment. Hooker was, besides, in the same position Burnside had endured at Antietam: his grand division had been broken up to bolster other commands. The commanding general could readily have perceived Hooker's reluctance as a fit of his famous pique, designed to rob Burnside of his last chance for victory. He told Hooker the assault must be continued; at that hour he still expected Franklin to advance along his whole front, and he dared not reduce the pressure on the right.

After Hooker departed, a telegram arrived from Hardie observing that Franklin would make another attack if he could, but he doubted there was time enough to form his troops—an opinion not shared by at least one division commander on Franklin's front. Burnside could only hope Hardie was wrong, for the alternative was to admit defeat. Burnside the gambler could not quit while he still had chips left.[34]

There are those who would hold that Burnside's reliance upon the infantry charge was an atavistic instinct, handed down from his Celtic ancestors, while one prejudiced observer at the Lacy house later characterized the repeated orders to advance as acts of increasing desperation. It is indeed possible that he was horrified by the tales of slaughter coming back from the bloody stone wall and could not bear the thought that all that sacrifice had been futile. Perhaps fatigue and stress were finally telling on him, but it was principally to aid Franklin's expected attack that Burnside continued to send men across the deadly plain below Fredericksburg. Looking back, a Confederate officer who had been with Jackson recognized that: in a speech to a group of Bostonians years later, Stonewall's ordnance chief pointed out that Burnside's persistence before Marye's Heights proved how much he expected of Franklin.[35]

Andrew Humphreys next confronted the wall, with his Pennsylvania division of the Fifth Corps. Here were some of the new men who made up such a large proportion of the army's bulk: all but two of these regiments were nine-month militiamen; only one had been in service longer than four months, and none had ever seen any action before. Nevertheless Humphreys, a stocky Old Army man who had attended West Point alongside Robert E. Lee, seems not to have doubted his men could capture the wall. In fact Robert E. Lee himself expressed fear that the continued pressure would crack his line.

The Pennsylvanians lined up on the edge of town. Humphreys led his second brigade across first, forming it in the protective shadow of the bluff and riding with it as it burst over the top toward the Confederate line. Halfway between the bluff and the wall lay the disorganized mass that had been the Second Corps, firing from the meager safety of that shallower depression. Humphreys's new troops, either misunderstanding their orders or fearing to go farther, lay down with the pinned troops and added to their sporadic and ineffective fire. Humphreys, his staff, and his brigadier rode brazenly about, until most of their horses were shot from under them, in a desperate effort to stop the men from firing and form them for a bayonet charge. Amazingly, they accomplished that feat, but their valiance proved futile: the brigade had lost so many men by the time it charged that the attempt was doomed. Some of the recruits came dangerously close to the wall, but fell back before the redoubled musketry and a flank fire from a battery on their right.

Convinced the refuse of the Second Corps posed the worst hindrance to his assault, Humphreys borrowed a courier's horse and started back to meet his other brigade, which he had ordered up. He found it waiting in the ravine behind the bluff. With twenty-two hundred men among them, these four regiments were only slightly smaller than the other brigade. The little general rode up and down their line, ordering the men to uncap their rifles and fix bayonets. He harangued them on the uselessness of small-arms fire against the entrenched enemy: their only hope was to get in among them quickly. He also forewarned them of the prone troops who filled the shallow depression before the stone wall. Ignore them, he advised; walk right over them. The fearless Humphreys then posted himself with the brigade commander, in front of the line, and in the twilight the nervous amateurs broke over the top with a frenzied cheer.

It was all for naught. The thousands of battle-weary men on the firing line were certain no charge could succeed. They waved the new men to the ground, yelled at them to give it up, even pulled at the skirts of their overcoats and deliberately tripped them, hoping to save their lives. They fragmented the charge, discouraging the bravest, ending any hope of success with their compassionate interference. Scattered companies pushed their way ahead, only to be forced back from the flaming wall because they were so few. His second horse down now, Humphreys could do no more to rally the brigade than any captain. Someone brought him a wounded colonel's animal, however, upon which he waved his first brigade back to the bluff and reformed it. When he reported the double failure, his corps commander ordered him to bring off his second brigade as well. The Pennsylvanians all gathered where their charge had begun and tallied the cost: neither brigade had been in action for more than fifteen minutes, but nearly a quarter of the division lay dead or wounded.[36]

During Humphreys's attempt, Charles Griffin's Fifth Corps division advanced to assist Sturgis's troops at the south end of the stone wall. Though Griffin's three brigades did not approach so close as the men they supported, their exposed position cost them nearly a thousand casualties in the final hour of daylight.[37] Nor did darkness end the carnage. Burnside had but two divisions on his right wing that were not yet committed to action—Sykes's division of Regulars and New Yorkers, which had nominally supported Humphreys's attack, and Getty's division of the Ninth Corps, holding the left end of town. Orlando Willcox, commanding the Ninth Corps, appears to have ordered Getty into the fray on his own initiative.

More than half Getty's men were new. The core of his command was Parke's original brigade, beefed up by six recently organized regiments. Willcox ordered the division to the extreme left of his front, near Hazel Run, in hopes of drawing enemy fire away from Humphreys's assault or, short of that, finding a soft spot in Lee's line. Getty marched his division out in two columns of brigade and halted them by the railroad track. His men had been watching the slaughter all day and were confident only that they would meet defeat or death. An officer in one regiment that had been with the army but four days looked at the scarlet sun teetering on the horizon and remarked, "I wish I could get up there and kick that thing down!"[38]

The first brigade crossed the railroad at dusk, commanded by Colonel Rush Hawkins. Hawkins had confounded his orders from Getty, leaving his own 9th New York zouaves to support a battery that needed no support. Thus his brigade moved out with just two small veteran battalions and three sprawling regiments of totally inexperienced recruits. The battle seemed almost to pause at Humphreys's repulse, and the brigade moved virtually alone against the Confederate position. The sides of the railroad cut offered brief shelter, but it could be used only for breathing room, as a place from which to spring.

At the word, the brigade came over the embankment in two lines, the left of the column struggling through swampy ground while the right stormed up the precipitous slope that shielded that end of the stone wall. Artillery and rifle fire lit up the night, and only darkness prevented the destruction of Hawkins's command. The fusillade diminished momentarily, long enough for a militiaman in the 25th New Jersey to scream they would all be captured. Illogical as that cry was, his wing of that regiment disintegrated. The left companies of the 13th New Hampshire moved ahead to fill the gap, but a few minutes later some of Griffin's confused Fifth Corps troops fired on the brigade from behind; the rest of the New Jersey regiment and the right companies of the 13th New Hampshire buckled at that, and the charge crumbled. Hawkins's brigade ducked behind the brow of a hill, where most of the Confederate artillery could not reach it. The second brigade never came forward. Darkness ended the frontal assaults, but the last news from the front was an inaccurate wire from Sturgis: "Our men only 80 paces from the crest & holding on like hell."[39]

Thus encouraged, still refusing to give in to sleep, Burnside prepared plans for a grand bayonet assault the next morning. To spearhead the attack he chose his loyal old Ninth Corps, which he intended to lead personally. Generally the commander of an army did not lead charges, but it was appropriate for him to use his personal popularity to lift the fighting spirit of his men, and Burnside was extremely popular with the Ninth Corps, as well as with other troops. General Couch, whom Burnside visited two hours after midnight, hinted at an ulterior motive for this decision. Couch lay on his bed at his headquarters in the city when Burnside came in to ask him about the details of the battle. The Second Corps commander, who had directed most of the fighting before Marye's Heights, spent an hour giving him the story. Couch thought Burnside appeared cheerful, but he sensed that his chief "wished his body was also lying in front of Marye's Heights." What Couch implied was that Burnside had sunk to the brink of suicide, as though he hoped to be killed in the charge. Yet McClellan has been criticized for failing to use just such a ploy to inspire his men at Antietam; nor were men like Albert Sidney Johnston, Robert E. Lee, or Phil Sheridan considered suicidal for leading—or attempting to lead—their men into battle. What happened to Couch's postwar recollection was the same thing that occurred to those of everyone who remembered Burnside after Fredericksburg: after years of exposure to the pejorative imagery of soldiers who blamed their defeat on a single man, he recalled his commander's every action in terms of sheer pathos.[40]

There is evidence that the atmosphere at the Phillips house did not droop so oppressive the night of December 13 as others have since suggested. Immediate eyewitness accounts are almost nonexistent; even Daniel Larned filled his journal after the withdrawal from Fredericksburg had cast a pall over Burnside's spirit. But the night after the fighting stopped, a New York colonel on duty at headquarters gave his wife an extremely optimistic rendition of the day's events. At 10:00 P.M. on the thirteenth Colonel John Crocker, who had spent the day on the roof with the generals, wrote that Burnside had proven himself "a great general & fully equal to his position." Crocker believed Burnside had won "some advantage" and would resume the work vigorously in the morning. He mentioned sympathy for the screaming wounded, whose cries carried over the river, but his account hardly described the moping dejection in which others later tried to paint the commanding general and his official household.[41]

The next day General Couch found himself buttonholed by George Getty, who had received orders to prepare his division for the bayonet charge. Getty practically begged Couch to ride across the river and advise Burnside against what he felt would be "a perfect slaughter."[42]

Getty spoke with good cause. The Confederates had spent most of the night digging new entrenchments, and the intimidating stone wall now sat before several tiers of rifle pits. The artillery that had wrecked so many brigades hid behind formidable embrasures, and many more eager muzzles bore upon the plain. Without Franklin's attack as a diversion, and probably even with it, no Union assault could come near the first Confederate line. No one saw this better than the foot soldiers of the Ninth Corps; still, Burns's division marched back from the far side of Hazel Run and took its position on the outskirts of town, lining up in a mass of brigade columns in resolute silence.[43]

The other side of the river, Burnside met with his subordinates. He presented them with his plan to lead the charge of the Ninth Corps. Old General Sumner, the most devoted of his officers outside his own staff, approached Burnside and said, as slowly and gently as possible, that they already knew of the plan. Not only was everyone familiar with it, there was not a general in the army who expected it to succeed. Sumner himself thought it would lead to disaster.[44]

With that reluctant admission Sumner did the country—and Burnside—the greatest service of his long career. No one else could have convinced the harried commander of the need to concede defeat. From anyone else it would have seemed to be either continued insubordination or the voice of inexperience, but Sumner was his heartiest supporter, whose judgment usually erred on the side of aggressiveness. Burnside could not ignore the advice: he called all the other commanders and put the question to them. Without a dissenting vote, they disapproved of the idea of another frontal assault. By now the fog had lifted, and Burnside went out to turn a glass on the imposing new Confederate works. That sight added to the opposition of his generals, he relented and agreed to cancel the orders, whereupon the discussion turned to what ought to be done.

Burnside determined for the time being to entrench on the outskirts of the city. Some in his council made reference to evacuating the western bank entirely, but General Couch objected on the grounds that such a complete withdrawal would be bad for both army morale and public opinion. Sumner concurred, and Couch and Hooker went back into the city to prepare to defend it.[45]

Fierce skirmishing continued until about noontime on the fourteenth. Franklin apprehended an attack on his left flank, which prompted him to leave his comfortable plantation house long enough to make his first circuit of his grand division's lines. Around eleven that morning Burnside rode over to make his own inspection there. It is perhaps indicative of how late he decided to scrap the Ninth Corps assault that he left Franklin near noon with the impression it was still scheduled; it was almost one o'clock that afternoon when Franklin asked Hardie to telegraph headquarters and learn whether he should cooperate with it.

After his look at the far side of the river, Burnside spent most of the day at the Phillips house, periodically conferring with his staff. The staff raised an uproar because word had just leaked in that General Banks had fitted out an expedition recently shipped to the Gulf Coast.

(This was probably the same army Lincoln had proposed landing on the Pamunkey.) It would have been more helpful to the Army of the Potomac had Banks taken his force—if indeed it was ready to fight—up the James River to threaten Richmond directly and draw much of Lee's strength away from Fredericksburg. At least one of Lincoln's cabinet officers felt the same, but Banks and twenty-odd thousand men headed for Louisiana to subdue a Mississippi River fort the Confederates intended to evacuate anyway. The staff suspected that Halleck had feared to return to McClellan's old lines on the James; it would have amounted to an admission that McClellan had been right, back in July. That was the biggest difference between Halleck and Burnside—as soon as he recognized them, the younger man made haste to admit his mistakes.[46]

At this juncture, Burnside was ready to accept altogether too much of the responsibility for the mistake that had been Fredericksburg. He remained too exhausted and too upset by the results of the battle to consider how materially Franklin's hesitation had assured defeat.

That afternoon the general slept for an hour in his secretary's tent. After seeing some officers in the house he again came to the tent to sleep half an hour, around 9:00 P.M. The rest of the evening his stomach troubled him, and the next day the secretary described him as "troubled and anxious all the morning." Generals came in and out, but Burnside spent hours alone.

Late on December 13 Burnside had sent Major William Goddard to Washington, to give Halleck the latest news and to report Burnside's intentions. The night of the fifteenth a message came back from Halleck, encouraging Burnside and expressing full confidence; it was accompanied by a telegram from Goddard, explaining that Halleck opposed a withdrawal but seemingly "favored your plan of operations." By that the aide must have meant continuing the assault, for when Goddard had last seen Burnside, that was his intention. Goddard wrote Burnside a private letter the following day, in which he described Halleck's opinion more candidly. The general-in-chief, despite all the subsequent information indicating no new assault would follow, opposed withdrawing across the river. That any garrison left in the city might be destroyed did not seem to matter to Halleck. With what Goddard characterized as "some flippancy," the Washington administrator remarked, "It's a damn sight better to be flogged than to retreat in the present condition of the country." Halleck still felt another attack would be "proper &

judicious," but, typically, he left Burnside the responsibility for determining where, when, and how to make that attack. Goddard confessed a general disappointment with Halleck, whom he had never met before, and he commented that when the news-hungry president interrupted their interview, Halleck never introduced Goddard or mentioned his mission.[47]

Goddard's letter must have struck the general with painful irony, for when it arrived he had already moved his last divisions back over the pontoon bridges. Sumner and Couch had urged he garrison the city permanently, but Hooker had intervened. The outpost was too indefensible, he said, for a small force to be able to hold it. Burnside, who seemed to agree, decided; with tears running into those famous whiskers he dictated orders to abandon Fredericksburg altogether. A miserable rainstorm helped to muffle the sound of his retreat, and by the dawn of December 16 the entire Army of the Potomac sat on the other side of the Rappahannock. The bloodstained bridges were gone.[48]

III

The severity of the defeat at Fredericksburg shook the war effort to its very footings. The governor of Maine wrote his friend, Vice President Hamlin, asking, "Hannibal, What does it mean?" Someone, the governor suspected, must have made an enormous miscalculation. In a proposal that might have driven Burnside's staff officers to apoplexy, he suggested rather tardily that a simultaneous attack ought to have been made up the James River. An enlisted man in the decimated 5th New Hampshire told his family, "The title of the Battle is Burnsides slaughter house!"[1] A brigadier whose prejudice against Burnside led him to insubordination said (after Burnside's death) that his competence was questioned "at every camp-fire" in the wake of the repulse. Everyone began to remember that he had not really had much faith in Burnside from the start—that the man seemed to lack much that a general needed to lead an army. One officer awaiting orders back in Washington noted, "Little Mac's friends are jubilant."[2]

To his credit, George McClellan did not share that jubilation. He expressed both admiration for Burnside's skillful retreat and sympathy for the almost subliminal prodding Burnside must have suffered from Halleck, which McClellan perceptively blamed for driving the new army commander into a battle on the enemy's terms. As might be expected, he concurred in the belief that Banks ought to have ascended the James. McClellan had spoken highly of Burnside to friends, but he had predicted that no general could effectively use so large an army. McClellan told one visitor, "He will do as well as anyone can with so great an army but our people do not appreciate the difficulties with which he will have to contend." It seemed Little Mac was, at least superficially, still a friend of Burnside's by late December, but events—and McClellan's motives—would soon change that: already General Parke and Mr. Larned had a fifty-dollar bet on McClellan's chances of becoming the next president.[3]

Despite retrospective comments to the contrary, not every soldier believed Burnside was to blame for the disaster at Fredericksburg. One young corporal who had fought under him since South Mountain, and had charged the stone wall, sensed the folks at home condemned the general, but the young man swore "he has the whole confidence of his soldiers who will follow wherever he leads." And a Massachusetts captain gave him backhanded praise: "Who have we got that is more capable of commanding our Army?" Even one of the Pennsylvania Reserves, who had suffered so badly on Franklin's front, admitted his division could have taken the Confederate position on Prospect Hill if it had been properly supported. Meade himself agreed, and so, eventually, did the Joint Committee on the Conduct of the War, a generally anti-McClellan clique which found Franklin culpable for failing to put enough men (or enthusiasm) into his assault. Because of the committee's bias against anyone tainted with "McClellanism," critics then and since have discounted the congressmen's coincidentally accurate determination, but President Lincoln seemed to take that line as well: when he later interviewed General Hooker after choosing him to command the army, he directed him to "put in all your men" in the next fight.[4]

Because Burnside did not immediately make Franklin's performance a public issue, some historians have concluded that his dissatisfaction with his left wing chief arose retroactively, dating from Burnside's removal from command of the Army of the Potomac. After all, Burnside first told the joint committee that Franklin only failed to carry Jackson's position because it was too strong—a gentler way of saying he employed too few troops. In private conversations the army commander spoke more pointedly. Major Goddard, who left Burnside the evening of December 13, went directly to Halleck and reported Burnside's distress over officers who displayed "a want of confidence or cordial coopera-tion." On December 16 Burnside's secretary wrote his brother-in-law that "Jealousies and political intrigues are greater enemies than an open foe" and added the general still believed the Confederates could be beaten "if he can rely on his officers."[5]

Lincoln soon had stronger reason to believe Franklin had not sup-ported his commander well enough. Only a week after the battle, Frank-lin and "Baldy" Smith, the Sixth Corps commander, went over Burn-side's head to suggest the army embark for the Peninsula again. They wrote the president, "The plan of campaign already commenced will not be successful." Not only did the letter imply a poor opinion of Burn-side and a willingness to resist or confound him, it pointed to a strain of inconsistency on Franklin's part, since he had been one of those to propose the withdrawal from the Peninsula in the first place.[6]

The bulwark of Franklin's defense was the attack order Burnside issued. He said it contradicted the program agreed upon the evening of December 12, arguing it reduced his grand assault to a reconnaissance-in-force. Had he really believed that, though, the orders that filtered down to Meade and Gibbon would not have directed them to *carry* their objectives.

In justice to Franklin, it must be recognized that Burnside's order did not clearly state the Left Grand Division should make an all-out assault directly behind the Hamilton house, but both the direction and vigor his attack should take must have become clear during the December 12 conference. Even in the event Franklin did not simply lose his bearings but actually misunderstood his objective, it ought to have occurred to him that he was expected to make the greatest effort, for Burnside had placed the preponderance of the army at his disposal. The only reason Franklin may have declined to interpret his attack orders liberally— aside from an active wish to subvert Burnside—was his fear of the ten-sion existing between the commander and his generals: he may have been afraid that, by technically overstepping his written instructions, he risked a court-martial in case of defeat. Such things had happened before—Fitz John Porter was enduring such a trial at that moment for exercising battlefield discretion—but Ambrose Burnside was not the man to fault a subordinate for an honest effort.[7] Still, an air of not necessarily mutual mistrust existed because of the openly expressed misgivings about Burnside's plan. As it was, Franklin suffered not for having exceeded the letter of his orders, but for having failed to do so.

The decision to assign James Hardie to Franklin's headquarters represented Burnside's desire to improve communications between himself and the chief of his left wing. Having no particular reason at that time to expect hesitation from Franklin, he probably never charged Hardie with authority to increase the strength of the assault nor suggested that Hardie report a feeble performance: the staff officer's function seems largely to have been to report frequently to headquarters, to give Burnside some notion of when to launch Sumner's attack.

Without instructions to that effect, Hardie would have been the last person to urge Franklin to act more aggressively, or to notify Burnside that his drive was understrength. Hardie was, in fact, much closer to Franklin than to Burnside. The two had been sixteen-year-old plebes together at West Point, had both graduated in the top third of their class, and had been at McClellan's elbow on the Peninsula campaign— Hardie as his assistant adjutant general and Franklin as a trusted division and corps commander. In an army whose officers tended to align themselves with McClellan or Hooker against Burnside, or vice versa, Hardie was a friend to both McClellan and Hooker.[8] Yet there existed far better grounds to send someone else to oversee Franklin's assault, if Burnside had such a motive in the back of his mind. Unknown to Burnside, and unnoticed by historians since, Hardie had no faith in his commander. More than three decades after Fredericksburg, one of McClellan's aides reported a remark made by one of the general staff shortly after Antietam: this "staff-officer of high rank and distinguished merit" told the other officers, "I was a year in the cadet corps with Burnside, and I was instructor at West Point when he graduated, and he served with me in the same battery, and I know him through and through, and he's a good fellow, but I tell you if he's in command of a battery it's just as much as he's fit for." No one on McClellan's staff matched all the criteria in that long sentence, but one—James Hardie— was a high-ranking staff officer of distinguished merit, had been an instructor of English grammar until the year before Burnside graduated from West Point, and had served in the same battery with him at Fort Adams. He had not shared a year as a cadet with him (though Burnside reported in during Hardie's final month at the academy), but if he mistakenly assumed Burnside was an 1846 alumnus, as the reference to being an instructor when he graduated would imply, then he would also have calculated that Burnside was a plebe during Hardie's last year. No one else on McClellan's staff came nearly so close to fitting that description, and if the long-silent aide spoke the truth, he could not have attributed the derogatory comment to anyone but the very man Burnside sent to help bring his plan to fruition—a man apparently already convinced the army lay in the hands of an incompetent from whom it needed to be protected.[9] Even if he could separate his personal suspicions from the job at hand, however, Hardie's evaluation of the tactical situation would have tended to mirror Franklin's—and Franklin did not fix his eye so much on victory as on avoiding the possibility of being whipped.

In his own mind, Ambrose Burnside appears to have blamed Franklin only for his failure to put enough punch into the assault made mostly by Meade's Pennsylvanians; it is difficult to determine whether he ever faulted the left wing commander for more, so silent did Burnside stay during the wartime and postwar debates. If he did not criticize Franklin for having missed the objective, Lee's extreme flank, it was because he probably never learned of it. Franklin himself at least seemed to believe Meade had driven almost directly for both Hamilton's Crossing and Captain Hamilton's house: that much emerges from his faulty map and from one of Hardie's afternoon dispatches, referring to some woods and a battery he erroneously supposed to be near Hamilton's house.[10] Quite possibly Burnside remained convinced Franklin had struck true as well, at least until he considered the matter dead.

The heaviest and bitterest criticism leveled at Burnside dealt with his repeated attacks on the stone wall. His stubbornness there has been ascribed to sheer desperation, and one modern writer equated him to a crazed bull, butting blindly at the taunting matador.[11] In fact it was probably only the communications lag between the Phillips house and "Mansfield," where Franklin was ensconced, that spurred him to keep the assaults going: even the telegraph, used for the first time on an American battlefield, might have failed to tell him of Franklin's progress in time to properly coordinate Sumner's attack. He thus made inefficient use of his army, but by the time the fighting began, Burnside found his choices severely limited. The terrain and a projection in Lee's line made the Telegraph Road the most appropriate target. Any elaborate flanking movement here would have thinned his line dangerously, even if the canal had not prevented such a tactic. Seemingly forgotten by those who excoriate Burnside for the assault against Longstreet's entrenched position are two important facts. First, Burnside had no prior warning of the riflemen hiding in the sunken road. He knew he had to overcome serious artillery fire, but for all of E. P. Alexander's promises to Longstreet, Confederate artillery was not what stopped the Union soldiers: almost every survivor records that it was the blinding sheets of musketry that put an end to each assault. But for those riflemen, the Yankees would have been safe from the belching cannon because the gunners could not depress their pieces sufficiently to bear on the front ranks.

With all the information Burnside had, therefore, his decision seems hardly so bizarre as most have insinuated, for the other salient point overlooked by his detractors is that such attacks were an established element of the tactical repertoire of the day. His generation had studied the science of war under men like Dennis Mahan, Henry Hunt (Burnside's own present chief of artillery), and one of his more critical division commanders, John Newton. New lessons given by expert marksmen armed with rifled muskets had not yet penetrated; soldiers more revered than Ambrose Burnside showed less ability to profit from experience that contradicted their West Point educations. Robert E. Lee's expensive assault at Malvern Hill, for instance, did not prevent him from repeating the mistake at Gettysburg, and U. S. Grant's fiasco at Cold Harbor followed two similarly bloody failures before Vicksburg.

Nonetheless, there is cause to believe Burnside labored under extreme physical and mental exhaustion. Due at least partly to his disinclination to sufficiently delegate the duties of his new position, he had been without a good night's sleep since he took command. His own loyal secretary documents both this and the digestive difficulties that arose at the time of the battle—symptomatic of severe anxiety. One of General Franklin's apologists recounts the secondhand tale of a staff officer who recalled that Burnside had exhibited signs of great nervous fatigue just before the battle; at the height of the fighting that same officer supposedly caught Burnside sneaking up to the attic of the Phillips house to steal a nap, complaining he was "dead with sleep." The story invites skepticism, for the author was rabidly partisan and did not reveal the staff officer's name, but if true, the anecdote illustrates the command-

ing general may have succumbed to stress. The combination of stress
and frustration can produce an irresistible urge to sleep, especially in
an individual already deprived of rest, or prolonged stress alone can
induce both apathy and a desire to sleep at the most critical moments.
Precisely that condition allegedly inhibited Stonewall Jackson the previous June: expected to attack the Union flank at White Oak Swamp,
Jackson instead ordered his troops into bivouac while he went to sleep.[12]

Apathy seems not to have been part of Burnside's problem. Apathy would not have allowed him to propose leading a frontal assault he
might not have survived; apathy would have prevented him from shed-
ding tears, as Larned said he did when he ordered the withdrawal from
Fredericksburg. His principal emotion at that juncture was not apathy, but frustration. More than one of his generals sensed it, expressing
enormous sympathy for a man so ill-used by fortune.[13]

Less than a week after the battle the inevitable detail of frock-coated
congressmen sauntered into General Sumner's headquarters, accompanied by the inebriated sergeant-at-arms of the Senate. While General
Patrick escorted the impaired functionary to his own cot for a long
snooze, the committee proceeded to investigate. They spoke with Burnside first, then with his grand division commanders. The testimony
revealed that all three of the subordinates had favored a full-strength
attack on the left. The better to wreak havoc on his opponent's army,
Burnside had chosen the classic combination that served him so well
at Roanoke, Newbern, and Antietam: a convincing frontal feint in conjunction with a decisive flank attack with his left. Although Burnside afforded Franklin no criticism whatever, the committee ultimately found
Franklin negligent, and indeed he was. It was he whose unfamiliarity
with the ground sent Meade astray; it was his failure to use his cavalry that allowed annoying artillery fire to delay Meade's attack and
distract Doubleday from supporting him; but for his McClellanlike paranoia and his disinclination to venture from headquarters for a glimpse
of the action, he could have put more weight into the misdirected assault when it began to promise success. Franklin tried to divert blame
to the critical pontoon delay; the congressmen nodded, but still pegged
him as their chief culprit. Any imprecision in Burnside's written orders
escaped these solons, but even Franklin did not complain of his battle
orders until months later, and then only in a desperate effort to exoner-
ate himself.

Nor did the committee cite Burnside for what may have been almost as crucial as Franklin's negligence: his failure to complete the crossing of the river the night of December 11, so as to attack early on the twelfth. Despite the risks of crowding and confusion, it appears at least in retrospect that Lee would not have molested him that night; had the plan of December 13 been worked the morning of December 12—even if Franklin had gone afield in the same manner—the Confederates who drove back Meade's breakthrough might not have been so handy.

After giving his testimony, Burnside returned to work at his headquarters. That afternoon his tubercular medical director, Dr. William Church, arrived from home. The good doctor brought newspapers that criticized President Lincoln, Secretary Stanton, and General Halleck for having pressured Burnside into making the unfortunate attack at Fredericksburg. That, Church said, was now the accepted story on the streets. It enjoyed nearly equal credence in the army.[14]

"I'll put a stop to that," snorted Burnside. Forgetting that his assignment in place of the cautious McClellan had implied a certain amount of pressure to move quickly, that Halleck had been hot for some action (though he carefully declined to order any), and doubtless ignorant that Lincoln had been complaining of his failure to make an attack just seventeen days after his appointment, Burnside penned a letter to the newspapers taking all the blame on himself. His horrified staff begged him not to do such an injustice to himself, objecting as well that it was inappropriate for him to leap into the press on behalf of the administration. Burnside at least concurred with the latter half of that argument, and asked the president's permission to see him immediately.

The next day, while General Hooker gave the congressional committee the best possible picture of Joe Hooker (to the detriment of Burnside), General Burnside went up the Potomac to speak with Lincoln. In a midnight interview the president greeted him nervously, but his anxiety turned to relief when he learned Burnside's mission. He offered no objections, so Burnside went back to Willard's to finish the letter. The following day an eager Edwin Stanton, having heard of this welcome document, pressed Burnside to submit it. Burnside replied the matter was between him and Lincoln, and none of Stanton's business. The penitent secretary later apologized, whereupon Burnside forgivingly mentioned he had already mailed it to the New York papers.[15]

In the form of an antedated official report that denied Burnside had

been ordered into the battle, Burnside's letter received wide circulation and helped redirect some of the fury of public indignation to the
field commander. The endless denunciations made the general ache,
but also gave him an odd sense of relief. Whether personally culpable
or not, he saw the responsibility as his. It was an apt sermon with
which his friend the Reverend Woodbury consoled headquarters a few
days later: "Well done, good and faithful servant," he began, taking his
text from the parable in the Book of Matthew which defines true faith-
fulness as the readiness to risk what the master has entrusted when
there is a promise of profit. Only the servant who sits upon the master's resources, conserving them but gaining nothing more, earns his
rebuke. That McClellan fit the role of the "wicked and slothful servant"
doubtless escaped none of those in Woodbury's little congregation.[16]

Burnside's assumption of blame actually revived some public confidence in him. The father of one of his staff officers wrote to say his
"frank & noble account" worked "a wonderful effect" on the country's
morale. Another thought Burnside's brave letter "absolutely saved the
government." But if any good followed the general's selfless gesture, it
was offset by a column from William Swinton of the *New York Times*,
who speculated Burnside had made his confession at the instigation
of government officials—thus invoking a private sample of Burnside's
rare "towering passions." Even some of those who accepted the letter
as genuine and spontaneous, and considered it "frank and manly," read
a tone of apology into it and felt it might have been better left un-
written. Burnside, for whom confidence in the administration seemed
of paramount importance, could not see it that way.[17]

Absolved of the opprobrium for having prodded Burnside unduly,
Henry Halleck promptly resumed chiding him for not moving on the
enemy. Reporting an increased Confederate presence in the Shenandoah Valley and before Fort Monroe the day after Christmas, Halleck
blamed it on "the inactivity of the Army of the Potomac. . . . This is certainly very disheartening." By now quite sensitive to such subtleties,
Burnside began preparing for a wide flanking movement—crossing the
Rappahannock several miles below town as he had planned once before.
Within two days of Halleck's shrouded barb he had issued the necessary
orders to his cavalry. On December 29 he ordered Hooker to arm and
provision his men for a lengthy maneuver approximating Hooker's own
proposal of nearly six weeks before.[18]

The general's subordinates had only begun foiling him, however. John Newton and John Cochrane, respectively division and brigade commanders under the critical Smith and Franklin, appeared in Washington on leave the afternoon of December 30, their only mission to convince someone of importance that Burnside was incompetent and his campaign must be halted. Despite the denials of all concerned, their pilgrimage must have been sanctioned by Franklin and his Sixth Corps commander: what else would have secured the furlough of two of a division's only three generals the day before an important movement? The same mutinous intent had spread like gangrene straight down the chain of command composed of those four men.

The two conspirators eventually reached the White House, where they shocked the president with accounts of widespread doubt about Burnside's capacity. Though he smouldered indignant at their insubordinate intrigue, Lincoln wrote Burnside a hasty note asking him not to make any important movements without first checking with the administration. Burnside answered immediately, if not cheerfully, that he would rescind the orders that had anticipated his intended campaign. Since the army would not be going anywhere, he said he would sail up to Washington, ostensibly to give the testimony Fitz John Porter had requested, but primarily to confer with the president.[19]

On the last day of 1862, while the western armies grappled in bloody combat in Tennessee, the embattled Burnside met with his commander-in-chief. Lincoln began by telling him of the challenge made against his qualifications as a commander. With justifiable heat Burnside asked who the complaining officers were, but Lincoln would not say. The general then explained the fundamentals of his latest plan—taking the army downriver, crossing, and coming around behind Lee's forces. Lincoln wanted to discuss it with Halleck and Stanton, and would neither approve nor disapprove the undertaking.

Burnside went on to say that, because of the failure at Fredericksburg, he lacked the confidence of his officers and the country, and he ought to be replaced. The president then asked his opinion of the soldiers' sentiment in regard to Stanton and Halleck. Sentiment—at least at headquarters—rose intensely critical of these two, and Burnside said so, but in a manner that did not satisfy his own preference for precision and justice in such topics.

Later that day Burnside testified before the court-martial trying

Porter. Porter, who may have been one of those McClellan friends who
derived smug gratification from Burnside's defeat, had no cause to
regret that general's appearance in the courtroom. Burnside attempted
to do the defendant the least damage the truth would allow. When
the day's proceedings ended, the defendant and his witness returned
together to Willard's, where Burnside spent another night of letter
writing. In the wee hours of January 1 he composed a formal appeal
for his own removal and more carefully restated his pessimistic view
of the army's regard for Stanton and Halleck, adding that Stanton had
probably lost the confidence of the civilian population, too—though he
recognized that his isolation with the army might have disqualified him
as a competent judge of that. He warned Lincoln, "It is of the utmost importance that you be surrounded, and supported by men who have the
confidence of the people, and of the army, and who will at all times give
you definite and honest opinions in relation to their separate departments, and at the same time give you positive and unswerving support
in your public policy." Burnside was sure he had lost the support of his
subordinates and felt he should "cheerfully give way" to someone else.
He wanted to retire to private life: this was the first time he articulated
the desire, but from the first day of 1863 (though he remained willing
to serve so long as his services were needed) he heartily wished himself
free of the army and its backbiting politics.[20]

In a conference the next morning with Lincoln, Stanton, and Halleck, Burnside gave the letter to the president, who read it silently but
returned it without a word. Lincoln asked Halleck to comment on Burnside's strategy. Halleck characteristically hesitated, asserting finally
that field operations were the prerogative of the field commander—
deftly skirting his responsibility to give Lincoln "definite and honest
opinions." The two tangled briefly over it, but finally the president let
it go. Burnside thus returned to the army without Lincoln's approval of
his proposed course, and with Halleck's very indefinite approval.[21]

Understandably agitated, Burnside fumed at his subordinates, demanding the names of the men who had gone behind his back to Lincoln.
No one would say, but an offhand remark of Franklin's led him to suspect Newton and Cochrane. He told a group of generals about his visits
with Lincoln, letting it out that he had asked to be removed from command, and he mentioned the four-way conversation with the president,
Stanton, and Halleck, apparently citing the letter. Within weeks Gener-

als Franklin, Smith, and William Brooks circulated a perverted version of the incident, insinuating Burnside openly called for the removal of both Stanton and Halleck.[22]

When he had calmed down, Burnside considered his alternatives: he could keep the army immobile, wasting a million dollars a day, accomplishing nothing, and satisfying no one; or he could override the administration and his own generals, raising the army's morale and health, improving public opinion of the war effort, and chancing victory with another campaign. Like the good and faithful servants of the parable, he chose the more aggressive horn of the dilemma.

Burnside notified Lincoln and Halleck that he had ordered the preliminary engineering on still another river crossing. He warned Halleck, though, that if his effectiveness as a commander had not been impaired before, it certainly was now: everyone knew the president had stopped him before because of the interference of Newton and Cochrane, and the knowledge further compounded the problems of confidence and cooperation among his subordinates. He forwarded to Lincoln his own undated resignation, which he invited the president to accept whenever he felt Burnside's actions were an embarrassment to him. Lincoln replied that he did not yet wish to replace him, and tried to soothe Burnside's battered nerves. "Be cautious," he wrote, "and do not understand that the government, or country, is driving you." Halleck responded with a letter that seemed half intended to relieve himself of any blame for the November pontoon fiasco, concluding the epistle by commenting, very Hallecklike, that it was all up to Burnside: he ought to use his army, and soon, unless something changed, which it might.[23]

These conflicting, confusing messages ought to have discouraged Burnside, but he intended to force the issue. Unless exceedingly unfavorable circumstances arose, he would pursue the offensive—facing either another battle or relief from the overpowering responsibility of a hobbled command.

It would have been better had Newton and Cochrane kept their mouths shut. For the entire week after Burnside originally intended to move, the weather remained cold but clear. A diarist noted but one day between December 30 and January 19, in fact, when it was "too muddy to march," but at some point during the winter an extended period of wet weather was inevitable.[24]

The sensation that he was free, one way or the other, brought the old Burnside back. An exhausting personal reconnaissance of the upper fords once again became "a fine ride of 15 or 18 miles." The day after that he rose before dawn, galloping past his shirttailed staff on that walleyed grey, roaring with glee at some practical joke Dr. Church would discover when he awoke. General headquarters even hosted a makeshift skating party during an especially severe cold snap. The general's appetite returned, and he resumed polishing off significant portions of the delicacies sent by his staff officers' relatives. He rode before the serried divisions in a review such as this army had not seen since Warrenton, wherein at least one Indiana officer glanced up at a general he considered fully as competent as any.[25]

The euphoria that followed this latest crisis lasted less than a fortnight. Burnside still faced the problem of scornful, potentially un-cooperative subordinates. Division and corps commanders—and espe-cially Hooker—were straining Burnside's patience with their discour-aging chatter. Early in January Burnside arrested General William Brooks—"Bully" Brooks, as he was known—for insubordination, but Brooks was only one of many officers whose malicious gossip infected the whole army. Desertions approached critical levels, as did resigna-tions. A Detroit lieutenant with the 24th Michigan tried to resign on the grounds of disagreement with the emancipation policy of the admin-istration; Burnside heard about it, ordered Franklin to send over the officer in question, and gave the young man as severe an upbraiding as he ever administered, for daring to sit in judgment on the government. To make his point, he threw the lieutenant aboard the guardship at Aquia and prepared a recommendation for his dismissal. As though in response, a Second Corps officer provoked his own court-martial when he proclaimed Burnside an "accursed abolitionist" in front of his own men and some other officers; he apparently made the charge because, unlike McClellan, Burnside would not speak out against the Emanci-pation Proclamation. The clamor against the general began to assume strong political overtones. Burnside's own secretary fell into an acrimo-nious argument with an old friend who criticized the general. It seemed only the earth and skies remained to defy him.[26]

Burnside distributed the orders for the movement; the army would begin a march around the Confederate left flank on Monday, January 19, on which day mistaken sources reported that Longstreet's corps had gone to Tennessee. The Eleventh and Twelfth corps moved down to supporting distance, and the Army of the Potomac rolled upriver like a gigantic earthworm, already convinced by men like Franklin, Smith, Brooks, and Newton that the mission was futile. One of Reynolds's senior staff officers, who happened to believe some of the derogatory continuum that pervaded the Left Grand Division, nevertheless felt Franklin, Smith, and their respective staffs had no right to denounce Burnside as they did. He found them "talking outrageously" about him the morning the movement began. Franklin's staff chattered openly about their chief taking over the army, a subject dear to Franklin's heart. General Hunt, the artillery commander, and General Reynolds both seemed to sense an excellent chance of success in Burnside's plan (as did General Meade, now in charge of the Fifth Corps), but the troops were discouraged by the dissident generals. Colonel Charles Wainwright thought Franklin "has completely demoralized his whole command, and so rendered failure doubly sure." He had talked so long and loud against Burnside and his plan, Wainwright wrote, "that he certainly deserves to be broken. Smith and they say Hooker are almost as bad." If Franklin was so skeptical about the maneuver, Wainwright felt, he had enough rank to enter a formal protest. Failing that, the honorable thing would be to ask to be relieved.[27]

As if the virtual mutiny among Burnside's generals were not enough to stymie him, it began to storm. The headquarters staff packed amid the fury: "It rains great guns," one noted in a hasty message home, "and blows a harricane." It continued so for three days. The mud deepened, columns of miserable troops dragged to a virtual halt in the suction, and those units that did manage to reach the crossing points sent up the familiar plaint that the pontoons had not arrived.[28]

The pontoons could not move at all—nor could the artillery, except by corduroying the roads. It was only too perfect for the doomsayers: nothing Burnside could do would go well. Hooker broadcast his denunciation of the commanding general. Those who had been carping all along could now crow; little did anyone reflect on the three weeks of relatively good weather in which, but for the intervention of Newton and Cochrane, the army might have moved.

Burnside heard of the despair, and of such things as Hooker's mutinous rhetoric, and called off what reporters already dubbed the "Mud March." He had had enough, and determined there would have to be some changes. Halleck had twice evinced at least passive support for

the notion of removing uncooperative subordinates—had flatly agreed
that complainers like Newton and Cochrane ought to be cashiered—so
Burnside compiled a list for the headsman. Either the officers on that
list would go, or he would. He telegraphed the president that he was
coming to Washington with important orders Lincoln must see.[29]

Ambrose Burnside has been roundly ridiculed for General Order
Number 8, which dismissed Generals Hooker, Brooks, Newton, and
Cochrane from the service and relieved five men of their positions—
Generals Franklin, Smith, Sturgis, and Ferrero, and Franklin's assistant adjutant general, Colonel J. H. Taylor. Had he issued that order
without consulting the president, it would not only have been preposterous, but illegal. All he did, however, was prepare for Lincoln's consideration those very orders Halleck had implied would be forthcoming if he
requested them. At least in the case of the dismissals, courts-martial
would have been in order, and eight senior subordinates constituted a
significant element of opposition, so Lincoln would of course be shocked.
In fact it seems Burnside hoped to shock him—to propose technically
difficult terms—but those terms would have been necessary for him
to continue in command. If the president wanted him to remain, the
removal of those men was a reasonable expectation.[30]

The journey to Washington was a comedy of painful errors. As General Meade observed not much later, Burnside appeared "to have the
very elements against him."[31] He wished to reach the White House by
midnight, January 23, so as to be back at Falmouth by eight o'clock the
next morning. Obviously he planned to sleep but little; as it transpired,
he slept not at all.

That evening Burnside, his private secretary, his devoted servant
Robert Holloway, and Henry Raymond of the *New York Times* crowded
into an ambulance. The driver was nearsighted. As Robert noted, he
was "a little deaf too." Between myopia, the darkness, and the accumulated woodsmoke and fog, they lost their way within a quarter mile.
Finally the teamster dropped the ambulance over a steep streambank
full of dead mules, and there it stuck. The passengers clambered out
in the mud to find the road, where they met a horseman who said he
had business at headquarters. Forgetting to identify himself, Burnside
asked the mounted man to ride back to a distant campfire to ask directions. The rider remarked rather insolently that they might ask for
themselves, and cantered away.

Returning to the ambulance, the five of them unharnessed the team and lifted the vehicle around manually, proceeding as best they could for the steamboat landing. At one point the road was blocked by a mired artillery wagon, and Burnside ordered everyone out to help. With a half-dozen privates, the old black man, an aristocratic scrivener, and the discomfited editor of the *Times*, the commander of the Army of the Potomac put his embroidered epaulette to the muddy wheel and heaved. Burnside alone could muster considerable strength, and the wagon finally moved.

When they arrived at Stoneman's Switch three hours later, the train for Aquia Creek had already departed. Burnside directed the telegrapher to call it back, but he said he could not. Suspicious of the operator, Burnside borrowed a lantern and started down the tracks on foot, his companions following. Two miles or more down the line they saw the train coming. Burnside signaled with the lantern, and the engineer stopped for them, but before reversing the locomotive to Aquia the general insisted on returning to Stoneman's Switch to arrest the telegraph operator.

It was about seven o'clock in the morning when their steamer docked at Washington. Burnside went directly to the White House, saw Lincoln, and told him he could not continue in command unless Order Number 8 met with approval. "I think you are right," the president said, and asked the general to return after he had had a chance to speak with Halleck and Stanton. Burnside joined his rested comrades at Willard's, said a premature goodbye to Mr. Raymond, and returned to Falmouth with the secretary and Robert. He may have napped an hour on the boat that afternoon. By midnight the three of them reached Washington again. Burnside went at once to the president, who sent him to Willard's for some sleep after arranging a ten o'clock interview with Halleck.[32]

After breakfast the next morning, Lincoln called Stanton and Halleck into his office and told them he had decided to replace Burnside with Hooker. When Burnside arrived at ten, the president broke the news to him. For all his dislike and distrust of Hooker, Burnside accepted the decision with overall relief. Assuming the resignation of his commission had been accepted, he asked if he might not go directly home. Not at all, they told him; they wanted him to take command of a new, expanded department consisting of North and South Carolina. Burnside had learned that his old friend John G. Foster had graciously asked for Burnside to come back and resume command at Newbern, but Burnside did not want to take Foster's assignment away. Besides, he argued, David Hunter had only recently been appointed head of the Department of South Carolina, and he was senior to Burnside. Nothing daunted, the three of them implored him to stay in the service for the sake of the country. Lincoln, at least, did not want the general to leave the army with an air of failure about him, and Burnside probably sensed that, but at last he talked them into a thirty-day furlough so he could think about it.[33]

Back at Willard's, Burnside found Mr. Raymond still in his room. He took the newspaperman aside and told him of the change. He said he knew Mr. Raymond would be inclined to defend him in the affair, but asked that in so doing he would not speak ill of Hooker, lest it weaken public confidence in him. He specifically asked that Raymond not mention Order Number 8, which would put the new commander in a particularly bad light just when he needed everyone's support. Perhaps straining to surmount his personal reservations about Hooker, the general told Raymond he was a fine officer who was bound to win the country a victory.[34]

Before he could begin his furlough, Burnside must return to Falmouth for the undeserved humiliation of turning the command over to Hooker. That evening, January 25, he and his two attendants stopped at the Lacy house to see General Sumner. Sick of all the bickering, Sumner had asked to be relieved of his command, and orders to that effect had come with Burnside. The next morning Burnside sent for Hooker, and by seven o'clock the man Burnside had recently thought merited hanging was in charge of the Army of the Potomac. Later that morning Burnside asked numerous officers to visit headquarters. He spoke to the assembled generals there, asked them (with what General Patrick considered an undertone of resentment) to give Hooker all their confidence and cooperation, and shook hands all around. By midday all the trunks were packed. The departing commander called on Sumner, who cheerfully agreed to accompany him and his retinue to Washington, and the "wretched, straggling old place" known as Falmouth was only a bitter memory. They all enjoyed a farewell celebration aboard the *Carrie Martin*, on the way up the Potomac, and bedded down comfortably at Willard's by evening.

The morning of January 27 Burnside, his secretary, and a few of the

New Yorkers on the staff boarded the train for home. By wire or earlier trains, word ranged ahead that Burnside was coming, and when the general climbed down at the New York terminal he stepped into a raging blizzard and a cheering crowd of well-wishers: apparently public opinion did not entirely coincide with that of the army.

Documenting this odyssey for Mrs. Burnside, who waited back in Rhode Island, the general's secretary chose that reception as a fitting close. With a wonderful capacity for melodrama, if not prediction, Mr. Larned announced, "Thus endeth the Drama of 'Burnside and the Army of the Potomac.'"[35]

The first battle of Bull Run. A. R. Waud's eyewitness sketch shows
Burnside, at center, directing his brigade (Library of Congress).

Burnside as a freshly minted brigadier general in the autumn of 1861,
as he was gathering the flotilla for his invasion of North Carolina
(author's collection).

John G. Foster as a major general, sometime after he commanded the first brigade of Burnside's division (Francis Trevelyan Miller, ed., *The Photographic History of the Civil War*, 10 vols. [New York: The Review of Reviews Co., 1912]).

Ashby's Harbor, where the Burnside expedition landed on Roanoke Island. The first Confederates watched them land from the trees at right (photograph by author, 1989).

A contemporary—and rather idealized—engraving of Burnside's
landing on Roanoke Island (J. T. Headley, *The Great Rebellion: A
History of the Civil War in the United States*, 2 vols.
[Hartford: American Publishing Company, 1862, 1866]).

The mouth of Slocum's Creek. Union troops sloshed ashore along the bank at right before advancing on Newbern (photograph by author, 1989).

Chatham, the Lacy mansion, overlooking Fredericksburg. Here Burnside had his headquarters during the Second Bull Run campaign (photograph by author, 1988).

John G. Parke, commander of Burnside's third brigade on Roanoke; he later served as his chief of staff and stand-in corps commander (Francis Trevelyan Miller, ed., *The Photographic History of the Civil War*, 10 vols. [New York: The Review of Reviews Co., 1912]).

Fox's Gap, over South Mountain, as photographed in 1922. In the foreground is the Old Sharpsburg Road. Reno was mortally wounded at the crest, just above the house at right (collection of Jim Clifford and Jack Burke).

Jesse Reno. His death at South Mountain was a severe blow to Burnside, whose style of command required dependable subordinates (Francis Trevelyan Miller, ed., *The Photographic History of the Civil War*, 10 vols. [New York: The Review of Reviews Co., 1912]).

The Rohrbach Bridge over Antietam Creek. The break in the fence is
a re-creation of the point through which the 2nd Maryland and 6th
New Hampshire burst into the wartime road, along the creek at left
(photograph by author, 1987).

The Rohrbach Bridge from the vantage point of the Confederate
defenders (photograph by author, 1987).

Burnside at Warrenton, November, 1862, mounted on Major, his
notorious bobtail. Note the curb bit and martingale, tack indicative of
a difficult horse (Francis Trevelyan Miller, ed., *The Photographic
History of the Civil War*, 10 vols.
[New York: The Review of Reviews Co., 1912]).

Fredericksburg from the Falmouth side of the Rappahannock, a day or so after the Army of the Potomac withdrew from the city (Francis Trevelyan Miller, ed., *The Photographic History of the Civil War*, 10 vols. [New York: The Review of Reviews Co., 1912]).

Captain Hutton arresting Clement L. Vallandigham in his home, May 5, 1863 (*Leslie's Illustrated*, May 23, 1863).

John Hunt Morgan, Confederate cavalier (Francis Trevelyan Miller, ed., *The Photographic History of the Civil War*, 10 vols. [New York: The Review of Reviews Co., 1912]).

Burnside's delirious reception at Knoxville, September 2, 1863 (Ben Perley Poore, *The Life and Public Services of Ambrose E. Burnside, Soldier—Citizen—Statesman* [Providence: J. A. & R. A. Reid, 1882]).

Fort Sanders, Knoxville. Note the narrow berm, or ledge, around the
foot of the parapet, which E. P. Alexander claimed was lacking
(Francis Trevelyan Miller, ed., *The Photographic History of the Civil
War*, 10 vols. [New York: The Review of Reviews Co., 1912]).

Robert B. Potter. Slight, serious, and courageous, he commanded the
Ninth Corps temporarily in Tennessee and led the second division
from the Wilderness until the end of the war (Francis Trevelyan
Miller, ed., *The Photographic History of the Civil War*, 10 vols. [New
York: The Review of Reviews Co., 1912]).

Orlando Bolivar Willcox, Burnside's classmate in the West Point class
of 1847. Assigned to Burnside at the start of the Maryland campaign,
he remained with him until the end (Francis Trevelyan Miller, ed.,
The Photographic History of the Civil War, 10 vols.
[New York: The Review of Reviews Co., 1912]).

Brigadier General Thomas G. Stevenson, killed by a sharpshooter at
Spotsylvania, May 10, 1864. His death left Burnside with only one
truly capable division commander (Francis Trevelyan Miller, ed., *The
Photographic History of the Civil War*, 10 vols.
[New York: The Review of Reviews Co., 1912]).

Spotsylvania. Confederate earthworks can still be distinguished by the rough vegetation curving from the foreground into the distance. On May 12, 1864, Burnside's extreme right captured the trenches in the middle distance but was driven back (photograph by author, 1988).

Bethel Church, where Burnside and his staff stopped on the afternoon of May 22, 1864 (photograph by author, 1988).

The North Anna River, near Ox Ford. The foliage at right conceals precipitous limestone cliffs (photograph by author, 1988).

The Battle of the Crater, by John Elder, showing Mahone's Virginia brigade counterattacking Ferrero's division (Clarence C. Buel and Robert U. Johnson, eds., *Battles and Leaders of the Civil War*, 4 vols. [New York: The Century Co., 1884–88]).

Mary Bishop Burnside, "a very quiet, ladylike, and exceedingly nice personage," according to George Meade, who also reported her to be "rather younger than I expected." Daniel Larned described her as "quite delicate." She died at age forty-seven (Ben Perley Poore, *The Life and Public Services of Ambrose E. Burnside, Soldier—Citizen— Statesman* [Providence: J. A. & R. A. Reid, 1882]).

Senator Burnside (Library of Congress).

Burnside the way the Army of the Potomac remembered him, in a
sketch by Charles W. Reed, of Warren's Fifth Corps
(Library of Congress).

Burnside the way Rhode Island remembered him: his equestrian
statue in Providence (photograph by author, 1989).

5

CHANTS OF OHIO

Burnside was not to enjoy a full month of uninterrupted relaxation. He had no sooner arrived in Providence, shed of most of his staff officers, than William Sprague asked the Rhode Island legislature to honor him with the hospitality of the state, including an invitation to address the joint houses of the general court. The representatives of a state short on prominent men lost no time: they adopted the official resolution within twenty-four hours, much to the discomfort of the shy fellow they meant to honor.[1]

Nor was the general's leisure encumbered solely by such public plaudits. His railroad paperwork had been piling up (in fact, this had been the nominal purpose of his leave of absence), and the Committee on the Conduct of the War wanted to hear more from him. Accompanied by Molly, Burnside returned to Washington and appeared in the committee chambers on February 7.

This time the congressmen were specifically interested in the difficulties Burnside had encountered with subordinates after Fredericksburg—particularly any who might have gone to the president behind his back. Burnside hesitated to blame or criticize individuals, not so much for the damage it might do to their reputations as to avoid further erosion of public confidence in men who still served in the army. Chairman Ben Wade assured him the committee would make nothing public that might have such a negative effect; Burnside therefore went into the matter of General Order Number 8 and its causes, a subject he still considered secret between himself and his immediate advisors. He voiced his suspicion of Newton and Cochrane as the insubordinate emissaries, and when Representative Daniel Gooch asked outright if Burnside felt his generals had not fully supported him in the battle of December 13, he admitted as much. In this official atmosphere he softened his criticism, insisting he suspected no deliberate bad faith or disobedience, but he left no doubt of his disappointment in Franklin's feeble effort or, for that matter, in Hooker's reluctance to make his twilight attack. These two, he accurately deduced, had prepared themselves more for failure than for success.[2]

When Burnside's testimony was over, the committee members escorted him onto the floors of the House and Senate, where his infectiously congenial personality earned a warm reception among the congressmen. Aside from John C. Frémont, Burnside was the highest-ranking advocate of emancipation in the army now; though his views were not so extreme as theirs and his scruples were deeper-seated, the Radicals took him to their bosoms. He stood as their potential champion, however unwillingly, and Democrats made much of it, undermining his nonpartisan demeanor.[3]

Even more damaging to Burnside's relations with conservatives in and out of the army was the joint committee's perfidious handling of testimony Burnside expected to remain confidential. Not only did the committee eventually publish its entire record, some of the members seem to have provided the newspapers with an inside glimpse of the proceedings. Three days after Burnside spoke to the group, the *New York Tribune* published an announcement of his "remarkable disclosures," adding that "imbecility, cowardice, apathy and treason met him at every turn."[4] References to treason early in 1863 often reflected upon George McClellan and his followers: Fitz John Porter was gone now—purged in part for his allegiance to McClellan—and Burnside's statements about Franklin may have struck the McClellan gang as another blow against one of their own.

By the time the *Tribune* article hit the streets, Mr. and Mrs. Burnside were back in New York for the wedding of Edward Neill, of the general's staff. Wednesday evening, February 11, Burnside and Parke joined an executive of the Sanitary Commission for dinner. Several other guests attended, male and female, military and civilian, but the former commander of the Army of the Potomac became the center of attention.

Some of those present still believed the authorities in Washington were responsible for the debacle on the Rappahannock, but Burnside disabused them of the notion one last time, repeating that he made the move without orders from anyone. He added that he expected to win the battle, too, until one of his staff brought word that another general (whom the dinner guests presumed to be Franklin) *"was doing all he could to make the attack a failure."* This was his strongest denunciation yet, far surpassing the version he gave the joint committee. He told his host that his first impulse was to ride over and shoot Franklin, but reason got the better of him. The diarist who recorded the dinner party lumped Franklin and Porter in the same light: "bad cases of blood poisoning and paralysis from hypertrophied McClellanism."[5]

The rest of the general's time was his own, but he had to devote much of it to private correspondence. Sprague pestered him about running for governor, now that the chief executive had abandoned the office for a seat in the Senate, but Burnside had already had bad luck in that line and probably felt his defeat at Fredericksburg had done nothing to increase his constituency. There came invitations to patriotic rallies, lectures, and more weddings, and his recent prestige brought a host of British relatives out of the woodwork. One distant cousin, ancient, semiliterate, and quite mistaken, wrote from Gilesgate Moor, near Durham, that she was his "Ant Eleasabeth"; she wanted to know if his father was still alive. A young Irishman, William Burnside, mistook the general for a native of the Emerald Isle; he asked his presumed kinsman's approval to join the Union army, though he offered to purchase his own commission after the European fashion.[6]

Assuming he was due back in Washington the day his leave expired, Burnside boarded a train for New York the evening of February 23. He notified army headquarters from the Fifth Avenue Hotel that he could come at any moment, but Halleck told him not to worry: there was, he said, "no cause for haste." Ultimately Burnside spent a full week in New York, working in the Illinois Central office and tending to some more personal affairs. The Christian Commission held a rally, for which he made a brief appeal; the father of one of his staff officers proposed establishing a fund for General Reno's widow and children, who were living on his dollar-a-day pension, and Burnside helped with that.[7]

Just as the general prepared to leave New York, D. Appleton and Company approached him about publishing his report on the battle of

Fredericksburg. He declined to allow it, citing the technicality that it violated orders to publish official reports without permission. He also implied he would not be willing to seek such permission. Assuming an attitude he would maintain thereafter, Burnside ignored the opportunity to tell his side of the story publicly because he did not wish to discredit those generals whose accounts were at odds with his. Unfortunately for his reputation then and since, those generals—particularly Franklin—did not reciprocate Burnside's air of unselfish neutrality.[8]

Burnside and his wife went to Washington by train on the first of March, while his staff sailed together from New York. When the general arrived in the city, he took his usual rooms at Willard's. George McClellan loitered in the capital that day, giving his own testimony to the joint committee, and he, too, lodged at Willard's. Significantly, the two old friends did not meet. Possibly the twenty-four hours of their common presence passed without either of them learning the other was there, but it would be a long-odds bet that no one in that famous lobby mentioned the fact to them; more likely, their final estrangement had begun.[9]

The rest of Burnside's entourage arrived Monday evening, March 2. No specific orders awaited them, for the administration had not yet made up its collective mind about the best place for Burnside. Rampant rumors, especially in the Ninth Corps, whispered about a new expeditionary force under his command: the news of Lincoln's January offer of the Department of the Carolinas had leaked out by now, fueling the flames of speculation. That prospect still survived, for the president wanted better cooperation on the coast of the Carolinas than John Foster and David Hunter seemed able to provide; a single department head would solve that discordance. Burnside resisted, nevertheless; he had no qualms about subordinating himself to a junior officer, but he consistently declined to put one of his seniors in that same position. Next, the War Department seemed inclined to saddle him with a command out West, as it had done to John Pope. Senator John Henderson led a powerful lobby that wanted Samuel Curtis removed from the Department of Missouri, and Henderson looked to Burnside for the job. Burnside balked again, but the president wanted Sumner for that place, anyway. Burnside spent most of his daylight hours at either the War Department or the White House; he refused to leave Washington even for an evening appearance at the Cooper Institute, as though afraid his superiors would decide upon an unsatisfactory assignment for him in his absence.[10]

The question of what to do with Burnside found its answer in a long letter from a general in Cincinnati. Seven months before, during the Confederate invasion of Kentucky, the War Department had gathered the states of Michigan, Ohio, Indiana, Illinois, and most of Kentucky together into the Department of the Ohio. Since that time, Horatio Wright had commanded the department. Wright had recently been pelting Washington with his suspicions of another impending invasion of Kentucky, and because his forces were so scattered he asked for ten thousand reinforcements in that state. Before Washington could respond, Wright learned the U.S. Senate had adjourned without confirming his appointment as a major general, which he understood to mean that his management of the department had not pleased that body. Public knowledge of the Senate rebuff would do little for his effectiveness, he reasoned, and he asked to be replaced by someone "who combines administrative ability in its most enlarged sense with military knowledge," closing his lengthy memorial with another call for the ten thousand reinforcements and a proposal to establish a reserve force of fifty thousand Bluegrass soldiers.[11]

Wright's suggested qualifications fit George McClellan better, but the Lincoln administration viewed Ohio as a perfect post for Burnside, offering sufficient scope for one of the ranking generals in the country. There, too, was a place for his Ninth Corps, the Ishmaels of the army, transferred away from the Army of the Potomac soon after Hooker took command. On March 16 Halleck handed Burnside confidential orders to take two divisions of the corps from General Dix, at Fort Monroe, and go to Cincinnati.[12]

Before he left Washington, Burnside endured a final round with the joint committee. By now those politicians were delving deep into the history of the Potomac army, inviting a number of officers up from the Rappahannock and taking advantage of administrative stragglers like Burnside. The ides of March saw General Meade checking in at Willard's for that purpose, and Burnside called him up to his room. Mrs. Burnside was there, and Meade found her to be "a very quiet, lady-like and exceedingly nice personage, quite pretty and rather younger than I expected to see." The two generals chatted at length with the ease that Burnside always instilled, but finally conversation turned to

Franklin, who had recently written Burnside to ask his help in correcting some critical newspaper accounts. Burnside had found nothing inaccurate in the articles, and he characterized what Franklin had requested as a "whitewash." Meade, who remained ignorant of some of the essential facts of the battle on the left, seemed to think Franklin would not get a fair shake; he was thoroughly convinced of that by the next afternoon, returning from a conversation with Ben Wade that suggested a prearranged conclusion against Franklin. Meade may not have been so far off the mark; it was the bias of the committeemen, in fact, that robbed their decision of the credibility it deserved.[13]

Three days later Burnside made his farewell appearance before that session's committee, answering questions about operations between January and September of the previous year. One of his more important revelations dealt with the condition of his troops after Antietam: they retained sufficient morale and organization, he said, to have renewed the fight on the eighteenth, and he had advised McClellan of the fact. Unbeknownst to Burnside, that flatly contradicted testimony McClellan had given seventeen days before—much to the delight of the chairman, who planned to have his report in type within a fortnight. The long friendship came to an end that afternoon; henceforth, Burnside and McClellan were enemies.[14]

Joe Hooker had sent the Ninth Corps away from the Army of the Potomac as he might have expelled a leper. Even he could not abide Baldy Smith, however, and so dispatched him to Fort Monroe in temporary charge of it. Burnside would have none of that, for he was the permanent commander of that corps, and instead he ordered Parke to Newport News for the command. On March 17 Burnside wrote his first order in this new capacity, announcing the resumption of his duties with the Ninth Corps and directing General Parke to transfer Getty's and Sturgis's divisions to a location he revealed only to Parke. That location was Baltimore. For reasons that may have been more personal than logistical, though, Getty's division remained behind; Willcox's division came on in its place, and the difficult Rush Hawkins disappeared forever from Burnside's life.[15]

Burnside lingered a few days in Washington and Baltimore. He had to arrange the transportation of his reduced corps with Quartermaster General Meigs and acquaint himself with the administration's wishes within his huge new department before venturing into it. Before Burnside left the capital behind, the War Department learned some disturbing news from Indianapolis. The ranking officer there, Colonel Henry Carrington, wrote both Lincoln and Stanton that Southern sentiment was growing in Indiana, especially since Congress had passed the first national draft law. There had always been an element of disloyalty in Illinois and Indiana, for much of those states had been settled by immigrants from the South—immigrants like Thomas Lincoln and Edghill Burnside; but Carrington charged there existed an active organization devoted to fomenting rebellion. The Knights of the Golden Circle, as he called them and counted them, numbered about 90,000. He alluded to large quantities of arms and explosives the group had hidden, and he accused Kentucky suppliers. Loyal citizens had been harassed by clusters of these Knights, Carrington said, and two hundred mounted men had ridden into one county seat just south of Indianapolis and "declared for Jeff. Davis." Twenty-odd miles from Ambrose Burnside's birthplace, one of Carrington's provost squads had triggered an alarm when it ventured into Rush County to arrest deserters: two hundred armed and mounted men had turned them back, or so they had reported. According to Colonel Carrington, Indiana already sat on the verge of open rebellion when the freshly enacted Conscription Act brought the state to a crisis.[16]

Neither Lincoln nor Stanton seems to have revealed the degree of Carrington's alarm to Burnside, and both appear to have discounted the colonel's views. The only effect Carrington's memorandum had on Burnside manifested itself in a telegram from Halleck: the secretary of war, Halleck said, wanted Burnside to go directly to Indianapolis from Cincinnati, for he feared the officer commanding there would cause trouble by "imprudence."[17]

Burnside and his staff left Baltimore by train Sunday evening, March 22. In 1843 a teenaged Burnside had made the trip from Cincinnati to Baltimore in most of a week; in 1863 it required little more than thirty hours of continuous rail travel. The cars stopped only twice between Sunday night and Tuesday morning—for breakfast at Altoona and a late lunch at Pittsburgh. Either word had reached western Pennsylvania that Burnside was on the way (which was still supposed to be a secret) or someone recognized the general's bald pate and whiskers. Such a crowd gathered at Pittsburgh that the staff could not navigate without a rolling diamond of armed guards; before Burnside boarded again, an impromptu choir of seminary girls serenaded him with "The Star Spangled Banner." The staff followed him back on the car when the last bar rang, waved wistfully to the gathered girls, and settled in for the last long stretch across Ohio. It was a rumpled, hungry, and poorly rested collection of officers who descended to the Cincinnati platform at five-thirty the next morning.[18]

Burnside found that one of Horatio Wright's final acts as commander of the department, undertaken while the Burnside administration still rattled across Pennsylvania, had been to denominate Indiana a separate district and assign Colonel Carrington to its command. In light of Stanton's warning, that news could not have been comforting, but Burnside had no opportunity for the desired pilgrimage to Indianapolis any time soon: the incursion into Kentucky that Wright had predicted appeared to have begun.[19]

The day Burnside's train pulled out of Baltimore, a detachment of John Morgan's cavalry under Colonel R. S. Cluke captured Mount Sterling, forty miles east of Lexington. Cluke took three hundred prisoners. The next day General John Pegram led fifteen hundred Southern cavalrymen against the garrison at Danville, forty miles southwest of Lexington; the Union defenders there fell back beyond the Kentucky River March 24. That same day the commander of the eastern district of Kentucky learned of a Confederate column moving against his headquarters at Louisa, on the West Virginia border. To Quincy Gillmore, commanding at Lexington, it seemed like nothing less than the invasion he, too, had long foreseen.[20]

Back in Cincinnati, Burnside and Wright were not so sure. Certainly it was nothing to ignore, but with what Burnside knew of Confederate dispositions, the estimates of enemy numbers were incredible. General Gillmore forwarded reports that credited Pegram with seven thousand men, while a brigadier at Lebanon guessed that twelve thousand Confederates had captured Danville, with General John C. Breckinridge at their head. Burnside delayed assuming command of the department for a day, but he held close to headquarters, telegraphing Halleck to know whether the last division of the Ninth Corps could not be sent out from Newport News; the Army of the Potomac could better afford to detach a division than this enormous department, he argued.[21]

Halleck's first telegram to Burnside as commander of the department came the next day, regretting an inability to send any more troops and directing him to concentrate his available forces in central Kentucky to repel the enemy. By that same evening, however, General Gillmore had changed his tune in a manner that boded well for Union forces. Only forty-eight hours after advising Cincinnati of a full-fledged invasion spearheaded by seven thousand men, he spoke of information corroborating his subsequent suspicion that the enemy in his front numbered fewer than thirty-five hundred. Another eight hundred approached Lexington from the east, he said, but he reserved a sufficient cavalry force to monitor that movement. Fifteen hundred more Confederates threatened Louisa, but these more realistic calculations defused the panic in Kentucky by nightfall of March 25.[22]

As soon as the first of his Ninth Corps began coming in, Burnside sent troops to Louisville; it had been from that direction that the most exaggerated reports of Confederate strength had come, and from Louisville the reinforcements could operate against Pegram's left flank. Burnside ordered Jeremiah Boyle, the general commanding at Louisville, to gather an offensive force at Lebanon for a cooperative movement with Gillmore. The afternoon of March 27 he telegraphed Gillmore to attack Pegram with his main body and send detachments against Cluke and Humphrey Marshall, who led the Southern troops before Louisa.[23]

The overrated invasion dissolved almost instantly. Even before Burnside's order for a general attack, Marshall's little army disappeared from Louisa. Julius White, in charge of the eastern district, sent a few hundred men after Marshall, but White's infantrymen could not keep up with their mounted adversaries. Cluke similarly withdrew before loyal Kentucky cavalry, and on March 28 General Gillmore went to the front to drive Pegram away. Still overestimating the size of Pegram's brigade—just as Pegram overestimated Gillmore's force—he chased the Confederates nearly fifty miles. Pegram drew most of his command up on Dutton's Hill, north of Somerset, on March 30, but after several hours of hammering, Gillmore cracked his line with an infantry assault. Two regiments from Louisiana and Tennessee found themselves cut off and had to scatter downriver to avoid the flanking column Boyle had sent from Louisville. The remainder of Pegram's horsemen rendezvoused on the outskirts of Somerset, forming another line nearer the Cumberland River. Gillmore decided not to attack this position, and during the night the fewer than one thousand remaining Confederate cavalrymen crossed to the southern bank of the river with 537 beef cattle—the real object of their raid. Some of Pegram's troops ferried themselves across at a settlement that would come to be called Burnside.[24] For the present, Kentucky was safe.

With the emergency resolved, Burnside had time to digest a letter Halleck supplied, outlining some general instructions for his new assignment. Like so many of Halleck's communications, this one maundered in ambiguity and self-contradiction: he suggested that Burnside could invade East Tennessee, or occupy the mountain gaps between Tennessee and Kentucky to deny Confederate access, or concentrate his troops in central Kentucky to thwart any future enemy forays there. Then he added that none of these courses was practical alone and said Burnside perhaps ought to gather an army near Lexington and send cavalry raiding into East Tennessee; also, he would have to guard the railroad from Louisville very closely, lest Rosecrans's Tennessee army go hungry after it ranged beyond the navigable portion of the Cumberland. Halleck plagiarized his ideas mostly from Wright's letter of March 15, but he proposed them in a sequence that would allow him to blame Burnside's discretion if things went wrong: yet, whichever option Burnside followed, Halleck could always point to the other suggestions he had made.[25]

An enclosure accompanying Halleck's general instructions became nearly as important as the instructions themselves. It consisted of a copy of a letter Halleck had written to Rosecrans, which he told Burnside to use as a guide to Halleck's attitude about the relation of the military with the civilian population. Halleck sent it in reference to Burnside's "treatment of the inhabitants of Kentucky," but he said Burnside's own judgment should prevail, as usual. Probably Burnside saw no reason to treat the residents of Kentucky any differently from those of Ohio or Indiana: all three states still held to the Union, all had disloyal elements, and all three had federal garrisons. Whatever applied to the citizens of Kentucky ought logically to have applied to all three.[26]

Halleck's letter to Rosecrans began with an approval of "more rigid treatment of all disloyal persons," and he defined loyal, neutral, and "avowedly hostile" citizens, outlining the measures the military should follow with each. For the manifestly hostile, Halleck proposed confinement or expulsion, and he felt the rules of war applied to any association such people had with the enemy—in other words, let them stretch hemp. Disloyal people had already cost the government much, he added, "and it is time that the laws of war should be more rigorously enforced against them. A broad line of distinction must be drawn between friends and enemies, between the loyal and the disloyal." The letter to Rosecrans concluded with that perennial caveat designed to protect Henry W. Halleck: as to the appropriate action in individual cases, Rosecrans would have to decide for himself.[27]

For the moment Burnside chose the third option of Halleck's "general instructions." He shuttled the first and second divisions of the Ninth Corps across the Ohio and scattered most of them in a wide arc around Lexington. He also organized Gillmore's troops into a single division, which he tentatively styled the fourth division of the Ninth Army Corps, as though to remind the War Department that Getty's detached division still belonged to him.[28]

With the enemy driven to the fringes of his department, Burnside thought it safe to leave Cincinnati for an introductory tour of some of the territory for which he was responsible. He remained in the city only long enough to wave appreciatively to some of his old troops, who cheered lustily as they passed his lodgings at the Burnet House.[29] That evening he departed with Robert, one orderly, and five staff officers on an inspection of northern Kentucky, one of the most vulnerable portions of his bailiwick. Since Burnside's duties included the protection of the railroads, the director of the Kentucky Central put his private car at the commander's disposal for the journey: the staff officers leaned comfortably into the plush upholstery, availed themselves of a well-stocked pantry, cooled their drinks with ice from the refrigerator, and hardly noticed the slow, ten-hour ride to Louisville.

Breakfast at the Galt House provided a pleasant improvement over the miserable fare served at the Burnet House. Burnside spent most of the day closeted with General Boyle, the native Kentuckian in charge of his state's western district. Boyle was a lawyer, not a professional soldier, but because of his familiarity with the state (and particularly with his district) Burnside hoped to keep him. The same seems not to have been true of General Gillmore, in the central district; Burnside arrived at Gillmore's Lexington headquarters the afternoon of April 2, after a glimpse of the defenses of Frankfort.

Native bourbon flowed freely in Lexington. The hotel keeper at the Phoenix House was a boisterous Unionist of the back-slapping persuasion, and he took an instant liking to Burnside. So did the general population; crowds followed him when he appeared on the streets. Neither Burnside nor any of his staff were teetotalers, but they quickly learned that a Kentuckian expected a man to comply when he was invited to drink, and they had to work hard to stay sober. To cap this difficulty, their hosts threw a punch party that evening: some of the headquarters heads were probably still throbbing early the next afternoon, when Burnside's special car started back to Cincinnati.[30]

The impressions Burnside gathered on this tour influenced his actions over the next few days. When he arrived back at the Burnet House, he found a wire from Halleck demanding that he relieve Boyle and send him directly to the secretary of war. Burnside objected immediately, so the War Department explained that Boyle had been bullying the ordnance officer at Louisville, who had reported the possibility of graft on Boyle's staff. Burnside countered that the officious ordnance officer had delayed the deployment of a cavalry regiment when Boyle needed to move against Pegram and had used some insubordinate language when responding to Boyle's requests. He had nothing against the lieutenant in question, Burnside said, but he deemed his independence of spirit a result of his official independence from department authority, for he reported only to the Washington bureau. The assistant secretary of war agreed to satisfy that deficiency, and in the end Boyle retained his command, but the correspondence cast him as a rather choleric individual.[31]

Henry Carrington also remained in command at Indianapolis, despite the administration's fears about his "imprudence." Burnside explained to the secretary of war that Wright had appointed Carrington, but the commander offered to remove him if the secretary wished. Stanton declined the opportunity, unless Burnside found it necessary.[32]

Burnside did want to change commanders in the District of Central Kentucky. There is no indication that he undervalued Quincy Gillmore's competence—Gillmore had been the only cadet ahead of Parke in the class of 1849—but his date of rank created an inconvenience: Orlando Willcox, whose division occupied the central district, outranked Gillmore by almost nine months. It would have been awkward to ask Willcox to serve under his junior, and equally awkward to ask Gillmore to become a subordinate in the district he once commanded, so Willcox's first orders put him in Gillmore's office.[33]

Early April was filled with fresh assignments and requests for the services of officers who were awaiting orders. Burnside secured Jacob

Cox for the army post at Columbus, and gave the District of Ohio to his West Point classmate John Mason. But Mason was a career soldier more suited to a military environment, while Cox had excellent political sense: barely a week later these two traded jobs. For the District of Illinois Burnside appointed General Jacob Ammen, who had graduated from the military academy when Burnside was eight years old. George Hartsuff, a young major general who had led a brigade under Burnside at South Mountain, wrapped up some court-martial duty to report for unspecified work in the Department of the Ohio. By April 11 Burnside formally announced his entire staff, lacking only the son of General Sumner, who was detained in New York by that old warrior's recent death.[34]

Some of the men Burnside named to his staff were General Wright's, whom he continued in positions where they had proven useful. Most of his staff from the old days had also joined him by now, including Lewis Richmond, Dr. Church, Charles Loring, and seven of his former aides-de-camp. The ever-present Daniel Larned had finally attained some rank; as a captain and assistant adjutant general he was technically Colonel Richmond's auxiliary, but he dealt directly with the general and so remained a private secretary.

Burnside promoted one former aide, Captain James Madison Cutts, Jr., to judge advocate of the department. Cutts had been with him in Maryland and at Fredericksburg, where he carried the first of Franklin's afternoon orders to attack with his entire force. A native of Washington City, Cutts was a great-nephew of Dolly Madison and a brother-in-law to the late Senator Stephen Douglas. He had practiced law in prewar St. Louis with a young Kentuckian named Basil Duke, who rode now with John Hunt Morgan. Captain Cutts was a bright prospect, but he suffered from a sharp temper and a touch of voyeurism. The afternoon before he was appointed judge advocate, someone caught him looking through the keyhole at the couple lodging next to him at the Burnet House; just before midnight of the same day, when the husband went downstairs, Cutts dragged a suitcase over to the door between their rooms and climbed on top of it to peek over the transom. The lady was undressing for bed; she saw Cutts, recognized him, and filed a complaint about the intrusion.[35]

As much as such an incident distressed Ambrose Burnside, the antics of Captain Cutts meant nothing alongside other problems coming to light in this new department. Not only were there the military difficulties of securing Kentucky against guerrilla forces, and the logistical impossibilities of an invasion of East Tennessee (toward which he sensed steady pressure), but it seemed the states north of the river harbored myriad enemies. To a degree this was literally true: to Burnside's astonishment he discovered that many Confederate prisoners enjoyed the freedom of communities where they were held, fettered only by their own promises not to escape, and he had to issue an order abolishing that practice. Yet Burnside apprehended an even greater threat from the civilian population. The draft law had certainly infuriated many citizens, and Democratic newspapers deleted few adjectives in their denunciation of the government's overweening usurpation of authority. This had led to the sacking of some newspaper offices—in at least one instance by a mob of soldiers—which only increased the invective of the surviving opposition. Colonel Carrington constantly alluded to the subject of what would come to be called a fifth column, and the accounts he sent from Indianapolis seemed to confirm his predictions. As though to underscore the "Copperhead" threat, local elections on April 7 resulted in big victories for the Democrats in southwestern Ohio.[36]

The situation seemed to call for swift action. In North Carolina, when he encountered similar problems, Burnside issued an order for the arrest of anyone who so much as "uttered one word against the Government of the United States." It was not an uncommon tactic during civil strife; Maryland had been saved for the Union with the help of such widespread, unconstitutional arrests. President Lincoln himself had issued a proclamation (only two days after his most famous one) subjecting all disloyal persons, their aiders and abettors, anywhere within the United States, to martial law. That was tough language, for it provided the death penalty for a wide range of crimes. This turned out to be unconstitutional as well, but that decision lay some years away. Lincoln's edict suspended habeas corpus for persons so arrested, and proclaimed that its strictures would remain in effect "during the existing insurrection." Burnside appears to have used Lincoln's own document, backed as it was by Halleck's firm letter to Rosecrans (and Halleck's instructions that this should be Burnside's guide), to compose General Order Number 38: anyone within his department found guilty of committing "acts for the benefit of the enemies of our country" would be subject to execution. This covered correspondence by secret mail, trying to pass through the lines to join the enemy, or harboring escaped prisoners. Those who declared sympathy with the Confederacy, it added, would either be tried as above or banished to the Southern lines. Now reaching beyond his earlier attitude as a War Democrat, Burnside assured Republicans at a Hamilton, Ohio, rally that he had the authority to decide what constituted disloyalty and to inflict the appropriate punishment. Milo Hascall, the general with whom Burnside had finally superseded Colonel Carrington, went a step further: criticism of the administration, he warned, would be considered tantamount to treason.[37]

Burnside hoped to discourage Southern sympathizers with the fear of brute force rather than with the use of it—as evidenced by his removal of Carrington. The colonel had become dangerously excited about his Copperhead theory, but Burnside tried to calm him, telegraphing, "There is no cause for alarm—the military power used prudently and quietly will settle it all." He finally replaced Carrington because he would not abandon his frantic appeals; like Stanton, Burnside became concerned over the colonel's "imprudence," fearing perhaps that he might answer a mob with a massacre.[38]

It was one thing to arrest dissidents in a conquered province and confine them indefinitely; it was quite another to try residents of a loyal state before military tribunals and set the penalty of death on the expression of a phrase or the passage of a letter. Still, Order Number 38 might have been the quiet solution Burnside envisioned had it not been for the provocation of one vocal opponent.

Initially Burnside's order met with far-reaching support. Rosecrans's chief of staff told a civilian friend he would enforce the order on Copperhead students at home; a league of loyal Kentuckians cordially approved it "in all its parts and parcels." But within days the provost marshals were inundated with the most unlikely prisoners. They arrested a man named Taylor on the charge of hiding Colonel George Hodge, of the Confederate army. In a day or two it became apparent that he had simply offered a home to Mrs. Hodge, his in-law, who had no knowledge of her husband's whereabouts: Abraham Lincoln did as much for his own wife's Confederate kin a few months later. A young subaltern in the 19th U.S. Infantry roused an immense amount of sympathy when his name appeared at the bottom of a letter to a Confederate officer. He and the woman who tried to carry the letter south both landed in jail, but his brother, his mother, and several prominent citizens peppered Burnside with testimonials to the boy's loyalty. He had been in the service since the very beginning of the war, and had stood beside his father when the old man was killed at Carnifex Ferry. The Confederate correspondent was merely an old schoolmate, and the letter smelled of nothing more than nostalgic regrets at the course of events. Jennie Moon, the girl who had the envelope in her pocket, made the round trip through the lines frequently, carrying such homely messages for relatives and friends.[39] According to the letter of Order Number 38, such people should be shot or hanged, without exception.

The embarrassment of imprisoning innocents like Mr. Taylor, Jennie Moon, and Lieutenant Lowe was an expected feature of such wholesale arrests, and every general who ordered them learned to put up with it. But this was not the only adverse effect of the new decree. Headquarters desks were quickly cluttered with oaths, paroles, appeals, testimonials, and offers of evidence, seriously impeding administration of the department. The dictatorial overtones of the order further infuriated the antiwar element as well and offended many War Democrats, almost worsening the situation it was meant to correct. Presumably not all Republicans favored the stern new policy, either: in the days after Lincoln's own firm announcement in the fall of 1862, one of his loyal supporters blamed the resulting arbitrary arrests for the Republican defeats in the New York elections that season. Worst of all the problems associated with it, any hesitation to prosecute the brutal promise of Burnside's order would impart an even greater impression of weakness than if it had never been issued: North Carolina Confederates could readily envision the shadow of the gibbet and might be intimidated by it; nominally loyal Midwesterners could not imagine such a thing, and the threat would mean nothing unless carried out. Fervent Unionists nevertheless expected rigorous enforcement. One man who signed himself "Union Defender" expressed unmitigated outrage that Burnside had released the wife of one Confederate officer. The woman, he fumed, had the gall to ride the streets of Covington with her mother, in an open carriage, laughing like the she-devil the anonymous informant thought she was.[40]

Most of the early attempts to enforce the order fizzled. A Confederate major from Louisville, captured before the publication of Order Number 38, was the first to escape. Burnside wanted to try him as a spy; the major's father, editor of the proadministration *Louisville Journal*, made a plea to Lincoln that eventually led to the officer's exchange.[41] Another Kentuckian, Thomas M. Campbell, was apprehended under compromising circumstances near his home, between Cynthiana and Paris. A military court convicted him of espionage and sentenced him to hang at Johnson's Island on May 1. Campbell's sister and his brother, himself a Union officer, visited Burnside and moved him to the verge of tears with their tale of divided family loyalties, so Burnside decided to do what he could. There seemed to be no question of the condemned man's guilt, but Burnside allowed him a stay of one week, later extended to a month, in which to unburden his soul and earn some sort of clemency. Campbell finally caved in, saving his own neck by implicating numerous other Kentuckians in a long and not very admirable affidavit, whereupon President Lincoln ordered Burnside to postpone the execution until further notice. Further notice never came: Campbell cheated the gallows, though he remained imprisoned at Johnson's Island until the last six weeks of the war.[42]

Those who had no influential friends or relatives did not always fare so well. Two convicted spies went before a firing squad just one month after Order Number 38 was published, and the event cast a pall over Burnside's entire day. Despite his gloom, he would not retreat from his firm policy: he was prepared to hang several men on the last Friday of May, but with what seemed a twinge of regret at the injustice of selective executions, he stayed the sentences of all of them when Lincoln reprieved Campbell.[43]

Democratic editors bent Burnside's resolve to their own advantage even before the first victims went to their deaths. The general may have had such journalists and politicians in mind when he included "declaring sympathy for the enemy" within the punishable offenses of his order, for Halleck had just warned him to monitor the conduct of Senator Lazarus Powell, the Democratic candidate for governor of Kentucky. Powell had reportedly advised secession before, and in fact Confederate operatives looked upon him as a valuable friend.[44]

It was not Powell who ultimately sabotaged Order Number 38, but an ex-congressman from Dayton, Ohio. Clement Laird Vallandigham, an old-school Democrat who wanted to be governor of his state, had become the principal Ohio spokesman for the opponents of Lincoln's war measures. Adamant against coercion, arbitrary arrests, emancipation, and the draft, he had spent most of the past two years railing against the government. Order Number 38 impelled him to a frenzy of fresh denunciation, fueled equally by righteous indignation and his desire to challenge the order personally. Recognizing that Burnside had worked himself into a corner, he hoped the general would either back down or strike the blow that could only enhance Vallandigham's notoriety.

As at Fredericksburg, Burnside was reduced to two unenviable choices; he characteristically opted for the offensive, asking Stanton if he might not exercise greater authority. "I shall try to do nothing indiscreet," he said. His provost marshal learned that Vallandigham planned to speak against the war at Mount Vernon on May 1, so when the swarthy orator stood on the platform that Friday he faced a huge crowd that included two Ohio army officers in citizen's dress. While Vallandigham spoke, they scribbled. In the course of his two-hour-long screed Vallandigham specifically repudiated Order Number 38 and urged the citizens of Ohio to resist—though only at the ballot box. He had even harsher words for General Hascall. On the evidence of the two officers' reports, Burnside arranged Vallandigham's arrest. A friendly Dayton resident telegraphed Cincinnati that the would-be candidate was at his First Street home the evening of May 4, and Burnside sent Captain Charles Hutton and a company of soldiers by special train. Hutton arrived very early May 5, forced Vallandigham's front door when the owner refused to open it, and announced his arrest. Hutton mispronounced the Dutch name, whereupon his prisoner said his name was not Vallan*dig*ham.

"I don't care how you pronounce it," Hutton replied, "that's the way you spell it—and you are my man." Within hours, the former U.S. representative relaxed in a cell at Kemper Barracks, near Cincinnati.[45]

Burnside obviously regarded the political situation north of the Ohio as a critical one, but this attempt to suppress dissension merely stiffened the opposition. Democrat newspapers flew into a twenty-four-point rage. No sooner did word of Vallandigham's arrest reach the streets than Dayton erupted in a full-fledged riot. A mob set fire to the office of the *Dayton Journal*, the local Republican organ, and Burnside sent a hundred men to quell the disturbance. By the time the soldiers arrived, the Phillips House was on fire, with women and children streaming from its doors. Captain Hutton led another guard detail to the office of the *Dayton Empire*, which had dared to publish a headline reading "Will free men submit? The hour for action has arrived." Hutton arrested the editor, John Logan, and his men found two hundred muskets and a swivel cannon in the printshop. This ominous discovery seemed to confirm the worst fears about Copperheads. These were too many weapons for a few printer's devils to use in defense of their shop; there must have been an uprising in the works. This evidence persuaded Burnside more than ever of the wisdom of his course, and without the least delay he brought Vallandigham before a military court.[46]

Even in his determination to crush the seditious element, Burnside had not lost his innate sense of justice. He might reach into the ranks of legitimate dissidents in his quest for traitors, or stretch the jurisdiction of military tribunals, but in all other respects he insisted upon fair play. Unlike others in his government, he refused to respond to anonymous complaints against individuals or to act upon any charge of disloyalty that failed to cite specific offenses and list witnesses. Nor did he resort to long pretrial confinements in miserable dungeons, as did some Washington officials: Clement Vallandigham's trial began the day after his arrival in Cincinnati, during which Burnside moved him to a comfortable but well-guarded room at the Burnet House. As far as Burnside was concerned, the accused was innocent, unless and until the military panel found otherwise. An administration supporter by the name of David Levin tried to send Vallandigham a pocket testament with the snide inscription, "Prepare to meet thy Maker"; Burnside intercepted it and responded to Levin with as much contempt as others felt for Vallandigham, reminding him that he was prejudging an untried prisoner and striking at a defenseless foe. He closed the letter with which he returned the testament in terms of bitter rebuke: "You—a worm of the earth, have dared to use the word of Almighty God as a means of expressing a personal hate; you have attempted with sacrilegious hands to use that blessed volume, whose every page breathes forgiveness, and love, to molest what you hoped were the last hours of a dying man."[47]

The military commission had no authority to determine whether Vallandigham had committed treason or sedition. Its sole purpose was to judge whether he had violated Order Number 38, and with what may or may not have been creative recollections of the context of his various statements, the witnesses were able to convince the officers that he had. Vallandigham protested (and the Supreme Court later agreed) that the military had no jurisdiction. The judge advocate, the prurient

Captain Cutts, later demonstrated regard for even the rights of those who rose in arms against the country, but he admitted he had no authority to decide the question of jurisdiction. On the second afternoon of the trial, therefore, the court found the accused guilty and sentenced him to confinement for the duration.[48]

An effort to have Vallandigham released on a writ of habeas corpus failed, but before Burnside could send him to the chosen prison—Fort Warren, in Boston harbor—President Lincoln decided it would be better to banish him into the Confederacy. It was a brilliant ploy, for while it removed Vallandigham from the area where he might do much harm, it also denied him the degree of martyrdom Fort Warren might have afforded; at the same time, it effectively associated the dissident's cause with that of the enemy. Burnside objected, however, with a logical argument of his own: the court had rejected the alternative of expulsion for some reason known only to its members, and presidential interference might be viewed either as tampering with a legitimate court or as recognition that the court was not legal. Lincoln nevertheless insisted upon the political expedient of exile. Burnside accordingly transferred the prisoner to Rosecrans's army, at Murfreesborough, Tennessee. On the morning of May 25, Mr. Vallandigham stood on the Shelbyville Turnpike and presented himself to an Alabama cavalry officer.[49]

The exile eventually made his roundabout way to Canada. As he had hoped, his party nominated him for governor in absentia, largely through sympathy over his arrest, but in the November elections he lost to John Brough by a landslide. While Burnside's critics have long blamed him for Vallandigham's nomination, suggesting the arrest backfired, none have observed how this course of events led many Ohioans to identify the Democrats with Copperhead subversion. Had the party fielded a less notorious antiwar advocate in 1863, the result might have been an uncooperative administration at Columbus; as it was, fewer Ohio counties went Democratic that fall than in any other state election during the war. Other factors were certainly involved—Gettysburg and Vicksburg, to name two—but Burnside's apparently injudicious policy actually helped put a Union governor in power at a critical crossroad. And while Burnside's arrest of an out-of-office politician and a newspaper editor is usually cited as further evidence of his incompetence, Edwin Stanton's efficiency is seldom questioned despite his orders for similar arrests in 1862 and his readiness to make them again in 1864. As in most other instances, Burnside's actions are habitually perceived in the worst light possible.[50]

Halleck had written Burnside a letter on May 20, explaining that his friends had predicted the Vallandigham case would do more harm to the political situation than good and adding that he would have interfered as little as possible in the civil affairs of loyal states (thus modifying his March epistle to Rosecrans). Burnside was already cognizant of the dangers of abusing military force: he had warned General Mason against it, more than a week before, while authorizing him to investigate a cabal of Columbus businessmen reportedly supplying the Confederacy. Some of his subordinates were more zealous, though, and late in May General Hascall delivered an Indiana editor to him along with a copy of one of his newspapers, which Hascall said violated Order Number 38. Prominent Indiana and Illinois politicians clamored for Hascall's removal, and in the course of discussion with them Burnside learned that none of Lincoln's cabinet had approved of his famous order or its enforcement. He wrote the president on the subject, insisting that any change in policy ought to be toward even stricter enforcement, but he offered once more to step aside if his administration of the department seemed imprudent to Lincoln. Lincoln replied rather curtly that he would tell Burnside when he wanted to replace him, but he informed him the cabinet supported Burnside's actions once they had been taken, only doubting their necessity. The response must have worked the desired effect, at least for the moment: that was the last heard of the Indiana editor, whom Burnside seems to have released.[51]

In the midst of the Vallandigham imbroglio, ghosts from the past winter arose to haunt Burnside. Late in March General Franklin made some supplementary remarks to the Committee on the Conduct of the War, defensively implying the defeat at Fredericksburg had been entirely Burnside's fault, charging for the first time that his battle order had transformed Franklin's grand assault into a virtual reconnaissance. The testimony made its way to Cincinnati in newspaper form as early as April 5, moving Captain Larned to remark, "Franklin begins to show his teeth." Burnside fretted over Franklin's self-serving misconstruction, even muttering about an uncharacteristic public response. Larned advised against a newspaper controversy. "I shall not get into a controversy," Burnside said, "but if it is necessary I will write one letter that will strip the hide off that man in about a minute." A few days later, the headquarters staff gasped to see a copy of Order Number 8 reprinted in the *New York Herald*. Since Lincoln had not approved it, the order had never been published, and no one beyond the president, the general, and a few staff members were supposed to know anything about it. Only two copies had been drawn, one of which Burnside put in his private papers, in Providence. Colonel Richmond had apparently forgotten the other at the Falmouth headquarters, where it must have fallen into Hooker's hands.[52]

A few days after the report of the joint committee made the papers, Franklin published his reply. So soon did it follow that he must have had most of the manuscript prepared beforehand. This thirty-two-page pamphlet served as the foundation for the argument that a stubborn and incompetent Burnside had sent the Army of the Potomac to needless slaughter. Burnside ignored most of it when he finally read it, expecting plenty of time for such debate after the war ended, but there was one passage he was not allowed to neglect: the misstatement that Burnside had told Franklin he called on Lincoln to remove him, Halleck, and Stanton because they had all lost the confidence of the country. Halleck asked Burnside about it on May 9. Burnside did not obtain a copy of Franklin's *Reply* until May 12, but he promised to answer it "briefly" as soon as time allowed. Halleck then pursued the matter with Franklin, who said Burnside had made the claim to him in the presence of General Smith and perhaps others. The obliging Smith and Bully Brooks sent corroborating letters. In 1866 Franklin wrote Halleck on the same subject, and Halleck remarked that Burnside had never made the answer promised in May of 1863; they had never discussed it again. Franklin pronounced Burnside crazy, and Halleck agreed that his memory was at least "unreliable."[53]

Burnside did begin the response to Halleck's inquiry. On May 24 he sat down with a few sheets of department stationery and sought to clarify the events around Franklin's accusation. He read Franklin's pamphlet for the first time just before putting his pen to the paper. "General Burnside" (Franklin had written) made a "request to the President to remove the Secretary of War and the General-in-Chief" from their positions. That was not quite the way it had gone, as Burnside proceeded to explain. He had written Lincoln in his January 1 letter that he considered it every official's duty to step out of the way whenever he had lost public confidence, and later he mentioned his personal opinion that both Stanton and Halleck had lost that confidence. The only person he recommended removing, however, was himself. When he related the incident to Franklin and the others later, they apparently missed the fine distinction, which was important by May because Franklin's tale threatened to create a new wave of doubt about Stanton and Halleck. Burnside's version is confirmed by a letter to the president dated January 5, in one copy of which he referred both to the January 1 letter and his conversation "in your presence" with "the gentlemen of whom we were speaking." The readiness of Franklin, Smith, and Brooks to give the story the damaging interpretation they did may have been partially influenced by the fact that each of them had been marked for the axe in Order Number 8.[54]

Save for one brief personal defense early in 1866—the postwar exposé for which he was willing to wait—this was the only rebuttal Burnside ever made to any of Franklin's accusations. Accelerating affairs in the Department of the Ohio forced him to lay the incomplete letter to Halleck aside; he never returned to it, partly because of his hesitance to create discord. As he explained to a friend back East, he had no desire to dredge up unpleasant, complicated topics for the mere assessment of blame. At a public dinner shortly after First Bull Run, he had made comments that inadvertently implied he had foreseen the disaster there and had warned McDowell about it, and he still felt miserable about it: those remarks, he wrote, were "one of the most ungrateful, sinful acts of my life" and terribly unfair to McDowell. Resurrection of the story of Fredericksburg, he feared, would lead to similar unintended injuries.[55]

For all the turmoil, every event in the Department of the Ohio did not turn unpleasant; Burnside even had leisure for personal business. Once during his stay in Cincinnati, the general made a visit to Liberty. His sister Ellen still lived in the family homestead there, and Benjamin returned home often. The "other" family, those British Burnsides, also required his attention again. Ambrose Burnside, nephew of the Durham "Ant Eleasabeth," sent him a baptismal certificate with his own name on it but a birthdate of May 22, 1779; he wanted to know if it belonged to the honored general. According to an accompanying letter from Edward "Burnsides," the Ambrose of the certificate had joined the British navy in the early part of the century, as had his son—also named

Ambrose—and neither had ever been heard from again. There had to be some familial connection: Ambrose was not so common a Christian name, and these people lived only a few miles from the Scottish border. Despite that, and the coincidence that the certificate indicated a birth-date only one day short of Burnside's own birthday, the general seems to have cherished no genealogical proclivities. With the amused endorsement that he was not eighty-four years old, he directed his secretary to simply return the document to its English owners.[56]

About the time of the Vallandigham trial, Burnside was gratified to learn that the fund begun for General Reno's family had grown to eleven thousand dollars. A week later he had a visit from a girl claiming to be Reno's own niece. There was something out of the ordinary about Miss Ella Reno, though: for the past year and a half she had been serving in the Union army. For five months she had ridden with the 5th Kentucky Cavalry, until they found her out; since then she had passed herself off for an infantryman of the 8th Michigan—a regiment that went up South Mountain with Willcox the day Reno died. This marked the fourth time, altogether, the young lady had been discovered masquerading as a man; for the present she condescended to wear feminine attire, but there was no indication this would be anything more than a brief interlude for the wiry imposter.[57]

The most delightful part of Miss Reno's visit for General Burnside was his ability to provide a hostess: Mrs. Burnside had arrived only a few days before. She and Mrs. Goodrich, the commissary's wife, made the long journey from the coast in hopes they could settle in for a few months.[58] Their sojourn would not be so long.

II

In the same letter in which he had criticized the Vallandigham arrest, General Halleck mentioned that Stanton wanted Burnside to take the field with his troops, reminding Burnside this was a "matter upon which I wrote you some time ago." That reminder appears to have been meant more for the record than for Burnside, for the only such suggestion Halleck had made consisted of one of the alternatives of his nebulous general instructions of March 23. Halleck became especially anxious for such a movement now, though, for intelligence said Joe Johnston was stripping Braxton Bragg's Tennessee army of troops for the relief of the Vicksburg garrison.[1]

Burnside had already begun planning the field operations. For some time he had been advancing troops toward the Cumberland, alarming his Confederate counterpart in East Tennessee: that man was none other than General Dabney H. Maury, the West Point comrade whose wedding Burnside had found so delightful. As early as May 4 Maury alerted the commander in southwest Virginia that Burnside seemed to be preparing for an invasion of East Tennessee. On May 15 Burnside sent Colonel Loring to confer with Rosecrans about a combined operation against Bragg and Maury, and the next day he asked Willcox to have one of his brigadiers report on the feasibility of taking and holding Cumberland Gap; three days later Burnside prodded Halleck again for Getty's division, which the general-in-chief had once promised to transfer back to him. Halleck declined, and after making a sarcastic remark about doing some damage to the enemy now or never, he added that he must withhold not only Getty's division but any reinforcements at all.[2]

The two divisions of the Ninth Corps and the troops Burnside had inherited from Wright were spread all over the department by May. Returns for the end of April showed nearly 58,000 men on the rolls. Fewer than 40,000 were present, and only 31,000 available for duty: of these, more than 5,000 lay fragmented over Ohio, Indiana, and Illinois, guarding prisoners in four major camps and doing provost duty. The rest were strewn the breadth of Kentucky, fanned out in a 400-mile arc from Henderson, near the mouth of the Wabash, to Louisa, on the Big Sandy. At least a dozen major paths offered the Confederates access into Kentucky's underbelly, and Burnside had to guard them all in addition to protecting his supply routes, all of which lay vulnerable to sabotage by disloyal Kentuckians. To concentrate his forces and still counter the perpetual threat of incursions required careful planning and synchronization.[3]

In order to facilitate concerted movements, Burnside organized his forces into a compact field army. Late in April he asked Halleck for permission to group the old department troops into a formal corps, but Halleck hinted it might be done in reward for "some important victory," otherwise not. Yet Stanton gave his blessing the very next day. Burnside took all the troops that had been in Kentucky when he arrived (save those he styled the fourth division, Ninth Corps) and consolidated them into the new Twenty-third Corps. This was the command he had wanted for George Hartsuff, and the burly young major general took charge of the corps despite recurring trouble from his South Mountain wound. Colonel Loring stopped at Louisville, on his way back to Cincinnati, to familiarize Hartsuff and General Boyle with the arrangements he and Rosecrans had made for the movement.[4]

In Lexington, Willcox worked frantically to ready his troops for the field. He remained awake all night Friday, May 22, and pressed every blacksmith shop in town into service to shoe the horses of the 2nd Tennessee Cavalry. At three o'clock Saturday morning he dispatched a long telegram to Burnside, explaining the difficulties of operating on the Cumberland River where Burnside planned to advance. So bad were the roads between Stanford and Somerset that supply wagons could carry only half-loads on good days and quarter-loads in bad weather. The greatest problem was forage, though it was nearly as hard to keep the men in rations. Samuel Carter, the brigadier in charge of the nominal fourth division, had had to call for double rations of onions and potatoes at Somerset to cure an outbreak of scurvy. A lack of wagons only worsened the supply problem: Willcox had only 293 to serve the 20,000 men in central Kentucky for whom he was responsible. "What," he wanted to know, "would Scott or Taylor have thought of that in Mexico?"[5]

After another futile appeal for Getty's promised division, Burnside put his army in position. From his desk in Cincinnati he ordered Willcox to push one division southwest to Columbia and another to Crab Orchard, to support Carter. Willcox learned of a Confederate division lurking in extreme southeastern Kentucky, which caused him some anxiety for his left, but his right flank was secure: Hartsuff was going to wheel a couple of regiments and a battery into Tennessee, where they would link with Rosecrans's left.

Burnside boarded a steamboat for Louisville May 25. He met with Hartsuff and Boyle, and with Andrew Johnson, military governor of Tennessee, who had shared Burnside's sartorial beginnings. Himself a native of East Tennessee, Johnson yearned to establish a Union presence in that loyal fastness. Burnside assured him of his own inclination to invade the mountainous region, but Halleck's refusal to send him Getty's division prevented him from stretching his lines that far.

Burnside did expect to cross into Tennessee without Getty, but only

west of the Cumberland Mountains. If he and Rosecrans joined forces
down there, he intended to put himself under Rosecrans, for though he
outranked him it would be Rosecrans's department: he made that clear,
to avoid any troublesome arguments, for he would have had a right to
claim the overall command.[6]

The prospect of an offensive always seemed to cheer Burnside, and
with his official obligations met, he and Mrs. Burnside attended a party.
Returning to Cincinnati, the general announced to Rosecrans that he
could begin their combined surge toward McMinnville and Chattanooga. Rosecrans said he planned to move within four days; he offered
to lend Burnside pack mules, to negotiate the bad roads below Somerset. On the last day of May Burnside had four divisions sitting along
the right bank of the Cumberland, ready to sweep closed the doors of
invasion and bend back the right flank of his old battery commander,
Bragg. Shortly after midnight, June 2, Rosecrans telegraphed that he
had begun his movement and wanted Burnside to advance Hartsuff's
wing to Carthage, Tennessee. The next day, just as Burnside prepared
to leave for the front, Halleck interrupted him with a telegram bordering on neurotic: only two weeks earlier, Halleck had interpreted
the reinforcement of Johnston's army as a good opportunity to strike
Bragg's weakened Army of Tennessee; now he saw it in terms of the
danger it held for Grant, and he wanted to know how many men Burnside could send him at Vicksburg. Burnside explained Rosecrans's reliance on his flank movement into Tennessee, adding that Rosecrans
was already under way and expected Burnside to abide by their plans;
if he were to renege on Rosecrans, he might be able to afford Grant
eight or ten thousand men. Despite the ill omen of Halleck's inquiry,
he went on to Lexington as though the Tennessee campaign remained
operative, but when he reached Lexington, he found another telegram
waiting for him, directing him to send Grant the eight thousand men.
Burnside complied immediately; a lady in Lexington watched sadly as
a long train of unused Ninth Corps ambulances streamed beneath her
window, following the troops back to Ohio River steamboats.

This disrupted the entire plan, for as Burnside had warned Halleck,
he could only detach those troops if he abandoned the Tennessee campaign. Knowing that, Halleck nevertheless wired Rosecrans, "If you
cannot hurt the enemy now, he will soon hurt you." Burnside assured
Rosecrans he would give what help he could, but the notion of an offen-

sive was out of the question. He barely had enough troops left to guard his long line, and any Yankees who crossed the Cumberland now would be sitting ducks.[7]

The first and second divisions of the Ninth Corps—formerly Willcox's and Sturgis's—numbered about eighty-six hundred effectives, so Burnside decided to send them. Reasoning that Hartsuff could handle affairs in Kentucky and that Grant might be able to use his help, if his plight was so great, Burnside asked if he ought not go with the reinforcements. Halleck responded that it was preposterous to suggest the commander of a department should leave his post to accompany a fragment of his force, perhaps forgetting he had expected Burnside to invade East Tennessee (which was outside his department) with less than a third of his army. Still, there was less logic in Burnside going to Vicksburg than to Knoxville. It was as though he itched for some action; the forbearance Cincinnati required of him had apparently driven him to the limits of frustration.[8]

It may have been a symptom of that frustration which surfaced in the days before he left for Lexington. Burnside had lately been much troubled by the vituperation of the opposition press as it rebuked the Lincoln administration for the draft law and intolerance of dissidents. He had previously prevented book dealers from distributing Pollard's *First Year of the War* (the Confederate version of events), so he was not likely to permit the wholesale denunciation of the government, and on June 1 he issued Order Number 84, prohibiting the circulation of the *New York World* within his department and suppressing the publication of the *Chicago Times*.[9]

The hue and cry over this infringement on the First Amendment was even louder than it had been after Vallandigham's arrest. Burnside had received indirect and anonymous threats against his life in May, but now his enemies grew bolder. One Chicagoan who dared to provide his name and address told Burnside he was "a most ignorant, narrow-minded and bigoted fool," citing the assassination of Marat and advising the general that the spirit of Charlotte Corday yet survived in America. One Ohio newspaper continued the Marat theme, publishing Charlotte Corday's courtroom confession as though it were a random filler, highlighting her admission that she had formulated the plot "since the arrest of the representatives of my people." Even friendly bodies like the Illinois House of Representatives condemned the suppression of the *Times*, and a petition against Order Number 84 made its way to President Lincoln's desk within forty-eight hours, signed by the mayor of Chicago, Senator Lyman Trumbull, Congressman Isaac Arnold, and a fistful of other prominent Illinois citizens. A year later Lincoln himself would suppress the *New York World* and the *Journal of Commerce*, throwing their editors in prison, but for now he decided this was an instance in which he could not support Burnside. The afternoon of June 4 Burnside revoked the order according to presidential instructions.[10]

With most of the Ninth Corps gone, Burnside was hard pressed to find troops to defend Kentucky. Now Hartsuff could not swing into Tennessee as easily as he had hoped, and Samuel Carter, commanding a division left at Somerset, feared an exaggerated enemy force across the river might overwhelm him.[11]

Since April, Burnside had been trying to recruit twenty thousand Kentuckians for one-year service in defense of the state, in accordance with an act approved by Congress in February. Stanton had finally authorized him to begin recruiting on May 2, but a month later Burnside was still haggling with the provost marshal general over the manner in which those troops should be raised. In the end, of the eighteen regiments Burnside advertised under the act, nine failed to complete their organization. Nine survived to be mustered in between July and January, but only the first of them took the field in time to be of any use to Burnside.[12]

Kentucky was not the only state where volunteers would no longer step forward. It was a problem across the North, and the solution seemed to be conscription, authorized by Congress in March. The very threat of conscription sparked outrage in parts of the Midwest, and the preliminary compilation of enrollment lists, begun in June, seemed to bring some counties to the brink of insurrection. Indiana nurtured the most determined resistance. Milo Hascall's days as district commander in Indianapolis had been numbered since Abraham Lincoln's erstwhile campaign manager joined the ranks of those complaining about his stern administration; once Burnside's invasion of East Tennessee hung fire, he replaced Hascall with Orlando Willcox. Willcox arrived as the state appeared ready to explode.[13]

General Willcox had not arranged the papers on his desk yet when he learned of the murder of a pair of government employees in southwestern Rush County. A federal marshal and a detective, escorting enrolling officers, were ambushed in their buggy by a couple of discontented farmers. In Sullivan County, on the Illinois border, fifty soldiers sent to arrest draft resisters had been driven away by about two hundred armed men. Five other counties hosted violent confrontations worth the district commander's attention, some of them as far north as Fulton County, fifty miles from the Michigan line.[14]

In Illinois, a mixed mob of several hundred, mostly Irish, attacked four officials in Chicago, bashing in one man's skull and roughing up the others. Ohio's resistance was concentrated in several northern counties around Mansfield, where some enrolling officers and marshals were mobbed or threatened away from their duties.[15]

Burnside's customary response—a show of force—was not an immediate option. Because of a threat to Mississippi River garrisons outside his department, he had already sent away his disposable troops in Illinois and Indiana; his Ohio forces were largely occupied with prisoners at Camp Chase and Johnson's Island. Willcox obtained a few men by transferring two thousand Confederate prisoners from Indianapolis to Camp Chase, thereby eliminating the danger of their liberation by rioters. He soon needed these extra men, for Sullivan County erupted again in mid-June with the murder of another enrolling officer. Burnside appealed to Stanton for authority to declare martial law (with its attendant summary justice) in certain Indiana counties, but when he proposed to use that authority, Willcox dissuaded him. Though he stood ready to back up the civil authorities with a few dozen bayonets, Willcox recognized that the excesses of some soldiers were partly responsible for the uprising, and that martial law would merely inflame a populace already enraged at military interference. He worked instead with Democrats who were willing to preach obedience to the law. Consequently, he managed to complete the draft enrollment with the deployment of fewer than three hundred men. Minor outbreaks of resistance continued into the end of June, but without further bloodshed.[16]

Burnside supported the Conscription Act both officially and privately. He took a classical view toward military service, explaining to a friend in Philadelphia that "a citizen though not in the field is none the less a soldier." But when the enrolling officers began taking the names of black men, he bridled in a fashion that belied his presumed subservience to the Radicals. He may have felt that, since Negroes did not enjoy the privileges of citizens, they did not bear the obligation of service, but

the argument he posed to President Lincoln was based on practicality
rather than justice. A proportional draft of the free black population,
he wrote the president, would yield but few soldiers and would deprive
the army of their impressed labor while simultaneously alienating the
white population in loyal slave states. Both he and General Boyle, a
native Kentuckian well acquainted with the Southern racial attitude,
wired the White House late in June to urge that the enrollment be re-
stricted to white men. Lincoln, admitting he did not fully understand
the issue, said he currently planned no draft of black men and declined
to stop the enrollments, until Burnside emphasized it was the enrollment alone that caused the trouble. It would create more difficulties in
Kentucky than any levy of blacks would be worth, and the states north
of the Ohio might pose even more opposition to Negro enrollments than
Kentucky.[17]

Down in lower Kentucky, Burnside still tried to lend Rosecrans
a hand with his reduced resources, but the loss of the Ninth Corps
seriously impaired his ability to operate on Rosecrans's left flank—as
Rosecrans's own chief of staff recognized. Burnside found he could not
even offer diversionary assistance; General Carter's first foray across
the Cumberland revealed fourteen Southern cavalry regiments near
Monticello. With only his own division on hand, Carter began to worry
whether it was not he who was in trouble. Fortunately for him, the
anxiety was reciprocal.

By now General Maury had been replaced by Simon Buckner—another of Burnside's old friends and a fellow legatee of the Kingsbury
estate—and Buckner wired into southwest Virginia again to warn of
another invasion. Spies reported the Yankees moving pontoons toward
Somerset, and Buckner guessed that Carter's raid on Monticello was a
feint, designed to cover the main crossing. As late as June 10, a week
after Burnside sent the Ninth Corps away and gave up his offensive,
Buckner reported his opponent struck the "same threatening attitude."
It was finally a loyal Republican newspaper that betrayed Burnside's
bluff: on June 16 Samuel Jones, commander of southwest Virginia, sent
Buckner news from the *Cincinnati Commercial* of June 10 which confirmed that much of Burnside's army had gone to Mississippi.[18]

By now Burnside had given Buckner something else to occupy his
mind. Falling back on another of Halleck's "general instructions" of
March, he gathered a small field force and organized a two-pronged

raid into East Tennessee. While Julius White led his garrison against Confederate salt works near Prestonburg, Kentucky, Burnside planned to have another detachment of fifteen hundred cavalry dash into Tennessee west of the Cumberlands, cut across the mountains, and wreak what havoc it could on the East Tennessee & Virginia Railroad. To lead the railroad raid, Burnside handpicked Colonel William P. Sanders of the 5th Kentucky Cavalry. Formerly a captain in the 6th U.S. Cavalry, Sanders was a tall, handsome man with a bushy beard. Fully as big as Burnside, he inspired confidence in most men by his mere presence. Both White and Sanders left their camps June 14, White starting from Louisa and Sanders from Mount Vernon.[19]

These two contingents had barely begun their missions when Burnside's staff quavered with a violent argument between the judge advocate and two aides. The staff was moving from the Fourth Street office to larger rooms on Ninth Street, and in the course of settling into the new building Captain Hutton appropriated a desk coveted by Captain Cutts. The mercurial Cutts cursed himself blue, and Hutton returned his insults in kind. Cutts stomped away, but within hours he received a challenge to a duel, transmitted somewhat reluctantly by Major Cutting. Cutts scorned both the offer and Captain Hutton, whom he characterized as a coward. Burnside arrested all three of them: Hutton for the challenge, Cutting for carrying it, and Cutts for his unbecoming conduct, his derogation of Captain Hutton, and the Peeping-Tom incident of April. All three went before a court-martial, and Burnside— disgusted in particular with Cutts—testified for the prosecution. Even during the trial (so Larned noted) Cutts "insulted" another lady at the Burnet House. The court-martial apparently shared Burnside's estimate of the case, for it sentenced Hutton to nothing more than an official reprimand, acquitted Cutting, and directed that Cutts be cashiered.[20]

During this domestic squabble Burnside heard from General White, who had not met with much success in his raid. On the fifth day of his expedition he adjourned near Paintsville, all of twenty-five miles from Louisa, calling for five hundred more infantry. Burnside could afford to send none: he had just ordered another thousand cavalry and a regiment of infantry from Somerset toward Jamestown, Tennessee, to distract Sanders's pursuers, and John Morgan was reported dangerously near the Kentucky border again. Burnside warned White his dawdling would alert the Confederates to his movement—which it already had—and though White was able to crawl another dozen miles in the next two days, he finally determined the enemy had prepared too well for him to attack the salt works. His dispatches to that effect were three days coming over the mountains, and before Burnside could give him any further orders, it began to rain. The deluge continued for more than a week, inundating the primitive road network, and White's troops went out of action for the remainder of June.[21]

The Confederates responded to Burnside's activities with some raids of their own. A couple of hundred Southern cavalry rode through Kentucky east of Lexington, almost reaching the Ohio River before a Union detachment from Mount Sterling overtook them and scattered them. Captain Thomas Hines, one of John Morgan's most daring subordinates, led a more alarming incursion just west of Louisville. Choosing eighty of the best troopers in the 4th Kentucky Cavalry, he started north from Tennessee in the middle of the month. He crossed the Cumberland, captured a mail coach, relieved a Union sutler of his stock of uniforms, and robbed a paymaster's train at Elizabethtown. When cavalry surprised his force the next day, Hines led it through the Yankee gantlet and struck northwest, for the Ohio River. The Confederates crossed to the Indiana shore below Leavenworth and assumed the personae of a militia unit known as the Indiana Greys.[22]

The purpose of Hines's raid remains something of a mystery. At the time, Burnside assumed he had come to burn the bridges of the New Albany and the Ohio & Mississippi railroads. In light of events during the following month, Hines might have been riding on reconnaissance for a more ambitious operation, or he may simply have been directed to create a diversion. Neither Hines nor Morgan ever filed a report, since both fell prisoner soon after, but one student of their careers insists Hines was making his way to the home of a powerful Indiana Copperhead, Dr. William Bowles. The excitable Colonel Carrington credited Dr. Bowles with a secret army of ten thousand men, and a partisan newspaper later reported that Hines's men asked often for Bowles. The doctor lived at French Lick, and the Confederates did ride in that direction, running into militia at Paoli, about ten miles from French Lick.[23]

Contemporary reports convinced Burnside that sympathizers assisted Hines with supplies and information. He pointed out to Halleck that enemy recruiters, spies, and couriers were more numerous in Illinois, Indiana, and Ohio than in the supposedly divided state of Kentucky. He could not resist making ironic comment on the administration's failure to support his conservative doctrine in those states when the same course seemed appropriate in the relatively loyal Bluegrass region.[24]

Conflicting reports reached Cincinnati. Boyle apprised Burnside of the little invasion June 19, two days after Hines crossed the river. His rather accurate assessment credited Hines with eighty to two hundred men, and Boyle shipped a hundred men downriver to block their return to Kentucky. Orlando Willcox ordered a mounted detachment south from Indianapolis, and home guard units roused themselves to repel the invaders. When Boyle departed for Danville to inspect his main body of troops, his assistant adjutant general forwarded Burnside a corruption of the original report, raising enemy strength to five hundred and advancing the date of their crossing to June 20. Mention of an encounter at Paoli suggests this was an amplified duplication of old news, but in Cincinnati, headquarters dealt with it as a strong new raid. Boyle's assistant promised to send another flotilla with three hundred men and two guns to counter the threat, but Hines had already been driven away: Boyle's first transport trapped him on an island in the Ohio. Some of the hundred men landed on the beach while others fired from the steamer's deck, and eventually the bulk of the Confederate company surrendered. Ten men escaped to the Kentucky shore with nothing but their drawers and revolvers, Hines among them.[25]

While Hines hovered like a wasp behind Burnside's ear, John Morgan occupied the greater part of his interest below Kentucky's southern border. Rosecrans warned that Morgan skulked near Lebanon, Tennessee, with about four thousand men on June 20, as though preparing to invade Kentucky again. Three days later he reported the cavalier riding across the Caney River, toward East Tennessee, with twenty-three hundred men. It occurred to Burnside that Morgan might be on the trail of Colonel Sanders, and since he had heard nothing from his own Kentuckian, he began to worry. His concern evaporated June 26, when word came that Sanders had reentered Union lines. His cavalry had accomplished what Rosecrans called "a fine thing" in East Tennessee. After dismantling the railroad from Lenoir's Station up to Knoxville, Sanders had demonstrated outside that city for one entire night, agitating Confederates as far away as Bristol, Virginia. Three major railroad bridges fell in flames behind him, including one 2,100-foot-long trestle at Strawberry Plains, north of Knoxville, and he had taken five hundred prisoners and ten cannon besides destroying some commissary stores. Buckner mobilized every Confederate in the department to capture him. Things looked grim for Sanders when he found his escape route barred at Rogers's Gap; he had to burn the captured artillery as well as the section he had brought with him, but he was able to sidestep to a more primitive road, brush aside a regiment of Confederate cavalry, and slip back to Kentucky. When all his detachments reached camp he tallied only nineteen casualties, most of them exhausted stragglers captured in the wake of his killing march.[26]

Now Burnside operated according to the "preferred" suggestion of Halleck's infamous, contradictory instructions of March—maintaining a concentrated force in central Kentucky while annoying East Tennessee with cavalry raids. As Sanders electrified the Confederates around Knoxville, however, Halleck again changed his mind. Remarking that two infantry divisions and one of cavalry had been detached from Bragg's army, the Washington administrator once more concluded: "This seems the proper time for an advance toward East Tennessee." In so doing, he overlooked his own observation of March, which had warned that an invasion of that region posed "almost insuperable obstacles," principally in the area of supply lines. These obstacles had not been removed, and John Morgan's henchmen were demonstrating just how vulnerable the Ohio River country would be if Burnside's army left Kentucky. Still, Halleck prodded. Burnside accommodated him to the extent of throwing a thousand of Carter's cavalry across the state line to Jamestown, but with Confederate raiding parties at every hand he dared do no more for the present. On the Fourth of July, while Grant accepted the surrender of Vicksburg and Lee prepared to retreat from Pennsylvania, both Halleck and Stanton wired Cincinnati to urge the importance of a strike into Simon Buckner's domain. Bragg was so weakened by detachments, they knew, that he had called on Buckner for help. Burnside offered that he, too, had been stripped of troops, and he had a long line to guard. He was as eager as anyone to invade East Tennessee, but he had another problem to solve first: Morgan and a force reported at four to five thousand had broken through his attenuated cordon two days before, rafting over the Cumberland at Burkesville, in the middle of Kentucky.[27]

Morgan thundered unhindered through Columbia, but met with a serious repulse at the bridge over the Green River on Independence Day. A battalion of two hundred Michiganders who had never seen more than a skirmish refused Morgan's invitation to surrender, driving him from the river road with five dozen casualties, including one of his more experienced colonels. Morgan bypassed this determined detachment and went on to capture the entire garrison at Lebanon. His division—its numbers overestimated, but still a substantial force—raided with virtual impunity barely twenty miles from Louisville when Burnside unfolded another telegram from Halleck: if he was to succeed with the occupation of East Tennessee, Halleck said, he must be quick. "There is no need at the present time of keeping large forces in Kentucky," he added. With commendable tact, Burnside replied that Halleck was dead wrong. How, he wondered, could he move his principal force over the mountains with Morgan free to disrupt his supplies and communications? He promised to start his East Tennessee expedition as soon as Morgan was "disposed of," but heavy rains impeded the pursuit.[28]

Captain Hines and his surviving squad of troopers had reappeared west of Frankfort on the first of July, capturing and destroying a passenger train. Burnside offered a reward of a thousand dollars from his own pocket for their capture, but the ethereal Hines vanished again, riding toward the Ohio. He met his commander at the bank of the river on July 8. It seemed as though they had prearranged the rendezvous from the moment of Hines's departure, three weeks before.[29]

Morgan commandeered two steamers at Brandenburg, and during the night he began ferrying his command over the swollen Ohio to Indiana. Union officials remained ignorant of his actual whereabouts until the gunboat *Springfield* happened by from Portland, Kentucky, the next morning. The impromptu ferries were still shuttling cavalrymen, and the ensign commanding the *Springfield* opened fire. Morgan's guns responded, and a fight sputtered for more than an hour. The last of Morgan's division crossed after the *Springfield* fled back upriver to spread the word. At New Albany her skipper reported ten thousand Confederates where there were not three thousand, and three batteries of heavy artillery, though Morgan had but one battery of field guns. General Boyle relayed more reliable information, but Burnside knew he had serious trouble on his hands. Halleck would have to fret for some time before any Union soldiers crossed the Tennessee mountains.[30]

III

During the organization of the Twenty-third Corps, Jeremiah Boyle's role had been redefined. Now he was in charge of a division within that corps, but he found it difficult to abandon his former responsibilities as commander of all western Kentucky. From the moment Morgan approached Louisville, Boyle acted as Burnside's intermediary with pursuing forces, and Burnside allowed him that authority. Burnside also told him to take whatever he needed from the federal ordnance department, and Boyle dipped liberally into those stores, ignoring the protests of the independent officer in charge of them.

In at least one instance, Boyle's overbearing manner served to hinder the chase, when he sent peremptory orders to the commander of another division without explaining his special authorization. Henry Judah, a man fully as self-important as Boyle, remained deep in Kentucky with several brigades that included a few cavalry regiments. Boyle demanded those mounted units, but Judah declined to obey orders that seemed not to descend the usual staircase of command, and Burnside had to telegraph directly to General Hartsuff to bring Judah into line. Boyle met similar difficulties over the gunboats at Louisville; there was still no interservice command structure, and Boyle lacked the winning personal warmth which had allowed Burnside to cement his alliance with Goldsborough and Rowan. When Boyle "ordered" gunboats down to shell Morgan's crossing, they remained tied to the docks. Not until Burnside wired more diplomatic requests to the local commander and the chief of his squadron did those floating forts become available.[1]

Judah finally released his cavalry regiments and sent them north under his senior brigadier, Edward Hobson. Hobson followed Morgan through the heart of Kentucky, but his leading horsemen reined up on the left bank of the Ohio in the wake of Morgan's successful passage. One of the commandeered steamboats drifted in flames on the far shore; the other lay undamaged and idle on the Kentucky side. Hobson ordered the surviving steamer up to Louisville, to ask for army transports, and Boyle immediately sent some down.[2]

The first Indiana town Morgan encountered was Corydon, and a local home guard unit was there to greet him. Haphazardly armed, some four hundred Hoosiers lined up behind a rail fence to demonstrate that

Confederates were not necessarily welcome, whatever differences these citizens might have with the central government. Morgan went into line and charged when he saw the resistance. The farmers emptied a few saddles: Morgan's own adjutant fell dead by the general's side. But the undisciplined militia was outnumbered and overmatched, and in a few minutes the affair was over. Three citizens lay dead, a dozen were wounded, and most of the rest fell prisoner to the raiders.[3]

Indiana's governor, Oliver Morton, grew frantic. While soldiers all along the Ohio presumed Morgan would try to recross into Kentucky, Morton cited unspecified information that convinced him the Confederate was headed straight for Indianapolis. Back in Cincinnati, Daniel Larned thought Morton "a confounded fool" and hoped Morgan would get him. Hundreds of Confederate prisoners (recently returned to Indianapolis) and Colonel Carrington's recent rantings about a Copperhead uprising must have tainted the governor's reasoning, but to aggravate his fears, he heard a false report that Morgan had sent a brigade to Paoli—alarmingly close to Dr. Bowles's supposed Copperhead headquarters at French Lick. Less easily disturbed, General Burnside consoled Governor Morton with the logic that Morgan was yet two days from the Indiana capital and unlikely to strand himself so deep in enemy territory. Also, he had come in too little force for an invasion; he would seek to cross the river sooner or later. The only questions were when and where.[4]

Morgan bored forty miles into Indiana, but as Burnside expected, that was as deep as he dared venture. At Salem he shrugged off another home guard detachment and assigned several squads to the burning of nearby railroad bridges. The main body dismounted and began appropriating food, forage, and supplies. This rather orderly impressment quickly degenerated into senseless, if relatively harmless, pillage, and a slower column moved out of Salem, burdened with frivolous plunder that included tableware, ice skates, and some caged canaries.[5]

In order to confuse his pursuers, Morgan cut a false trail back to the Ohio. Traveling southeast from Salem, he created the impression he would attack New Albany, just across the river from Louisville. General Boyle arranged a gathering of two thousand Indiana militia to repel him, and Burnside gave Boyle permission to arm them and Louisville's volunteers from the arsenal there. The wire between Cincinnati and Louisville fell ominously silent shortly after this transmission.[6]

Hobson's three partial brigades, about twenty-five hundred men, all rode on the Indiana shore by first light of Friday, July 10, some thirty miles behind Morgan. Boyle, Burnside, and Hartsuff looked frantically for Judah, who had wandered astray in the vicinity of the Green River with the rest of his division. Willcox put a regiment and a battery aboard a train at Indianapolis, but he feared to let them depart lest Morgan veer back toward the city and capture them. Thus the little Confederate division galloped across southeastern Indiana with no serious opposition. There was another brief exchange with some home guards outside Pekin, after which the raiders turned away from the river road toward Vernon, in Jennings County. Late on the night of July 11 an Indiana militia general arrived in Vernon with a few troops, and when Morgan sent in a demand for surrender, the militiamen defied him. At 2:00 A.M. July 12 the bulk of the Confederate troops bypassed Vernon, riding toward Madison, another river town. Ten miles south, Morgan reined his column east again.[7]

Burnside and his staff found fighting Morgan by telegraph worse than a battle in the field. They could apply no system to the shuffling of strange and unpredictable troops across whole counties; it was like a chess game played by mail, without benefit of a board of one's own. Reports of Morgan's whereabouts came in a confetti of little telegraphic notes, many of them contradictory, and the Cincinnati office gave little credence to any save those of reliable officers who had personally seen or fought with the grey wraith. The customary difficulties of such long-distance maneuvering were, unknown to Burnside, complicated by an expert telegrapher attached to Morgan's staff. George Ellsworth, nicknamed "Lightning" for his nimble fingers, periodically tapped into the wires along Morgan's route, taking Burnside's orders off the line or sending false information and instructions to Union authorities. Even genuine sightings seemed irregular, though, describing a sawtooth pattern—a zigzag route that led Larned to believe Morgan was running scared, dashing blindly toward the safety of the Ohio. In fact these southerly detours were false trails, intended to lure pursuers away. Morgan planned to continue as far east as he could, perhaps to the shore opposite West Virginia and possibly (according to one of his deserters) to Lee's army, which he still expected to find in Pennsylvania.[8]

Neither Burnside nor any of his subordinates really believed the deserter's statement; it sounded too audacious even for Morgan. Instead,

Burnside anticipated he would cross at Lawrenceburg when he left the road to Madison, so there he sent Willcox's Indianapolis troops. The only strategy Burnside could follow was to get a line of battle across Morgan's path—preferably volunteers, but militia if necessary—to slow the raiders' pace until Hobson could overtake them.[9]

The Confederates grew visibly weary. Their column accordioned until it required five hours to pass a single point, and side trips for delicacies widened the line of march from its original column of fours. From the 2:00 A.M. sidestep around Vernon they rode nearly sixty roundabout miles July 12, levying a tribute from the town of Versailles before camping near Sunman. Early the next day the point riders trotted across the Ohio border into the town of Harrison. A few of them cleaned out the post office there, relieving Postmaster Clarke of a fat wallet in the process.[10]

The day before, Burnside had asked Governor Tod to call out 20,000 Ohio militia in the southern part of the state, principally around Cincinnati. On July 13, while citizens who had reconnoitered Morgan's force announced 11,000 men and 8 guns under his command, Burnside imposed martial law on Cincinnati, Covington, and Newport. Shops closed, and the city assumed an eerie quiet for a Monday morning. Burnside's decree included none of the usual restrictions on the travel of civilians; with the broad hint that every man was needed, he said he expected none would abandon the city during its peril. Just in case Ohio courage did not match the crisis, though, he closed all the barrooms. Perhaps it was as well he did, for many an unoccupied city resident would have been looking for some such diversion: where Burnside planned on 5,000 militia from Cincinnati alone, the entire county provided fewer than 1,500. Three regiments at Lawrenceburg, Indiana, constituted his only real defense for the city, and he ordered them up. Their route along the river paralleled Morgan's, ten miles to the north.[11]

The timid Cincinnati shopkeepers need not have troubled themselves about Morgan, for he had no intention of attacking the city. He feinted north, toward Hamilton, then ducked back through the outskirts of Cincinnati, riding slowly but singlemindedly eastward. He saw no Union soldiers, for Burnside had drawn his few troops into a tight perimeter; even the headquarters staff loaded their carbines and revolvers and placed them in easy reach. Morgan marched into and through the night without a shot fired, his path chosen by reluctant guides plucked from their beds at midnight. As Burnside peered into the darkness, the Confederates passed around him in an arc less than twenty miles from his office. In the morning Morgan made a demonstration against Camp Dennison, northeast of the city, but with Burnside's encouragement the lieutenant colonel in charge there put up a good bluff. His garrison consisted of a green artillery battery, some militia, and a few recently exchanged prisoners, totaling fewer than two thousand men, most of them unarmed. He put them all in line, and Morgan thought again about assaulting the camp. Hobson's cavalry dogged three or four hours behind him; finally he rode around the little bastion, making his way to Williamsburg by afternoon. There, for the first time since they left Indiana, the exhausted Southern horsemen stepped down to sleep. That same day, Lee's army completed its retreat back into Virginia.[12]

The Confederates had one advantage over General Hobson, for they were able to sift the countryside for the best fresh horses and leave their broken-down mounts behind. Hobson actually seemed to be losing ground now, and Burnside became more anxious than ever to impede Morgan's progress. He alerted the militia in southern Ohio to stand in his way, and sent troops up the Ohio River from Cincinnati and Covington. General Judah had finally surfaced, so Burnside put him on a steamboat bound for Portsmouth with a couple of cavalry regiments. Colonel Sanders, Burnside's own raider, galloped out from Cincinnati with parts of two Michigan regiments to reinforce Hobson directly. For insurance, Burnside also kept one brigade aboard boats, patrolling the Ohio alongside the line of Morgan's advance.[13]

In the middle of Morgan's sprint across southern Ohio Burnside fell ill, for the second time in a month. He had been so sick at the end of June that Molly considered returning from Providence to nurse him, and now he took to his bed again. This time he lay flat on his back for two days, and he lost twenty pounds that week, but his correspondence with the commanders of the pursuit never flagged. By the time he regained his feet, he found news to cheer him: Hobson rode but fifteen miles behind Morgan, who neared Jackson, Ohio; Ohio militia blocked his route east, and Judah approached from the south. It looked like the end of the line for John Morgan.[14]

Morgan gained some time when he burned the bridge over the Scioto River canal, and before Hobson arrived in Jackson, the Confederates had disappeared behind the smokescreen of the burning railroad depot there. Worn out as they were, the raiders managed to surprise and capture an entire militia regiment before streaming toward Pomeroy, on a bend in the Ohio. Hobson, satisfied the inexperienced home guards could never hold Morgan for him, shook off a couple of dependable regiments to race around him and bring him to bay. First he dispatched August Kautz and two Ohio regiments, later adding Colonel Sanders and his tiny brigade.[15]

The net closed in from all sides. From the new state of West Virginia came Burnside's old English and ethics professor, Eliakim Scammon. Scammon had sewn on well-deserved brigadier's epaulettes since Antietam, and he rode down the gangplank at Gallipolis at the head of four veteran regiments. He spun a web of pickets around that town, positioned a couple of thousand militia within that cordon, and steamed upriver to Pomeroy with the better part of his brigade. Morgan tested the Gallipolis pickets and took some prisoners, but he judged Scammon's defenses too strong to attack. At the outskirts of Pomeroy he showed a bit more desperation, lashing out at the Ohio regiment under Rutherford B. Hayes; the Buckeyes volleyed just once and the Confederates reeled upriver, twenty men fewer. Kautz, who had personally outdistanced all but two hundred of his chasseurs, finally caught up with the fugitives as they tried to cross the river at Buffington Bar, near Portland. Outnumbered as he was, he attacked. Sanders arrived to help, and his Michiganders pitched into the enemy with their Spencer repeaters. Soon they could hear navy gunboats tossing their shells at the disconcerted raiders. Worn to a frazzle and hopelessly outgunned, the Confederates fled upstream in considerable disorder.[16]

Not far ahead of them waited General James Shackelford, with part of Hobson's reinforced cavalry command. Hobson's orders had placed Shackelford astride the principal river road, and when Morgan saw these Yankees, there was nothing for him to do but deploy for a fight. Shackelford put parts of five Kentucky regiments in front, so the final clash was entirely a Bluegrass affair; when his three central regiments surged forward in a charge, a flurry of white linen suddenly speckled the Confederate line. Basil Duke, Morgan's second in command, came forward and surrendered that part of Morgan's division on the field, including Colonel Dick Morgan, the general's brother. Morgan himself nearly made it across the river, but he turned back when he saw his men giving up. This raid, sanctioned by no Confederate authority and

specifically limited to Kentucky by Bragg, would cost Morgan a great
deal, but the opprobrium of abandoning most of his command to the
enemy was more than Bourbon pride could endure. He swam his horse
back to the Ohio shore, rallied several hundred survivors, and escaped
by an obscure path.[17]

General Hobson found himself robbed of the glory at the hour of victory. Though Burnside had specifically appointed him to lead the chase,
and though he had followed his prey more than eight hundred miles,
the obstinate Henry Judah arrived at the last moment and insisted on
taking charge. He stood senior to Hobson in rank and was his division
commander in the official new hierarchy of the Twenty-third Corps,
but those organizational charts meant little in the context of this Ohio
free-for-all: here, most of the Union commanders operated on an equal
footing. Not so with Judah, a man who styled his whiskers (and apparently his personality, as well) after Napoleon III. He assumed command
over Hobson's indignant objection, accepted all the prisoners in his own
name, and telegraphed Burnside news of the "defeat" of Morgan's men.[18]

Certainly it was a defeat, but it was not Morgan's destruction. With
his remaining few hundred men, Morgan sped north. Scammon, patrolling both sides of the Ohio now, rousted Morgan's camp on the Hocking
River that same night, and the raider pushed on in the darkness, following the banks of the Muskingum into the middle of the state. General
Shackelford followed him with some of Hobson's men, outdistancing his
communications with both Hobson and the overbearing Judah, who remained behind to bring in the prisoners. Hobson frothed over the stolen
credit, but Burnside's telegrams made it clear he knew who had really
brought Morgan to ground. So did the people of Ohio: near the spot
where Judah intersected with him and took his command away now
stands the town of Hobson.[19]

The fagged and ragged remnant of Morgan's shattered division was in
no shape to defend itself. Many of the Confederates had lost their arms,
and those who clung to their weapons were nearly out of ammunition.
They still herded a gaggle of prisoners—mostly tenderfooted militia,
captured Saturday night—and at every halt officers would ride to the
roadside to scribble paroles for them. Morgan's acting adjutant pulled
out of the line of march the second morning after the fight at Buffington
Bar and wrote a parole for Lieutenant C. B. Lewis. The Southerner
used a pencil stub, spreading a scrap of paper on the pommel of his

saddle, and the scowling home guard lieutenant walked away, minus his sword and sixty dollars in greenbacks. Morgan plodded on, and as Lewis limped back toward Pomeroy he accumulated a tattered entourage of Confederate stragglers who meekly surrendered to him rather than face the retribution of a civilian mob.[20]

Reports from men like Lewis implied Morgan was, if not done for, at least rendered harmless. Though Burnside continued to keep in touch with the pursuit and organized local defense forces by telegraph, he relaxed a bit when the first boatload of prisoners arrived. The evening of July 21 he shed his uniform for a boiled shirt and a frock coat, combing out his famous whiskers for the wedding of another of his staff officers. But the festive atmosphere did not long survive: on the streets of Cincinnati there were crowds gathering. Roused by the news of bloody draft riots in New York City, antiwar crowds went through the Victorian ritual of alternately cheering for their hero, Vallandigham, and groaning for their nemesis, Burnside. Men who had failed to respond to Burnside's call for militia chanted their opposition to any military service, yet criticized the general at the same gatherings for his failure to corral Morgan sooner.[21]

The complaining public may have been somewhat chastened when long queues of dejected prisoners marched from the Cincinnati wharves to accommodations on land. As a temporary convenience, Burnside locked Morgan's officers in the Cincinnati jail. Captain Cutts, awaiting the final outcome of his court-martial, resented this felonlike confinement of bona fide prisoners of war, among them his own former colleague Basil Duke. Cutts attacked Burnside for this "barbarity" with tactics both fair and foul. He sent the general a straightforward, vigorous objection, but he preceded it with a cowardly private telegram to President Lincoln, in which he caricatured Burnside as a mindless maniac; he suggested Joe Hooker be sent to replace him, implying Burnside lacked courage as well as sense and warning that Burnside would disgrace himself, the president, and the country, "as he did at Fredericksburg." The general had lost all respect for Cutts by now, and though he planned to remove the Confederates to a regular prison camp, it was not because of the captain's ravings. Neither, for that matter, did Lincoln reply to Cutts's partisan and personally vindictive message.[22]

Shackelford finally caught up with Morgan's sleeping survivors forty miles west of Wheeling, West Virginia. The morning of July 24 he drove them several miles east, but the raiders stalled him by burning bridges. Morgan, long since apprised that Lee no longer roamed Pennsylvania, seemed determined to ford the Ohio into what he still stubbornly called the state of Virginia, and he led his tatterdemalions toward Steubenville, across from what had been the Old Dominion's panhandle. As they spurred freshly stolen mounts across the Jefferson County line, the Confederates raced into the arms of one of Burnside's most antagonistic colleagues.[23]

William Brooks, whom Burnside had recommended for dismissal in Order Number 8, was now in command of the Department of the Monongahela, with headquarters in Pittsburgh. Burnside had warned him of Morgan's approach on July 23, in order that he might prepare to defend his side of the Ohio, but Brooks responded by transporting himself, uninvited, into Burnside's department. He made temporary headquarters at Steubenville and posted three regiments of Pennsylvania militia on the Ohio side, reporting his presence to Burnside only after arranging a warm reception for Morgan. Where another officer might have carped at such an infringement of his territory, Burnside forwarded a couple of cavalry regiments by rail and offered to make them subject to Brooks's orders. On Saturday, July 25, Brooks wired that Morgan seemed to be falling into the trap; Burnside refrained from making the token suggestions that would have put him in the position of overall commander, simply wishing Brooks success.[24] It was a routine correspondence they exchanged, with no hint of rancor: only the closest scrutiny of the circumstances reveals Brooks's presumptuous interference and Burnside's predictably generous surrender of the reins.

Morgan stabbed at Steubenville that Saturday, but the Pennsylvania militia repulsed him. Even without the militia Morgan would not have escaped, for Burnside had sent light-draft gunboats upriver with infantry aboard, which ought to have impeded Morgan long enough for Shackelford to come up behind him. Shackelford finally cornered him anyway, using the two cavalry regiments Burnside had sent by train. On Sunday, near New Lisbon, the Kentucky raider at last surrendered his dwindling force to Major George Rue of the 9th Kentucky Cavalry and Major W. B. Way of the 9th Michigan Cavalry. Brooks's proximity, and Burnside's subordination of his prerogative to efficiency, deprived Burnside of much of the official notice he deserved for orchestrating the long and complicated pursuit. For instance, though the 9th Kentucky formed part of Hobson's brigade, operating under Shackelford's immediate orders, Rue reported the capture directly to Bully Brooks; so did Major Way. Brooks, in turn, telegraphed the adjutant general in Washington of the end of Morgan's raid, bypassing Burnside entirely and affording the department commander only an ex post facto copy of Rue's report as a token deference to propriety. Shackelford complained of Rue's insubordinate usurpation, but Burnside let it go, wiring Shackelford to bring the prize home by the first train; Morgan's capture was gratification enough, regardless of who gained the glory. Thus did Burnside go virtually unrecognized for the destruction of the second-most-troublesome Confederate cavalry force west of Virginia.[25]

At first Burnside intended to send Morgan and his staff to Johnson's Island, where he had finally incarcerated Duke and the other officers captured at Buffington Bar, but Halleck had other plans for the cavalier. Because Confederate authorities hesitated to exchange the officers of a Union brigade captured on a raid into Alabama and Georgia, Halleck decided to lodge Morgan and his principal officers in the cells of the Ohio state penitentiary, at Columbus. Prison barbers, intent more on humiliation than hygiene, shaved both their faces and their heads, over Burnside's own objection. Doors of densely crosshatched wrought iron slammed shut on the Morgan brothers, Duke, Colonel Cluke, Captain Hines, and a couple of dozen others whose names had haunted Burnside from both sides of the Ohio since the first day of spring.[26]

Morgan's capture freed an amazing number of troops for other duty. Some fifty-five thousand militia returned to their homes from Ohio alone, and Burnside ordered several thousand troopers from his main force, the Twenty-third Corps, back into Kentucky.

"I can now look after the other work you desire done," he told Halleck.[27]

6

TWICE ACROSS THE CUMBERLAND

I

By "other work," Burnside alluded to the long-postponed invasion of East Tennessee. When Halleck took the Ninth Corps away in June, he implied the East Tennessee campaign would have to wait until those troops returned, and though he did not specify when, he did indicate they would come back. Lately he had been badgering Burnside about the invasion, though, even during the hunt for Morgan. Now he demanded a count of the men Burnside could spare for the operation. With the Ninth Corps still detached, and much of his cavalry scouring Ohio, Burnside could find only six thousand available men. So inferior a force would be pretty vulnerable south of the Cumberland, he noted, but once the Ninth Corps arrived or Morgan was run down, he would have the men available to assure their supply line, at which time he would start them off. Halleck responded that that was not good enough. Reversing his earlier promise, he warned that the Ninth Corps might never be returned to him. Revealing an appalling ignorance of both the devastation Morgan's raid had wrought on civilian morale and the demonstrated incompetence of the militia, Halleck went on to tell Burnside East Tennessee was more important than checking "petty raids" like Morgan's. "The militia and Home Guards must take care of these raids," he wrote, evidently intending no irony.[1]

Yet another discouragement impeded a movement out of Kentucky. Colonel John Scott, the Louisiana cavalryman, burst into eastern Kentucky again before Morgan gave up the ghost. He brought a brigade of horsemen and two batteries, partly to create a diversion for Morgan's frenzied retreat. Burnside, however, feared the raid had more to do with the Kentucky elections scheduled for August 3. Charles Wickliffe, a Peace Democrat, campaigned against Thomas Bramlette, colonel of a Union regiment, in a fiery gubernatorial race that no longer included Senator Powell. In order to prevent Scott from intimidating Unionists and swaying the election, Burnside again imposed martial law. Although Scott's brigade was scattered and driven back into Tennessee before the election, Burnside maintained control for the civil authorities until the polls closed. Not unlike Lincoln's "monitoring" of the Delaware elections, Burnside's attempt to guarantee the democratic process resulted in nothing less than an election rigged for the Union ticket. General Boyle, himself a candidate for Congress, simply jailed his opponent; he also promised that anyone who voted for Wickliffe would be considered a rebel—a hefty threat, in light of Order Number 38. The names of opposition candidates were frequently stricken from the ballot in the more crucial counties, or voting on the Wickliffe ticket ended by military edict, and anyone who declined the rigorous oath of allegiance went under arrest until the election was over. In some places the voting was suspiciously unanimous, and a Union landslide of nearly four to one testified to the extent of military interference. What Burnside had feared Scott would do, he did himself, and one newspaper complained the administration "carried the election at the point of the bayonet."[2]

Despite Halleck's doubts about the Ninth Corps, Lincoln had personally telegraphed Burnside it would come back, but when Grant did not immediately release it, Lincoln felt constrained to explain the delay. He assured Burnside the corps would be coming up the river soon, but the first week of August passed without word from his old troops. Burnside therefore excluded them when he recalculated his strength for Halleck on August 4: he had about twenty-three thousand men below the Ohio, of whom seventeen hundred were detached to Rosecrans. Five regiments were packed for mustering-out, but with Morgan locked up he thought he could collect twelve thousand men for an expedition into East Tennessee. He could only accomplish that, he cautioned Halleck, by weakening the railroad garrisons, and if those garrisons had not been so strong before, Morgan and Scott could have done a great deal more damage than they did. How about Getty's division? he asked again.[3]

After months of stalling, Halleck responded instantaneously that

Getty was not going to rejoin Burnside—not now, not ever. He ordered Burnside to gather his twelve thousand men and move immediately on Knoxville. Rosecrans would be waiting somewhere to the southwest, and the two forces would connect. The final sentence of Halleck's order carried the sting of the schoolmaster's switch: "The Secretary of War repeats his orders that you move your headquarters from Cincinnati to the field, and take command of the troops in person."[4]

Burnside flew into one of his white-hot rages at Halleck's insinuation he had either disobeyed orders or was too lazy or timid to leave the comfort of his city quarters. His pen racing with indignation, he scrawled an indiscreet reply, denying Stanton had ever given such an order before and reminding Halleck that he had been within reach of his forwardmost troops in early June, when Halleck himself had taken away his mobile force and ordered him to stay where he was. Burnside finished with a few acerbic observations on Halleck's tone and his generally uncooperative attitude. Apparently Captain Larned or Colonel Richmond balked while transcribing the insubordinate letter and counseled Burnside to modify the message, for the general worried his way through several versions. Twenty-four hours passed before an edited draft went to the wire, softer than the original but still full of outrage.[5]

Halleck's tone may have stemmed partly from the frustration of coordinating the movements of two armies hundreds of miles away, each circumvented by independent problems—he grew equally short with Rosecrans; but Halleck came to be famous for less creditable motives. Like McClellan in Maryland, he seems to have worked at creating a correspondence designed to shift responsibility for a stalled campaign from his own shoulders; certain inconsistencies in his official report of the East Tennessee campaign support such a notion. Halleck also appears to have carried a grudge against Burnside, not having forgotten (as Burnside had) about William Franklin's assertion that Burnside had called for Halleck's removal. Sarcasm and innuendo from army headquarters could do nothing but harm, whatever the cause; Burnside's staff concluded Halleck's contrary and condescending demeanor was meant to prompt Burnside's resignation or, better yet, to drive him to some blunder for which he could be removed.[6] Once again, Burnside felt that he went into battle with enemies behind as well as before him.

For all his apprehension about jeopardizing Kentucky and fielding a force too small to protect itself, Burnside quickly exchanged notes with

Rosecrans. Each made his plans according to the other's itinerary. Just as Burnside was packing to leave Cincinnati, he learned that harbingers of the Ninth Corps were debarking at Cairo. The two divisions overspread a convoy of steamboats in the Mississippi, stretched out between Memphis and the Ohio River, but they were not the divisions they had been. In June Burnside had loaned Grant more than eight thousand men; after a grueling campaign to Jackson, Mississippi, barely six thousand of them returned. Worse yet, most of those six thousand came back too sick for any but the lightest duty. General Parke himself had a touch of fever, one of his aides was so emaciated and fragile looking that Captain Larned did not recognize him, and one of the division commanders lay on his deathbed.[7]

Burnside left the city blissfully unaware of the condition of his old corps. It was three o'clock of a muggy Monday morning, August 10, when he closed up his overpriced rooms at the Burnet House. He, Larned, and Robert, with another servant and one aide, boarded the Ohio River ferry in the twilight. The sun broke over the horizon as the ferry chugged across, and nine o'clock had not yet sounded when their train pulled into Lexington. Larned smiled contentedly when he heard the general direct their driver to the Phoenix House, with its back-slapping proprietor and good food. Burnside notified Washington of his arrival, checked on the position of troops in the Twenty-third Corps, retabulated his strength, and finally accepted an invitation to a soirée at the home of Mrs. Henry Duncan. Her brother-in-law had been on Morgan's staff, but Mrs. Duncan was a thoroughgoing Union lady. She surprised the general with a band to serenade him. Such a tribute traditionally demanded a little speech, but Burnside had not come ready; he stumbled through a few quickly improvised platitudes so clumsily that one Lexington lady accustomed to soaring Southern rhetoric made wry comment to those at her elbow, in the corner of the room.

"We did not get him to make speeches," said one of the other women. "We got him to fight—and he can do that."[8]

The next day was a busy one for Burnside. In the morning he rode the train to Louisville, where he and Boyle discussed how to defend Kentucky without most of the Twenty-third Corps. He telegraphed from there to Indianapolis, hoping Willcox could spare him some troops, and inquired about the progress of the Ninth Corps. When he returned to Lexington, he found a packet of telegrams, including one from the

War Department, chastising him for permitting Boyle to draw on the Louisville armory during Morgan's raid. In the same pile of mail lay a message from Adjutant General Lorenzo Thomas, authorizing him to raise as many Negro regiments as he could, though Burnside had already advised Washington that the organization of black soldiers would only alienate whites in the Ohio River country. Neither communication seemed to require an answer, so he went straight to a special train scheduled to carry him to Nicholasville. Their engine derailed not far from the city, however, so he and his companions had to transfer to a civilian passenger coach. It was late evening when they arrived in Nicholasville, and the weather had turned extraordinarily cool. The little headquarters family found some horses and rode the six miles to Camp Nelson under a threatening sky. Hastened by the overcast, dusk had already settled by the time they dismounted.[9]

Initially an armed camp of instruction, Camp Nelson was on its way to becoming one of the U.S. Army's largest supply depots. The general put up in the residence of a Mrs. Bonner, a local woman whose home happened to be within the range of the camp. It sat on the lip of a magnificent ravine that plummeted to the Kentucky River. From this sylvan setting, within sight of picturesque Hickman's Bridge, Burnside tried to coordinate the convergence of his divisions and to organize a supply system for their trek over the bottomless mountain roads. Supplies were his greatest anxiety from the very start. Even Halleck had warned him at the outset how difficult they would be to gather, and Orlando Willcox had corroborated that when he tried to advance beyond the Cumberland ten weeks earlier. A general who had campaigned in the area before sent him some helpful suggestions from the army under Rosecrans, to which General Boyle added some of his own. Still, bureaucratic bungling delayed the transportation of supplies even to Camp Nelson and other central Kentucky locations that enjoyed good roads, and the Ninth Corps reinforcements seemed to be going in every direction but the one Burnside wanted. As he wrestled with these problems, the general seemed to become unusually agitated.[10]

Burnside had expected to be on the march by now, and in order to expedite his advance he decided to take only as much food as his wagons could carry. He would let his men live off the countryside when that ran out; there would be no resupply until enough additional troops arrived to secure the lines of communications. Bold as that decision was,

Burnside immediately felt better for it—much as he had revived when he determined to make his last advance across the Rappahannock, in January. It would have freed him to move almost at once, had it not been for the matter of horses. Nearly half the little army he intended to field consisted of cavalry or mounted infantry, and the quartermasters were aggravatingly slow coming up with remounts for the animals that had been worn out during the recent raids. Nor were they any better at alleviating that perennial shortage, forage: this, too, had to be carried in as much quantity as possible, and the wagon teams would probably eat more than half of each load on the way. Burnside optimistically told Rosecrans on August 13 that he might be able to start three brigades of cavalry and one infantry division within two days.[11]

The news that John Parke had reached Cincinnati further improved Burnside's mood, and for a couple of days the staff remembered the jovial old chief they had known in Newbern. He perched one of Mrs. Bonner's daughters on his extra horse and trotted her down to see a review of the garrison; the following day he presented his officers with the contents of a large fruit basket given him by the Shaker community just downstream, gleefully handing out the produce himself; the next night he and his staff attended a dance, the music supplied by black callers and fiddlers, and the general broke them all down with his boundless energy. He came in for a disappointment after the festivities, though, for when they returned to Mrs. Bonner's there sat Parke, pale and weak. He looked as sick as they had ever seen him, and he told them the rest of the corps enjoyed no better health. Sorry now that he had ordered Parke down from Cincinnati, Burnside sent him back the next morning. Though he ought to have taken medical leave, Parke remained in the city a while, culling the Ninth Corps for its few able men and sending them on to Kentucky. His occasional reports grew gradually worse, instead of better, describing units with two-thirds of their muster rolls on the sick list and officers dying on the job from chills and fever. The corps would obviously not be able to follow Burnside south any time in the near future.[12]

On August 16 Rosecrans swept his army forward in an arc that stretched from Sparta, Tennessee, into Alabama. Burnside's share of their agreed-upon program consisted of covering Rosecrans's left flank, which he expected to accomplish by occupying the Confederates of East Tennessee. Still delayed by a shortage of fresh mounts—the avail-

able supply of which had been requisitioned down from Louisville by
Rosecrans—Burnside could only push his forces toward the banks of
the Cumberland, threatening the enemy until he dared cross in real
strength.[13]

To relieve the pressure on the miserable roads his troops would have
to travel, he spanned his soldiers into five columns across a front more
than a hundred miles long. The deeper into Kentucky and Tennessee
they traveled, the closer they would converge, the five columns meld-
ing into three the far side of the Cumberland and into two before they
crossed the Tennessee line, finally reuniting at the seat of Morgan
County. The timetable of the various detachments represented a compromise between mobility and cohesiveness. Burnside was especially
anxious about spreading himself too thin after he crossed the mountains: while it was his duty to shield Rosecrans's left flank, he had no
one to guard his own left but himself.

The same afternoon that Rosecrans rolled forward, Burnside and his
staff rode the fifteen miles from Camp Nelson to Danville. Burnside
had a final conference with Boyle there the next day: they spoke mainly
of the surveying and construction of a railroad line from the Bluegrass
down to Knoxville, which Boyle agreed to supervise after Burnside's
departure. During the course of their meeting they stepped out on the
balcony of the Sneed House to review Hascall's division as it passed by.
Shortly after lunch, Burnside said goodbye and galloped off for Crab
Orchard, overtaking Hascall's men and passing them at the head of his
escort—seventy-five cavalrymen, all riding white horses. The general
wore a checkered shirt and his trademark slouch hat with the crown
belled out, and the soldiers hooted affectionately at his gaudy attire.
Just before dinnertime Burnside directed his retinue to the side of the
road, near Stanford. For the first time since the march from Warrenton, nine months before, he and the staff camped together in the open
air. Their horses kicked into a hornets' nest before the evening ended;
George Fearing, an aide Daniel Larned considered a "most conceited
snob," was stung unmercifully.[14]

Hornets notwithstanding, Burnside reached Crab Orchard shortly
before noon of August 18. There he sat for three days, pounding the
telegraph key late into the night, looking for his horses and forage. The
staff sat out the delay under the sound roof of the Spring Hotel, but
everyone had to take his meals at the Crab Orchard Hotel, which failed

to satisfy Captain Larned's epicurean palate. The menu and the rigorous travel were not the total of Larned's discomforts: he had clipped his hair almost razor short for the campaign, and he suffered endlessly from Burnside's jibes about his enormous ears. The secretary consoled himself with a bath in the nearby mineral springs.[15]

Though the food, forage, and transportation had not yet been delivered, Burnside told Hascall to move out on August 20. He could afford to leave Rosecrans unprotected no longer. Headquarters followed the easternmost column (and its herd of two thousand beeves) out of Crab Orchard on the afternoon of August 21. Almost immediately did the roads narrow to bumpy dirt tracks over steep hills, the grades worsening with every mile. A hot sun lathered the teams as they struggled up the mountainsides under heavy burdens that included five thousand new rifles for anticipated volunteers. Even on their horses, Burnside's staff was four hours climbing a dozen miles to Mount Vernon. Only a quarter of the distance to their first major landmark, the Cumberland, the office-softened aides went to bed exhausted that night, camped discouragingly near the foot of the next morning's first hill. Already the pace of the march took its toll: Captain Larned awoke dreadfully ill at dawn, perhaps a bit sunstruck, and by the next morning Burnside decided to return him to Cincinnati.[16]

As everyone had predicted, the trail grew even worse below the Cumberland. Hartsuff sent word back from the front that he had never seen such terrible roads. He had more bad news, as well: the local inhabitants had been expecting him for days. That meant they had no hope of surprising the enemy, but instead rather good reason to anticipate an ambush. In fact, Burnside's tent did not yet stand south of the river when Simon Buckner learned of his approach from a spy. That operative was overimpressed with the Yankees' numbers, nearly tripling Burnside's forces for the benefit of his employer, but the exaggeration merely prompted Buckner to take greater precautions.[17]

Buckner, who had effectively become a corps commander under Bragg in a recent reorganization, had the unenviable job of guarding all East Tennessee with a force much too small. He counted forty-three mountain passes that required protection, each of them dependent upon the security of the others. Between Loudon and the Virginia state line he had about as many men as Burnside could muster in his mobile force, but he had the advantage of two railroads that could speed him reinforcements from either Bragg's army or Samuel Jones's Department of Western Virginia. Bedford Forrest also commanded a crack Confederate cavalry division at Kingston, directly in the way of Burnside's march. Rather than try to meet the invaders head-on, Buckner divided his forces. He left a small brigade of infantry near the northern end of his department, within reach of General Jones, and detailed twenty-five hundred men under John Frazer to hold Cumberland Gap; he massed the rest of his infantry below Knoxville and concentrated his cavalry toward Kingston, near Forrest. He left most of East Tennessee open for Burnside, from Knoxville to Jonesborough, hoping to pounce upon him from both sides or from behind once he occupied the region. As early as August 25 he detected an inviting lapse between Rosecrans and Burnside, wiring Richmond that now was the time to swing between them and destroy their armies individually.[18]

Bragg preferred to curl his right wing back and solidify his own position; he ordered Buckner even farther south. Aware now of Yankees within thirty miles of Knoxville, Buckner sent a telegram to Cumberland Gap through Abingdon, ordering Frazer to give up the gap and fall back on Jones's forces. When the message passed through Abingdon, Jones saw it and interfered, countermanding Buckner's instructions. With almost half of all the troops Jones could spare for field operations, Frazer sat idle in the isolated pass where so many settlers had crossed into frontier Kentucky.[19]

As he lumbered into Tennessee, Burnside shaved off a pair of cavalry detachments to confuse the enemy. They prodded at Knoxville through two different gaps in the Cumberlands, neither of which Burnside planned to use, while the main force continued south.

Forage already grew rather scarce. There was little to be had in this border area, and certainly not enough for Burnside's preponderance of mounted troops and his many wagon teams. The people here, never well-to-do, had been left destitute by the war. Many farms had been abandoned as neighbors took vengeance on one another over political differences. Burnside put his troops on half-rations, and they pilfered so freely from the remaining mountain folk that he had to resort to the medieval penalty of branding on the cheek to discourage them. Still, he worried most that the Confederates would use their rail connections to send an overpowering force against him from either Bragg or Lee— just as Buckner had proposed. The East Tennessee & Virginia Railroad line caused Burnside the greatest anxiety: it offered a direct conduit for troops from anywhere in North Carolina or Virginia, against whom he could have no forewarning. Until the first brigades of the Ninth Corps could make their way down from Kentucky, he could hope for no assistance in the event of such an attack.[20]

Screening Burnside's advance was the cavalry division commanded by Brigadier General Samuel Carter, a U.S. Navy captain presently serving in the army. Carter's qualifications included his capacity to lead men and the fact that he was a native of these mountains. He sent a brigade each toward Kingston, Knoxville, and Loudon. Those horsemen who approached Kingston and the "capital" of East Tennessee, Knoxville, met with almost no resistance, but when General Shackelford tried to cross the bridge at Loudon he ran into John Pegram's cavalry, well dug in. There was a sharp fight, but when Shackelford began dropping shells across the river, the Confederates saddled up. Burnside, who had accompanied this column, could not get his men over in time to save the bridge. Colonel Sanders had failed to burn that structure in June, but Confederates put their own brands to it now; by nightfall its blazing trusses had dropped into the Tennessee.[21]

Both Bragg and Buckner expected Burnside to continue southwest, to join Rosecrans. That would have left East Tennessee, with its vital rail link to Virginia, in Southern hands. Reporting September 2 that none of the Union columns had crossed the Cumberland Mountains, Buckner wired his new commander, "The best hopes are entertained of this concentration." By that same evening, Buckner's "best hopes" were dashed: Burnside's cavalry had turned up outside Knoxville.[22]

In light of Henry Halleck's later insinuation he intended for Burnside to join Rosecrans from the outset, it is interesting the Confederate commanders were so anxious for that very prospect. The worst scenario Bragg might have envisioned would include Burnside occupying the Upper Tennessee Valley, cutting him off from direct communication with Lee and threatening his right, while Rosecrans used the Lower Tennessee to supply a flank movement around Bragg's left. Such a combination would force Bragg to evacuate Chattanooga and fall back into Georgia, abandoning the South's major east-west railroad system. Small wonder, then, that he and Buckner hoped for the Army of the Cumberland and the Army of the Ohio to meet in his front. Despite Bragg's hopes and Halleck's future distortions, the original plan was the

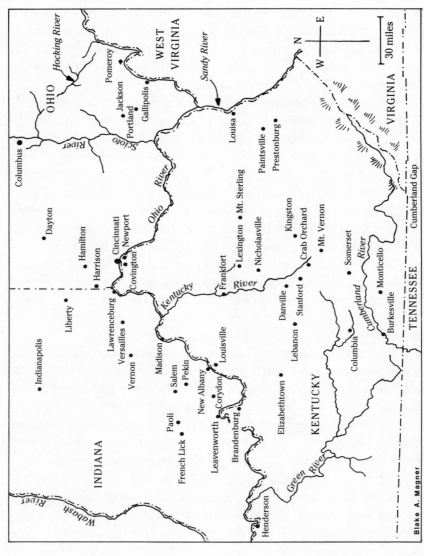

Map 8.
Kentucky

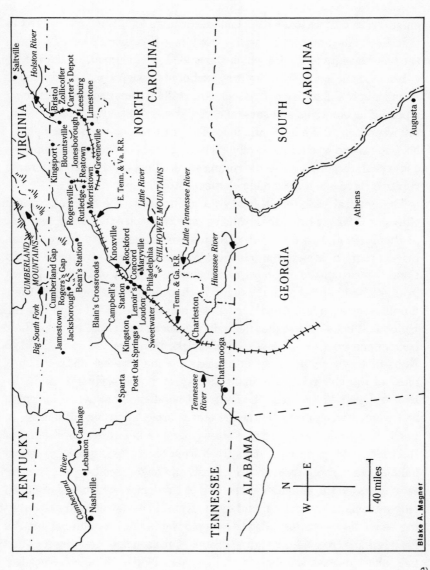

Map 9.
East Tennessee

Blake A. Magner

one carried out: as Rosecrans flanked Bragg's left, Burnside moved to take Knoxville and connect with—not join—Rosecrans's left. That was the basic assignment with which Burnside left Cincinnati in August.[23]

Burnside accomplished the first part of his assignment September 2. A brigade of Carter's cavalry took Knoxville without a shot, capturing a pair of locomotives and several cars besides military supplies which, unfortunately, did not include food. The trains stood momentarily useless, for there was no point along the captured section where supplies could be gathered, but the idle rolling stock symbolized the considerable rupture Burnside had made in Confederate transportation.[24]

The general rode into the city the next day at the head of Samuel Gilbert's infantry brigade. For more than two years these people, most of them devoted to the United States government, had been virtual prisoners in their own communities. With Confederate troops to shield them, secessionist neighbors had mounted a reign of terror. Known loyalists had been shot and hanged in their own front yards, and their families were driven from their farms; men who decided to fight for the Union had been required to flee into Kentucky and Ohio, turning their backs upon wives and homes. Many of the refugees had gravitated to Knoxville, where the prospect of assassination was less distinct. Thus most of the city rose in jubilant paroxysm at the arrival of their deliverer. One resident described outright pandemonium, with older men and women weeping for joy while others crowded around Burnside to touch him or his horse. Five dozen young ladies lined both sides of the road, holding national flags fresh from secret hiding places; people handed the passing troops water, fruit, and baked goods. The greeting far surpassed the delirium at the city of Frederick, which had endured only a week of occupation, and even after Burnside reached the building he would use as his office the people would not leave him alone. All day civilians trooped through in groups, a brazen few stepping forward to shake hands as the more timid gawked. Not until he consented to make a public address would they let him return to work, so he agreed to speak the next day. The following afternoon he mounted the balcony of the Mansion Hotel with a few hastily concocted notes, impressing the East Tennesseeans with his eloquence no more than he had the ladies at Mrs. Duncan's party, but they cheered him nonetheless. If he stammered through his remarks, one eyewitness observed, he was "an honest, noble man. He had a heart, and spoke from it." It was his valiant effort to free them that mattered: a quarter-century later one East Tennessee native recorded that the name of Burnside still commanded reverence in the region.[25]

Burnside's first concern was to discover the location of the enemy. He sent a few hundred cavalry and part of White's division south of the Tennessee from Loudon to look for the tail of Buckner's retreating column; Buckner had withdrawn to Charleston, and White's reconnaissance found the country free of Confederates for more than fifty miles down the line of the Tennessee & Georgia Railroad. While the cavalry accompanying White secured the desired contact with Rosecrans's videttes, Burnside put the two captured trains to use by loading a mixed brigade of dismounted cavalry and infantry on them and running them up to Morristown, where they captured some additional cars. Burnside had warned the leader of this expedition, Colonel John W. Foster, about guarding the stations along his route against the Confederates slipping behind him and cutting him off; Foster (no relation to General John G. Foster) became so exuberant over his easy progress that he continued all the way to Carter's Depot, beyond Jonesborough. He demanded the surrender of the Confederate garrison there, but without success. The Confederate commander, Alfred Jackson—unenviably called "Mudwall"—retreated to Bristol, where he quickly initiated a counterexpedition. With fewer than nine hundred men at hand, he followed the Yankees back to Jonesborough when they withdrew. Foster left garrisons in blockhouses at the various stations, and by September 8 he posed himself back at Morristown, halfway between Jonesborough and Knoxville. As Burnside had warned him, the Confederates circled some cavalry below his forwardmost unit at Limestone Station and tore up about six miles of track, burning a small bridge in the process. The stranded infantrymen, comprising most of the 100th Ohio, knew nothing of the destruction until they found themselves under attack by Jackson's dismounted troopers. They fell back to the safety of the blockhouse at Limestone Station, but Jackson brought up a battalion of North Carolina infantry and some artillery. Foster came chugging up the line with some reinforcements, but a weak engine and the length of mutilated track sealed the fate of the isolated outpost. The entire garrison surrendered before noon.[26]

Meanwhile, Burnside orchestrated tenfold retribution. John Frazer, first ordered to hold Cumberland Gap, then to evacuate it, had finally been told to hold it at all hazards, so he was still there when Burnside's roving cavalry radiated up from Knoxville. Frazer had four infantry regiments and an artillery battery on the spot and a regiment of horse scouting south, toward Knoxville. It was a formidable garrison, by the standards of Confederate strength in East Tennessee, and it was imperative to the security of the region that Burnside drive it away or capture it. He proposed to capture it.

Before leaving Kentucky, Burnside had directed the organization of an independent brigade intended to move on Cumberland Gap from the north, under one John DeCourcy. DeCourcy had been the colonel of an Ohio regiment since the early days of the war, and more than a year ago he had led another brigade into the gap, holding it for two months. It was because of his knowledge of the terrain that Burnside chose him, not for his charm: DeCourcy was a pompous whiner who could be extremely uncooperative.[27]

DeCourcy left Crab Orchard with four Ohio and Tennessee regiments on August 25. By September 7 he had reached Cumberland Ford, complaining every step of the way about deficiencies in quartermaster, commissary, and medical supplies, incidentally threatening to resign when it looked as though he might have to subordinate himself to a division commander. By now he knew that General Shackelford had arrived on the south side of the gap, and he sent word back to Lexington promising to expose the "culpable negligence of certain departments" if someone—namely Shackelford—leisurely captured the prize ahead of him. He ran low on ammunition and food, he said, because "the commissary and quartermaster officers at Crab Orchard have not been sober for many days." Otherwise, he argued, he would already have captured the place.[28]

Shackelford and DeCourcy finally penned Frazer into the gap. Shackelford demanded his surrender, simultaneously warning Knoxville the Confederates had up to four thousand troops in front of him. Frazer's cavalry regiment had been separated from him and driven away, so he was down to about twenty-five hundred men again, but Burnside hurried up from Knoxville in the van of an additional infantry brigade. Meanwhile Shackelford, the ranking officer at the scene, directed DeCourcy to cover the road to Harlan and keep his scouts out. DeCourcy snapped back that he was perfectly familiar with the approaches to the gap and had been in military service too long to be told his business. With none-too-subtle allusion to his "independent command," he implied Shackelford could mind his own business, after which he sent Frazer a series of his own requests to surrender.[29]

Burnside pushed the infantry relentlessly, covering the sixty rugged miles from Knoxville in a phenomenal fifty-two hours. He found Shackelford's negotiations with the besieged badly confused by DeCourcy's repeated meddling. Burnside sent his senior aide to Frazer at once, advising him to dismiss all other flags of truce but his own, giving him one hour to surrender his post. Burnside's name at the bottom of the message would normally have meant that the bulk of his army was present: that was probably just the impression he wished to create. After a couple of days of stalling, therefore, Frazer hauled down his flag. Colonel DeCourcy pulled in his pickets as soon as the surrender was announced, allowing several hundred of the Confederates to escape. By the time Burnside's guards herded up the garrison, barely two thousand prisoners remained.[30] Frazer asked the favor of a parole for his men; Burnside had it in his heart to grant it, but Halleck ordered otherwise. Washington believed the Confederates were forcing paroled but unexchanged Vicksburg prisoners to fight Rosecrans, and for the moment the cartel was essentially suspended. Rather than confront his prisoner with this unpleasant and unproven accusation, apparently, Burnside cited the technical fact that Frazer did not hold independent field command and lacked the authority to guarantee his side of the agreement. On the morning of September 10 the Confederates made the 1,500-foot descent into the valley below and started the long walk north. With them went Colonel DeCourcy, under arrest for insubordination. If the Southern prisoners were not out of the war for good, DeCourcy was.[31]

The only Confederates facing Burnside now were the few thousand under Sam Jones between Saltville, Virginia, and Jonesborough. Having left Knoxville before the little fiasco at Limestone Station, Burnside did not realize this little contingent kept up the contest: he considered East Tennessee conquered. The morning of September 10, he stopped to look back on a week of solid success. The loyalists of Tennessee were liberated; the rebellion here seemed over. He had known no such feeling for more than a year, and since he had grown tired of the sort of professional cannibalism practiced by men like DeCourcy (and Halleck), Burnside concluded this would be a fitting moment to hang his Tiffany sword over the mantle. With the characteristically humble observation that someone else could do his job as well as or better than he, he asked President Lincoln to let him go home. Impressed with the sincerity of the plea, Lincoln nevertheless insisted he still needed the general. With obvious disappointment, Burnside replied he would remain as long as absolutely necessary.[32]

When he returned to his office in Knoxville, Burnside found a note from Thomas Crittenden, a corps commander under Rosecrans, who said Rosecrans had taken Chattanooga. Bragg, he added, had retreated apace toward Rome, Georgia—fully sixty miles south of Chattanooga. Less encouraging intelligence came from reliable Unionists near Bristol, who heard that Confederates there had been ordered to retake East Tennessee at all costs: reinforcements for that purpose could easily shuttle from Virginia. Corroborating that report, Colonel Foster said citizens told of ten or fifteen thousand Confederates at Jonesborough. Foster himself remained skeptical, doubting more than two thousand of the enemy, but he had heard rumors of a corps of Lee's army coming down to help; his freshest dispatch had also remarked that his pickets northeast of Greeneville were driven in with "considerable fighting."[33]

After the customary two-day communications lag, Burnside read Halleck's September 11 congratulations for the capture of Knoxville and Cumberland Gap. The general-in-chief ordered him to seize the mountain gaps along the North Carolina border and bar the enemy's passage from Virginia, reiterating "connect with General Rosecrans, at least with your cavalry." Halleck authorized him to enlist every loyal soldier he could find in East Tennessee, which Burnside was already beginning to do. Rosecrans prepared to seal off northwest Georgia, Halleck added, and once the troops had established a solid defensive line, Washington would decide whether the next offensive operation should go down into Georgia or up into Virginia.[34]

These orders perfectly described Burnside's interpretation of his position. That part of his cavalry under Colonel Byrd had already made contact with Rosecrans below Athens, Frank Wolford's cavalry kept an eye on activities east of the French Broad, part of Foster's brigade stood watch over the upper Smokies, and Shackelford was moving his own cavalry and the remainder of Foster's into position to drive the enemy out of Jonesborough and into Virginia.

By September 13 Burnside grew reasonably certain that Robert E. Lee had sent heavy reinforcements to Bristol: railroad transportation had certainly been leaving Bristol in heavy volume, and rumor had it that Richard Ewell's entire corps—Stonewall's old command—was on the way. Such troops as those demanded far greater respect than the undisciplined detachments Buckner had left behind, so Burnside gravitated his main body toward Greeneville. The enemy still concentrated at Jonesborough, but General John S. Williams had taken over for Jackson, who remained in a subordinate capacity. His arrival implied that Williams had reinforced Jonesborough with a command of his own, but in fact he had come alone.[35]

The rumors reaching Knoxville had their genesis in the departure of James Longstreet's corps from Lee's army. Rolling stock had indeed rumbled out of Bristol to make the transfer, but it was not for East Tennessee these veterans were bound: on September 9 they boarded the cars for Bragg's army, via Augusta, Georgia. Their destination was especially difficult to predict because, aside from intelligence sources hinting at Jonesborough, Burnside's army would have been the more logical target. He had a smaller army, his flank lay unprotected, and his supply route was particularly precarious. The more direct rail line from Lee's army also posed less risk to the Confederates. Unknown to Burnside, General Lee concurred with him in that regard: he had only sent Longstreet to Georgia because of Bragg's mistaken assumption that Rosecrans and Burnside would combine forces against him. Had he known Burnside was moving on Knoxville, Lee wrote his president, he would have sent the corps there to contest the occupation of East Tennessee, vital as it was to the integrity of Confederate communications.[36]

Burnside wondered if he would be able to defend himself against a superior force made up of the cream of the Confederate army. He had responsibility for guarding nearly two hundred linear miles of front with the three small divisions of the Twenty-third Corps and a couple of independent brigades—between twelve and fifteen thousand men. Native volunteers, most of them deserters from the Confederate army, were coming into his various camps by the score, so his acting quartermasters began breaking open the boxes of extra rifles to arm them. Burnside ordered White's infantry division up from Loudon to Knoxville, and Hascall's from Concord to Greeneville. He looked for the advance of the Ninth Corps to reach Cumberland Gap every day, which would free another brigade to oppose the supposed Jonesborough host, but dawn after dawn he heard no word from his old corps. In desperation, he sent a courier back through Kentucky to push forward any spare troops that might remain in Indiana.[37]

Two Confederate deserters came into Colonel Foster's lines the afternoon of September 15, bringing welcome news: they said their forces at Jonesborough consisted of only half a dozen regiments and three batteries under Williams and Jackson—four thousand men, they estimated. This information struck Burnside as more of a stay of execution than a pardon, though, for the same two deserters had heard that Ewell was on the way. Later that day or early the next, Burnside also heard from his old friend Jacob Cox, whom he had left at his Cincinnati office. On the first anniversary of the fight at South Mountain, Cox wrote to warn him of a Confederate concentration against General Scammon, another of their Maryland cohorts. Scammon was in the Kanawha Valley of West Virginia, beset by as many as thirteen regiments. Cox interpreted it as a mere demonstration, or diversion, meant to draw Burnside back to the Ohio, which Burnside could remedy with a thrust from East Tennessee into Virginia.[38]

If Burnside had any reservations about moving against Jonesborough before, he had none now. Should Ewell's or any other troops be on the way from Lee's army, Burnside's interests dictated he strike before they arrived; so much the better if it took the heat off Scammon.

The next day Foster reported the enemy had fallen back five miles, and he asked if a reconnaissance-in-force would not be appropriate for the morning. Burnside had undertaken just such a maneuver when he opened two out-of-date dispatches from Halleck. The first, dated September 13, reminded him of the importance of hurrying his reserve forces down from Kentucky—as if he were not already striving to do just that—and ordered him to slide his infantry down toward Chattanooga to "connect" with Rosecrans, who might leave the city to fight Bragg. The second message was a day newer, and did not take the form of an order but advised he "should re-enforce General Rosecrans with all possible dispatch," citing a belief the enemy was gathering to fight. Halleck made no mention of Confederate reinforcements, but sometime that same day Burnside received a plea from Rosecrans, announcing that both Longstreet and Joe Johnston's Mississippi army had combined to crush him.[39]

Burnside was surprised and perhaps a bit skeptical about all of this:

the last he had heard, Bragg was in headlong flight into Georgia. Rosecrans was at least correct about Longstreet, though; he arrived in Atlanta in time to join Bragg in a tandem attack. Bragg struck Rosecrans along Chickamauga Creek, in northern Georgia, on September 19.

Because a flare-up of General Hartsuff's old wound made it difficult for him to take the field, Burnside exchanged places with him, leaving the younger man to the office duty at Knoxville while he started up to Greeneville to lead the troops. Halleck's missives overtook him on the road the morning of the seventeenth. He sent a courier to the wire at Cumberland Gap with Halleck's answer: "Orders to go below will be obeyed as soon as possible." Since his troops were already in position to attack Jonesborough in superior numbers, he would oversee the battle and send his largest force toward Chattanooga as soon as the shooting stopped. In the meantime he repeated his orders to rush the Ninth Corps into Tennessee and directed Hartsuff to send whatever troops were not in contact with the enemy downriver, to a collection point from which they could all start for Chattanooga. Halleck read Burnside's reply September 18 and again urged him to give Rosecrans "all the aid in your power." He added that none of Ewell's corps seemed absent from the Army of Northern Virginia. Telegraphic communications between Cumberland Gap and Knoxville commenced on the nineteenth, so Burnside saw Halleck's reply during one last, hasty visit to Knoxville before his attack. Halleck still hid the immediacy of the crisis—Rosecrans could, it seemed, have bought a good deal of time with a retreat. Burnside had already turned around White's division, part of Hascall's, and Wolford's cavalry brigade and marched them back toward Knoxville, on the first leg of the journey to Chattanooga. He could do no more for the moment, for the enemy had increased his force at Jonesborough to a reported six thousand by the addition of a Virginia brigade from Lee's army, and Burnside had only about that many troops on the scene. To assure that such a reduction in his advantage did not result in disaster, Burnside returned to the front to direct an immediate attack with his remaining resources.[40]

Satisfied the infantry and cavalry he had sent Rosecrans were all he could spare, Burnside started up the rail line again toward Virginia. He changed at Morristown on Monday, September 21, when another of Halleck's messages caught up with him. This carried a more alarmed tone, indicating for the first time that Rosecrans was under actual attack, but it also implied he had not yet found it necessary to give up the southern bank of the Tennessee River. By now Rosecrans had been pushed back to Chattanooga, where he was relatively safe, but thanks to the communications delay neither Burnside nor the authorities at Washington knew this. Burnside had heard nothing from Rosecrans since September 16; he could do nothing but obey the spirit of both Halleck's orders— to hold the line of the Holston River and simultaneously give Rosecrans all the aid in his power. Byrd's cavalry brigade still hugged Rosecrans's flank, and with Wolford's reinforcements, and White's and Hascall's infantry, there would be about eleven thousand men on hand. Deducting the brigade at Cumberland Gap, that took more than half of Burnside's entire strength. Halleck had not yet made clear that East Tennessee should be abandoned, either. Burnside understood such a retreat was unthinkable; therefore he assumed he should help Rosecrans while still covering his original territory. The only way he could manage that was to leave a provost detail in Knoxville and protect his own threatened left with the balance of his troops. He did precisely that, stripping the Cumberland Gap garrison for picket guards. Burnside explained it would take some time for even those men he was sending to arrive near Chattanooga, for some critical bridges were out, but he promised to forward the Ninth Corps to Rosecrans, too, whenever it arrived. If he could rout or capture the Confederates at Jonesborough, Burnside might also be able to afford another brigade or two for Chattanooga, so he continued north with that object still in mind.[41]

When Burnside arrived at the front that night, he found the Confederates concentrated around Carter's Depot and Zollicoffer, a few miles up the line. Burnside formulated his battle plan during the night. Before dawn he sent Colonel Foster's cavalry brigade in a wide arc around the enemy's left, to strike Jones's headquarters at Zollicoffer. When those horsemen were well on their way, he sent a flag of truce to General Williams, at Carter's Station, with a message warning he intended to fire on the nearby villages, offering an opportunity to evacuate the civilians. This courtesy amounted to no more than a bluff, that Williams might read "Headquarters, Army of the Ohio" on the letterhead and presume, as Frazer had, that Burnside's entire army confronted him. The ruse worked. During the night Williams learned of Foster's flanking movement and fell back on the other Confederates at Zollicoffer.[42]

Late that same evening, or in the predawn hours of September 22,

Burnside was finally apprised of the Union defeat at Chickamauga. A courier who had had to cover forty miles of the rail line on horseback because of burned bridges delivered a personal message from President Lincoln. In a single sentence written the morning of the twenty-first, the president cut through all the vague and self-protective instructions Halleck had provided: "Go to Rosecrans at once with your force, without a moments delay." This was a command Burnside could understand; it left no room for misinterpretation.

Burnside outlined his situation for the president. As soon as he heard from Foster, whom he could hardly abandon, he would leave a small force to guard against any resurgence of the enemy's fighting spirit and start the balance of his men south. He had hoped to capture Jones altogether, but considering the president's note, that project would have to wait. Preceding his returning troops on horseback and by train, Burnside arrived in Knoxville on Wednesday, September 24. That day or the next came another message from Halleck, warning that Bragg may already have foiled what—for the first time—Halleck called Burnside's "junction" with Rosecrans. It was, Halleck advised, no longer safe south of the Tennessee River. Any reinforcements for Rosecrans would have to travel on the north bank.[43]

This posed a couple of problems. White's infantry division and the two cavalry brigades were already south of the Tennessee, where they encountered a solid wall of Confederate cavalry; Burnside ordered White to withdraw to the right bank, at Loudon. The other difficulty was that the railroad crossed the river there, and if Burnside should move on the north bank he would have to go overland again, his lifeline open to all the old dangers offered by mountains, bad roads, and Confederate cavalry. Stores of food and supplies already dipped too low to accumulate another wagon train such as the one that brought him down from Kentucky, and the countryside was picked clean. The only course Burnside could follow was to move along the railroad in sufficient force to defy Bragg. That required most of his army, including the cavalry, three thousand of which rode wornout horses. Replacements for those horses, two thousand more head of beef, and some more new rifles for the volunteers were on the way to Knoxville from Kentucky.[44]

For more than a week the president had urged Halleck to move Burnside down to assist Rosecrans, and despite Burnside's repeated assurances he was doing so, his every successive acknowledgment came

from a point still farther from Rosecrans. Nor could Lincoln understand why Burnside's principal force was stranded above the Holston
River by burned bridges when it had been below the Holston originally.
Burnside's apparently contrary behavior had driven Lincoln to the only
instance of profanity War Department telegraphers ever heard from
him. On September 19, while the president stood by the key, it started
clicking with Burnside's answer to Halleck's messages of nearly a week
before. Hoping it would report progress toward Chattanooga, Lincoln
instead read that Burnside would leave Knoxville for Greeneville, in
the opposite direction, to attack Jonesborough, which lay yet farther in
the wrong direction.

"Damn Jonesborough," Lincoln had sputtered. He could be very sarcastic, as he had demonstrated with McClellan after Antietam, and
when he read Burnside's lengthy explanation for his delays, he scrawled
a rather nasty letter in reply, opening with "Yours of the 23rd is just
received and it makes me doubt whether I am awake or dreaming."[45]

The president's unusual aggravation revealed that he failed to understand a number of circumstances concerning Burnside. First, he seems
not to have taken into account the primitive communications that connected the Army of the Ohio with Washington. Messages had to travel
west to Covington or Cincinnati, then south to Cumberland Gap, sixty
mountainous miles from Knoxville. Seldom was there a complete telegraph circuit, and most dispatches required at least two days to transmit: Halleck's September 13 wire took three and a half days. Any orders
containing the least ambiguity could easily have caused the lapse of a
week or ten days while they were questioned and clarified, and it is not
at all unfair to characterize Halleck's initial instructions as ambiguous.
Probably unknown to Lincoln, Halleck had transmitted the president's
most earnest wishes in the form of requests and advice rather than
orders, nor were even those requests altogether precise. Halleck directed Burnside to push his troops forward into "East Tennessee" and
to move his infantry "toward" Chattanooga "as rapidly as possible." He
followed that with another note advising Burnside he "should" bolster
Rosecrans "with all possible dispatch," which allowed considerable room
for interpretation of the word "possible." As late as September 18 the
tone of the general-in-chief continued advisory and nebulous, referring
to "all the aid in your power" but stopping short of ordering him to send
his entire force, and even his urgent message of the twenty-first lacked

the sense of an order, merely remarking that "Rosecrans will require all the assistance you can give him to hold Chattanooga." At no time did Halleck relieve Burnside of his considerable responsibility for holding East Tennessee—as Lincoln appears to have intended—instead repeatedly ordering him to "hold some point near the upper end of the valley" and send the remainder of his force to Rosecrans. Maintaining such a presence in northeast Tennessee required a series of garrisons at Cumberland Gap and between Knoxville and the Virginia line; that left Burnside too few men either to bull his way south of the Tennessee to Chattanooga or to guard his supply line over the bad roads north of the Tennessee. Halleck's admonition to hold upper East Tennessee simply confirmed Burnside's understanding of Lincoln's solicitous attitude toward the region, further departing from the president's current intention.[46]

Lincoln was also unaware that, as Halleck's first two messages made their way into the Cumberland Mountains, Burnside had already begun shifting the weight of his army from the southern end of his line to its northern extremity. Encouraged by Crittenden's overoptimistic news that Bragg was safely on the run, and anxious to eliminate the threat Jones represented, he had ordered White's and Hascall's infantry divisions to Greeneville. Both these units had camped north of Knoxville when Halleck's first appeal arrived, and the only remaining connection between the Army of the Cumberland and the Army of the Ohio was Byrd's cavalry. On September 17, White's troops lay 120 miles from Rosecrans, and the cavalry under Shackelford and Foster was nearly 200 miles away, while Lincoln believed Burnside massed his main body between Knoxville and Loudon. That impression may have been deliberately left with him by Halleck, who knew nothing of Crittenden's erroneous telegram but seemed anxious, after the humiliating defeat at Chickamauga, to create the illusion he had long ago ordered Burnside to combine his army with that of Rosecrans. In fact, even if Burnside had abandoned all of East Tennessee the morning of September 17, even if he had ignored his own supply line and the threat of Jones at his rear, and even if he had overcome the Confederates who stood to resist him to the south, he could never have supplied Rosecrans a single rifleman before the disaster of September 20. The bulk of his troops would have arrived long after the defeat, in an exhausted condition and without supplies; East Tennessee would have been lost for nothing, and Burnside's army would only have further taxed Rosecrans's already strained supply line. No one has ever pointed out what a fortuitous event it was that Burnside could not comply with Halleck's and Lincoln's wishes.

The final element Lincoln failed to consider when he gave vent to his temper was that Burnside's whereabouts did not necessarily coincide with that of his troops; as Frazer and Williams had supposed, a department commander would ordinarily either accompany the largest part of his army or establish headquarters in a central location, but, at least partly because of Hartsuff's condition, Burnside did not follow the custom. When he wired, "I go to Greeneville tonight," he did not mean he would take the entire Army of the Ohio. Actually, the farther northeast Burnside traveled, the nearer to Chattanooga the preponderance of his troops moved: he had only four cavalry brigades and four infantry brigades in East Tennessee, exclusive of the garrison at Cumberland Gap, and when he first heard Rosecrans might be in trouble, only one cavalry brigade rode south of Knoxville. Almost immediately he ordered back White and Colonel Wolford's horsemen, so that within four days half his army occupied Loudon and Athens. As soon as Jones retreated to Virginia, Hascall's division also moved south of Knoxville, leaving only two cavalry brigades to keep Jones in check. With the exception that he did not move south from Loudon—which he could not safely do— Burnside had obeyed Halleck's directions to the letter.[47]

With his customary disinclination to offend people, Lincoln never sent the biting letter of September 25. His intervention in the chain of command implied a certain disapprobation, however, and Burnside went over the previous week's correspondence to find out where he might have gone wrong. When he detected a note of reproach in Halleck's use of the word "delay," he submitted a summary of his military position, his supply situation, and his interpretation of Halleck's orders to date. What, he wished to know, did the administration want? Should he abandon East Tennessee?

Both Lincoln and Halleck responded, essentially, that he ought to hold what he had and reinforce Rosecrans besides. This was no help at all. Burnside felt he could get no specific orders, so he developed three specific plans for approval. The first required the abandonment of East Tennessee and a complete junction of Burnside's twenty thousand men with Rosecrans by the roads north of the river. This would allow him to do without his vulnerable supply line, carrying only provisions enough to reach Rosecrans. The second option entailed slinking south of the river from Loudon and attacking Bragg's right wing with about fifteen thousand, leaving the other five thousand to face Jones. The final alternative called for a combined force of cavalry and infantry, twelve thousand strong, which would cross the river and circle south of Bragg's right flank, cutting his railroad connection from Dalton to Atlanta and destroying the machine shops and powder mills along the way, dashing finally to the Atlantic coast—living off the land in a march to the sea. The last bold maneuver would draw off a sizable force of the enemy from Chattanooga; it might have been the brainchild of John Hunt Morgan. Halleck fairly ridiculed it.[48]

Burnside wired the three proposals to both Rosecrans and Halleck. Halleck responded in his habitually ambiguous manner, refusing to do much more than repeat his vague and unworkable instructions of the past month. His sole remark upon Burnside's long proposition was the dry rejoinder that "distant expeditions into Georgia are not now contemplated." He did offer that Rosecrans no longer required Burnside to go directly to Chattanooga, but merely to hold a force ready to go to his aid if he should call for it.[49]

Whatever Burnside did, other than sit tight, might very likely result in disaster; should that happen, it was just as likely that he would be found at fault. He therefore desired an unequivocal order on which he could base his movements. Such a thing was impossible for Henry Halleck to produce: he was too thorough a bureaucrat to assume the responsibility. In a fit of exasperation similar to Lincoln's, Burnside scribbled Halleck a personal reprimand for his indefinite and frequently contradictory orders. On the one hand he told Burnside to hold all of East Tennessee, from Loudon to Bristol, with a force barely sufficient; on the other he wanted him to send every available man to Rosecrans. "The impression is left upon those who did not know our force, and situation," Burnside explained, "that you know that I was strong enough to do more for Rosecrans than I have done, and that I was tardy in obeying your orders." He concluded with the reminder that he would be happy to be relieved if Halleck deemed him incompetent or insubordinate.[50]

Like Lincoln's furious letter to Burnside, this one never went into the dispatch pouch. Just as Burnside signed it, a communication arrived from Rosecrans, who had only now received his copy of Burnside's three plans. He wanted him to adopt the first, abandoning East Tennessee and reinforcing him directly, and soon—contrary to Halleck's recent statement. Burnside wired this information to Washington, asking if it should be done. With infuriating stubbornness, Halleck still refused to stick his neck out. "I can only repeat former instructions," he persisted. "I cannot make them plainer."[51]

Halleck really meant that he *would* not make them plainer, and he thereby achieved precisely what Burnside feared: he covered himself, leaving the impression Burnside had been strong enough to assist Rosecrans but had been slow to obey. This interpretation has since prevailed. Grant had been even slower to respond—for equally good reasons—but that is largely forgotten, and the scapegoat of Fredericksburg has come to serve similar duty for the failure at Chickamauga.

One of the staff officers of the Army of the Cumberland even charged, decades later, that Burnside deliberately withheld his assistance because he feared his superior rank would create a confusion in command; he purported that Hartsuff, who was junior to Rosecrans, offered to avoid that problem by leading the reinforcements himself.[52] The story is altogether implausible. In the first place, Hartsuff was too ill to leave the Knoxville office. Besides, Burnside had already resolved the issue of rank with his June letter subordinating himself to Rosecrans once they joined forces; his later readiness to act as a corps commander under General Meade proved his sincerity.

Few students of Chickamauga have failed to find Burnside partly to blame for the drubbing Bragg gave Rosecrans. None, however, seems to have considered the precise chronology of the complete correspondence between Washington and Knoxville, or the condition of affairs within Burnside's sphere of responsibility.

The controversy over Chickamauga had barely begun, but the participants were forced by their common enemies to postpone the debate. Joseph Wheeler's Confederate cavalry, which had so far confined White to the vicinity of Loudon, splashed across the Tennessee River early in October, cutting between Rosecrans and Burnside. Rosecrans, whom one observer considered too nervous to command an army, began to hail Burnside for help again. White had sent Burnside a report about the crossing, but since Burnside had not received it, he asked Rosecrans if his sources might not be mistaken. Incensed, Rosecrans replied, "If you don't unite with us soon, you will be responsible for another catastrophe, I fear." Reference to "another catastrophe" may have been Old

Rosey's way of blaming Burnside for his recent defeat, or perhaps he alluded to Wheeler's capture of a large number of wagons, supplies, and several hundred troops. Rosecrans suspected Wheeler's raiders would circle behind Burnside's army, cut off his supplies and communications, and combine forces with Sam Jones, in Virginia: that is what he told Burnside, and he sent the same warning to Halleck in a telegram remarkably derogatory of Burnside.[53]

Rosecrans sent three more messages to Knoxville over the next five days, complaining constantly of Burnside's failure to respond. The Confederates had poised a strong force just below White's videttes to help Wheeler break through, and dispatch bearers had to negotiate hostile territory; few of them made it, and Burnside seems not to have received Rosecran's more desperate appeals. The Confederate cavalry did not circle Burnside after all, instead veering behind Rosecrans and disrupting his own communications, finally recrossing the Tennessee at Muscle Shoals, Alabama.[54] Though no one commented upon it, Wheeler's raid demonstrated just how vulnerable Burnside's lifeline would have been had he heeded Rosecrans and Halleck and stretched himself thin along the north bank of the river.

Emboldened by the withdrawal of the greater part of Burnside's troops, which he presumed had gone to Chattanooga, Sam Jones proposed to retake East Tennessee and break up the recruiting camps full of North Carolina and Tennessee tories. He sent John Williams back toward Jonesborough with a brigade of cavalry, but he put Major General Robert Ransom in charge of the entire operation. Ransom, just down from Richmond, had two brigades of infantry, one of them from Lee's army. He told Williams to spread out his cavalry and start down the railroad in the direction of Knoxville as though he were screening the advance of a large army, while Ransom himself moved against Cumberland Gap with his infantry. Williams thought he heard Ransom say he should not advance beyond Bull's Gap for the present. A veteran of Scott's campaign to Mexico City, Williams dutifully rolled his regiments south on what he hoped would be a similar expedition, sweeping up little Union garrisons along the way.[55]

The Ninth Corps, such as there was left of it, had finally arrived from Kentucky. Robert Potter had come down with Edward Ferrero's first division and Simon Griffin's brigade of the second: nineteen depleted regiments amounting to perhaps six thousand men. As Ransom and

Williams left Jonesborough, Orlando Willcox arrived at Cumberland Gap with three thousand untrained men in four regiments—six-month volunteers from Indiana.

Burnside recognized a new field officer in Ferrero's division; this young man had been one of his signalmen in North Carolina and a line officer under him in Virginia, and Burnside asked the effective strength of his regiment like an old friend inquiring after the family. The major recited some disappointing figure. The general, possibly thinking of Willcox's throng of Hoosiers, told him they were worth more than a thousand new men.[56]

Burnside ordered both Potter and Willcox up to Morristown, just below Bull's Gap. Williams, who believed Ransom still made his way to Cumberland Gap, assumed his own mission was to create a diversion for that attack; thus he felt much gratified to find so many Yankees piling up in front of him when he reached Bull's Gap. First came Ferrero's division, rattling up the rickety railroad from Knoxville. A brigade of Hascall's division, already on duty at Morristown, lined up with them. Then Shackelford drew up two cavalry brigades. Finally came Willcox and his rookies, from Cumberland Gap.

Unbeknownst to Williams, his demonstration no longer served any purpose: Ransom had fallen back into Virginia. As in the case of General Frazer just before his capture, General Jones short-circuited the usual channels and directed Williams to push the Federals beyond Bull's Gap, if possible. Williams reported rumors of heavy Union reinforcements, but Jones scoffed at the notion, attributing them to disloyal citizens bent on discouraging him. When Williams added up the several brigades arrayed against his one, Jones simply told him to fight as long as he could. Considering that Williams had fewer than two thousand cavalry to face Burnside's twelve thousand or more, that might not be very long.[57]

Burnside started for Bull's Gap the morning of October 9, expecting to contend with equal numbers. The train took five hours to cover the forty miles to Morristown; after that the general and staff rode their horses to the front. Shackelford deployed to skirmish with the enemy, but evening came without an engagement. The night turned cold, and Burnside had to huddle with his staff in a lean-to of overlaid shelter halves, with a fire blazing at the open ends. They all ate crosslegged in the firelight, Burnside in the middle.

The next day Burnside rose early. He and his jangling attendants passed the Ninth Corps about nine that morning. It was the first time these troops had seen their old commander since March, and they went wild. Caps flew into the air and fell like so many flocks of starlings, and the hills echoed with lusty cheers. Burnside reciprocated the greetings by uncovering his bald dome, riding bareheaded for fifteen minutes at a time.[58]

Shackelford began pushing Williams by ten o'clock. The Confederate had to broaden his front to a width of two miles, but he made a stubborn resistance. Burnside again chose Foster's cavalry to swing around behind the enemy's line, but because of Williams's ruse, he thought this was Jones's entire army before him, and he gave Foster too wide an arc to follow. Foster could not cover the additional expanse of muddy roads before Burnside decided to attack with his infantry. It was about half past three in the afternoon when Burnside stopped near Blue Springs and ordered Potter to bring up a division to break the Confederate line, and it was five o'clock before the first of Ferrero's three brigades stood ready to go in. Its path lay over a harvested cornfield and open pasture, while the defenders had the protection of the woodline. When Burnside gave the word, the infantry lurched forward with a confident yell, but Burnside turned his back to them. "I can't see those brave boys fall," he muttered. This was the first time he had sent Ninth Corps troops into battle since Fredericksburg.[59]

Burnside might as well have watched, for Williams fell back quickly. He retreated through the night, with skirmisher firing lighting the darkness at his heels. At Greeneville a few hundred infantry under Jackson reinforced him, and together they met Foster the next morning. Foster had not yet reached his destination and had not prepared his ambush; neither was Williams in the state of disorganized rout Foster had anticipated. In short order the Confederates sent Foster's unsupported cavalry packing.[60]

That same morning Burnside started for Greeneville himself, passing between occasional clusters of citizens who alternately cheered him and fell to their knees in prayer. A courier dashed up with word of Foster's fight, and Burnside spurred his wild-eyed bobtail into a gallop, splashing through the mud, jumping fences, and cutting across fields. A second messenger brought him back to a walk, though, with news the Confederates were on the retreat again. Union infantry was wearing out, and Burnside realized Williams's retreat moved too quickly for a strong force of foot soldiers, so he directed the cavalry to take over the pursuit.

The roadway was littered with the refuse of the Confederate withdrawal. Burnside followed it as far as Greeneville, Andrew Johnson's hometown. With a group that included Parke and General Potter, Burnside ate his lunch in the home of Governor Johnson's married daughter. That afternoon he went up the line to Rheatown and camped for the night.[61]

Williams fought another sharp skirmish October 12, after which he fell back to Jonesborough, then to Blountsville, just south of the Virginia border. The paucity of his force was apparent now, so Burnside left the cavalry to counter any more forays, with a brigade of infantry at Jonesborough and Willcox's short-term men at Greeneville. He ordered the rest, including the Ninth Corps, back to Knoxville, and he returned there himself the next day, not a little disappointed that he had not been able to bag Williams's entire brigade. His staff reflected bitterly that the whole affair would have been unnecessary had Burnside been permitted to use White and Hascall to neutralize Jones three weeks before.[62]

During Burnside's absence at the front, belated news of Rosecrans's call for reinforcements must have reached Knoxville, for a sudden panic infected the civilian population at the rumor Burnside might go to Chattanooga. Two former congressmen petitioned President Lincoln in the names of Christianity, Humanity, God, and Liberty not to forsake the loyalists of East Tennessee. They, like Burnside, supposed the Confederates would exact a terrible vengeance on those who had rallied to the flag if they were permitted to reoccupy the region. The day after that anguished telegram went to Washington, Rosecrans wired again for assistance, reminding Burnside he had not heard from him in ten days. Halleck also suggested he shift his weight to Kingston so he could better cooperate with Chattanooga. The general-in-chief, who once reproved Rosecrans for telegraphing too frequently, now complained that Burnside reported too seldom. Perhaps Burnside's silence was a result of his flimsy and vulnerable lines of communications, at least at first; but as his various exchanges with Rosecrans and Halleck became evermore frustrating, it is possible he shut the two of them out in disgust. When Halleck's last directive arrived, Burnside was already considering sending Lincoln a peremptory resignation. His old intestinal ailment troubled him often now, he had suffered all the abuse he intended to endure for his failure to do the impossible, and he did not want to be remembered as the man who gave Knoxville over to the Vandals.[63]

It was probably the rising star of Ulysses Grant that prevented Burnside's departure from the army at this juncture. Just as he pondered his resignation, he learned Grant had been appointed to command the Military Division of the Mississippi, embracing the Armies of the Ohio, Cumberland, and Tennessee. The creation of this new administrative stratum interposed a level of command between Burnside and Halleck; it also obviated direct communication with Rosecrans—who was deposed anyway. Here was a man Burnside thought he could work with. An immediate glow warmed the hearts of those in the Knoxville headquarters, and the general looked forward to a fresh start with his new chief. "Please rely upon my full and cordial support," he told Grant.[64]

II

The first thing Grant wanted to know was Burnside's strength and how his men were distributed. The Ninth Corps and Willcox's six-month men gave him almost 15,000 infantry, 8,600 cavalry, and more than 100 fieldpieces in East Tennessee. Such numbers might have puzzled army headquarters, considering Burnside's continual complaints of insufficient manpower, but the figures represented those men who were present, regardless of whether they were sick or detached for fatigue or other duty. His effective strength was much lower, with most of that encumbered by the responsibility of guarding various strategic bastions. Nearly 2,000 men and 13 of the guns defended Cumberland Gap; some 9,000 cavalry, infantry, and artillery manned 4 garrisons between Morristown and Jonesborough; 6,000 provided reconnaissance and an initial defense force at and below Loudon; more than 3,000 held the vicinity of Knoxville; and a substantial number of men were required to convoy the wornout supply teams on their pathetic journeys over the mountains. All Burnside could muster for a mobile force was fewer than 5,000 men of the Ninth Corps. He proposed to post them at Kingston, where Halleck had recently been urging him to locate his surplus troops.[1]

Some of the guards strewn along the northern end of the railroad were fresh recruits from the Smoky Mountains. Burnside had hoped for as many as 10,000 of these volunteers, and by the middle of October he had realized a healthy portion of that estimate: 3,000 men had already enlisted for three years of service, and another 2,500 had signed on as home guards. Burnside had brought thousands of weapons over the gaps for these loyalists—as Bragg had done for Confederate sympathizers, more fruitlessly, during the Kentucky invasion of 1862—and they stood present for duty despite a lack of uniforms. Mustering officers swore in at least one new regiment from each side of the state line: the 2nd North Carolina Mounted Infantry and the 13th Tennessee Cavalry. Hundreds of Tennesseeans also joined Burnside's Midwestern regiments, in which many had peripatetic relatives. Unionists in the mountains of North Carolina had been escaping into Kentucky for months, and now they returned to Knoxville in droves. Certainly, the loyal element was more pronounced here than it had been on the North Carolina sounds.[2]

Grant, unlike Halleck, Rosecrans, and even Lincoln, understood Burnside's precarious position in East Tennessee: situated at the end of a 200-mile wagon ride from his supply base, his teams rawboned and dying in the traces, vulnerable from both flanks and innumerable mountain passes. Grant thus sounded less impatient and critical. Burnside's staff, and presumably the general himself, appreciated the new chief's courteous tone. Grant recognized that Burnside's best hope lay in the Armies of the Tennessee and Cumberland breaking Bragg's siege of Chattanooga; that would simultaneously remove the greatest threat to his flanks and open the Tennessee River for a supply route all the way to Knoxville. Also realizing that the railroad from Louisville and Nashville was already overtaxed by the appetite of the forces at Chattanooga, Grant did not continue Rosecrans's lament over Burnside's failure to join him; he might stay where he was, for the present.[3]

Even staying where he was proved difficult. In order to keep watch over Bragg at the same time he maintained communications with Chattanooga, Burnside established cavalry outposts on both sides of the Tennessee below Loudon. At Philadelphia, on the Tennessee & Georgia Railroad, sat Frank Wolford's brigade of cavalry: three Kentucky regiments and the 45th Ohio Mounted Infantry. These were ordinarily dependable men, many of them armed with breechloaders that included Burnside carbines and some Henry repeaters. Neither their experience nor their ordnance availed them much good on October 20, however.

They were low on ammunition, and a combination of overwork and their belief the Confederates had recently retreated below the Hiwassee River may have rendered them less alert than usual. Their last scout along the Hiwassee could not have been long completed when Carter Stevenson moved his Confederate division across that river and launched a two-brigade cavalry attack on Wolford's camp. Some of the Southern horsemen made their way behind the forward Union outpost undetected, and though the Kentuckians and Buckeyes fought valiantly, they were taken front and rear. Wolford tried to turn the tables on his assailants by circling two regiments behind the enemy's frontal assault, but the two leapfrogging regiments became pinched between the first wave of Confederates and their supports. More than two hundred of that wing were captured, and for a time it seemed Wolford's entire brigade would be gobbled up. His troopers had shot up most of their remaining ammunition, and his six-gun battery had fired its last round, when Wolford gathered the survivors in a desperate charge for freedom up the Loudon road. With sabers and revolvers alone they cut their way through, dragging four or five prisoners with them, and bolted headlong for the safety of White's earthworks outside Loudon. Wolford left behind nearly five hundred men, most of them captured, as well as all his loaded supply wagons, ambulances, the six howitzers, and his teams. The loss afforded Henry Halleck a wonderful opportunity to point out his earlier admonition against operating south of the Tennessee, and he made great use of it in the annual report he was then composing.[4]

The same force that captured Philadelphia diverted a few companies to destroy the ferry over the Tennessee at Kingston; the commander of Burnside's brigade at Post Oak Springs heard the roar of Wolford's fight just before this little column challenged his pickets, and a citizen told him these cavalrymen were the vanguard of Bragg's army. It all seemed logical to that officer: the Union armies at Chattanooga were too strong and well protected to overcome, so Bragg had swung his bulk against the Army of the Ohio. That warning reached Burnside's office October 21, but he seemed to give it little credit. The next day Burnside paused in the midst of a letter to Lincoln and Grant on the subject of that new railroad from Louisville to Knoxville, which he hoped would allow him to issue new camp equipment, reinstate full rations, and reclothe his troops, when a message came tapping in from a staff officer at Loudon: eight thousand Confederate infantry and artillery had just appeared below Philadelphia; the officer had seen them with his own eyes.

As soon as Burnside had that information, he gave his staff orders to be packed in half an hour, but they did not start for Loudon until October 23. They boarded the train in a torrential downpour, with the headquarters paperwork tucked protectively under their rubber ponchos. Burnside rode in the locomotive, carrying a well-deserved gift for Colonel Sanders in his pocket: Edwin Stanton's announcement that the president had appointed Sanders a brigadier general.[5]

The road to Loudon was little more than thirty miles long, but because of the ferocity of the storm the engineer dared do no more than crawl, apprehensive of coming too quickly on a washed-out section of track. They were hours making Loudon, where the nude stone piers of the burned railroad trestle rose from the water. Rain still lashed the earth savagely, and the poor visibility of day had given over to total darkness, but Burnside insisted on finding White's headquarters; he slogged away from the depot with two aides. Two hours later the three of them returned, their cavalry boots veneered to the very knees with mud. White had reported no significant movement of the Confederates at Philadelphia, so Burnside told the rest of the staff they could bed down for the night. It was yet too miserable to think of pitching tents, and even a search for a suitable house would have left them drenched, so they decided to remain in their railroad car. No one had eaten in fourteen hours, and the cry went up for Paul, the general's chef. To their immense surprise and pleasure, this inveterate forager came down the aisle with a sizzling pan of beefsteak, some boiled chicken, hardtack with butter on it, and a pot of hot coffee. Where he had found the food or cooked it, no one asked; each officer stuck a candle stub on the arm of his seat and went to work on the food. When the last bone had gone out the windows someone produced a deck of cards, and with the rain still pounding the roof of the car, a foursome of whist bid back and forth until two o'clock in the morning. By then the candles had flickered out, and the aides pulled their coats about themselves and slumped down for what sleep they could get, crowded two in a seat.[6]

Down at Chattanooga, George Thomas had replaced Rosecrans. Learning of Stevenson's movement, he asked Burnside if he needed any help, offering either to send reinforcements or assume control of a longer section of the Tennessee, so Burnside could shorten his line and compact his forces. Burnside responded gratefully that he had no use for reinforcements, as he could barely feed the men he had.

As if the threat from the south were not alarming enough, Burnside awakened to a wire from Halleck after midnight on Sunday, October 25. The Army of Northern Virginia had forced its Union counterpart, under George Meade, to retreat toward Washington, then had withdrawn south of the Rappahannock. Halleck suspected the feint was designed to cover the detachment of still more of Lee's army to the southwest, to reinforce either Bragg or Jones. Halleck's latest intelligence corroborated this: he was certain Ewell's corps had gone to Tennessee with twenty or twenty-five thousand men, and since spies had not reported his passage through Richmond, Halleck assumed he had traveled by way of Lynchburg, which would have put him on the line to Abingdon. Ultimately this information proved to be false, but after more than a month of urging Burnside to work his forces down toward Chattanooga, Halleck reversed himself and said he should move them back in the direction of Abingdon.[7]

Burnside woke Captain Larned at 2:00 A.M. to write dispatches to Shackelford and the other commanders up north, then he called a council of war with Parke, Potter (whose corps he had redirected to Loudon instead of Kingston), White, and Sanders—whom he placed in command of all the cavalry around Loudon. Larned watched the generals' conference from outside the tent, writing a letter to his sister. He knew as much as anyone about this disconcerting new development, and he predicted Burnside would return to Knoxville so as to remain equidistant from each beleaguered flank. The generals, however, must have come to the conclusion that Ewell's corps was not the worse threat; perhaps they reasoned that an advance by the Army of the Potomac would prompt Lee to call him back, if indeed he came at all. Burnside's own information indicated that Longstreet had command of the Confederates across the Tennessee River. That meant there would be a good many of them, that they would be well commanded, and that they would be among the best in the Southern army. This was the front he must face.[8]

Having made his decision, Burnside could do nothing more but wait. The night waned clear; fair weather came at a premium now, so Burnside lay his preoccupations aside and joined his staff in some predawn songs around the campfire. Larned especially remembered the general's basso profundo carrying the lower octave of "Watchman Tell Us of the Night."

Monday was Mrs. Burnside's birthday. The general spent the entire day in his tent, ill again, and Parke was down with his own recurring fever. Shackelford renewed the anxiety over the Ewell rumor in the afternoon, transmitting citizen reports of reinforcements at Abingdon that included at least a brigade from Lee's army. On Tuesday Shackelford added that he knew of sixteen thousand Confederates around Abingdon, but he said most of them had already been there; through civilian contacts within his perimeter, and their relatives and acquaintances inside Sam Jones's lines, Shackelford determined that Jones had received no more than two thousand reinforcements. Relieved at least for the moment of the need to fight on two fronts at once, Burnside told Grant he did not believe the tale about Ewell, but in order to consolidate his forces he ordered White's men north of the Tennessee River. Both the Tennessee and the Holston were too rain-swollen for the enemy to cross, so he chose to leave a light guard on the riverbank and move back to Lenoir's Station. At the same time, he telegraphed President Lincoln about his troublesome Mexican malady; he warned he was growing weaker from it, intimating he might become unfit for command at some point.[9]

Later that day Shackelford modified his earlier report: while he stood by his estimate of enemy numbers, he thought they might be on the move, in the direction of Kingsport and Rogersville. There were reportedly four Confederate brigades beyond Bristol. Willcox wrote from Greeneville that he, too, had spies who mentioned the column marching on Kingsport and Rogersville, but he had heard they were working themselves into position for an attack on Knoxville, from behind. This, Burnside told Grant, was particularly bad news: he could little afford to retreat far from Jonesborough or he would lose his supply line through Cumberland Gap. He could change his base to Kingston, and pull back all his troops and supplies in the upper valley, but it would be a pity to abandon these loyal people and their recently harvested sustenance after such a long struggle to hold the country. He could spare no men to repel the thrust up north, for new reports counted some twenty thousand Confederate infantry near Loudon, with another fifteen or twenty thousand on the way. Burnside still appears to have doubted such numbers, but he could not deny he faced a considerable legion of Confederates, or that they already made tentative demonstrations against Loudon itself.[10]

Burnside stood watching in a cold drizzle as White's, Potter's, and Sanders's divisions pulled back to Lenoir's Station. Behind them trailed a ragtag collection of civilian refugees on horseback, in two-wheel carts, and afoot. One brigade lingered at the river to dismantle the pontoon bridge and to do something about the locomotive and cars stranded on the left bank. This little train had been carried across the river in pieces and laboriously rebuilt as a means of supplying the outpost at Philadelphia, but there was neither time nor conveyance to retrieve it. A volunteer engineer worked up a head of steam in the boiler, slid it in reverse, opened the throttle, and rode to within a few yards of the burned-out bridge; moments after he jumped, the cars toppled into deep water. The firebox hissed one final objection, the river smoothed over the fresh grave, and the Yankee soldiers on the north bank felt they had witnessed the death of an old friend. A few moments later some Confederate horsemen appeared opposite, with a white flag. They came across in boats on some trumped-up mission that included, Burnside thought, determining how strong the Union forces here were.[11]

Burnside remained at Lenoir's Station October 29, orchestrating an orderly withdrawal of Shackelford's and Willcox's troops by telegraph at the same time that White posted his pickets opposite Loudon. He suspected this might be the end of the year's campaign: October's heavy rains had so thoroughly diluted the roads and deepened the rivers that the Confederates would have a hard time molesting him before cold weather settled in. Accordingly, he let it slip that Lenoir's might be their winter quarters, depending on the movements from across the river. The next day it rained yet again, further broadening the natural protection provided by the Tennessee. After lunch Burnside put his staff on the train, telegraphed the servants at Knoxville to warm the fireplaces at headquarters and prepare dinner, and told the engineer to take them up the line. It was a raw day, inside the car and out, but both Parke and Burnside felt a little better. Earlier the general had written Molly he would be home for good in November, but now Captain Larned doubted he would have to resign—at least from illness. Burnside was almost his old self again when they reached headquarters late that afternoon: no fires had been kindled, nor had any food been prepared, and the general lit into the servants in a way that proved to his staff officers he was on the mend.[12]

Though the Army of the Ohio could have evacuated East Tennessee at any moment, via Jacksborough or Cumberland Gap, and though communications were still complete between Knoxville, Chattanooga, and Kentucky, the headquarters staff already began to suffer from the military equivalent of claustrophobia. "We are actually cut off from the civilized world," Captain Larned complained. A certain lethargy seized some of the officers, who seemed depressed by the prospect of a long winter between two formidable foes. To overcome their torpor, Burnside had a big bell mounted in the house, which Paul rang for breakfast every morning at eight o'clock. It lasted only a few days before some layabed stole it, but Paul substituted a big iron pan and kept the grumbling young aides to the schedule their chief required.[13]

For all the anxiety, life at headquarters was not yet exactly Spartan. Though Burnside was willing to share the rigors of camp life whenever necessary, and to sleep in the same mud as his soldiers, he appreciated comfort. At Knoxville he and his staff lived in the home of an East Tennessee mandarin named Crozier, with all the Greek Revival splendor the region could provide. They ate their meals in a formal dining room, on a polished table and clean tablecloths, with silver service enough for everyone. The house was lighted with gas, but they had a healthy supply of tallow candles for leisure reading in some out-of-the-way room: the departed Crozier (a Confederate sympathizer) had also left his eclectic library for the amusement of his more literate enemies. When Burnside's New York and New England assistants tired of literature, they played whist. Paul found beef aplenty, and a young Yankee mechanic kept a steady supply of flour pouring in for the whole army from one commandeered mill at Lenoir's. Loyal folk, still fearful the Federal troops might depart, deluged Burnside with gifts of pastries and fruit. It was actually a delightful sojourn, aside from the perpetual fear of encirclement, and it took a New Haven dandy like Daniel Larned to remark that this was their worst department yet.[14]

Through the first week of November the news from White's front indicated no immediate threat from that direction. Burnside's information about Longstreet's arrival was prophetic but premature; it probably had its inception in a similar rumor rife in the Confederate camp, which in turn might have risen from a suggestion Jefferson Davis had made

to Bragg in late October. Conscious of a growing disaffection between
Bragg and Longstreet, the Confederate president proposed Bragg send
Old Pete up to "expel" Burnside from East Tennessee and occupy the
area himself, holding a position from which he could assist either Bragg
or Lee as events dictated. Bragg concurred, and Longstreet's first brigades unloaded at Sweetwater Station, below Philadelphia, on November 6. He brought some fifteen thousand men with him, and Bragg
loaned him another five thousand of Joe Wheeler's cavalry. Reports of a
significant movement reached General Sanders, at Maryville, as early
as November 5, but Sanders remained skeptical because his civilian
scouts were so prone to panic. By the time the operator transcribed
Sanders's telegram from the Knoxville key, however, Burnside's attention had already been drawn to the other end of his line.[15]

Up at Greeneville, Orlando Willcox had been watching for the Confederate troops seen near Kingsport. He, too, seemed reluctant to believe his informers. He suspected his spies had exaggerated a guerrilla
foray, for his detachment of home guards on the Virginia border had
reported no enemy activity. Colonel Israel Garrard held Rogersville
with his 7th Ohio Cavalry, a Tennessee regiment of mounted infantry,
and a battery of artillery, and Willcox assured Burnside that no significant expedition could pass that way without Garrard's knowledge.
The next day, though, Willcox heard that two thousand enemy cavalry seemed to be trying to flank his advance detachment at Leesburg,
below Jonesborough. The Confederate column traveled without wagon
trains, for greater speed, and herded a few beeves on the hoof. This
brigade, commanded by another West Point graduate named William
Jones, nicknamed "Grumble," was but one of two converging on Willcox,
but it had no interest in Leesburg. Another brigade of John Morgan's
old division left Kingsport after Jones was well on his way, and on the
morning of November 6 they fell on Garrard's somnolent camps, putting
Garrard and the 7th Ohio to their heels. Garrard galloped up to the
commander of the Tennesseeans, hatless and obviously agitated, and
told him to spread out his regiment to hold the enemy, who were coming
from the rear. Garrard thereupon retreated across the Holston with the
survivors of his own regiment, while the Tennessee rear guards tied
their horses to trees and prepared for the last ditch. The second Confederate column soon struck them from behind. The Tennessee major
recognized a hopeless situation and surrendered his entire regiment

and the artillery battery. Garrard fled back to Morristown with barely half the 7th Ohio behind him. Still flustered, he wired Burnside that he had been "totally defeated," which was true enough—he had lost nearly seven hundred men, most of them veteran troops—but he finished with the erroneous and alarming information that the enemy had chased him west of Bull's Gap.

Had so large a Confederate column really taken Bull's Gap, it would have meant that Shackelford, Willcox, and the tenuous supply line from Cumberland Gap were all cut off. As it happened, Garrard spoke too soon. Grumble Jones had neither the strength nor the inclination to go farther than Rogersville; he only wished to frighten the Yankees into pulling back from Greeneville, and that he managed to do nicely. Moments after learning of Garrard's disaster, Burnside ordered Willcox and Shackelford to work their way back to Bull's Gap and defend it. General Parke commented, with remarkable understatement, that they might "have some trouble" if that position were lost. Burnside cautioned Sanders to keep a sharp watch now: once news of Jones's success reached Loudon, the enemy there would be likely to increase his pressure.[16]

Despite the ominous gatherings on his flanks and the deterioration both of his resupply teams and the roads they had to travel, Burnside had not lost his taste for the offensive. Recently he had reminded Grant of his old idea about a cavalry raid on Bragg's rear, through North Carolina and Georgia; in contrast to Halleck's mocking rejection, the new commander liked it. On the same day as Garrard's surprise, Grant told Burnside to collect all the cavalry he could spare for a raid on the railroad, either the Chattanooga line to Atlanta or the Georgia Railroad, between Atlanta and Augusta. Burnside called on Sanders for men. Though he was busy guarding the Little Tennessee, and many of his horses were badly worn out, Sanders thought he could afford to detail a thousand or twelve hundred troopers. Burnside reasoned that no more than that ought to go through the mountains, or they would not be able to carry enough provisions without slowing their pace dangerously; if Grant wanted, however, Burnside thought he might be able to scrape up as many as two thousand men.

This reply did not reach Grant immediately. Sometime Saturday night, November 7, the telegraph line to Chattanooga went dead. That augured ill for the detachment at Loudon, but Sanders could find nothing out of the ordinary. Still, Burnside told him to employ his own little army of spies to expand his observation, not only in Longstreet's direction but on the far side of the Chilhowee Mountains, where some Confederate Cherokees were thought to be lurking.[17]

In order to assure Sanders of both an escape route and a means of mutual support with the infantry at Lenoir's, Burnside adopted the cavalryman's suggestion of building a temporary bridge at that point. The bridge from Loudon was already in use, and Burnside had no more pontoons or materials, but he did have one officer on the Ninth Corps staff who could manage the thing. Potter's assistant inspector general, Lieutenant Colonel Orville Babcock, had graduated third in the West Point class of 1861; he was a Vermonter with an uncommon share of Yankee ingenuity. Without a chain, a rope, a stick of lumber, or a nail, Babcock went to work on the pontoons for the bridge. He repaired an idle sawmill to cut green timbers and planks; he approached the artificers of the cavalry and artillery field forges for his wrought-iron work, including corner brackets and nails, and when the blacksmiths had time they obliged him; for rope lashing he spun raw cotton and wove the strands; in lieu of chains to drag logs to his mill, he twisted lengths of telegraph wire into cable. The citizens around Lenoir's refused to lend, rent, or sell their draft animals to him, and his men had to move nearly everything by hand. By November 7, though, he reported the pontoon boats finished. He guessed his mill might have one good working day left in its wheezy boiler, during which he planned to mill out the planks and balks. While he complained of a lack of the most essential materials, he commented that there was not an artisan whose services he needed who could not be found in the ranks: the diversified background of the old Burnside division once again served the country well.[18]

Still, Babcock could not finish the project in time for Sanders. Before he could saw the bridge planks, the incessant rains threatened to trap the cavalry in the triangle between the Holston, the Little Tennessee, and the Little rivers. Sanders thereupon moved his headquarters and most of his cavalry over the Little River to Rockford, about fifteen miles below Knoxville, but his videttes still roamed the banks of the Little Tennessee.

All of Burnside's cavalry suffered for lack of remounts. Shackelford could saddle up fewer than three-quarters of his men, and the wet weather helped ruin the hooves of Sanders's horses: large numbers began rubbing their pasterns together with the symptoms of "scratches," and a good many were probably limping around with undiagnosed thrush. The only replacements Burnside could offer were little better off. One herd delivered to Rockford included more than a hundred horses the quartermasters pronounced wholly unfit; the 12th Kentucky drew ninety-two of them, two of which died before the regiment even reached camp.[19]

By November 12 the telegraph to Chattanooga had been repaired. Among the backlog of messages that poured into the Knoxville office lay one from Grant, dated the eighth: he planned to make an assault on the left of Bragg's position at Lookout Mountain, in hopes of drawing Longstreet back from Burnside's flank. Thomas had already objected to such an attack, also citing exhausted horses, which prevented him from moving his artillery; Grant nevertheless insisted he would press Bragg as soon as William Sherman arrived from Memphis with the Army of the Tennessee. So far Sherman had only reached Fayetteville, but if Burnside could hold on a little longer, the crisis would be ended. Burnside promised to keep his position as long as he could, but warned that his jaded cavalry left him vulnerable to raids on his attenuated supply line. Grant already planned to send a navy-escorted supply convoy from Nashville to the Big South Fork of the Cumberland, which Burnside could reach through Jacksborough. The extraordinary rainfall had momentarily raised the river deep enough for such a mission, if only he could find some gunboats to escort the steamers.

Late that evening, two visitors appeared at Burnside's headquarters. One was Colonel James H. Wilson, of Grant's staff, and the other Charles A. Dana, the assistant secretary of war. Grant had sent them up from Chattanooga with the same information contained in the telegram, dispatching them as soon as he discovered the wires were interrupted. The two found no evidence of impending action from across the river.[20]

There would soon be action enough. The next day, Friday the thirteenth, Confederates moved into Loudon in full force, planting batteries that could reach White's works on the far shore. Union pickets at Huff's Ferry, on an oxbow in the river a few miles downstream from Loudon, saw a few Confederates poling across on what looked like a flatboat. It seemed as though the fireworks were about to start; Burnside was certain of it. While he still enjoyed communications with Grant, he wired that he thought it best to concentrate his forces and fight Longstreet, drawing him back toward Knoxville so as to stretch his supply line from Bragg's army. That would also prevent Longstreet from reinforcing Bragg in good season, should Grant attack him. No reply to that self-sacrificing offer came that day.[21]

Sometime after midnight on November 14, Longstreet lurched across the Tennessee at Huff's Ferry with his infantry and artillery, his own teams so used up that the extra caissons lumbered along behind confiscated oxen. Confederate foot soldiers wrestled a pontoon bridge into the cold water by hand, for the sake of quiet, while that infantry detachment rowed over to try to capture the Huff's Ferry pickets. Wheeler's cavalry marched up the east side of the Tennessee, following an arc he hoped would put him between Sanders and Knoxville. More Confederate horsemen bore to Longstreet's left, in pursuit of Byrd's brigade, at Kingston.[22]

Longstreet's flatboat-borne rangers missed their prey, so breathless Yankee pickets carried word of the crossing to White's headquarters. White jostled his telegraph operator out of bed and had him pounding brass before he was fully awake. A flurry of clicking raised the Knoxville operator, several frantic messages coming in before dawn. White's pickets had fallen back half a mile, to the sound of planks going down on pontoons; an officer sent down to investigate the report found the bridge nearly complete. Troops in line near the crossing could hear Confederate bugles signaling their cavalry to advance. The enemy was a mile and a half away, and White wanted to know whether he should dispute the crossing or confront them after they had crossed. He needed to know quickly, before dawn revealed his puny force. If Burnside wanted him to fight, he said, he ought to have the help of Potter's Ninth Corps.

Burnside did not believe he wanted to contest the crossing. It might be the easier option, but if he were to discourage Longstreet now, the Confederates would probably only return to Bragg's army and put Grant in a vice. Rather than risk that, Burnside ordered White to retire toward Lenoir's Station. He simultaneously directed Potter to send his trains up to Knoxville, break up the machine shops and grain mill, and either send his pontoon bridge up by the railroad or destroy it. Finally, he sent Potter a few hundred cavalry and an extra battery, the only troops he could spare.

By now Grant's approval of Burnside's course had come in: he should draw Longstreet as far away as possible, to the outskirts of Knoxville, even, but with no undue haste. Grant added that East Tennessee was of the utmost importance, and if Burnside could hold it for another week, all would be well.

That seemed to offer an excellent solution. If the Army of the Ohio simply moved to the east side of the Holston by the bridges at Lenoir's and Knoxville, abandoning the supply line and the railroad, sending Willcox back to Cumberland Gap, it could easily survive a week or more. Burnside calculated he could raise three weeks' sustenance in Blount and Sevier counties, though Parke guessed it would be more like ten days' supplies. Colonel Wilson, the visitor, shrank from the idea of giving up the army's umbilical, commenting that Grant did not want him to include the capture of his entire army in his plans—a point on which Wilson was very nearly wrong, for Grant told Burnside to defend East Tennessee even at the sacrifice of "most of the army." If Grant could actually have secured Burnside's relief in the promised week, the seemingly harebrained plan would have been ideal, for Burnside would have been safe behind the unfordable river, in abundant circumstances, while Longstreet would have been drawn into the picked-over vacuum on the other bank. But even John Parke objected to the maneuver, and there was no one then in Tennessee whose judgment Burnside respected more than Parke's. In the end it was fortunate Parke prevailed, for it took Grant longer to polish off Bragg than he anticipated.[23] When this discussion broke up, Burnside started for Lenoir's himself.

Before leaving the city, Larned put together the general's books and paperwork to send it all back to Cincinnati. Made uneasy by this precaution, Larned did not share his chief's optimism. To his sister he wrote that by the time she read his letter he would be gone—whether to Libby Prison or Kentucky he could not say. He told his brother the same: "Probably we will have to fly or be captured tomorrow." For once Larned underestimated his chief. Hanging his head out the cab of a locomotive hurtling south, the man with the whiskers had no thought of flight.[24]

The 35th Massachusetts had begun its day at 3:00 A.M., when officers had crept through the camps around Lenoir's whispering, "Turn out without noise and stack arms on the color line." Two hours later these veterans of South Mountain and Antietam were told to pack their belongings and prepare to strike their tents at a moment's notice, much to the dismay of those who had built huts and installed chimneys at the hint of winter quarters. The disgusted privates spent the forenoon sprawled about their former camp, some watching the northward parade of wagons and the arrival of White's men, some of them reading the first issues of W. G. Brownlow's new loyalist paper, *The Knoxville Whig and Rebel Ventilator*, which had recently gone into circulation at the exorbitant rate of fifteen cents a copy. These Bay State troops still waited there in the early afternoon, when a locomotive and tender squealed to a halt in their midst. The first of four men to leap from the tender was General Burnside, followed by Edward Ferrero. Within fifteen minutes, Burnside issued orders for what one Massachusetts man called "the fighting portion of the army" to face about.[25]

Colonel Wilson and Mr. Dana were the two other men on the tender. Here they bade Burnside goodbye: they were headed back to Grant's army by the same roundabout route over which they had come, on horseback. For all anyone at Lenoir's knew, their way might already be barred by Southern cavalry, so their farewell assumed a solemn tone. As he left the station, Undersecretary Dana harbored some misgivings about the coming confrontation. He thought he detected an unsettling lack of experience in the upper echelons of the Army of the Ohio. Hartsuff had finally gone down to a sickbed, and in his place at the head of the Twenty-third Corps sat a relatively green brigadier. The commander of the Ninth Corps, Potter, had been a mere colonel eight months before. Other than Burnside, the only obviously competent man with the army was Parke—whom Dana considered wasted in his role as chief of staff.[26]

It was true that both Burnside's corps and most of his divisions and brigades were under men new to such responsibility; it was a problem with which his Ninth Corps had labored since its inception, and one which would continue to hamper its performance. But if Mr. Dana had been able to foretell the outcome of the campaign that began as he departed, he would have changed none of the players.

Burnside's worst worry had come from the east side of the Holston. Wheeler's cavalry had circled around Maryville and surprised the garrison there, scattering the 11th Kentucky Cavalry. Sanders had quietly withdrawn most of his troops north of the Little River, though, and the Confederate plan to capture his entire force failed miserably. Wheeler took only 151 prisoners, while Sanders thundered down at the head of a brigade that blunted Wheeler's drive. The Kentuckian was heavily outnumbered, but just as Burnside arrived at Lenoir's, Sanders reported, through Parke, at Knoxville, that he was in no trouble and could retire slowly and safely to the works across the river from Knoxville. The message found Burnside shortly after he bounded off the tender, and he quickly understood that he could afford to delay his return to the city. Only then did he order Potter to send Ferrero's division back down toward Loudon, to help one of White's brigades challenge the Southern spearhead, discommoding the lounging Massachusetts regiment. It had begun to rain hard again when the troops started south.[27]

White had perhaps fifteen hundred men on the scene; half his regiments had gone to Kingston to support Byrd's cavalry brigade, with which they were now cut off from the rest of Burnside's force. Ferrero's division may have numbered three thousand, and for a time after he joined White there were enough Yankees to deal with Longstreet, even to drive his skirmishers backward a mile and a half. At last the Confederate artillery and darkness stopped the Union advance, and the Federals lay down in dense timber while the rain pelted them relentlessly. Dry wood appeared in the hands of certain foragers as though by magic, and the aroma of boiling coffee seeped through the green, rotting smell of the drenched forest floor. Burnside gave orders for a night attack, planned first for nine o'clock and then for midnight, but as more and more of Longstreet's men crossed the river, it became apparent that White and Potter alone could not make an impression upon them. After midnight, when the rain had finally stopped, Potter decided he had better bring his other little division down from Lenoir's— five wiry regiments, under a colonel. Those two demi-brigades crawled from wet blankets at one-thirty on the Sabbath morning and staggered south, still half-asleep. Darkness aggravated the usual accordioning of the march, and men who tried to maintain their momentum against knee-deep mud careened into those ahead of them who had stopped. Lightly grasped muskets flew like chaff in these collisions, cracking other men on the heads, and because of the suction of the mud nearly everyone lost his balance at one time or another and fell (usually sitting) in the yellow quagmire. Thick overcast shrouded the stars and the light of the fingernail moon, and the soldiers could barely see their own equipments; they found their way by the cursing of the men ahead. Day was just breaking when they took their position on high ground near

Loudon, every pair of pants coated to the waistband with the amber
pâte of Tennessee's topsoil.[28]

White's lead brigade withdrew from before Longstreet's crossing
that morning. The Confederate corps started after it, but as White retreated past Loudon, Potter's tiny second division stepped across the
road behind it and blocked the way. Behind this rear guard of veteran New Englanders, Pennsylvanians, and Marylanders, the various
wagon and artillery trains of the Army of the Ohio struggled through
axle-deep mud toward Knoxville. Horses and mules weakened from
weeks of poor feed strained at sodden old harness, and beast or leather
frequently broke. Cold, moist air muffled the occasional snap of some
merciful quartermaster's revolver. Ferrero assigned an entire regiment
of infantry to push and drag each piece of his two artillery batteries.
Burnside began to see the futility of so desperate an exodus under such
a burden, but so short were his rations at Knoxville that he dared leave
nothing behind that the courage of his infantry might salvage. Colonel
Joshua Sigfried, commanding Potter's rear guard, managed to stave off
Longstreet's advance for several hours with but a regiment of Massachusetts skirmishers, but by midafternoon he discovered Confederate
troops sneaking around his right. The trains and the main body had all
reached the momentary safety of Lenoir's Station, so Sigfried herded
in his skirmishers, formed a column of march with a screen of flankers
on either side, and trotted after the rest of the army.[29]

Longstreet now divided his infantry into two columns. One division,
under Micah Jenkins, continued the pressure on Potter, following by the
road along the railroad. Another, commanded by Lafayette McLaws,
marched to the road linking Kingston to Campbell's Station, farther up
the railroad. The positions of McLaws and Jenkins formed an isosceles
triangle with Campbell's Station, the rail station at the apex. The roads
to Knoxville converged just below there, and if McLaws reached that
intersection first, he would have Burnside trapped. Burnside was a bit
closer to Campbell's Station than McLaws, but the Confederates could
let their supply trains fall behind without losing them, while Burnside
could not.

Longstreet made a faint push at Lenoir's Station late in the evening,
but Potter's artillery and infantry quickly dissuaded him. General Potter's headquarters escort arrived during the night. These four com-

panies of Indiana cavalry raised the number of Burnside's immediate effective force to about eight thousand—about half the size of Longstreet's infantry alone. With the Hoosiers came Colonel John Hartranft, an able veteran whose regiment was in the same division as Sigfried's. Hartranft outranked Sigfried by months, so when Burnside directed Potter to send someone up to secure the junction below Campbell's Station, Potter put Hartranft in charge of his depleted second division and sent him. He gave him the few hundred cavalry, urging him north in all haste.[30]

Most of Burnside's men had not slept during the night, but had lain cold and wet on their arms in anticipation of an attack. William Humphrey's three Michigan regiments were the best-rested at Lenoir's, and they took over the rear guard, backpedaling slowly and skirmishing with the Confederates all the way.

Looking about him in the cold, dense fog that morning, Burnside decided the precious wagon train would be the death of his army if he did not shuck it. He issued Potter and White field orders to destroy most of their vehicles and baggage, directing them to turn the teams over to the artillery. Guns and caissons rolled a little better with a dozen or sixteen horses in front of them, but men still had to throw their shoulders against muddy iron tires from time to time. Unable to burn the saturated wagons, pioneers went at the spokes of the wheels with axes, but their destruction fell short of complete. Perhaps impelled by the approaching backs of Humphrey's Michiganders, the saboteurs threw down their implements and followed the line of retreat. When Longstreet arrived he found scores of wagons in park formation, loaded with supplies he needed.[31]

Hartranft's two miniature brigades wrestled seven fieldpieces the eight long miles to the strategic intersection. Four of the guns were those heavy, 20-pounder Parrotts commanded by Samuel Benjamin. Benjamin had begun the war as a lieutenant in charge of those big rifles, and a lieutenant he still was. So he would remain, except for a couple of brevets, while the nominal captain of his battery rose to the command of an infantry division. Benjamin never complained, for all of that, because he loved the artillery and enjoyed a fight.

Hartranft beat McLaws to the intersection by less than an hour, turning back down the road to Kingston in order to buy the main column plenty of room. Taking a cue from the Confederate General Williams, he sent a couple of hundred cavalry forward in a single long skirmish line, such as might have cleared the advance of the entire army. He told the horsemen to charge the enemy when they first saw them. This they did, and their brazen tactic convinced McLaws to bring up the rest of his division before proceeding farther: he stopped a tad over two miles from the road junction.[32]

Back on the road to Lenoir's, Humphrey fought a savage delaying action. His 17th Michigan held the dismal honor of covering the rear of the rear guard while Jenkins's Confederates pushed and shoved the beleaguered Yankees, trying to bring them to a stand. Late in the morning, as the 17th approached the banks of Turkey Creek, Jenkins threw most of his South Carolina brigade against it. The single regiment reeled under repeated volleys, but held long enough for Humphrey to bring the 2nd and 20th Michigan in on its right. This thin line, fewer than nine hundred men, crouched behind a rail fence on the edge of the woods bordering the creek. Here they stayed, until Humphrey learned the remainder of the baggage train lay safely beyond Campbell's Station. Some of their officers encouraged them from horseback, and the audacity cost at least one Michigan colonel his life. When Humphrey finally gave his men permission to withdraw, they did so in echelon, the three regiments sliding backward and sidestepping before the withering musketry in dreadful grace. At the same time, McLaws brought most of his strength down on Hartranft.[33]

White's remaining brigade had dug in beyond Campbell's Station by now. The pitiful remnant of trains sat behind him, and Potter made arrangements to pull back to White's line. First, though, he had to send another brigade forward to help Humphrey and Hartranft. David Morrison's brigade of Ferrero's division, three more regiments, squeezed into the angle between the roads. The Union brigades falling back on those roads connected on Morrison's left and right, forming one long line across the junction. Jenkins threw two brigades against Humphrey and Morrison; Humphrey managed to withdraw in perfect order, and Morrison's regiments did a half-wheel to the left to meet the assault. When all these troops had worked their way back to the station, Potter put his last brigade on the extreme right. White remained in reserve, and the artillery they had so jealously saved wheeled up hub-to-hub to face the infantry assault everyone expected. A grey line of battle did appear, but a few shells from Benjamin's rifles and one of the smaller batteries broke it up and drove it away.[34]

Another road led to Campbell's Station from Potter's left, and when he asked his Indiana escort to scout it, they found Confederates marching in their direction, looking to turn that flank. Burnside had already prepared for that event, however. A few minutes after hearing of this discovery, Potter met a courier with Burnside's order to withdraw to a less vulnerable hilltop a thousand yards behind. First he sent the batteries back in relays, keeping a few guns in position all the time. Next he ordered his reserves to fall back—two of Hartranft's regiments, one of them completely out of ammunition. The rest of the Ninth Corps and White's troops marched back under cover of the fire of their long-range batteries, and by four o'clock in the afternoon Potter's new line of battle was established, bristling once more with artillery. Confederate infantry formed again, but McLaws and Jenkins were never able to co-ordinate their assaults of some three brigades each. Jenkins tried again to dislodge the Federals from their new position, but a few shells scattered his men "like nine-pins"—as a Massachusetts man remembered. Artillery dueled back and forth, but Burnside's men suffered almost as much from the premature explosion of Benjamin's shells as from enemy fire. Dark foiled Longstreet's plans as it had the night before. Instead of being brought to its knees, the Army of the Ohio had lost barely three hundred men—most of them from Humphrey's three Michigan regiments.[35]

As it grew dark, Burnside lined his remaining ordnance wagons along the Knoxville road, and while his weary infantry started north again, the wagoners distributed ammunition to those who needed it. A strong picket line deceived the Confederates, and Yankees who entered their second or third night without sleep began the sixteen-mile trudge toward what they hoped would be safety. Officers on horseback nodded in the saddle, and many a foot soldier later claimed he slept in the ranks while on that march.

Now Burnside began to worry again whether Knoxville would still offer sanctuary. Wheeler's cavalry had threatened to roll over Sanders and his poorly mounted men and take the city from behind. Burnside wired Parke he wanted the city held "by any means in your power." If the enemy shelled the place, Parke should send the citizens to their cellars; if Wheeler attacked, Parke could punch loopholes in the houses and garrison them with the armed but ununiformed Tennessee recruits. To Burnside's relief, though, Wheeler had disappeared from south of the river. With great difficulty, he had crossed to Longstreet's side of the river too late to bag Burnside's army.[36]

When Burnside and his staff first arrived in Knoxville at midnight, they still wondered whether the place could be held. Confidential messengers from headquarters had already notified the more prominent Unionists that the army might have to evacuate. Those who had capitalized on the Union takeover, like Mr. Brownlow of the *Whig and Rebel Ventilator*, lost no time mounting up for the healthier climate of the Bluegrass.[37]

In 1863, most of Knoxville perched atop a half-mile-wide plateau between two creeks, standing 150 feet over the Holston. The railroad to the north squared off the city's boundary. East Knoxville, across First Creek, occupied two hills: Flint Hill rose near the river; nearer the railroad and some eighty feet higher was Temperance Hill. East of (and higher than) both of these was Mabry's Hill, on the Dandridge Road. West of town, the University of East Tennessee sat on another plateau beyond Second Creek. Most of a mile downriver, a stream called Third Creek creased the table-land again, on its way to the Holston.

The road from Kingston and Campbell's Station cut perpendicularly across Third and Second creeks. Simon Buckner's retreating Confederates had left but two meager fortifications behind when they evacuated—a small bastion on Temperance Hill and a half-finished fort northwest of the university. Burnside's chief engineer had borrowed the engineer battalion of the Twenty-third Corps to bring these up to defensible condition, and by the time the first of Potter's exhausted infantry staggered up the pike, the forts were ready.[38]

The five thousand drained men left under Potter and White marched all night. They began straggling into Knoxville before dawn. Commissaries handed out rations of beef and hardtack in the darkness, and the men lay down for a couple of hours' rest before the sun rose. At the first hint of day, staff officers prodded them to their feet and led them to their assigned positions on the perimeter, where they began work on a ring of shallow rifle pits, anchored on the river and connecting the two fortified positions. They did much of their digging with bayonets and plates, for the supply of picks and shovels was limited: most of them had been abandoned to the enemy at Lenoir's, when the work parties absconded.[39]

Burnside sent Sanders's brigade down the Kingston road dismounted, with orders to cover the tail end of the retreating column. He asked the tall Kentuckian to delay the enemy long enough to allow for the construction of stronger works. Sanders had fewer than a thousand men left, but with these and another small provisional brigade, he left the city on foot, his men armed with an assortment of breechloading and repeating carbines. He met Longstreet's skirmishers several miles out of Knoxville and spread his men out to face them, slowing the Southern approach to a crawl. By late afternoon Sanders had backed onto a hill half a mile west of Third Creek, and there he decided to make a stand. He sheared off the two-regiment provisional brigade to guard the Clinton Road, on his right, while his men fashioned a rail breastwork on the hill. At nightfall he still held the hill.

Near midnight, Burnside called Sanders away from his troops for a conference at headquarters. Orlando Poe, Burnside's chief engineer, joined them; Burnside wanted to know, mainly for Sanders's information, how long it would take Poe to complete sufficient works to insure Knoxville's defense. Poe said he thought a substantial line could be finished by noon the next day. Burnside asked Sanders if his men could hold that long, and the cavalryman promised they would. His word was enough for Burnside, who ended the meeting there. Sanders and Poe had been classmates at West Point; they shared the same quarters that night, but a courier woke Sanders before dawn. Poe never saw him alive again.

E. P. Alexander, Longstreet's artillery chief, dared not waste much of his ammunition on the position Sanders had fortified: he had too little as it was, and might need all of it for a siege. He unlimbered two Napoleons in a position behind a brick house, only a few hundred yards from the Union breastwork, from which they threw solid shot that sent the fence rails flying like so many pencils. The Yankee cavalrymen would flinch and start to run at every shot, but Sanders kept them in line by little more than personal example, standing upright behind the piled rails with his upper body in full view of the Confederate riflemen and gunners. Marksmen in the cupola of the brick house raised particular havoc, and Sanders sent back a request for Lieutenant Benjamin to silence them with his long-range Parrotts. The Parrotts sat in the half-finished star fort, a mile and a half from the Confederate sharpshooters, but with a combination of skill and luck Benjamin aimed a single gun at the house and put a round straight through their hideaway, wrecking it so badly they could no longer use it.

Noon passed, but Sanders still clung to his hilltop, fighting in full view of the men in Knoxville. Perhaps he meant to maintain his position until dark, both to allow his men a safer withdrawal across the open plain behind them and to give Poe more time to ready the defenses, but by midafternoon his troopers had been shelled beyond endurance. A pair of particularly good shots from the Napoleons scattered the horsemen, and two South Carolina regiments sprinted toward them. Sanders rallied his men again, but rifle fire felled him. As an impromptu stretcher team hurried him back to the city, still alive, his little brigade fell apart.[40] From this point forward, it would be a textbook siege.

As the last of his men scurried inside the pale, Ambrose Burnside did not succumb to the dejection which ought to have accompanied the closing of the trap. He revealed no hint of the despair some attributed to him at Fredericksburg. Halleck needled Grant about relieving Knoxville, assuring him Burnside would not fight and could be expected to surrender (giving the lie to his self-proclaimed supportive attitude), but Grant thought Burnside might have been the only man not especially alarmed at his plight. Grant himself could take some of the credit for this optimistic outlook, for in replacing Henry Halleck as Burnside's immediate superior he had removed the perpetual anxiety over orders contrived to throw responsibility on the subordinate in the event of disaster. Unlike General Halleck, whose conflicting instructions seemed designed more to please those above him than inform those below him, Grant was willing to take responsibility for the orders he issued. That had become clear November 15, when he told Burnside to hold East Tennessee even at the cost of most of his army. Also unlike Halleck, Grant never hesitated to encourage a dangerous course of action if it promised a fair chance of success: when Burnside pulled inside the protection of the forts, he found a message from Chattanooga telling him, "You are doing what appears to me exactly right." Grant had a reputation, too, for quick, decisive action, and when he assured Burnside that he would immediately either draw Longstreet off or send a force to relieve him, Burnside could believe him. For the first time in fourteen months, he could trust the next man above him. Late on November 18 he sent one last message to both Grant and Lincoln before the telegraph key fell silent, comforting them with the opinion that he could beat back anything Longstreet sent against him.[41]

Burnside put most of his faith in his old Ninth Corps and in Orlando Poe. Captain Poe had been in the topographical engineers since 1856. As a volunteer colonel he had commanded a brigade under Burnside, at Fredericksburg and in Kentucky, but an expired appointment as brigadier general had dropped him back to his preferred occupation, if not his preferred rank. Poe had already prepared a makeshift defense with the battalion of engineers he himself had organized back in Kentucky; when the retreating troops came in from Lenoir's, he assigned each brigade to the construction of a length of line along the high ground around Knoxville, and he worked them until they dropped. After that, he impressed the labor of every male contraband in the city and of all the white citizens, loyal and otherwise. The Unionist civilians dug with a will, Poe noted, while others "worked with a very poor grace, which blistered hands did not tend to improve."[42]

A skirmish line held the Confederates at bay while the fatigue crews scrambled to perfect their improvised fortifications. Burnside stood at the breastworks with them, alternately observing the work and scanning Longstreet's position with a telescope. Evidently a Southern officer was doing the same thing, and saw this obviously important Union soldier standing by the sheltered battery rising near First Creek. In a moment, a distinctive team of white horses emerged from the ridge beyond the railroad to drop a rifled cannon into battery, and the gun threw three quick rounds at Burnside. The first perforated a tent, scaring the wits out of a lounging resident, while the second crashed through the door of a nearby house. The last shell passed uncomfortably close to Burnside's telescope. The former artillery lieutenant bared his teeth in passing aggravation and waved a gunner away from the piece in the closest lunette. He triangulated with the quadrant for an instant, nodded to the private holding the lanyard, and watched his shot land perfectly. The white horses disappeared into the woods, dragging their injured cannon after them.[43]

General Sanders died November 19, at about the same hour that President Lincoln spoke to a crowd in a Gettysburg cemetery, and late in the evening half a dozen division and brigade commanders joined Burnside and Parke around the raw grave, to pay their respects to the

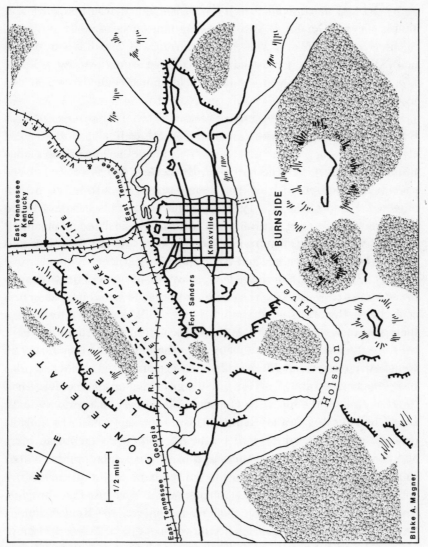

Map 10.
Knoxville

Blake A. Magner

man who had mortgaged the city with his life. It was a somber and simple service. General White likened it to the burial of Sir John Moore, in the Napoleonic Wars, where "Not a drum was heard, nor a funeral note." White's analogy must have been a little overdrawn: the soldiers in a nearby regiment were wakened from much-needed sleep by the mournful dirge of a brass band.[44]

Improvements on the perimeter resumed the next morning. At first Burnside and Poe disagreed about the length of line they should enclose. Remarking that he could muster only about twelve thousand rifles (aside from a few hundred recruits), Burnside opted to cut the works short at Temperance Hill and run them straight down to the river. Poe objected. He pointed to Mabry's Hill, which had the advantage of elevation over both Temperance and Flint hills, and he insisted on including it. That would rob Longstreet of an excellent artillery position, and even if the Confederates could take Mabry's by storm, it would prove a Pyrrhic victory, while the defenders could simply withdraw to prepared works on Flint Hill. That line of argument swayed Burnside, and soon the earthworks wound around Mabry's Hill. A series of forts, protected batteries, and deep rifle pits eventually reached from Flint Hill, over the northern end of the plateau, to the incomplete star fort, and back down to the river. All the rifle pits were protected by chevaux-de-frise—sharpened stakes driven into the ground at an angle of forty-five degrees against the direction of attack. The stakes included two thousand Confederate pikes left behind by Buckner; they created a difficult obstacle once the engineers wired them together. By damming First and Second creeks, Poe also managed to create ponds that prevented Longstreet from assaulting much of the northern part of the town.[45]

The star fort remained the strongest single work. At Poe's suggestion, Burnside named it Fort Sanders in honor of the Kentuckian. It had an 8-foot ditch around it, and the parapet stood 12 feet and more above the surrounding terrain. The truncated star ran almost 400 feet along its northern and southern fronts, and nearly 100 yards on the side facing Third Creek. The northwest bastion of Sanders was the most vulnerable spot in the entire line, though. It formed a salient that would diffuse the defenders' fire, diluting its effect, and that face of the fort invited no protective fire from any other portion of the defenses. With the help of Simon Buckner and the railroad superintendent at Knoxville, Poe devised a means of improving the strength of the point.

Earlier that year, Buckner's soldiers had cleared a pine forest from before the fort, leaving stumps a foot tall. Poe accepted the donation of several reels of old telegraph wire from the railroad yard, and under cover of darkness his men wound the wire around all those stumps, weaving an entanglement both treacherous and virtually invisible. Poe placed Benjamin's four big Parrotts inside the fort, alongside six Rhode Island Napoleons. For infantry support he chose two of Ferrero's brigades: Christ's and Humphrey's. Humphrey's was the brigade Poe had previously commanded.[46]

Lieutenant Benjamin, who had had to abandon some of his caissons in the rush to save the intersection below Campbell's Station, complained to Burnside's ordnance officer that he was dangerously short of shell for the Parrotts. That staff officer had destroyed an arsenal outside Knoxville before Longstreet arrived, but he had rescued the machinery and carted it back to the city. He rigged a metalworking shop with this equipment, operating it with water power from one of Poe's dams, and one of his more inspired and important projects involved manufacturing ammunition for Benjamin from an oversupply of Hotchkiss shells for the James rifles. These were 3.8-inch projectiles. Presumably after removing the powder charge, he locked them into one of the salvaged lathes and turned some two hundred of them down to the 3.67-inch diameter Benjamin needed.[47]

Forage grew nearly as scarce as ammunition. For a time, the south side of the river remained open for the gathering of such supplies, and a pontoon bridge still linked the city with the cavalry commands camped there. Confederates upriver built a heavy log raft, intending to float it down to break the bridge, but word of the plan drifted downstream first—in a bottle sent by a loyal citizen, claimed one officer—and Captain Poe and Babcock teamed up to build a boom across the Holston to catch it. The boom also served to trap smaller rafts of food, sent down by Union inhabitants along the French Broad River. Still, the massive herds of lame, half-starved horses, mules, and cattle required more grain and hay than Knoxville could ever provide; this had been one of Burnside's reasons for wanting to cross south of the Holston during the invasion. One thing plentiful in the city was salt, so Burnside had all the beeves butchered and preserved. In an effort to further reduce the drain on livestock sustenance, he directed his quartermasters to cull all the used-up animals from the teams, lead them to the river, and shoot them, rolling their carcasses into the stream. He also cut the garrison's rations of bread and meat, and within four days he had to withhold coffee and sugar altogether, conserving the tiny remainder for the hospitals.[48]

The enemy was in little better condition. As Burnside had planned, Longstreet had come fully forty miles from his closest railhead, faced with the same poor roads that had plagued the Army of the Ohio for ten weeks. Food ran short, as it almost always did in the Confederate army, but so did all the nonmilitary essentials. Neither Longstreet's quartermaster nor commissary departments had enough wagons; the implements captured at Lenoir's Station comprised almost all of the intrenching tools. The only spare horseshoes available were those the farriers could wrench from the hooves of Burnside's dead horses along the road, or fish out of the river.[49]

None of these impediments turned James Longstreet from his purpose. He concentrated his infantry north and west of Knoxville, from the mouth of Third Creek to the East Tennessee & Kentucky Railroad. He posted Wheeler's cavalry on the northeastern quadrant of the city, barring the regular route to Cumberland Gap. The crackling of skirmishers filled the daylight hours, especially in front of Fort Sanders, and occasionally a Union regiment would sally out to destroy some sharpshooter's lair. Humphrey's brigade became a favorite source for these missions. His 17th Michigan crawled out under cover of night and burned a house from which several of the Sanders garrison had been shot, losing in the course of the attempt a lieutenant whose name was memorialized by a battery. Someone, no one ever determined who, chose Humphrey's 2nd Michigan for a foolhardy assault on a troublesome Confederate salient. The salient could not have been held had it been taken, and the regiment lost more than half its 160 men and its major, who died in the hands of the enemy. Fort Byington took the major's name, and Battery Galpin that of one of his dead lieutenants. The Southern marksmen plied their trade with frightful success, suggesting the nomenclature of nine more forts and batteries around the city as they methodically dropped field and company officers. Two more of Humphrey's Michigan officers fell in one day, including the commander of one of his regiments, shot from a distance of half a mile.[50]

Despite the severed wires, Burnside still managed to send word of his situation to Grant. Willcox yet held the vicinity of Cumberland Gap with a motley garrison equivalent to two brigades each of infantry and cavalry, plus five batteries, and his scouts worked their way cautiously to Knoxville, probably crossing the Holston well upstream and traveling the relatively unimpeded left bank. By these intrepid carriers did Burnside relay irregular information to Chattanooga. The journey from Knoxville back to the gap, combined with the circuitous transmission by telegraph through Cincinnati, Louisville, and Nashville, assured at least a two-day delay, and sometimes the dispatches were never received. On November 21 Burnside wrote Grant he had more than a week's half-rations of bread and two weeks of beef and pork, with forage enough for the moment, but these glad tidings seem never to have arrived in Chattanooga. As late as November 23, Grant expressed extreme uneasiness over whether Burnside could hold out ten days longer, and at midnight of November 24 he remained sufficiently anxious to send Willcox special instructions to encourage Burnside's resistance for a few more days.[51]

According to one of the dispatches that did reach Grant, Burnside seemed no longer so optimistic about his chances of repelling Longstreet. He feared less that his army would be starved out than that the enemy might now be strong enough to overpower him. Indeed, Longstreet had issued orders for an assault on Fort Sanders already, but had postponed the attack. The very night Burnside sealed his apprehensive note to Grant, the Confederate crossed two brigades of Texas, Alabama, and Arkansas troops to the south side of the Holston, shuttling them over out of range on flatboats. He directed them to occupy an eminence known as Cherokee Heights, which towered over University Hill and Fort Sanders. There he hoped to mount artillery capable of reducing Sanders, after which he would assault it with infantry. Colonel Alexander, the artilleryman, rowed over with the promiscuous little flotilla and accompanied the two brigades up the heights, but once there he pronounced the range too great for what little artillery ammunition he had.

Rather than give up this high ground, Longstreet decided to use it to support an attack on Burnside's unobstructed southern approach. He brought up another piece of plunder from Lenoir's—Orville Babcock's pontoon bridge—and placed it beyond the reach of Union artillery. On November 25 the two Confederate brigades came down from Cherokee Heights and struck the three smaller hills across the river from

Knoxville. Most of Shackelford's cavalry met them, plus one of Milo Hascall's infantry brigades, and together they put the Southerners to flight. Burnside sent over Hascall's other brigade just as a precaution, but that marked the extent of the threat from that direction. That night, Burnside and Captain Poe made a personal reconnaissance of the terrain on the left bank before designing another line of fortifications.[52]

From his precarious vista atop Missionary Ridge, Braxton Bragg grew impatient with what seemed a feeble attempt to reduce Knoxville. Pestered for reinforcements, he started two more divisions to Longstreet's assistance. One of the brigadiers in those divisions was Alexander W. Reynolds, the former U.S. Army officer who had caused Burnside his ten-year wrangle over the missing quartermaster funds. (The dispute had finally been settled in Burnside's favor only five months before, when the United States comptroller decided Reynolds had embezzled the money.)[53]

Bragg followed these reinforcements with his own chief engineer, Danville Leadbetter, who carried orders to speed up the operation. General Leadbetter arrived the night after the failed assault south of the river. His presence did not produce immediate results, for he and Longstreet spent three days discussing proposed assaults on Fort Sanders, Mabry's Hill, and across the river, despite ominous rumors of fighting around Chattanooga. All the while these two tramped around Burnside's lines, the Yankee engineers moved dirt, logs, and guns into ever-more-formidable configurations: Burnside grew stronger every time James Longstreet had to cancel his plans. For the major general inside the city, it was a pleasant reversal of the roles he and Longstreet had played nearly a year before.[54]

III

The name of Ambrose Burnside is seldom associated with the tremendous victory Grant won at Chattanooga in late November of 1863, but without the near self-sacrifice of the Army of the Ohio that victory might not have been possible, and certainly it would not have been so devastating. Burnside's offer to use his army as live bait further reduced Bragg's force—already somewhat inferior to Grant's—by a total of about twenty-three thousand men, setting the Confederate Army of

Tennessee up for an overwhelming attack from three sides. On November 23 George Thomas moved out to capture high ground in the frog of the horseshoe-shaped heights around Chattanooga, and the next day Joe Hooker flung two corps against the western heel of that horseshoe, wresting Lookout Mountain from Bragg's left hand. On November 25 Sherman put his army on the eastern flank of those heights, and Thomas struck Bragg's center. The Confederate advantage of position was far more intimidating than Lee's had been beyond Fredericksburg, but unlike the men of the Army of the Potomac in 1862, Thomas's soldiers had not been discouraged by skeptical superiors who pronounced the heights impossible to carry. Union infantry stormed the steep slope of Missionary Ridge and drove Bragg's troops away in total (and virtually shameless) retreat.

Grant took a few more days to wrap up his victory. He ordered Gordon Granger to race the Fourth Corps to Burnside's relief, but when Grant returned from directing the pursuit after a four-day absence, he found Granger had not yet left Chattanooga; nor did he appear inclined to go. Grant therefore sent Sherman to Knoxville, with Granger as his subordinate. He also wrote a note to Burnside, explaining that three columns were coming to his assistance and that he ought to hold out "a few days longer." (Fifteen days had already passed since his "seven days more" dispatch of November 14.) Colonel Wilson and Undersecretary Dana carried this message to Colonel Byrd, at Kingston—also carrying a duplicate, copied by a secretary and signed by Grant. Grant intended only the duplicate for actual delivery to Burnside; the one in his own hand (Wilson told Byrd) was meant to find its way to Longstreet. Grant and Longstreet had been close friends in prewar days: Grant supposed Old Pete would recognize his penmanship, regard the message as genuine, and abandon the siege.[1]

Upriver, at Knoxville, Burnside had no inkling of the events at Chattanooga until long afterward. Longstreet had intercepted some rumors, and certain cavalry reports corroborated them. This information, and the arrival of Bushrod Johnson's infantry division from Bragg and two cavalry brigades from Sam Jones, at last persuaded Longstreet to strike. In the rain and fog of November 28, Lafayette McLaws moved three brigades to the front, northwest of Fort Sanders. Poor visibility postponed the attack yet again, but late that same evening McLaws forced his skirmishers ahead, capturing the Union picket line. He en-

countered a touch of luck in the form of a demoralized recruit from the
8th Michigan, who scampered into Confederate lines to give himself
up. His officers considered this private a poor soldier, and he confirmed
their judgment that night, giving the enemy an unsolicited but accurate description of Union defenses all the way from Fort Sanders to
the river, with a list of all the regiments in line and their approximate
strengths.[2]

Inside Fort Sanders were perhaps 350 men, including some from all
three of Ferrero's brigades, but most of them belonged to Humphrey.
Morrison's brigade held the rifle pits left of the fort as far as the
river; Benjamin Christ's four regiments were entrenched from Second
Creek to a point just short of Sanders; and Humphrey's battered brigade covered the environs of the fort itself. Though all the regimental
commanders outranked him, as well as most of the company and battery commanders, Lieutenant Benjamin exercised supreme authority
in Fort Sanders by virtue of Burnside's special orders. Because of the
nighttime skirmishing, the lieutenant suspected an attack was in the
offing, though those around him doubted it. Benjamin nevertheless bade
the corporal of the guard wake him early November 29, and in the cold
moonlight he posted grumbling men along the ramparts.[3]

Fourteen Southern regiments lay trembling in their cotton uniforms
as the morning wore on toward twilight, their bayonets already rattling
on the muzzles of their rifles. Under brigadiers now dead, these men
had slaughtered Burnside's men before Marye's Heights. Four Mississippi regiments here had slowed the crossing of his entire army along
the Fredericksburg waterfront. If these stalwart soldiers reflected on
the irony of their situation, collected as they were to assault the same
sort of works from which they had repelled these same opponents, at
least none of them yet kenned another painful similarity to that earlier
battle: just as Burnside's men had been brutally surprised by the existence of the sunken road at Fredericksburg, Longstreet knew nothing
of the deep ditch around Fort Sanders. His chief of artillery had made
a reconnaissance only two days before, in which he had been unable to
distinguish any such ditch, and Longstreet himself thought he had seen
a Yankee amble down into the swale on the western face of the fort,
emerging on the other side with no perceptible effort. Others had reported watching dogs trot across places where the ditch was supposed
to be. Citizens had reported Fort Sanders was constructed by leveling

a hill, with the earth for the parapet coming from the crown of the hill; that suggested there might be no ditch at all. Officers from Johnson's division, just up from Bragg's army, agreed: they had served in Knoxville under Buckner, and they all maintained there was no regular ditch, though perhaps there were some irregular pits and depressions. None of these men had seen Knoxville since Samuel Benjamin's improvements began, though, and General McLaws was suspicious. He had no tools or materials in his entire division for the construction of scaling ladders: when first ordered to make the canceled assault of November 21, he had suggested distributing fascines to the men—bundles of sticks, or in this case of straw—with which to fill up the ditch, but Longstreet had replied sarcastically that fascines would be of more use as protection from bullets than to fill the ditch.[4]

Colonel Alexander had carefully planned his preparatory bombardment, but Longstreet robbed him of it when he decided to precede the attack with but three signal guns. In futility and frustration, Alexander aimed these three pieces to drop their projectiles inside Fort Sanders, and his gunners stood in the freezing drizzle with the lanyards in their hands. At the first glimmer of light the trio of corporals snapped their wrists, and Alexander watched the fuses of his shells spin through the sky like shooting stars until they exploded in midair. The three brigades of Georgians and Mississippians jumped to their feet while the thwarted Alexander poured the fire of a dozen guns on the target, getting in what licks he could before his own men neared the fort. The artilleryman was pleased at the accuracy of this fire, but it only made him rue the loss of a major barrage all the more. For all the direct hits on Fort Sanders, however, its traverses were so skillfully constructed that only one man was wounded.[5]

Lieutenant Benjamin had his men tucked under the lip of the parapet, not a head showing, his guns standing triple-shotted with canister. He had not positioned a single gun in the northwest bastion, for there the ditch was deepest and there he fervently hoped the enemy would attack. Like Longstreet, he doubted the invulnerability of the western face of the fort; two fieldpieces waited to sweep the ditches lengthwise if Confederates chose to fill them.

The second hand of Benjamin's watch did not complete two full revolutions between the moment he saw the enemy appear over a crest, eighty yards away, until the first of them fell in the ditch. Their front line faltered and toppled at the telegraph wire, but their ranks massed so closely that those behind rolled on over the fallen, chanting a breathless "hep-hep-hep" as they trotted. Because they attacked this unprotected point, only one of Benjamin's gunners could bring a muzzle to bear on them. They tumbled into the ditch by the hundreds and tried to circle around the fort, but the flank guns belched bucket after bucket of canister into them.[6]

At this point the ditch dropped eleven feet deep, and at ground level the parapet rose another thirteen feet at a 45-degree angle. Colonel Alexander later complained the Union engineers had inconsiderately neglected to leave a berm, or ledge, at the base of the parapet, from which attackers might propel themselves up the steep face. Actually there was such a berm, but the freezing rain of the night before had coated the slope with ice. Only by a primitive sort of mountaineering or acrobatics could any of the Southerners reach the embrasures. Yet some of them did reach it: many of them, in fact, though virtually every man who did fell victim to a Federal rifleman. At least three color bearers tried to plant the Stars and Bars on the top of the work; all of them lost their flags and either their lives or liberty. A New York sergeant burst from one embrasure and dragged a Mississippi color sergeant back in with him, flag and all. Musketry rang strangely hollow, its customary crash muffled by the lingering fog.[7]

Adjacent defenders lay what covering fire they could, but few of the troops on either side of the fort had a direct view of the Confederates teeming on the northwest face. The few hundred Yankees inside the ramparts were essentially on their own, their only ally the depth of the ditch beyond the parapet. They were outnumbered about eight to one, and the available rifles could not always match the numbers of those able to clamber up to the brow of the fort. Another sergeant in the 79th New York exchanged his musket for an axe at one point, and a Massachusetts major watched him cleave open the skulls of three Southern boys before he took up his rifle again. After three-quarters of an hour of such carnage the collective nerve of the attacking column had been shattered. There was simply no one left with the courage to scale the wall. Three Confederate colonels lay dead in the trench, while another cradled a shivered arm that no surgeon could save. The commanders of two Georgia regiments were less seriously wounded, but out of action.

If the survivors of the three brigades could not advance, neither would they retreat. Some still tried to work their way around to the fort's flanks, but canister blasts swept the ditch at every attempt. The tubes of the guns inside the fort could not be depressed enough to fire on the crowd milling beneath them; despite Burnside's special purchase of patented hand grenades in Cincinnati, there were none in the fort, but Lieutenant Benjamin cooly substituted for that deficiency. Calling for case shot and shell, he cut the fuses short with his pocket knife, lit them with the cigar clenched in his teeth, and tossed them over the parapet like shotputs. The blasts provoked chaos in the crowded ditch. Benjamin thought he detected a fresh assault after he first tried this trick, but so shuffled and confused were all the Confederates that this last attempt could have been nothing more than an impulsive act of desperation by those who found the ditch too hot. At last the broken and beaten remnant surged back through a crossfire from Ferrero's other brigades and disappeared over the low ridge whence they had come, leaving over six hundred men behind.[8]

Benjamin pulled a couple of hundred prisoners into the fort, as well as the three flags and about a thousand discarded rifles. He had killed and wounded far more Confederates than the number of men he commanded. A bit later the lieutenant colonel of the 8th Michigan strolled over to find blood running like a brook in the ditch and the dead corded upon one another in heaps. Inside Fort Sanders, Benjamin's entire loss amounted to only eight men killed and five wounded. "I know of no instance in history," Captain Poe commented, "where a storming party was so nearly annihilated."[9]

With the day barely begun, Longstreet ordered back the reserve brigades he had intended to send in after the capture of the fort. These supporting troops had not yet withdrawn from the crest in front of Fort Sanders when a staff officer brought the Confederate commander news of Bragg's rout at Missionary Ridge. From that moment it was plain to James Longstreet that he could not continue the siege. A short time later Burnside gratified him with the immediate offer of a flag of truce to bury his dead and recover his wounded. The speed with which Burnside made the suggestion demonstrated humanitarian motives, but his generosity in surrendering the wounded to their friends was not altogether unselfish: they would only have depleted his food and medical supplies, and their repatriation served to hamper Longstreet the more.[10]

Burnside knew he had won a great victory. He had battered and demoralized most of McLaws's division and foiled a general assault with almost no loss to himself. The battle had been fought and won under the direction of a mere subaltern, whose rank entitled him to the command of nothing more than a pair of cannon. The only disturbing element of the entire affair seems to have been forgotten in the euphoria of the triumph: with unusual frankness, Lieutenant Benjamin accused General Ferrero of hiding himself in a bombproof during the whole battle. "I did not see him outside," the lieutenant reported, "nor know of his giving an order during the fight."

In retrospect, Benjamin's indictment rings true enough. Ferrero's own account implied he had a role in the battle, but his ambiguous rendition was not substantiated by those of his brigade commanders. Of all these reports, the only one Burnside saw (at least before the war ended) was Benjamin's, and even that did not reach him until after he relinquished command of the department. A court of inquiry should have weeded Ferrero out, but none ever convened. Burnside may have considered it beyond his authority by that time; he may also have weighed the possibility that Benjamin was mistaken, or that his charge amounted to an indiscreet manifestation of a certain jealous arrogance that pervaded his report. Burnside held the lieutenant in high esteem, but official action on his insinuation could have been very damaging to the younger man's career. Whether through administrative technicality or Burnside's customary magnanimity, Ferrero escaped to skulk another day.[11]

Two days after the bloody fray, Grant's decoy messenger let himself fall into Longstreet's hands. No record of the courier's fate survives, and quite possibly he died for his ruse in some Dixie prison pen the following summer, but the sacrifice of his freedom did not have the immediate effect Grant wanted. Rather than hurrying away from Knoxville at the news of Sherman's approach, Longstreet decided to dawdle there as long as he could, to draw Sherman away from Grant as Burnside had lured him away from Bragg. Therefore, Burnside did not yet know that his campaign had substantially succeeded, or that the siege was about to be raised. His men continued on half- and quarter-rations, enduring bitterly cold nights without overcoats and with shoes which had fallen nearly or completely apart. But the next day, December 2, Grant's duplicate dispatch found its way into the Crozier mansion, and a collective sigh of relief echoed through headquarters: no longer need the commissary stores be hoarded; no more need Burnside agonize about the possibilities of annihilation or surrender.[12]

At the same time Grant's letter came through from the south, a courier slipped in from the north with news that must have struck Burnside as bittersweet. Based on the October 27 letter in which Burnside had outlined the health problems so acute at that time, President Lincoln had chosen to replace him. The decision might have been welcome six weeks before, but now Burnside savored the taste of victory under an agreeable superior, and he might have been willing to continue in Tennessee. The decision, however, had been made long since, though this was Burnside's first inkling of it. His replacement would be his old friend from the North Carolina campaign, John G. Foster. Foster had reached Cumberland Gap the day after Longstreet assaulted Fort Sanders, and with Willcox's two small divisions he started south, but he dared not approach too recklessly, with Longstreet's big corps squarely across his path.[13]

In the foggy forenoon of December 3 one of Burnside's staff noticed that much of the Confederate artillery had been removed from the south side of the Holston. The enemy pickets before Fort Sanders had also dwindled from a hundred to only three or four, and strange noises drifted toward Union lines from the Southern camps: brass bands were honking, apparently in a fruitless attempt to disguise the sounds of teamsters driving cattle and wagons. The eerie cacophony continued into the afternoon, carrying all the more clearly into Union lines once the fog lifted. It all portended the end of the siege, and the next night Longstreet filed his infantry north in a chilling downpour. Federal pickets ventured forth the morning of December 5 to find the Confederate works empty, so Burnside mounted what cavalry he could to chase after the retiring enemy. Later that day an orderly delivered a note from Sherman, who had marched his column up the east side of the Holston: Sherman had twenty-five thousand bone-weary men at Maryville; as badly as they needed rest, they could be in Knoxville in twenty-four hours if Burnside wanted them. He did not need them, Burnside responded, but Sherman himself was welcome to come up for a visit.[14]

Sherman did visit, and he dragged General Granger along. Colonel Wilson also rode ahead, and Mr. Dana. Sherman had had a miserable journey. His men had left Chattanooga a week before with only a blanket apiece and short rations, picking up what extra food they could find in a landscape already stripped, and they had suffered through a severe cold snap. Even Sherman had had to ask for lodging in a private home one night, to avoid freezing to death. Still, on he had driven his troops and Granger's, expecting to find Knoxville closely invested and garrisoned by an army of walking skeletons. When he and his entourage crossed the pontoon bridge into Knoxville, he noticed a pen of cattle—the freshest proceeds of foraging along the French Broad—and he began to scowl at what seemed abundant supplies, sneering especially at Burnside's comfortable quarters. When his host sat him down to a fine dinner of roast turkey with full trimmings, Sherman could no longer restrain himself: he told Burnside he had heard Knoxville was starving, and he was exasperated to find he had pushed his men so far for no reason. The misunderstanding arose from Burnside's November 23 dispatch to Grant, in which he calculated a total reserve of ten or twelve days' supplies. That would have meant his last cracker would be consumed no later than December 5—the day before. Burnside tried to calm Sherman with the explanation that his provisions had been made to last by resorting to partial rations. On November 28 Burnside had informed Grant that his supplies were further enhanced by continued (and unexpected) access to the relative abundance of the French Broad River, but if Grant ever received that message it came too late for him to tell Sherman, who had already departed. Perhaps as a matter of hospitality, Burnside neglected to say how thoroughly the staff had ransacked the city to provide Sherman with the delicacies on his plate; he ought to have done so, for the irascible Sherman remained disgruntled, almost disappointed. This false impression filtered down through Sherman's ranks and leaked homeward, and within a fortnight a Ninth Corps major complained of the public perception of the siege. Reading newspapers and his first shipment of mail since early November, the major found Northern reaction to their recent plight quite passive; in a letter to his parents he lamented that "the feeling seemed prevalent that we were safe enough at Knoxville, living like princes."[15] Misinformation like that did nothing for either Burnside's reputation or the morale of his men.

After inspecting Burnside's fortifications, "a wonderful production" which he considered "nearly impregnable," Sherman asked Burnside if he wanted to use his troops to deal with Longstreet. Weighing the advantage of numbers against the difficulty of subsisting so many men in that isolated region before winter rains raised the rivers to steamboat depth, Burnside finally decided to ask only for Granger's two divisions. Granger wailed piteously about the condition of his corps; he begged and blustered against the order leaving him at Knoxville. Unmoved by the display, Sherman left him behind. No doubt Sherman did not offer his own troops a second time, for neither did he want to stay. Five days before, he had told Grant "East Tennessee is my horror. . . . Burnside is there and must be relieved, but when relieved I want to get out, and he should come out too." Occupation of the area was a mistake, in his eyes.[16]

Like Abraham Lincoln, Burnside held precisely the opposite view: East Tennessee must not only be contested, but retained. Accordingly, he put John Parke at the head of a field force with which he expected him to follow Longstreet out of the state. Rather than use Granger's footsore men, he gave Parke the undernourished but rested troops from his Ohio army. There were only about eight thousand who could make the march, but they left Knoxville the next morning, as Granger's corps tramped across the Holston to take their places. With this substitution accomplished, Sherman turned back to Chattanooga.[17]

Burnside anticipated Longstreet would march steadily northeast until safely positioned near Jonesborough or Bristol, especially since Grant's dummy dispatch implied there were forty thousand Yankees arrayed against him. But, even deprived of Bragg's cavalry force and short some thirteen hundred casualties, Longstreet was determined to linger as long as possible, siphoning Union strength from elsewhere. In that respect, at least, Grant's trick backfired, encouraging Longstreet by exaggerating the success of his diversion. He marched for five consecutive days, with Parke in weary pursuit; both armies suffered for the want of shoes, food, and clothing. They crawled like two great delegations of peasants, on their way to petition opposing emperors. Longstreet finally met with Ransom's mixed force at Rogersville, just beyond the road to Cumberland Gap, and here he stopped and faced about. Parke also halted, establishing his own headquarters at Rutledge, and their pickets studied each other in the vicinity of Bean's Station, where the roads from Rogersville and Cumberland Gap intersected. A few days later Longstreet learned of Sherman's departure: armed with that news and Robert Ransom's few thousand reinforcements, he lashed at Parke December 14, driving him all the way back to Blain's Crossroads and forcing him to call up Granger. Rain and cold momentarily suspended the hostilities, and there ended Longstreet's counterattack.[18]

By then General Burnside was gone from Tennessee. Foster arrived in Knoxville December 11, and Burnside left the next day with most of his staff, perhaps satisfied, finally, to take his leave of a troublesome department after the successful operations of November. Behind lay the loyal city, twice redeemed, the fortuitous retreat from Loudon and Campbell's Station (which even his opponent characterized as "very cleverly conducted"), and the significant but seldom-recognized contribution to the stunning Union victory at Chattanooga.[19]

No one could say what lay ahead—save for the miserable trek back through Kentucky. Burnside and his officers returned by way of Big Creek Gap, through Jacksborough, over roads churned so rough his wagons all broke down in the mountains, one by one. Somewhere he obtained an old Concord stagecoach to carry all their luggage; the staff filled the interior and loaded up the roof and baggage compartment, and what they could not carry on this or pack on their saddles they left behind. Local hostlers could provide only mules to pull the stage, and it took ten of them to budge it.

The motley procession reached the Cumberland River three rainy days out of Knoxville, at dark. Burnside thought they should wait for daylight to make the treacherous crossing, but during the night someone told him the river was rising so fast it would be impassable by morning. He roused everyone, and at midnight he led the procession into the ford, which ran diagonally across the current. It was too dark to distinguish the telltale ripples, and the staff only found its way by following close to the leader, who picked his way carefully. Everyone came out safely on the north bank, but not without a soaking. Burnside sent Captain French on to find dry lodging, and the commissary roused a nearby resident. That house already overflowed with soldiers, however, and as French spoke with the owner he recognized Jacob Cox descending the stairs. Cox was on his way to Knoxville, for a field command. He and his staff welcomed a soggy, chilled Burnside and his officers to a warm fire and coffee, over which they discussed the thrilling events of November; they sat up all night, but at the first hint of dawn Burnside made ready to leave. His clothes had not yet dried as he swung into the saddle and waved his arm for the crazy, topheavy coach.[20]

Despite the rigors of the road, Burnside arrived at Cincinnati December 18 in robust health. Artillery saluted him from Newport Barracks; a band serenaded him from the street below the Burnet House balcony, and he responded now with the obligatory little address, dedicating his victory in East Tennessee to the private soldiers who had made it possible. So anxious was he to go home that he left the city the same evening, on the ten o'clock train for New York. The acerbic editor of the *Cleveland Plain Dealer* noted his passage through that town, with spiteful humor, the next morning.[21]

Molly met the general on his way east; they endured a formal reception committee at Albany, and when they arrived in New York, a group of Burnside supporters sponsored a grand public dinner at the Fifth Avenue Hotel. Here the general first heard the Sallie Ward story, when one of his hosts recounted it. It seemed that once, when the future of the Army of the Ohio looked particularly hopeless, an aide brought word to the White House that the sound of firing had been heard from the direction of East Tennessee. The news was probably the result of Willcox's report of heavy firing, sent during the battle for Fort Sanders. Lincoln apparently received this dispatch while he sat in conference with some cabinet officers, and he said he was "glad of it," prompting those around him to ask why that was a cause for satisfaction. Lincoln responded with an anecdote about Sallie Ward, a neighbor of days gone by, who had a houseful of children. Whenever someone told her he had heard one of her offspring crying somewhere, she would gleefully reply, "Ah, there's one of my children that isn't dead yet."[22] The tale was amusing enough in its original context and might even have been construed as complimentary, but it did not long survive in that light. Those who believed Burnside capable of nothing productive soon bent the story to conform to their own prejudices: reciting it in a revised version, which dated it during the Chickamauga campaign, they insinuated Burnside had been sluggish and uncooperative. Had that been the original intent, the story would never have been introduced at a celebration in Burnside's honor.

Captain Larned accompanied the Burnsides to Rhode Island for the holidays. He noted the general seemed extremely tired, now that he was home. After all, he had been under considerable strain since the middle of October, and he had suffered an undue amount of pressure from his superiors for a month previous to that. For the first time since 1860, Burnside relaxed before his own fire at Christmas and read about the war from afar. From newspapers he learned Foster's army experienced greater need of horses and food than when Burnside had left. Longstreet still clung to East Tennessee with his own half-starved army, but if Union forces could not expel him they at least had no difficulty maintaining their own position. Burnside had no way of knowing that Longstreet had asked to be relieved after Knoxville, just as Burnside had after Fredericksburg and the Mud March, but Burnside did not need that particular detail to reflect pleasantly upon the contrast between his situation at the beginning of 1863 and the commencement of 1864. His sense of redemption, even resurrection, was further heightened shortly after Congress convened: only four times during this war had the Senate and House of Representatives combined in a resolution presenting their thanks to individuals for great service to the nation, and in January of 1864 the two houses agreed to express their official gratitude a fifth time, to Ambrose Burnside and the men under his command.[23]

They held a little New Year's party in Providence. Mrs. Burnside presented gifts all around, and when the wine glasses were empty, the general and the local members of his staff boarded the train for New York. They established temporary headquarters at the Fifth Avenue Hotel, and the next day Burnside and Larned took the night train to Washington. With what little sleep those wobbly, overused tracks allowed, the general went straight to the War Department to discuss his next assignment. He remained in the capital several days while the secretary of war tested first one, then another proposal. Initially he wanted Burnside for the Department of Missouri again, and rumors of that choice radiated as far as New York. Missouri had been a curse on its commanders. It served as no graveyard for the discredited, like the Department of the Northwest, for despite its isolation, it could be extremely volatile. The inhabitants had divided into factions more violent and vindictive, if possible, than in Kentucky and Tennessee, and if it was not probable a commander would drop into obscurity there, it was because he was likely to get into a good deal of trouble. The department required a man of both military sagacity and delicate political finesse, and it spoke well for the administration's opinion of Burnside that he remained a candidate after the political crisis of the spring of 1863. It might have been because he knew his firm style would meet with disapproval that Burnside objected to the appointment, or he may have felt justifiably put-upon to be chosen for a third consecutive political hotspot. What he really wanted was a field command, even a subordinate position. During his brief furlough he had written a letter to that effect to his own former subordinate, George Meade. Meade's handling of the Army of the Potomac had resulted in some brutal journalistic criticism, and Burnside consoled him with a mixture of praise and sympathy, backing that vote of confidence with the assurance that he, the former army commander, would be proud to serve under Meade at the head of a corps.[24]

For all the commendable humility that allowed Burnside to make that offer, his nature seemed best fitted to independent command. While he had failed at the head of an army of 120,000—a job for which almost no one was prepared in 1862—his greatest triumphs had been achieved in North Carolina and East Tennessee, where he was unfettered by immediate supervision; those armies were small enough that he could inspire his men by his profound presence and courage. Jacob Cox, who knew him better than most of his contemporaries, felt that subordination sapped Burnside of the sense of personal responsibility which elicited his fullest energy and creativity. Without that feeling of ultimate accountability, Burnside was also less inclined to remove subordinates who demonstrated a want of capacity. In the end it was this flaw that most harmed him.[25]

The Missouri idea went back into a drawer—William Rosecrans finally drew that post. Next came the possibility of returning to the Department of the Ohio. Down in Knoxville, General Foster complained of ill health, asking if someone might not come down to replace him. Governor Andrew Johnson wanted Burnside back and appealed personally to President Lincoln. "He is the man," Johnson wrote, "the people want him; he will inspire more confidence than any other man at this time." Burnside agreed to consider it; he liked it better than Missouri. Yet the president did not name him to that department, either. Grant apparently never knew Burnside was available for reassignment: his first choices were James McPherson and John Schofield, but Parke outranked both of them. Parke seemed capable to Grant, but he preferred Baldy Smith and suggested Smith's expired appointment as a major general could be reissued from its original date, answering both the question of seniority and—Grant thought—ability. It is not altogether certain Grant would have approved of Burnside's reappointment, had he even known it was under consideration, since he now blamed Burnside for the continued presence of Longstreet's corps in East Tennessee: forgetting the supply problem and apparently forgiving Sherman's reluctance to serve there, Grant held that Burnside ought to have used Sherman's extra troops to drive Longstreet back into Virginia. Grant seems to have softened his judgment later, though, when Foster's replacement remarked that East Tennessee was the safest place for Longstreet, whose supply shortfall rendered him relatively innocuous.[26]

Stanton's third proposal to Burnside was a Lincolnesque compromise: it specified no location or objective beyond that of recruiting the Ninth Corps to fifty thousand men for "special service." The order suggested a grand independent command suitable for one of the senior generals in the United States Army, but its vagueness gave no room for objections. It would be a tremendous undertaking, for at that juncture the Ninth Corps numbered fewer than four thousand men present for duty, but Burnside's affection for his old corps was overpowering; he readily accepted, rushing back to New York to begin the task.[27]

Fewer men would volunteer now than at any time since Fort Sumter. The War Department further hampered Burnside with an order confining him to New York, Pennsylvania, Michigan, and New England, "so far as the regiments from those States in the Ninth Corps are concerned," and by the requirement to fill up all his old 1861 regiments before starting any new ones; Stanton also denied him all the 1862-vintage regiments of the Ninth Corps in East Tennessee. Since the Ninth Corps had no regiments from Maine or Vermont, and only three from the populous state of New York, the combination of these restrictions left Burnside little hope of ever approaching the fifty thousand mark. It looked as though the administration were using Burnside's considerable popularity with the veterans of the North Carolina campaign to garner as many reenlistments as possible. That was perfectly legitimate (though Stanton could have been honest enough to say so), and the eligible veterans flocked to reenlist. But if the Ninth Corps was ever to reach the anticipated capacity, it would need access to other sources of troops. On January 26 Burnside dispatched Major James Van Buren, his senior aide-de-camp, with a personal letter to the secretary of war. In it, Burnside asked for the 1862 regiments which had served with him since South Mountain, none of which were yet eligible to reenlist, and for Getty's long-lost third division of the Ninth Corps, which he had not seen since leaving the Army of the Potomac. He suggested a number of other things, including the addition of a new division of Negro regiments—indicative of an important evolution in his attitude toward black recruiting—and the authorization of fourteen new regiments in New York, Vermont, and Maine. The old regiments had already mustered as many reenlistments as they ever would, he argued, and without these modifications he could never accumulate the desired force. Van Buren presented the letter to Stanton the next day.[28]

New regiments were a great bugaboo with Edwin Stanton. They were popular among state governors, for they offered a wonderful opportunity to repay political favors with field commissions. Burnside countered that drawback with a proposal to withhold the field commissions until all the companies of the new regiments were full, which would avoid the problem of ghost regiments and would encourage the various governors to complete the new units quickly. The plan did not overcome Stanton's innate prejudice against new regiments. He remarked to Major Van Buren that Burnside had been dispatched to carry out the wishes of the War Department but had ended up adopting the views of the governors. That was hardly true, as Van Buren pointed out, but Stanton refused to give in: it hindered the replenishment of the old, reliable regiments to start fresh ones, for recruits naturally gravitated to the new organizations, seeking the comfort of heavy artillery, the glamor of cavalry, or the security of a new infantry regiment that was unlikely to be thrown into action soon. Neither would the secretary permit the 1862 regiments to leave Knoxville: with the reenlisted regiments all home on furlough, those men made the backbone of the East Tennessee garrison. He allowed for the possible reattachment of the third division (only when the rest of the Ninth Corps had completely filled up) if the military situation permitted (which was another major consideration), and he saw no difficulty assigning a black division once the individual regiments were complete. Though his decisions all made sense, Stanton's reply to each point seemed deliberately designed to offer Burnside the greatest possible incentive for raising as many troops as he could from the constituency with which he was most popular.[29]

Before long, however, Secretary Stanton realized, as Burnside did, that all the 1861 volunteers who were going to reenlist had already done so. Early in February the U.S. provost marshal general began authorizing the advertisement of new regiments. In New York alone, he dedicated four regiments specifically for Burnside's corps; in Massachusetts the 56th, 57th, 58th, and 59th regiments had been opened for recruiting all winter, initially with the understanding they would be composed largely of discharged veterans, and Burnside won the use of all four; Maine began raising a couple of new infantry regiments, and Vermont came up with one, all of them earmarked for Burnside. Simon Griffin wrote from New Hampshire that his old 6th regiment had blossomed to five hundred men with new recruits, and a Michigan colonel asked if his freshly recruited regiment could attach itself to Burnside's force. John Bross, a veteran Illinois captain named to command the 29th U.S. Colored Troops, expressed satisfaction that his new regiment would form part of the all-black division under Burnside.[30]

Ambrose Burnside thus found himself pressed directly into the recruiting service. Newspapers applauded the idea of using his considerable reputation (Army of the Potomac critics notwithstanding) to strengthen the army. Nor was he the only famous officer so employed that winter. Winfield Hancock, recuperating from his Gettysburg wound, had also come north with orders to raise fifty thousand men for "special duty" with the Second Corps. He and Burnside even went into direct competition with each other. Late in February a Boston newspaper regurgitated the appeal to fill up all the old regiments before initiating new ones, and the Burnside faction took umbrage: the Second Corps had more old Massachusetts regiments than the Ninth (which had left most of its Bay State representation in North Carolina), so the editorial logic would benefit Hancock at the expense of Burnside, who had to rely on those four new regiments. Burnside's man in Boston suspected the newspaper piece was the work of one of Hancock's assistants, a convalescent brigadier and former journalist named Francis Barlow. Hancock also had the leisure to linger in Boston, and his presence seemed responsible for the desertion of an aggravating number of prospective Ninth Corps recruits to Hancock's camp. The situation appears to have caused some jealousy and hard feelings between the respective staffs, though Burnside kept his usual distance from such emotions.[31]

Burnside had already sent most of his staff officers to their home states to facilitate recruiting. Lieutenant Colonel Loring manned the Boston office, Major Cutting circled the shore of Lake Michigan, Captain Goddard worked Providence, and Captain DeWolf set up shop in

Concord, New Hampshire. In some states Burnside was able to install more exalted proxies, such as General Potter, whose services he requested for New York, and General Edward Harland, of the old 8th Connecticut, whom he brought up from Newbern to take care of the Hartford office. With these advance men preparing the crowds, he scheduled a marathon of public appearances. He left one assistant adjutant general at the New York office, took his wife's arm, and started for Boston, where Colonel Loring's parents hosted them for a few days. On February 3 the general led the Massachusetts legislature in a body to the recruiting camp at Readville, where they reviewed four thousand new men; the next day he and Mrs. Burnside lunched with Governor Andrew, Edward Everett, Oliver Wendell Holmes, and an assortment of other Brahmins; the afternoon of February 5 they attended a formal dinner in Burnside's honor at the Revere House. Burnside curried the politicians whose help he needed, had a few words with gathering crowds, then departed for similar functions in Providence. Next he went up to New Hampshire to meet Governor Joseph Gilmore, a corpulent old politico who had squelched his own military aspirations when he waved the wand of patronage too freely. Mrs. Burnside had tired by now and returned home, but the general continued on to Portland and Augusta, Maine. These jaunts of a few days each consumed most of February.[32]

The letter Major Van Buren had delivered to Stanton in January included a pair of good campaign plans, each of which indicated both Burnside's desire to return to the field and the theater where he most wanted to serve. The suggestions outlined strikes at the Weldon Railroad, Lee's seaboard lifeline, and Wilmington, the Confederacy's last operable Atlantic seaport. Either required him to return to the North Carolina sounds. By war's end both operations had been accomplished by other generals, but for the present the War Department hesitated to make any commitments. As if to reinforce the notion of a return to North Carolina, however, Stanton approved of Burnside's choice of Annapolis as a mobilization center for his burgeoning new corps. Captain French went down to inspect the accommodations in mid-March. He found a sleepy little city overcrowded by war: the buildings vacated by the naval academy had been converted to hospitals, and all the other government buildings were full. Camp Parole, built to house unexchanged Union prisoners, might provide shelter for five thousand men (French guessed), but that was only a fraction of the numbers he expected. He proposed using the barracks at Camp Parole for the newest troops, who had not yet received tents, evicting them as they drew their shelter halves. That expedient worked for a time, but the crush of recruits quickly outstripped the capacity of the Quartermaster Department to ship canvas. A couple of weeks after French's inspection there were not enough tents to go around. A new colonel of U.S. Colored Troops complained to the New York Union League that Colonel Hartranft, commanding the post at Annapolis, refused to issue the black recruits their tents because he needed them for white soldiers.[33]

By now, Ulysses Grant had been promoted to lieutenant general, with supreme command of the armies of the United States. He came east to confer with the Washington authorities, and on March 11 Stanton invited Burnside down from New York to meet him. Despite their former association, Burnside and Grant had not yet crossed paths. Given the brevity of Grant's stay—he started back to Nashville early the next day—their interview must have been brief, but it allowed Burnside time enough to persuade the new general-in-chief to release the rest of the old Ninth Corps troops from East Tennessee: no sooner had Grant arrived in Nashville than he ordered them to Annapolis under Orlando Willcox. Two days later Grant complied with another of Burnside's requests, relieving John Parke of his field command and directing him to join Burnside. While Parke sped back to New York alone, Ninth Corps infantry and artillery started toward Cincinnati on foot, the gunners leaving their cannons, caissons, and teams behind. The infantry consisted mostly of regiments mustered in the summer of 1862, each of them swollen to four or five hundred rifles now by dint of heavy bounties; Willcox estimated he led six thousand of them out of Knoxville.[34]

These administrative worries out of the way, Burnside undertook another round of personal appearances, this time in the Midwest. While his staff oversaw the processing of the first arrivals at Annapolis, the general's train turned west at Philadelphia. He stopped in Harrisburg March 17, and in Pittsburgh the following day. Three days lapsed between his visit there and his arrival in Chicago, suggesting a stopover at the old home place in Liberty. When he reached the city whose newspaper he had suppressed, he spoke to the board of trade, which organized a reception for him. He refused to apologize for his heavy-handed administration of the previous spring, offering still to smite those enemies behind him as lustily as those in front. The cause of the Union could not fail, he told these businessmen, because it was just. Like most of Burnside's early public utterances, the speech oozed with routine patriotic rhetoric—except for one sentence, in which he revealed his impression that he had endured a disproportionate share of difficult assignments: "Probably very few of the general officers in the army have seen more dark hours than I have," he said. Could he have but known he had not seen the last of those dark hours, he might not have continued his duties with such cheerful optimism.[35]

The day after the Chicago speech Burnside traveled first to Detroit and then to Cleveland, where officials reorganized the 60th Ohio Infantry for the Ninth Corps from among men paroled with the Harpers Ferry garrison in 1862. Just one year ago Burnside had passed through this city in the opposite direction, on his way to the Department of the Ohio; he had been under a bit of a cloud then, but as the train rattled east he radiated victory and hope. When he arrived in Washington he reported to Halleck on the considerable progress he had made recruiting infantry, asking for another half-dozen batteries to complement his expanded force. Confident he could do little more to raise troops, and worn out after ten days on the cars, he retreated to Providence for a few days' rest.[36]

His sojourn at home was brief, for returns tallied far fewer than the fifty thousand men he and the War Department wanted. Early in April he resumed pleading with the public at large and prodding the authorities, petitioning Grant again for the return of the old third division, Getty's, the remnants of which were presently strewn all over North Carolina and southeastern Virginia. Grant left the bare possibility open, but promised nothing. Nor would he tell Burnside his specific plans, advising him only to be ready to move from Annapolis by April 20 and to keep news of the movement a secret. In fact, Grant had already decided to use Burnside's corps in Virginia, alongside Meade's Army of the Potomac, but the only other soldier aware of that right now was Grant's old friend, William Sherman.[37]

7

AGAIN VIRGINIA'S SUMMER SKY

I

Annapolis, in April of 1864, was not the sleepy shellfishing town Ambrose Burnside had first seen nearly three years before: the rails from there to Washington and Baltimore rattled endlessly with carloads of soldiers, provisions, and new equipment. The old-timers of the original Ninth Corps remembered this as the emotional capstone of their service: they were hardy veterans now, many of them just returning from long reenlistment furloughs; they had a new camp on fresh ground; they looked forward to a new assignment, possibly amid scenes of past glory, in the Carolinas. Best of all, the beloved Burnside had come back to lead them.

Perhaps Burnside shared the euphoria of these halcyon days, despite his underlying desire to leave the army. The nucleus of his old corps and their immediate reinforcements formed a command a bit smaller than the coastal division he had assembled here in 1861, but the men were much fonder of his familiar face than they had been of the virtual stranger of that first expedition. Their cheers came more spontaneously. The camp wore a contented holiday air, unlike the frenetic let-us-get-on-with-it attitude that had prevailed in the first winter of the war. Uniforms sparkled dark and new, the enemy lay a hundred miles away, and these old soldiers were happy to have it so. Their new tents glowed like so many giant lanterns in the moonlight as they plugged lighted candles into the sockets of their bayonets and sang the songs that took them home.[1]

Burnside arrived at the City Hotel with Molly April 13, but he had to leave her in their rooms immediately to organize a review of the troops for General Grant, who came to Annapolis that same day. Some noticed a difference in this review that hinted at an important change in the way the army would be used. Everyone expected to pull on white gloves and parade around the Maryland landscape for Grant, as they had had to do for McClellan and the rest, but these fancy-Dan affairs were a thing of the past: Grant had them fall in where they camped, while he and Burnside rode around them at a canter, assessing them without making them march. With Grant, one marched only to reach the battlefield; to a greater and more final degree than when Burnside had assumed command, the pomp was out of this war.[2]

The corps broke camp April 23. With palpable disappointment, men at the rear of the line of march watched the head of the column turn away from the waterfront: Burnside was not the only man in the Ninth Corps who entertained visions of the North Carolina coast, and those happy images crumbled as the leading color guard and its blaring band turned down the road to Washington. Now speculation shifted to the mission of defending the capital, and people from Washington to New York who thought they enjoyed privileged information assumed the corps would settle into the commodious forts around the city while the Army of the Potomac tended to Lee.[3]

The afternoon of the third day's march from Annapolis brought the head of the column to the outskirts of Washington. Burnside rode ahead, then sent back an aide to warn the brigade commanders to spruce up their ranks for a little parade; it seemed the citizens of the city had come out to see the troops.

Crowds bordered the route of the march, applauding and waving, for it was not every day that an entire corps of seasoned soldiers strode through town. Congressmen and their families filled the Capitol grounds; government employees joined thousands of private citizens to cheer them along down Pennsylvania Avenue; cabinet officers and bureaucrats hung from the windows of the White House and various department headquarters. The men picked up their feet and involuntarily straightened their shoulders. Ahead, on the balcony of Willard's Hotel, stood a pair of tall men they all recognized. One was the burly, bushy Burnside; the other, lankier observer, was President Lincoln himself. Every man craned his neck to see the two, and the commander of each regiment saluted as his guidons passed beneath the balcony. Only the officer leading the 51st New York forgot to raise his hand in tribute, for just as he approached the dignitaries his brother, a grizzled volunteer nurse named Walt Whitman, stepped from the throng to join him.[4] Brass bands echoed after the muddy pantlegs as they disappeared down the avenue. At last the cheering died away, and the column moved toward the Potomac bridges to its new assignment.

That new assignment, the exhilarated soldiers quickly learned, would be in Virginia: not the fringe of Virginia abutting the District of Columbia, but the brutal, bloody Virginia of Lee and Longstreet. Those veterans who had served in the Virginia army in 1862 and early 1863 harbored uncomfortable apprehensions about soldiering again with the Army of the Potomac, for it was headed by a fractious set of generals whose cliquish attitudes filtered down to the very privates: many of those men regarded Burnside and his corps as perennial outsiders. As one New York captain wrote late that summer, Burnside's men felt "our Corps never had a fair chance since we came in this Army."[5]

Burnside himself appears not to have suffered from this paranoia in April of 1864, but such misgivings would not have been unjustified. In the year since the door had closed between him and George McClellan, Little Mac had submitted his report of service as the army commander, which he had revised to throw the onus of his ultimate failures on Burnside. During the winter McClellan published that report, complete with its deliberately manufactured indictment of his old friend, as something of an advance campaign biography. That report made the rounds of corps and division headquarters as the Virginia days lengthened into spring, confirming McClellan partisans in their prejudice against Burnside, tainting even the opinions of some who previously recognized the true causes of Burnside's own downfall. Charles Wainwright, artillery chief for one of Meade's corps, swallowed McClellan's story whole. He not only deemed Mac a great man after finishing the book (precisely as McClellan hoped), he praised him for the restraint with which he alluded to "the great failures of his subordinates to do their duty, as in the case of Sumner at Williamsburg, and Burnside at Antietam."[6] McClellan's misrepresentations would have a profound effect on Burnside's reception.

As it rolled onto the Sacred Soil once again, the Ninth Corps gathered strength almost magically, like Antaeus. The skeleton divisions of

"Burnside's Travelling Menagerie" were already swollen with new recruits, including those entire regiments of newcomers, but more reinforcements awaited them at Alexandria or hurried from behind to overtake them. Twenty more regiments soon aligned themselves at the morning muster, all but two of them brand-new organizations. None had ever been in battle as regiments. These accessions doubled Burnside's strength, but between the new regiments and the rookies in the old ones, the Ninth Corps could not boast three tried veterans out of every ten men. All nine of the brigade commanders were colonels.

Early in May Grant maneuvered the Army of the Potomac toward the fords of the Rapidan River, east of Lee's winter works, hoping to be able to skirt past the Confederates and gain the shorter road to Richmond. He held the Ninth Corps independent of that army, out of respect for Burnside, who outranked every man in it—including George Meade, its commander. For the moment, Grant left the corps to guard the supply line, the Orange & Alexandria, and Burnside made his headquarters at Warrenton Junction while the last of his reinforcements caught up.

Among the new units straggling into the Ninth Corps camps were two heavy artillery regiments, each of them twice the size of the biggest veteran infantry regiment. The reorganized 2nd Pennsylvania was, in actuality, perfectly new; the 14th New York had been in the process of organization since the previous summer, but it had enjoyed the comfort of coastal forts until wrenched from the casemates and armed with rifles. A couple of regiments of dismounted New York cavalry came limping along behind the transmogrified artillerymen.

The most talked-about troops in all of Virginia were those in Burnside's fourth division—seven regiments freshly raised, every man of them black except for their officers. They had come from occupied Southern plantations, where the work force had been cast adrift; from free Northern enclaves; and from Canada, at the termini of the Underground Railroad. They were the first U.S. Colored Troops the Army of the Potomac had ever seen, and few who did see them failed to write home about them. A man on Meade's staff expressed astonishment that the federal government would jeopardize these innocents by throwing them into combat against Lee's Confederates; he preferred to see white men fight their own battles. Some of the erstwhile slaves might have argued whether this were altogether a white man's fray.[7] The sight of these armed black men represented the great transformation wrought

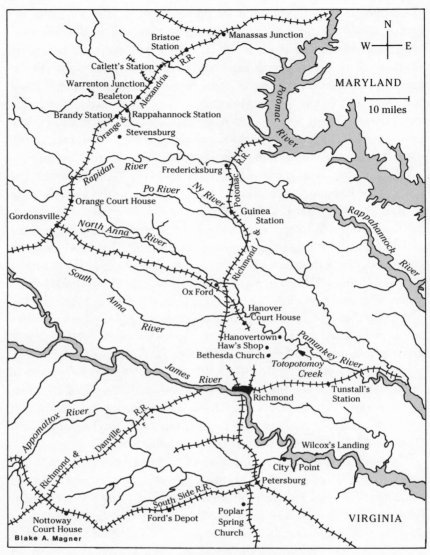

Map 11. The Eastern Theater, 1864

by a war that had already changed many things and many men; their presence in the Ninth Corps marked one of the men so changed, signifying as it did Burnside's final reevaluation of his prewar politics. The Democratic principles which allowed him to return fugitive slaves to loyal Tarheels early in 1862 had given way beneath the larger burden of reunion by the end of that year; his pragmatic accommodation of racial sensitivities, evidenced by his reluctance even to enroll potential black conscripts in Kentucky in 1863, had now evolved into a remarkably egalitarian perspective. If emancipation were not yet a fact, he considered it inevitable, and once the slave was free, Burnside was ready to call him a man: George McClellan was not the only Democrat with whom he had broken.

Grant had consolidated Meade's army into three large wings—the newly replenished Second, the Fifth, and the Sixth corps. In the warm, grey predawn light of May 4, all three corps roosted near or headed for the crossings of the Rapidan. As soon as the Army of the Potomac splashed across, and troops from Washington came down to replace Burnside's railroad guards, Grant wanted the Ninth Corps to start for the fords. Commanders of some of the new regiments—particularly the dismounted cavalry—doubted whether their men could complete an average day's march.[8]

Grant gave Burnside his cue that morning. Elements of the corps lay as far behind as Bristoe Station and Manassas Junction, but Burnside put some of them on the road by 7:00 A.M. By early afternoon most of the Ninth Corps was in motion, except for some railroad guards who remained unrelieved. The day turned extremely hot and dusty. A traffic jam forced a halt of several hours at Brandy Station, but those waiting had to stand in ranks under the sun, and the stop offered no refreshment. Just before two o'clock a wire reached Warrenton Junction directing Burnside to commence a forced march, requiring the troops farthest back to make a night march. A courier had to relay that cable ahead to Burnside, who had proceeded to Rappahannock Station, but as soon as he read it (at four o'clock) he quickened his pace. He directed his black division to reach Warrenton Junction that night— fifteen more miles—and to press on for Germanna Ford early in the morning. Darkness, bad maps, and bad roads created confusion, and progress slowed to a crawl. The Negro division did not even arrive at Catlett's Station, a few miles short of Warrenton Junction, until daybreak on May 5. One division that had started earlier made Bealeton sometime after midnight, while parts of another marched within a half-dozen miles of the ford—at the cost of having to countermarch six miles because of a wrong turn. These most advanced fragments of Burnside's corps camped at two o'clock in the morning. One veteran officer recorded this as the hardest march he ever made, and counted only fifty men around the campfires of four companies in his regiment. Other outfits straggled the same, he noted. Officers had pushed them to their "utmost strength," one well-experienced man said.[9]

The following day's march was even worse. While most of the Army of the Potomac partook of a long siesta in the vicinity of the gutted Chancellor house, the exhausted men of the Ninth Corps rose early, leaning briskly into the highway toward Germanna Ford and a lone pontoon bridge Grant had left for them. Few of those with Burnside that day forgot the severity of that march when they came to tallying up their experiences years later. "We hurried on at a dog trot," one captain remembered, without respite even to make coffee. They halted only for the ranks to close up, or for batteries or ammunition trains to give way, with but little chance to swig from a warm canteen or gobble some hardtack on the move. Part of the second division halted for an hour near Stevensburgh; when the bugles blew, the ranks "seemed to melt down like snow upon hot iron," as one observer described it. When the vanguard came in sight of the Rapidan that afternoon, a shout went up that spoke more of relief than enthusiasm. The brigades congregated at the bridgehead, shuffling tediously across, fanning out on the opposite heights to guard against any Confederate resistance.[10]

During that day, Grant had run into trouble. Lee, aware of the attempt to slip around his flank, slammed broadside into the Union advance. Briefly stunned, blue columns ground to a halt and backed into line of battle. Those divisions that had just left their leisurely bivouac at Chancellorsville arrested their progress, rested some more, and finally turned toward the fighting. The antagonists grappled all afternoon May 5 in the snarl of undergrowth known locally as the Wilderness, sparring along the turnpike and the plank road that ran west to Orange Court House. When the fighting broke off at dark, Grant began planning a major assault for the morning, by which time he hoped to have the added weight of the Ninth Corps.

By dark, Burnside had all of his corps in position near the old Spotswood Tavern except the black division. The last leg of the long march had been the worst of all, from the bluffs along the ford to the tavern. It was only some three and a half miles, but they covered it at what one man remembered as "almost a double-quick. I can safely say that the brigade never saw an hour's march like that one," he judged, "before or since." But still there came no rest for the weary: Grant feared the Confederates would try to turn his right, so Burnside's men had to remain under arms. His third division moved out on the firing line, to relieve a Sixth Corps division. A few men slunk away for a quick bath in Flat Run, but the majority of the footsore, hungry, sunstruck troops clung to their muskets and stood in their sweat-soaked wool uniforms, staring toward the woods where rattling volleys kept rolling to and fro. Not until 10:30 that night did regimental commanders pass the word to lay down and sleep, without unrolling blankets. Most of these men had marched forty miles in the past thirty-six hours, with an average of less than four hours' sleep.[11]

Meanwhile, Burnside had gone to see Grant, who made his headquarters near Wilderness Tavern. The two armies had been fighting a divided battle, with Winfield Hancock on the left, facing A. P. Hill's Confederate corps, and Gouverneur K. Warren and John Sedgwick standing against Ewell on the right. The battle on Hancock's front rode up and down the Orange Plank Road; that on the right raged perpendicular to the Orange Turnpike. Grant wanted to position the Ninth Corps in the woods between these two fronts, so Burnside could swing right or left as the situation required. Grant told him to rouse his troops at two, and he set four-thirty as the hour for the attack. That hour stood until someone else later expressed doubt whether this would allow Burnside's drained soldiers enough time to claw their way through the tangled undergrowth. The objection seems to have come from Meade's own corps commanders, who had been in the brush all afternoon and knew what he would be up against. Grant, however, worried that Lee would strike first, or that Longstreet's corps would come up from Gordonsville, and he declined to postpone the assault more than half an hour.[12]

There is a story—not a particularly convincing one, but a story nevertheless—of another conference between Meade and his corps commanders. No one mentioned the incident except a young ordnance officer, who seems to have learned it secondhand and failed to record it for nearly half a century, by which time all the potential witnesses had died. According to that lieutenant, when Burnside took leave of Meade and the others he threw back his shoulders and said: "Well, then, my troops shall break camp by half-past two." When Burnside was safely out of earshot, Meade's chief engineer, James Duane, ostensibly commented, "He won't be up—I know him well." The incredible portion of the tale is not that Duane would make so disparaging a comment behind Burnside's back, for that is the way most of Burnside's critics attacked him. Duane had good reason to find fault with Burnside: it had been Duane who led Burnside's staff to the wrong ford at Antietam, and Duane who sent the all-important pontoon dispatch to Harpers Ferry by slow-moving regular mail, back before Fredericksburg. Duane was a McClellan partisan, too, and the McClellan clique based its defense of Little Mac on Burnside's supposed incompetence. Burnside may have had a reputation for moving slowly, but it was not altogether deserved. He was the man who had gotten a jump on Bobby Lee between Warrenton and Fredericksburg, and the man who had just moved his corps twice as far as the Army of the Potomac had marched, in less time. The myth of the lethargic Burnside had begun with the deliberate fabrication of the 8:00 A.M. Antietam attack order in McClellan's 1863 report—a report on which James Duane had assisted. Duane's snide remark would have been perfectly logical; what is not quite kosher about the anecdote is the claim that Burnside said he would break camp at 2:30. Like the fictional Antietam order, it seems contrived to fix the blame for ensuing delays on Burnside. In fact, Burnside had some of his troops awake as early as 12:30, and most of the reports written soonest after the Wilderness put the hour of march at 2:00 A.M. [13]

Three of the men who led Burnside's divisions had commanded regiments under him in North Carolina. Thomas Stevenson and Robert Potter, both Boston-born, had the first and second divisions, respectively; his most experienced commander was Orlando Willcox, of the third division; in charge of the black troops of the fourth division was Edward Ferrero, the dancing master who showed the white feather at Knoxville. Burnside grouped his dismounted cavalry and heavy artillery regiments into a provisional brigade—the "awkward squad," or "Company Q" of the corps, under Colonel Elisha G. Marshall—which remained behind to guard the ford while Willcox and Stevenson followed Potter down the road. The corps had made what Grant later called "a remarkable march," most of the new men somehow keeping up with the veterans, but now their fatigue became a significant factor in the total darkness of a new moon, as they traversed strange roads in the flotsam of an embattled army. They were groggy and did not know where they were going. It was not that far to their assigned position—less than four miles—but, unlike the Confederate reserves against whom they raced, they had to march parallel to and just behind their own line of battle, so every step of the way they were bucking artillery, ammunition, and ambulance trains that choked the few existing roads. It was, paradoxically, not until Potter's division turned onto an even-more-primitive road near the Lacy house, where the weald grew thick and full of the smoke from brushfires, that the troops found the going easier. There were no Confederates in sight, and so easily did they penetrate the Wilderness that Potter and others around him feared a trap. By now the appointed hour of five o'clock had arrived. According to a man in the 6th New Hampshire, his regiment filed into Potter's skirmish line at "daylight," which was about 4:50 A.M.: one of his officers scribbled "5 P.M." into his diary, meaning 5:00 A.M. Those observations coincide very nearly with the recollection of one of Meade's staff, who remembered Potter coming on the field about 5:30. As Meade's corps commanders had warned, the Wilderness was hard going, and Burnside's would not be the only troops to show up later than expected during this battle. They would, however, be the only ones with the excuse of physical exhaustion.[14]

Burnside made his headquarters where the woods road opened out of the Lacy field, where couriers could most easily find him. The density of the Wilderness confused Burnside's arrangement of his assault, and staff officers frequently reported back to consult with him. Occasionally a division commander himself would gallop back to confirm some particular, and all of this coming and going led the McClellanized Colonel Wainwright to frown on Burnside's staff work. The cause of all the headquarters traffic probably lay in Burnside's maps. Captain Larned ordered some from the engineer department May 3, after learning the army's destination, but if any were delivered by dawn of May 6 they were poor guides to Spotsylvania County. One of Meade's aides later made a special complaint about the accuracy (and durability) of all the maps supplied to the Army of the Potomac that spring, and about the map for this particular region specifically.[15]

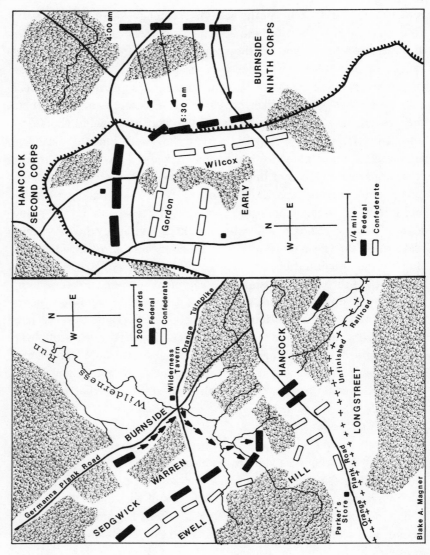

Map 12.
The Wilderness and
Spotsylvania

While Burnside's men bushwhacked toward their indistinct goal, Hancock had begun his attack and was driving A. P. Hill's corps before him. He held back one division to answer Longstreet's expected arrival on his left flank, but he threw in the rest of his wing. He anticipated Burnside would fall on Hill's left and probably collapse the Confederate line, but a staff officer from Meade reined up to say Burnside had only one division up and it had not yet come into position.

"I knew it," Hancock sputtered. "Just what I expected. If he could attack now, we would smash A. P. Hill to pieces." Possibly Hancock's outburst merely manifested that special contempt in which the Army of the Potomac had come to hold Burnside: that was the light in which Meade's man took it. But if that was Hancock's meaning, he had occasion to nibble some humble pie four weeks hence, when similar conditions caused his own corps to arrive too late for an assault at Cold Harbor. An interpretation more complimentary to both Hancock and Burnside is that Hancock harked back to the warning he and the other corps commanders had given Meade the previous evening—that five o'clock was too early for Burnside to be able to fight his way through the crush of men and vegetation with his somnambulent troops. These generals at the front knew better than Grant or Meade how tough the going was in the Wilderness. James Wadsworth's fresh division had made a march even shorter than the one proposed for Burnside, and through some of the same terrain, the afternoon before; Wadsworth had taken several hours to cover the ground in broad daylight and even then fell short of his destination. One Second Corps general found it "very difficult" to maneuver in the woods after dark, and it was almost entirely in darkness that Grant expected Burnside to move.

Potter's two brigades worked their way down the muddy track toward Parker's Store, apparently without much guidance from general headquarters. General Warren, the Fifth Corps commander, sent an ordnance officer (he of the council-of-war tale) to guide Burnside's troops. This young aide merely reported that Warren had sent him to help; he seems not to have so much as pointed in the appropriate direction, and because the preoccupied general did not immediately recognize him, the lieutenant accompanied him no farther. Misinterpreting Burnside's bleary, sleep-robbed expression for haughty condescension, he simply rode away.[16]

Willcox's division supported Potter's, one brigade on either side of the road, but Stevenson's division did not follow: successive orders from Grant had broken it up to buttress the ends of Hancock's line. One of Stevenson's brigades, under Daniel Leasure, went astray through what one of the division's more self-righteous staff officers characterized as Leasure's incompetence, so the entire division floundered until nearly nine o'clock. The fourth division remained well in the rear, guarding the supply trains by Grant's own order: Burnside would not have the use of these men again for weeks. As Burnside's corps gravitated into battle, it consisted of fewer than a score of regiments under Potter and Willcox.

Potter put Simon Griffin's New England brigade into line of battle. Griffin, short two of his six regiments that day, moved behind a heavy screen of skirmishers guarding his front and his left flank. The rumble of fighting echoed ominously from either side, and finally Griffin's skirmishers ran into resistance on their own front. They pushed the Confederates steadily for an hour or so, then tried to feel the enemy's strength on the far side of a clearing near the Chewning farm, but Stephen Ramseur's North Carolina brigade trotted into the breech from Ewell's corps and drove them back to the edge of the woods. General Potter came up and began forming Griffin's men for a charge across the open ground, but a courier interrupted him with Grant's order for all Burnside's troops to sidestep a mile to the left and come up on Hancock's right. Not only had Potter pointed his men in the wrong direction to accomplish Grant's original objective of crumpling Hill's flank; now there was real trouble on Hancock's line. Longstreet had finally arrived, back from Tennessee and fresh from Gordonsville, and his brigades scattered the division on Hancock's right. Grant wanted Burnside to wheel to the left and destroy Hill's flank all the more, but for the more defensive purpose of saving Hancock from total rout.[17]

It was midmorning by now. Grant sent Burnside his senior aide-de-camp, Lieutenant Colonel Cyrus Comstock, to lead the Ninth Corps into the desired position. Comstock had been Burnside's chief engineer at Fredericksburg, but his service prior to that was of some significance. He had served on McClellan's staff on the Peninsula and in Maryland, and virtually ever since his graduation from West Point in 1855 he had been closely associated with James Duane. He had perhaps undue respect for Duane's judgment, and Duane judged Ambrose Burnside absolutely worthless. It should therefore not be too surprising that Comstock complained in his diary that Burnside's corps came into line perpendicular to Hancock's right "after long delay," but that delay and the fact that the head of the corps emerged from the woods in the wrong position were at least partly Comstock's responsibility. Potter had first to extricate his brigades from a fight, which consumed considerable time; then his division and Willcox's lead brigade had to sidle to the left a mile and a half to connect with the battered division on Hancock's flank. Straightening the lines in thickets so dense one regiment had to crawl fifty yards on hands and knees required perhaps half an hour, so the clock may have swung toward eleven before Potter's line of battle groped forward again. He necessarily advanced even slower than before, for he reported moving literally blind in the undergrowth, and since no one could be certain whether they were on course, the skirmishers picked their way with extreme caution. They knew only that Longstreet's corps swarmed somewhere on the field, and that the angle of Burnside's line to Hancock's left the Ninth Corps flank wide open.[18]

Potter struggled through the endless brake until he struck the flank of those Confederates thrashing Hancock. Because of the poor visibility, he failed to realize the enormous advantage he might have had, and the enemy line found time to curl back to receive his attack. Potter was not the only officer uncertain of his position: he and Burnside, riding together, came upon an isolated fragment of Hancock's wing—General Stevenson, with about a hundred members of his detached division—lost in the brush.

Burnside noticed just then that Simon Griffin's brigade stood organized and waiting behind Potter's busy skirmishers. It is perhaps a measure of his sensitivity to the element of time that he stepped out of character to interfere with Potter's management of his troops.

"Let Griffin attack," he half ordered, half suggested. Potter unleashed the brigade, and the New Englanders stepped through the remnants of Hancock's right flank, their bright accoutrements and Annapolis-new uniforms contrasting sharply. They surged into the budding tangle of the Wilderness, but their attack ran into marshy ground, on either side of which were Confederate riflemen, dug in. Griffin pressed forward and took some works in front, but a fierce counterattack drove him back. Visibility, already occluded by the thick vegetation, diminished further in the sulphurous haze of gunfire and smoke from brushfires it had sparked. The advance through the woods had somewhat disorganized

Griffin's men, and they were a little disoriented when the Confederates hit them. They fought gamely enough for a few minutes, but their leaders fell quickly and the encounter turned into a melee. Griffin had his horse shot from under him and saw two of his aides killed; the commander of one of his new regiments fell wounded; the colonel of the 11th New Hampshire was captured, and his lieutenant colonel was killed. Back came the Maine, New Hampshire, and Vermont boys, streaming through the brush and taking others with them. Willcox's first brigade stepped in to steady the line, and he called for assistance from his second brigade. It all looked pretty bleak for a time, but they had saved Hancock's flank.[19]

The battle stabilized by midafternoon, though Burnside held a position more vulnerable than he could observe. His four remaining brigades, further reduced by heavy drafts for wagon guards, dangled disconnectedly in the void between the two Union wings, more than a mile from Warren on the right and at least half a mile from Hancock's recoiled line. Immediately in front of Burnside sat six Confederate brigades, while a full division of Georgians and Carolinians stretched unopposed to his right. Unintimidated—or perhaps only unaware of his predicament—Burnside visited Hancock and urged him to mount a new attack with his corps. Reclining on a cot to relieve the persistent pain from his old wound, Hancock refused, citing a perceived threat to his left flank.[20]

Grant laid plans for an evening assault across the entire front, but before he could spring it the Confederates came at them again, breaking up Mott's division of Hancock's corps and seizing some rifle pits. Without waiting for orders, Burnside moved out on his front and took some of the heat off Hancock, who eventually patched up his line. The Wilderness wrought the same disruption on Lee's assault as it had on the Union attack, and by dark the armies withdrew to their makeshift entrenchments, from which they glared at each other throughout the next day.[21]

Stalemated in the Wilderness, Grant tried again to slip around Lee's right flank. He sent the Army of the Potomac toward Spotsylvania Court House, retaining Burnside's corps to cover the rear and guard the army's wagon train, which had parked near the Chancellorsville battlefield. Burnside located his headquarters at the Aldrich house, on the Catharpin Road. Grant proposed he move from there to Alsop's, on the road from Fredericksburg to Spotsylvania Court House, by roads well in the rear of the fighting. The lieutenant general advised him to keep two divisions free to attack the vicinity of the courthouse, stipulating that he wanted white divisions for that duty: even Grant seems to have concluded very early that black troops were good for little but guard details.

Grant realized by the evening of May 8 that Lee had beaten him to Spotsylvania, so he warned Burnside not to proceed beyond a place called "Gate," along the Fredericksburg road. Gate was identified on Grant's map, and apparently on Meade's, but Burnside found no such location on his, though his advance troops were already astraddle the place Grant intended. Therefore, when he received Grant's order to reconnoiter the roads to Spotsylvania the next day, Burnside had no idea whether he lagged behind Grant's expectations or had already gone too far. It happened he had pushed too far.

Impelled by Grant's unintentionally confusing order, Burnside sent Willcox browsing ahead. He did so rather nervously, for his reduced corps lay dangerously isolated on the left wing. Willcox ran into Confederate videttes near the Gayle farm. They fell back before him, and he backed them up to the Ny River, where a strong force of dismounted cavalry struck him head-on. Willcox brazenly crossed the bridge there without orders and threw out a line of battle, sending back an appeal for support. Burnside promised him Stevenson's first brigade and relayed Willcox's findings to Grant.

Now it was Grant's turn to be puzzled. Not supposing the Ninth Corps had advanced so far, he interpreted the information as an attempt to turn the Union left: for a time thereafter a note of panic pervaded headquarters correspondence. Grant told Burnside to have his lead division dig in and hold its position as long as possible, and Burnside forwarded hold-to-the-last-ditch orders to Willcox, who came slightly unglued, questioning whether Burnside had received his assessment of the situation up front. Where, he asked, was that brigade of Stevenson's?

Willcox was not in so bad a predicament as he thought: a low-hanging fog veiled a perfect lack of Confederate supports. Stevenson came up just after noon, by which time Willcox's fight had subsided to picket fire.[22] The whole first division crossed the Ny to cement the hold on the bridge, and Willcox sent back fidgety reports of enemy movement, but Lee's right was much weaker than Willcox apprehended. Still, Burnside called Grant's attention to the distance between the Ninth Corps and the Army of the Potomac, and the commanding general sent one of Hancock's divisions to fill the void.

The morning of May 10, Grant organized an assault on Lee's line with part of the Army of the Potomac, instructing Burnside to cooperate with a strong demonstration in his front. The Ninth Corps commander accordingly rode up to the front, bringing Potter's division to beef up the attack. When he arrived at the Ny, he encountered an ambulance carrying General Stevenson's body to the rear: he had been killed by a sharpshooter. Burnside was visibly moved by the loss of this subordinate— more so, perhaps, than when Sanders died in Knoxville, and nearly as badly as the evening Reno was killed. Before the summer ended, Stevenson's absence would cost him far more than personal grief.

For the present, Colonel Daniel Leasure took over the first division. Charles Mills, a staff aide who criticized Leasure's performance in the Wilderness, wrote his mother about his new chief, commenting, "I had a favorable opinion of him, but I can't say that I retain it."[23] His assessment is not conclusive, for Mills had something nasty to say about everyone he met (except perhaps the worst general ever to blight the Ninth Corps), but Burnside's reluctance to use the first division under Leasure does hint at a lack of general confidence.

While he made his dispositions for the afternoon, Burnside worried about the Second Corps troops on his right. There were not enough of them to do more than baste Burnside's wing to the main body, and they consisted of Gershom Mott's division, which had not done well in the Wilderness. Glancing at that division and the length of line it had to fill, Burnside sent a man to Grant, asking if he ought not leave a Ninth Corps division at the bridge to support Mott. Grant's reply made it obvious he wanted Burnside to put everything he had into his effort on the left, though it was so late he doubted if Burnside could bring up that last division. Burnside nevertheless hurried that division to the front. He chose to break up Leasure's division, however. The commander of Leasure's bigger brigade was prostrate with sunstroke, and his successor was one of those inexperienced new field officers, so Burnside gave it piecemeal to Willcox. That left Leasure in command of little more than his original brigade. The Pennsylvania colonel's days with the Ninth Corps were numbered: two days later a lieutenant colonel complained of having to take command of his brigade in battle because

Leasure was "not to be found," and two days after that Leasure went home, pleading illness, never to return.[24]

Grant's scenario included a massed assault by twelve regiments on Lee's center, with Burnside pressing his right and Mott driving in between. Burnside may have misconstrued Grant's instructions, putting more emphasis on his use of the word "reconnaissance" than his off-hand reference to Burnside's "attack," and though Potter and Willcox drove the enemy steadily backward, nothing resembling a battle materialized. Potter approached within five hundred yards of Spotsylvania Court House, flanking Lee's line, but darkness and unfamiliar terrain again prevented Burnside from recognizing his advantage. On the right, Grant's massed assault had failed and been driven back. Mott's advance also fizzled, some of his regiments thrown into headlong flight, and Burnside pictured himself in a tight spot. He directed his men to resort to the shovel; by then it was ten o'clock at night and too late to advance farther, anyway. Grant's own staff liaison with the Ninth Corps seemed to understand, but from his distant headquarters Grant blamed Burnside. Perhaps he was persuaded by the disparaging comments of Meade's officers; they wasted no opportunity to point out Burnside's every shortcoming, and the sheer volume of opinion may have worn away Grant's usual fairmindedness. When next the army moved, he resolved to send another staff officer to Burnside's headquarters, with specific orders to prod him.[25]

Grant scheduled the next attack for the predawn hours of May 12. In order to take advantage of the high ground, the Confederates had been forced to leave an angular protrusion in their lines. With the weaponry of the day, this presented a singular weakness because it diffused the defenders' firepower instead of concentrating it. The same principle had lured Longstreet's attack to the salient at Fort Sanders. Grant crowded Hancock's entire Second Corps in front of that inviting bulge, told Burnside to attack it from the east, and positioned part of the Sixth Corps to go in on Hancock's right.

Grant sent his senior aide, the critical Cyrus Comstock, to ride herd on Burnside; the envoy's mission became apparent from the start. As if to mitigate the effects of Comstock's presence, Grant also dispatched a friendlier member of his staff to accompany him—Colonel Orville Babcock, of Burnside's East Tennessee cadre.[26]

After the fighting of May 10, Burnside had withdrawn his isolated corps to the north side of the Ny River, nearly back to the Gate which had eluded him in past days. Here, on the eleventh, arrived a new commander for Stevenson's division: Thomas Crittenden, the long-haired Kentuckian whose premature news of Braxton Bragg's rout had led Burnside into some trouble. A full major general, Crittenden had held that rank longer than anyone in the Army of the Potomac, Meade included. That seniority explains his assignment to the Ninth Corps, for rank was a prime consideration in placing officers; besides Grant, Burnside alone outranked Crittenden. About midnight on Wednesday, Crittenden bedded down in the same house as Burnside. No one slept much more than two hours: by 2:30 each headquarters was abustle with preparations for the 4:00 A.M. movement.

Thick clouds obscured whatever grey light the sky might have afforded at that hour. May 11 had been rainy, and the Ninth Corps moved forward through a steady drizzle. Heavy mists covered Burnside's advance but also slowed it: no one knew which fog-shrouded thicket or swale shielded the enemy's line. Burnside had made no special reconnaissance, for which he may have had several reasons. First, Grant's order for the attack never left general headquarters until four o'clock Wednesday afternoon, and if it required as much time to deliver as other messages, it did not reach Burnside until near dark—too late for an effective appraisal of the terrain. Besides, Burnside initially understood he would be expected to attack toward the courthouse, over territory he already knew; not until nightfall of May 11 did he learn from Colonel Comstock the new direction Grant intended him to take. Grant had also warned the Ninth Corps commander to prepare his assault "with the utmost secrecy, and veiled entirely from the enemy." Sending out men in the pitch dark who might draw Confederate attention, while gathering topographical information of dubious quality, could be construed as disobedience of those orders: Colonel Comstock's face was evidence enough that Grant suddenly questioned Burnside's adherence to his instructions. For his part, Comstock suggested no reconnaissance.[27]

Potter's division led off, followed by Crittenden and Willcox. The corps filed down the Fredericksburg road, crossed the Ny bridge, and broke into columns of brigades. Simon Griffin's New Englanders once more took the front line, three regiments abreast, as the drenched divisions disappeared into the woods to the west. They slogged through streams and a boggy ravine while a hint of light began to glow behind the haze; when they had left their bivouac more than a mile behind (some said two miles), a dull, damp popping announced they had flushed the Confederate pickets. The enemy's main line lay a quarter-mile beyond those outposts, protected by a couple of intervening rifle pits.

One of Potter's batteries briefly softened the indistinct earthworks before Griffin's infantry swung forward. Hancock's corps had already captured the tip of the salient, and as the regiments on Potter's right assailed the near side of that prominence, Hancock's men pushed jubilantly ahead of them, sending several thousand prisoners to the rear. As a consequence of having charged en masse, however, the Second Corps was badly jumbled, and before long a determined Confederate counterattack began driving it back.

Potter's men, meanwhile, carried the rifle pits. Griffin's brigade had struck the Southern line at an angle, the New Hampshiremen on his right flank climbing up the parapet and fighting toe-to-toe for the works. Eventually the Granite Staters drove the Confederates from their trenches, clambering over and capturing a section of artillery. They were not inside those trenches long. The same counterattack that pressured Hancock back into the salient met Griffin obliquely, overlapping his left, and he had to demand some fancy footwork from his troops to wheel them into line to meet it. Veterans pushed recruits into place, and a thin semblance of a battle line greeted the onrushing Southerners.[28]

Both Grant and Hancock sent Burnside a flurry of urgent requests to close the gap between his corps and the Second. Hancock's disheveled mass had fallen back well beyond the right of the Ninth Corps, and Burnside could join with him only by groping along the works to his right. He had already committed his first and second divisions, and he soon needed Willcox to support Crittenden's beleaguered left. The provisional brigade of involuntary infantrymen stood guard over the Fredericksburg road, stationed there for want of cavalry to prevent the entire army from being flanked, and could not safely move up to assist. Burnside battled for twice the length of trenches Hancock held, and so found it difficult to stretch his troops toward him. Griffin's brigade, his nearest element, was already heavily involved in an effort to repel the counterattack against Hancock, and could hardly shoulder arms and shift to the right.

Hancock's assault had been successful because of the surprise he had gained, and because the Confederates had withdrawn their artillery from the exposed salient. For all the remarkable coordination Burnside had been able to maintain, after advancing farther and over more unfamiliar terrain than Hancock, Burnside did not share that surprise. The Confederates he faced were both alert and well supplied with artillery. At eight o'clock Grant ordered him to drive forward with all his might, adding almost pedantically, "That is the way to connect." Given the angle at which Burnside hit the enemy's line, that was not necessarily the way to connect: had Burnside been able to break straight through in that manner—and he had a devil of a time trying—his flank would have fluttered in midair, and he would have left Hancock behind. About this time Hancock sent a courier to Burnside, belatedly reporting exaggerated success on the Second Corps front, boasting seven thousand prisoners and thirty cannon taken. Hancock's earlier pleas, and the stubborn resistance before the Ninth Corps, both seemed to belie Hancock's encouraging dispatch. It may be a token of Burnside's frustration at this juncture that Hancock's report and Grant's eight o'clock note were crumpled into tight little wads.[29]

Though Colonel Comstock was in a position to understand Burnside's plight, he still annoyed the general with frequent suggestions. Burnside, who cannot have been unaware that Comstock meant to push him, snapped at last that he would "command his own divisions." Then, sorry to have hurt the young man's feelings, he promptly apologized. About 9:00 Potter reported he had tied his right to Hancock's left, but Grant continued to send Comstock orders to coax Burnside; Comstock returned occasional telegrams describing the situation on the left. The lieutenant general's attitude may have deteriorated somewhat by now, as both Warren and Horatio Wright, the new head of the Sixth Corps, failed to meet Grant's expectations on the right. Irritated at these serial disappointments, the supreme commander grew testy. Not satisfied the Ninth Corps carried its share of the fight, he directed Burnside at 10:20 to strip away a division for Hancock's use and "push the attack with the balance." He ended that communication with the curious admonition to "see that your orders are executed." At that, Burnside turned on Comstock and charged him with sending captious accounts of his management of the corps. Comstock denied it, but they wrangled over it for some minutes.[30]

The battle at the salient degenerated into a deadly donnybrook. Hancock's badly shuffled corps took a long time regaining some of its organization; the Sixth Corps went in on Hancock's right and quickly dissolved into a like throng, while the Confederates threw in every man they could spare. The combatants clubbed and bayoneted each other over the logs that topped the breastworks, and the dead fell like cordwood in the trenches. Rain periodically came in torrents, saturating everything, but it failed to douse the blazing rifles.

Thanks to Burnside's activity on the left—as Grant recognized much later—Lee could not divert sufficient forces to the salient to recapture it and drive Hancock away. At the time, though, Grant expected Burnside to do much more. In accordance with the lieutenant general's order to give Hancock a division, Burnside directed Willcox to disengage and march to the opposite flank of the corps, but he simultaneously petitioned Grant to rescind the order, pleading extreme pressure on his own front; before Willcox moved, Grant gave in.

Burnside had enough trouble as it was, but had Willcox been withdrawn there would have been a great deal more. He countermanded Willcox's marching orders and told him to make a vigorous attack on the extreme left, to take more pressure off Hancock. Willcox readied his brigades, but because of his anxiety for his left he took plenty of time to arrange a concentration of artillery to cover his flank in case he had to retreat. Lieutenant Benjamin, still corps artillery chief, placed several batteries in position to sweep the field the third division had to cross. Willcox still balked, complaining his left was too vulnerable, but Burnside understood that Hancock, Warren, and Wright needed this diversion at any cost. He told Willcox to go in, regardless of the consequences. By the time Willcox moved out it was almost two o'clock; he advanced under cover of some tall pines, but had gone only a few hundred yards when a battle line of North Carolinians emerged from an oak thicket on his left. These Confederates engulfed his flank, capturing the 17th Michigan almost whole—only four dozen men escaped. The 51st Pennsylvania was also nearly swallowed up, and both regiments lost their colors. Just then two more brigades opened on the Yankees from the works in front. Willcox disentangled the survivors and withdrew to his original position, his troops so dazed that only Benjamin's massed artillery prevented the Confederates from overrunning them. Perhaps Burnside's worst loss of the day was Lieutenant Benjamin himself. He ended the engagement with a ragged wound in the neck, but managed to clutch the gash closed until the crisis had passed. When the thunder of the big guns subsided, he consented to be carried to the rear, out of the war. Ahead of him lay an overdue promotion to captain, a Medal of Honor, and an early grave.[31]

The trenches blazed with pointblank rifle fire the rest of that rainy day and into the night, but no ground was gained and nothing was lost but lives. The firing did not slacken until well after midnight, when Lee withdrew to a more compact line of works across the base of the salient. That night Burnside and his staff slept the same as their men— with nothing but rubber blankets to shield them from the downpour— but they did not sleep as long as the privates. Grant warned Burnside to have his men awake and under arms by 3:30 the next morning, anticipating a counterattack, so the generals arose that much earlier.

No counterattack materialized. A steady skirmishing began the next morning and continued for five days, interrupted on the Ninth Corps front only by a brief and fruitless reconnaissance-in-force on May 16.

Headquarters during those five days consisted of a tent fly spread in the pine forest, back of the trenches. Paul, Burnside's accomplished chef, no longer traveled with the mess, and since Robert was not much of a cook, they endured slim pickings at the general's table. Burnside and his entourage ate regular-issue rations on a poncho stretched over the pine needles. Their baggage wagon lagged far in the rear, so no one had changed his shirt since May 8. Captain Larned had not shaved since he left Washington, and by the end of the fighting at Spotsylvania the general's famous whiskers were beginning to disappear amid the prodigious stubble on his chin.[32]

On May 18 Grant decided to try another grand assault on the lines across the bottom of what was now called the Bloody Angle. Each of the Union corps still in front of it forwarded a couple of brigades, to batter against those works so heavily studded with cannon. Warren's Fifth Corps had leapfrogged southeast, and Lee had sent much of his army to follow him; the abandoned Angle now sat before the extreme left of the Confederate army. Grant imagined it weak enough to crack.

To spearhead his portion of the assault, Burnside again chose Simon Griffin's brigade of Potter's division. He placed it alongside the first brigade of Crittenden's division, which had a newly assigned brigadier named James Ledlie. Ledlie had been a civil engineer in New York. To date, his service had been largely administrative: except for a stint as

John Foster's chief of artillery in the Goldsborough campaign of 1862, he had done little but garrison duty on the North Carolina coast. General Foster had recommended him, though, which carried a good deal of weight with Ambrose Burnside. Nevertheless, Ledlie had already watched his first appointment as brigadier general expire without congressional approval, and now he apprenticed under a second appointment. It would have been better for all concerned had he taken the hint the first time: Stephen Weld, the colonel he superseded, was better qualified to lead a brigade.[33]

For all of that, Ledlie's incompetence is not what prevented his brigade from reaching the enemy line on May 18. Richard Ewell's Confederate trenches were so closely defended by artillery that no troops from the Second, Sixth, or Ninth corps could touch them. Burnside's men tried three times before he gave up. Union troops drew back to their own defenses and resumed the constant crackling fire that had characterized their sojourn near Spotsylvania Court House. Late that night, staff officers brought orders for the men to pack up their traps and move south: the Second Corps had already pulled out of line, and long before sunup on May 19 Burnside's men followed in its wake.[34]

Once again the Ninth Corps took its place on the extreme left of the army, a mile or more southeast of Spotsylvania and north of the Po River. The corps burrowed in around the Quisenberry house that morning. Two regiments of Regulars ventured out to get the lay of the land, and the next day Ledlie's entire brigade cleared its front in a circuitous reconnaissance. Other scouting parties hiked down to view the approaches to the Po, preparatory to an advance farther south.

Grant ordered Burnside to start south from his works on Friday, May 21, taking the Telegraph Road across the Po at Stannard's Mill. Potter sent Curtin's brigade toward the mill that afternoon. According to one diarist in that brigade, they left their entrenchments about four o'clock, running into stiff resistance about a mile down the Telegraph Road. Curtin had to fall back into line of battle. Eventually he drove these Confederates across the river, but they stopped him on the north bank with fierce shellfire. Potter scouted around for a ford, but Burnside was not about to give someone else an opportunity to blame him for wasting time against a fortified river crossing—as McClellan had recently done. Grant had offered him an alternate route in the event of such resistance; apparently dissuaded at the outset by Curtin's encounter, Burnside quickly determined to follow that second option. The added mileage of the other route required him to come to his decision without much hesitation, and before Potter could finish his reconnaissance, Burnside ordered him to follow the path of least resistance at once.[35] Potter sent his other brigade back to Smith's Mill, where it arrived in a driving thunderstorm and turned east, toward the Richmond, Fredericksburg, & Potomac Railroad. The rest of the corps trailed behind as Simon Griffin's New Englanders staggered through the darkness along winding Virginia farm roads. Not until dawn did the command draw up for a nap: General Burnside and his staff had ridden ahead to the railroad to pitch their tents, and there the exhausted infantrymen fell out. This was Guinea Station, in plain view of the plantation office where Stonewall Jackson had died, a year before.[36]

While the troops rested, Burnside cantered ahead to establish a new headquarters on the line of march. At a conspicuous crossroads he found a solid brick chapel known as Bethel Church. Here, unknown to Burnside, was where the first memorial service had been held for his West Point classmate, Jackson. The staff officers found water and bathed themselves for the first time in a fortnight, taking advantage of the passing trains to plunder their own baggage. Some of the staff unrolled blankets in the aisles and slept, but Burnside sat in a pew and meditated quietly.

Meade's staff discovered him thus, while the Ninth Corps infantry plodded by. Some wag in the ranks taunted the officers in the church doorway: "My house is the house of *God*," he quoted, "but you have made it a den of thieves." One of Meade's aides noticed Burnside seated inside "like a comfortable abbot," but he seemed to concur with the private about Burnside's staff. He was particularly amused by a handful he described as the "unmistakeable New York *bon ton*, arrayed in soldier clothes."[37]

Meade departed after a brief visit, but later that day Burnside found him with Grant, resting on the porch of a roadside home. The elderly lady who owned the house sat nearby, though defiantly aloof. Union infantry trudged past in seemingly endless numbers. Burnside saw the woman as he climbed the stairs; ever the gentleman, he presented his respects to her before speaking to Grant, doffing his high-crowned hat and bowing low. In a conversational tone, he supposed she had never seen so many Yankees. She allowed that she certainly had—in the Confederate prisons in Richmond. Grant's and Meade's aides roared with amusement, slapping their thighs at the expense of the commander of the supernumerary corps.[38]

The next day they resumed the hot, dusty road south, and the predominantly new soldiers of the Ninth Corps straggled shamefully. These laggards had been pestering civilians so much in the past couple of days that Grant sent Burnside an order to put a trustworthy regiment behind his corps, to hurry up the slow and shoot the looters. No looters needed to be shot that day, but a stream of footsore and weary riflemen dragged behind. One general thought he perceived a lack of discipline in the corps, which may have arisen from the attrition of good officers: except for Griffin and Hartranft, whose names had just gone in for promotion, Ledlie was the only brigadier in command of a brigade—and he would prove to be no prime specimen. The same officer who detected loose discipline also found the various Ninth Corps staff organizations "worthless," a fault that could cripple the best body of troops, but the principal problem was probably the extraordinary number of new organizations in Burnside's command. All three corps of the Army of the Potomac struggled with a heavy proportion of recruits that spring, but none of them bore the burden of perfectly green regiments, complete with new field and company officers: the assorted command structures within the Second, Fifth, and Sixth corps were all established, with veteran officers in charge. Not so with the Ninth Corps: more than a third of Burnside's remaining regiments—probably half his white troops—were brand-new, while a couple were less than one year old. Therein lay the problem. Edwin Stanton may have been more justified than even he knew when he hesitated to authorize new units. It was Burnside's misfortune to have had the fewest old regiments on which to build his new corps.[39]

May 23 was Burnside's fortieth birthday. His assigned goal for the day was the North Anna River, where Lee had originally wanted to meet him in the late autumn of 1862. The river offered particular defensive advantages from the south bank, where five crossings rippled the water. Upstream, at Jericho Mill, Grant ordered a pontoon bridge thrown across for the Fifth and Sixth corps, and there both he and Meade made their headquarters. A little over a mile downstream existed a ford, at Quarle's Mill, as yet unknown to Union soldiers, and an old, abandoned ford lay just below that. Still another mile or more down the river was Ox Ford, which would be Burnside's responsibility, and the same distance farther on stood Chesterfield Bridge, on the Richmond Stage Road. Hancock would use the bridge; half a mile down from there sat the rail crossing of the Richmond, Fredericksburg & Potomac line— also in Hancock's domain.

Hancock reached the North Anna first. Warren next arrived at the Jericho ford and began crossing, with Wright's Sixth Corps right behind him. The Ninth Corps had the longest march, and came up too late in the day to attempt a crossing. The last of Burnside's divisions did not form up on the heights above Ox Ford before nine o'clock.[40]

Once it became apparent Grant intended to cross his troops at the bridges farthest up- and downstream, Lee responded by folding the wings of his army back in a wedge, anchoring his flanks on marshy ground and another bend in the river. With Burnside's usual luck, the apex of that wedge pointed at Ox Ford. Equally customary was the ill fortune represented by two escaped slaves, who waded to the Union side and spread the false news that Lee had retreated from all the fords and bridges and was on his way to the South Anna River. These contrabands also mentioned the Quarle's Mill fords, and general headquarters relayed that information to Burnside, in case Ox Ford proved too difficult.

Militarily, Ox Ford happened to be the most difficult crossing of all. The ravine the North Anna had carved into Virginia limestone stood steepest here, the river bottom slippery-smooth bedrock; the southern bank was, and still is, a challenge to any but athletes. Confederate breastworks scowled from the brow of that bank, abristle with bayonets and cannon.

The morning of May 24 Burnside tested the ford, finding the enemy presence and natural impediments too great a combination. Grant told him he must get across somehow, for Warren, Wright, and Hancock had all gone over to the right bank; three miles separated these two segments of the army, and the Ninth Corps had to fill that void. Grant still seemed to operate under the delusion that Lee had retreated south. Following Grant's instructions, Burnside sent Potter's division over Chesterfield Bridge to join Hancock and started Crittenden across near Quarle's Mill.

The Quarle's Mill ford was deep. One man noted that evening how the water had reached "up to are middles," and Burnside heard that many of those who crossed here slipped and fell, soaking their cartridge boxes. It took fully four hours to wade six thousand men to the other side. At least one veteran officer emptying his boots on the right bank looked back at the river and wondered whether another Ball's Bluff might not be in the making.[41]

It was Crittenden's job to clear Ox Ford by sweeping downstream on that side, but he made the mistake of sending Ledlie's brigade across first. By the time the first brigade had struggled over the treacherous ford, according to one eyewitness, Ledlie had thoroughly liquored up. Starting from the south bank with nothing but his four Massachusetts regiments and two little battalions of Regulars, Ledlie proceeded downstream. The Confederate rear guard he probably expected to overpower turned out to be a main-line defense, grizzled Southerners staring at him from behind shotted cannon and substantial rifle pits. In his animated state, Ledlie scoffed at the works and ordered a perplexed company commander back to require assistance from Crittenden. Crittenden listened dumbfounded as this captain (not even a staff officer) demanded three regiments in Ledlie's name: one on each flank, and one in reserve. That would have given Ledlie the bulk of the division, committed without the division commander's slightest involvement. Perhaps wondering who was subordinate to whom, Crittenden returned the reluctant messenger with the news that the other brigade had not yet crossed, and with instructions for Ledlie to restrain himself unless he saw a sure thing.

Too late. Ledlie had formed for a charge and would listen to no superfluous warnings. With a wiggle of his sword, he sent fifteen hundred men against A. P. Hill's Confederate corps. The uneven contest lasted a remarkably long time, but after a couple of hours of brutal punishment the lone brigade fell back in disorder, a flag lost and one of the more experienced regimental commanders dead on the field. Three of Ledlie's staff were gone, as well as his brigade guidon-bearer. Crittenden took control as soon as he could reach the field, but a thundershower complicated things for him by lifting the river too high for anyone to escape.[42]

Learning the strength of the enemy at Ox Ford, Burnside took it upon himself to disobey the letter of Grant's orders to the extent of retaining Willcox's division on the north side. Still unaware of Lee's wedge formation, he concluded the Confederates might be interceding a force between the halves of the Union army. At the same time, he put some men to work on a makeshift bridge at Quarle's Mill, for the evacuation of the first division.

Crittenden dug in alongside Crawford's division of the Fifth Corps, which had come downriver, but the Confederates missed a good opportunity to batter this stranded wing. Once Grant had formulated a more accurate image of the enemy's position, he approved both Burnside's initiative in withholding Willcox and his construction of the bridge.[43]

With the Ninth Corps sandwiched between different elements of the Army of the Potomac, and separate couriers delivering duplicate instructions to Burnside and Meade where one would suffice, Grant reassessed his cumbersome deference to Burnside's rank. He may also have come to realize, as Meade already did, that the bewhiskered Rhode Islander's humility was genuine, and that he might not bridle (as most generals would) at the thought of serving under a man who had earlier been a fledgling division commander under him. As Burnside bedded down that night, with his corps scattered to the four winds, he received a dispatch from Grant: hereafter, the Ninth Corps would compose part of the Army of the Potomac, and Burnside would report directly to General Meade. Burnside responded with a characteristic note expressing satisfaction at what he considered a sensible decision.[44]

Daniel Larned hardly saw it that way: he preferred working directly with Grant. As a man through whose hands Ninth Corps correspondence passed, he found Meade's communications condescending and occasionally downright spiteful. He thought it a bad omen the order for consolidation should come just as the corps was broken up and dispersed throughout the army; it seemed too much like the first step in a plan to dissolve the corps and eliminate Burnside.

General Burnside nevertheless rose bright and cheerful the next morning, greeting Grant with the same attitude of heartfelt gratification when he rode by Ninth Corps headquarters. The lieutenant general was pleased and—given the intense jealousy of most officers for their rank—perhaps a bit surprised.[45]

An instance of such jealousy flared the following day. Isolated from everyone but Warren's Fifth Corps, Crittenden received Meade's order to take his directions from that corps commander for the present emergency. Crittenden had been a major general commanding a division back when Warren had charge of a regiment. He nominally agreed to submit, but he wrote Burnside a terse note complaining of the situation, asking to be relieved. Burnside smoothed his hackles, and for a time the conflict subsided. Meade himself was several months junior to Crittenden, however, and the proud Kentuckian departed the corps in less than a fortnight.[46]

Meade, whose greatest admirers credit him with all the diplomatic finesse of a wolverine, began almost immediately to test Burnside's great patience. Only minutes after Grant assigned the Ninth Corps to his army, Meade detached two of Burnside's three remaining divisions to abutting corps, leaving the ranking general in the Army of the Potomac in command of nine regiments. That annoyed only Burnside's staff, for it all made sense to the general. But the next day Meade seemed to go out of his way to insult Burnside's intelligence, asking whether he had entrenched Willcox's division before Ox Ford—which he naturally had, after two anxious days there.

Lee's position was too strong for Grant to carry, and while the two armies faced each other here, the Confederate railroad system strained itself to shuttle reinforcements to the Army of Northern Virginia. Grant soon learned of them. With no hope of defeating Lee where he sat, he determined to draw him from his impregnable works with another sashay around the Southern right flank.[47]

The Union army began its withdrawal May 26. Enemy skirmishers had to be kept at a distance, as discovery of the movement could have led to disaster: in his arrowhead formation Lee might easily have held off one of Grant's divided wings with a fraction of his troops, simultaneously driving the other wing into the river with the bulk of his army. Thus, when Confederates came snooping near Potter's division on Hancock's front, Potter launched an attack that pushed them out of sight of Hancock's works. He lost about four dozen men in the process, including another good colonel—Henry Pearson, of the 6th New Hampshire. That made five regimental commanders Simon Griffin's brigade had lost in three weeks, all of them experienced officers.[48]

Everyone passed safely back to the left bank that night, the Ninth Corps concentrating at Mount Carmel Church, several miles north of the river. Just after dawn the next morning, Meade and his staff reined up at Burnside's headquarters. Meade began at once to tear into Burnside for allegedly blocking Warren's line of march south of the river, and for failing to provide brigades to guard the fords. On such occasions,

Meade's delivery usually deteriorated into the most offensive profanity.
A staff officer told of the time he damned his army commander, Joe
Hooker, up and down; another watched as he cursed himself into a
frenzy at a private he caught stealing corn, coming to his senses only
after he had staggered the soldier with a blow to the head. Meade obviously knew better than to raise his hand to Burnside, but his invective
soared to its usual crescendo.

Burnside was ready for him, though: he had just received a dispatch
on the same subject, in which Meade had accused him of making a report "inconsistent with the fact," and if anything could put an edge on
Ambrose Burnside's temper it was an insinuation he had not told the
truth. He sailed right back into Meade with evidence that no Ninth
Corps troops were south of the river, that the desired brigades were
guarding the fords at that very moment, and that Warren's information was, itself, incorrect. Their respective staffs glared at each other,
but even one of Meade's aides saw the logic in Burnside's explanation,
and Meade dropped the matter, though he uttered nothing resembling
an apology. This made an inauspicious beginning for their new association.[49]

II

The North and South Anna rivers come together above Hanover Court
House to become the Pamunkey, which had served McClellan as a
supply line in the early days of the war. Now, two years later, Grant
resorted to the same artery, building his supply depot on the ruins of
McClellan's, at White House Landing.

The Ninth Corps followed the rest of the army the evening of May 27,
and its three white divisions marched for most of the next two days
and nights. They splashed over the Pamunkey during the night of
the twenty-eighth, coming to rest near Hanovertown. Meade ordered
Burnside to anchor his left on Haw's Shop, a couple of miles southwest
of Hanovertown. The extreme right of Hancock's corps lay half a mile
to the rear of Haw's Shop, leaving an inviting hiatus for some adven-
turesome Confederate division. Burnside surveyed the landscape, then
sent an officer to Meade's headquarters to ask whether he ought not
connect with Hancock by falling back. Meade responded with orders

for Hancock to move up, perhaps to spare the jaded foot soldiers of the Ninth Corps, who had been forty-eight hours on the road. Burnside found the position of the Second Corps far stronger than the ground near Haw's Shop, and pressed the point as carefully and respectfully as he could, but Meade told him rather peremptorily to stay where he was while Hancock moved up. This tart reply may have brought on a brief and uncommon spell of irritability recorded by Burnside's amanuensis: the general returned to his tent and remained in it, very quiet, while his staff visited a nearby house and its family of proud but ragged Confederate women.[1]

The corps crossed Totopotomoy Creek May 30, amid spurts of skirmish fire, pushing ahead the next day over extremely rough ground. So thick and irregular was the terrain that the various corps could not keep properly aligned. Adjoining divisions could not see each other, and whenever one general moved his troops, he would often unwittingly abandon his neighbor's flank. Operating on a single road with a narrow front, Burnside received periodic notes from army headquarters advising him the flank of either the Second or the Fifth corps hung in the air: most of these messages took an accusative tone, blaming Burnside, so he would jockey his men about to oblige. In at least one instance, though, Meade ordered him to advance and connect with a Second Corps division already at his right hand; in another it was Warren who advanced his corps, without giving Burnside any notice of his intention. Warren, to whom Meade all but ordered Burnside to subordinate himself, also raised a tempest over two Ninth Corps brigades that did not relieve his men quickly enough to suit him. The complaint caused unnecessary problems between Burnside and headquarters and contributed greatly to General Crittenden's determination to leave this army—for the two brigades in question were his.[2]

By noon of June 1, the Army of the Potomac occupied a line running generally southeast from the Pamunkey and Totopotomoy Creek, with the Second Corps on the northern end, the Ninth Corps on its left, Warren's Fifth Corps left of that, and Wright's Sixth Corps on the extreme left of the army. That evening Meade directed Hancock to leapfrog the Second Corps all the way to Wright's left, to the vicinity of a crossroads known as Cold Harbor. Hancock began by pulling a division out of line on Burnside's right, opening a gap between Burnside and the balance of the Second Corps. Having too few men to fill the breach, Burnside refused his right—swung it back, like a gate, to protect his flank. He sent word of the change to Meade, since his new position isolated Hancock's remaining divisions. Meade's reply is a tribute to his antagonistic spirit. He received Burnside's dispatch not as the vital information that it was but as a complaint, or an excuse for some shortcoming, and though he could not deny Hancock had made a mistake by withdrawing from the middle of the line instead of from his exposed flank, neither did he refrain from the sarcastic but pointless observation that Burnside knew Hancock had begun the shift, implying he ought to have been prepared for even that injudicious maneuver. Meade may simply have misunderstood Burnside's concern, but while he may not have been looking for excuses to chastise his new subordinate, he seemed unwilling to do anything that might turn their relations toward a more positive course. Perhaps he felt threatened by the assignment of his former superior and viewed him as a potential competitor, to be kept in his place.[3]

The next day, June 2, Warren sidled down the line to the left, below Bethesda Church, and Meade told Burnside to bunch his divisions up behind Warren and follow. The Ninth Corps had not a single mounted cavalryman in its ranks to help screen the movement of the infantry, and when Crittenden started his rearguard division after the others, he pulled in his pickets, who might have served that purpose. Willcox noticed the omission, warned corps headquarters, and Burnside instantly told him to get some of his own men out there. Just as Willcox posted a Michigan regiment, the Confederates swept out of the woods at them, slamming broadside into Crittenden's division as it marched south. The Michigan men stood alone across a crucial crossroads while Crittenden swung his brigades into line to repel the attack. Potter's and most of the rest of Willcox's divisions were already out of range, behind the Fifth Corps, and Warren's sidelong movement had caused a rift between his corps and Crittenden's division. Warren's right flank thus invited assault, and Confederates spilled behind his northernmost brigade. More of them, led by Burnside's old roommate Henry Heth, also dashed beyond Burnside's right and tore up telegraph wires, carrying several hundred prisoners with them when they retreated. Both Burnside and Warren passed a few tense moments, until together they marshaled enough pressure to drive the enemy back at both points on the punctured line; when it was all over, the Ninth Corps stretched northeast from Bethesda Church, at a protective right angle to the rest of the army.

Warren blamed his misfortune on the "sudden giving way of the Ninth Corps," but he shared the responsibility with Crittenden, whose premature removal of his pickets may have sparked Lee's attack. This deadly cotillion called for Burnside to cast off behind the line and face his corner, to protect the flank: Warren began his movement—essentially an allemande left—with Crittenden still in mid-pirouette, sundering the set and allowing the enemy to break in.[4]

Crittenden's sloppy performance revealed his lack of enthusiasm for his command, but it also highlighted a flaw in Burnside's professional demeanor. Since his first days as a troop commander, he had demonstrated a preference for background management. Not unlike Robert E. Lee, he usually designed the strategy his division, corps, or army would follow, discussed it with his subordinates, then allowed them to command their own men with minimal interference once the shooting began. Such had been the key to his victories in North Carolina, but this policy required cooperative, confident lieutenants like Foster, Reno, and Parke. One doubtful supporter like William Franklin or James Longstreet could lose a battle under a system like that, and a single incompetent could court disaster. The best and the bravest in the Union army were dropping at an ever-accelerating pace, and the dross rose inexorably to the top: this ran precisely contrary to the progression in the industrial environment Burnside knew, and eight weeks later the lesson would have to be pounded home a little harder. Henceforth, the successful generals would be those who stared over the shoulders of the men just below them.

Grant had planned for a major assault for the morning of June 2, but the various corps—particularly Hancock's—could not come into line on time. Hancock did not arrive until more than an hour after the time of Grant's proposed attack, citing excessive darkness, heat, dust, bad roads, poor maps, a poorer guide, and exhausted troops—everything that had delayed Burnside in the Wilderness. Grant then postponed the attack until late afternoon, but the sortie against Warren and Burnside finally persuaded him to wait until the next morning. By then the Confederates had completed their trenches, and they were virtually invulnerable.[5]

At cockcrow of June 3, three corps surged ahead from the left of
Meade's line: the Second, Sixth, and the Eighteenth corps, this last
newly arrived from below Richmond. Southern firepower staggered
them, and the assault stalled in the open terrain in front of Lee's intimidating works, with enormous Union casualties for the brevity of
the attack. On the Ninth Corps front, Burnside sent Potter and Willcox into the first line of rifle pits, where they saw their men frightfully
shot up. Potter's reduced division lost about eight hundred, including a
score of officers, while contesting those shallow pits with Confederates
in main-line works only yards away.

In order to support the principal attack, Burnside arranged a renewed assault for the early afternoon—perhaps remembering a diversion he had wanted his left-wing commander to make at Fredericksburg. As at Spotsylvania, Willcox devoted a great deal of time to the
positioning of his artillery and infantry, while Potter's exposed men
waited impatiently under raking fire in the rifle pits. Willcox did not
declare himself ready until two hours beyond the time Burnside had
appointed. Late as it was, and despite the uncertainty of success, Burnside still hoped to make the attack: he knew little of affairs on the left,
but supposed his assault would assist the other three beleaguered corps.
Warren proposed sending in some troops, too. Then came orders from
Meade to suspend everything: the three corps on the left had lost much
and gained nothing, and Grant saw no sense in continuing the operation. Willcox and Potter held what they had, their riflemen digging in
with tin cups and bayonets, though Jubal Early's corps kept up a furious
fire all the rest of the day. Burnside and his staff slept with their boots
and spurs on that night, anticipating an attack in the dark, but by dawn
of June 4 Early had pulled back, leaving enough dead to convince Potter
he had gotten the best of the brawl. The rest of the army could not say
the same: Grant lost more men at Cold Harbor than Burnside had at
Fredericksburg, most of them before works as strong as the infamous
stone wall.[6]

Burnside endured more trying hours between Saturday, the day after
the grand assault, and Sunday morning. Shortly after breakfast, Warren apprised him that Meade had ordered the Fifth Corps to shift to the
left again, and he asked Burnside to move similarly, to avoid another
debacle like that of June 2. In the course of their discussion, they agreed
that everyone would benefit if the Ninth Corps simply evacuated its un-

opposed lines and skipped around Warren to replace the Second Corps division he was supposed to relieve: not only would that obviate the dangerous accordioning of the battle line, it would save Fifth Corps troops the unnecessary disruption of their rest. Burnside and his staff rode to find Meade, to ask (among other things) if he approved of the idea. They found him eating lunch at the headquarters of the Eighteenth Corps.

This corps consisted of troops drawn from the coast of North Carolina, many of them men Burnside had left behind with Foster in 1862. It chanced that the new commander of that corps was Baldy Smith, whose dismissal Burnside had demanded in Order Number 8. Dining with Smith and Meade, as luck would have it, was Bully Brooks, another object of the same unexecuted order. Brooks served as a division commander under Smith, as he had at Fredericksburg, and while Burnside had forgiven them their lack of support in that battle, they had not forgiven him his indictment of them. As Burnside consulted with Meade, Smith and Brooks glowered, liptight.[7]

Meade concurred with Burnside's plan, so by four o'clock Potter and Willcox marched to relieve David Birney's Second Corps division. Meade, unfortunately, had not advised his own chief of staff of the changed itinerary, so Burnside's supply train, which had been directed to his former position under the old orders, arrived too late for his men to draw rations. His infantry had already started, but rather than send all the supplies back, he transferred what he could into his own corps wagons. That left him short of vehicles, and he had to turn his wounded over to the care of Sheridan's cavalry.

At last, in the evening, Burnside had to confer with Smith about the specific entrenchments each would occupy. Smith showed him where to put his divisions, but as Burnside led them in he noticed that Smith had designated positions held by one of his own divisions, as well as Birney's. So reduced was the Ninth Corps that Burnside required both Potter and Willcox just to fill Birney's works, while Crittenden would have to spread himself alarmingly thin to man the trenches Smith had uncovered. Later Burnside confronted Smith about abandoning his portion of the line, but that overstuffed general replied he "did not . . . think it necessary for those troops to wait to be relieved by others when I ordered them away." Burnside, perhaps puzzled that a general would consider it prudent to leave such a void in the defensive line, reminded Smith that the battered Ninth Corps was too small for the

length of trenches dumped in its lap; Smith responded with a perfectly
nasty note suggesting Burnside had reneged on a promise, advising
him to take it up with the army's chief engineer. The chief engineer,
once again, was the same James C. Duane—now a major—who, like
many others on Meade's staff, held Burnside in contempt. Smith felt
quite safe depending upon Duane for arbitration.[8]

Warren had been acting rather proprietary over Crittenden, and he,
rather than Burnside, ordered the first division down to fill Smith's vacuum. Crittenden could not safely occupy the trenches until the next
morning, and Burnside had a sleepless night easing his other two divisions into the dark and dangerous works. The enemy lay close enough
to hear all their clatter, and sudden activity frequently invited an artillery exchange. During this long, apprehensive night Burnside let it slip
that he had become "perfectly disgusted" with the treatment accorded
him and his corps in this army. That was a noteworthy admission for so
patient and obedient a soldier, but it came nowhere near describing the
indignation of his staff, who felt too many in the army imposed on their
chief's good nature.[9]

Burnside returned from a midnight visit to Meade to find his staff
hunkered around a cracker box, on which sat their telegraph key, under
an intermittent staccato of artillery and small arms. He offered the
operator a half-candle borrowed from headquarters to transcribe his
messages, but the night was rainy and unseasonably cold, and before
long the candle sputtered out, leaving them to translate Morse code by
memory, in total darkness. A little later, some inattentive pioneer up
the line felled a tree across the loosely run wire, jerking the transmitter
key off the box and over the trench. The noise of a night attack almost
simultaneously echoed from an indistinguishable direction, and the officers all went groping out on the vulnerable side of the works, clawing
the soggy red soil for the telegraph apparatus. Finally, Burnside sent
all but a few necessary officers back to the corps trains, while he and
the unlucky few shared the danger of field headquarters. The chilling
rain defied those who were inclined to sleep, and anyone who did nap
was roused by a startling reveille: just before dawn a sudden flurry of
shells snapped the headquarters flagpole and ventilated a nearby tent.
Later in the morning another barrage so threatened his little group that
Burnside chose a more protected position. Safety was but a relative

quality at the front; the staff had barely occupied the new headquarters when a bullet came zipping through the tent wall and drilled a water pail beside one of Burnside's aides.[10]

Despite the occasional shell or the perforation of camp equipage, the battle line remained fairly stable for the next few days, and the headquarters household found time to relax a bit and recognize just how bloody and arduous the campaign had been. Burnside reflected on the horrors of the past five weeks but finally confided to his secretary that, for all he had endured since the Wilderness, it had not been as hard on him as that first independent operation at Hatteras Inlet, where every day had threatened the complete destruction of his little armada.

During this breathing spell, Burnside also had the leisure to read some New York newspapers, wherein he discovered some accounts particularly disparaging to the Ninth Corps. William Swinton, of the *Times*, was responsible for at least one of them. Swinton had earlier fueled Burnside's wrath by insinuating the general took responsibility for the battle of Fredericksburg because the War Department had asked him to. The reporter traveled now with Grant's staff, in return for which privilege he had promised to refrain from corresponding with his newspaper: he had broken his word, and presently he violated the dictates of common sense as well, by wandering into Burnside's camp. The general promptly arrested him and threatened to have him shot as a spy the next day. Burnside's gesture was obviously all bluff, designed to frighten the columnist, but it probably saw a measure of success before Grant rescued his perfidious guest. Even Grant was not amused with the reporter, for his articles were frequently read behind Confederate lines, but with seeming mercy he reduced Swinton's "sentence" to banishment from the army. The newspaperman took his revenge on Burnside two years later, in his history of the Army of the Potomac.[11]

The welcome respite from pitched battles encouraged Mathew Brady to come out to Cold Harbor with his camera equipment. The Ninth Corps staff lined up twenty strong behind the general, who conjured up something resembling a smile. When that sitting was over, Brady conspired with his assistant to take a candid shot of himself with Colonels Richmond and Goodrich, the three of them gathered around Burnside as he perched on a comfortable grain sack with a newspaper.[12]

Brady's pictures record a deceptive impression of inactivity. Headquarters hangers-on had been scurrying for two days to pack their belongings, while the secretaries sent private correspondence back to Washington. Into the baggage wagons, once again, went the fresh clothing, the tents, the razors and strops—all that made life in the field bearable. The Army of the Potomac was going to move, quickly and stealthily, away from its maze of entrenchments; it was going to cross the James River. Despite the common expectation that the river posed an insurmountable barrier, despite political fears about returning to McClellan's rejected plan of 1862, the blue behemoth slunk away in the twilight toward the broad and beautiful water.

Burnside had met with his division commanders before the cameramen came, announcing some organizational changes. He reduced Colonel Marshall's formerly independent brigade by half, transferring the two dismounted cavalry regiments to Potter's and Willcox's depleted divisions. He attached the two heavy artillery regiments, under Marshall, to the first division, denominating it the third brigade. Army headquarters took the two regiments of Regulars from James Ledlie's brigade that morning, sending them to the Regular division of the Fifth Corps, but Meade made up the loss by the addition of a large new regiment from New York. All these changes left the Ninth Corps even more topheavy with inexperienced regimental organizations than before.

Equally significant was the departure of Thomas Crittenden, who had finally insisted upon being relieved. James Ledlie, who had so impetuously thrown his troops against Lee's works on the North Anna, rose to division command as the senior brigadier. Burnside had not witnessed the North Anna attack; he seems to have credited Ledlie with courage instead of rashness, and at least officially he held him in high regard. Nor was he alone in that judgment: one officer who would come to despise Ledlie wrote home from Cold Harbor, extolling the brigadier's capacity and courage.[13]

The Army of the Potomac began its movement that evening, when Burnside's three white divisions left camp in numerical order. His corps had the longest route, swinging in a wide arc some twenty miles back to Jones's Bridge, on the Chickahominy. The yawning column kept moving all night, then spent much of the daylight on June 13 waiting for the army's wagon train to untangle itself at Tunstall's Station, continuing afterward through the choking dust to Jones's Bridge. Night had come again when Burnside's troops bivouacked on the north bank of the Chickahominy, lulled to sleep—if any of these exhausted men needed lulling—by the steady drumming of Wright's Sixth Corps on pontoons, audible from three-quarters of a mile away.[14]

Early the next morning the Ninth Corps itself rumbled over that bridge and struck for the James. By noon the lead brigades rested within three miles of the big river, and Burnside led his staff into the yard of a substantial plantation. The owner, a judge descended from an old Virginia family, occupied a prison cell at Fort Monroe, but his wife greeted Burnside gracefully, apologizing for not having prepared herself for visitors. A Miss Tyler stayed in the house with her—a niece of President Tyler who had recently fled her own home when Colored Troops ransacked it. She asked Burnside if he would not make his headquarters over there, and he dispatched several of his staff through the intervening windbreak of oaks to investigate the possibility.

The house was a mess. Furniture had been destroyed where convenient, and overturned where not; mattresses lay slashed and gutted; the extensive library had been scattered, books and manuscripts ripped to shreds. Using the home as a command post would at least prevent further depredations, and at first Burnside agreed to stay there until his corps should move away. According to his corps engineer, Major James St. Clair Morton, Meade wanted Burnside to cross the James at Wilson's Wharf, and the Tyler home sat convenient to that place. Meade had also told Morton that Burnside would not be able to cross before June 16, but either Meade or Grant had changed his mind, preventing Burnside from acceding to Miss Tyler's request. Now Grant wanted the Ninth Corps to cross several miles upriver, at Wilcox's Landing, opposite Windmill Point. Burnside left a guard at the Tyler house, proceeding to Wilcox's Landing at the head of his column.[15]

By daylight of June 15, Hancock's corps had alit on the south side of the James, and engineers worked feverishly on an immense pontoon bridge shored up by steamboats. Grant's grand design included moving Smith's Eighteenth Corps against Petersburg, Richmond's sister city, from City Point—where, like the Second Corps, it had been transported by ship. Hancock, Burnside, and the rest of the Army of the Potomac would meanwhile come up from Windmill Point. Petersburg was lightly defended, and Smith could have taken it himself when he arrived there, about 1:30 the afternoon of the fifteenth. Instead, he frittered away the rest of the day reconnoitering the virtually empty Confederate works around the city.

Hancock waited until midmorning that day for sixty thousand rations supposedly coming downriver from Ben Butler's supply depot at Bermuda Hundred; Grant had personally arranged the transfer of the food, but it never reached Hancock. The Second Corps thus started late and hungry, and Hancock soon found that his map was worse than useless. Only by commandeering some slaves for guides could he find his way. The roads ran powder-dry, with hardly a well or waterhole along the way. The men suffered terribly from thirst, and when their stomachs told them to fall out to cook their evening meal, their officers hurried them on in response to an appeal from Smith. The day had grown dim before Hancock's first regiments arrived behind the Eighteenth Corps, which had finally occupied an encouraging section of the Petersburg works. Smith relieved his men with Hancock's, and everyone rested.[16]

Burnside passed that same afternoon feeding his men from the supply wagons, but about six o'clock Meade ordered him to put his command over the bridge and follow Hancock. Willcox's and Potter's divisions started immediately, and Ledlie's brought up the rear. Into the hot breath of the Virginia night they strode, into the barely subsided dust of Hancock's wake. It was a killing march they made: men who had never before fallen out dropped by the roadside, unable to bear the heat, the pace, or the dust. Not until morning could they stop to cook anything, one veteran regiment whittled down to a pair of color bearers and three riflemen. A little coffee, perhaps some salt pork and hardtack, and off they lurched again for the front.

The head of the Ninth Corps reached Hancock about ten o'clock that morning, having covered more than twenty-two miles in the past fifteen hours. Burnside conferred with Grant's staff engineer, who decided the Ninth Corps ought to go in on Hancock's left, facing Harrison's Creek. By one o'clock the corps stood in line, ready to go. It had been more than thirty hours since most of these men had slept.[17]

With the help of the Greek choruses at the various headquarters, Grant had apparently interpreted the events of the previous six weeks as proof that Burnside could not be trusted to throw his weight into a mission. Neither did he seem overly impressed with Smith anymore, for he issued special orders for Hancock, the junior of the three, to assume command of the troops before Petersburg. He may have been wise to do so, misguided prejudgments aside, for even if Burnside's combative nature had driven him to assault the deceptively imposing works, his attack might have been rendered a failure by the jaundice and skepticism of Smith, Hancock, Brooks, and the rest.

Hancock decided, after much reconnaissance, on an evening attack in the center, his own Second Corps charging for the heights topped by a house owned by one Mr. Hare. Smith would support him with two brigades on the right, and Burnside with two on the left. Griffin's and Hartranft's brigades, Burnside's best, accordingly formed ranks. By late afternoon Meade arrived and took charge. He approved Hancock's plan, and at six o'clock he sent some twenty-five thousand blue uniforms rolling toward Petersburg. On the Confederate side, even with the recent reinforcement of two divisions, General Pierre Beauregard had no more than ten thousand men to oppose them. The Confederate defenders fell back a bit, fighting savagely to establish a new line, trying after dark even to recapture their lost ground. In the end they settled into fresh works a little nearer Petersburg, hoping only for the arrival of the Army of Northern Virginia.[18]

Still, neither Burnside nor his men found rest. In preparation for another assault the next morning, Potter's division crept Indian fashion into a ravine, only rods from the enemy picket line on the ridge near the Shand house. The troops packed away their cups and canteens and uncapped their rifles, to prevent accidental noises that might alert the men at the top of the ravine. Thirteen regiments crawled into that brushy defile, Griffin's brigade in front, and Ledlie's division stood in reserve behind them.[19]

It was still dark when Potter sent his men over the top. They cleared the ridge in a few spectacular minutes, taking four guns, six hundred prisoners, and five flags—including one belonging to the 44th Georgia, which had had an adjutant named Addison Burnside, now more than a year dead on the field of Chancellorsville. One Confederate general grudgingly admitted it was "a very neat and well managed affair." It made a fine beginning for Bunker Hill Day.[20]

Bushrod Johnson's Confederate division took to its heels in near panic, but the successful assault broke down Potter's organization. Heavy fire began to buffet his line—dropping his own horse from under him—and Potter signaled his men to dig in beyond the captured works.

Now would have been an opportune time for Ledlie to dash over Potter and smash the desperate enemy, but Ledlie had disappeared. His men, he later explained, were caught up in the fallen timber of that still-dark ravine.

After daylight, Burnside had Willcox prepare for another attack to the left of Potter's new line. As usual, Willcox wanted to arrange artillery support, and though the Confederates had already enjoyed considerable leisure to bolster their works, he wasted more time questioning the exact point Burnside wanted him to attack. Burnside's engineer, Major Morton, had to walk out on the field with a compass and demonstrate to Hartranft the direction he was supposed to take. Morton finally led the attacking column himself, to assure it did not veer astray; he died at the head of it, but for all his valiant efforts the assault went wrong. The leading brigade met the indistinct objective at an oblique angle, its left flank dangerously exposed to raking fire, and the regiments disintegrated. Nearly half of Hartranft's command melted away in a few minutes, some of his refugees fleeing through the lines of the Second Corps. Willcox complained the artillery did nothing to help him, intimating that Samuel Benjamin's successor did not quite fill the missing lieutenant's shoes.[21]

Perhaps to redeem himself for his morning failure, General Ledlie asked Burnside to try his division in a similar attack. Ledlie's subordinates, getting wind of this transaction through the staff grapevine, did not appreciate the offer: as Lieutenant Colonel George P. Hawkes led his 21st Massachusetts into the works from which Willcox had sprung, he sensed an unusual apprehension among his men. He was pretty nervous himself, having witnessed Willcox's brutal repulse.[22]

Ledlie's division was already rather thinned out. Colonel Marshall had been wounded earlier in the day, and now only one brigade could field even a full colonel. Ledlie reported thirty-two casualties before his men even moved out. When it advanced, the first division suffered as badly from those batteries on the flank as had the third, but, charging full-tilt across that canister-swept plain, the first and second brigades reached the opposing rifle pits within minutes, flailing promiscuously with the bayonet and rifle stock. To their surprise, the assailants found themselves in possession of the first line, but the Confederates maintained a vigorous fire from stronger works, and Southern cannon still rained iron on them without much interference from Union batteries.

Presently the senior officer sent back for help, and Ledlie promised it soon, but all the help he had was Marshall's brigade—those two big, new, heavy artillery regiments. At the moment, they suffered nearly as great a fire as the two brigades actually engaged; to Burnside's disgust, no one could make them move forward.[23]

Ledlie did not function very well this afternoon, either. The commander of one of his regiments heard Ledlie was drunk, and that his staff had hidden him away. This rumor is given substance by a first division staff officer, a lieutenant who croaked about being left in virtual command of the division—transmitting Burnside's orders and confirming they were carried out—while Ledlie vanished from headquarters for several hours. A field officer from one of the front-line brigades came looking for Ledlie and finally found him in a stupor, safely out of harm's way. These two brigades fought from late afternoon until about 10:00 P.M. without Ledlie's promised support, running out of ammunition before they finally withdrew under a concentrated counterattack. In something over five hours, they lost 838 men; fewer than 600 rallied together after the retreat.[24]

Everyone with the Ninth Corps had taken quite a beating. Willcox had tried to help Ledlie when Ledlie seemed unable to help himself, throwing in a brigade that took the colors of the 35th North Carolina (which had done so poorly against Burnside at Newbern). Willcox lost his brigade commander and one of his regimental colors before this attack, too, came pouring back. He wanted to send in his other brigade, but Burnside shook his head: the corps had taken enough punishment for one day.[25]

Most of the Union army lay down to sleep shortly after midnight, but the Confederates spent the night pulling back the better part of a mile, to a set of works prepared during the day's fighting. When groggy Union divisions stumbled forward at dawn on June 18, they fell against abandoned entrenchments. Orlando Willcox led the way this bright morning, supported on the left by Crawford's Fifth Corps division and on the right by a lagging division of the Second Corps, under Francis Barlow.

The Union soldiers quickened their pace, splashing across the various branches of Harrison's Creek, over the ridge beyond, across fields, and into a wood. Willcox's exuberant men entered the grove supposing the Confederates had evacuated, expecting to emerge on the other side to find the outskirts of Petersburg open to them, but when they left the cover of the little forest, they hitched up abruptly. The railroad cut of the Petersburg & Norfolk line gaped at them from across an open field, beyond that lay another brushy ravine, and a couple of hundred yards the other side of the ravine stood more of those devilish fieldworks, with Beauregard's men and a fresh division from Lee's army milling behind them. All the glow and giddiness went out of Willcox's troops, but they slid forward anyway. When Crawford caught up on his left and Potter had come up behind, Willcox sent Hartranft ahead to take the railroad cut. Crawford joined in the assault, and Yankees soon crouched behind the raw, steep slope of that antebellum engineering achievement.[26]

Barlow did not advance so far, and Beauregard's fortifications curled around Willcox's right here, so he endured a vicious crossfire. He tried to convince Crawford and Barlow to attack the enemy line in concert with him, because he felt compelled to get out of the cut, but though Crawford was willing enough, Barlow demurred.

That happened about noon. Willcox's men took what cover they could, bearing a gale of shell for another three hours while the high command pondered. Perhaps the successive hammerings before an intrenched enemy had forged a belated respect for earthworks in Grant and Meade, for it was not until 3:00 P.M. that Meade issued an astonishing order: whereas no one seemed able to cooperate with anyone else, each corps should attack whenever and however it damn well could. The attack was, literally, to go willy-nilly.[27]

Since Barlow still declined to help him, Willcox asked Potter to come up on his right. The troops in the cut gouged footholds in the soft clay, without which they could not breast it, and after another two hours of troop joggling, the line bolted forward once more. Willcox recorded "men falling at every step," as the two best divisions of the Ninth Corps descended the slope to Taylor's Creek and worked their way up the other side. A brigade that had lost its commander the previous evening lost two more now, and Colonel John Curtin fell wounded in Potter's division, leaving yet another brigade to a lieutenant colonel.

More of Lee's troops crowded onto the parapets behind the red fortifications, and Lee himself fought the field, so it was only at a tremendous cost of life that Willcox seized and held a position a hundred yards short of those blazing breastworks. Potter came as close as he could: no other Federal division approached so near the Confederate line as his, and nothing this side of hell could bring his men any closer. When darkness finally allowed them the opportunity, the vulnerable Yankees dug some works of their own. Willcox reported another 1,231 casualties for that day; at nightfall he had fewer than 1,000 men left in his division.[28]

Burnside again neared physical exhaustion. He had been on the field constantly for three days, with even less sleep than the harried infantrymen. This time, at least, he recognized the problem and left the direction of the corps to General Parke. One of Meade's staff officers found Burnside that afternoon, reclining against a tree at Fifth Corps headquarters, leisurely damning the heavy artillerymen to General Warren's staff while Warren dozed on a cot.

"Worthless," Burnside judged them. "In the attack last night I couldn't find thirty of them." His customary generosity soon overcame his fury, however, and he reasoned, "They didn't enlist to fight, and it is unreasonable to expect it of them." His forgiving nature took in Meade, as well. For all the insults and innuendo of the army commander's correspondence, Meade had issued an order congratulating the Ninth Corps for its superhuman efforts of the last few days, prompting Burnside to remark, "He is irascible, but he is a magnanimous man."[29]

That evening began the siege of Petersburg. No more would the blue host batter against those formidable defenses. It had been a brutal three days; even Meade's aides were critical. Theodore Lyman felt "there has been too much assaulting this campaign!" Lyman recognized the fatal consequence of the army's aggressiveness: "The best officers and men are liable," he wrote, "by their greater gallantry, to be first disabled; and of those that are left, the best become demoralized by the failures, and the loss of good leaders; so that, very soon, the men will no longer charge entrenchments and will only go forward when driven by their officers." Sometimes they would not go forward then—Hancock's highly touted corps had balked in the final attack on Petersburg.[30] It may have been no coincidence that the corps to advance the farthest was the one that did not feel itself a part of this army, the one that had something to prove about itself and its beloved commander.

The extra effort had been very costly to the corps. In four days of fighting, the Army of the Potomac had lost nearly ten thousand men. Except for the Second Corps, which was particularly decimated June 18—and which counted 83 regiments to Burnside's 39—the Ninth Corps had borne the most losses, even though it was the smallest corps

operating before Petersburg during those battles. Five brigade commanders had been wounded out of action, including three more with
valuable experience. Only two of seven brigades still fought under the
same men who had led them across the Rapidan. The irreplaceable engineer, Major Morton, lay among the dead. Numerous other competent
staff officers had fallen at both brigade and division level. Willcox alone
had just lost three field officers commanding regiments, and after the
initial battle for Petersburg, it was more common than not to find Ninth
Corps regiments led by captains, many of them mere boys. Even most
of the colonels who suddenly vaulted to brigade command were only a
few months removed from civil life.[31] The zenith of the Ninth Corps had
passed.

III

The sun had hardly risen on Sunday, June 19, when Robert Potter, son
of the Episcopal bishop of Pennsylvania, began planning a means of
driving the enemy from the most recent fortification in his front. Potter's division held the fresh trenches west of Taylor's Creek, where he
and Willcox had dug in like badgers the previous evening. Warren's
Fifth Corps lay to the left, the Second Corps immediately to the right.

In the red glow of dawn Potter detected a protrusion in the Confederate line, a redoubt shielding a battery. The little fort loomed less than
a hundred yards away, and the general thought it might be possible to
tunnel under it and blow it up. He scribbled a note to that effect and
sent it to Burnside.[1]

Five days later—days during which Confederate sharpshooters
picked off three dozen men per diem in the Ninth Corps alone—Potter
composed a more formal proposal for a gallery under that battery. His
48th Pennsylvania consisted largely of Schuylkill County coal miners,
and its commander was himself a mining engineer. The Pennsylvanians
had discussed such a project for days, independently of Potter's observation, and with a little help from general headquarters they guessed
they could reach the objective in two or three weeks.

Burnside called for Potter's miner that evening. Lieutenant Colonel
Henry Pleasants, a self-assured widower of thirty-one, dazzled Burnside with an ingenious proposal, offering simple solutions to every engi-

neering obstacle Burnside could pose. At noon the next day, a hundred or so Pennsylvanians gathered in the gulley behind Potter's picket line and began tunneling toward history.[2]

One thing Pleasants had not calculated was the amount of dirt his men would carry out of the mine. So fresh and dark was it that he feared Confederates might take notice of it from some treetop or signal tower, so he provided his men with cracker boxes in which to haul the refuse to scattered points ever-farther behind Potter's main line, where others from the 48th cut brush and trees to cover it. The precaution consumed much labor, but the location of the mine remained undetected, despite Confederate countermines and the treachery of Union deserters.

By June 28, after three full days of digging, the miners had burrowed 130 feet into the earth—about a quarter the distance to the center of the fort. Potter optimistically expected they would continue to progress 40 feet a day, but the farther stooping soldiers had to carry those cumbersome cracker boxes, the less they could tunnel. Pleasants could have built some wheelbarrows with a few small wheels and an armload of lumber, but he could appeal for no such luxuries from Meade's headquarters. In fact, Meade thought Pleasants was a crackpot. He and his chief engineer, Major Duane, flatly doubted such a long mine could be dug, and they told Burnside so. Of the forty basic mining tools Duane had listed in a manual he wrote for engineer troops, he provided not a one to Pleasants, nor any material.[3]

About this time there developed a revealing misunderstanding among some of Meade's staff. His provost marshal, Marsena Patrick, took it into his head that Meade had approved the mining operation and put it under the direction of Colonel Henry Burton, who had charge of the siege train. Whether anyone else succumbed to that misapprehension is not clear, but when Baldy Smith asked Grant to transfer Burton to the Eighteenth Corps, Patrick immediately assumed Smith's main game was to disrupt Burnside's project. Perhaps Smith knew nothing of the mine then, or of the mistaken role attributed to Burton, but it came naturally for one high-ranking officer to rate Smith's spitefulness toward Burnside higher than his devotion to the war effort.[4]

Pleasants had to scavenge the Ninth Corps camps for lumber to shore up his gallery, and when he had picked them clean he asked Burnside for passes to send a couple of companies into unoccupied territory, where he confiscated a lumber mill and turned out some green timbers to cart back to Petersburg. At one point the ribs of his tunnel sank into a soft vein of marl, and Pleasants raised his trajectory sharply to avoid it, leveling off again when the shaft ran into drier clay and sand. Both the digging and the timbering went more easily thereafter; with the end in sight, Pleasants ordered six tons of powder and a thousand yards of safety fuse from Meade's chief of artillery.[5]

Up on the earth's surface, trouble brewed. At Grant's request, Meade asked for Burnside's opinion about the feasibility of an attack on the enemy in his front. Cautiously, Burnside explained that his sector was probably the best spot to make an assault, but he thought it would be better to await completion of the mine. If Grant insisted on an immediate offensive, though, Burnside felt it had no better chance of success than before his works, especially "if it is left to me to say when and how the two other corps shall come in to my support." That curious qualification may have been Burnside's way of adverting to the last attack at Antietam, when success hung on McClellan's failure to send promised reinforcements: it was an understandable concern, but he might have chosen more diplomatic language. His apprehensions about Burnside's ambition reinforced, Meade shot back with a gruff reminder that he, not Ambrose Burnside, now commanded the army. Burnside instantly apologized for the unintended affront, explaining himself so humbly the army commander thanked him for his apology and promised to do all in his power to promote "harmony and good feeling" among his corps commanders and himself.[6] The good-hearted Burnside may have fallen for the rhetoric, but those who knew Meade best would have chuckled at the very thought.

The mine neared completion by the middle of July. Pleasants wanted to double-check his progress, so as not to overshoot the fort, but when he approached Meade's engineers for the loan of their theodolite, they suddenly could not spare it. Refusal of the instrument came some time after the mine passed the maximum length Duane had said it could reach without collapsing or smothering the men, by which time the availability of the theodolite may have become a function of Duane's pique. Burnside had to send to Washington for an older model of the same device, with which Pleasants crawled out on the picket line and braved enemy sharpshooters fifty paces away to draw an accurate reading.

While the mine neared the point where Pleasants wanted the main gallery to fork right and left into chambers for the powder magazines,

Burnside planned an assault to follow the detonation and chose the troops to lead it. It was not a difficult decision, for his three white divisions had been decimated in the fighting of May and June. The fourth division, Ferrero's black troops, consisted of nine large, fully officered regiments. These men had seen little action since they were reattached to the corps, but neither had they ever been asked to charge impossible fortifications, and Burnside felt they would be least inclined to waver. The white men, he feared, would advance only as far as they felt safe before digging in. Ferrero's division it would be.[7]

Ferrero had an objection, however. It seemed his division had been used as laborers by every corps to which Grant had loaned it in the past weeks; General Warren in particular had overworked them day and night to build better breastworks for white troops. Ferrero implied he would have no time to train his men if they had to slave for other corps, and Burnside turned his inspector general loose on the case. A few days later, Burnside assured Ferrero that the duties of his division would hereafter be left up to him.[8]

The black troops began sprucing up for the big show and practicing the complicated footwork necessary to carry out Burnside's plan. Like more than half the regiments in Burnside's corps now, the Negro battalions were all new—most were mustered in that spring—and their training had languished while they dug trenches and guarded wagons. For Burnside's purposes, they would at least have to master a right or left wheel in double column, which was difficult enough for veteran troops. The nine black regiments (including two that joined after the corps left Annapolis) had nearly two weeks in which to prepare. By the time Pleasants had finished the mine and filled it with powder, they knew their parts well. They needed only to be unleashed, as soon as the dust settled.[9]

Meade decided—perhaps through Duane's suggestion—that Pleasants had called for too much powder. The ordnance department therefore delivered a disappointed Colonel Pleasants four tons of explosives where he expected six, but that irked him much less than the fuse. The thousand yards of safety fuse he requisitioned came to hand in the form of common blasting fuse, cut into short lengths, so he had to splice it every few feet. This particular gaffe had nothing to do with availability, for Henry Hunt's own inspector of artillery ordered the fuse directly from New York, where it was manufactured. To compensate for the uncertainty of so many splices, Pleasants laid three lines of fuse in a trough of open powder. At six o'clock on the evening of July 28 he reported the entire contraption set to explode.

While the sappers lugged some eight thousand sandbags into the mine to tamp the magazines, more difficulty arose between Meade and Burnside. Meade had asked for Burnside's plan of attack, which consisted of advancing Ferrero's division as soon as the mine exploded, each brigade shaving off one regiment to sweep the Confederate trenches perpendicularly while the rest fanned out and seized the gravestone-studded hill behind Blandford Church and the Jerusalem Plank Road. Two days after Burnside submitted the plan, he visited army headquarters, where Meade flabbergasted him with a refusal to let the black troops make the assault: they were too inexperienced, and he did not trust them. Burnside argued, to no avail. Meade stood resolute, adding he would allow no fancy maneuvers in front of the enemy; the attacking column would drive straight for Cemetery Hill, without detaching flank guards.[10]

Burnside fought for the use of the Colored Troops as earnestly as he dared. At last Meade relented somewhat and agreed to put the question before Grant, promising to present the lieutenant general with both sides of the debate. Burnside apparently believed him and did not insist upon arguing his own case, but Meade's objectivity fell short of complete, and when he raised the subject at general headquarters he gave Burnside's argument a faint show. He never even revealed Burnside's plan to Grant, representing his own orders for the implementation of that plan as the original design; nor could he forbear adding the weight of political expediency to the discourse when his own objections seemed to fail, reminding Grant of the backlash which might follow any disaster that befell the black division.

Burnside's interview with Meade took place on Thursday, and the attack was set for Saturday, before dawn. When Burnside heard nothing from Meade by Friday morning, he suspected Grant had authorized his original plan. He was so confident, he packed all his baggage for the journey into Petersburg. Toward noon, as he sat in his tent discussing the attack with Potter and Willcox, Burnside looked up to see Meade stoop inside the flap, at the head of a retinue of staff officers and corps commanders. Meade was abluster with the news that Grant had sustained him: white troops must lead the charge for Cemetery Hill.[11]

Burnside was more devastated this time than before. He fairly begged Meade to reconsider, but he might have saved his breath. Finally he acknowledged the order, bowed his head, and promised to do his best. When the crowd of officers left his tent, Burnside sent for Ledlie. That general came along presently, and they all began to present their opinions about who should lead. Potter's and Willcox's divisions were closest to the mined fort, and theirs had been the more effective units during the spring campaign. Ledlie's men were the freshest, though; since June 17 they had been farther away from those deadly sharp-shooters than the other divisions, and perhaps they were less jumpy. The four generals wrangled over the issue for several hours, returning repeatedly to the conclusion that Ferrero's men should make the assault. Robert Potter seems to have expected his dependable division to win the honor by default, emaciated as it was, but he did not demand the advanced position. Finally, only twelve hours before the mine was to be blown, Burnside reached the same pinnacle of frustration that led Meade to issue his preposterous attack-at-will order of June 18: he threw three scraps of paper into a hat—probably his own, with that deep crown—and told the other three to turn their faces away and draw. Ledlie fished out the odd lot.[12]

Despite the initial skepticism about the mine at army headquarters, great preparations ultimately attended its explosion. Grant sent Hancock's Second Corps and several thousand cavalry on a foray north of the James, to draw Lee's forces away; then the Second Corps raced back to the trenches on Burnside's right, while the cavalry galloped around to the extreme left, to threaten Petersburg from the southwest. Warren stripped his trenches and massed most of his troops on Burnside's left, ready to go to his support. Edward Ord (who had replaced Baldy Smith), brought the Eighteenth Corps over from Bermuda Hundred to back up Burnside, and even a division of the new Tenth Corps marched from the Army of the James to join Ord behind the works of the Ninth Corps.[13]

Apparently to counter the lack of good brigade commanders, Burnside had recently consolidated Ledlie's ten regiments into two brigades. At one o'clock on the morning of July 30, Ledlie filed those brigades into the covered way that zigzagged toward the trenches in front of the enemy fort. They were a dejected lot. Until a couple of hours before, these soldiers had expected Ferrero's black regiments to lead the charge: they themselves entertained only the vaguest notion of what was expected of them, and they had little confidence in James Ledlie. For that matter, so did James Ledlie. These past few weeks he had worked hard to have his resignation accepted, perhaps as much to evade further combat as to avoid the humiliation of watching his commission go unconfirmed by Congress a second time, and on this eve of his last battle he again relied upon a heavy draught of artificial courage.[14] In a few hours this bilious brigadier would come to epitomize the weakness in Ambrose Burnside's laissez-faire style of management: a little meddling on Burnside's part would have been most welcome just now.

Meade's formalized orders called for Burnside to ready his parapets for the passage of his troops and to render his infantry obstructions passable. In front of Ledlie's division, fatigue details piled up sandbags to form a couple of stairways, and in other locations they leveled the parapet somewhat, but Burnside did not insist his division commanders remove their own defensive impediments. So close were the lines here that the only works of that nature were abatis—hardwoods dropped in place, their tangled tops facing the enemy line. Rifle and artillery fire over the past six weeks had splintered those trees, so a line of men would have little difficulty passing through them. Anyone who ventured out to chop up what remained of them would take his life in his hands, even at night, but Burnside seemed even more concerned about the signal those echoing axes might have given the Confederates on that portion of the battle front. Thus, the abatis remained. Each division, however, would follow a regiment of acting engineers armed with axes and spades, whose duty it would be to clear away any obstacles and throw up new trenches wherever they were needed.[15]

One other obstruction Burnside allowed to remain was a tall stand of pine, which obscured the view of the only Union battery that bore on a shallow depression south of the mined redoubt. The army artillery chief, Henry Hunt, reminded Burnside of that copse the afternoon of July 28, but Burnside feared this, too, would alert the enemy, and the pines still stood as the sliver of waning moon rose July 29.[16]

General Potter moved his division to Ledlie's right via another covered way; he put Griffin's brigade in front. Consistent with his usual poor judgment, Ledlie placed his second brigade at the head of his column, under the recently recovered Colonel Marshall. Marshall's command was composed of one battered battalion from Maryland, an incomplete New York regiment with a single day of combat to its credit, and those two thoroughly demoralized regiments of heavy artillerymen. Even their comrades in the first division noticed the artillerymen's aversion to this sort of work: in an appraisal eerily similar to Burnside's private comment about the "heavies," one regimental historian remarked simply, "They had not enlisted for it." [17]

The night air hung hot and dense. Across the way, in the four-gun fort, a regiment of South Carolinians got what sleep they could in the muggy summer darkness. General Stephen Elliott commanded the line here; in one of those little ironies of war, Elliott's father was, like General Potter's, an Episcopal bishop, though in his case the bishop of South Carolina. Elliott's men had heard rumors of Yankee mining, supposedly along a projecting portion of the trenches like theirs, but countermines had uncovered no such tunnel, and the sweating Southerners did not dream what awaited them.

Burnside moved his headquarters from the other side of Harrison's Creek to Fort Morton, a few hundred yards behind the front lines. Named after the late Major Morton, this fourteen-gun battery commanded a good view of the mined fort and the hill beyond. Like a hermit crab, General Meade occupied Burnside's empty headquarters at Harrison's Creek. Grant joined him there. From that position they could see nothing of the impending battle, but telegraph wire connected them with the other corps commanders. [18]

Most of the officers, from company level to the top, stayed awake all night, while the men catnapped as well as they could. Ledlie had reconnoitered the ground with his brigadiers, but they need not have bothered: so late did they learn their brigades would lead the assault that it was pitch dark by the time they had their little look—the new moon was only three days away. Besides, the three officers did not pass beyond the parapet. Even if the opposing works had not been so close, Ledlie's senior brigadier could not have clambered out there: General William Bartlett, in command barely a week, had just recovered from his fourth wound, the first of which had cost him a leg; his cork replacement did not adapt him for scurrying about on midnight expeditions. [19]

Colonel Pleasants won the honor of lighting the fuse. Headquarters scheduled the explosion for 3:30 A.M., so he fired the ends of the three wires at 3:15. Five minutes later Meade sent Burnside a suggestion to hold off a bit, since it was so dark, but it was already too late for that, and Burnside told him the mine would have to go off as expected. Still, 3:30 came and passed without the detonation. Though Pleasants had accurately estimated about fifteen minutes of burn time, he waited until after 4:00 to send someone in to examine the problem, to be absolutely certain the fuses had failed.

At 4:15 Meade dispatched a note inquiring about the delay. At that very moment, Pleasants sent a sergeant into the gallery, then a lieutenant. Since Burnside did not yet know the difficulty, he withheld his reply to Meade. Five minutes later came another query, and two aides from Meade's staff reined into Fort Morton to see what was wrong. Burnside still had no idea, despite having sent Major Van Buren down to the mouth of the mine. Soon a third dispatch came from Meade, immediately followed by a fourth, telling Burnside to attack anyway if the charge could not be exploded. Major Van Buren spared Burnside that gruesome prospect when he returned about then with news that the failed fuse had been revived; the two aides went back to Meade with word the charge was expected to go off at 4:45. In fact, it erupted one minute earlier.[20]

The explosion grumbled out of the earth in what seemed slow motion, causing the ground to tremble for several hundred yards in all directions before throwing the fort, its guns, and its garrison into the sky. With a surprisingly muffled roar, what would later have been called a mushroom cloud rose about a hundred feet high, taking with it the terrified debris that had been a regiment of infantry and a battery of artillery. Fully five minutes passed before chunks of wood, metal, men, and dirt stopped falling. Only then did the dust and the rotten sulphur smoke begin to settle around what soon came to be known as the Crater.

Almost immediately, 164 guns and mortars opened on the Confederate lines from previously established positions. The delay occasioned by the faulty fuse actually proved beneficial, in that it gave all these artillerymen some light by which to shoot. Now, at least, they could avoid shelling their own assaulting column.

Ledlie ordered his division over the top as soon as the clutter stopped falling, after which he retired to a bombproof. Some of his men had to be reformed, for they had scattered to the rear when the earth began raining on them; they soon rushed up the sandbagged staircases, though, yelling at the top of their lungs. Axmen quickly chopped the abatis away and leveled the chevaux-de-frise on the Confederate parapet; then the acting engineers in Ledlie's division poured into the exploded fort and began reversing the face of the enemy trenches.[21]

All of this took little time, contrary to the later findings of a court of inquiry. A captain in the Regulars guessed it was three to five minutes after the explosion before he heard Ledlie's men cheering; an officer in the Fifth Corps could make out their voices "a few minutes" after the blast. A colonel in Bartlett's brigade saw the first of Marshall's men moving to the attack within five minutes of the actual eruption, and another Regular on Ledlie's staff remembered years later that it took no more than ten minutes to reform the men of the first division and move them up.[22]

The enemy could reply but feebly to Ledlie's attack. The bulk of the Army of Northern Virginia remained north of the James, keeping watch over Hancock's now-empty trenches, and those Confederates left on this length of the line were all badly shaken by the catastrophe. Only a skeleton force of infantry lay right and left of the Crater, so Ledlie's men ran into nothing more than light resistance. Accustomed to seeking shelter from every shot, however, they drove straight into the gaping hole created by the explosion, and there they stayed. Some of Ledlie's engineer regiment began digging a covered way from the Crater back to their own works. Officers tried to form their regiments in the soft sand and clay, but the irregularities of the Crater and the steep, crumbling sides prevented most of them from presenting an effective battle line. Their men seemed more inclined to inspect the damage, and to help extricate surviving Confederates, than to fight. When Bartlett's mostly Massachusetts brigade crowded in behind Marshall's, the situation merely worsened. The headlong charge for the crest of Cemetery Hill petered out just beyond the western slope of the Crater.[23]

Here again surfaced the specter of James H. Ledlie. For more than a dozen decades, veterans and students of the Crater battle have blamed this bogging-down of the first division on such factors as the defensive conditioning of the Ninth Corps after six weeks on the front lines, or on the absence of a division commander in the Crater. Certainly these entered into it: Burnside admitted both these problems contributed to the ultimate catastrophe. The principal reason for the failure of Ledlie's division to capture Cemetery Hill, however, may be that Ledlie never told his brigade commanders they were expected to do so. Men who attended those brigade conferences the late afternoon of July 29 claimed to have heard no mention of moving beyond the captured works, and one recorded that General Bartlett specifically told his regimental commanders to stay there—that another division would dash beyond them to take the high ground. If that is true, Ledlie conveyed a bizarre interpretation of his instructions. Potter and Willcox, who were both present when Burnside explained the duties of each division, understood the corps commander's orders perfectly, so it is doubtful such a misconstruction was Burnside's fault.[24]

Perhaps Ledlie was already slightly drunk when he arrived—late—at corps headquarters: pungent breath warranted little notice in 1864, for drinking on duty was neither prohibited nor particularly frowned upon. The Ninth Corps chief himself was not averse to taking a glass for refreshment, and one colonel mentioned sharing a couple of pints of cider on ice with a shirt-sleeved Burnside one blazing July day, the two of them surrounded by the corps supply of crated alcohol. Ledlie was a special case, however—known for tipping a bottle to fortify his courage. In such an impaired condition he may not have properly digested his orders, or in the long interim between his departure from corps headquarters and his meeting with his brigadiers he may have primed himself too well to pass those orders along undistorted. No one ever asked Ledlie about it: he avoided a court of inquiry by means of a strategic furlough, and resigned before the Committee on the Conduct of the War could call him. The two brigade commanders who might have shed light on the matter spent the rest of the war in Southern prisons.[25]

Before long, some of Marshall's regiments began losing men to rifle fire from up and down the Confederate line, and they clung all the tighter to their sheltered positions. A few Confederate marksmen took them from the rear because of a shallow concavity of the line here; had Meade allowed Burnside to implement his original plan, that thin but irritating fire would have been checked by the regiments detailed to move perpendicularly down those hostile trenches.[26]

Not long after Ledlie's vanguard advanced—and probably ahead of the bulk of the first division—Simon Griffin led his brigade into the fracas on Ledlie's right. Smoke and dust still hung thick, causing confusion that was compounded when the commander of one of the front-line regiments fell dead. Griffin's battle line came up against the unexploded trenches north of the Crater, driving the still-stunned defenders back a bit. Instead of taking this opportunity to push for the crest, Ledlie's men began climbing up into the works Griffin had just taken, mingling with his men.

Potter and Griffin had previously discussed the possibility of resurrecting Burnside's plan for a flanking regiment to sweep the enemy trenches. Griffin sent one of his new Maine regiments up the line to do that, and the Mainers advanced into the area behind the Confederate works. Eventually their colonel looked back and noted Ledlie did not take advantage; his regiment seemed to suffer all the punishment, and for nothing, so he stopped where he was and asked for new orders. Potter, meanwhile, sent Burnside information which the absent Ledlie could not—that the first division seemed unwilling to advance. Burnside replied that Potter might as well move if Ledlie could not. He gave similar instructions to Willcox, who threw Hartranft's brigade in on Ledlie's left. Burnside could not fathom why the first division was unable to move in the face of so little opposition, but he anticipated his old reliables would quickly overcome any obstacles.[27]

It was around 5:15. Enemy musketry had picked up, and now the Confederates wheeled some fieldpieces into place. Ledlie's division still squatted in the Crater. Griffin finally disentangled his brigade sufficiently from the others to form it on the far side of the enemy works. To support it, Potter sent two regiments from his other brigade straight up the trenches, past the point the Mainers had reached, to try to silence an especially troublesome battery by Blandford Cemetery. Then Griffin went forward, but canister from that cemetery battery weakened the force of his attack, and a concentrated volley from a few hundred of Elliott's surviving South Carolinians drove him back. Hartranft met no better luck on the left. He seized less than a hundred feet of trenches, the rest of his brigade spilling into the Crater and the relatively undamaged southern wing of the fort.[28]

Burnside's inspector general wrote him a note from the front line, corroborating Potter's fear that Ledlie's men could not be made to advance, but the courier to whom he handed it knew nothing of Burnside's move to Fort Morton. He carried the message all the way back to the old headquarters at Harrison's Creek, where it fell into Meade's hands. The army commander suspected Burnside was aware of the first division's stubbornness; it irritated him to have to learn this important news accidentally, and he insisted quite gruffly that Burnside push forward all his own men and Ord's Eighteenth Corps. Burnside, who could hardly

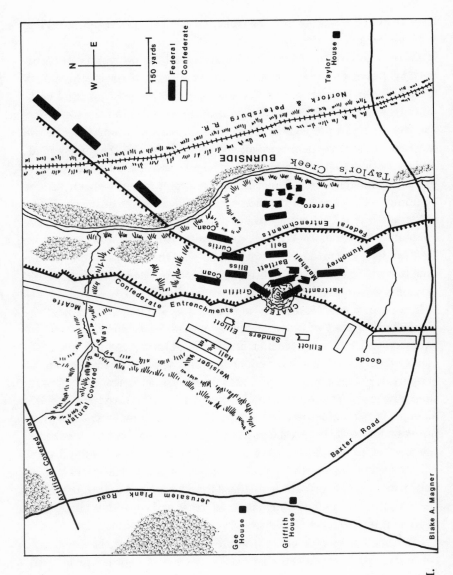

Map 13.
The Crater, 1:00 P.M.

Blake A. Magner

Federal
Confederate

150 yards

N
E
W

Taylor House

Norfolk & Petersburg R.R.

BURNSIDE

Taylor's Creek

Ferrero

Federal Entrenchments

Coan
Curtis
Bell
Humphrey
Bliss
Bartlett
Marshall
Hartranft
Griffin
CRATER

Confederate Entrenchments

McAffe

Way

Natural Covered

Artificial Covered Way

Elliott
Sanders
Elliott
Goode

Hall
Weisiger

Jerusalem Plank Road

Gee House

Griffith House

Baxter Road

see for the smoke, answered he would advance as rapidly as possible. Ord tried to move, but found his way blocked by the rest of Zenas Bliss's brigade of Potter's division, part of which still filled the covered way. Casualties were coming back now, too, further choking that artery: Ord's advance was stymied.[29]

Soon after six o'clock, Meade sent to know whether the Fifth Corps ought to go in on Burnside's left. At that point, everyone still assumed that Warren faced well-defended entrenchments, and that a direct assault would be costly. With so many troops already crowded into a front less than a thousand feet wide, Burnside advised simply forming Warren's men in readiness to attack, pending the proper moment. Then he and Warren went personally into the jammed covered way to see for themselves what was happening: smoke still hovered too thick for accurate observation from Fort Morton.

Their visit to the front showed that one of the greatest impediments to the advance of Burnside's corps was the enfilading fire of infantry and a single gun south of the Crater. Union artillery might have silenced the gun, had pioneers taken the axe to those intervening pines.

Warren rather wished Burnside would order his Fifth Corps in on the left, or so he testified a couple of weeks later. This sudden subordinate attitude of Warren's seems wonderful, considering his customary condescension, but Burnside had no orders giving him specific authority over other corps, and Meade's jealous reminder of July 3 had implied he would have no such control. He therefore declined to act without consulting army headquarters.[30]

Meade grew increasingly impatient with the lack of information from the front. Ordinarily General Parke, the corps chief of staff, might have mollified the army commander with frequent messages, but Parke had taken sick leave again. Burnside had appointed his temporary replacement, Julius White, only the night before. White, one of Burnside's division commanders in East Tennessee, had just arrived with a general assignment to the corps. Burnside offered him Parke's job more as a courtesy, to give him something to do, than because he did well at such work; White sent but one communication to Grant all day July 30, and none to Meade. Thus, when the Fifth and Ninth corps commanders returned to Fort Morton, Burnside found another snappy, sarcastic message from Meade, answering his suggestion about Warren with the reminder that the Fifth Corps had been ready to move for three hours, pointing out the need for haste. Burnside replied he was aware of that necessity and was doing all he could. Meade promptly responded with a demand for the specific problem that prevented his advance. "I wish to know the truth," he added, recollecting the surprise information about Ledlie's nonperformance, "and desire an immediate answer." Burnside did answer immediately—that General Meade's remark was unofficer-like and ungentlemanly, in that it implied Burnside was less than truthful. Meade requested Burnside return a copy of his allegedly offensive dispatch, intimating he would need it as evidence for official charges.[31]

In obedience to those earlier orders to put in all his troops, Burnside sent word for Ferrero to take in his black brigades. The staff officer who delivered the order discovered Ferrero in the bombproof hospital of the third division. With him sat Ledlie, who had lingered there since his own division moved forward, alternately complaining he was sick and that he had been struck by a spent bullet. Ferrero said he would advance as soon as the other troops (presumably Ledlie's) were out of the way, but Burnside's aide returned with several more orders to push ahead, finally carrying one directing Ferrero to charge right over the white troops. At last Ferrero went out to transmit the instructions, but not before one of the surgeons gave him a bracer of rum. Ledlie likewise took a tumbler, and after the alcohol had a chance to stir him he took up lodging elsewhere.[32]

For all their inexperience, and despite having stood perspiring for two hours in the covered way while processions of screaming wounded squeezed by, and even with the dreadful volleys of canister and mus-ketry that now crisscrossed everything between the Crater and the Union works, the black brigades trotted out by the flank and streamed without hesitation toward the swirl of smoke and men. Many of them de-toured into the Crater, but others leaped over the captured trenches and went to their work. Behind them came some of John Turner's division of Tenth Corps troops, who followed on their heels.

With some of the black troops and the help of part of Turner's, General Griffin prepared to make another assault on Cemetery Hill. Turner faced a brigade to the right, to quell the vicious fire from that direction, while Griffin's line struggled resignedly ahead. Willcox, meanwhile, had sent in his other brigade to suppress that one-gun battery and widen the breach: more than half this brigade panicked at one devastat-ing volley and broke, but three Michigan regiments actually wrested a length of trenches from the Southerners and sent a few dozen prisoners to the rear.

At that particular moment the Confederates' first reinforcements arrived, forming in the swale behind the Crater, joining a few hundred of Elliott's Carolinians, who had rallied there. Just as the black and white assault began, William Mahone flung a brigade of Virginians against it.[33]

The Negro troops, still the most organized on the field, had the fore of this advance, and the Virginians tilted toward them with the blood of the Furies welling in their eyes. The colonel of one of the Virginia regiments saw black soldiers walking over the bodies of dead Confederates and felt, as never before, the rage to kill swelling in his breast. The sheer ferocity of these eight hundred Virginians drove the bigger blue line back to the meager cover of a cavalier trench at the rear of the Confederate works, but the Virginians fired a point-blank volley into that brimming ditch and plunged into it with their bayonets, the echo of their Rebel Yell skirling above the slaughter.

The stunned blacks bolted. They disrupted their comrades behind them when they fled, stabbing friends with their bayonets as they ran, carrying white troops with them to the rear. Officers flailed at them with their swords, to no purpose: the enemy seemed to take no prisoners, and these former slaves and sons of slaves ran for their lives. Confederate artillery completely covered their escape route to the Union lines, and Mahone's charge bore down on the right of the clustered Yankee force, so the flight carried south, toward the Crater. Federals packed so close when they ducked into the trenches near there that many could not raise their arms. A number of troops, including some of Ledlie's, who had worked their way up into those works, found themselves cut off and captured. Confederates gestured menacingly for them to crawl out of the trenches, hurrying them to the rear, occasionally dispatching one of their black prisoners.[34] It was not yet nine o'clock.

When he saw his troops reeling from Mahone's counterattack, Burnside called for help. He asked Meade to send in the Fifth Corps now, meaning probably to have Warren attack the works along his front. A signal officer nesting in a Ninth Corps tower had reported the Confederates were stripping their right to reinforce the Crater, and Mahone's counterattack verified the observation, so Warren could expect to find the way almost clear. The Confederate line was, in fact, dreadfully thin in that sector because of Mahone's departure, and Warren's attack could very possibly have succeeded, but information from the front convinced George Meade the battle was already lost. Grant performed a personal reconnaissance, trotting up to the covered way without pausing to announce himself at Fort Morton. He reached the front in time to see Ferrero's men repulsed, and directed Meade to call off the entire operation. That fit Meade's mood precisely; instead of accommodating Burnside in regard to Warren's attack, he wired Burnside to bring his own divisions back to the old line.[35]

With Ord trying to keep up, Burnside turned his horse's head for the old Ninth Corps headquarters and spurred him into a full gallop. As he had probably anticipated since early July, this was Antietam all over again: a solid push in support of his troops would have broken the back of Confederate resistance, but at the critical juncture, that support was withheld. Burnside leaped from his lathered gelding and confronted Meade with words unmixed, his ample forehead ablaze with indignation; he still smarted, no doubt, over the insulting telegram, and he knew Meade would turn his insubordinate response against him if the day did not end in victory. This was one of his rare rages, and staff eyebrows climbed as he thundered at Meade over the order to withdraw. The past months of sarcasm and condescension had finally brought him to full boil. He maintained the assault would succeed if it were continued, meaning that Warren's advance should also proceed. Meade asked Ord what he thought, but Ord shook his head. At that, Meade's resolve stiffened, and he reiterated the order to pull back the troops.[36]

Burnside cooled enough to relay the order to White, who telegraphed back with the advice they should hold the Crater permanently, incorporating it into the Union trench system. The lay of the land made that rather foolhardy, and when Meade refused, Burnside did not press the point. He did ask—and receive—permission to postpone his withdrawal until dark, when the Confederate crossfire might have subsided.

By headquarters dictum, Burnside's well-planned assault was a failure. Grant had already saddled up and returned to City Point, and now Meade rode back to his own headquarters. All the troops supporting the Ninth Corps on the right and left drew back to their camps and trenches. Ord and Burnside continued to wrangle over the lost opportunity at the Harrison's Creek headquarters, Burnside snarling at the white-haired Ord for his failure to back him up in front of Meade, insisting he could have accomplished much with the Eighteenth Corps and Turner's division. Ord replied just as savagely that he could not move his men—that he was "held by the throat"—perhaps unaware that his troops were no longer blocked, that only a single, small regiment stood in the way of his assault on Burnside's right.[37] Wrought back to full fury, Burnside turned next on Grant's perennial observer, Colonel Comstock, who lingered behind his chief. Like many officers with Grant and Meade, Comstock had ridiculed Burnside freely, and now he worried some of his comments might have made their way back to their subject. Perhaps they had. Comstock tried to calm him, but Burnside told him to go back to Grant's camp and never return; if the lieutenant general had need of a spy at Ninth Corps headquarters, he could send someone else.[38]

The scene at Harrison's Creek lasted until nearly noon. The troops in the Crater had degenerated into a mob, dense and disorganized; they could do almost nothing to defend themselves. Some Massachusetts men kept to their work on the sap coursing from the Crater back to the Union line, but Potter's acting engineers had thrown aside tools and taken up rifles to cover the helpless mass teeming in that blasted hell-hole. Willcox began three more covered ways from the old line to the Crater, levying refugees from Ferrero's division to work on them.[39]

Unhindered now by concern for his flanks, William Mahone concentrated all his attention on the Crater. Burnside's order to withdraw reached that cauldron about 12:30, when the dust and sun had long since emptied every canteen. The heat drove some men literally mad. Brigade commanders on the scene—Hartranft, Griffin, and Bartlett, whose cork leg had been shattered—agreed they could never withdraw the uncontrollable throng in good order. They begged for a decent covering fire on the flanks of their position, under which everyone might flee in a single mass, but every corps commander save Burnside had been ordered to stand down. Burnside had committed his entire corps; he could offer the desperate brigadiers nothing but artillery support.[40]

The Confederates made a second advance on the Crater, but the attack sputtered out before Burnside's field guns and a few hundred determined riflemen who graced the rim. Convinced no covering fire would be forthcoming, the senior officers on the front line decided to encourage everyone to run for it anyway, in a wholesale rush that might condense casualties. As the Federals were about to begin that bolt for freedom, a final Confederate charge swept down on the Crater. It met little concerted opposition. White rags danced wherever men could find them, while about half the demoralized blue multitude dashed helter-skelter back to the Union lines. The rest, the equivalent of a full brigade, marched the other way as prisoners.[41]

General Potter, whose men had done the most fighting, sent Burnside a startling assessment. Regimental officers advised him his division was virtually annihilated and could not possibly hold its former stretch of the trenches. Willcox thought he could take a share of the line, but the fragments of Ledlie's two brigades could do nothing more than go into camp. Burnside borrowed Ord's troops to fill the gaps in his front while he worked frantically to reorganize the depleted brigades in the first, second, and fourth divisions. His corps alone had lost nearly four thousand casualties; almost half his regimental commanders and two good brigadiers were gone, as well as a disproportionate number of the best veterans in every unit. Never again would the Ninth Corps distinguish itself on the battlefield.

While Burnside struggled to regroup, Meade sent several inquiries about the situation at the Crater. Disgusted at the way Meade had left him to fend for himself, Burnside flung the dispatches to the ground one after the other, growling that he would answer no such insulting message. There could have been but one result after all his support was withdrawn, he reasoned, and Meade ought to know what that result was. Not until midmorning the next day, when both he and his line were a little more stable, did Burnside give Meade an outline of affairs. He suggested in that same message that they seek a truce to bury the dead and collect the few score of wounded between the lines, but while Meade supplied a letter requesting such a truce, he directed Burnside not to use it unless the Confederates declined an informal armistice. It seems Meade wished to avoid the admission of defeat that went with an appeal for a truce. Burnside attempted the informal arrangements Meade wanted, but the local Confederate commander would have nothing to do with it. The afternoon of July 31 slipped away while the required letter made its way to General Lee, who forwarded it to Beauregard; the truce did not begin until the next morning. By that time, without water in the broiling sun, most of the wounded had died.[42]

Meade also asked for an account of casualties in the Ninth Corps, but

Burnside had a hard time sifting through the exaggerated reports and rumors emanating from his shocked and disorganized divisions. The truce attempt distracted him, but in the afternoon he tallied a figure of nearly ten thousand men available for duty. Finally, after dinner, he sent Meade an estimated loss of forty-five hundred, "the greater portion of which was made [sic] after the brigade commanders in the crater were made aware of the order to withdraw." It seemed to Meade that Burnside blamed the order to withdraw for most of the Ninth Corps casualties, so he sent back a demand for an explanation of that accusative comment. Burnside responded with a tart reply to Meade's chief of staff: "Please say to the Cmdg. Genl. that the latter part of my dispatch means just what it says and inasmuch as it is very distinct the requiring of an explanation seems to be superfluous. He knew the state of affairs by my written and verbal reports when he ordered a withdrawal and he knows the state of affairs now." Either on his own hook or by the advice of his staff (probably on his own, since the most judicious members of his staff were not present), Burnside modified the final draft of that angry note somewhat, though he maintained to the end that Meade's withdrawal order precipitated the hasty and costly retirement from the Crater.[43]

After a good deal of preliminary grumbling, Meade finally created— rather than called—a court of inquiry to investigate the disaster. He appointed four officers to form the court; when he learned he had no such authority, he asked Grant to use his influence with Lincoln, that the president might legitimize his appointments. He simultaneously preferred charges against Burnside for insubordination, as a result of the "ungentlemanly" dispatch and the blowup at the Harrison's Creek headquarters. An inquiry suited Burnside just fine, though he admitted he had exceeded the bounds of military courtesy, but he was justifiably shocked to hear the appointments to the court: Winfield Hancock, Nelson Miles, Romeyn Ayres, and Edmund Schriver. Not only were all four men members of the Army of the Potomac and friends of Meade, but Hancock had (unknown to Burnside) previously expressed a lack of confidence in the Ninth Corps commander. Hancock, Miles, and Ayres had all led troops in the very battle for which they were to assess blame, and Schriver was Meade's own inspector general. Given the general dislike for the Ninth Corps in the Army of the Potomac, these appointments did not bode well for Burnside. Unassigned officers, or those from other armies, would normally compose such a board, but when Burnside made that suggestion to the president, Lincoln told him not to worry.[44]

The court convened between August 8 and September 8, but it did not meet every day. In fact, in the midst of the investigation, Winfield Hancock led his corps into a fight at Reams's Station from which it fled in ignominious rout, every bit as shameful as anything that happened at the Crater.[45] Hancock was Hancock, though, and Burnside was Burnside, so Reams's Station went uninvestigated while the Crater inquiry resumed four days later. In twelve full days of interviews, the court heard everyone from General Grant to a subaltern in one of the black regiments. Even court member Ayres stepped down to respond to questions, revealing in the process that he had already judged the issue. Major Van Buren kept a notebook during the inquiry, jotting down the correspondence Meade submitted and doodling on the back pages during the boring testimony of the first two days. When Burnside came in, later on the second day, Van Buren told him that some of Meade's submitted dispatches pertained to their hostile exchange after the battle: these had nothing to do with determining responsibility for the defeat, and since Meade had brought him up on separate charges over them, Burnside was naturally upset to see them here. He entered a formal objection, at which Van Buren scribbled the words "Schriver cross" in his notebook; Colonel Schriver, Meade's inspector, sat as judge advocate. Meade countered with his own objection, and the court rejected Burnside's complaint, illogically deciding the post-assault correspondence was pertinent and citing the technicality that Burnside ought to have objected the moment Meade offered the material, instead of at the end of the day—notwithstanding Burnside had been absent when the dispatches came into evidence.[46]

The court's findings were predictable enough: it attributed the preponderance of responsibility for the failure to Ambrose Burnside and his corps. Principally, the court noted Burnside's failure to level the parapets in his front, so a broad column of assault could sweep across the Crater, despite Burnside's explanation that he feared alerting the enemy and getting the working parties shot to pieces. The four officers also deemed Burnside negligent for failing to push Ledlie's division beyond the Crater, and for not withdrawing it in favor of another when it would not advance, even though evidence demonstrated that Ledlie failed not only to command his division, but to acquaint Burnside with its reluctance to advance. The court seemed to overlook the extremely narrow front at the Crater, which precluded the withdrawal of individual divisions without pandemonium. Ledlie, Ferrero, and Colonel Bliss drew deserved censure for remaining behind while their commands attacked, and the court took Orlando Willcox to task for what it characterized as an insufficient effort, presumably because his division was not destroyed. The only court criticism even remotely associated with Meade was the suggestion that some officer near the battlefield ought to have exercised authority over all the attacking forces. In a roundabout manner, that could be construed to mean Burnside should have been able to call on Warren and Ord at will, echoing his July 3 request to "say when and how" the other corps would support him; it could also have implied Meade ought to have been on the spot, to react instantly to new developments. If the latter were the case, those arbiters showed their superior officer extreme lenience compared to the opprobrium they attached to Ledlie, Ferrero, and Bliss for a similar absence.[47]

Whether conscious of it or not, the four officers of the court operated under a bias that prevented them from finding the true cause of the tragedy. Their primary criticism was perfectly lame: sufficient openings had been made in the parapet to pass through a company at a time, which could quickly have combined in regimental or brigade formations. Potter moved behind a wide front of skirmishers, for all the supposed hindrance of the earthworks; nor did Willcox find the parapets a significant problem. The lack of division commanders in the Crater also assumed inflated importance in the court's decision: their absence contributed to the defeat only insofar as time was lost giving them orders which they simply passed along to brigadiers. There were, besides, what amounted to acting division commanders in the Crater, any one of them superior to James Ledlie. Considering Ledlie's reliance upon Dutch courage, his presence would have been a decided liability. Potter and Willcox remained within a hundred yards of their embattled divisions, which was close enough for most purposes. Normally they would have been on hand to manage the withdrawal, but by then the massed soldiers were so disorganized no one could have untangled them.[48]

The battle of July 30, 1864, was actually lost July 29, at the instant George Meade told Burnside he could not use his fresh black troops

or his plan employing divergent flank guards. That threw Burnside
back on his three combat-weary white divisions. They could still make
a spirited stand-up fight—Simon Griffin's brigade proved as much—
but they had developed a debilitating taste for their fieldworks during
the fruitless assaults of May and June. The previous spring, any one of
Burnside's divisions might have sprinted through or around the Crater
by the flank, veered into a column of assault, and taken the hill behind
Blandford Church, but no longer. The bravest lay dead on too many
battlefields this side of the Rapidan, while most of those who survived
had the habit of keeping their heads down. As a Confederate general
put it, "In assaulting breastworks, & particularly in assaults which fail,
the leaders are thinned out & the shirkers are most apt to survive."
Even poets who never saw a battle recognized the problem, mourning
the loss of so many courageous souls:

> Brave, brave were the soldiers (high named to-day) who lived
>   through the fight;
> But the bravest press'd to the front and fell, unnamed,
>   unknown.[49]

Yet in the end it was not that defensive trait itself which brought
disaster, but Burnside's awareness of it. That awareness led to the long
and inconclusive discussion with his division commanders, which culmi-
nated in a frustrated reliance upon chance. Chance put the one man in
the critical spot who could not be trusted there—James Ledlie. Burnside knew nothing of Ledlie's weaknesses, nor, apparently, did anyone
else outside the first division, but therein is the crux of the problem.
Burnside believed in a loose rein, for horse or man: that philosophy
is as evident in the discretion he allowed subordinates as in the way
he bridled at Colonel Comstock's obvious surveillance of his own headquarters. Closer monitoring of his corps might have exposed Ledlie's
incompetence before it was too late. That shortcoming, combined with
Meade's meddling, supplanted a division almost certain to win the day
with one led by a man equally certain to lose with any troops.

By the time the court presented its findings, Burnside was gone. The
morning after his third and last day of testimony, he packed his belongings and prepared for a twenty-day leave. For all the brass bands,
champagne, and gaiety that marked his departure, he may have sus-

pected he might not return, but he looked forward to a vacation from the poisonous jealousy and prejudice of the Army of the Potomac.[50]

Though he spent much of his furlough on railroad business, Burnside made time for pleasure. Late in August he and Molly rode the train up to Dover, New Hampshire, changing there for a series of stages that took them through the White Mountains. His niece had written him of the grand scenery there a couple of years earlier, and he seemed ever since to have planned this excursion. But for an occasional demand for a speech, the couple enjoyed a very private vacation.[51]

By the end of the month a refreshed Burnside came home. A few days before his leave expired, he asked Grant where he should await orders, but Grant replied that he ought not return to his corps just then—the board of inquiry had only recently found him responsible for the Crater disaster. The reply itself was telling enough: its import became more apparent with each passing week, and toward the end of September Grant ordered Burnside to return his staff officers to duty with the corps. That should have been the closing of the book; it was plain the general-in-chief wanted Burnside out of the war. The ever-hopeful Burnside would not give up, though, and ventured south in mid-November, asking permission to visit the army. None too cordially, Grant replied, "You are authorized to visit headquarters," and Burnside sailed down to Petersburg, apparently unaware that Grant was on his way north to visit his wife in New Jersey. The former Ninth Corps commander stopped first at those headquarters to see John Parke, who commanded in his absence. A military train scheduled to take him to his appointment with Grant at City Point failed to depart on time, and an hour later Grant and his staff boarded their steamer. Burnside, meanwhile, climbed into the cab of a returning locomotive in a vain attempt to overtake them. He missed Grant again at Fort Monroe and Baltimore, returning finally to Washington without having seen him. With that uninformed and unfair attitude now endemic in the Army of the Potomac, Colonel Comstock remarked that Burnside "as usual was behind time and got left."[52]

Burnside had wanted to discuss the discomfort he felt collecting his army salary without doing any duty, and he broached the topic with the president before returning to Providence, offering once more to resign his commission. He complained that the combination of the court of inquiry finding and his continued inactivity put him back under a cloud.

Lincoln, who seems to have believed the general had been wronged, refused to accept his resignation and begged his indulgence.

Either the night before or the evening after his conference at the White House, Burnside encountered a Southern lady who boasted of some standing in her native community. They fell into conversation, perhaps at Willard's. Too chivalrous to hold a lady's politics against her, the general was also apparently too naive to recognize that otherwise respectable refugee women had been driven to outright prostitution by economic necessity, and toward the end of the evening he offered to escort her to her chambers. Somehow she persuaded him beyond her door, but when she began to turn down the gas he saw her scheme and fled.[53]

His appetite for the iniquitous capital sated, Burnside remained at home until unemployment again drove him to see the president. He and Lincoln talked over the attack on Wilmington, Burnside's spring brainchild. The highly regarded assistant secretary of the navy, Gustavus Fox, lobbied for either Burnside or Quincy Gillmore to lead the expedition, for they both had experience in such campaigns; Fox thought Burnside particularly well fitted because of his good relations with previous naval collaborators. The assignment finally went to Ben Butler, for political reasons, and he made a bad fist of it.

In January Burnside met with the president again, coming away this time with an apparent promise of a command "forthwith." General Grant thought to put him in temporary charge of the Middle Department, consisting of the relatively dull states of Pennsylvania, Delaware, Maryland, and West Virginia; he asked Stanton to give him the place, but Stanton ignored the request, assigning instead an obscure brevet brigadier general.[54]

Personal disaster struck just as Burnside began his last conversation with Lincoln. Molly's older brother and two of her nieces had sailed from New York as Burnside left for Washington, bound for philanthropic work among the freedmen of South Carolina. Their steamer, the *Melville*, went down in heavy seas January 12, and all three perished. Burnside rushed home as soon as he heard the news.[55] Shortly after he arrived, he learned that Butler's successor on the Wilmington expedition had captured Fort Fisher, closing the port. That ended any practical hope that Burnside might be able to end the war on a positive note, so he turned to the preparation of his official service report. This chronology would constitute the only personal defense of his military career. He had spent past furloughs collecting subordinate reports— the more damaging of which he had not yet seen, because their authors withheld them—and in the last winter of the war he began work. None of these reports saw print in his lifetime, nor could he have expected at the time that they ever would, but this limited medium offered all the vehicle he wanted in which to set a few records straight. His irrepressible, Quakerlike confidence in ultimate justice, which had somehow survived the bad example of the Army of the Potomac, seemed to convince him that his solitary, handwritten report would lead the muse of history aright.[56]

Some were not so shy as Burnside about repairing his reputation. During the winter, on the motion of Burnside's friend, Senator Henry Anthony, Congress decided to assign the Joint Committee on the Conduct of the War to the Crater debacle. Just before Christmas the congressmen interviewed Burnside, after which they went down to Petersburg for a day to take testimony from the other pertinent corps and division commanders still on duty with the army. Meade assumed the inquisitors had roused at Burnside's urging and predicted their investigation could only backfire on him, uncovering his incompetence and further absolving Meade. Unlike the court of inquiry, however, the committee was not unduly influenced by Meade and bore no prejudice against Burnside. They questioned Meade, Grant, General Hunt, Major Duane, and a couple of staff officers never called by the court of inquiry. Like all good politicians, they went home by the holidays, but they took transcripts of the proceedings of the court of inquiry to study. When Congress reconvened, the committee had the benefit of two more witnesses the military court had not seen—Colonel Pleasants and General Turner, the only division commander who had actually gone into the Crater. The members mulled the accumulated material for another fortnight or so, and early in February Chairman Ben Wade initialed their conclusions. The true cause of the Crater defeat, they decided, was Meade's interference with Burnside's plan. Had he left Ferrero's division to lead the attack, with detachments sweeping up the enemy lines to quell the flank threat, the plan ought to have worked. Both Grant and General Warren had told them as much. The only criticism the committee tendered Burnside was for the manner of choosing the lead division by lot. They perceived no misjudgment in his choice of the first division, given the veto of Ferrero's, but thought the method of choosing improper.[57]

The Joint Committee on the Conduct of the War was principally composed of Radical Republicans, who adopted Burnside as a protégé because he had so assiduously avoided the McClellan intrigues, to the point of alienating McClellan and his faction. The congressmen were therefore inclined his way, but their opposing bias did not throw them so far from the target as Hancock's court. They may have failed to notice Burnside's loose hand with his division commanders, or that he had retained subordinates who no longer measured up to that sort of discretion, but the initial court of inquiry had missed much more than that.

Early in February Burnside mentioned to Grant that he had not been assigned to the Middle Department, and the general-in-chief said he had nothing else to offer. That lack may have been unrelated to the joint committee investigation, for its conclusions were not published until four days later, but once Grant had that report in hand, it was even more certain he would have no command for Burnside for a long time to come. Taking Meade's side, he suggested a court-martial for Burnside might clear the army commander's name.

"I suppose General Burnside's evidence has apparently been their guide," he remarked to Meade, "and, to draw it mildly, he has forgotten some of the facts." To come to such a conclusion, Grant himself must have forgotten a few facts, among them his own testimony. "General Burnside wanted to put his colored division in front," he had told the committee, "and if he had done so I believe it would have been a success." He had also testified he knew Ledlie would finally lead the charge, but he did nothing about it though he thought Ledlie the worst general Burnside had. Meade pushed for no court-martial: he had already preferred charges against Burnside which had come to nothing. He said he would be satisfied just to have the court of inquiry proceedings published, to counter those of the committee, and eventually the transcripts of both bodies appeared in the same little volume. The dual publication, however, did not constitute the great vindication Meade had hoped it would.[58]

Burnside resumed his lodgings at the Fifth Avenue Hotel, so as to be near his railroad affairs, working periodically on his report. Others also tried to clear up their records as the war ground to its obvious conclusion, as the general found in a letter from Vincent Colyer. The trouble-making Christian Commission man from the Negro school at Newbern asked Burnside for a letter corroborating, among other things, that Colyer had arrived in North Carolina with hospital supplies and had worked at his own expense. Colyer had recently published a pamphlet detailing his exploits there, describing the closing of the school and blaming Governor Stanly for his woes. Burnside had already written to Stanly, pointing out Colyer's misrepresentations, and though he provided Colyer with the desired letter, he included in it his corrections of the do-gooder's little memoir; thus, if Colyer wanted to use Burnside's letter for some self-gratifying purpose, he would also have to present a contradiction of his pamphlet.[59]

Even at home in supposed disgrace, Burnside still wielded enough influence that people hounded him for recommendations. Cousin James Burnside, a Veteran Reserve Corps captain with much time on his hands, asked Cousin Ambrose to put his good name on James's application for a permit to bring ten thousand pounds of cotton and fifty thousand pounds of tobacco through the lines. If James received the permit, he did so without his cousin's help. General Burnside had a policy against recommending relatives: he had violated that policy but once, in the case of a nephew sutler named H. S. Gould, and he had come to regret it.[60]

As spring once more promised action, the idle general made one final attempt to secure an assignment. On March 23 he wired Secretary Stanton a brief offer that might have been pathetic had it not defined how completely Burnside subordinated pride and ego to his country's service: "If I can be of any service to General Grant or General Sherman as a subordinate commander or aide-de-camp, or as a bearer of dispatches from you to either of them, I am quite ready." The image of so senior a major general serving as an aide, or bearing dispatches, was perhaps too much for Stanton's image of such an officer's dignity. Grant forced Lee out of Richmond and virtually ended the war at Appomattox without Stanton so much as acknowledging Burnside's telegram.[61]

On the last afternoon of Abraham Lincoln's life, Burnside mailed a final resignation, enclosing with it a letter congratulating Edwin Stanton for his part in the victory. He added that he would soon have to visit Philadelphia, and if the president and Stanton pleased, he would be happy to continue on to Washington for a farewell audience. The desperate hand of John Wilkes Booth prevented a reply and precluded any goodbyes to Burnside's fellow former Hoosier.[62]

Four days later Burnside made his last visit to the president, leaning over the open casket in the East Room before filing into a seat alongside Grant, Goldsborough, Andrew Johnson, and scores of other dignitaries to hear the funeral sermon. Though he sat with the military giants of America, he wore civilian clothes; Johnson accepted his resignation that same afternoon, perhaps as a result of Burnside's personal request, dating his acceptance retroactively to April 15, 1865—precisely four years after Burnside had opened Governor Sprague's offer to command the 1st Rhode Island.[63] For Ambrose Burnside and Abraham Lincoln, the Civil War ended at the same moment.

EPILOGUE: THE UNDISCOVER'D COUNTRY

The senator held himself tall and straight, but his appreciative palate and sedentary occupation had finally combined to force his waistband to the same breadth as his formidable shoulders. His step measured a brisk pace, but his wraparound whiskers and the thick fringe of hair over his ears gleamed so white he looked older than his fifty-seven years. His two nieces emerged from the Providence train station with him, just finished with a summer at his cottage near Bristol, and as he hailed a hansom in his rolling baritone there were few on the street who failed to recognize him.

This was Monday afternoon, September 12, 1881, which, if Ambrose Burnside stopped to remember, marked the nineteenth anniversary of his triumphant entry into Frederick, Maryland; it was also exactly twenty years since he received permission to raise his coast division, but past events probably did not enter his mind today. Nearly every public man preoccupied himself these days with the fate of President Garfield, shot ten weeks since, and with the political ramifications that might attend his death.[1]

At the time of the last presidential assassination, Burnside thought his public service was over, but in the intervening sixteen years he had devoted more time to the business of his state and country than he had spent on military duty. Less than a year after he resigned his commission, the people of Rhode Island elected him their governor with an astounding threefold majority. Twice had they reelected him, with the inevitably diminishing mandate each time, but even at the last with a margin that still approached two to one. As his final term ended, he hoped once again to retire to private life: there seemed no logical place for him in politics, for he did not care to continue as governor and the state had two senators in their prime—his friend Henry Anthony and

young William Sprague. It may have been Burnside's availability for
office, in part, that sparked Senator Sprague to make an enemy of him.
The two had recently taken opposite sides on the issue of President
Johnson's impeachment, and Burnside, perhaps the most popular man
in Rhode Island, was a friend of the Brown and Ives families, who com-
peted with Sprague for control of the state. Once he had been safely
reelected, the chisel-toothed Sprague attacked Burnside with all the
venom of a spoiled brat. In the spring of 1869, one month after he began
his second term, he took the Senate floor on the pretext of some unrelated tax bill and launched into a denunciation of the performance of the
1st Rhode Island Regiment and its colonel at First Bull Run. He characterized Burnside as incompetent at best, and a coward at worst; his
men, whom Sprague had been proud enough to accompany in 1861, had
been a craven collection of misfits. Sprague's attack aroused a barrage
of rebuttals from the Senate itself, not the gentlest of which came from
Senator Anthony, who asked Sprague to listen to some of his own 1862
proclamations honoring Burnside. All the rhetoric seemed to confirm
Burnside in his decision to leave politics.[2]

Governing a state as small as Rhode Island remained a part-time job
just after the Civil War, and Burnside spent most of his spare time
on railroad work. One of his investments, the Cairo & Vincennes line,
tottered on the brink of bankruptcy as his third gubernatorial term expired, and in the summer of 1870 he traveled to London in a vain effort
to sell enough bonds for the completion of the railroad. The Franco-
Prussian War had degenerated into the siege of Paris before he arrived,
and the old soldier could not resist the chance to observe that European conflict. Late in September he crossed the channel and entered
the Prussian lines at Versailles. There he found a few other Americans,
among them cocky little Phil Sheridan, and he met Count Bismarck,
who granted him a permit to enter the besieged city. In Paris he spoke
with the United States ambassador and Jules Favre, head of the provisional French government. Favre asked Burnside to carry a message
to Bismarck, who selected Burnside, also, to take his reply back into
the city. Sheridan, as vain a man as ever lived, cynically supposed Bismarck's purpose in this mediation was to ply Burnside's own vanity and
elicit information on the city's defenses, but Burnside would have recognized the guise of a spy; besides, he favored the French. His humani-

tarian mission between the belligerents failed to achieve the armistice he desired, and in mid-October he returned to England.[3]

Billy Sprague's long run of good fortune came to an end in 1873. During that year he lost his influential father-in-law, Chief Justice Chase, and the Panic of 1873 swept away most of his wealth; with his money went his comely wife, who began a flirtation with a better-heeled senator.[4]

Burnside also ran into financial difficulties in the early seventies. It seemed, for instance, that the Treasury Department would never cease hounding him over quartermaster funds, and in March of 1872 the auditors presented him with a bill for more than $37,000 in shortfalls. A mining venture with Henry Heth had already failed. In 1874 he invested heavily in a New Jersey company that lost a quarter of its $400,000 capital in the first year. But when the Rhode Island General Assembly next discussed senatorial nominations, the legislators declined to reelect William Sprague; in January of 1875 they chose fifty-year-old Ambrose Burnside. He took his seat March 5, 1875, alongside both of Abraham Lincoln's vice presidents, Hannibal Hamlin and Andrew Johnson. Vice President Henry Wilson, who as a senator had occasionally corresponded with the young commander of the North Carolina expedition, administered the oath; among the sitting senators was Burnside's sometime friend, sometime critic, Oliver P. Morton.[5]

Burnside remained interested in the events of the war, though he dwelt upon them far less than most politicians. He hosted at least one staff reunion, in 1867, and on another occasion he delivered a 44-page address to the Society of the Burnside Expedition and the Ninth Army Corps. He accepted an invitation to Knoxville for the Fourth of July celebration in 1874, and the citizens there welcomed him as deliriously as in 1863. The following Memorial Day, Burnside stood atop the rostrum in the Antietam National Cemetery and spoke, once again, of his belief that the lowest private in the ranks deserved the same praise as the most successful general: each had given his all, and no man could do more. A decade later, George McClellan would stand on that same spot and gratefully accept a much larger measure of credit for saving the Union.[6]

That summer of 1875, Brown University awarded Senator Burnside an honorary degree, and President Grant spent a couple of days relaxing at Edghill, Burnside's summer place near Bristol. Burnside spoke for his shy guest when local folk called on the reluctant president for an address, and he introduced the Ohio-born Grant to the mysteries of a New England clambake.[7]

Much of the joy went out of Burnside's life the next spring. After years of delicate health, Molly Burnside fell into her final illness just as the congressional session opened; she died March 9, at the age of only forty-seven. In his grief, the senator withdrew into his work, and within days of the funeral he sat on the impeachment of Grant's secretary of war.[8]

Burnside's Senate career demonstrated the political metamorphosis the Civil War had wrought upon him. In his early years as a sound Democrat, he may not have sympathized with the peculiar institution, but he acknowledged the property laws pertaining to it. Even during his administration of the Department of the Ohio he sided with conservatives on the issue of raising Negro soldiers in places like Kentucky. He had none of the popular illusions about the natural inferiority of black men, however, which allowed him finally to champion the use of U.S. Colored Troops in 1864. It was perhaps this egalitarian instinct that brought him the attention of the Radicals and forged him to the Republican party after Appomattox. He did not share the scheming vindictiveness of some of the Radicals, and it could only have been the desire to see justice done the former slaves that set his sentiments against President Johnson in the impeachment trial of 1868. That crisis proved a watershed for many a public American: thereafter, Burnside did not often find himself across the fence from the Jacobins.[9]

He did not, however, follow in political lockstep; his beliefs merely coincided with Republican political strategy. While Radicals may have supported the Fifteenth Amendment as a means of securing Republican voters, Ambrose Burnside fought for a bill allowing black applicants special admissions privileges at West Point, arguing a case that sounded much like an affirmative action policy from another century. Unlike many Republicans, though, Burnside resumed cordial relations with former Confederates. They were always welcome at his Washington rooms, and he did not shirk from defending them on the floor of the Senate when right required it. Now and then he challenged powerful fellow Republicans, notably Oliver Morton.

Burnside chaired the Committee on Education and Labor, served on the Committee on Military Affairs, and won the chair of the Committee on Foreign Relations at the beginning of his second term. In 1878 he proposed reforms that threatened to fracture the army's ossified officer corps, disrupting the status quo so objectively that old friends, secure in the service, howled at him. As though to testify to his exalted opinion of the enlisted man, Burnside also supported a bill providing pensions for noncommissioned officers after thirty years; yet he simultaneously argued for more stringent investigations of disability claims—sheer heresy in the wake of the Civil War.[10]

Perhaps the best-known of Burnside's senatorial stands concerned the case of Fitz John Porter. In 1878, the disgraced general made another in a long series of attempts to have his 1863 court-martial reversed and his dismissal revoked. Porter had been found guilty of disobedience of John Pope's orders to assault Jackson's right flank at Second Bull Run. He had been convicted more on the evidence of telegrams revealing his contempt for Pope than for the actual omission, and now he wished to overturn the conviction with Confederate reports, unavailable during his trial, which demonstrated that his reluctance to attack was proper and judicious. The issue first went before an army review board and eventually reached Congress in the form of a bill. The politicization of what should have been a judicial matter upset Burnside. In 1862 he had willingly testified in Porter's behalf, but late in 1880 he argued that new evidence only justified a new trial—not the outright reversal of the decision by legislative fiat. Procedure may have been the foundation of his argument, but there was a little more to it than that.

In a speech to which he had obviously given some thought, Burnside remarked he could forgive former United States officers who had gone over to the Confederacy, for they had followed a course based on conscience; Porter, on the other hand, had put "the benefit of one man ahead of that of his country," and this Burnside found less easy to forgive. The "one man" he referred to was not Porter himself, but George McClellan: during the past eighteen years Burnside had come to realize that McClellan finally put patriotism, honor, and personal friendship behind his private ambitions, subordinating both truth and his affection for Burnside to his lust for fame, and his principal ally in this endeavor was Fitz John Porter. Exactly how much Burnside knew remains a puzzle, but he appears to have had a hint of Porter's contribution to his estrangement with McClellan.[11]

Porter's appeal found no resolution for another six years, when a Democratic majority assured him success. He resumed his place on the muster rolls as a colonel on the retirement list and began collecting a pension—something for which even Burnside was not eligible.

Congress adjourned the week President Garfield was wounded, and Burnside went home to Edghill, where he passed the life of a gentleman farmer. He managed a growing herd of tawny Alderney cattle there, and stabled all his horses near the house. For harness, he kept a lively gelding named Dick, who shared Burnside's taste for speed so well that he overturned the carriage in the early days of the recess, bruising the senator and respraining his weak ankle. Still alive at Edghill was Major, the brigandish bobtail Jacob Cox had so feared. Major was nearly thirty, but few besides Burnside dared climb on his back.[12]

As the summer of 1881 drew to a close, the inevitable houseful of visitors wandered homeward. The last to leave were the Bishop girls, grown ladies now, and their uncle escorted them to the Providence station, dropping them at their grandmother's house on Benefit Street. From there he directed the cab driver to Senator Anthony's house, where he enjoyed an afternoon's conversation followed by dinner, lingering until after dark. Anthony offered the junior senator his carriage, but the night held clear so Burnside walked back to the station.

Robbie, Robert Holloway's son, met him at the Bristol terminal with a buggy. They arrived at Edghill late. Robbie brought Burnside his dressing gown and slippers, but though he dressed for bed he walked the house for some time, complaining of pains in his chest. Robbie told some of the other servants, who came in their nightclothes to ask if they could call the doctor. Burnside said to wait, as it was too late, but at dawn they found him still about, too uncomfortable to sleep. Robbie ran for Dr. Barnes, who arrived from Bristol after ten o'clock.

Quite worried by now, Burnside threw himself on the bed with the remark that something should be done for him quickly, asking for morphine as the doctor tested his erratic pulse. No one remembered him saying anything more, though he obviously suffered great pain. At five minutes before eleven o'clock, his heart ceased to beat altogether.[13]

Two days later the citizens of Bristol crowded into St. Michael's Church to hear a memorial service for their famous neighbor, after which a special train carried the casket to Providence, to lie in state at City Hall. The funeral drew hundreds to the First Congregational

Church the following day, September 16. The pallbearers included George Fearing, the aide who found that hornets' nest on the way into East Tennessee, and John Parke, still wearing both a general's uniform and those Burnside whiskers. Major Van Buren and Dr. Church were dead these fifteen years, and Daniel Larned's duties as an army paymaster bound him to the West Coast. Also absent from the mourners was George McClellan, who, on this very date in 1862, had written the reprimand that began the gradual breakup of his friendship with Burnside: even had he not been vacationing in France, he probably would not have come.[14]

Three ministers offered eulogies. Augustus Woodbury, who had ferociously defended the general against his army of detractors during the war, remembered now his thoroughly unselfish nature. He recounted an instance, after Fredericksburg, when he urged Burnside to make a public response to his critics. Burnside refused, Woodbury said, rather than embroil the army in greater controversy. "I have simply to do my duty," he had said. "I can safely leave any claim that I have to the judgement of future years and the justice of my fellow countrymen." The story rang true: Burnside had written almost the same words to Jonathan Sturges in 1863.[15]

With that allusion to the greatest flaw in Burnside's public life—his trust in the essential goodness and honesty of men—the Reverend Woodbury resumed his seat. The hearse started from the church ahead of a long column of representatives from city and state government, the Providence Board of Trade, Brown University, the Loyal Legion and the Grand Army of the Republic, and a number of private societies and labor groups. Headed by the pallbearers and the governor, the procession turned at Olney Street toward Swan Point Cemetery.[16] There, with leaves already blowing red and brown into the raw grave, John Parke said goodbye to the most honest and loyal comrade he ever knew.

NOTES

ABBREVIATIONS

AEBP

Ambrose E. Burnside Papers, Generals' Reports and Books, Records Group 94, National Archives.

B&L

Buel, Clarence C., and Robert U. Johnson, eds. *Battles and Leaders of the Civil War.* 4 vols. New York: Century Co., 1884–88.

CCW

Report of the Joint Committee on the Conduct of the War. 3 parts. Washington, D.C.: Government Printing Office, 1863.

Crater Report

Report of the Committee on the Conduct of the War on the Attack on Petersburg, on the 30th Day of July, 1864. Washington, D.C.: Government Printing Office, 1865.

CV

Confederate Veteran magazine.

OR

War of the Rebellion: A Compilation of the Official Records of the Union and Confederate Armies. 128 vols. Washington, D.C.: Government Printing Office, 1880–1901. (Series 1 unless otherwise indicated.)

OR Atlas

Atlas to Accompany the Official Records of the Union and Confederate Armies. Washington, D.C.: Government Printing Office, 1891–95.

ORN

Official Records of the Union and Confederate Navies in the War of the Rebellion. 31 vols. Washington, D.C.: Government Printing Office, 1894–1927. (Series 1 unless otherwise indicated.)

RIHS Papers

Ambrose E. Burnside Papers, Rhode Island Historical Society, Providence, R.I.

SHSP

Southern Historical Society Papers.

USAMHI   United States Army Military History Institute, Carlisle Barracks, Pa.

USMA Archives   United States Military Academy Archives, West Point, N.Y.

USMA Library   United States Military Academy Library, West Point, N.Y.

USMA Records   United States Military Academy Records, Records Group 94, National Archives, Washington, D.C.

PROLOGUE

1. Poore, *Life of Burnside*, 50–51.

2. Ibid., 18–23.

3. Ibid., 23–25; Samuel Bigger to Albert S. White, August 15, 1842, Ambrose E. Burnside cadet application file, USMA Records; "Circumstances of the Parents of Cadets, 1842–1879," USMA Archives. The four economic categories were indigent, reduced, moderate, and independent.

4. Poore, *Life of Burnside*, 25–26, 256; Richmond (Indiana) *Palladium*, January 17, 1867; "History of Union County Schools, 1804–1906," Union County Public Library; Samuel Bigger to Secretary of War, August 13, 1842, Burnside Cadet application, USMA Records. Poore misspells Haughton's name "Houghton."

5. Poore, *Life of Burnside*, 28–29; Albert S. White to J. C. Spencer, August 25, 1842, Joseph Totten to Albert S. White, August 26, 1842, O. H. Smith and Albert S. White to Secretary of War, March 3, 1843, petition of the Indiana legislature, and Ambrose Burnside's letter of acceptance, March 17, 1843, all in Burnside's cadet application, USMA Records.

6. This and all following information on Burnside's academic achievement and deportment from "Merit Book, 1836–1853," and "Register of Delinquencies, 1843–1847," USMA Archives.

7. Gallagher, *Fighting for the Confederacy*, 166; "The Memoirs of Brigadier-General William Montgomery Gardner," Special Collections, USMA Library.

8. Heth, "Memoirs," 7.

9. Poore, *Life of Burnside*, 53; Hannah Gill to Burnside, May 27, 1862, Box 1, AEBP.

10. Poore, *Life of Burnside*, 53, 57; Returns from Regular Army Artillery Regiments, Second Artillery, reel 11, and Third Artillery, reel 19.

CHAPTER ONE

I

1. Woodbury, *First Rhode Island*, 62.

2. Ibid., 63–64; *OR* 2:671, 691, 715–16; Albert G. Bates to "My Darling, beloved Edith," June 19, 1861, transcript in the Wiley Sword Collection, USAMHI.

3. Eckert and Amato, *Ten Years in the Saddle*, 111; Returns from U.S. Military Posts, 1800–1916, Las Vegas, N.M., 1848–1851, reel 602.

4. Burnside to F. Burt, October 3, 1853, box 1, AEBP.

5. Poore, *Life of Burnside*, 64–65; Cullum, *Biographical Register*, 2:318.

6. Returns from Regular Army Artillery Regiments, reels 19, 20.

7. Smith, "Oxford Spy," Union County Public Library, 3–4; Poore, *Life of Burnside*, 73–74. Lottie Moon's exploits seem to be largely of her own invention, and many of her accounts of Civil War activities defy logistical possibility or social probability: see, for instance, Marsh and Marsh, "Ballad of Lottie Moon." The origin of the altar episode appears to be Poore's gravestone biography; it is not unreasonable to suppose that Lottie Moon herself—then living in New York and engaged in writing—responded to Poore's appeal for information about the general's life with her imaginative recollection.

8. Poore, *Life of Burnside*, 60–64; Returns from Regular Army Artillery Regiments, reel 20.

9. Burnside to F. Burt, October 3, 1853, A. W. Reynolds to Thomas S. Jesup, December 30, 1853, and W. H. S. Taylor to Burnside, September 18, 1856, all in box 1, AEBP; Report of J. M. Brodhead, U.S. Comptroller, June 4, 1863, box labeled "Official Q.M. Papers," RIHS Papers. Captain Reynolds won reinstatement to the army in 1857, after Buchanan took office, but he went over to the Confederates when Texas seceded, apparently without the formality of a resignation. Elected colonel of the 50th Virginia, he was captured at Vicksburg and ended the war as a sidelined brigadier commanding Athens, Ga. See Report of J. M. Brodhead, just cited, and Confederate Compiled Service Records, General and Staff Officers and Nonregimental Enlisted Men, reel 209.

10. Poore, *Life of Burnside*, 77–78; Edwards, *Civil War Guns*, 114–15.

11. Poore, *Life of Burnside*, 78–82.

12. Burnside to George B. McClellan, May 4, 1858, reel 5, McClellan Papers; Cullum, *Biographical Register*, 2:318; promissory note to Bristol Fire Arms Co. from A. Van Valkenburgh & Co., dated July 9, 1856, with endorsement of Mechanics Bank, New York, indicating payment was refused, January 12, 1857, and undated bankruptcy offer of A. Van Valkenburgh to Bristol Fire Arms Co., all in box 22, AEBP.

13. Patent certificate dated March 25, 1857, and design dated April 28, 1858, Burnside Collection, Special Collections, USMA Library.

14. Burnside to McClellan, May 4, 1858, and McClellan to Ellen Marcy, undated (but 1859), reel 5, McClellan Papers.

15. Woodbury, *Ninth Army Corps*, 10; Cullum, *Biographical Register*, 2: 318–19; Burnside to McClellan, June 14, 1860, reel 5, McClellan Papers; Nathaniel Bishop tombstone, Swan Point Cemetery, Providence, R.I.

16. Woodbury, *Ninth Army Corps*, 13–14; Poore, *Life of Burnside*, 93–95; Stone, *Rhode Island in the Rebellion*, 283.

17. Woodbury, *First Rhode Island*, 26, 51–52; Stone, *Rhode Island in the Rebellion*, 286; Poore, *Life of Burnside*, 98–101; *Register of Officers and Cadets* (1844), 4.

18. Woodbury, *First Rhode Island*, 52, 57, 59; *OR* 2:689, 691, 715.

19. Fitz John Porter to McClellan, April 15, 1861, reel 5, McClellan Papers.

II

1. Rhodes, *All for the Union*, 17, 30; *OR* 2:734.

2. Rhodes, *All for the Union*, 21–22; Woodbury, *First Rhode Island*, 70; *OR* 2:330, 393, 397.

3. Boatner, *Civil War Dictionary*, 418–19; *OR* 2:383.

4. Rhodes, *All for the Union*, 39–40; Haynes, *Second New Hampshire*, 7–8.

5. Haynes, *Second New Hampshire*, 19–20; *Providence Evening Press*, July 17, 1861.

6. Haynes, *Second New Hampshire*, 20–21, 24–25; Woodbury, *First Rhode Island*, 79–81.

7. Haynes, *Second New Hampshire*, 21–22; *OR* 2:312–14, 743–44. A New York soldier in Andrew Porter's brigade remembered being allowed to forage liberally at Fairfax; another New Yorker in Tyler's division attributed the destruction of Germantown to the 2nd Wisconsin. See Fairfield, *27th N.Y.*, 10, and Meagher, *Last Days of the 69th*, 6. Burnside's respect for private property became famous, especially among Southerners. It was therefore sad that, while Burnside was preoccupied with a tactical nightmare at Fredericksburg, troops under him conducted the most memorable pillage of the war—aside from Sherman's rampage in Georgia and the Carolinas.

8. *OR* 2:308, 318, 324, 329–31; *CCW* 2:39; Eckert and Amato, *Ten Years in the Saddle*, 293.

9. Haynes, *Second New Hampshire*, 22; *OR* 2:326, 348, 362. One of Andrew Porter's staff officers, riding behind Burnside's brigade, tried to blame Burnside for Tyler's delay, later citing it alongside another delay popularly—and incorrectly—attributed to Burnside, at Antietam. See Eckert and Amato, *Ten Years in the Saddle*, 295.

10. Woodbury, *First Rhode Island*, 88–89; *OR* 2:331, and 51(1):23; Haynes, *Second New Hampshire*, 23–24; *CCW* 2:161.

11. Woodbury, *Second Rhode Island*, 31; Haynes, *Second New Hampshire*, 24; *OR* 2:319, 558–59; Eckert and Amato, *Ten Years in the Saddle*, 295; E. P. Alexander, *Memoirs*, 30.

12. *OR* 2:319, 395–96, 559, 563; Rhodes, *All for the Union*, 36. One witness has Hunter riding in a carriage because of lameness (Woodbury, *Second Rhode Island*, 31).

13. Woodbury, *Second Rhode Island*, 34–35; *OR* 2:396, 559; Eckert and Amato, *Ten Years in the Saddle*, 297; Carter, *Four Brothers in Blue*, 11; Muster Roll of Company D, 11th Mississippi.

14. Fairfield, *27th N.Y.*, 12, 15; *OR* 2:389. The uniform of the 11th Mississippi is depicted in the photographs of two original recruits in *CV*, April, 1899, 180.

15. *OR* 2:319, 559.

16. Roelker, "Letters of William Ames," 13–14; *OR* 2:396, 401; Haynes, *Second New Hampshire*, 31–32.

17. *OR* 2:393, 396–97, 401–3; Haynes, *Second New Hampshire*, 32–34.

18. *OR* 2:397; Rhodes, *All for the Union*, 34; Haynes, *Second New Hampshire*, 37; Woodbury, *Second Rhode Island*, 36–38.

19. *OR* 2:397.

20. Rhodes, *All for the Union*, 34–35; Woodbury, *First Rhode Island*, 138–40.

21. *OR* 2:360, 376–77, 385, 387, 398-99, 428; *B&L* 1:194. In a letter written only three days after the battle, one enlisted man in the 2nd Rhode Island corroborated Burnside's account of forming to cover the retreat of the army. Corporal Samuel English told his mother how "the R.I. regiments, the New York 71st and the New Hampshire 2nd were drawn into a line to cover the retreat" but added that a panicky officer alarmed the troops, who finally fled in perfect confusion. The letter is published in Rhodes, *All for the Union*, 34. Oddly enough, Burnside granted Porter the fact that he rose naturally to command of the division "by virtue of your superior rank" (*OR* 2:398), yet Burnside seems to have ranked Porter by several days. Burnside's commission as colonel ought to have dated from the mustering ceremony of May 2, while Porter's appointment as colonel of the 16th U.S. Infantry came on May 14. Porter was promoted to brigadier general, to rank from May 17, but that date of rank was retroactive, and he did not assume his new role until sometime after Bull Run. See Boatner, *Civil War Dictionary*, 661. Even Burnside's note of apology and explanation, written August 3, is addressed to Porter as "Colonel" (*OR* 2:398).

III

1. McClellan, *Own Story*, 66; *B&L* 1:660; William Sprague to McClellan, August 2, 1861, reel 5, McClellan Papers.

2. *B&L* 1:660.

3. McClellan, *Own Story*, 87.

4. Returns from Regular Army Artillery Regiments, reel 20; *OR* 5:35; *B&L* 1:632–34, 660, 673. By 1880 Burnside remembered this interview was in October (*B&L* 1:660), but in March of 1863 he testified it was in early September

(*CCW* 3:333). Correspondence (*OR* 5:36) agrees. Burnside was in New York on the project as early as September 20. See Burnside to Seth Williams, September 20, 1861, reel 5, McClellan Papers.

5. *B&L* 1:660–61; Poore, *Life of Burnside*, 124; *OR*, ser. 3, 1:535–36, 551, 553–54, 562; R. Cornell White to Burnside, July 21, 1862, box 2, AEBP; Burnside to Randolph Marcy, October 26 and November 6, 1861, reel 13, McClellan Papers; D. R. Larned to "My Dear Sister," August 18, 1862, Larned Papers.

6. J. Baldwin Taft to Burnside, December 7, 1861, box 5, AEBP. Flag Officer Louis M. Goldsborough testified that, until his intervention in November, 1861, Burnside's command was intended for use on the York River (*CCW* 1:631).

7. *OR* 4:608, 611–12, 623–24; *B&L* 1:639–40. It was probably no coincidence that, except for a brevet after the fact, Hawkins never did become a brigadier general.

8. *OR* 4:609.

9. *New York Times*, November 8 and December 3, 1861.

10. *CCW* 1:631; *ORN* 6:421–22.

11. *New York Times*, November 9, 1861; Benjamin F. Burnside to AEB, October 6, 1861, box 22, AEBP; Burnside to McClellan, June 14, 1860, reel 5, McClellan Papers.

12. Benjamin F. Burnside to AEB, August 27, October 6, and November 20, 1861, and March 2, 1862, AEB to Benjamin F. Burnside, February 1, 1862, and Benjamin F. Burnside's recommendations and notice of termination, February 1, 1862, signed by W. W. Waters et al., all in box 1, AEBP; L. Eastabrook to Benjamin F. Burnside, September 17 and October 14, 1861, box labeled "Official Q.M. Papers," RIHS Papers.

13. Benjamin F. Burnside to AEB, March 2, 1862, box 1, Andrew Burnside to AEB, November 10, 1862, and Edward D. Burnside to AEB, November 12, 1862, with AEB's endorsement, box 3, and AEB to James O. P. Burnside, January 16, 1865, box 21, AEBP.

14. *New York Times*, November 22 and 23, 1861.

15. Burnside to Seth Williams, November 19, 1861, reel 13, McClellan Papers; Boatner, *Civil War Dictionary*, 301–2, 618–19, 691.

16. Burnside to Randolph Marcy, December 3, 1861, and to Seth Williams, December 7, 1861, reel 13, McClellan Papers.

17. Burnside to Seth Williams, December 16 and 24, 1861, reel 14, McClellan Papers; *OR* 4:704; D. W. Mitchell to Burnside, January 2, 1862, and George W. Cullum to Burnside, January 6, 1862, box 1, AEBP; Poore, *Life of Burnside*, 271–72. During the summer of 1861, Burnside tried to discourage his old friend Buckner from his course with the Confederacy, even interceding with President Lincoln to earn the promise of a commission, but Buckner still joined the Confederate army when Kentucky's neutrality was violated. See Perry, "Buckner and McClellan," 296–97.

18. Richmond, *The Richmond Family*, 361; *Souvenir of Gen. Lewis Richmond*, 9.

19. Learned, *The Learned Family*, 214; Henry Howe to D. R. Larned, December 9, 1861, Larned Papers; Stephen G. Hubbard and John Woodruff to Burnside, December 9, 1861, box 1, AEBP.

20. Burnside to Seth Williams, December 11, 1861, reel 14, McClellan Papers; *New York Times*, December 10, 1861; Thomas Nixon to Burnside, January 8, 1862, box 1, AEBP.

21. Burnside to Seth Williams, December 16, 1861, reel 14, McClellan Papers; D. R. Larned to "Dear Henry," December 18, 21, and 27, 1861, Larned Papers; Burnside's hotel bill, January 8, 1862, box 5, and sundry petitions from applicants and contractors, box 1, AEBP.

22. *New York Times*, December 30, 1861; *ORN* 4:489, 493–94, 500; D. R. Larned to "Dear Henry," December 27, 1861, and to "My Dear Sister," January 3, 1862, Larned Papers.

CHAPTER TWO

I

1. *B&L* 1:661–62; Traver, *Battles of Roanoke*, 8.

2. *B&L* 1:661–62; J. R. Magruder to Burnside, January 9, 1862, Thomas J. White to Burnside, January 9, 1862, and Ezra Sheckell to Burnside, January 16, 1862, box 1, AEBP.

3. Roe, *Twenty-fourth Massachusetts*, 42; *B&L* 1:663.

4. *OR* 4:717; *B&L* 1:662.

5. *OR* 9:352–53. As consistently as possible, place names will be rendered as they were most commonly spelled during the Civil War, hence Newbern, Goldsborough, etc. It was not until 1891 that a city official persuaded the Geographic Branch of the Department of the Interior to accept *Newbern* as the appropriate spelling of his community's name, but even before the end of the century the North Carolina general assembly undid his labor by adopting the present spelling, *New Bern*. See Watson, *History of New Bern*, xiv. In either case, the verbal emphasis is upon the first syllable.

6. *B&L* 1:662; Burnside's hotel bill for December 19, 1861, through January 8, 1862, box 5, AEBP; *OR* 4:576.

7. *B&L* 1:663.

8. Gangewer diary, January 9, 1862.

9. Draper, *Recollections*, 43–47; *B&L* 1:662; William F. Draper to George Draper, January 12, 1862, Draper Papers; Roe, *Twenty-fourth Massachusetts*, 46.

10. *B&L* 1:663–64.

11. Ibid., 664.

12. Stick, *The Outer Banks*, 89, 296; Jackman, *Sixth New Hampshire*, 28; Burnside to Randolph Marcy, November 26, 1861, reel 13, McClellan Papers; Traver, *Battles of Roanoke*, 10. A 1989 conversation with the harbormaster at

the Ocracoke end of the Hatteras ferry indicated the name "Swash" has been applied to several nearby inlets over the past couple of centuries, including Hatteras Inlet, the eighteenth-century channel closed by the British wreck, and Portsmouth Inlet, below Ocracoke Island.

13. Oliver S. Coolidge to his father and sister, January 15–17 and 21–22, 1862, Coolidge Papers, Duke University, cited in Sauers, "Burnside's Campaign," 132, 136.

14. *OR* 9:108; Draper, *Recollections*, 47–50; William F. Draper to Lydia Joy, January 28, 1862, Draper Papers. A man Burnside sent back to Washington learned that the party responsible for the inaccurate tales of drowned men was "our friend Rawlings," who remains otherwise unidentified. See F. Sheldon to Burnside, February 2, 1862, box 1, AEBP.

15. *B&L* 1:665; *OR* 9:355–57.

16. *OR* 9:355; *B&L* 1:666; Newbern *Daily Progress*, January 27 and 29, 1862.

17. *OR* 9:354–56; F. Sheldon to Burnside, February 2, 1862, box 1, AEBP; *Providence Journal*, August 5, 1862. Burnside commented to Daniel Larned during the brutal spring campaign of 1864 that he still regarded the dismal days at Hatteras as his worst of the war (Larned to "My Dear Sister," June 9, 1864, Larned Papers).

18. *OR* 9:356–57; Newbern *Daily Progress*, January 27 and 29, 1862; *B&L* 1: 665.

19. Stick, *The Outer Banks*, 89, 295; Roe, *Twenty-fourth Massachusetts*, 47–49.

20. Roe, *Twenty-fourth Massachusetts*, 46.

21. *OR* 9:75, 359; *ORN* 6:537; Draper, *Recollections*, 50.

22. Wise, *End of an Era*, 3, 27, 38, 48–50; *OR* 9:127–29, 150.

23. *OR* 9:128, 132–35, 143.

24. Ibid., 129; *ORN* 6:594–96.

25. *OR* 9:75, 81; *ORN* 6:551–52; Draper, *Recollections*, 52.

26. *OR* 9:76, 176; *ORN* 6:594–96; Burlingame, *Fifth Rhode Island*, 20; Barney, *First Three Months in the Army*, 25–26. The colonel of the 31st North Carolina, in charge of the Confederate pickets, inflated the boat's party to "about fifteen men," of whom he claimed his men killed 3 and wounded 1: *OR* 9: 176. Total naval casualties on the Union side at Roanoke numbered only 14, of whom only 3 were killed; Confederate losses of 143 killed, wounded, and missing were almost entirely accumulated in the land battle of February 8. See *OR* 9:173 and *ORN* 6:554, 581.

27. *OR* 9:76, 86, 97; Seagrave diary, February 7, 1862; Robertson, "Roanoke Island Expedition," 340. Description of the Ashby cabin is from Draper, *Recollections*, 54.

28. *OR* 9:81, 151, 171–77; Wise, *End of an Era*, 181–82; Sauers, "Laurels for Burnside," 21; Gangewer diary, February 11, 1862.

29. *OR* 9:80, 86, 98.

30. Welch, *Burnside Expedition*, 38. The modern road from Ashby's Harbor runs parallel to the wartime track, but a little east of it, and is thus a bit longer at 1.2 miles.

31. Foster saw "about 2000 men." Shaw's entire force at the 3-gun battery consisted of 2 companies of the 46th and 8 of the 59th Virginia, about 450 strong together; 8 companies of the 31st North Carolina, perhaps 370 men; and Company B, 8th North Carolina, with as many as 60 muskets. By the end of the assault here Foster had all of his brigade save the 24th Massachusetts and 1 company of the 27th, all of Reno's brigade, and the 4th Rhode Island and 9th New York, of Parke's—for a total of perhaps 7,000 men (*OR* 9:86, 174–77, 180, 358). Burnside thought he landed 7,000–7,500 men altogether (*CCW* 3:337).

32. Emmerton, *Twenty-third Mass.*, 49.

33. Avery, *The Marine Artillery*, 6, 9.

34. *OR* 9:86–87, 98, 106, 172; Emmerton, *Twenty-third Mass.*, 50; Drake, *Ninth New Jersey*, 44–46; Traver, *Battles of Roanoke*, 24; *B&L* 1:643–44. The 9th New York later took great credit for storming the battery, but it seems Reno's men had already cleared the barricade before they attacked. Sauers devotes an entire appendix to this controversy in his dissertation, 572–84, and points out that the zouaves' light casualties (seventeen wounded) do not testify to the desperation of their charge.

35. *OR* 9:87, 99.

36. D. R. Larned to "Dear Henry," February 9, 1862, Larned Papers.

37. *OR* 9:93, 107, 109, 141.

38. Ibid., 362; J. Hal Elliott to Burnside, February 22, 1862, and A. Sinclair Flandrall to Burnside, February 13, 1862, box 1, AEBP.

39. Pollard, *The Lost Cause*, 212–13; Newbern *Daily Progress*, February 11, 1862; Jones, *War Clerk's Diary*, 66.

40. *OR* 9:74.

II

1. Hawkins's Report, dated February 11, 1862, is in box 1, AEBP.

2. Wise to Burnside, February 11, 1862, and Burnside to Wise, February 12, 1862, box 1, AEBP; *OR*, ser. 2, 1:51, 166–67.

3. D. R. Larned to "My Dear Sister," May 15, 1862, Larned Papers; *OR*, ser. 2, 2:184–85.

4. Roe, *Twenty-fourth Massachusetts*, 70–72.

5. *OR* 9:160–61, 193–96; *B&L* 1:646–47. There must have been a certain Unionist population in the vicinity, for on February 12 the colonel of the 59th Virginia wrote from Winton that "there are, of course, some traitors," one of whom was killed by the men of that regiment while fighting them from within his home at Newby's Bridge (*OR* 9:192). Hawkins, who had been so sure of great Union sentiment the previous September, later tried to claim he never

believed in the tale of Winton loyalists, though that spring he himself met with a group of 250 such loyalists only forty miles away. See *OR* 4:607–9 and *B&L* 1: 646, 659.

6. Alfred Holcomb to "Dear Father and Mother," February 13, 1862, Holcomb Letters.

7. *ORN* 6:656–57; Barney, *First Three Months in the Army*, 30; *OR* 9:194.

8. Draper, *Recollections*, 59.

9. *OR* 9:110, 161.

10. Ibid., 241–43, 424.

11. Chase, *Battery F, First Rhode Island*, 20–22; Burlingame, *Fifth Rhode Island*, 30; *OR* 9:369. The original of Thomas's March 10 dispatch is in box 23, AEBP, and the naval signals are penciled on the reverse of that sheet.

12. Seagrave diary, March 11, 1862; Jackman, *Sixth New Hampshire*, 35.

13. Seagrave diary, March 11, 1862; Burlingame, *Fifth Rhode Island*, 30–31; Niles diary, March 9, 1862; *OR* 9:261.

14. *OR* 9:201; J. F. Farnsworth's and Henry Wilson's recommendations, Seth Williams to Burnside, February 3, 1862, and H. H. Helper to Burnside, April 22, 1862, all in box 1, AEBP. After the war Harvey Hogan Helper published a reconstruction newspaper in Raleigh (Bailey, *Helper*, 199).

15. Sinclair departed Fisher's Landing about 1:00 P.M.; the last of the Union troops landed at Slocum's Creek about 2:00, and none are reported to have been put ashore at Fisher's Landing. See the reports of Branch, Colonel Sinclair, and Captain Robert Williamson, *OR* 9:242–43, 262, and 208, respectively. The trouble with the 35th North Carolina was chiefly in its colonel. Less than six weeks later Sinclair was defeated for reelection to that office because of his poor performance (Jordan and Manarin, *North Carolina Troops*, 9:354, 358), and seven decades afterward a centenarian Confederate veteran still scorned his former commander: "I did not think much of it when he left us exposed to danger and found a safe place for himself," he told one listener (statement of Daniel Franklin Aman, aged 103, *CV*, September 1930, 339).

16. Draper, *Recollections*, 60; Roe, *Twenty-fourth Massachusetts*, 78–80; *Philadelphia Weekly Press*, September 1, 1886, cited in Sauers, "Burnside's Campaign," 293.

17. Emmerton, *Twenty-third Mass.*, 62–63; Parker, *51st Regiment*, 99–102.

18. Parker, *51st Regiment*, 99.

19. Burlingame, *Fifth Rhode Island*, 31; Niles diary, March 13, 1862.

20. Burlingame, *Fifth Rhode Island*, 32; Parker, *51st Regiment*, 99; Draper, *Recollections*, 60.

21. Draper, *Recollections*, 60; Burlingame, *Fifth Rhode Island*, 32.

22. *OR* 9:201–2, 208.

23. Parker, *51st Regiment*, 102–3; Emmerton, *Twenty-third Mass.*, 63.

24. Burlingame, *Fifth Rhode Island*, 34; Gangewer diary, January 31, 1862; *OR* 9:202.

25. *OR* 9:246–48; Crawford, *Fort Sumter*, 450, 452. Crawford erroneously supposed that Meade died in July of 1861.

26. *OR* 9:202–3, 205, 212, 224; Emmerton, *Twenty-third Mass.*, 63–64.

27. *OR* 9:212–13, 242.

28. *ORN* 7:117–18; Burlingame, *Fifth Rhode Island*, 38.

29. Parker, *51st Regiment*, 103–4; *OR* 9:224–25.

30. *OR* 9:225–26, 267.

31. Ibid., 203, 221, 226.

32. Burlingame, *Fifth Rhode Island*, 36; *OR* 9:234.

33. Henry C. Heisler to "Dear Sister," March 24, 1862, Heisler Papers; *OR* 9:204, 213, 234, 248.

34. Roe, *Twenty-fourth Massachusetts*, 86; *OR* 9:213.

35. *OR* 9:204, 221, 260; Barney, *First Three Months in the Army*, 41–42; Parker, *51st Regiment*, 106–7.

36. Roe, *Twenty-fourth Massachusetts*, 86–87; *ORN* 7:109.

37. Roe, *Twenty-fourth Massachusetts*, 87.

38. *OR* 9:204, 235.

39. Ibid., 204; *ORN* 7:109; Sprague, "Burnside Expedition," 441.

40. D. R. Larned to Mrs. A. E. Burnside, March 23 and 25, 1862, Larned Papers.

41. Sauers, "Burnside's Campaign," 289, 301, credits Branch with about 4,000 men and Burnside with 10,000. Commander Rowan officially calculated 7,500 enemy troops, allowing for 11,500 Union soldiers, commenting the fortified Confederates should have whipped the Yankees "out of their boots" (*ORN* 7:118). Sauers's figures may be more accurate, though Burnside himself estimated he had only about 7,500 men ashore at Newbern when congressmen asked him about it one year later (*CCW* 3:334, 337). Branch lost 165 killed and wounded, and 413 captured or missing; Burnside's casualties totaled 471, all but one of whom were killed or wounded (*OR* 9:211, 247).

III

1. O. W. Holmes to Burnside, March 30, 1862, Jennie M. Wilson et al. to Burnside, March 31, 1862, John Stover to Burnside, March 20, 1862, and Official Resolution of the R.I. General Assembly, April 16, 1862, box 1, AEBP.

2. Draper, *Recollections*, 62, 66–67.

3. Seagrave diary, March 15, 1862; *OR* 9:199–200.

4. *OR* 9:207, 369–70, 373; Lorenzo Thomas to Burnside, March 15, 1862, box 1, AEBP.

5. Garnett, "Cruise of the Nashville," 331–32; *ORN* 7:138.

6. *OR* 9:281–82, 293; Draper, *Recollections*, 69.

7. *OR* 9:200, 370.

8. Niles diary, March 18, 1862; *OR* 9:269, 372–73; William McKinley to "Dear

Wife," March 23, 1862, McKinley Collection; D. R. Larned to "My Dear Sister," March 24, 1862, Larned Papers.

9. *OR* 9:296–97; Burnside to Hawkins, March 22, 1862, marked "Not sent," letterbook labeled "March–June, 1862," RIHS Papers.

10. D. R. Larned to Mrs. A. E. Burnside, March 23, 1862, and to Henry A. Howe, March 31, 1862, Larned Papers; Green, *New Bern Album*, 37; Cox, *Reminiscences*, 1:451–52.

11. *Newbern Progress*, April 9, 1862; D. R. Larned to "My Dear Helen," April 7, 1862, Larned Papers.

12. *OR* 9:375, 381.

13. Chase, *Battery F, First Rhode Island*, 27–28; *OR* 9:332.

14. *OR* 9:375, 384; copy of Surgeon J. H. Thompson's dismissal, Larned Papers. Fourteen months later, Burnside recommended the penitent doctor for reinstatement (Burnside to Edwin M. Stanton, June 12, 1863, box 8, AEBP).

15. *OR* 9:453–55.

16. D. R. Larned to Henry A. Howe, March 31 and April 2, 1862, Larned Papers; *OR* 9:295–334.

17. *OR* 9:305, 376–77; *OR Atlas*, plates CXXXVII and CXXXVIII.

18. Years later Hawkins said he was led astray by a treacherous guide, whom he ordered taken into the woods and shot. He made no mention of such a guide in his official reports, offering no excuse whatever for his delay. Reno referred to "the treachery or incompetency" of Hawkins's guide, but said nothing of any execution. Confederate General Huger, however, wrote Robert E. Lee of a member of the North Carolina militia who was forced to guide the South Mills expedition; that militiaman escaped during the "confusion" of the landing below Elizabeth City, Huger said. If that man was the treacherous guide, Hawkins bore the responsibility both for letting him escape and, afterward, for losing his own way. The story of duplicity and execution fits into a pattern of fanciful recollections that grace Hawkins's later writings. See *B&L* 1:655–56; *OR* 9: 305, 309–11, 313–15, 464.

19. *OR* 9:305–7; *B&L* 1:655–66.

20. *OR* 9:307, 309–11, 316–17. Hawkins, whom Reno nevertheless praised for exceptional personal bravery, appears to have made the unadvisable charge in a desperate effort to redeem himself and, perhaps, to steal the glory from Reno's troops, who had done most of the fighting.

21. Ibid., 306.

22. Ibid., 326, 374, 377–79, 466–67, 470; Jackman, *Sixth New Hampshire*, 48. The navy did succeed in blocking part of the Albemarle and Chesapeake Canal (*ORN* 7:277).

23. D. R. Larned to "My Dear Sister," April 22, 1862, Larned Papers.

24. *OR* 9:284–85, 294.

25. D. R. Larned to "My Dear Sister," April "22" and May 15, 1862, Larned Papers.

26. William Phillips to Burnside, January 2, 1862, Hannah Gill to Burnside,

May 27, 1862, both in box 1, Marie L. Willcox to Burnside, June 4, 1862, and Jane C. Kingsbury and John Cunningham to Burnside, July 1, 1862, all in box 2, AEBP.

27. R. B. Marcy to Burnside, April 14, 1862, box 1, AEBP; *OR* 9:273–75, 376–80, 389; McClellan, *Own Story*, 245. One sick private could not even get a convalescent furlough because an attack was expected daily and every man might be needed (Henry C. Heisler to "Dear Sister," May 2, 1862, Heisler Papers).

28. Wise, *End of an Era*, 210; *OR* 9:388.

29. *OR* 9:380–81, 389.

30. Ibid., 377, 379, 384, 388–91; D. R. Larned to "My Dear Sister," May 18, 1862, Larned Papers. Burnside was extremely solicitous of his sick and wounded men and frequently visited the hospitals. After the battle of Newbern he met John Hope, a Massachusetts soldier wounded in the leg, who remembered the general from his days in Burnside's artillery company, during the Mexican War. Burnside dug into his own pocket for ten dollars, so Hope might supplement his diet with fresh fruit and vegetables, and gave him another five when he sailed for home. See Charles Reed to Burnside, April 8, 1863, box 6, AEBP. He also played host to the mother of one of Reno's dead, who came down to recover her son's body, and donated ten dollars to start a purse for her (*Newbern Progress*, May 29, 1862).

31. *OR* 9:380, 396–97; Green, *New Bern Album*, 54; Sauers, "Burnside's Campaign," 509, 511; Brown, *Edward Stanly*, 206–7.

32. *OR* 9:394; Woodbury, *Ambrose Everett Burnside*, 16; Cox, *Reminiscences*, 1:356–57.

33. *Newbern Progress*, April 5, 1862; *OR* 9:395–96, 399–402; Colyer to Burnside, May 31, 1862, box 1, Burnside to Stanly, January 16, 1865, and Burnside to Colyer, January 25, 1865, box 20, AEBP.

34. *OR* 9:394, 398; D. R. Larned journal, June 21, 1862, Larned Papers.

35. *OR* 9:398–99; Nevins and Thomas, *Diary of Strong*, 3:230.

36. *OR* 9:398–99, 404; McClellan, *Own Story*, 403; D. R. Larned to "My Dear Sister," June 11 and 16, 1862, Larned Papers.

37. D. R. Larned to "My Dear Sister," June 16, 1862, Larned Papers; Burnside to McClellan, June 13, 1862, reel 25, McClellan Papers. While Burnside did not invent his tonsorial style, he made it popular with scores of officers under his command, including Generals Foster and Parke, Colonels Stevenson and Osborn of the 24th Massachusetts, and his assistant adjutant general, Lewis Richmond.

38. Woodbury, *Ambrose Everett Burnside*, 25; Stone, *Rhode Island in the Rebellion*, 310; *Newbern Progress*, June 21, 1862; D. R. Larned to "Dear Sister," June 16, 1862, Larned Papers. A few days later Burnside received a pair of slippers from Mr. Larned's sister. He showed them to General Parke, asking him if he didn't wish he were a major general so he could have such nice slippers. Parke replied he would be glad to take the slippers as a brigadier

but he would be damned if he would have any sword presentations, whereupon Burnside slapped him on the head with the slippers. See D. R. Larned to "My own darling Sister," June 20, 1862, Larned Papers.

39. *B&L* 1:665.

40. *OR* 9:81–83, 109, 172, 211, 241–47, 358.

CHAPTER THREE

I

1. *OR* 9:385, 409; Roe, *Twenty-fourth Massachusetts*, 130; Barrett, *Civil War in North Carolina*, 128.

2. *OR* 9:404–7; Jackman, *Sixth New Hampshire*, 52–53.

3. *OR* 9:405, and 11(3):322; Loving, *Letters of George Washington Whitman*, 58–59.

4. D. R. Larned to "My Dear Sister," July 16, 1862, Larned Papers; Poore, *Life of Burnside*, 154.

5. D. R. Larned to "My Dear Sister," July "21" (25?), 1862, Larned Papers; McClellan, *Own Story*, 449; *CCW* 1:637–39; *OR* 11(3):337–38.

6. *CCW* 1:650. The exact date Burnside was first offered command of the army has never been determined, but his visits to Washington just before and just after the Harrison's Landing conference are generally accepted as the two most likely occasions. Manuscripts recently published seem to point to the latter stop in the capital, July 26 and 27. See Sears, *Papers of McClellan*, 376–78, wherein he cites McClellan's July 30 letters to Samuel Barlow and Mrs. McClellan; in these McClellan reveals he was apprised that day of the Burnside offer, speaking of having "positive information" and saying "the command was for two days persistently pressed upon" Burnside. The positive source was doubtless Burnside himself, relaying the news through an intermediary, and his return to Fort Monroe about July 28 would have allowed McClellan to hear of it by July 29 or 30. Had the offer been made just before the generals set out for Harrison's Landing, Burnside would probably have told his friend during that meeting. In his testimony to the Committee on the Conduct of the War (*CCW* 1:638–39), Burnside said Halleck was ready to renege on his promise to McClellan as soon as they reached Washington, yet it was not until August 3 that Halleck notified McClellan he would have to come back from the Peninsula; what prompted him to delay so long was, perhaps, Burnside's refusal to take control of the army. Burnside spoke only that once about the offer, and he did that reluctantly (*CCW* 1:650).

7. *OR* 11(3):337–38, 346, and 12(3):473–74; John P. Hatch to his father, August 9, 1862, Hatch Papers; Sparks, *Inside Lincoln's Army*, 116–17.

8. *OR* 11(1):80–81, and 12(2):5; *CCW* 1:452; Barrett, *Civil War in North Carolina*, 128–29.

9. *OR* 11(3):333, and 12(3):524; D. R. Larned to "Dear Henry," August 2, 1862, Larned Papers.

10. Jackman, *Sixth New Hampshire*, 62; Maury, *Recollections*, 73–75. There emerged a postwar story that the wedding party of young officers trod Marye's Heights during a visit to Fredericksburg, concluding unanimously that 20,000 men could have held the position against any force that might assail it (Hopkins, *Seventh Rhode Island*, 56). The tale is hardly credible, for several reasons: Marye's Heights was then an obscure and uninteresting spot, and the wedding guests were lodged in the opposite direction from Fredericksburg, leaving little reason for them ever to have gone there; the anecdote also reflects all too conveniently on Burnside's 1862 assault; and, given the military thinking and the ordnance of the day, the heights would have been deemed even more susceptible to a grand infantry assault in the 1840s than in the 1860s, when it was still not considered necessarily foolhardy—until, of course, after the attempt had failed. I am indebted to Robert K. Krick, chief historian at Fredericksburg and Spotsylvania National Military Park, for introducing me to the Maury connection and the tale from Hopkins.

11. D. R. Larned to "Dear Henry," August 7, 1862, Larned Papers.

12. Townsend, *Rustics in Rebellion*, 224–32; George H. Allen, *Forty-six Months*, 124–25; George E. Bates to "Dear Cousin Albert," August 11, 1862, Marvel Collection.

13. John P. Hatch to his father, August 9, 1862, Hatch Papers.

14. *OR* 12(3):565–66, 569.

15. Ibid., 566, 569; Walcott, *Twenty-first Massachusetts*, 126–27; Burnside to Halleck, August 13, 1862, box 2, AEBP.

16. Eby, *A Virginia Yankee*, 70, 72–73; Walcott, *Twenty-first Massachusetts*, 127; *OR* 12(3):571.

17. *OR* 2:753, and 12(3):572; D. R. Larned to "Dear A(melia)," August 15, 1862, and to "My Dear Sister," August 18, 1862, Larned Papers.

18. D. R. Larned to "Dear A(melia)," August 15, 1862, and to "My Dear Sister," August 18, 1862, Larned Papers.

19. D. R. Larned to Mrs. Burnside, August 19, 1862, Larned Papers; *OR* 12(3):590.

20. *OR* 12(3):594, and 12(2), supplement:938; Weld, *War Diary*, 129. Even President Lincoln worried about Porter's influence with McClellan. See *OR* 11(3):154.

21. D. R. Larned to "My Dear Sister," August 25, 1862, and to "Dear Henry," August 26, 1862, Larned Papers; *OR* 12(3):660.

22. *OR* 12(2), supplement:1003.

23. Ibid., and 12(3):661, 699–700, 732–33.

24. Jackman, *Sixth New Hampshire*, 78–84; Walcott, *Twenty-first Massachusetts*, 142–44; *OR* 12(3):734–36.

25. *OR* 12(3):731–33, 957–58. Even junior officers and enlisted men in the

Ninth Corps were appalled at the "accursed jealousy toward brother soldiers" rampant in the Army of the Potomac, the more so because of the cordiality and affection existing between most of the officers of their own corps, "all owing to the magnanimous and open-hearted spirit with which our general had administered his command." See Walcott, *Twenty-first Massachusetts*, 124.

26. *OR* 12(3):724, 732–33, 758.

27. Ibid., 774, 994; Poore, *Life of Burnside*, 158; Welles, *Diary*, 1:91.

28. Walcott, *Twenty-first Massachusetts*, 163–66.

29. Pope testified at Porter's court-martial that he challenged Porter about the Burnside dispatches the night of September 2, and until now that statement has not been contradicted; see *OR* 12(2), supplement:838–40. I am grateful to Stephen Sears, however, for pointing out that Pope's December testimony was mistaken, and that he probably referred to a letter Porter had written to Census Bureau official J. C. G. Kennedy in mid-July (reel 30, McClellan Papers). But during the court-martial Burnside mentioned warning Porter of his poison pen, and by the time Porter was notified of formal proceedings against him three days later, Pope knew of those dispatches, too. For Burnside's remark on Porter's tone, see *OR* 12(2), supplement:1003.

II

1. *OR* 12(3):799, 814–16, and 19(2):196–97; *CCW* 1:639.

2. *OR* 19(2):169.

3. Welles, *Diary*, 1:104–5, 110, 124; *CCW* 1:650.

4. Raymond, "Extracts," 423.

5. *OR* 19(1):416 and (2):198.

6. Boatner, *Civil War Dictionary*, 205, 707, 816, 926; Cox, *Reminiscences*, 1:264.

7. *OR* 19(2):290.

8. Lord, *Ninth New Hampshire*, 43–44; *Register of Officers and Cadets* (1844, 1845, 1846), 20–21, each volume; Cox, *Reminiscences*, 1:110.

9. Bailey diary, September 10–12, 1862.

10. Jackman, *Sixth New Hampshire*, 98; Walcott, *Twenty-first Massachusetts*, 187; Elmer Bragg to William L. Bragg, September 14, 1862, Bragg Collection; Spooner, *Maryland Campaign*, 12.

11. *OR* 19(1):178, 416, 822–23; *B&L* 2:583–84; Poore, *Life of Burnside*, 164; D. R. Larned to "Dear Sister," October 3, 1862, Larned Papers; Strother, "Recollections," 275–76.

12. *B&L* 2:603; Bloss, "Lost Dispatch," 84–86.

13. *OR* 19(2):603–4.

14. Ibid. (1):209, 417; Bailey diary, September 13, 1862; Strother, "Recollections," 277.

15. *B&L* 2:560; *OR* 19(1):53.

16. Sparks, *Inside Lincoln's Army*, 143; *B&L* 2:585.

17. Cox, *Reminiscences*, 1:280; *B&L* 2:585–86.

18. *B&L* 2:586–87; *CV*, January 1898, 27.

19. *OR* 19(1):428. McClellan refers to his easy marches in his October report in *OR* 19(1):26.

20. Cox, *Reminiscences*, 1:287; *OR* 19(1):214, 267, 417, 427–28; Robinson diary, September 14, 1862.

21. *OR* 19(1):50, 267, 417, 428–29; Cox, *Reminiscences*, 287–89; Sparks, *Inside Lincoln's Army*, 143. When McClellan wrote his final report the following August, after he had decided upon Burnside as the scapegoat for his failure in Maryland, he exercised the same passive voice employed by Hooker to create the illusion Burnside was a mere spectator. It is therefore not clear under what circumstances the order to Hooker was issued. In the 1880s, when Burnside was safely dead, McClellan boldly asserted that Burnside had had nothing to do with Hooker's orders, implying that the original idea had not even been his (*Own Story*, 582–83). Had that been so, McClellan would have certainly objected to Burnside's report of September 30, 1862, in which he took credit for the movement: McClellan saw the report, but did not object. McClellan's own father-in-law and chief of staff, Randolph Marcy, helps to corroborate that Burnside—rather than McClellan—directed the battle, for Marcy's messages to McClellan from the front describe the movements Burnside said he ordered, and these messages would have been unnecessary had McClellan been present. A note from Burnside to an obviously absent McClellan also announced "I have thrown Hooker's on the right." See undated correspondence (but September 14, 1862), reel 32, McClellan Papers. Meade's report referred to Burnside's personal direction of Hooker's divisions, but Hooker's did not. With his usual magnanimity, Burnside did not reveal Hooker's audacious hesitation until compelled to do so months later by the sheer insolence of Hooker's own report. See *OR* 19(1):213–16, 267, 417, 422–23. Finally, one of McClellan's staff noted that the headquarters group including McClellan did not even depart for the battlefield until about 2:00 P.M., after Hooker's arrival at Bolivar (Strother, "Recollections," 277).

22. At least one Confederate, the sergeant major of an Alabama regiment, surrendered voluntarily as Hooker advanced, and Burnside apparently interviewed him personally. The following March that deserter, then living in New York, asked Burnside for a corroborative letter, evidently so he could be excused from enrolling for the draft. Burnside's certification of the man's claim, dated March 18, "1862" (1863), is in box 1, AEBP.

23. *B&L* 2:572–77; Strother, "Recollections," 278.

24. *OR* 19(1):442, 460; Lord, *Ninth New Hampshire*, 74–76; Committee of the Regimental Association, *Thirty-fifth Massachusetts*, 28–30; Cox, *Reminiscences*, 1:291.

25. Cox, *Reminiscences*, 1:291; Eby, *A Virginia Yankee*, 107.

26. Strother, "Recollections," 278; McClellan, *Own Story*, 583; D. R. Larned to "Dear Henry," October 4, 1862, Larned Papers; Hammond, *Diary of a Union*

Lady, 179. The last source is the published diary of Maria Lydig Daly, whose brother, Philip Lydig, served on General Parke's staff and—by extension— on Burnside's. McClellan later used Burnside's supposed approbation of the Halleck telegram as evidence he did not consider his own participation worth mentioning, and he had the nerve to criticize his then-dead friend for not having approached as near the battle as the commanding general, when the most logical position for the commander of a divided wing was a point convenient to both halves. That point was Pleasonton's knoll: there Burnside was, and that was as close to the battle as McClellan himself came. See McClellan, *Own Story*, 583, and *OR* 19(2):289.

27. *OR* 19(1):53, and (2):290, 297, 420; Sears, *Landscape Turned Red*, 170– 71; McClellan, *Own Story*, 584, 616; Cox, *Reminiscences*, 1:381.

28. McClellan, *Own Story*, 584–86; Parke to Lorenzo Thomas, February 4, 1864, Letters Received by the Commission Branch of the Adjutant General's Office, reel 1.

29. Cox, *Reminiscences*, 1:297; *B&L* 2:558; Robinson diary, September 15, 1862; Elmer Bragg to Mrs. William L. Bragg, September 17, 1862, Bragg Collection; Walcott, *Twenty-first Massachusetts*, 194. Understandably, the exhausted Yankees did not dig very deep graves for their fallen foes: forty years later the skeletons of Confederate dead were still turning up under farmers' plows, and half a century after the fighting, battlefield visitors were still able to find human remains on the surface of the ground (*CV*, October, 1911, 484).

30. *OR* 19(2):296, and 51(1):837; Walcott, *Twenty-first Massachusetts*, 194; Cox, *Reminiscences*, 1:297.

31. McClellan, *Own Story*, 586; *OR* 19(2):308, and 51(1):837; Cox, *Reminiscences*, 1:298.

32. *OR* 19(1):53, 215, and 51(1):834; Burnside to McClellan, July 15, 1862, cited in McClellan, *Own Story*, 472.

33. As mentioned above, Stephen Sears's research has cast considerable doubt on the long-held belief that Porter knew of Burnside's passing of the damaging telegrams as early as September 2. When the court of inquiry was called on September 5, however, Porter would have been anxious to learn what evidence stood against him, and surely must have asked Burnside about the wires. The court of inquiry had essentially been suspended now, but even in the unlikely event Porter considered his troubles over, he would naturally have resented Burnside's failure to observe the confidentiality of the McClellan clique.

34. McClellan to Ellen Marcy, undated (circa 1859), reel 5, McClellan Papers.

III

1. *OR* 51(1):837–38.
2. Sears, *Young Napoleon*, 291–92. McClellan's most careful biographer to

date herein concludes that he actually wanted Lee to effect his retreat into Virginia, in order to allow the Army of the Potomac time to reorganize before advancing to the kill. If that is true, McClellan's critical messages to Burnside on September 15 and 16 are nothing less than deliberate contrivances, meant to throw Burnside in a bad light.

3. Cox, *Reminiscences*, 1:298; McClellan, *Own Story*, 586.

4. Cox, *Reminiscences*, 1:304; *OR* 19(2):307–8; *B&L* 2:632; McClellan, *Own Story*, 587.

5. Cox, *Reminiscences*, 1:303–4; *B&L* 2:632–33.

6. Schenck, "Burnside's Bridge," 10. It bears noting that Schenck's conclusions are drawn from rather superficial research: he employed only five sources, of which only one Confederate memoir and the *OR* were not secondary works. From the latter documents he used none of the correspondence, relying almost exclusively upon McClellan's second report; therefore some of his most essential facts were distorted. For all of that, Schenck's article marked the beginning of the myth that Burnside lost the day at Antietam through his own petulance.

7. *OR* 19(1):443, 450, and (2):314; Nevins, *Diary of Battle*, 306. Six days later Sturgis remembered making his movement on the morning of September 16, but he must have been mistaken; most other sources, including many from within his division, agree the shift was made between afternoon and sundown. See, for instance, Walcott, *Twenty-first Massachusetts*, 197; Committee of the Regimental Association, *Thirty-fifth Massachusetts*, 37; Bailey diary, September 16, 1862.

8. *OR* 19(2):308, 314. The troops Burnside saw were probably part of Ewell's division, under A. R. Lawton, arriving on the Harpers Ferry Road (Ibid., [1]:967).

9. D. R. Larned to "My Dear Sister," October 9, 1862, Larned Papers.

10. *B&L* 2:632–33; Cox, *Reminiscences*, 1:307; *OR* 19(1):30.

11. *OR* 19(1):888–89, 914.

12. Ibid. 51(1):844.

13. Ibid. 19(1):31, 129, 419, and 51(1):844; *B&L* 2:647; *Letter of the Secretary of War*, 209. In this report, finished August 4, 1863, McClellan first changed the time of Burnside's attack order to 8:00 A.M. The pertinent drafts of McClellan's *Own Story* manuscript are on reel 71, McClellan Papers. In one manuscript version, McClellan tried to simultaneously excuse himself for his vague order and to cast blame on Burnside. "The attack on the right," he wrote, "was to have been supported by an attack on the left with the hope of something more *than a division*" (italics added). By the next draft even McClellan realized how lame that sounded, and he scratched out the final three words.

14. McClellan, *Own Story*, 603.

15. *B&L* 2:651; *OR* 19(1):419, 453, 471–72. It is now commonly believed that the creek could have been crossed anywhere, the principal authority for that theory being Henry Kyd Douglas of Stonewall Jackson's staff. "One thing is

certain," he recorded at the end of the century, "they might have waded it that day without getting their waistbelts wet in any place" (*I Rode With Stonewall*, 172). Those who accept that statement because of Douglas's relative familiarity with the area ignore much evidence, not the least of which is Douglas's inability to see the creek on the day of the battle, or for many months before or after it. Though it had been a dry summer, and the creek appears low in photographs taken four or five days after the battle, it had rained most of the night before. Antietam Creek drains a sizable chunk of Washington County; it rises rapidly and can be positively intimidating. In more than two hours of searching, Crook found but one difficult place to cross, and even at Rodman's crossing a lieutenant of the 4th Rhode Island found the stream "breast deep" (Spooner, *Maryland Campaign*, 21). The monument to the 11th Connecticut, approved and erected by men who were there, shows Colonel Kingsbury less than halfway across the creek but already wetting his waistbelt. A zouave who crossed with the 9th New York at Snavely's ford described himself emerging on the far side "soaking wet from my waist belt down" (*B&L* 2:661). It should be apparent that, outside the shallowest of the fords, Antietam Creek was certainly impassable to organized bodies of troops under accurate, point-blank rifle fire on the seventeenth of September.

16. *OR* 19(1):429–30, 444; Jackman, *Sixth New Hampshire*, 104; Cox, *Reminiscences*, 1:340.

17. Lord, *Ninth New Hampshire*, 109–10.

18. Captain Duane supervised the drawing of an official map of the Antietam battlefield shortly after the fighting ceased; while he clearly indicated the ford used by Hooker on the right, he failed to label any fords on Burnside's front. Either Duane was uncertain of their locations or, knowing a controversy might develop over them, deliberately refrained from committing himself. Under no circumstances could he have considered them too unimportant to denote. See *OR Atlas*, plate XXVIII, map 2.

19. Spooner, *Maryland Campaign*, 21–22; *B&L* 2:661.

20. Cox, *Reminiscences*, 1:342–43.

21. Sacket's letters, added posthumously (and with his name misspelled) to *McClellan's Own Story*, 609–11, merit some skepticism. Sacket was either McClellan's unflagging supporter or an obsequious flatterer, as evidenced by his fawning letter to McClellan after his elevation to general-in-chief of the army—a letter promptly followed by Sacket's appointment as inspector general (Sacket to McClellan, November 11, 1861, reel 13, McClellan Papers). If Sacket was the third or fourth messenger to Burnside, then the time he claims to have arrived at Burnside's position—about 9:00 A.M.—is demonstrably false. So, too, is the comment that he remained with Burnside more than three hours before the bridge was carried, because barely three hours elapsed between the receipt of the first order and the capture of the bridge. Both statements appear deliberately coordinated with McClellan's insistence that he sent Burnside's first attack order at 8:00 A.M., which has already been controverted. Sacket

did, however, tell the same story to at least one other officer (N. H. Davis to McClellan, January 31, 1876, reel 38, McClellan Papers).

22. Biddle, "Recollections," 468.

23. Loving, *Letters of George Washington Whitman*, 67–68; *OR* 19(1):890.

24. Walcott, *Twenty-first Massachusetts*, 201; Committee of the Regimental Association, *Thirty-fifth Massachusetts*, 45; *OR* 19(1):425, 451.

25. *B&L* 2:653. Just as he had accused his friend of keeping an unseemly distance from the fighting at South Mountain, McClellan asserted that Burnside never crossed the bridge (*Own Story*, 604). Not only does Cox contradict this (*Reminiscences*, 1:345), but an eyewitness from one of the illustrated newspapers sketched Burnside with his troops, on the bluff, in the midst of the fighting. See Pratt, *Civil War in Pictures*, 70–71.

26. *OR* 19(1):891, and (2):312.

27. Cox, *Reminiscences*, 1:345; *B&L* 2:654.

28. Brunson, *Pee Dee Artillery*, 6–7; "Last Colonel of Artillery," 225; *B&L* 2:661–62.

29. *OR* 19(1):453, 456, 468; *B&L* 2:655–56; Spooner, *Maryland Campaign*, 23–26.

30. *New York Tribune*, September 19, 1862; Poore, *Life of Burnside*, 172–74.

31. Walcott, *Twenty-first Massachusetts*, 203; Committee of the Regimental Association, *Thirty-fifth Massachusetts*, 46–50; Loving, *Letters of George Washington Whitman*, 68; Elmer Bragg to William L. Bragg, September 22, 1862, Bragg Collection.

32. Elmer Bragg to William L. Bragg, September 22, 1862, Bragg Collection; *OR* 51(1):844; *B&L* 2:660.

33. McClellan, *Own Story*, 607; affidavit of James Bucklin, in Ballou, *Services of Maj.-Gen. Ambrose Everett Burnside*, 2:57–59.

34. D. R. Larned to "Dear Sister," October 3 and 9, 1862, and to "Dear Henry," October 4, 1862, Larned Papers. Burnside told the Committee on the Conduct of the War that he did see McClellan the night of September 17, asked for troops, and left a staff officer to bring McClellan's decision about the morning attack (*CCW* 1:642). In his memoirs (*Own Story*, 607), McClellan dates that request on the eighteenth, early in the morning. Burnside may have mistaken the hour of that early morning visit, putting it before midnight, or he may have determined to avoid mention of McClellan's refusal to see him the night of the seventeenth, to protect an old friend whose treachery was not yet obvious.

35. McClellan, *Own Story*, 607, 610–11; Strother, "Recollections," 285; Eby, *A Virginia Yankee*, 112; *OR* 19(1):66.

36. *OR* 19(1):32, 66–67, 373–74.

37. Ibid., (2):330.

38. Schenck, "Burnside's Bridge," 10; Cullen, "Beau Ideal of a Soldier," 9; *OR* 19(1):31; Sparks, *Inside Lincoln's Army*, 152.

39. It ought to be remembered that Hooker's grand division was reduced from six infantry divisions to two at Fredericksburg, yet he was neither ex-

pected to relinquish his wing command nor criticized for his failure to do so. The order removing Hooker from Burnside's control (*OR* 19(2):297) specified, moreover, that the detachment was temporary.

40. Rather than defending his faulty reconnaissance, Captain Duane covered for it with the same charge McClellan employed: that Burnside ignored an early morning attack order. Duane was spreading this fabrication as early as June 26, 1863 (Eby, *A Virginia Yankee*, 187), while McClellan was working on his second report. He and the deposed general collaborated on parts of the report; both stood to profit if the blame could be foisted on Burnside.

41. Lord, *Ninth New Hampshire*, 131.

CHAPTER FOUR

I

1. Basler, *Works of Lincoln*, 7:549; Longacre, *Letters of Edward King Wightman*, 48.

2. D. R. Larned to "My Dear Sister," October 3 and 9, 1862, and to "Dear Henry," October 4, 1862, Larned Papers; Hammond, *Diary of a Union Lady*, 179.

3. Albert D. Richardson to Sydney Gay, September 27, 1862, Sydney H. Gay Papers, Columbia University Library, quoted in Nevins, *War for the Union*, 2: 225.

4. D. R. Larned to "Dear Henry," October 16 and 25, 1862, Larned Papers.

5. *OR* 19(1):182; Cox, *Reminiscences*, 1:359–61; Sears, *Young Napoleon*, 366.

6. Hahn, *Towpath Guide*, 120; Circular Order dated September 22, 1862, and Hawkins to Burnside, September 23, 1862, box 2, AEBP.

7. D. R. Larned to "My Dear Sister," October 9, 1862, Larned Papers.

8. McClellan's precise location during the raid is a mystery. The president of the B&O Railroad wrote of providing a special car by which McClellan would be reunited with his family about that time (J. W. Garrett to McClellan, October 8, 1862, reel 33, McClellan Papers). Burnside's secretary located McClellan in Philadelphia (D. R. Larned to "My Dear Sister," October 12, 1862, Larned Papers). It would have been extremely difficult for McClellan to have reached Philadelphia undetected and almost as much so for him to have made the round trip between the evenings of October 8 and 10, when his whereabouts are unaccounted for. Possibly he was sequestered nearby with his wife, aboard the special train mentioned by Mr. Garrett.

9. D. R. Larned to "My Dear Sister," October 12, 1862, Larned Papers; Blackford, *War Years with Jeb Stuart*, 173–74; *OR* 19(2):420, 424, 485.

10. *OR* 19(1):2, and (2):381, 533, also 21:131–33.

11. Longacre, *Letters of Edward King Wightman*, 69.

12. D. R. Larned to "My Dear Sister," October 27, 1862, Larned Papers; *OR* 19(2):484, 494–95, 498–99.

13. D. R. Larned to "My Dear Sister," November 4, 1862, Larned Papers; John G. Parke to A. V. Colburn, November 6, 1862, reel 34, McClellan Papers; *OR* 19(2):509.

14. McClellan, *Own Story*, 646; Cox, *Reminiscences*, 1:389; D. R. Larned to "My Dear Sister," November 4, 1862, Larned Papers.

15. *OR* 19(2):113–15, 532; *OR Atlas*, plate VII, map 1; Nevins, *Diary of Battle*, 119.

16. Memorandum of movements "for tomorrow," Burnside to A. V. Colburn, November 6, 1862, and John G. Parke to Colburn, same date, reel 34, McClellan Papers; Hopkins, *Seventh Rhode Island*, 28.

17. Hopkins, *Seventh Rhode Island*, 28; Cogswell, *Eleventh New Hampshire*, 21–22.

18. Burnside to A. V. Colburn, November 6, 1862, reel 34, McClellan Papers; D. R. Larned to "My Dear Sister," May 28, 1862, Larned Papers; Tyler, *Recollections*, 56.

19. *B&L* 3:104–6; *Chicago Tribune*, September 6, 1875 (page mislabeled "September 5"); McClellan, *Own Story*, 651–52, 660; Boatner, *Civil War Dictionary*, 95.

20. Assorted correspondence, reels 32–34, McClellan Papers; *OR* 19(2):344–542; D. R. Larned to "Dear Henry," October 16, 1862, Larned Papers.

21. Nevins, *Diary of Battle*, 122; Welles, *Diary*, 1:179.

22. Tyler, *Recollections*, 56–57; McClellan, *Own Story*, 661.

23. Rebecca Woodbury to Burnside, November 10, 1862, box 3, AEBP; Sparks, *Inside Lincoln's Army*, 174–75.

24. Henry C. Marsh to his father, November 25, 1862, Indiana Division, Indiana State Library; *New York Times*, November 12, 1862.

25. Howard, *Autobiography*, 1:314; *B&L* 3:106.

26. *OR* 19(2):546; McClellan, *Own Story*, 646, 660.

27. See Loving, *Letters of George Washington Whitman*, 150, for evidence the Rappahannock was unfordable even well upstream at that time.

28. Haupt, *Reminiscences*, 160; Herman Haupt to Mrs. Haupt, November 15, 1862, Haupt Family Papers.

29. *OR* 19(2):579–80, 583, and 21:84.

30. Lord, *Ninth New Hampshire*, 206–7; *OR* 21:84–85, 792–95. Woodbury testified to the Committee on the Conduct of the War that Halleck had finally told him of the movement, whereupon Woodbury asked to have it delayed five days; Halleck, Woodbury said, refused. Halleck apparently forgot Woodbury's request, for he put all the blame upon him in his communications with Burnside (*OR* 21:172, 792; *CCW* 1:665, 675). Even Hooker reported hearing either Halleck or Meigs tell Burnside not to worry about the pontoons—that they could be in Fredericksburg in three days (*CCW* 1:671).

31. *OR* 21:101–3, 1013–14.

32. Ibid. 19(2):575, and 21:47; Elmer Bragg to William L. Bragg, November 21, 1862, Bragg Collection; Thompson, *Thirteenth New Hampshire*, 24.

33. *OR* 21:104, 773–74; *New York Times*, November 13, 1862.

34. *OR* 21:103, 790–91, 800; *B&L* 3:70, 121–22.

35. Sparks, *Inside Lincoln's Army*, 181; D. R. Larned to "Dear Henry," November 22, 1862, Larned Papers; Basler, *Works of Lincoln*, 5:509–10.

36. D. R. Larned to "My Dear Sister," November 27, 1862, Larned Papers; Angle and Miers, *The Living Lincoln*, 515–16; Sparks, *Inside Lincoln's Army*, 182–83.

37. D. R. Larned to "My Dear Sister," November 27, 1862, Larned Papers.

38. *OR* 21:87–88, 1033; Thompson, *Thirteenth New Hampshire*, 27–34; *B&L* 3:129; Sumner to Burnside, November 23, 1862, box 3, AEBP.

39. *New York Times*, December 6, 1862; William F. Draper to Lydia Draper, November 8, 1862, Draper Papers.

40. Longacre, *Letters of Edward King Wightman*, 75; Poore, *Life of Burnside*, 64.

41. Howard, *Autobiography*, 1:321; *B&L* 3:107–8, 129; Sparks, *Inside Lincoln's Army*, 186. Rush Hawkins later wrote that he and another colonel met Burnside alone after the council and warned him of the disaster that would surely follow the planned assault (*B&L* 3:126–27). Burnside would not have been likely to ask the colonel's opinion, as Hawkins claimed he did, for the commanding general seems to have disliked Hawkins for the same traits that turned him against Hooker: Hawkins was, for instance, one of the few officers whose promotion Burnside had never seen fit to recommend. Hawkins waited until both Burnside and the other witness had died to reveal his powers of prophecy, and his story smells of self-serving invention.

42. Meade, *Letters*, 1:351. Something never considered is that Burnside's repeated protests that he was incapable of commanding the army may not have been based entirely on his judgment of his own military capacity. In 1862 there were basically two types of officers in the Army of the Potomac: those who loved George McClellan and considered him the only man who could command the army, and those who did not. A great many of the former—Burnside among them—held key positions in that army, and there was the ever-present possibility that many of them, either because of a lack of confidence or out of pure spite, would fail to give McClellan's successor the support and cooperation necessary for efficient command. In the end it was precisely that factor, rather than his fancied incompetence, which destroyed Burnside's effectiveness.

43. Meigs, "Relations of Lincoln and Stanton," 458, 461; Donald, *Inside Lincoln's Cabinet*, 112.

44. William Church to Burnside, October 11, 1862, box 3, AEBP.

45. D. R. Larned to "Dear Henry," November 22, 1862, and to "My Dear Sister," November 27, 1862, Larned Papers.

II

1. Sparks, *Inside Lincoln's Army*, 187.

2. *OR* 21:106–7, 168, 170–71, 177–80.

3. General David Birney, who commanded a Third Corps division loaned to Franklin on December 13, submitted the only two maps on which the road to Hamilton's Crossing is named: on both maps it is mislabeled "Road to Bowling Green." See *OR Atlas*, plate XXX, maps 3 and 4.

4. *B&L* 3:73; Confederate Compiled Service Records, Records Group 109, National Archives; *OR* 21:588, 643. No fewer than eighty-five different Burnsides served at least one enlistment in Confederate service, including four of the general's Georgia and Florida cousins who laid down their rifles at Appomattox. See *SHSP* 15:224–25, 309–10. Corresponding Union records in the National Archives reveal at least a score of Burnsides, all Midwesterners, none of whom fought at Fredericksburg.

5. *OR* 21:168–70, 183, 191; *SHSP* 32:269–71.

6. *B&L* 3:121; *OR* 21:282–83, 335; Stiles, *Four Years Under Marse Robert*, 129–30; Longacre, *Letters of Edward King Wightman*, 87.

7. *OR* 21:64, 219, 449, 630. Another factor discouraging Burnside from crossing Franklin to clear out the skirmishers was time: it would have taken him several hours to cross, prepare a bridgehead defense, and work a division upriver in broad daylight without leaving it open to a counterattack that might cut it off. See Stonewall Jackson's note to D. H. Hill (ibid., 1060) for evidence that the Confederate high command was uncertain of where Burnside planned to attack as late as the evening of December 12.

8. *B&L* 3:143–47.

9. *OR* 21:107–8; Sparks, *Inside Lincoln's Army*, 188.

10. *B&L* 3:108; Blackford, *War Years with Jeb Stuart*, 195; Charles D. Chase to Charles Chase, January 11, 1863, Chase Family Papers; Robinson diary, December 12 and 13, 1862; Cogswell, *Eleventh New Hampshire*, 45.

11. Longacre, *Letters of Edward King Wightman*, 87; *OR* 21:109; Jacob L. Greene, *Franklin and the Left Wing*, 12–13; *B&L* 3:133; *CCW* 1:652.

12. *OR* 21:71, 89; Sparks, *Inside Lincoln's Army*, 189; James A. Hardie to Burnside, March 12, 1863, box 6, AEBP; *CCW* 1:707–8.

13. *CCW* 1:707–8; *OR* 21:643, 663, 669, 674.

14. *B&L* 3:134; Stackpole, *Drama on the Rappahannock*, 171. Though he consulted but few sources and made conspicuously uncritical use of them, Stackpole's analysis is brutally disparaging of Burnside.

15. Whan, *Fiasco at Fredericksburg*, 53; Nevins, *Diary of Battle*, 145. The hypothesis that Franklin was meant to turn right on the road to Hamilton's Crossing also explains the apparent contradiction that he was, on the one hand, to hold his entire command in readiness for a movement down the old Richmond road and, on the other, to send at least one division to take Prospect Hill. As

Franklin tried to explain it later, this would cause the two forces to diverge; if Burnside wanted him to take the road to Hamilton's Crossing, however, and simply succumbed to a general misapprehension that the road there was the old Richmond road, the smaller force Franklin was to send out would merely range ahead on the same route the rest of the Left Grand Division would follow.

16. *OR* 21:90; *CCW* 1:707–10; Hardie to Burnside, March 12, 1863, box 6, AEBP: Franklin probably meant that the official copy—the one Burnside told Hardie he would transmit by telegraph—arrived by courier.

17. Jacob L. Greene, *Franklin and the Left Wing*, 16–17; *B&L* 3:134–35; *OR* 21:91, 454; Nichols, *Toward Gettysburg*, 155–56; Nevins, *Diary of Battle*, 147–48. David Birney felt Franklin had plenty of men to carry the entire crest; his use of barely one-sixth of his force led Birney to the incorrect conclusion that the assault was a mere diversion. See *CCW* 1:706.

18. *OR* 21:90.

19. Ibid., 510–11; Nevins, *Diary of Battle*, 143.

20. *OR* 21:71; *B&L* 3:133; Sumner to Burnside, November 23, 1862, box 3, AEBP; Philadelphia *Weekly Times*, April 26, 1879. While he only expressed it to his diary, John Reynolds's chief of artillery criticized Franklin's failure to follow this route. Apparently unaware that Burnside's orders indicated almost exactly what he proposed, Colonel Charles Wainwright insisted he would have advanced toward the Massaponax, driving in the enemy skirmishers, then would have turned to make an oblique attack on Lee's right, directly at Hamilton's house. "Thirty guns would have silenced those of the enemy on the crest, and afterward have covered our right flank," he wrote the day after the battle. He continued to record that he would have put another thirty guns on the left— which, with the guns on Stafford Heights, would have neutralized any attack from across the Massaponax. As things turned out, it might have been better had that militia-trained colonel had command of Franklin's wing. See Nevins, *Diary of Battle*, 145. If, as Franklin later insisted, the orders of December 13 were a radical change from the plan of December 12, Franklin must have perceived his part of the December 12 scheme as a frontal assault: that it was not is borne out by Baldy Smith's *Century* article two decades later. As quoted in the text, Smith recalled that the Left Grand Division was to deploy "in columns of assault on the right and left of the Richmond road, carry the ridge, and turn Lee's right flank at any cost." Columns of assault right and left of the road would indicate the direction of attack was parallel to, rather than perpendicular from, the stage road, and such a movement would have turned Lee's right by making his position untenable. Smith's reference to carrying the ridge, however, epitomizes the geographical difference between Burnside's order and the interpretation Franklin and Smith later tried to impose upon it. Burnside told Franklin to seize "the height near Captain Hamilton's," meaning that he was to advance beyond Lee's right, sweep behind it, and strike the end of the ridge *nearest* Hamilton's house. After the discussion of December 12 it seems unlikely Franklin fell victim to so subtle an ambiguity: more credible is that

he misjudged his distance in the fog or fell short as a result of poor reconnaissance. Support for the argument of shoddy or insufficient reconnaissance can be found in the rather inaccurate map Franklin submitted in his defense. Published in a now-rare pamphlet which Franklin printed privately, it is reproduced in *OR* 51(1), between pages 1032 and 1033. The map depicts Meade's division advancing almost directly on the Hamilton house (which it did not do), suggesting Franklin at least suspected he was supposed to hit the extreme end of Lee's line. The First Corps artillery chief also made reference to General Franklin's failure to inspect even his occupied lines, much less the ground beyond, attributing the omission to Franklin's "natural laziness." See Nevins, *Diary of Battle*, 145, 147. Six days after the battle Burnside told the Committee on the Conduct of the War that he wanted Franklin to put his forces "in rear of their extreme left" [*sic*], meaning Lee's right (*CCW* 1:655).

21. *OR* 21:463, 480, 510–11, 631. Meade testified to the joint committee that his division was the smallest in the First Corps; Reynolds said it was the largest. Both were wrong, but Meade's estimate of 4,500 men was 2,000 shy of the December 10 morning report total (*CCW* 1:691, 698, 702).

22. *OR* 21:511–12, 632; *OR Atlas*, plate LXIII, map 7; D. R. Larned's notes on the battle of Fredericksburg, Larned Papers.

23. Caldwell, *Brigade of South Carolinians*, 92–94.

24. *CCW* 1:667; Herman Haupt to Mrs. Haupt, December 13, 1862, Haupt Family Papers; D. R. Larned's notes on the battle of Fredericksburg, Larned Papers; *OR* 21:91–94, and ser. 3, 3:294.

25. Bartlett, *Twelfth New Hampshire*, 41–42; Thompson, *Thirteenth New Hampshire*, 45; Sparks, *Inside Lincoln's Army*, 189.

26. *B&L* 3:79, 111. It has been suggested that reconnaissance could have overcome the stoppage at these bridges, but that was not possible without sacrificing the element of surprise; Burnside's strategy now relied partly upon Lee anticipating no major assault here, in hopes he would strip the position.

27. *OR* 21:131, 287; *B&L* 3:111; Cory, *Private's Recollections*, 25; Seville, *First Delaware*, 56–57.

28. *B&L* 3:111–13; Child, *Fifth New Hampshire*, 153–54.

29. *B&L* 3:113; Walcott, *Twenty-first Massachusetts*, 241; Cogswell, *Eleventh New Hampshire*, 54; Lord, *Ninth New Hampshire*, 196–97; Lapham, *Recollections*, 28–30.

30. *OR* 21:92–93, 139–42, 362–63; Franklin to Meade, March 25, 1863, Letterbook, Meade Letters, Historical Society of Pennsylvania, cited in Cleaves, *Meade of Gettysburg*, 92.

31. *OR* 21:128. Franklin partially quotes the order (which he denied having received when he spoke to the joint committee) on pages 23 and 24 of his pamphlet (Franklin, *Reply*).

32. For a detailed analysis of Franklin's attack, see A. Wilson Greene, "Opportunity to the South." Longstreet told Lee that Franklin offered his only danger (*B&L* 3:81), and one roundabout source has it that Lee admitted to

Meade, when they met at Appomattox, that Franklin could have crushed the Confederate right with a better effort (Nevins, *Diary of Strong*, 4:24).

33. *New York Times*, December 17, 1862.

34. Franklin, *Reply*, 4; *B&L* 3:114; *OR* 21:92. David Birney later testified there was definitely enough time to mount a second assault after Meade had been repulsed (*CCW* 1:707).

35. McWhiney and Jamieson, *Attack and Die*, 174–91; William Allen, "Fredericksburg," 138. McWhiney and Jamieson credit Celtic heritage with the popularity of the reckless infantry charge, citing Celtic attacks at the battles of Telamon (225 B.C.), Bannockburn (1314), and Culloden (1745). Not only was Burnside's ancestry wholly Celtic, his own great-grandfather, Robert Burnside, had taken part in the disastrous charge at Culloden (Poore, *Life of Burnside*, 18). The witness at the Lacy house was correspondent William Swinton of the *New York Times*, who wrote his uncomplimentary memoirs of Burnside after two run-ins with him, in one of which Burnside arrested him and threatened to have him shot as a spy for violating orders against newspapermen wandering into camp. See Swinton, *Campaigns*, 251; Grant, *Memoirs*, 2:143–45; Circular Order expelling William Swinton and "Mr. Kent" from the Army of the Potomac, July 6, 1864, box 19, AEBP. Newman, "Essential Sleep," 67–68, observes that the sleepless person takes fewer facts into consideration when making decisions and becomes "befuddled" when important decisions have to be made. By this time Burnside was operating under a burdensome "sleep debt."

36. *OR* 21:430–33, 443–44; *B&L* 3:81; Ted Alexander, *126th Pennsylvania*, 43–44.

37. *OR* 21:136, 404–5.

38. Ibid., 311–12; Thompson, *Thirteenth New Hampshire*, 50.

39. *OR* 21:312, 332, 340–44; Thompson, *Thirteenth New Hampshire*, 50, 53, 60; D. R. Larned to "My Dear Henry," December 16, 1862, Larned Papers.

40. *B&L* 3:117. A similar bias, though probably much less unconscious, tainted William F. Smith's memoirs of Burnside, which picture him in a state of uncontrollable anguish and self-condemnation just after the battle (ibid., 128); by then Smith carried not only the standard prejudice about Burnside's capacity that he helped to create, but an enormous personal grudge as well.

41. John S. Crocker to Mrs. Crocker, December 13, 1862, Fredericksburg and Spotsylvania National Military Park. My thanks are due A. Wilson Greene, of the park staff, for apprising me of Crocker's letter.

42. *B&L* 3:117.

43. Longacre, *Letters of Edward King Wightman*, 90–92; Blackburn, *Diary of Ralph Ely*, 48.

44. *CCW* 1:653.

45. Ibid., 653, 659; *B&L* 3:117–18; Sparks, *Inside Lincoln's Army*, 190.

46. *OR* 21:120–21; Nevins, *Diary of Battle*, 145; D. R. Larned's notes on the battle of Fredericksburg, Larned Papers; William Goddard to Burnside, December 17, 1862, box 3, AEBP; Welles, *Diary*, 1:192.

47. *B&L* 3:117–18; D. R. Larned's notes on the battle of Fredericksburg, Larned Papers; William Goddard to Burnside, December 16, 1862, box 3, AEBP.

48. *B&L* 3:118; *OR* 21:66; D. R. Larned's notes on the battle of Fredericksburg, Larned Papers; Pearce, *Diary of Henry A. Chambers*, 76.

III

1. Israel Washburn to Hannibal Hamlin, December 17, 1862, Washburn Papers; Rodney H. Ramsey to "Dear Father," December 24, 1862, Miscellaneous Civil War Letters, New Hampshire Historical Society.

2. Cochrane, "The Army of the Potomac," 57; *B&L* 3:106; Fleming, *Letters of Alexander Hays*, 285.

3. Sears, *Papers of McClellan*, 533–34; Joseph C. G. Kennedy to Burnside, December 1, 1862, box 4, AEBP; D. R. Larned to "Dear Henry," December 8, 1862, Larned Papers.

4. Elmer Bragg to William L. Bragg, December 23, 1862, Bragg Collection; William F. Draper to "My Dear Father," January 9, 1863, Draper Papers; Truxall, *Respects to All*, 35; *CCW* 1:55, 67, 691–93; *B&L* 3:120.

5. See, for instance, T. Harry Williams, *Lincoln and the Radicals*, 267–68, for the theory of belated disappointment in Franklin; William Goddard to Burnside, December 16, 1862, box 3, AEBP; D. R. Larned to "My Dear Henry," December 16, 1862, Larned Papers.

6. Basler, *Works of Lincoln*, 6:15.

7. Jacob Cox was very specific about this point of Burnside's character. "He never found fault with a subordinate for assuming responsibility or acting without orders, provided he was assured of his honest good purpose in doing so. In such cases he would assume the responsibility for what was done as cheerfully as if he had given the order." See Cox, *Reminiscences*, 1:451. Cox's testimony is corroborated by Burnside's conduct with other subordinates throughout the war; that trait contributed substantially to the decline of his reputation, which is precisely why such generosity was scarce among commanders.

8. Boatner, *Civil War Dictionary*, 374; *B&L* 3:241; *OR* 5:23 and 11(2):114.

9. Biddle, "Recollections," 468; *Register of Officers and Cadets* (1846), 23; Returns from Regular Army Artillery Regiments, Third Artillery, reel 20. Shortly after Fredericksburg, Hardie left the Army of the Potomac for New York, to help McClellan prepare his final report—the one that turned so critical of Burnside (*Memoir of James Allen Hardie*, 34).

10. See Hardie's 1:25 message, *OR* 21:92.

11. Swinton, *Campaigns*, 251; Adams, *Our Masters the Rebels*, 134.

12. *Register of Officers and Cadets* (1846), 20, and (1847), 22; D. R. Larned's notes on the battle of Fredericksburg, Larned Papers; Jacob L. Greene, *Franklin and the Left Wing*, 25–26; Bartley, *Fatigue*, 43; Dowdey, *Seven Days*, 201–2. Dowdey's conclusions about Stonewall Jackson's 1862 performance are

not unchallenged. See A. Wilson Greene, "Jackson on the Peninsula."

13. D. R. Larned to "My Dear Henry," December 16, 1862, Larned Papers; *B&L* 3:117; Meade, *Letters*, 1:348.

14. Sparks, *Inside Lincoln's Army*, 194; *CCW* 1:67, 660, 662–63, 667; *New York Times*, December 19, 1862; Nevins, *Diary of Battle*, 149.

15. Raymond, "Extracts," 424; D. R. Larned to "My Dear Sister," December 23, 1862, Larned Papers.

16. *New York Times*, December 23, 1862; *OR* 21:66–67; D. R. Larned to "Dear Henry," December 26, 1862, and to "My Dear Sister," December 28, 1862, Larned Papers.

17. J. Van Buren to Burnside, December 23, 1862, box 3, AEBP; Hammond, *Diary of a Union Lady*, 212; Raymond, "Extracts," 424; Frederick D. Williams, *Letters of James A. Garfield*, 201.

18. *OR* 21:886–87, 895–96, 899.

19. *CCW* 1:730–46; Basler, *Works of Lincoln*, 6:22–23; *OR* 21:900; Burnside to Fitz John Porter, December 30, 1862, letterbook labeled "Dispatches, December 26, 1862–January 20, 1863," RIHS Papers.

20. The date of the New Year's Eve conference is established by the secretary of the navy, who met Burnside on the White House portico the morning of December 31 (Welles, *Diary*, 1:211). *CCW* 1:717–18; Nevins, *Diary of Battle*, 156 (for evidence of army feeling about Halleck and Stanton); D. R. Larned to "My Dear Uncle," January 1, 1863, Larned Papers; *OR* 12(2), supplement: 1002–6, and 21:941–42. Burnside's January 1 letter to Lincoln is nowhere published, and T. Harry Williams refers to the curious deletion of even the mention of that letter as though to question its existence (*Lincoln and His Generals*, 203). The text of the letter is, however, preserved in Mr. Larned's hand in a letterbook entitled "Copies of Private & Important Dispatches & Letters," RIHS Papers.

21. Basler, *Works of Lincoln*, 6:31; *CCW* 1:718–19.

22. *OR* 21:1006–11; Meade, *Letters*, 1:344. In the late spring of 1863 Generals Franklin, Smith, and W. T. H. Brooks—all by then bitter enemies of Burnside—claimed he had said he stated his thoughts about Stanton and Halleck to Lincoln in the presence of the other two. Meade, who was part of that conversation but who was still then Burnside's friend, did not make that case when he wrote home about it. Burnside probably referred to passing the letter to Lincoln while Stanton and Halleck were there. On the basis of this misunderstanding, Halleck, complaining that Burnside never responded to his query on the subject, characterized Burnside's memory as "unreliable," while Franklin suggested Burnside was "crazy." What they meant to say was that he had lied, which he had not. Probably, with the possible exception of Smith, neither did they: Burnside likely told the story with unintended ambiguity. His account of the conversations with Lincoln and the passing of the letter are in an unfinished draft in his own handwriting, dated May 24, 186– (1863), box 8, AEBP. This was to have been his reply to Halleck's question, but because of impending

military movements and a growing mistrust of Halleck's good faith, he never finished it.

23. *OR* 21:944–45, 953–54; Burnside to Halleck, January 4, 1863, letterbook for December 26, 1862–January 20, 1863, RIHS Papers; Basler, *Works of Lincoln*, 6:46.

24. Thompson, *Thirteenth New Hampshire*, 94–102.

25. D. R. Larned to "Dear Henry," January 9 and 16, 1863, and to "My Dear Sister," January 15, 1863, Larned Papers; *CCW* 1:719; David E. Beem to "My Dear Wife," January 18, 1863, Beem Papers.

26. Sparks, *Inside Lincoln's Army*, 199, 204; Raymond, "Extracts," 420–21; Burnside to Franklin, January 18, 1863, letterbook for December 26, 1862–January 20, 1863, RIHS Papers; Howard, *Autobiography*, 2:181; D. R. Larned to "My Dear Sister," January 20, 1863, Larned Papers.

27. Nevins, *Diary of Battle*, 157–61; Meade, *Letters*, 1:347–48. Considering the evidence of Smith's participation in the Burnside denunciation, and his demonstrable attempts to undercut the commanding general, his own account of this period is most amusing. "I had felt sympathy for Burnside and did what was possible to stem the tide of opinion," he recorded in his brief autobiography. This memoir, written for the eye of Smith's daughter (and after Burnside's death), alternates tales of Burnside's incompetence with instances of General Smith's own generosity toward his unfortunate superior. Not only would Smith have us believe he defended Burnside after Fredericksburg, but that he stood guard outside his tent for two hours during the Mud March, so the exhausted commander could sleep, and that he said nothing to General Grant about Burnside's capacity during the Knoxville campaign, specifically because of their private quarrel, though Smith admitted "in my opinion his merits were below zero." A critical reading of Smith's recently published autobiography raises serious doubts about his overall veracity. See Schiller, *Autobiography of William F. Smith*, 62–65, 81–82.

28. D. R. Larned to "My Dear Sister," January 20, 1863, Larned Papers; *OR* 21:976–77, 979–80, 986, 989–90.

29. *OR* 21:122, 998; Raymond, "Extracts," 422–23; *CCW* 1:718.

30. Raymond, "Extracts," 703–4.

31. Meade, *Letters*, 1:348.

32. D. R. Larned to Mrs. A. E. Burnside, January 28, 1863, Larned Papers; Basler, *Works of Lincoln*, 6:77.

33. *OR* 21:1009; *CCW* 1:721–22.

34. Raymond, "Extracts," 707–8. Rumors of Order Number 8 were already rife in the army (Nevins, *Diary of Battle*, 161), apparently because of loose-lipped officers on Burnside's staff; Colonel Goodrich, the commissary, spilled the story to General Patrick the day Burnside left the front (Sparks, *Inside Lincoln's Army*, 207–8).

35. D. R. Larned to Mrs. A. E. Burnside, January 28, 1863, Larned Papers;

Sparks, *Inside Lincoln's Army*, 208; Nevins, *Diary of Battle*, 131 (for a description of Falmouth).

CHAPTER FIVE

I

1. Governor Sprague to the Senate and House of Rhode Island, February 2, 1863, and Resolution of the State of Rhode Island, February 3, 1863, box 5, AEBP.

2. *CCW* 1:716–25. This testimony may have sealed the professional fate of Newton and Cochrane. The latter saw the light and resigned a few days later, his commission languishing without confirmation; Congress also refused to confirm Newton's promotion, and despite service at Gettysburg, he finished the war in virtual exile, as the commander of Key West and Dry Tortugas. See Boatner, *Civil War Dictionary*, 161, and *OR* 41(3):880.

3. *Detroit Free Press*, February 9, 1863.

4. *New York Tribune*, February 10, 1863.

5. Poore, *Life of Burnside*, 203; Nevins, *Diary of Strong*, 3:296–97. Poore seems to confuse this visit to New York with Burnside's January 27 return to that city from the Army of the Potomac.

6. Sprague to Burnside, February 13, 1863, and "Eleasabeth" Burnside to Ambrose E. Burnside, January 5, 1863, box 5, and William J. Burnside to Ambrose E. Burnside, January 22, 1863, box 6, AEBP.

7. D. R. Larned to "Dear Henry," February 23, 1863, Larned Papers; Halleck to Burnside, February 28, 1863, and Charles G. Loring to Burnside, February 24, 1863, both box 6, AEBP.

8. Burnside to D. Appleton & Co., February 28, 1863, box 6, AEBP.

9. D. R. Larned to "My Dear Sister," March 4, 1863, Larned Papers; Sears, *Papers of McClellan*, 540; *CCW* 1:431–41.

10. D. R. Larned to "My Dear Sister," March 4 and 6, 1863, Larned Papers; Loving, *Letters of George Washington Whitman*, 87; Beale, *Diary of Edward Bates*, 279; *Philadelphia Inquirer*, March 10, 1863.

11. *OR* 23(2):105, 134, 142–46.

12. Ibid., 147.

13. Meade, *Letters*, 1:358–60.

14. *CCW* 1:637–42, and 3:333–37.

15. *OR* 23(2):149–50, 25(2):44, and 32(2):468.

16. Ibid. 23(2):363–67.

17. Halleck to Burnside, March 21, 1863, box 11, AEBP.

18. D. R. Larned to "My Dear Sister," March 24, 1863, Larned Papers.

19. *OR* 23(2):168–70.

20. Ibid., (1):164, 168, 171–72, and (2):165.

21. Ibid., (1):166, 171, and (2):164, 169–70.

22. Ibid., (1):168, and (2):172–75.

23. Ibid., (1):168–69, and (2):175–77.

24. Burnside to Jonathan Sturges, June 7, 1863, box 8, AEBP; *OR* 23(1): 169–70, 172–75, 196.

25. *OR* 23(2):162–64.

26. Ibid., 164. The letter Halleck enclosed was in response to an appeal Rosecrans endorsed (ibid., 54–56) for stricter management of disloyal citizens in Kentucky and Tennessee because of the great number of Confederate sympathizers there.

27. Ibid., 107–9.

28. The designation of the fourth division, Ninth Corps, appears only on the abstract of returns from April and May, 1863 (ibid., 299, 379).

29. Cogswell, *Eleventh New Hampshire*, 69.

30. D. R. Larned journal, April 4, 1863, Larned Papers.

31. *OR* 23(2):188, 206, 210, 215–16.

32. Ibid., 216–17.

33. Ibid., 227.

34. Ibid., 216–18, 220, 231–32.

35. *OR* 21:128, and 23(2):231–32; Charges and Specifications against Captain James M. Cutts, Jr., and Cutts to Burnside, July 23, 1863, box 21, AEBP; *New York Herald*, November 21, 1856.

36. *OR*, ser. 2, 5:463; *Ohio State Journal*, March 7, 1863; *Cleveland Leader*, March 28, 1863; *Dayton Empire*, March 14 and April 11, 1863. One close student of the phenomenon argues that Carrington exaggerated the secret society theory to account for his own injudicious actions (Klement, "Carrington and the Golden Circle Legend").

37. *OR* 9:380, and ser. 2, 5:480, 485; Basler, *Works of Lincoln*, 5:436–37; *Ohio State Journal*, April 21, 1863.

38. Burnside to Carrington, April 20, 1863, Letterbook #1, Army of the Ohio, RIHS Papers. Carrington's correspondence alone pegs him as a doomsayer. On March 19, 1863, he notified the adjutant general of the U.S. Army "the next ten days are of the utmost significance. I know the danger, and speak from actual knowledge of the organization that puts us in peril." Three months later, after he had been relieved of the Indianapolis command, he wrote his next superior, "I assure you that there will be depredations upon the Indiana and Illinois border from men who never had connection with the rebel army." He said he knew such a campaign was "to be inaugurated the latter part of June." He insisted, "I am no alarmist," but like a Millerite recalculating Judgment Day he added, "I have been surprised that the movements did not commence earlier." The movements he described never did commence. See *OR*, ser. 3, 3: 76, 410.

39. Frederick D. Williams, *Letters of James A. Garfield*, 271; Resolution of the Central Union Club of Kentucky, April 13, 1863, and James Taylor to Burnside, April 16 and 17, 1863, both in box 6, Thomas O. Lowe to Burnside,

April 15, 1863, statement of Manorah Lowe, April 11, 1863, and letters of Henry Brown, Thomas E. Momas, S. G. Spees, and John W. Hall to Burnside, all April 13, 1863, and all in box 21, AEBP. Lieutenant Lowe was later released and returned to duty, earning citations for gallantry at Chattanooga and in the Atlanta and Nashville campaigns (*OR* 31[2]:461, 45[1]:602, and 49[2]:974). His brother, however, was a fierce critic of the Lincoln administration: see Thomas O. Lowe's letter in the *Dayton Journal*, May 7, 1863. Jennie Moon was the sister of Lottie Moon, Burnside's supposed former fiancée, and her arrest may have inspired Lottie to the postwar fiction that it was she, herself, whom Burnside arrested for carrying contraband mail. In "The Ballad of Lottie Moon," Thomas and Marlene Marsh recount Lottie's tale with apparent credence: she is supposed to have appeared at Burnside's headquarters wearing a disguise, but he recognized her anyway, after which he imprisoned her and her sister in the Burnet House for three months. Daniel Larned, who detailed all the social, political, and military affairs at the Burnet House, made no mention of the sisters or of Lottie's former relationship with Burnside in any of his voluminous journal entries or correspondence. Burnside would probably not have kept such information to himself even if he had been able, and Larned's ignorance of Lottie casts doubt on both her wartime recollections and her earlier romantic episode with Lieutenant Burnside.

40. Nevins, *Diary of Strong*, 3:268–69; parole of Mrs. W. B. Phillips, May 2, 1863, and "Union Defender" to Burnside, May 3, 1863, box 7, AEBP.

41. *OR* 23(2):230, 49(2):581–82, and ser. 2, 5:520.

42. Ibid., ser. 2, 5:544, 685, 7:512, and 8:226, 289; D. R. Larned journal, May 5 and 14, 1863, Larned Papers; statement of Thomas M. Campbell, May 10, 1863, box 21, AEBP.

43. D. R. Larned journal, May 14, 1863, Larned Papers; *OR*, ser. 2, 5:556–57, 707.

44. *OR* 23(2):230. A Confederate colonel, while reporting to his secretary of war on informants and intelligence matters, specifically mentioned Powell taking his Senate seat in Washington (ibid. 5:978).

45. D. R. Larned journal, May 5, 1863, Larned Papers; *OR*, ser. 2, 5:555, 635–42, and ser. 3, 3:147.

46. D. R. Larned journal, May 5, 1863, Larned Papers; *OR*, ser. 2, 5:556–57; *Ohio Statesman*, May 7, 1863; *The Crisis*, May 13 and 27, 1863.

47. *OR*, ser. 2, 5:557; Burnside to David Levin, May 7, 1863 (copy), Larned Papers.

48. *OR*, ser. 2, 5:634, 645–46. For Cutts's sentiments on the subject, see his appeal on behalf of Basil Duke, July 23, 1863, box 21, AEBP.

49. *OR*, ser. 2, 5:656–57, 665–66, 705–6.

50. Klement, *Limits of Dissent*, 252; *OR*, ser. 2, 7:367, ser. 3, 2:321–22, and 4:426–27. For maps diagramming the results of wartime elections in the Midwest, see Gray, *Hidden Civil War*, 61, 109, 152, 205.

51. *OR* 23(2):369, and ser. 2, 5:664, 717; John S. Mason to Burnside, May 11,

1863, with Burnside's endorsement, and Milo Hascall to Burnside, May —, 1863, box 7, AEBP. The editor was D. E. Van Valkenburgh, of the Plymouth *Weekly Democrat*.

52. D. R. Larned to "Dear Henry," April 5 and 24, 1863, Larned Papers.

53. Franklin, *Reply*, 17; *OR* 21:1006–12.

54. Burnside's unfinished draft, dated May 24, 1863, box 8, AEBP; *OR* 21: 944–45.

55. *OR* 21:1011–12; Burnside to Jonathan Sturges, June 17, 1863, box 8, AEBP.

56. Poore, *Life of Burnside*, 207; Ambrose Burnside and Edward Burnsides to Ambrose E. Burnside, April 10, 1863, box 6, AEBP.

57. H. S. Olcott to Burnside, May 6, 1863, box 7, AEBP; D. R. Larned journal, May 14, 1863, Larned Papers.

58. D. R. Larned to "My Dear A———," May 13, 1863, Larned Papers.

II

1. *OR* 23(2):337, and ser. 2, 5:664–65.

2. Ibid. 23(2):331, 338, 813–14, and ser. 2, 5:665.

3. Ibid. 23(2):299–300, 330, 333. Reports of Confederate forces gathering for another invasion of Kentucky were almost daily fare (ibid., 329–32, 335–36, 339–40, 342, 360, 362–64.

4. Ibid., 352, 357, and ser. 3, 3:147, 164.

5. Willcox to Burnside, May 23, 1863, box 7, AEBP; *OR* 23(2):361. Despite more than 20,000 men listed "present" on his rolls, Willcox had only 16,531 effective troops, only a portion of whom he could deploy for offensive maneuvers (*OR* 23(2):300).

6. *OR* 23(2):331, 355–56, 359–60, 372; D. R. Larned journal, May 30, 1863, Larned Papers.

7. D. R. Larned journal, May 30, 1863, Larned Papers; *OR* 23(2):373–74, 376, 383–84, 883.

8. *OR* 23(2):384, 386–87.

9. J. R. Hawley to Burnside, May 19, 1863, box 7, AEBP; *OR* 23(2):381.

10. "A friend" to Burnside, undated (May, 1863), and John F. Worth to Burnside, June 3, 1863, box 8, AEBP; *Cleveland Plain Dealer*, June 4, 1863; *OR* 23(2):385–86, ser. 3, 3:252, and 4:388. Rosecrans also stopped the circulation of the *Chicago Times* in the Department of Missouri in February of 1864 (*OR* 34[2]:363), but he was not overruled.

11. *OR* 23(2):387, 389.

12. Ibid., ser. 3, 3:39, 125, 147, 187, 242–43, 358; Dyer, *Compendium*, 1195, 1210–12.

13. *OR* 23(2):369; Willcox to Burnside, June 17, 1863, box 8, AEBP.

14. Willcox to Burnside, June 17, 1863, box 8, AEBP; *OR*, ser. 3, 3:338–39, 347.

15. *Chicago Tribune*, June 26 and 27, 1863; *OR*, ser. 3, 3:349–50.

16. *OR* 23(2):420, 435–36, and ser. 3, 3:370–71, 391–92, 396–97; *Louisville Daily Democrat*, June 16 and 18, 1863.

17. Burnside to Jonathan Sturges, June 17, 1863, box 8, AEBP; *OR*, ser. 3, 3:416, 418–20.

18. *OR* 23(2):387, 421, 864–65, 872, 875.

19. Ibid., (1):386, and (2):430–31, 438; D. R. Larned journal, June 29, 1863, Larned Papers.

20. D. R. Larned journal, June 25 and July 8, 1863, and D. R. Larned to "My Dear Sister," July 16, 1863, Larned Papers; Charges and Specifications against Captain James M. Cutts, Jr., box 21, AEBP. Ironically, President Lincoln exchanged the sentences Cutts and Hutton received. Perhaps at the request of Cutts's father, a U.S. Treasury official, he reduced the captain's punishment from dismissal to a presidential reprimand that was, in the end, downright friendly; but because the Articles of War provided no other punishment but dismissal for challenging another to a duel, he increased Hutton's punishment from a reprimand to cashiering, dating his dismissal September 28 but reinstating him October 30. Cutts continued in the army, but was still a captain doing duty with his Regular Army regiment by Appomattox. Decades later he received a Medal of Honor for unspecified gallantry in the Virginia campaign of 1864. See Basler, *Works of Lincoln*, 7:538–39; *OR* 42(2):849, and 46(2):738. After the war Cutts appealed to Burnside for a recommendation for brevet promotion based on his war service; his immodest sixteen-page letter must have persuaded the forgiving Burnside, for by October of 1866 Cutts was a brevet lieutenant colonel (Cutts to Burnside, November 13, 1865, box labeled "Correspondence & Miscellaneous," RIHS Papers; *OR*, ser. 2, 8:967).

21. *OR* 23(2):433, 439–41, 454, 507.

22. Ibid., 439; Horan, *Confederate Agent*, 24–25.

23. *OR* 23(1):443, and (2):398; Horan, *Confederate Agent*, 25–27; *Madison Courier*, June 24, 1863, cited in Horan, *Confederate Agent*, 25. The *Courier* may have exaggerated or invented the Confederate inquiries to discredit Bowles, a political opponent; Carrington's report is equally suspect.

24. *OR* 23(2):397–98.

25. Ibid., (1):444; Horan, *Confederate Agent*, 27.

26. *OR* 23(1):384–89, and (2):440, 447–48, 459.

27. Ibid., (2):163, 438, 440, 514.

28. Ibid., (1):633–34, 645–46, and (2):517.

29. Horan, *Confederate Agent*, 28; *OR* 23(1):632.

30. Joseph Watson to Leroy Fitch, July 9, 1863, box 9, AEBP; *ORN* 25:242; *OR* 23(2):711.

III

1. *OR* 23(1):711–14, 721, 725; *ORN* 25:249; James A. Hardie to Boyle, July 23, 1863, box 10, and Hardie to Burnside, August 11, 1863, box 11, AEBP.

2. *OR* 23(1):658–59.

3. *Annals of the War*, 250; Dyer, *Compendium*, 990.

4. *OR* 23(1):716–17, 721–22; undated fragment of a letter, Larned Papers. Governor Morton's paranoia probably stemmed from a statement made by the captain of one of the steamers Morgan commandeered: he said Morgan asked him what the Hoosiers would think of him going to their capital and capturing the governor. See *Cincinnati Daily Commercial*, July 11, 1863.

5. *Annals of the War*, 250–51; Quisenberry, "Morgan's Men," 98–99.

6. *OR* 23(1):718.

7. Ibid., 656, 719–20, 730, 733; Dyer, *Compendium*, 990.

8. *Annals of the War*, 251; Mosgrove, "Following Morgan's Plume," 113; D. R. Larned to "My Dear Sister," July 12, 1863, Larned Papers; myriad reports in regard to Morgan, box 9, AEBP; *OR* 23(2):722.

9. *OR* 23(2):730.

10. Mosgrove, "Following Morgan's Plume," 116–17; *B&L* 3:635; *OR* 23(1):744; A. S. Clarke to Burnside, July 29, 1863, box 10, AEBP.

11. *OR* 23(1):737, 744–45, 816; *Cincinnati Daily Commercial*, July 14, 1863.

12. *B&L* 3:635; D. R. Larned journal, July 22, 1863, Larned Papers; *OR* 23(1):746, 749; *Annals of the War*, 252–53.

13. Mosgrove, "Following Morgan's Plume," 118; Theodore F. Allen, "Federal Account," 57; *OR* 23(1):664, 752, 756.

14. D. R. Larned to "Dear Helen," June 25, 1863, and to "Dear Henry," July 26, 1863, Larned Papers; Mrs. Burnside to General Burnside, June 27, 1863, box 8, AEBP; *OR* 23(1):756–57.

15. *OR* 23(1):660, 662, 672–73.

16. Ibid., 662, 666, 677–78.

17. Ibid., 640, 661–62; *B&L* 3:635; *Annals of the War*, 255–66; Mosgrove, "Following Morgan's Plume," 119–20.

18. *OR* 23(1):661, 776.

19. Ibid., 642, 678, 777.

20. Ibid., 673; C. B. Lewis to Burnside, July 28, 1863, box 10, AEBP.

21. D. R. Larned journal, July 22, 1863, and Larned to "Dear Henry," July 26, 1863, Larned Papers; *Cincinnati Daily Commercial*, July 24, 1863.

22. Cutts to Burnside, July 23, 1863, box 21, AEBP; *OR* 23(2):545. Cutts sent his wire to Lincoln within hours after his removal as Burnside's judge advocate, indicating the vengeful motives of the dispatch (*OR* 23[2]:545).

23. *OR* 23(1):642; *Annals of the War*, 253.

24. *OR* 23(1):793, 797, 802.

25. Ibid., 636, 667, 675–76, 795, 805, 808.

26. *OR* ser. 2, 6:153, 174.

27. *OR* 23(1):636, 816.

CHAPTER SIX

I

1. *OR* 23(2):384, 553, 558. Halleck was giving way to executive pressure for the East Tennessee invasion. Responding to a memorial from two citizens of that region, Lincoln wrote that Rosecrans and Burnside were coming to their relief. He never sent the letter, out of fear the secret might reach the enemy, but the movement was important to him (Basler, *Works of Lincoln*, 6:373–74).

2. *OR* 23(1):828–42, and (2):572; Coulter, *Civil War in Kentucky*, 176–78; *Louisville Daily Democrat*, August 4, 5, and 7, 1863; *Cleveland Plain Dealer*, August 7, 1863.

3. *OR* 23(2):561, 591–92.

4. Ibid., 593.

5. Ibid., 593–94. The various drafts of Burnside's reply, dated August 5 and 6, survive in box 11, AEBP.

6. D. R. Larned to "My Dear Henry," August 6, 1863, Larned Papers.

7. *OR* 30(3):17, 30; D. R. Larned to "My Dear Sister," August 2, 1863, Larned Papers.

8. D. R. Larned journal, August 10 and 11, 1863, Larned Papers; *OR* 23(2): 603. The Burnet House charged exorbitant rates to army officers. Larned's bill for a month was $114.63, and Burnside's $581.75. See D. R. Larned to "My Dear Sister," May 6, 1863, Larned Papers.

9. D. R. Larned journal, August 11–13, 1863, Larned Papers; *OR* 30(3):18; James Hardie to Burnside, August 11, 1863, and Lorenzo Thomas to Burnside, August 10, 1863, box 11, AEBP.

10. D. R. Larned journal, August 11–13, 1863, Larned Papers; George H. Thomas to Burnside, April 20, 1863, box 6, AEBP; *OR* 30(3):17–18.

11. *OR* 30(3):22, 72.

12. D. R. Larned journal, August 13 and 15, 1863, Larned Papers; *OR* 30(3): 45, 72.

13. *OR* 30(3):63, 72, 356.

14. D. R. Larned journal, August 16 and 17, 1863, and Larned to "My Dear A———," May 13, 1863, Larned Papers; *OR* 30(3):64.

15. *OR* 30(3):72; D. R. Larned journal, August 18–20, 1863, and Larned to "My Dear Sister," August 20, 1863, Larned Papers.

16. *OR* 30(2):94–95, and (3):717–18; D. R. Larned journal, August 21–23, 1863, Larned Papers.

17. *OR* 30(3):128, and (4):554.

18. Ibid., (4):512, 526, 537, 546, 554. Buckner's available forces, northeast of Burnside's column, consisted of about 3,400 men under Generals Frazer and

A. E. Jackson, plus whatever troops Samuel Jones could spare from southwestern Virginia; west and south of Burnside, he eventually gathered "about 9000" more (ibid., 587), and Forrest's cavalry division was within easy supporting distance. Before the end of August, Buckner was also reinforced by Alexander Stewart's infantry division.

19. Ibid., 571–72, 616.

20. *OR* 30(2):548, and (3):169, 195, 262, 904; Burnside to Halleck, October 3, 1863, box 12, AEBP.

21. *OR* 30(3):333, and (4):587; White, "East Tennessee," 302–3.

22. *OR* 30(4):587.

23. Halleck's orders of August 6 were to "endeavor to connect with the forces of General Rosecrans" (ibid. 23[2]:593). On September 11 he repeated this portion of the order: "Connect with General Rosecrans, at least with your cavalry" (ibid. 30[1]:34). Burnside had effected that connection September 7. In his report of November 15, 1863, however, Halleck refers to "a junction between the two armies of Burnside and Rosecrans," which he said "had been previously ordered"—previous, he implied, to September 9. There is considerable difference between a "connection" and a "junction," which implies the outright consolidation of the two forces, and Halleck gave Burnside nothing even resembling an order to join Rosecrans with his main body until September 14; Burnside did not receive it until September 17. See ibid. 30(3):638, 718.

24. Ibid. 30(3):333.

25. White, "East Tennessee," 304; Rule, "Loyalists of Tennessee," 477–78; Kniffen, "East Tennessee Campaign," 418. For an extensive but bitterly partisan account of the ordeal of loyal East Tennesseeans, see Brownlow, *Sketches*.

26. *OR* 30(2):590–92, 643–44, (3):358–59, 401, 433–34, 436, and (4):607.

27. Ibid. 10(1):72–74, and 52(1):438.

28. Ibid. 30(3):169, 435–36.

29. Ibid., (2):548–49, 596–97, 617–18, and (3):380.

30. Ibid., (2):617–21, 635, and (3):501. It was Frazer's report, written in captivity, that documented DeCourcy's negligence (ibid., [2]:614).

31. Ibid., (2):621–24, (3):943, and ser. 2, 6:280; Chapman, "A Georgia Soldier," 232. At the end of the century one of DeCourcy's officers tried to demonstrate that Burnside arrested the colonel out of jealousy, because DeCourcy reached the gap first. Neither his conclusion nor his premise had any foundation. See McFarland, *Surrender of Cumberland Gap*.

32. *OR* 30(3):523, 554, 717.

33. Ibid., 523, 525, 557, 592.

34. Ibid., 555.

35. Ibid., 618, 717, and (4):618.

36. Longstreet, *Manassas to Appomattox*, 436; Lee to Jefferson Davis, September 14, 1863, *SHSP* 12:324.

37. *OR* 30(3):639–40, 660, 691–92.

38. Ibid., 638–39, 661.

39. Ibid., 617, 638, 691, 717–18.

40. *OR* 30(2):550, (3):718, 731, 755–56, and (4):653, 659; Cox, *Reminiscences*, 1:534; White, "East Tennessee," 306. In his official report (*OR* 30, [2]:550), Burnside remembered receiving Halleck's first dispatch the evening of September 16, but his own dispatch of the next morning makes no mention of it, while his later message of September 17 acknowledges both. His report, submitted more than two years later, was probably in error.

41. *OR* 30(3):770. In his reply to Halleck, Burnside wrote: "It does not seem possible for me to successfully withdraw my forces from the presence of Jones if [*sic*] he should be beaten back or captured." Logic would indicate he meant to say "*unless* he should be beaten back or captured."

42. Ibid., (2):550, 592–93, 605, and (3):786.

43. Ibid., (2):550, 605, and (3):785, 808–9; Basler, *Works of Lincoln*, 6:469–70.

44. White, "East Tennessee," 306; *OR* 30(2):585, and (3):718, 904–5.

45. Basler, *Works of Lincoln*, 6:480–81; Bates, *Lincoln in the Telegraph Office*, 202.

46. *OR* 30(3):617, 638, 731, 769–70, 905, and (4):25, 114. Lincoln wrote Burnside September 27, "East Tennessee can be no more than temporarily lost" if he joined Rosecrans, but as late as October 5 Halleck wired him to "leave sufficient force in the upper end of the valley to hold Jones in check." See ibid., (3):905, and (4):114.

47. Ibid., (2):579. Burnside was not the first subordinate Halleck tried to sacrifice in order to escape criticism himself. A couple of weeks after the capture of Fort Donelson, he stuck a similar knife in U. S. Grant's back. See Catton, *Grant Moves South*, 195–97.

48. *OR* 30(3):904–6, 954, 955.

49. Ibid., 25.

50. Burnside to Halleck, October 3, 1863, box 12, AEBP.

51. *OR* 30(4):72, 96, 114.

52. Kniffen, "East Tennessee Campaign," 429. Kniffen does not cite the source of Hartsuff's alleged comment, nor the context in which it was made— if it ever was; his article appeared years after both Burnside and Hartsuff were dead.

53. Shanks, *Personal Recollections*, 258; *OR* 30(4):50, 79, 96.

54. *OR* 30(2):722–25, (3):922, and (4):230–31, 270, 350. Some period maps use the spelling "Mussel Shoals."

55. Ibid., (2):605–6, 639–40.

56. Ibid., 551, and (4):73, 96; William F. Draper to Lydia Joy Draper, September 30, 1863, Draper Papers.

57. Draper, *Recollections*, 119; *OR* 30(2):557, and (4):731, 733.

58. D. R. Larned journal, October 21, 1863, Larned Papers.

59. Ibid.; *OR* 30(2):551, 640–41.

60. *OR* 30(2):641.

61. D. R. Larned journal, October 21, 1863, Larned Papers.

62. *OR* 30(2):552, 641–42; Draper, *Recollections*, 121–22; D. R. Larned to "Dear Henry," September 29, 1863, Larned Papers.

63. *OR* 23(2):255–56, and 30(4):401, 428, 469; D. R. Larned to "My Dear Sister," October 18, 1863, Larned Papers. Burnside had apparently mentioned his intention to resign several days before, for on October 14 General White asked pointblank whether the rumor he would do so was correct (White to Burnside, October 14, 1863, box 12, AEBP).

64. *OR* 30(4):404–8. One theory holds that Rosecrans was marked for removal since the battle of Chickamauga but was retained in command to satisfy the voters in his home state, Ohio, until after the October elections. On October 13 Burnside's old nemesis, Vallandigham, was trounced in his gubernatorial bid; the results of the election were generally known by October 14, and the order for Rosecrans's relief was dated October 16 (Shanks, *Personal Recollections*, 262).

II

1. *OR* 31(1):680.

2. Ibid. 23(2):950–52, and 31(1):681; Dyer, *Compendium*, 1472, 1641.

3. Grant, *Memoirs*, 2:44; D. R. Larned to "My Dear Sister," November 2, 1863, Larned Papers. The watercourse from the mouth of the French Broad River to the Little Tennessee River was considered part of the Holston River in 1863; today it is called the Tennessee River, which is officially formed by the confluence of the Holston and the French Broad. See Montgomery, "Nomenclature of the Upper Tennessee," 46–57.

4. *OR* 30(2):564, and 31(1):6–12, 682, 688. Burnside relayed Wolford's report of the Confederate retreat to Edwin Stanton even as Wolford was fighting for his life (ibid. 31[1]:681).

5. Ibid. 31(1):682–83, 687, 701–2; D. R. Larned journal, October 22, 1863, and Larned to Mrs. Burnside, October 31, 1863, Larned Papers.

6. D. R. Larned journal, October 22, 1863, and Larned to Mrs. Burnside, October 31, 1863, Larned Papers.

7. *OR* 31(1):687, 718; D. R. Larned to "My Dear Sister," October 25, 1863, Larned Papers.

8. D. R. Larned to "My Dear Sister," October 25, 1863, Larned Papers.

9. D. R. Larned to Mrs. Burnside, October 31, 1863, Larned Papers; *OR* 31(1):730, 745–46, 756–58.

10. *OR* 31(1):758–59, 771, 778–79.

11. D. R. Larned to Mrs. Burnside, October 31, 1863, Larned Papers; Committee of the Regimental Association, *Thirty-fifth Massachusetts*, 174; Hawkes diary, October 28, 1863.

12. Hawkes diary, October 29, 1863; Larned to Mrs. Burnside, October 31, 1863, and to "My Dear Sister," November 2, 1863, Larned Papers; Committee of the Regimental Association, *Thirty-fifth Massachusetts*, 175.

13. D. R. Larned to "My Dear Henry," November 2, 1863, and to Mrs. Burnside, November 7, 1863, Larned Papers.

14. D. R. Larned to "My Dear Sister," November 2, 7, and 8, 1863, to "Dear Henry," November 2, 1863, and to Mrs. Burnside, November 7, 1863, Larned Papers. A sketch of the Knoxville headquarters appears in Poore, *Life of Burnside*, 217, and a description of its comforts in Sherman, *Memoirs*, 1:396. The owner was John H. Crozier, a lawyer who favored secession (*B&L* 3:737; Eighth U.S. Census, Knox County, Tennessee, reel 1259).

15. Longstreet, *Manassas to Appomattox*, 480–83; *OR* 31(3):62, 110, and 52(2):554–55.

16. *OR* 31(1):551–54, 558–60, and (3):47, 63, 67.

17. Ibid., (3):45–46, 66–67, 105–6, 116–17, 127–28.

18. Ibid., 76–77.

19. Ibid., 78, 110, 117.

20. Ibid., 88, 93, 127; Grant, *Memoirs*, 2:49–50.

21. *OR* 31(3):138–39.

22. *B&L* 3:746; *OR* 31(1):456–57, 540.

23. *OR* 31(1):260, (2):30, and (3):145–46, 148–50; Wilson, *Under the Old Flag*, 1:283–84.

24. D. R. Larned to "My Dear Sister," and to "Dear Henry," November 14, 1863, Larned Papers.

25. Committee of the Regimental Association, *Thirty-fifth Massachusetts*, 176–77.

26. *OR* 31(1):260, 273.

27. Ibid., 332, 540–41, and (3):147; Draper, *Recollections*, 126.

28. *OR* 31(1):332, 337; Draper, *Recollections*, 126; Committee of the Regimental Association, *Thirty-fifth Massachusetts*, 178. The sixth regiment of Hartranft's division, the 11th New Hampshire, had remained in Knoxville (Cogswell, *Eleventh New Hampshire*, 199).

29. *OR* 31(1):332, 350, 378; *B&L* 3:746; Committee of the Regimental Association, *Thirty-fifth Massachusetts*, 179.

30. *OR* 31(1):332–33, 481; *B&L* 3:732–33; Longstreet, *Manassas to Appomattox*, 490–91.

31. Draper, *Recollections*, 127; *OR* 31(1):350, 378; Longstreet, *Manassas to Appomattox*, 491–92. Humphrey had detached a fourth regiment to guard the supply train as it made its way back to Knoxville. See Cutcheon, "Recollections," 5.

32. *OR* 31(1):333.

33. Cutcheon, "Recollections," 6–7.

34. *OR* 31(1):333, 526; Draper, *Recollections*, 128–29; Committee of the Regimental Association, *Thirty-fifth Massachusetts*, 182.

35. *OR* 31(1):288–90, 333–34, 483, 526–27; *B&L* 3:733; Draper, *Recollections*, 129; Committee of the Regimental Association, *Thirty-fifth Massachusetts*, 182–83.

36. Committee of the Regimental Association, *Thirty-fifth Massachusetts*, 184; *OR* 31(1):542, and (3):157; G. W. Doughty to Burnside, November 18, 1863, box 13, AEBP. Wheeler did not say how he crossed the unfordable river; he must have done so in commandeered boats.

37. *OR* 31(1):274–75, and (3):157; Humes, *Loyal Mountaineers*, 246.

38. *OR* 31(1):300–301; *OR Atlas*, plate XLVIII, map 2, and plate CXXX, views 1–4.

39. Committee of the Regimental Association, *Thirty-fifth Massachusetts*, 185. Two days later, with the Ninth Corps reunited at Knoxville, Potter reported a total strength of only 4,483 officers and men—the size of one average division (Potter to Burnside, November 20, 1863, box 13, AEBP).

40. *B&L* 3:737–38, 747.

41. *OR* 31(3):163, 177, 182; Grant, *Memoirs*, 2:58.

42. *OR* 21:52, and 31(1):296.

43. Committee of the Regimental Association, *Thirty-fifth Massachusetts*, 187–88.

44. Ibid., 188; White, "East Tennessee," 316.

45. *OR* 31(1):295–96, 298, 301; Draper, *Recollections*, 131–32.

46. *OR* 31(1):298–99, 324.

47. Ibid., 324.

48. Ibid., 275–76; *B&L* 3:739.

49. *OR* 31(1):459, 476–77, 480.

50. Walcott, *Twenty-first Massachusetts*, 287; Cutcheon, "Recollections," 10–13; *OR* 31(1):363–67. Colonel Humphrey reported Ferrero ordered him to make the hopeless sortie on the Confederate salient; Captain Poe knew nothing about it and later tried without success to determine who ordered it (*B&L* 3:740). Ferrero reported he "received instructions" for the sortie (*OR* 31[1]:352) but never said from whom. His report, submitted after Burnside left the department, seems deliberately vague. The attack was perhaps his own ill-conceived notion.

51. *OR* 31(1):269, 405, and (3):240; Grant, *Memoirs*, 2:64, 75.

52. *OR* 31(1):269, 277, 297–98, 459.

53. Ibid., 532–33; Report of J. M. Brodhead, June 4, 1863, box labeled "Official Q.M. Papers," RIHS Papers.

54. *OR* 31(1):460, and (3):736.

III

1. Grant, *Memoirs*, 2:92–94; *OR* 31(3):273.

2. *OR* 31(1):486–89; David Morrison to Edward Ferrero, November 30, 1863,

box 13, AEBP. Johnson's division was one of the two Bragg originally ordered to reinforce Longstreet; he called the other back.

3. *OR* 31(1):342–44, 356, 358–59, 364. The size of the Sanders garrison is a matter of dispute. Benjamin claimed, "We were not 250 strong in the fort" (ibid., 344). Captain Poe estimated 375 infantry in and around the fort, for a total of no more than 440, including the artillery (*B&L* 3:742–43). The commander of the 20th Michigan named the same regiments as Poe, and the same approximate strengths, coming to a total of "about 320 to 340 men" who apparently included neither the artillerymen nor forty of the 2nd Michigan who were just outside the fort (Cutcheon, "Recollections," 14). Both Poe and Cutcheon missed a company of the 100th Pennsylvania stationed inside the fort (*OR* 31[1]:364).

4. *B&L* 3:748; *OR* 31(1):484, 487–88, 490–91.

5. *B&L* 3:748–49; *OR* 31(1):344.

6. *OR* 31(1):342–44; Cutcheon, "Recollections," 16.

7. *OR* 31(1):299, 319, 353, 491; Cutcheon, "Recollections," 16.

8. Draper, *Recollections*, 141; *B&L* 3:749, 752; *OR* 31(1):344; Committee of the Regimental Association, *Thirty-fifth Massachusetts*, 193; Walcott, *Twenty-first Massachusetts*, 288. Burnside's ordnance officer bought 140 grenades the previous August (W. H. Harris to D. R. Larned, August 5, 1863, box 11, AEBP).

9. *OR* 31(1):299, 344, 475; Blackburn, *Diary of Ralph Ely*, 67.

10. Longstreet, *Manassas to Appomattox*, 505–7.

11. Burnside handled the affair by failing to commend Ferrero directly in his own report, written late in 1865. See *OR* 31(1):278, 344, 353–54, 356, 358–59, 364.

12. Ibid., 278, 462; Longstreet, *Manassas to Appomattox*, 509. During the siege the defenders of Knoxville were reduced, for instance, to bread made from Indian corn meal, ground up cob and all (Cox, *Reminiscences*, 2:84).

13. *OR* 31(1):278–79, and (3):166, 283, 327; Cox, *Reminiscences*, 2:76.

14. Charles G. Loring to Burnside, December 3, 1863, box 22, AEBP; *OR* 31(1):278; Longstreet, *Manassas to Appomattox*, 511; *B&L* 3:750.

15. Sherman, *Memoirs*, 1:395–96; *OR* 31(1):269–70; Poe, *Personal Recollections*, 46–47; William F. Draper to "My Dear Parents," December 22, 1863, Draper Papers.

16. Sherman, *Memoirs*, 1:396, 409–10; *OR* 31(3):297.

17. *OR* 31(1):278, and (3):353; Sherman, *Memoirs*, 1:410. Burnside assumed Longstreet would voluntarily leave Tennessee for Virginia, where rations and other supplies would be more certain; it was a logical deduction, but incorrect.

18. Longstreet, *Manassas to Appomattox*, 511–15; *OR* 31(1):326–29; Dickert, *Kershaw's Brigade*, 318.

19. *OR* 31(1):279.

20. Cox, *Reminiscences*, 2:75–76.

21. *Cincinnati Daily Commercial*, December 19, 1863; *Cleveland Plain Dealer*, December 19, 1863.

22. Poore, *Life of Burnside*, 222–24; *OR* 31(3):272.

23. D. R. Larned to "Dear Henry," January 2, 1864, Larned Papers; *OR* 31(1): 281, 467–68, and 32(2):71–72.

24. D. R. Larned to "Dear Henry," January 2, 1864, Larned Papers; Cleaves, *Meade of Gettysburg*, 265.

25. Cox, *Reminiscences*, 2:40.

26. D. R. Larned to "My Dear Sister," January 5, 1864, Larned Papers; *OR* 32(2):79, 149–50; Grant, *Memoirs*, 2:113.

27. D. R. Larned to "My Dear Sister," January 8 and 10, 1864, Larned Papers.

28. *OR* 33:363, 428–29.

29. Ibid., 443–44; Van Buren to Burnside, January 27, 1864, box 15, AEBP.

30. *OR*, ser. 3, 4:79–80; Anderson, *Fifty-seventh Massachusetts*, 3–4; Houston, *Thirty-second Maine*, 33–34; Dyer, *Compendium*, 1654; Simon Griffin to Burnside, March 2, 1864, Dorus M. Fox to Burnside, March 3, 1864, and John Bross to Burnside, March 16, 1864, all in box 16, AEBP.

31. *Philadelphia Inquirer*, January 16, 1864; *OR* 33:373, 427; Charles G. Loring, Jr., to Burnside, March 1 and 7, 1864, box 15, AEBP.

32. Loring, Cutting, Goddard, and DeWolf to Burnside, various dates in March, 1864, box 16, and John Andrew to Burnside, January 25, 1864, box 15, AEBP; *Boston Evening Transcript*, February 2–5, 1864; *OR* 33:542; D. R. Larned to "Dear A——," February 4, 1864, Larned Papers; Burnside to E. M. Neill, February 17 and 25, 1864, Thomas R. Hayes to Burnside, February 19, 1864, and Mrs. Burnside to E. M. Neill, February 23, 1864, all in box 15, AEBP. For a review of Governor Gilmore's brief military career, see Marvel, *Race of the Soil*, 4.

33. *OR* 33:427–28; W. H. French to Burnside, March 16, 1864, and W. Silliman to George Bliss, March 30, 1864, box 16, AEBP.

34. Grant, *Memoirs*, 2:116; Edwin M. Stanton to Burnside, March 11, 1864, box 16, AEBP; *OR* 32(3):67, 74, 80, 102.

35. Poore, *Life of Burnside*, 226–30.

36. Dyer, *Compendium*, 1525; *OR* 33:741; D. R. Larned to "My Dear Sister," April 13, 1864, Larned Papers. Burnside's itinerary is reconstructed from his numerous telegrams to Assistant Adjutant General Edward M. Neill, box 16, AEBP.

37. *OR* 32(3):246, and 33:803, 807–8, 815. For the month of April Burnside reported 27,487 men assigned to the Ninth Corps, of whom 19,250 were present for duty (ibid. 33:1045). As late as April 25, when the Ninth Corps passed through Washington, the attorney general of the United States had no idea where it was bound (Beale, *Diary of Edward Bates*, 360).

CHAPTER SEVEN

I

1. Cogswell, *Eleventh New Hampshire*, 265–67; Hopkins, *Seventh Rhode Island*, 161–62; Draper, *Recollections*, 152. Besides numerous regimental histories, the requests Burnside received from men who wanted to serve with him attest to the respect and affection he inspired. Aside from such requests cited in the last chapter, see T. W. Egan to Burnside, January 22, 1864, W. D. Mann to Burnside, January 22, 1864, and H. B. Titus to Burnside, January 25, 1864, all in box 15, AEBP.

2. Loving, *Letters of George Washington Whitman*, 112–15; D. R. Larned to "My Dear Sister," April 13, 1864, Larned Papers; Elmer Bragg to "My Dear Sister," April 20, 1864, Bragg Collection; Cogswell, *Eleventh New Hampshire*, 265–70.

3. Cogswell, *Eleventh New Hampshire*, 265–70; Beale, *Diary of Edward Bates*, 360; Nevins, *Diary of Strong*, 3:433.

4. Elmer Bragg to William L. Bragg, April 28, 1864, Bragg Collection; Cogswell, *Eleventh New Hampshire*, 280–87; Loving, *Letters of George Washington Whitman*, 117.

5. Loving, *Letters of George Washington Whitman*, 131.

6. Nevins, *Diary of Battle*, 330–31.

7. Agassiz, *Meade's Headquarters*, 102.

8. *OR* 36(2):363.

9. Ibid., 380, 387, 426; Weld, *War Diary*, 284–85; Jackman, *Sixth New Hampshire*, 213; Cogswell, *Eleventh New Hampshire*, 315.

10. Jackman, *Sixth New Hampshire*, 213–14; Cogswell, *Eleventh New Hampshire*, 316, 319.

11. Cogswell, *Eleventh New Hampshire*, 327–32.

12. *OR* 36(1):904, and (2):404–5, 424–25.

13. Schaff, *Wilderness*, 225–26; Cogswell, *Eleventh New Hampshire*, 333; *OR* 36(2):927, 934, 972. The conference of Meade's corps commanders probably took place without Burnside. A musician in Potter's division recorded in his diary that he was awakened at one o'clock that morning to move to the front (Bailey diary, May 6, 1864).

14. Grant, *Memoirs*, 2:193–95; *OR* 36(1):18, 927; Anderson, *Fifty-seventh Massachusetts*, 35; Jones diary, May 6, 1864; Schaff, *Wilderness*, 231–32.

15. Nevins, *Diary of Battle*, 352; D. R. Larned to J. C. Woodruff, May 3, 1864, box 16, AEBP; Lyman, "Uselessness of Maps," 79–80.

16. Agassiz, *Meade's Headquarters*, 94–95; Schaff, *Wilderness*, 231–32; *OR* 36(1):407, 611, 615. Hancock's late arrival at Cold Harbor on June 2, though equally as understandable as Burnside's tardiness at the Wilderness, was largely responsible for a postponement of Grant's attack that allowed Lee time to make his works impregnable, setting the stage for the Union disaster that followed.

17. Charles J. Mills to "Dear Father," May 7, 1864, Mills Letters; *OR* 36(1): 611, 615, 927–28, 1081, and (2):441: Jackman, *Sixth New Hampshire*, 215.

18. *OR* 5:24, 11(1):124–25, 19(2):308, 36(1):928, 934, and (2):442, 460–61; Sumner, *Diary of Cyrus Comstock*, 215, 230, 264. In his *Wilderness Campaign*, Edward Steere accepts the Schaff-Duane assessment of Burnside without question, simply repeating their unfounded references to the "Sluggard of Antietam." This is hardly uncommon among historians, and the jaundiced memoirs of Army of the Potomac officers tend to guide the most persistent scholar in that direction. But Steere does Burnside the additional injustice of claiming he spent five hours—from 9:00 until 2:00—moving two miles from the fight with Ramseur to the relief of Hancock's right (413). Burnside's acute angle of march backward and forward not only increased the distance, he was not even in touch with Hancock's flank until 10:00 A.M., according to Comstock (*OR* 36[2]:460). Given half an hour to form his brigades and post skirmishers, he probably did not begin to advance until 10:30; at 12:30 Comstock reported Burnside's leading brigade had been "smartly engaged" for fifteen minutes, meaning he was actually less than two hours coming up, rather than five (*OR* 36[2]:461). Considering the "impenetrable undergrowth" Potter described, and the precarious position of Burnside's right flank, he was not so unreasonably slow as the anxiety at headquarters may have made it appear.

19. *OR* 36(1):927–28.

20. Agassiz, *Meade's Headquarters*, 96–97.

21. Lyman, "Uselessness of Maps," 79.

22. *OR* 36(1):943, and (2):546–48, 580–85.

23. Ibid., (1):908–9, and (2):610; Charles J. Mills to "Dear Mother," May 11, 1864, Mills Letters.

24. *OR* 36(1):148, 908–9, 920, 954, and (2):610–11; Hawkes diary, May 12, 1864.

25. *OR* 36(1):909, and (2):613–14, 629; Agassiz, *Meade's Headquarters*, 108–10; Horace Porter, *Campaigning With Grant*, 94–95. Comments about Burnside at Army of the Potomac headquarters were seldom flattering, and McClellan's publication of his "revised" report only worsened the situation. Colonel Wainwright, who read the report in March, assessed Burnside's May 6 tardiness with the remark, "Burnside somehow is never up to the mark when the tug comes." Since Burnside had never had much trouble holding up his end of a schedule before, Wainwright could only have been swayed by the false accusations in McClellan's account of the Maryland campaign; it is worth noting that by May 14 Wainwright was also complaining of the sluggish marches of his own corps in the Virginia tangle (Nevins, *Diary of Battle*, 352, 355, 370–71). Cyrus Comstock also later admitted disparaging Burnside at headquarters: "He is not competent to command a corps, & I have spoken freely of him—" (Sumner, *Diary of Cyrus Comstock*, 285).

26. *OR* 36(2):629, 643. Twenty years later, Grant had decided Burnside was not to blame for the lost opportunity of May 10 (*Memoirs*, 2:225). The conde-

scending Comstock was a poor choice for an emissary.

27. Charles J. Mills to "Dear Mother," May 14, 1864, Mills Letters; *OR* 36(1): 909, and (2):643.

28. Charles J. Mills to "Dear Mother," May 14, 1864, Mills Letters; Jones diary, May 12, 1864; Horace Porter, *Campaigning With Grant*, 102; Hopkins, *Seventh Rhode Island*, 169–70; *OR* 36(1):928; Jackman, *Sixth New Hampshire*, 241–43; Committee of the Regiment, *Thirty-sixth Massachusetts*, 165.

29. *OR* 36(1):676–79. The original of Grant's eight o'clock directive, and apparently the only copy of Hancock's news to Burnside, are preserved in box 17, AEBP. Both have been laboriously smoothed.

30. Cyrus B. Comstock diary, May 12, 1864, Comstock Papers; *OR* 36(2): 663, 672–73, 679.

31. Grant, *Memoirs*, 2:232; *OR* 36(1):910, 944, 958, 1020; Charles D. Todd diary, May 12, 1864; Lane, "Truth of History," 74–75, 78–79; Parker, *51st Regiment*, 548; Cullum, *Biographical Register*, 2:781–82.

32. D. R. Larned to "My Dear Sister," May 13, 1864, and to "My Dear Henry," May 17, 1864, Larned Papers; *OR* 36(2):681.

33. Boatner, *Civil War Dictionary*, 474; *OR* 18:59.

34. *OR* 36(1):910–11, 917, 928–29.

35. Ibid., 911–12, 929, and (3):18, 64–65; Hopkins, *Seventh Rhode Island*, 177. As usual, some have tried to blame Burnside's failure to seize the Stannard's Mill bridge for Lee's successful withdrawal to the North Anna, but one student of the campaign has pointed out that Warren's Fifth Corps could have reached the mill a couple of hours earlier, before such Confederate strength accumulated—had Meade not rerouted it. See Matter, *If It Takes All Summer*, 339. Mr. Matter wonders whether Burnside knew how heavily the bridge was defended when he ordered Potter to abandon the Po crossing (*If It Takes All Summer*, 340); the length and volume of Curtin's fight (Hopkins, *Seventh Rhode Island*, 177) must have led Burnside to that deduction.

36. *OR* 36(1):911–12; D. R. Larned to "My Dear Sister," May 22, 1864, Larned Papers.

37. *OR* 36(1):912–18, 919; D. R. Larned to "My Dear Sister," May 22, 1864, Larned Papers; Agassiz, *Meade's Headquarters*, 120. The Jackson service is commemorated by a plaque on the church wall.

38. Grant, *Memoirs*, 2:250–51; Horace Porter, *Campaigning With Grant*, 136–37.

39. Sparks, *Inside Lincoln's Army*, 376; *OR* 36(1):153–64. Twelve of Burnside's thirty-five white regiments were new that spring, while two more had been organized in mid-1863; not one in the Second, Fifth, or Sixth corps was of later vintage than 1862.

40. *OR* 36(2):730, and (3):96, 118–19, 134–35.

41. Ibid., (3):148–49, 167–68; Whitney diary, May 24, 1864; Coco, *Letters of Charles J. Mills*, 89–90.

42. Weld, *War Diary*, 296–97, 311; Anderson, *Fifty-seventh Massachusetts*,

98–103; Committee of the Regimental Association, *Thirty-fifth Massachusetts*, 238–40.

43. *OR* 36(3):148–49, 166–68.

44. Ibid., 169.

45. D. R. Larned to "My Dear Henry," May 25, 1864, Larned Papers; Horace Porter, *Campaigning With Grant*, 144–45.

46. *OR* 36(3):170, 197–99.

47. Ibid., 199, 808.

48. *OR* 36(2):929, and (3):831–32. Perhaps the only thing that prevented the Confederates from attacking Hancock's weaker wing or Crittenden's exposed division on May 24 was an intestinal ailment that sent Robert E. Lee to his bed. See Dowdey, *Papers of Lee*, 739.

49. *OR* 36(3):256–57; Nevins, *Diary of Battle*, 116, 219; Agassiz, *Meade's Headquarters*, 128.

II

1. D. R. Larned to "My Dear Sister," May 30, 1864, Larned Papers; *OR* 36(3): 271–72, 309–10.

2. *OR* 36(3):356, 358, 391, 404, 407–9.

3. Ibid., (1):344, 913, and (3):462–63.

4. Ibid., (1):543–44, 913–14, 942, and (3):500–501, 504, 867; Agassiz, *Meade's Headquarters*, 140–41. Despite the assumption Crittenden's carelessness precipitated the attack, Lee seems to have planned it from the moment he discovered Hancock's departure. See Lee to James Seddon, June 2, 1864, *SHSP* 7: 292.

5. *OR* 36(1):344, and (3):867–69. In the wee hours of May 6 Burnside's corps marched at the very moment of the new moon, while Hancock's march of June 1–2 preceded the new moon by two days, so Hancock actually had a little more light than Burnside. See "It Was a Full Moon When . . . ."

6. *OR* 36(1):914, 930, 946, and (3):547–51; D. R. Larned journal, June 9, 1864, Larned Papers; *B&L* 4:249.

7. *OR* 36(3):575–76, 584; Agassiz, *Meade's Headquarters*, 149.

8. *OR* 36(3):585–88, 617–22; D. R. Larned to "My Dear Sister," June 5, 1864, Larned Papers.

9. D. R. Larned to "My Dear Sister," June 5, 1864, Larned Papers.

10. D. R. Larned journal, June 9, 1864, Larned Papers.

11. D. R. Larned to "My Dear Sister," June 15, 1864, Larned Papers; Grant, *Memoirs*, 2:143–45; Circular Order dated July 6, 1864, expelling Swinton and a Mr. Kent, box 19, AEBP; Swinton's *Campaigns*, the earliest account of that army, handles Burnside with brutal sarcasm.

12. D. R. Larned to "My Dear Sister," June 15, 1864, Larned Papers; Frassanito, *Grant and Lee*, 189–90.

13. D. R. Larned to "Dear Henry," June 11, 1864, Larned Papers; *OR* 36(3):

619, and 40(1):228–31; Charles J. Mills to "Dearest Mother," June 11, 1864, Mills Letters.

14. *OR* 36(3):765–66, and 40(1):521–22.

15. D. R. Larned to "My Dear Sister," June 15, 1864, Larned Papers; James St. Clair Morton to Burnside, June 15, 1864, box 23, AEBP. The black troops who sacked the plantation were probably those of Edward Hinks, of the Eighteenth Corps: his 1st, 10th, and 22nd U.S. Colored Troops operated in that vicinity in late May 1864, and some of them engaged in "foraging." See *OR* 36(2):165–67.

16. Horace Porter, *Campaigning With Grant*, 198; Grant, *Memoirs*, 2:293–96; *OR* 40(1):303–4, 705.

17. *OR* 40(1):522, and (2):67–68; Hopkins, *Seventh Rhode Island*, 190–91; Lord, *Ninth New Hampshire*, 455–56; Coco, *Letters of Charles J. Mills*, 104.

18. *OR* 40(1):306, 502, 545, and (2):90–91; *B&L* 4:541–42.

19. Bosbyshell, *The 48th*, 157–58.

20. *OR* 40(1):522, 530; Gallagher, *Fighting for the Confederacy*, 428. Some of Potter's front-line regiments were not properly credited with the capture of men, guns, and flags, as those trophies went to the rear in the custody of supporting troops, who claimed them for themselves (Bosbyshell, *The 48th*, 158).

21. Agassiz, *Meade's Headquarters*, 166; *OR* 40(1):545, 571–72, 577.

22. Hawkes diary, June 17, 1864.

23. *OR* 40(1):522–23, 532–35, 540; Agassiz, *Meade's Headquarters*, 168.

24. Hawkes diary, June 17, 1864; Coco, *Letters of Charles J. Mills*, 101–2, 114–15, 151; Weld, *War Diary*, 312; *OR* 40(1):533–35.

25. *OR* 40(1):472, 572–73. Samuel Crawford's Fifth Corps division had also moved up to support Ledlie, under the supposition he had taken the main Confederate line, but found he was only in the skirmishers' rifle pits. That division claimed to have captured an entire North Carolina regiment and sent it to the rear, and Crawford accused Ledlie of taking the immediate credit for it; it may also have been Ledlie whose troops misappropriated Potter's battle trophies (ibid., 472).

26. *B&L* 4:542–44; *OR* 40(1):572–73.

27. *B&L* 4:543; *OR* 40(1):572, and (2):167, 179.

28. *B&L* 4:543; *OR* 40(1):572–73, and (2):179–81.

29. D. R. Larned to "My Dear Sister," June 20, 1864, Larned Papers; Agassiz, *Meade's Headquarters*, 168.

30. Agassiz, *Meade's Headquarters*, 148; *OR* 40(2):168; Roe and Nutt, *First Heavy Artillery*, 172–75.

31. *OR* 40(2):218–40.

III

1. *OR* 40(2):220.

2. Ibid., 396–97; *Crater Report*, 17, 126; Bosbyshell, *The 48th*, 163.

3. *Crater Report*, 126–27; Coco, *Letters of Charles J. Mills*, 138; Bosbyshell, *The 48th*, 166; *OR* 40(2):484, 528.

4. Sparks, *Inside Lincoln's Army*, 389–90.

5. Bosbyshell, *The 48th*, 167–68; *Crater Report*, 127.

6. *OR* 40(2):608–9, 629, 630.

7. Ibid., (1):558; *Crater Report*, 17, 126–27.

8. *OR* 40(3):304–5.

9. *B&L* 4:563.

10. *Crater Report*, 15–18, 127; Agassiz, *Meade's Headquarters*, 196; *OR* 40(3):266. For whatever the possibility is worth, the fuse (like the powder) may have passed through the hands of Lieutenant Morris Schaff, the ordnance officer who had so low an opinion of Burnside (*OR* 40[3]:266).

11. *Crater Report*, 17, 42, 98, 125; Agassiz, *Meade's Headquarters*, 201.

12. *Crater Report*, 15–18; Potter, Letter.

13. *OR* 40(1):133–34, 699.

14. Ibid., 535; Weld, *War Diary*, 339, 344, 353; Coco, *Letters of Charles J. Mills*, 128, 130, 133.

15. *Crater Report*, 170–71; Hopkins, *Seventh Rhode Island*, 198; Committee of the Regimental Association, *Thirty-fifth Massachusetts*, 266–67.

16. *OR* 40(3):566; *Crater Report*, 111.

17. Committee of the Regimental Association, *Thirty-fifth Massachusetts*, 276; Dyer, *Compendium*, 1469; Agassiz, *Meade's Headquarters*, 199.

18. Boatner, *Civil War Dictionary*, 48, 262; Bernard, *War Talks*, 193–94; Agassiz, *Meade's Headquarters*, 197.

19. *Crater Report*, 143; *B&L* 4:549. Burnside gave Ledlie his orders with dusk at least four hours away: only Ledlie's own procrastination could explain his failure to conduct a daylight reconnaissance.

20. *OR* 40(1):557, and (3):656–57; *Crater Report*, 153–62.

21. Weld, "The Petersburg Mine," 208; *OR* 40(1):280, 535; Committee of the Regimental Association, *Thirty-fifth Massachusetts*, 268; *Crater Report*, 194, 222.

22. *Crater Report*, 224; Charles H. Porter, "The Petersburg Mine," 230; Weld, "The Petersburg Mine," 208; *B&L* 4:551.

23. McMaster, "Battle of the Crater," 20; Weld, "The Petersburg Mine," 209.

24. *Crater Report*, 17, 165; Anderson, *Fifty-seventh Massachusetts*, 219–21; Osborne, *Twenty-ninth Massachusetts*, 315–16; Newberry, "The Petersburg Mine," 3:123.

25. General Potter described waiting for Ledlie to appear at the July 29 conference in *Crater Report*, 98; Nevins, *Diary of Battle*, 433; Weld, *War Diary*, 311. For an account of alcohol abuse in Civil War armies, see Street, "Under the Influence."

26. *B&L* 4:552.

27. *Crater Report*, 99; *OR* 40(1):574.

28. *OR* 40(1):574, 579; *Crater Report*, 100.

29. *Crater Report*, 144, 186.

30. *OR* 40(1):707, and (3):657–59; *Crater Report*, 163–64, 183.

31. *OR* 40(3):612, 659–60, 664.

32. *Crater Report*, 206–7, 221–22.

33. Ibid., 122, 196; *OR* 40(1):586; Cutcheon, "Twentieth Michigan," 135.

34. Stewart, "Charge of the Crater," 80–82; Weld, *War Diary*, 353–54; Weld, "The Petersburg Mine," 211–12; Louis Bell to George Bell, August 12, 1864, box 3, folder 7, Bell Family Papers.

35. *OR* 40(3):636–62. Jedediah Paine's signal tower dispatches, recorded on these pages, have no times marked upon them. The originals of those same memoranda, preserved in box 18, AEBP, are in ink, while notations such as "between 6 & 7," "7 to 8," "9–," and "9.30" are penciled in. Burnside himself may have estimated the times he received them in the course of preparing for the court of inquiry.

36. *Crater Report*, 145; Agassiz, *Meade's Headquarters*, 200.

37. *OR* 40(3):661–62, 666; Agassiz, *Meade's Headquarters*, 201.

38. Sumner, *Diary of Cyrus Comstock*, 285; Sparks, *Inside Lincoln's Army*, 406.

39. *OR* 40(1):575, and (3):663; Committee of the Regimental Association, *Thirty-fifth Massachusetts*, 271; Hopkins, *Seventh Rhode Island*, 199.

40. The original of Burnside's order to withdraw is in box 18, AEBP. Folded twice into a rectangle the size of a business card, its edges are still red with the clay that clung to Griffin's, Hartranft's, and Bartlett's thumbs. In testimony to the brutal work of the mortars the Confederates trained upon the Crater, one face of the order is flecked with a black gob that appears to be dried blood.

41. *OR* 40(3):663–64.

42. Ibid., (1):529, 539, 542, 546, 576, and (3):691, 700–702, 821.

43. Ibid., (3):701–2, 705–6. The more acerbic reply that was not sent (Burnside to A. A. Humphreys, July 31, 1864) is copied into a letterbook labeled "July 30, 1864, Mine Operations," RIHS Papers.

44. *OR* 40(1):18, 171; *Crater Report*, 26.

45. A personalized account of Hancock's defeat at Reams's Station can be found in Billings, *Tenth Massachusetts Battery*, 242–54.

46. J. L. Van Buren's field journal, August, 1864, RIHS Papers; *Crater Report*, 150–51, 180.

47. *Crater Report*, 231–32. Meade's own provost marshal thought the commanding general would fare worse: the day after the battle, Marsena Patrick wrote, "If the matter be investigated nothing but Grant's presence will save Meade—" (Sparks, *Inside Lincoln's Army*, 407).

48. *Crater Report*, 186, 191, 197. One of Ledlie's staff officers wrote his father, "Some day or other, I will tell you a good deal about" Ledlie (Coco, *Letters of Charles J. Mills*, 142).

49. Gallagher, *Fighting for the Confederacy*, 407; Whitman, "The Bravest Soldiers," *Leaves of Grass*, 385.

50. Agassiz, *Meade's Headquarters*, 211–12. The prejudice accorded the Ninth Corps by the rest of the Army of the Potomac may have contributed to the continued survival of incompetents like Ledlie by imposing a siege mentality wherein Burnside was more defensive of his officers than critical of them.

51. *Portsmouth [N.H.] Morning Chronicle*, August 26 and September 1, 1864; Anna Bishop to Burnside, July 21, 1862, box 2, AEBP.

52. *OR* 42(2):603, 641, 1076, and (3):624; Sumner, *Diary of Cyrus Comstock*, 296; Simon, *Papers of Grant* 12:317–18.

53. Nevins, *Diary of Strong*, 3:518, 521.

54. G. V. Fox to Burnside, January 1, 1865, box 20, AEBP; Nevins, *Diary of Strong*, 3:546; *OR* 46(2):190, 300.

55. *Providence Journal*, January 10 and 13, 1865.

56. On Burnside's efforts to obtain withheld reports, see Seth Williams to Burnside, December 30 and 31, 1863, box 14, Daniel Butterfield to Burnside, January 25, 1864, and James A. Hardie to Burnside, January 30, 1864, box 15, Ira Spaulding to Rufus Ingalls and Ingalls to Burnside, both January 30, 1865, box 20, AEBP.

57. *Crater Report*, 1–10, 95, 125; Meade, *Letters*, 2:253.

58. *OR* 46(2):353, 497–98; *Crater Report*, 124–25. Grant's assessment of Ledlie came after that brigadier's more obnoxious traits became well known; at the time of the battle, Grant probably knew no more of Ledlie than Burnside did.

59. Colyer to Burnside, January 20, 1865, Burnside to Stanly, January 16, 1865, and Burnside to Colyer, January 25, 1865, box 20, AEBP.

60. James Burnside to Green Adams, December 1, 1864, Ambrose Burnside to James Burnside, January 16, 1865, box 21, and Ambrose Burnside to Montgomery Meigs, December 8, 1862, box 4, AEBP.

61. *OR* 46(3):96.

62. Burnside to Stanton, April 14, 1865, Letters Received by the Commission Branch of the Adjutant General's Office, 1863–1870, reel 143.

63. Nevins, *Diary of Strong*, 3:589; Special Order Number 175, announcing Burnside's resignation, dated April 19, 1865, box 7, Burnside Collection, Generals' Papers, Records Group 94, National Archives.

EPILOGUE

1. Poore, *Life of Burnside*, 386.

2. Ibid., 266–73, 278–84; Byrnes and Spilman, *The Providence Journal*, 181; Nevins, *Diary of Strong*, 4:208.

3. Poore, *Life of Burnside*, 285–92; Sheridan, *Memoirs*, 2:427–29; Nevins, *Diary of Strong*, 4:325.

4. Boatner, *Civil War Dictionary*, 789; Knight, *Sprague Families*, 58–74.

5. Poore, *Life of Burnside*, 296, 313–14; Treasury audit, March 12, 1872, bond agreement for Manhattan Bleaching and Dying Co., August 21, 1874, and capi-

tal statement of same, all in box labeled "Correspondence & Miscellaneous," RIHS Papers; Heth, "Memoirs," 9. Burnside found "great fraud" among Department of the Ohio quartermasters when he arrived there, but some of it apparently escaped him. See Burnside to Montgomery Meigs, June 17, 1863, Letterbook #2, RIHS Papers, and court martial proceedings against Captain H. J. Latshaw, A.Q.M., box 22, AEBP.

6. Poore, *Life of Burnside*, 297–303, 316; Douglas, *I Rode with Stonewall*, 176–77. Burnside's lengthy speech and assorted correspondence on the staff reunion are in the Correspondence & Miscellaneous box, RIHS Papers.

7. Poore, *Life of Burnside*, 317–21.

8. Ibid., 322.

9. Welles, *Diary*, 3:357; Nevins, *Diary of Strong*, 4:208.

10. Poore, *Life of Burnside*, 320, 332, 358–59, 366–67, 372–81; William W. Burns to Burnside, January 4, 1879, Special Collections, USMA Library.

11. *OR* 12(2), supplement:1002–6, 1051; Ropes, "Case of Fitz-John Porter," 351; Poore, *Life of Burnside*, 362–63.

12. Poore, *Life of Burnside*, 308, 385–86.

13. Ibid., 386–89.

14. Ibid., 392–400; Sears, *Young Napoleon*, 397–98; Woodbury, *Ninth Army Corps*, 496–500; Learned, *Learned Family*, 214.

15. Poore, *Life of Burnside*, 402–5; Burnside to Jonathan Sturges, June 17, 1863, box 8, AEBP. See also Woodbury's letters to the *Providence Journal*, December 18, 1863, and January 6, 1864.

16. Poore, *Life of Burnside*, 408.

BIBLIOGRAPHY

MANUSCRIPTS

Dartmouth College Library, Hanover, N.H.
  Elmer Bragg Collection
  Oscar D. Robinson diary
Fredericksburg and Spotsylvania National Military Park,
    Fredericksburg, Va.
  John S. Crocker Letters (photocopies)
  Charles J. Mills Letters (partial typescripts of USAMHI collection, below)
Indiana Historical Society, Indianapolis, Ind.
  David E. Beem Papers
  Alexander B. Pattison diary
Indiana State Library, Indianapolis, Ind.
  Indiana Division
    Henry C. Marsh letter
Library of Congress, Manuscript Division, Washington, D.C.
  Cyrus B. Comstock Papers
  William Franklin Draper Papers
  John Porter Hatch Papers
  Lewis M. Haupt Family Papers
  Henry C. Heisler Papers
  Daniel Reed Larned Papers
  George B. McClellan Papers
  William C. McKinley Collection
  Peter H. Niles diary
  Israel Washburn Papers
National Archives, Washington, D.C.
  Ambrose E. Burnside Collection, Generals' Papers
  Ambrose E. Burnside Papers, Generals' Reports and Books
  Confederate Compiled Service Records, General and Staff Officers and
    Nonregimental Enlisted Men, microcopy M-331
  Eighth Census of the United States, microcopy M-653

Letters Received by the Commission Branch of the Adjutant General's
    Office, microcopy M-1098
Muster Roll of Company D, 11th Mississippi
Returns from Regular Army Artillery Regiments, microcopy M-727
Returns from U.S. Military Posts, 1800–1916, microcopy M-617
U.S. Military Academy Records
New Hampshire Historical Society, Concord, N.H.
    John Batchelder Bailey diary
    Bell Family Papers
    Charles Chase Family Papers
    Josiah N. Jones diary
    Miscellaneous Civil War Letters
      Rodney H. Ramsey letter
Rhode Island Historical Society, Providence, R.I.
    Ambrose E. Burnside Papers
Union County Public Library, Liberty, Ind.
    "History of Union County Schools, 1804–1986" (typescript)
    Smith, Ophia D., "Oxford Spy Wed at Pistol Point" (disbound article)
U.S. Army Military History Institute, Carlisle Barracks, Pa.
    Civil War Miscellaneous Collection
      Henry Gangewer diary
      Alfred Holcomb Letters
    Civil War Times Illustrated Collection
      William Seagrave Collection
    George P. Hawkes diary
    William Marvel Collection
      George E. Bates letter
      Julius Whitney diary
    Massachusetts Manuscripts
      Charles J. Mills Letters
    Wiley Sword Collection
      Albert G. Bates Letters
    Charles G. Todd diary
U.S. Military Academy, West Point, N.Y.
    U.S. Military Academy Archives
      "Circumstances of the Parents of Cadets, 1842–1879"
      "Merit Book, 1836–1853"
      "Register of Delinquencies, 1843–1847"
    U.S. Military Academy Library, Special Collections
      William Wallace Burns Collection
      Ambrose E. Burnside Collection
      "The Memoirs of Brigadier-General William Montgomery Gardner"
      (typescript)

NEWSPAPERS

Boston Evening Transcript
Chicago Tribune
Cincinnati Daily Commercial
Cleveland Leader
Cleveland Plain Dealer
Columbus, Ohio, *Crisis*
Dayton Empire
Dayton Journal
Detroit Free Press
Louisville Daily Democrat
Newbern *Daily Progress*
    (Confederate)
Newbern Progress (Union)
New York Herald

New York Sun
New York Times
New York Tribune
Ohio State Journal
Ohio Statesman
Philadelphia Inquirer
Philadelphia Weekly Press
Philadelphia Weekly Times
*Portsmouth [N.H.] Morning
    Chronicle*
Providence Evening Press
Providence Journal
Richmond, Ind., *Palladium*

BOOKS AND ARTICLES

Adams, Michael C. C. *Our Masters the Rebels*. Cambridge: Harvard
    University Press, 1978.
Agassiz, George R., ed. *Meade's Headquarters, 1863–1865, Letters of Colonel
    Theodore Lyman*. Boston: Atlantic Monthly Press, 1922.
Alexander, E. P. *Military Memoirs of a Confederate*. New York: C. Scribner's
    Sons, 1907.
Alexander, Ted, ed. *The 126th Pennsylvania*. Shippensburg, Pa.: Beidel
    Printing House, 1984.
Allen, George H. *Forty-six Months with the Fourth R.I. Volunteers in the
    War of 1861 to 1865*. Providence, R.I.: J. A. & R. A. Reid, 1887.
Allen, Theodore F. "Federal Account of the Morgan Raid." *Confederate
    Veteran*, February, 1898, 56–58.
Allen, William. "Fredericksburg." *Papers of the Military Historical Society
    of Massachusetts* 3:122–49.
Aman, Daniel Franklin. Statement. *Confederate Veteran*, September,
    1930, 339.
Anderson, John. *The Fifty-seventh Regiment of Massachusetts Volunteers in
    the War of the Rebellion*. Boston: E. B. Stillings & Co., 1896.
Angle, Paul M., and Earl Schenck Miers. *The Living Lincoln*. New
    Brunswick, N.J.: Rutgers University Press, 1955.
Annals of the War. Philadelphia: Times Publishing Company, 1879.
*Atlas to Accompany the Official Records of the Union and Confederate
    Armies*. Washington, D.C.: Government Printing Office, 1891–95.

Avery, William B. *The Marine Artillery with the Burnside Expedition.*
    Providence, R.I.: N. Bangs Williams & Co., 1880.
Bailey, Hugh C. *Hinton Rowan Helper, Abolitionist-Racist.* University:
    University of Alabama Press, 1965.
Ballou, Daniel Ross. *The Military Services of Maj.-Gen. Ambrose Everett
    Burnside in the Civil War.* 2 parts. Providence: Rhode Island Soldiers
    and Sailors Historical Society, 1914.
Barney, C. Henry. *A Country Boy's First Three Months in the Army.*
    Providence, R.I.: N. Bangs Williams & Co., 1880.
Barrett, John G. *The Civil War in North Carolina.* Chapel Hill: University of
    North Carolina Press, 1963.
Bartlett, Asa W. *History of the Twelfth Regiment New Hampshire Volunteers
    in the War of the Rebellion.* Concord, N.H.: Ira C. Evans, 1897.
Bartley, S. Howard. *Fatigue—Mechanism and Management.* Springfield,
    Ill.: Charles C. Thomas, 1965.
Basler, Roy P., ed. *The Collected Works of Abraham Lincoln.* 9 vols. New
    Brunswick, N.J.: Rutgers University Press, 1953–55.
Bates, David H. *Lincoln in the Telegraph Office.* New York: Century
    Co., 1907.
Beale, Howard K., ed. *The Diary of Edward Bates, 1859–1866.* Washington,
    D.C.: Government Printing Office, 1933.
Bernard, George S. *War Talks of Confederate Veterans.* Dayton, Ohio:
    Morningside Bookshop, 1981.
Biddle, William F. "Recollections of McClellan." *The United Service*, May
    1894, 460–69.
Billings, John D. *History of the Tenth Massachusetts Battery.* Boston: Hall
    and Whiting, 1881.
Blackburn, George M., ed. *With the Wandering Regiment: The Diary of
    Captain Ralph Ely of the Eighth Michigan Infantry.* Mount Pleasant:
    Central Michigan University Press, 1965.
Blackford, W. W. *War Years with Jeb Stuart.* New York: Charles Scribner's
    Sons, 1945.
Bloss, John M. "Antietam and the Lost Dispatch." In *War Talks in Kansas.*
    Kansas City, Mo.: Kansas Commandery of the Military Order of the
    Loyal Legion of the United States, 1906.
Boatner, Mark Mayo. *The Civil War Dictionary.* New York: David McKay
    Co., 1959.
Bosbyshell, Oliver C. *The 48th in the War.* Philadelphia: Avil Print Co., 1895.
Brown, Norman D. *Edward Stanly, Whiggery's "Tarheel" Conqueror.*
    University: University of Alabama Press, 1974.
Brownlow, W. G. *Sketches of the Rise, Progress, and Decline of Secession.*
    Cincinnati, Ohio: Applegate & Co., 1862.
Brunson, Joseph W. *Historical Sketches of the Pee Dee Light Artillery.*
    Winston-Salem, N.C.: Stewart Print, 1927.

Buel, Clarence C., and Robert U. Johnson, eds. *Battles and Leaders of the Civil War*. 4 vols. New York: Century Co., 1884–88.

Burlingame, John K. *History of the Fifth Rhode Island Heavy Artillery*. Providence, R.I.: Snow & Farnham, 1892.

Burrage, Henry S. "The Retreat from Lenoir's and Siege of Knoxville." *Atlantic Monthly* 18 (1866):21–32.

Byrnes, Garrett D., and Charles H. Spilman. *The Providence Journal: 150 Years*. Providence, R.I.: Providence Journal Co., 1980.

Caldwell, J. F. J. *The History of a Brigade of South Carolinians First Known as "Gregg's" and Subsequently as "McGowan's" Brigade*. Dayton, Ohio: Morningside Press, 1984.

Carter, Robert Goldthwaite. *Four Brothers in Blue*. Austin: University of Texas Press, 1978.

Catton, Bruce. *Grant Moves South*. Boston: Little, Brown & Co., 1960.

Chapman, R. D. "A Georgia Soldier, C.S.A." *Confederate Veteran*, June, 1930, 230–32.

Chase, Philip S. *Organization and Service of Battery F, First Rhode Island Light Artillery, to January 1st, 1863*. Providence, R.I.: N. Bangs Williams & Co., 1880.

Child, William H. *A History of the Fifth Regiment, New Hampshire Volunteers, in the American Civil War, 1861–1865*. Bristol, N.H.: R. W. Musgrove, 1893.

Cleaves, Freeman. *Meade of Gettysburg*. Norman: University of Oklahoma Press, 1960.

Cochrane, John. "The Army of the Potomac." In *Personal Recollections of the Rebellion*. New York: New York Commandery of the Military Order of the Loyal Legion of the United States, 1891.

Coco, Gregory A., ed. *Through Blood and Fire: The Civil War Letters of Major Charles J. Mills*. [Gettysburg, Pa.]: n.p., 1982.

Cogswell, Leander W. *A History of the Eleventh New Hampshire Regiment, Volunteer Infantry, in the Rebellion War*. Concord, N.H.: Republican Press Association, 1891.

Committee of the Regiment. *History of the Thirty-sixth Regiment, Massachusetts Volunteers*. Boston: Press of Rockwell & Churchill, 1884.

Committee of the Regimental Association. *History of the Thirty-fifth Regiment, Massachusetts Volunteers, 1862–1865*. Boston: Mills, Knight & Co., 1884.

Cory, Eugene A. *A Private's Recollections of Fredericksburg*. Providence: Rhode Island Soldiers and Sailors Historical Society, 1884.

Coulter, E. Merton. *The Civil War and Readjustment in Kentucky*. Gloucester, Mass.: Peter Smith, 1966.

Cox, Jacob D. *Military Reminiscences of the Civil War*. 2 vols. New York: Charles Scribner's Sons, 1900.

Crawford, Samuel W. *The History of the Fall of Fort Sumter*. New York: S. F. McLean & Co., 1898.

Cullen, Joseph P. "The Very Beau Ideal of a Soldier." *Civil War Times Illustrated*, August, 1977, 4–10, 38–44.

Cullum, George W. *Biographical Register of the Officers and Graduates of the U.S. Military Academy*. Boston: Houghton, Mifflin & Co., 1891.

Cummings, Charles M. *Yankee Quaker, Confederate General: The Curious Career of Bushrod Rust Johnson*. Rutherford, N.J.: Fairleigh Dickinson University Press, 1971.

Cutcheon, Byron M. "Recollections of Burnside's East Tennessee Campaign of 1863." War Paper Number 39, Commandery of the District of Columbia, Military Order of the Loyal Legion of the United States.

———. "The Twentieth Michigan Regiment in the Assault on Petersburg, July, 1864." *Michigan Pioneer and Historical Society* 30:127–39.

Dickert, D. Augustus. *History of Kershaw's Brigade*. Newberry, S.C.: E. H. Aull Co., 1899.

Donald, David W., ed. *Inside Lincoln's Cabinet: The Civil War Diaries of Salmon P. Chase*. New York: Longman's, Green & Co., 1954.

Douglas, Henry Kyd. *I Rode with Stonewall*. Chapel Hill: University of North Carolina Press, 1940.

Dowdey, Clifford, ed. *The Seven Days: The Emergence of Robert E. Lee*. New York: Fairfax Press, 1978.

———. *The Wartime Papers of Robert E. Lee*. New York: Virginia Civil War Commission, 1961.

Drake, J. Madison. *The History of the Ninth New Jersey Veteran Vols*. Elizabeth, N.J.: Journal Printing House, 1886.

Draper, William F. *Recollections of a Varied Career*. Boston: Little, Brown & Co., 1908.

Dyer, Frederick H. *A Compendium of the War of the Rebellion*. Des Moines, Iowa: Dyer Publishing Co., 1908.

Eby, Cecil B., ed. *A Virginia Yankee in the Civil War: The Diaries of David Hunter Strother*. Chapel Hill: University of North Carolina Press, 1961.

Eckert, Edward K., and Nicholas Amato, eds. *Ten Years in the Saddle: The Memoirs of William Woods Averell*. San Rafael, Calif.: Presidio Press, 1978.

Edwards, William B. *Civil War Guns*. Harrisburg, Pa.: Stackpole Co., 1962.

Emmerton, James A. *A Record of the Twenty-third Regiment Mass. Vol. Infantry*. Boston: William Ware & Co., 1886.

Fairfield, Charles B. *History of the 27th Regiment N.Y. Vols*. Binghamton, N.Y.: Carl & Matthews, Printers, 1888.

Fleming, George Thornton, ed. *Life and Letters of Alexander Hays*. Pittsburgh, Pa.: Gilbert Adams Hays, 1919.

Franklin, William B. *A Reply of Maj.-Gen. William B. Franklin to the*

Report of the Joint Committee of Congress. New York: D. Van
Nostrand, 1863.

Frassanito, William A. *Grant and Lee: The Virginia Campaigns, 1864–1865.*
New York: Charles Scribner's Sons, 1983.

Gallagher, Gary W., ed. *Fighting for the Confederacy: The Personal
Recollections of General Edward Porter Alexander.* Chapel Hill:
University of North Carolina Press, 1989.

Garnett, Theodore S., Jr. "The Cruise of the Nashville." *Southern Historical
Society Papers* 12:329–34.

Grant, U. S. *Personal Memoirs of U. S. Grant.* 2 vols. New York: Charles L.
Webster & Co., 1886.

Gray, Wood. *The Hidden Civil War: The Story of the Copperheads.* New York:
Viking Press, 1942.

Green, John B., III. *A New Bern Album.* New Bern, N.C.: Tryon Palace
Commission, 1985.

Greene, A. Wilson. "Jackson on the Peninsula: Failure or Scapegoat?" *Civil
War* 18:6–19.

———. "Opportunity to the South: Meade Versus Jackson at Fredericksburg." *Civil War History,* December, 1987, 295–314.

Greene, Jacob L. *Gen. William B. Franklin and the Operations of the Left
Wing at the Battle of Fredericksburg, December 13, 1862.* Hartford,
Conn.: Belknap & Warfield, 1900.

Hahn, Thomas F. *Towpath Guide to the Chesapeake & Ohio Canal.* N.p.:
American Canal and Transportation Center, 1985.

Hammond, Harold Earl. *Diary of a Union Lady, 1861–1865.* New York: Funk
& Wagnall's Co., 1962.

Hassler, Warren W., Jr. *Commanders of the Army of the Potomac.* Baton
Rouge: Louisiana State University Press, 1962.

———. *General George B. McClellan: Shield of the Union.* Baton Rouge:
Louisiana State University Press, 1957.

Haupt, Herman. *Reminiscences of General Herman Haupt.* Milwaukee:
Wright & Joys Co., 1901.

Haynes, Martin A. *A History of the Second Regiment, New Hampshire
Volunteer Infantry, in the War of the Rebellion.* Lakeport, N.H.:
n.p., 1896.

Heth, Henry. "The Memoirs of Henry Heth." *Civil War History,* March, 1962,
5–24.

Hopkins, William P. *The Seventh Regiment Rhode Island Volunteers in the
Civil War, 1862–1865.* Providence, R.I.: Providence Press, 1903.

Horan, James D. *Confederate Agent, A Discovery in History.* New York:
Crown Publishers, 1954.

Houston, Henry C. *The Thirty-second Maine Regiment of Infantry
Volunteers.* Portland, Maine: Southworth Brothers, 1903.

Howard, Oliver O. *Autobiography of Oliver Otis Howard*. 2 vols. New York: Baker & Taylor Co., 1907.

Humes, Thomas W. *The Loyal Mountaineers of Tennessee*. Knoxville, Tenn.: Ogden Brothers & Co., 1888.

"It Was a Full Moon When . . . , A Researcher's Guide to Civil War Moon Phases," *Blue & Gray Magazine*, July, 1987, 35–37.

Jackman, Lyman. *History of the Sixth New Hampshire Regiment in the War for the Union*. Concord, N.H.: Republican Press Association, 1891.

Jones, John B. *A Rebel War Clerk's Diary*. New York: Sagamore Press, 1958.

Jordan, Weymouth T., Jr., and Louis H. Manarin, eds. *North Carolina Troops, 1861–1865*. 11 vols. Raleigh: Division of Archives and History, 1983.

Klement, Frank L. "Carrington and the Golden Circle Legend in Indiana During the Civil War." *Indiana Magazine of History*, March, 1965, 31–52.

———. *The Limits of Dissent*. Lexington: University Press of Kentucky, 1970.

Kniffen, Gilbert C. "The East Tennessee Campaign, September, 1863." *Papers of the Military Historical Society of Massachusetts* 7:411–32.

Knight, Benjamin, Sr. *History of the Sprague Families of Rhode Island*. Santa Cruz: H. Coffin, 1881.

Lane, James H. "The Truth of History." *Southern Historical Society Papers* 18:71–80.

Lapham, Oscar. *Recollections of Service in the Twelfth Regiment, R.I. Volunteers*. Providence: Rhode Island Soldiers and Sailors Historical Society, 1885.

"Last Colonel of Artillery, A.N.V." *Confederate Veteran*, May, 1917, 224–26.

Learned, William Law. *The Learned Family*. Albany, N.Y.: Weed-Parsons Printing Co., 1898.

Lee, Robert E. Letter to James A. Seddon. *Southern Historical Society Papers* 7:292.

———. Letter to Jefferson Davis. *Southern Historical Society Papers*, 12: 267–68.

Letter of the Secretary of War, Transmitting the Report of the Organization of the Army of the Potomac, and of its Campaigns in Virginia and Maryland, Under the Command of George B. McClellan, from July 26, 1861, to November 7, 1862. Washington, D.C.: Government Printing Office, 1864.

Longacre, Edward G. *From Antietam to Fort Fisher, The Civil War Letters of Edward King Wightman, 1862–1865*. Rutherford, N.J.: Fairleigh Dickinson University Press, 1985.

Longstreet, James. *From Manassas to Appomattox*. Secaucus, N.J.: Blue & Grey Press, n.d.

Lord, Edward O., ed. *History of the Ninth Regiment, New Hampshire*

Volunteers, in the War of the Rebellion. Concord, N.H.: Republican Press Association, 1895.

Loving, Jerome M., ed. *Civil War Letters of George Washington Whitman.* Durham, N.C.: Duke University Press, 1975.

Lyman, Theodore. "Uselessness of the Maps Furnished to the Staff of the Army of the Potomac Previous to the Campaign of May 1864." *Papers of the Military Historical Society of Massachusetts* 4:79–80.

McClellan, George B. *McClellan's Own Story.* New York: Charles L. Webster & Co., 1887.

McFarland, Robert W. *The Surrender of Cumberland Gap, September 9, 1863.* Columbus, Ohio: Press of Nitschke Brothers, 1898.

McMaster, Fitz William. "The Battle of the Crater." *Southern Historical Society Papers* 10:119–30.

McWhiney, Grady, and Perry D. Jamieson. *Attack and Die, Civil War Tactics and the Southern Heritage.* University: University of Alabama Press, 1982.

Marsh, Thomas O. and Marlene T. "The Ballad of Lottie Moon." *Civil War* 21: 40–45.

Marvel, William. *Race of the Soil: The Ninth New Hampshire Regiment in the Civil War.* Wilmington, N.C.: Broadfoot Publishing Co., 1988.

Matter, William D. *If It Takes All Summer: The Battle of Spotsylvania.* Chapel Hill: University of North Carolina Press, 1988.

Maury, Dabney Herndon. *Recollections of a Virginian in the Mexican, Indian, and Civil Wars.* New York: Charles Scribner's Sons, 1894.

Meade, George. *The Life and Letters of George Gordon Meade.* 2 vols. New York: Charles Scribner's Sons, 1913.

Meagher, Thomas F. *The Last Days of the 69th in Virginia.* New York: Irish American, 1861.

Meigs, Montgomery. "The Relations of President Lincoln and Secretary Stanton to the Military Commanders in the Civil War." *American Historical Review*, January, 1921, 285–303.

Memoir of James Allen Hardie, Inspector-General, United States Army. Washington, D.C.: Privately printed, 1877.

Montgomery, James R. "The Nomenclature of the Upper Tennessee River." *The East Tennessee Historical Society Publications*, no. 28 (1955): 46–57.

Mosgrove, George Dallas. "Following Morgan's Plume Through Indiana and Ohio." *Southern Historical Society Papers* 35:110–20.

Nevins, Allan. *The War for the Union.* 4 vols. New York: Scribner's, 1959–71.

———. ed. *A Diary of Battle: The Personal Journals of Charles S. Wainwright, 1861–1865.* New York: Harcourt, Brace & World, 1962.

Nevins, Allan, and Milton H. Thomas, eds. *The Diary of George Templeton Strong.* 4 vols. New York: Macmillan Co., 1950–52.

Newberry, Walter C. "The Petersburg Mine." In *Military Essays and*

Recollections. Chicago: Illinois Commandery, Military Order of the Loyal Legion of the United States, 1899.

Newman, A. S. "Essential Sleep—Personal Need, Military Duty." *Army*, September, 1986, 67–68.

Nichols, Edward J. *Toward Gettysburg: A Biography of John F. Reynolds*. University Park: Pennsylvania State University Press, 1958.

Official Records of the Union and Confederate Navies in the War of the Rebellion. 31 vols. Washington, D.C.: Government Printing Office, 1894–1927.

Osborne, William H. *The History of the Twenty-ninth Regiment of Massachusetts Volunteer Infantry*. Boston: Albert J. Wright, 1877.

Parker, Thomas H. *History of the 51st Regiment of P.V. and V.V.* Philadelphia: King and Baird, 1869.

Pearce, T. H., ed. *Diary of Captain Henry A. Chambers*. Wendell, N.C.: Broadfoot's Bookmark, 1983.

Perry, Leslie J. "Buckner and McClellan." *Southern Historical Society Papers* 24:295–301.

Poe, Orlando M. *Personal Recollections of the Occupation of East Tennessee and the Defense of Knoxville*. Detroit: Ostler Print. Co., 1889.

Pollard, Edward A. *The Lost Cause; A New Southern History of the War of the Confederates*. New York: E. B. Treat & Co., 1867.

Poore, Ben Perley. *The Life and Public Services of Ambrose E. Burnside, Soldier—Citizen—Statesman*. Providence, R.I.: J. A. & R. A. Reid, 1882.

Porter, Charles H. "The Petersburg Mine." *Papers of the Military Historical Society of Massachusetts* 5:223–39.

Porter, Horace. *Campaigning With Grant*. New York: Century Co., 1897.

Potter, Henry C. Letter. *Century* 35:481.

Pratt, Fletcher. *Civil War in Pictures*. Garden City, N.Y.: Garden City Books, 1955.

Quisenberry, A. C. "Morgan's Men in Ohio." *Southern Historical Society Papers* 39:91–99.

Raymond, Henry W., ed. "Extracts from the Journal of Henry J. Raymond." *Scribner's Monthly* 19:57–61, 419–24, 703–10.

Register of the Officers and Cadets of the U.S. Military Academy, West Point, New York. N.p., 1844–47.

Report of the Committee on the Conduct of the War on the Attack on Petersburg, on the 30th Day of July, 1864. Washington, D.C.: Government Printing Office, 1865.

Report of the Joint Committee on the Conduct of the War. 3 parts. Washington, D.C.: Government Printing Office, 1863.

Rhodes, Robert H., ed. *All for the Union, A History of the 2nd Rhode Island Volunteer Infantry*. Lincoln, R.I.: Andrew Mowbray, 1985.

Richmond, Joshua Bailey. *The Richmond Family, 1584–1896*. Boston: Privately printed, 1897.

Robertson, James I., Jr. "The Roanoke Island Expedition: Observations of a Massachusetts Soldier." *Civil War History*, December, 1966, 321–46.

Roe, Alfred S. *The Twenty-fourth Regiment Massachusetts Volunteers, 1861–1866*. Worcester, Mass.: The Twenty-fourth Veteran Association, 1907.

Roe, Alfred S., and Charles Nutt. *History of the First Regiment of Heavy Artillery, Massachusetts Volunteers*. Worcester and Boston: The Regimental Association, 1917.

Roelker, William Greene, ed. "Civil War Letters of William Ames." *Rhode Island Historical Society Collections*, January, 1941, 5–24.

Ropes, John C. "The Hearing in the Case of Fitz-John Porter." *Papers of the Military Historical Society of Massachusetts* 2:351–85.

Rule, William. "The Loyalists of Tennessee in the Late War." In *Sketches of War History, 1861–1865*, vol. 2. Cincinnati: Ohio Commandery of the Military Order of the Loyal Legion of the United States, 1888.

Sauers, Richard A. "General Ambrose E. Burnside's 1862 North Carolina Campaign." Ph.D. thesis, Pennsylvania State University, 1987.

———. "Laurels for Burnside: The Invasion of North Carolina, January–July, 1862." *Blue & Gray Magazine*, May, 1988, 8–20, 44–62.

Schaff, Morris. *The Battle of the Wilderness*. Boston: Houghton Mifflin Co., 1910.

Schenck, Martin. "Burnside's Bridge." *Civil War History*, December, 1956, 5–19.

Schiller, Herbert M., ed. *Autobiography of Major General William F. Smith: 1861–1864*. Dayton, Ohio: Morningside, 1990.

Sears, Stephen W. *George B. McClellan, the Young Napoleon*. New York: Ticknor & Fields, 1988.

———. *Landscape Turned Red: The Battle of Antietam*. New York: Ticknor & Fields, 1983.

———, ed. *The Civil War Papers of George B. McClellan: Selected Correspondence, 1860–1865*. New York: Ticknor & Fields, 1989.

Seville, William P. *History of the First Regiment, Delaware Volunteers*. Wilmington: Historical Society of Delaware, 1884.

Shanks, William F. G. *Personal Recollections of Distinguished Generals*. New York: Harper & Brothers, 1866.

Sheridan, P. H. *Personal Memoirs of P. H. Sheridan*. 2 vols. New York: Charles L. Webster & Co., 1888.

Sherman, W. T. *Memoirs of Gen. W. T. Sherman*. 2 vols. New York: Charles L. Webster & Co., 1891.

Simon, John Y., ed. *The Papers of Ulysses S. Grant*. 15 vols. Carbondale: Southern Illinois University Press, 1967–89.

Souvenir of Gen. Lewis Richmond. N.p., 1895.

Sparks, David S. *Inside Lincoln's Army: The Diary of Marsena Rudolph Patrick, Provost Marshal General, Army of the Potomac.* New York: Thomas Yoseloff, 1964.

Spooner, Henry J. *The Maryland Campaign with the Fourth Rhode Island.* Providence: Rhode Island Soldiers and Sailors Historical Society, 1903.

Sprague, Augustus B. R. "The Burnside Expedition." In *Civil War Papers Read Before the Commandery of Massachusetts, Military Order of the Loyal Legion of the United States,* vol. 2. Boston: R. H. Gilson Company, 1900.

Stackpole, Edward J. *Drama on the Rappahannock.* Harrisburg, Pa.: Military Service Pub. Co., 1957.

Steere, Edward. *The Wilderness Campaign.* Harrisburg, Pa.: Stackpole Co., 1960.

Stewart, William H. "The Charge of the Crater." *Southern Historical Society Papers* 25:77–90.

Stick, David. *The Outer Banks of North Carolina, 1584–1958.* Chapel Hill: University of North Carolina Press, 1958.

Stiles, Robert. *Four Years Under Marse Robert.* New York: Neale Publishing Co., 1903.

Stone, Edward W. *Rhode Island in the Rebellion.* Providence, R.I.: George H. Whitney, 1864.

Street, James, Jr. "Under the Influence." *Civil War Times Illustrated,* May, 1988, 30–35.

Strother, David Hunter ("A Virginian"). "Personal Recollections of the War." *Harper's New Monthly Magazine,* February, 1868, 275–91.

Sumner, Merlin E., ed. *The Diary of Cyrus B. Comstock.* Dayton, Ohio: Morningside, 1987.

Swinton, William. *Campaigns of the Army of the Potomac.* New York: Charles B. Richardson, 1866.

Thompson, S. Millett. *Thirteenth Regiment of New Hampshire Volunteer Infantry in the War of the Rebellion, 1861–1865.* Boston: Houghton, Mifflin & Co., 1888.

Townsend, George A. *Rustics in Rebellion: A Yankee Reporter on the Road to Richmond.* Chapel Hill: University of North Carolina Press, 1950.

Traver, Lorenzo. *Battles of Roanoke Island and Elizabeth City.* Providence, R.I.: N. Bangs Williams & Co., 1880.

Truxall, Aida C., ed. *Respects to All: Letters of Two Pennsylvania Boys in the War of the Rebellion.* Pittsburgh, Pa.: University of Pittsburgh Press, 1962.

Tyler, Mason Whiting. *Recollections of the Civil War.* New York: G. P. Putnam's Sons, 1912.

Waite, Otis F. R. *New Hampshire in the Rebellion.* Claremont, N.H.: Tracy, Chase & Co., 1870.

Walcott, Charles F. *History of the Twenty-first Regiment Massachusetts Volunteers*. Boston: Houghton, Mifflin & Co., 1882.

War of the Rebellion: A Compilation of the Official Records of the Union and Confederate Armies. 128 vols. Washington, D.C.: Government Printing Office, 1880–1901.

Watson, Alan D. *A History of New Bern and Craven County*. New Bern, N.C.: Tryon Palace Commission, 1987.

Welch, William W. *The Burnside Expedition and the Engagement at Roanoke Island*. Providence, R.I.: N. Bangs Williams & Co., 1890.

Weld, Stephen M. "The Petersburg Mine." *Papers of the Military Historical Society of Massachusetts* 5:207–19.

———. *War Diary and Letters of Stephen Minot Weld, 1861–1865*. Boston: Massachusetts Historical Society, 1979.

Welles, Gideon. *Diary of Gideon Welles*. 3 vols. Boston: Houghton Mifflin Co., 1911.

Whan, Vorin E. *Fiasco at Fredericksburg*. University Park: Pennsylvania State University Press, 1961.

White, Julius. "Burnside's Occupation of East Tennessee." In *Military Essays and Recollections*, vol. 4. Chicago: Illinois Commandery, Military Order of the Loyal Legion of the United States, 1907.

Whitman, Walt. *Leaves of Grass*. New York: New American Library, 1954.

Williams, Frederick D., ed. *The Wild Life of the Army: Civil War Letters of James A. Garfield*. [East Lansing]: Michigan State University Press, 1964.

Williams, T. Harry. *Lincoln and His Generals*. New York: Alfred A. Knopf, 1952.

———. *Lincoln and the Radicals*. [Madison]: University of Wisconsin Press, 1941.

Wilson, James Harrison. *Under the Old Flag*. 2 vols. New York: D. Appleton & Co., 1912.

Wise, John S. *The End of an Era*. Boston: Houghton, Mifflin & Co., 1899.

Woodbury, Augustus. *Ambrose Everett Burnside*. Providence, R.I.: N. Bangs Williams & Co., 1882.

———. *General Halleck and General Burnside*. Boston, 1864.

———. *Major General Ambrose E. Burnside and the Ninth Army Corps*. Providence, R.I.: Sidney S. Rider & Brother, 1867.

———. *A Narrative of the Campaign of the First Rhode Island, in the Spring and Summer of 1861*. Providence, R.I.: Sidney S. Rider, 1862.

———. *The Second Rhode Island Regiment: A Narrative of Military Operations*. Providence, R.I.: Valpey, Angell, & Co., 1875.

———. *The Soldier, Senator, Man*. Providence, R.I.: E.L. Freeman & Co., 1884.

SOURCES AND ACKNOWLEDGMENTS

As far as possible, this work has been based on primary sources. Unlike most of his contemporaries, Ambrose Burnside did not prepare a face for the faces he would meet, and his surviving correspondence is much more limited than, for instance, that of George McClellan. What few private letters he left, save a handful in the McClellan Papers, are contained in the Burnside Papers of the National Archives, which also holds the bulk of his official paperwork; the Rhode Island Historical Society preserves a somewhat smaller collection of Burnside material, most of it related to military or business affairs. These two sets of papers remain virtually untouched by historians. The greatest single source for personal information on Burnside is the Daniel Reed Larned Papers, in the Library of Congress; Larned was close to the general from December of 1861 until the siege of Petersburg, and his letters and journal vibrate with his evaluations of Burnside the man. The relative shortage of personal papers enforced a reliance upon other period manuscripts, newspapers, edited diaries and memoirs—often disagreeably tainted by time and motive—and, as a last resort, regimental histories. Secondary histories, unless pertaining to collateral or incidental topics, are generally cited only for comparison or criticism.

Of all the debts I have accumulated in four years of work on Burnside, none exceeds the one I owe A. Wilson Greene, of the Fredericksburg and Spotsylvania National Military Park. Not only did he offer living proof of another soul who doubted the traditional estimate of Burnside, he read and carefully criticized about a third of the manuscript, vastly improving at least that third. He and his colleague at Fredericksburg, Chief Historian Robert K. Krick, allowed me the run of their holdings and untangled some confusing technical matters for me. Bob's encyclopedic knowledge of things Confederate also yielded sources I might otherwise have missed.

Thanks to Michael Pilgrim, and particularly to Michael Musick, my trips to the National Archives were much more worthwhile than they otherwise would have been; their patience and persistence in my behalf transformed a labyrinthine quest into a few productive visits. Fred Baumann similarly aided me at the Library of Congress. Suzanne Christoff, curator of the U.S. Military Academy Archives, guided me through her own department and the West Point

Library's Special Collections, suggesting several sources with which I was unfamiliar, and Archivist Richard Sommers offered equally generous assistance at the U.S. Army Military History Institute. Michael Winey, of the institute, was his accommodating old self in the matter of photographs, while David Keough, another member of the staff, provided a couple of good tips on Rhode Island politics. I am grateful to Cynthia Bendroth, of the Rhode Island Historical Society; Stephen Cox and William Copeley, of the New Hampshire Historical Society; and Paul Brockman, of the Indiana Historical Society—as well as one anonymous employee of the Indiana State Library—for assorted and sundry courtesies attending my use of their manuscript collections. I am indebted to several local librarians, whose familiarity with their holdings served me well, namely the late Leatha Riley of the Union County Public Library, Liberty, Indiana; Emily Miles, reference librarian at the New Bern–Craven County Public Library, New Bern, North Carolina; and Amy Gardner of the Conway Public Library, Conway, New Hampshire, who seems never to tire of my interminable requests for interlibrary loans.

Michael Cavanaugh, of Cinnaminson, New Jersey, sent me Burnside-related material whenever he encountered it, and Blake Magner, from Westmont, New Jersey, put his customary extra effort into the maps for this volume. Richard Sauers, whose Ph.D. dissertation covered Burnside's North Carolina campaign, took the time to forward me some information not contained in that work. Peter Guay, of Honolulu, provided me with material on the effects of fatigue and sleeplessness from a military perspective, and Stephen Sears—known to anyone who ever heard of George Brinton McClellan—saved me from a number of egregious errors through his intimate acquaintance with the McClellan Papers. William Frassanito, equally conversant with Civil War photography, instantly put his finger on a particular image of Burnside I coveted. Gary Gallagher, of Pennsylvania State University, offered overall encouragement when I most needed it by opening one rather large door that might otherwise have stuck.

Perhaps my most unusual acknowledgment goes to three marines at the Cherry Point Air Station in North Carolina. Major M. J. Kerrigan organized my visit to the mouth of Slocum's Creek, now part of that installation, gathering the pertinent topographical maps; Master Sergeant Charles Finney gave me a guided tour of the southern approaches to New Bern; and Lance Corporal Brixey Lewis braved mud, ticks, and at least one cottonmouth moccasin to show me the terrain where Burnside's expedition landed that miserable thirteenth of March, 1862.

INDEX